# The Yale Leibniz

**Daniel Garber and Robert C. Sleigh, Jr.**

**General Editors**

The Yale Leibniz is a series of books containing texts and translations of the works of G. W. Leibniz. Each volume contains both the original language text and an English translation on facing pages. The original language text is up to the highest standard of modern textual scholarship. Some texts will be reprinted from the *Samtliche Schriften und Briefe,* in progress under the general editorship of the Akademie der Wissenschaften; others are taken from editions that meet the high standards of that edition. Some texts will be edited or re-edited from the manuscripts and early printed sources, with the cooperation of the editors of the Akademie edition. The translations are newly commissioned with the aim of making the texts more easily available to both students and scholars.

The series is intended to produce neither a complete edition of Leibniz's writings nor a comprehensive selected works edition. Although there will be uniform standards of editing and translation, each volume is intended to be independent, a collection of texts that constitute a natural unit. The focus of the series is Leibniz's philosophical thought, but this is interpreted broadly enough to include not only his metaphysics and epistemology but also his theology, his physics, and even aspects of his mathematics.

Each volume will be edited and translated by a scholar selected from the best of the international community of scholars working on late seventeenth-century philosophy.

G. W. Leibniz

# The Labyrinth of the Continuum

Writings on the Continuum Problem, 1672–1686

Translated, Edited, and with an Introduction

by Richard T. W. Arthur

New Haven and London: Yale University Press

Published with the assistance of the Ernst Cassirer Publications Fund.

Designed by Sonia Shannon.
Set in Times Roman type by The Composing Room of Michigan, Inc., Grand Rapids, Michigan.
Printed in the United States of America by Sheridan Books, Ann Arbor, Michigan.

**Library of Congress Cataloging-in-Publication Data**

Leibniz, Gottfried Wilhelm, Freiherr von, 1646–1716.
   [Selections. English & Latin. 2001]
   The labyrinth of the continuum : writings on the continuum problem, 1672–1686 / G. W. Leibniz ; translated, edited, and with an introduction by Richard T. W. Arthur.
      p.    cm. — (The Yale Leibniz)
   Original Latin text with English translation on facing pages.
   Includes bibliographical references and indexes.
   ISBN 0–300–07911–7
   1. Philosophy.   I. Arthur, Richard T. W., 1950–  II. Title.
   B2558 .A78   2001
   193—dc21
                    2001017973

A catalogue record for this book is available from the British Library.

*To my father, Geoffrey Arthur, for instilling*
*in me a love of language;*
*and to my mother, Lorna Arthur,*
*a love of hard work*

# Contents

# Preface

My attention was first drawn to the importance of this part of Leibniz's *Nachlass* by some quotations from the dialogue *Pacidius to Philalethes* given by Nicholas Rescher in his *Philosophy of Leibniz* (Englewood Cliffs, N.J.: Prentice Hall, 1967). Intrigued by these snippets, I set about translating larger fragments, until I had most of the dialogue. Since then, the process of extrapolation to the present volume of texts and translations, abetted by the encouragement of friends and colleagues, has been more or less inexorable.

The central problem of the collection, that of the composition of the continuum, is one whose importance Leibniz repeatedly stressed throughout his career. My aim has been to gather together and present in English translation a selection of the manuscripts he wrote on this subject between 1672 and 1686, most of them previously untranslated.

The original language texts are drawn from the authoritative *Akademie* edition of Leibniz's works, as explained in more detail in the Note on the Texts and Translation below. In making the translations, my aim has been to produce a readable English text that at the same time conveys the original's meaning as accurately as possible. No doubt it is the aim of all translators to strike some such happy balance between accuracy and fluency. But judgments concerning where the fulcrum should be placed differ from one age to another, as I was reminded on reading the preface of Henry Crew and Alfonso De Salvio's 1914 translation of Galileo Galilei's *Discorsi*. They criticize their predecessor Thomas Weston's 1730 translation for its overliteralness, when theirs, by modern standards, often verges on paraphrase. This remark probably reveals enough about my own attitude to translation, but I'll risk being more explicit. What I have aimed for is not a prose that could be mistaken for that of a contemporary anglophone—it is, I think, too Latinate for that—but an English that is reasonably fluent and modern, yet still recognizably Leibniz's style.

I have tried to render all important words and their cognates as consistently as I could, to the extent that English will allow. As an aid to this, I have followed the lead of Edwin Curley and others in providing a Glossary/Index. This contains a record of my translations of key terms and phrases, as well as a defense of them, and has the dual merit of providing a kind of running commentary on translation issues while keeping these apart from the textual concerns dealt with in the notes.

The scholarly notes are not intended to be comprehensive, nor could they be, given the extraordinary range of Leibniz's interests and sources. But I have done what I could to link these pieces with his other writings, particularly his earlier ones. The modest introduction and notes I had orig-

inally planned gradually gave way to something more substantial, as the fragmentary nature of the material seemed to demand progressively more substantiation. The resulting introductory essay has grown to the extent that the status of an intended companion volume is now moot. In any case, it has been rendered less necessary by the publication in the interim of Philip Beeley's *Kontinuität und Mechanismus* (on the philosophy of the young Leibniz in its context within the history of ideas). This fine work is highly recommended to all those interested in the origins and historical context of Leibniz's thought on the continuum who can read German.

## On the Selection of Texts

I have endeavoured to make the selection as comprehensive as possible, within certain limits. These have been dictated partly by the subject itself. The writings chosen are, broadly speaking, philosophical, bearing on the metaphysical problem of the continuum and its implications for mathematics and physics, rather than on Leibniz's advances during this period in mathematics or physics per se. But partly too I have been constrained to minimize the overlap with other planned volumes in the series.

Thus Leibniz's mathematical discoveries are clearly of crucial relevance to the development of his views on the continuum. By 1673 he had discovered the infinite series that now bears his name, and by early 1676 had all the vital ingredients of his differential and integral calculus. But the creation of the calculus does not automatically solve the problems of the infinite: in fact it leaves the ontological status of the infinite and the infinitely small still very unclear. Had Leibniz's differentials been indivisibles, for instance, then this solution to the mathematical problem would have carried over straightforwardly into metaphysics, and could have been used as a justification for atomism. But (as Leibniz gradually realized) the fact that infinitesimals or differentials can themselves have differentials, and so on to infinity, and the fact that the same whole can be resolved into different infinite sums of differentials by different "progressions of the variables," refute a simple identification of infinitesimals as indivisible parts of the continuum. Similarly, the fact that there are infinite geometric series that add to a finite sum disproves the notion (confidently advanced by both Galileo and Gassendi) that an infinitely divided whole must issue in infinitely small parts; yet this is not enough in itself to disprove the idea of indivisibles. Thus while Leibniz's mathematical discoveries are of the greatest import for his solution to the continuum problem, they do not themselves contain that solution. Accordingly, I have included none of Leibniz's strictly mathematical writings of the period, which are in any case planned for later volumes in the Yale Leibniz Series, but only

those texts where Leibniz discusses the implications of these results for the continuum problem.

Much the same applies to Leibniz's writings on physics of this period. Such writings as his notes on the first dialogue of Galileo's *Two New Sciences,* his "On the Cohesiveness of Bodies," and "On Matter, Motion, Minima, and the Continuum" clearly bear directly on the continuum problem and are thus included. Others whose bearing on it is less direct are not. For example, "Three Primary Axioms" (Aiii48) and "On the Secrets of Motion" (LH 35 XIII, 3, sheet 81), both dating from the summer of 1676, contain announcements of his physical axiom that the entire effect is equippollent to its cause, which he later claims is the thread that guided him out of the labyrinth; but there is no mention of the continuum in either piece. Similarly, "Mechanical Principles" (Aiii6) includes a discussion of the relativity of motion; but unlike "Space and Time Are Really Relations," "Motion Is Something Relative," and "Motion Is Not Something Absolute," all of which I have included, it does not explore the metaphysical implications of this.

Even with these restrictions, however, there were some delicate editorial decisions to be made. For given the broad sense in which Leibniz construed the continuum problem, there is little that he wrote on philosophy in this period that does not have some bearing on it. Most of Leibniz's philosophical writings between December 1675 and December 1676, for instance, concern to some extent either the infinite, atoms, or the nature of substance, space, and time; and since a selection of these constitutes the first volume in the Yale Leibniz Series, *De Summa Rerum: Metaphysical Papers, 1675–1676,* translated and edited by G. H. R. Parkinson (abbreviated here as DSR), this immediately presented a problem of potential overlap. Caught between the desire to preserve the integrity of my volume and the wish to avoid unnecessary duplication of his, I have opted for a delicate compromise. Two pieces from 1675–76 that concern the problem of the continuum throughout seem invaluable for understanding the progress of Leibniz's thought between 1673 and 1676: Aiii58 ("On Matter, Motion, Minima, and the Continuum"); and Aiii76 ("On the Plenitude of the World"); these I have reproduced in their entirety. As for the others, I have excerpted only those passages containing significant developments in Leibniz's thought on the continuum (as with the selections from Aiii60, 36, 71, and 74), referring the reader to DSR for the full context of these selections; I likewise defer to DSR for other pieces or passages on the continuum (in particular, Aiii85: "A Chain of Marvelous Demonstrations . . .") not included here.

I should also say something in explanation of the choice of the dates de-

termining this collection, 1672–86. For Leibniz had already devoted considerable energy to the continuum problem before 1672, and the solution he had achieved by 1686 was not so final as to preclude continuing attempts at refinement in his later writings, and even toying with a quite different alternative solution, as in the correspondence with Bartholomew Des Bosses. But the culmination of Leibniz's early work on the continuum was the account published in his short tract *A Theory of Abstract Motion* (1671), which together with its companion volume *A Theory of Concrete Motion,* their forestudies, and related manuscripts clearly constitute a substantial work in themselves and are to appear as a separate volume in the Yale Leibniz Series (Leibniz's First Physics). Consequently, it seemed natural to begin my volume with Leibniz's Paris writings (1672–76), which undergo a rapid development away from his youthful views as his understanding of the mathematical, physical, and metaphysical issues becomes increasingly sophisticated. Nevertheless, since some familiarity with his earlier theory of the continuum is indispensable for understanding Leibniz's starting point in the period of 1672–76, I have included relevant extracts from his early writings in an appendix of supplementary texts.

As for the cutoff at 1686, it is true that Leibniz wrote a good deal on the continuum problem after this date, especially in his correspondence. But (with the exception of the Des Bosses correspondence), this was almost always in a didactic mode, referring to his past labors. The manuscripts collected here, on the other hand, were composed during the formative period of his philosophy, and have a good claim to represent his concerted attempt to solve the continuum problem. By 1686 the characteristic features of Leibniz's mature solution are in place: the denial of atoms and vacua in matter and the espousal of an atomism of substance, the realization of the ideal character of continuous quantities such as space, time, and primary matter, the argument for the phenomenality of body and motion from the fact of their infinite dividedness, recognition of the relational nature of motion, and the proposal that, consequently, a substantial form or force is needed to underpin the reality of body and motion. Moreover, 1686 is a natural watershed in Leibniz's career, marking the year when he writes the first public account of his new system in the so-called *Discourse on Metaphysics,* his first publications on the calculus, and *Brevis Demonstratio . . . ,* the opening salvo of his attack on Cartesian physics.

## Acknowledgments

My debts are numerous. First, thanks to series editors Dan Garber and Bob Sleigh for their generous support and encouragement over the years while this work was in progress, and without which it would probably not have

appeared. I am grateful to the anonymous readers of Yale University Press for their helpful criticisms, and to Yale editors Judith Calvert, Otto Bohlmann, Susan Laity, and Joyce Ippolito for their advice. I owe much to those at the Leibniz-Archiv in Hanover, most especially to Reinhard Finster and Heinz-Jürgen Hess for their material support and superb hospitality, to the late Albert Heinekamp for his kindness, and to Herbert Breger for stimulating discussion of Leibniz's views on continuity. I also owe thanks to my home institution, Middlebury College, for the two academic years (1989–90 and 1994–95) in which the book was composed, and to the National Endowment for the Humanities for a Fellowship for College Teachers and Independent Scholars (FB-26897-89) in the first of these years. I am grateful to the Institute for the History and Philosophy of Science and Technology at Victoria University in the University of Toronto for their hospitality in accepting me as a visiting research fellow for 1994–95 and helping to make my stay a collegial and productive one. I would also like to thank the staff of the E. J. Pratt Library of Victoria University, and of the Centre for Renaissance and Medieval Studies, for facilitating my research in the University of Toronto's labyrinthine library system. In Middlebury, Mike Stineman helped me by scanning much of the Akademie Latin, and Carol Sampson assisted in the final assault of preparing for the press.

I also have debts to individual scholars too numerous to mention. I am grateful to G. H. R. Parkinson for all I have learnt from his example; to Edwin Curley for his painstaking reply and patient advice about translating Spinoza, to Massimo Mugnai and Bob Sleigh for kindly making available to me material from the new Akademie edition, to Alberto Portugal for finding me the Spanish quote from Borges, and to Jonathan Bennett for sage advice on how to translate a tricky French phrase. I am deeply indebted to Christia Mercer and Glenn Hartz for taking the time to read over drafts of my introductory essay and offer many helpful comments. Christia also gave me valuable early advice on translation, much encouragement, and the benefit of the insights contained in drafts of her new book on Leibniz's early metaphysics. I also want to thank Samuel Levey, whose penetrating questions suggested new angles on the very problems of interpretation that I was wrestling with in the introduction and helped me considerably in clarifying my own thoughts.

Finally, a thank you to my family for their support and forbearance for the long period in which this arduous task was in progress: particularly to my parents-in-law Giovanni and Rina Colussi, for their help in looking after our twins, and most of all to my wife, Gabriella Colussi Arthur, for her unstinting advice, love, and help.

## Abbreviations

**A** = *Gottfried Wilhelm Leibniz: Sämtliche Schriften und Briefe,* ed. Deutsche Akademie der Wissenschaften (Darmstadt and Berlin: Akademie-Verlag, 1923–). Cited by series, volume, and page, e.g. A VI.ii: 229, or series, volume, and piece number, e.g. A II.i N68, or both, A II.i N60: 504; except in the case of Series VI, volumes iii and iv (from which all my selections are taken: see Note on Texts and Translation above), where the series number is omitted: they are abbreviated **Aiii** and **Aiv,** resp. Thus Aiii60: 473 denotes piece number 60, page 473, in Series VI, volume iii, whereas Aiv312 denotes piece 312 in volume iv. For single-page pieces, I have omitted the page number (e.g. Aiii52, Aiv360); when the piece number has just been given, I cite by page numbers alone.

**AG** = *Leibniz: Philosophical Essays,* ed. and trans. Roger Ariew and Daniel Garber (Indianapolis: Hackett, 1989).

**AT** = *Oeuvres de Descartes,* 12 vols., Nouvelle présentation, ed. Ch. Adam & P. Tannery (Paris: J. Vrin, 1964–76). Cited by volume and page, e.g. AT VIII.1, 71.

**BA** = *The Complete Works of Aristotle,* 2 vols., Revised Oxford Translation, ed. Jonathan Barnes (Princeton: Princeton University Press, 1984).

**C** = *Opuscles et fragments inédits de Leibniz,* ed. Louis Couturat (Paris: Alcan, 1903; reprint ed. Hildesheim: Olms, 1966).

**CSM** = *The Philosophical Writings of Descartes,* 2 vols., ed. and trans. John Cottingham, Robert Stoothof, and Dugald Murdoch (Cambridge: Cambridge University Press, 1985). Cited by volume and page, e.g. CSM.i.235.

**DSR** = *G. W. Leibniz, De Summa Rerum: Metaphysical Papers and Letters, 1675–1676,* ed. and trans. G. H. R. Parkinson (New Haven: Yale University Press, 1992).

**EN** = Galileo Galilei, *Opere,* Edizione Nazionale, ed. Antonio Favaro (Florence, 1898).

**G** = *Die Philosophische Schriften von Gottfried Wilhelm Leibniz,* 7 vols., ed. C. I. Gerhardt (Berlin: Weidmann, 1875–90; reprint ed. Hildesheim: Olms, 1960). Cited by volume and page, e.g. G.vi.264.

**GM** = *Leibnizens Mathematische Schriften,* ed. C. I. Gerhardt, 7 vols. (Berlin and Halle: Asher and Schmidt, 1849–63; reprint ed. Hildesheim: Olms, 1971). Cited by volume and page, e.g., GM.ii.231.

**L** = *Gottfried Wilhelm Leibniz: Philosophical Papers and Letters,* 2d ed., ed. and trans. Leroy Loemker (Dordrecht: D. Reidel, 1969).

**LB** = *Leibniz Briefwechsel* (manuscripts): Niedersächsische Landesbibliothek, Hanover; as catalogued in Eduard Bodemann, *Der Briefwechsel des Gottfried Wilhelm Leibniz* (Hanover, 1889; reprint ed. Hildesheim: Olms, 1966).

**LH** = *Leibniz Handschriften* (manuscripts): Niedersächsische Landesbibliothek, Hanover; as catalogued in Eduard Bodemann, *Die Leibniz-Handschriften der Koniglichen offentlichen Bibliothek zu Hannover* (Hanover, 1895; reprint ed. Hildesheim: Olms, 1966).

**NE** = *New Essays on Human Understanding,* ed. and trans. Peter Remnant and Jonathan Bennett (Cambridge: Cambridge University Press, 1981).

**PW** = *Gottfried Wilhelm Leibniz: Philosophical Writings,* ed. G. H. R. Parkinson, trans. Mary Morris and Parkinson (London: J. M. Dent & Sons, 1973).

**SC** = *The Collected Works of Spinoza,* vol. 1, ed. and trans. Edwin Curley (Princeton: Princeton University Press, 1985).

**SO** = *Spinoza Opera,* 4 vols., ed. Carl Gebhart (Heidelberg: Carl Winters, 1924). Cited by volume and page, e.g. SO.ii.49.

**Ve** = *Gottfried Wilhelm Leibniz: Vorausedition zur Reihe VI— Philosophische Schriften,* in der Ausgabe der Akademie der DDR (Münster: Leibniz Forschungsstelle, 1982–), 10 fascicules. This is a

preliminary edition for the use and benefit of scholars, from which the selections in Part III here were originally taken. Although these pieces are now cited by their number in the new edition of *Aiv* (see above), the corresponding Vorausedition piece and page numbers are given in the leading footnote for each piece.

# A Note on the Texts and Translation

For Parts I and II, the original language text is that of the Akademie edition, Series VI, volume iii (available in most research libraries); for Part III it is that of volume iv of the same series, recently published in six substantial parts, A–F, totaling some 3,000 pages. I had originally availed myself of the preliminary edition of this volume, the so-called Vorausedition, but I was prevailed upon to delay publication until the appearance of the official edition so I could key all my referencing to it.

I have not reproduced all Leibniz's deletions, insertions, and replacements that are carefully recorded by the Akademie editors at the bottom of each page, but only those I judged to represent philosophically significant changes. And rather than clutter the printed page with these, I have tucked them away in footnotes in translation only, leaving readers interested in the original Latin to consult the Akademie editions. Text that Leibniz had crossed out is | enclosed within bold vertical bars |; deletions within deletions are {enclosed within curly brackets}. Restorations and corrections of Leibniz's text, whether due to unintended omissions or to inadvertent grammatical and other mistakes, are [enclosed within square brackets]. Conjectural reconstructions of the text where it is broken off or scarcely readable are <enclosed within diamond brackets>.

Given the unfinished nature of most of this material, there were other editorial decisions to be made concerning its presentation. Few of these pieces were written out in fair copy, an exception being *Pacidius to Philalethes* (Aiii78). But even there a substantial section of the fair copy was corrected, and, since the suppressed passage (including Leibniz's marginal comments) is of considerable interest, I have followed the Akademie editors in reproducing this as an insert in different type. Similarly, the enunciation of discoveries in "A Specimen of Discoveries" (Aiv312) is interrupted by a long Note on Firmness and Fluidity, which I have again presented as an insert in different type. The punctuation in the original language texts is Leibniz's own.

In the translations I have taken some liberties with punctuation and paragraphing, as can be seen by comparison with the Latin texts. Thus I have found it expedient to break up long sentences and paragraphs whenever it seemed that this would aid in making the translation more readable. Leibniz in any case punctuated according to a different system than ours, often using commas where we would use periods, sometimes writing qualifying clauses as separate sentences. Also, as the Akademie editors observe, Leibniz often uses a comma or semicolon to connect the phrase preceding it with the appropriate predicate. Leibniz's capitals are generally not preserved in the English translation. He systematically capitalized

such words as *Ens, Mens,* and *Angelus;* in the translation, only proper terms, such as the 'World Soul', 'God', 'the Earth', 'the Sun', are capitalized. Occasionally I have italicized words—such as those introducing categories in inventories—where it appears that Leibniz either inadvertently did not underline, and would have done so on editing, or used capitalization instead. I use "quotation marks" for quotations and titles, and 'single inverted commas' to denote words that are merely mentioned.

Leibniz made substantial comments on other authors. These he gave sometimes as footnotes, as in his annotations on the excerpts from Spinoza (Aiii19), sometimes embedded in the text (+ between these markers +), as in his annotations on Cordemoy (Aiv346). He also made many marginalia, some by way of textual additions or footnotes, but many as notes to himself for correcting the texts. Those that seem to have been intended as insertions or replacements for sections of text (as is the case for some fragments related to Aiv312), I have inserted accordingly; otherwise all Leibniz's marginalia are presented here as footnotes at the bottom of the page, numbered sequentially with the prefix L, as L1 etc. All my editorial notes, on the other hand, are given as endnotes, with normal numbering, and may be found at the end of the book.

Leibniz's titles, where they exist, are standardized and given in italic capitals and small capitals at the head of the text and within quotation marks in the table of contents. The other original-language titles, standardized and set in boldface on the verso pages, are generally those given them by the Akademie editors. Exceptions are 21, 27, and 28, where I have given what I judge to be more appropriate titles in square brackets, and 2, 5, 8, 17, 18, and 33, where I have used the English titles instead of the Akademie German. The English titles are translations of the originals except for Leibniz's notes and annotated excerpts (2, 5, 8, 17, 18, and 33), and for certain selections (18, 31, and 32), where the titles are my own. A date for each piece is given below the title: dates or parts of dates in square brackets are editorial conjectures for time of composition; dates or parts of dates without brackets are those entered by Leibniz himself. All dates are given New Style, i.e. according to the Gregorian calendar, which was ten days on from the older Julian calendar. During the period of this collection, this calendar was already in use in France while Leibniz was there (1672–76), although not in England or Germany. (Thus the *Pacidius,* which was written before Leibniz left England, and dated "Oct. 1676" according to the Julian Calendar still in use there, was written between 29 October and 10 November 1676, NS.)

## Introduction

"A mí, bárbaro inglés, me ha side deparado revelar ese misterio diáfano."
—Jorge Luis Borges, *Ficciones*

### 1. The Labyrinth

For Leibniz the problem of the continuum was central to metaphysics, and he never tired of stressing its importance. "Only Geometry," he wrote in 1676, "can provide a thread for the Labyrinth of the Composition of the Continuum, of maximum and minimum, and the unassignable and the infinite, and no one will arrive at a truly solid metaphysics who has not passed through that labyrinth."[1] The enthusiasm for geometry is not hard to understand: when he wrote this, Leibniz was putting the finishing touches to his seminal contribution to mathematics, the infinitesimal calculus. But the estimate of the continuum problem as vital to a successful metaphysics is typical, and similar statements abound in his writings. The most celebrated of these appears near the end of his life in the preface of his *Theodicy* of 1710. There the problem of the composition of the continuum is described as the second of the "two famous labyrinths" in which the human mind is wont to lose its way: it "consists in the discussion of continuity and the indivisibles which appear to be elements there, and where the consideration of the infinite must enter in."[2]

The first labyrinth—that concerning "the great question of free will and necessity, especially in the production and origin of evil"—is of course the subject of the *Theodicy* itself, the only full-length book that Leibniz managed to publish in his lifetime. Yet he had long intended to write on both labyrinths. In 1676 he had written a plan for an encyclopedic work, whose prospective sixth and seventh entries were to be "The first Labyrinth: on Fate, Fortune and Freedom," and "The second labyrinth: on the *composition* of the continuum, on time, place, motion, atoms, the indivisible and the infinite";[3] and even as he was finally presenting his conclusions on the first labyrinth in the *Theodicy* thirty-four years later, he continued to cherish the hope that he would find the opportunity to "declare himself" similarly on the second.[4] This he never did; his lifelong ambition to write a treatise on the labyrinth of the continuum remained unfulfilled.

That is a pity. An account by Leibniz himself of how he had emerged from his labyrinth with "a true conception of the nature of substance and matter" would have been hugely illuminating of his monadology, and perhaps much else in his mature philosophy. But he published not so much as an article on the subject, and scholars have had to make do with the terse formulations scattered about in his works, chiefly those in the *New System*

xxiii

and in certain passages of his correspondence with Antoine Arnauld, Burcher de Volder, Nicolas Rémond, and Bartholemew Des Bosses.[5] These are typically to the effect that the continuum involves indeterminate parts, and is consequently ideal, whereas the actual is a result or assemblage of discrete units; that in ideal things the whole is prior to the parts, whereas in actuals the parts are prior to the whole; and that "it is the confusion of the ideal and the actual that has embroiled everything and produced the labyrinth of the composition of the continuum."[6]

These remarks are enigmatic, to say the least, and judging from the efforts of those who have tried to understand them from Leibniz's time to the present day, they are sorely in need of further elaboration.[7] Moreover, their very brevity has tended to encourage the suspicion that Leibniz never really found a satisfactory solution, and that his repeated allusions to the labyrinth and its dangers were little more than rhetorical flourishes.[8] This suspicion has been compounded by prevailing views on the generation of Leibniz's mature system. Two interpretations have dominated for most of the twentieth century. According to one, Leibniz's mature philosophy emerges as a natural consequence of his logical discoveries in the period, particularly the predicate-in-notion principle. According to the other, it was precipitated by his advances in dynamics. Each of these interpretations engages aspects of his mature conception of substance, but neither connects in an obvious way with the problem of the continuum, thus making his claims for the centrality of the latter to his emergent conception of substance appear overblown.

The volume of writings presented here will, I hope, allay such misgivings. For between his arrival in Paris on a diplomatic mission in 1672, and the emergence of his mature philosophy in articles and letters published in 1686, Leibniz mounted a sustained assault on the problem of the continuum. In the manuscripts he penned in this period, one finds him wrestling with the problem of the infinite division of matter, and whether this issues in "perfect points"; how this relates to the infinitesimals of his calculus, and to infinite series; whether motion is truly continuous, or interrupted by rests; and what all these matters entail for the hypothesis of atoms and the void, and the nature of body and substance. One finds him developing a sophisticated theory of infinity, in which it is distinguished into three differing orders or "degrees"; tackling directly the problem of the unboundedness of the world; advocating a radical and original view on the nature of infinite aggregates; and integrating this with his denial of infinite number on the one hand, and the phenomenal nature of body and matter on the other.

These are not polished essays, however. One or two of them might per-

haps have been written with publication in mind, but the majority are little
more than "thinking on paper," often scribbled on the backs of bills or
whatever scraps of paper came to hand.[9] They are nuggets of philosophical experimentation[10] whose conclusions are usually provisional, and
sometimes even retracted later in the same piece. Nor is the overall line of
argument easy to discern. Views are triumphantly proclaimed, then later
quietly abandoned, with rarely any explicit mention of what has been
found unsatisfactory about them. To give just one example, the thesis that
motion is interrupted by rests, rejected in 1671, is reconsidered briefly in
April 1676 ("On Motion and Matter," Aiii68), to "see what would follow."
What does follow, he concludes, is nothing less than that "the cause of
things . . . is at last made clear in an admirable way, as well as production
out of nothing." This view is then elaborated at length later that year in
Leibniz's considered study of the problem, the *Pacidius Philalethi,* where
it is advanced with much fanfare—only to disappear completely from his
writings thereafter, with no explanation. Other notions undergo a quieter
development; for instance, that of a point as an infinitely small but actual
part of a continuous body in 1671, which eventually bifurcates into the
mathematical fiction of a "differential" insofar as it is infinitely small, and
the endpoint of a line insofar as it is an actual phenomenon. And some
seem to be just philosophical dead-ends, like the notion of the "unbounded" stationary universe, discussed at length in the first half of 1676.

The result is an array of arguments and themes of such bewildering intricacy that it is hard not to regard them as constituting a labyrinth in themselves. Here I find myself irresistibly reminded of a short story by the Ar-
gentine writer Jorge Luis Borges (himself a keen admirer of Leibniz's
metaphysics). In "The Garden of Forking Paths," Ts'ui Pên bequeaths his
heirs a labyrinth, which no one can locate, as well as a pile of mutually
contradictory draft manuscripts that no one can understand. The solution
to this double enigma turns out to be that "the book and the maze are one
and the same thing."[11] Ts'ui Pên's heirs, expecting a concrete labyrinth in
the grounds of his estate, were instead left an intellectual one (on branch-
ing time). In the case of Leibniz, it is more nearly the other way around.
The labyrinth he continually alludes to is more concrete than most have
supposed: not merely the abstract intellectual problem of the continuum,
but the actual maze of arguments he was embroiled in, spelled out in the
pile of manuscripts he left for posterity.

No doubt this maze of argument is very different from anything Leibniz
might have written had he fulfilled his intention to compose a treatise on
the subject. There is no sustained line of argument, no easily discernible
explanation for his changes of position. Yet I think that in a way this is

quite apt to the subject. The baroque intertwining of themes and arguments reflects the implicate or fractal nature of reality itself, as Leibniz conceived it, where there is a "world of infinitary creatures" enfolded into any part of matter, however small. And although the result is complexity itself, perhaps this requires no apology: the baroque, after all, *is* Leibniz's sensibility, as Gilles Deleuze has persuasively argued.[12] It is also more faithful to the openness of his style of philosophizing, there being virtually no thesis he is unwilling to consider if its relevance and consistency can be established. Indeed, there is an engaging frankness and spontaneity about his changes of mind displayed here that Leibniz could never have duplicated in a formal treatise, and, to the degree that he might have been successful in reducing his ideas to a more logical order, he would inevitably have masked their fascinating and tortuous development.

Of course, the labyrinthine nature of Leibniz's argument makes the task of introducing it extremely difficult. His path to its eventual solution is of such intricacy as to defy adequate summary in a book twice the length of this. Accordingly, what I shall offer here is something decidedly more modest. After setting Leibniz's problem in context, and giving a brief sketch of his first attempt at a solution to the continuum problem, I shall simply follow a few representative strands of his thought on the subject through some of their twists and turns, with no claim to completeness. I am well aware of how much of relevance this will leave unsaid. A decent commentary on even a short piece like "On Motion and Matter" would run into a sizable chapter. And I shall leave great veins of subject matter unmined: most notably, Leibniz's sophisticated theory of the infinite (and its relation to Spinoza's views), and the connection of the doctrine of *petites perceptions* with the analysis of geometrical figures as fictional entities approximated arbitrarily closely by polygons. I have tried to avoid entering scholarly controversies, usually relegating my disagreements with other scholars to occasional footnotes. (The reader should be aware, however, that much of what I say here runs contrary to accepted opinions about Leibniz's views, especially on the status of aggregates, corporeal substances, and space.) My aim is only to give some foretaste of the richness of his thought on the continuum, and if this aids in the appreciation of the importance of the problem to Leibniz's philosophical development, I shall be well content.

## 2. The Problem of the Continuum

Narrowly conceived, the problem of the continuum is purely mathematical. It concerns the *composition* of continuous quantities: whether a line, for instance, is composed of indivisibles (either points or infinitely small

line elements), or of divisible parts (either finite line segments only, or infinitesimal ones)—or, indeed, whether it is composable at all. But Leibniz's contemporaries and predecessors understood the problem as pertaining not just to purely mathematical entities, but to all supposedly continuous things. In this wider sense, the continuum problem is that of the composition of anything continuous: Is matter infinitely divisible, or does it have indivisible first elements or atoms? Is motion composed of an infinity of instantaneous tendencies to move? Is space composed of points, or time of instants or moments?[13]

Such questions had been much discussed in the early seventeenth century[14] and played a central role in the thought of many of its greatest thinkers. Thus a challenge problem issued by Jean-Baptiste Poysson in 1635 concerning whether an infinitely divisible magnitude could nonetheless be contained in a mathematical point attracted responses from many of the leading lights of the time, including Marin Mersenne, Pierre Gassendi, Jean-Baptiste Morin, Tommaso Campanella, and Ismael Boulliau.[15] And according to Lynn Joy's fascinating account, the appeal to mathematics in some of the responses to Poysson's problem encouraged Gassendi to undertake the detailed exposition of Epicurean atomism (with its distinction between mathematical and physical points) that was to become the cornerstone of his philosophy.[16] Meanwhile his great rival Descartes, despite dismissing the problems of the infinite as being beyond the capacities of our finite minds (and criticizing Galileo's efforts accordingly), had clearly committed himself to the rejection of indivisibles; but despite this, he had posited the actual division of matter to infinity (into "actually indefinite particles") as a necessary condition for variations of motion in a continuous plenum, thus bequeathing an unresolved tension to later Cartesianism. And in those parts of the *Two New Sciences* to which Descartes had taken exception, Galileo had proposed that continuous matter was composed of infinite indivisibles, and had suggested that the primary cohesion of bodies could be explained in terms of the indivisible voids between them, holding them together as a result of nature's repugnance to the vacuum. Likewise, he had analyzed continuously accelerated motion as containing increasing intensive "degrees of velocity" at each instant, and as accruing by the addition of instantaneous *momenta;* just as Descartes too had found a way of treating motion at an instant in terms of the *conatus ad motum,* or instantaneous tendency to move. Thomas Hobbes, finally, had seen in this notion of *conatus* or endeavour the nub of the new natural philosophy, and in his system it functions as the crucial link that allows him to build a materialist psychology from his physics.

It is this broader conception of the continuum problem that Leibniz in-

herits. As already indicated above, for him the labyrinth of the continuum concerns not just the composition of mathematical entities, but the whole complex of problems concerning the infinite divisibility of matter, the unboundedness of the universe, the existence of atoms, and the continuity of motion. But from the beginning he also saw the problem as intimately connected with the nature of incorporeal substances—souls or minds—and it is this further aspect that gives the problem its peculiar Leibnizian twist. The connection arises from the *indivisibility* of substance, a property it shares with the geometrical indivisibles advocated by Bonaventura Cavalieri and others as a foundation for the burgeoning proto-calculus methods of the seventeenth century, where the divisible line or surface is generated by the motion of an indivisible point or line. For Leibniz, who was already convinced that extended matter is not self-subsistent, but dependent on an incorporeal principle of motion, the inference must have appeared irresistible: continuous body too must be composed of indivisible substantial points, each containing within it an incorporeal principle of motion. And it seems that, whatever changes his concept of substance subsequently underwent, once Leibniz had worked out a theory of the continuum on this basis in the years 1670–71, the analogy between indivisible point and substance remained constitutive. But before examining this theory it may help to discuss Leibniz's views on the continuum from before 1670.

According to his later testimony, Leibniz first began to doubt the Scholastic philosophy he had learned in school as early as 1661, when, at the tender age of fifteen, he was in his first year of university in Leipzig.[17] Soon afterwards, he became completely enchanted with the new philosophy, particularly the atomist philosophy of Gassendi.[18] It is not known how deeply or accurately he understood Gassendi's position on the continuum, but the influence of at least two features he admits to adopting at that time are still discernible later on: first, obviously, Gassendi's rehabilitated atoms and void; and second, his (and Rodrigo de Arriaga's) doctrine that motion is not truly continuous, but interrupted by small intervals of rest (see Appendix 2e).[19] Also worth noting is the fact that Gassendi conceived his atoms as elements of matter that God has not only rendered indivisible, but also, as is often forgotten, endowed with active force. Thus, given the customary Aristotelian construal of substance as something which acts, they would have qualified as individual substances. This may have been relevant to Leibniz's original espousal of Gassendism; certainly, when he returned to atoms in 1676, he regarded them as indivisible only by virtue of a mind informing them, maintaining that "whatever acts cannot be destroyed" and that only minds could properly be said to be active. But exactly how Leibniz's early Gassendism became displaced is a very complex

matter, and I shall return to the question of his changing views on atoms below.

At any rate, by the time Leibniz left university in the late 1660s, he was firmly committed to finding a rapprochement between Aristotle and the moderns. Like his teachers Jacob Thomasius and Erhard Weigel, he maintained that an Aristotelian account of substance was not only compatible with the new mechanistic physics of Descartes, Galileo, Hobbes, and Gassendi, but essential for its proper foundation.[20] As Christia Mercer and R. C. Sleigh have argued,[21] his first explicit arguments for this were given in the course of a theological project he had undertaken in 1668 on behalf of Boineberg in Mainz, the *Catholic Demonstrations,* in which he sought to reconcile Catholicism and Protestantism by providing a metaphysics acceptable to both. Substance, he argues there, "is that which has a principle of action within itself" (A VI.i: 508; L 115). But every action of a body is a motion, since every action is a variation of essence, the essence of body is being in space, and variation of being in space is motion (A VI.i:508; L 111, 113, 115–16). Therefore a body can be substantial only if it contains within itself a principle of motion. But, Leibniz claims to have demonstrated in Part I of the *Demonstrations* (i.e. in the *Confession of Nature Against the Atheists* of 1668) that "no body has a principle of motion within itself apart from a concurrent mind" (A VI.i: 508; L 116). Thus the substance of body is union with a sustaining mind, this mind being the human mind for humans, and the universal mind (God) for all bodies lacking reason. Consequently, transubstantiation can be explained in terms of Christ's mind being substituted for the universal mind as the concurrent mind of the bread and wine.[22]

With this account of individual substance in place, Leibniz was confident that the compatibility of Aristotle with the new mechanical philosophy could be demonstrated; and although his construal of the nature and status of the minds of non-rational substances would undergo continual revision, the idea that mechanism requires a foundation in individual substances whose principle of activity is mind forms the starting point for all his further attempts on the continuum problem. The reconciliation project is very evident in the 1669 Letter to Thomasius (Appendix 1a) and the double fragment "On Primary Matter" of 1670–71 (Appendix 1d). If Aristotle's primary matter is identified with Descartes's subtle matter, then form may be reinterpreted as figure, the combination of matter and form giving figured matter, or determinate bodies. For primary matter and subtle matter alike are infinitely divisible and indeterminate; each lacks form and motion in itself, and acquires them only through motion. This, Leibniz explains, allows for a reconciliation between the continuity of primary/

extended matter insisted on by Aristotle and Descartes, and the discreteness of the inhomogeneous secondary matter appearing to the senses. For
"so long as matter is continuous, it is not cut into parts, and therefore does
not actually have boundaries in it"; actually existing matter, on the other
hand, has boundaries separating one part from another. As we shall see,
this essential distinction between primary matter as something indeterminate, and secondary matter as actually divided into determinate parts, i.e.
into bodies of various shapes and sizes, is basic to many later elucida-
tions.[23]

It is easy to see how this distinction works if secondary matter consists
of atoms separated by the void. But, Leibniz claims, the parts of secondary
matter may be regarded as discrete even if there is no void between them.
Here he invokes Aristotle's distinction between continuity and contiguity:
the parts of a thing whose adjacent extremities are together are *contiguous,*
i.e. merely touching; whereas those whose adjacent extremities are one
and the same boundary are *continuous* (see Appendix 2a). On this reading,
even the Cartesian *plenum* is discrete insofar as it is comprised of contiguous parts, notwithstanding the continuity of extension conceived prior to
any division.

Further, as Leibniz explains, this allows another major point of concili-
ation between Aristotle and the moderns to be brought to the fore: the constitutive role of motion. For according to Descartes, the differing parts of
extension are individuated by their differing motions. Thus without motion there would be no division into shapes or forms, and thus no individual corporeal substances. In the Cartesian philosophy, however, there is a
lack of resolution at this point, since the ontic status of motion is that of a
mere mode of matter. Already in his *Confession of Nature Against the
Atheists* of 1668, Leibniz had seized on this an opportunity for a proof of
divine existence, which follows by a version of Aristotle's Prime Mover
argument. For only *mobility* follows from the nature of a body as a being-
in-space, but not actual motion; and to say one body's motion is caused by
another's, and so on without end, is to give no reason for any body's motion. So bodies cannot have motion unless one assumes an incorporeal being, that is, God (L 111, 112). By the time of his April 1669 letter to
Thomasius, however, Leibniz claims to have a better argument,[24] one he
will return to in 1676. This is that a body only exists at each assignable instant of its motion, and is nothing in between. The cause or principle of its
motion must therefore be an incorporeal being that creates it at each assignable instant of its motion, i.e. motion depends on a continual creation
by God.[25]

Interestingly, when Leibniz published this letter early the following

year (1670) as an appendix to his preface for an edition of *De veris principiis* of Marius Nizolius, one of the few changes he made in the published version was to delete both references to the doctrine of continual re-creation. As Sleigh and Mercer have argued, this is a symptom of a crucial change in his philosophy of substance in that year. In the *Confessio* of 1668 Leibniz was already trying to parry the objection to his account of non-rational substance as a union of body with the divine mind—that it would imply "that there is one substantial form for all bodies, the concurrent divine mind" (A VI.i: 512; L 118). The reply he gives there is that "although the divine mind is the same, the concurrent divine mind is not." Instead there is a different concurrent mind specific to each body, which may be identified with the Platonic idea of that body. But the idea of a thing in the divine mind cannot be a cause of motion, so it is necessary for God to cause motion directly, as in the continuous creation account just described. As Mercer has argued in detail, however, this has the unfortunate consequence that the cause of motion does not follow from the essence of body. Thus motion is no more essential to body, or deducible from its nature, than it is in the Gassendist and Cartesian mechanical philosophies he is opposing.[26]

Things are otherwise, however, in Hobbes's philosophy, which Leibniz studied assiduously in the late 1660s and 1670, where the rigid Cartesian divide between wholly active mental substance and wholly passive matter is breached by the notion of *endeavours*. In Hobbes's scheme, these allow the elements of psychology to be cast in material form: all emotions, thoughts, and judgments are complexes of desires and aversions, these being nothing but endeavours towards and away from their object.[27] Leibniz appears to have been powerfully persuaded by this idea of the foundational role of endeavours. Unsurprisingly, though, given his project of basing bodies on minds, his interpretation of the significance of this is the inverse of Hobbes's. For if the figures and magnitudes of bodies depend on motion, as he believed he had proved, and motions are composed of endeavours, then all mechanical explanations are insufficient that are not ultimately founded on the mentalistic notion of endeavour.[28] Moreover, if he could show that endeavour is the essence of body, he would have solved the problems afflicting his theory of substance mentioned above; for at any given moment, the endeavour would simply be the principle of motion or "mind" of the body. But since endeavour cannot last in a body for more than a moment, the mind of a body is momentary, as opposed to true minds, which are able to sustain and compare endeavours. These considerations seem to have led him to his first explicit theory of the continuum, to which I now turn.

## 3. Leibniz's First Solution

Leibniz's first systematic account of the continuum appears in the *Theory of Abstract Motion* (hereafter TMA), which he presented to the French Académie des Sciences in 1671.[29] It is without doubt an eclectic account, an attempted synthesis of Hobbes's idiosyncratic definitions of "point" and "endeavour," Descartes's indefinitely divided matter, and Cavalieri's method of indivisibles, supported by an appeal to curvilinear infinitesimals and the Scholastic doctrine of "signs." The continuum, he says, has actually infinitely many parts; yet there are no minima or "things having no magnitude or part." But again, "there are indivisibles or unextended things, otherwise neither the beginning nor end of a body or motion is intelligible." Now even where this account has not been dismissed as plainly contradictory, it has usually been regarded as an embarrassing piece of juvenilia that Leibniz was happy to relinquish as soon as he had learnt some mathematics.[30] This is not the place to attempt a defense of the consistency of Leibniz's early theory. But it can be granted some measure of exoneration by pointing out how a number of its features survive his invention of the differential and integral calculus and continue more or less intact into his mature philosophy.

First, there is the doctrine of the actually infinite division of matter. This is upheld by Leibniz throughout his intellectual career, although his later argument for it (spelled out particularly clearly in Aiv266, "Created Things Are Actually Infinite") is independent of the theory of the continuum, narrowly conceived. But in 1670–71, the doctrine of "worlds within worlds to infinity" is held to be a consequence of continuity. Because of the infinite divisibility of the continuum, he says in the *Theory of Concrete Motion* (hereafter TMC) that it is certainly possible that smaller things will have proportionately the same qualities as larger ones, and so on to infinity, so that "there will be *worlds within worlds to infinity*" (see Appendix 1b). By this Leibniz appears to mean that the continuum is not only divisible into infinitely many parts, but consequently actually divided into them, so that every part contains further parts within it, right down to infinity.

Now this is, of course, a very heterodox interpretation of infinite divisibility, and a surprising one given Leibniz's desire to show the compatibility of Aristotle's philosophy with the moderns'. For Aristotle had explicitly denied that the infinite divisibility of the continuum entailed its composition out of indivisibles. Indeed, he had denied the actual infinite, so that, on the standard interpretation of his teaching, the infinitude of the parts of the continuum is a merely potential one.[31] Eventually, as we shall see, Leibniz will come around to an essentially Aristotelian construal of

continuity in terms of a potential for unlimited division, even while upholding the actual infinite.[32] But in 1671 he explicitly opposes the interpretation of the parts of the continuum as potential, and in the TMA he reveals his grounds for contradicting the Aristotelian view: *"There are
actually parts in the continuum, . . . and these are actually infinite,* for the
indefinite of Descartes is not in the thing, but the thinker." This alludes to
Descartes's argument in his *Principles of Philosophy,* on which I shall say
more below (in Section 6), according to which there must somewhere be
"a division of certain particles of matter to infinity," "a division of matter
into actually indefinite particles."[33]

Thus Descartes's "actually indefinite particles" are interpreted as infinitely small actuals. Here one might see the influence of Galileo, who
urged that the continuum is indeed infinitely divided into infinitely small
indivisibles (see Appendix 2b, EN 71–72). But Leibniz's actual parts are
not Euclidean points, or things having no parts. Unlike Galileo, who conceives his indivisibles as *parti non quante* (unquantified parts), Leibniz
conceives his as *quantities,* although ones smaller than any that can be assigned.[34] Their having quantity is crucial to the idea that they can be compared, so that, at a given instant, the endeavour (or instantaneous tendency
to move) of a faster motion may be greater than that of a slower motion;
and correspondingly, given the assumed equality of instants, that one point
may be greater than another. This notion of unassignable quantities that
are comparable to each other, although infinitely smaller than (and thus in-
comparable with) anything finite, is a second feature of the early theory
that remains intact in Leibniz's later thought. But it does not so much survive his invention of the calculus as spawn it: the unassignable lines and
times of Leibniz's early theory will metamorphose into the differentials of
his calculus. This continuity of conception can be seen most clearly in
Leibniz's characterization of a circle in terms of "an *infinitangular polygon*" that is not equal to a circle in magnitude, even though it has an equal
extension, the difference being "smaller than can be expressed by any
number," or "unassignable."[35]

This is not to say that this development takes place without any con-
comitant change in interpretation of the "unassignables"; far from it. In the
TMA they are constituent parts of the geometrical continuum, and, by extension, of reality itself (as is made explicit in the canceled fragment of "A
Demonstration of Incorporeal Substances" (Aiii3$_4$) given below).[36] Later,
of course, Leibniz will deny not only that anything actual can be continuous, but also that anything continuous can have actual (as opposed to
merely potential) parts. Yet even as he is developing this position, as we
shall see, Leibniz already comes to doubt that there are any infinitesimal

*fictions*

parts in reality. Indeed, his interpretation of infinitesimals as fictions is in place already in 1676, at the very time he is putting the finishing touches to the essential structures of the calculus itself. But in order to appreciate this contrast, a little more needs to be said about his earlier interpretation, as outlined in the TMA.

For there is a third feature of the early work that remains constant in these pages (again under an evolving interpretation): the denial of *minima* in the continuum. As mentioned above, this seems at first sight to be at odds with his upholding of *indivisibles;* for what else is a minimum but a last part that can be divided no further? Actually, Leibniz will soon cede precisely this point, but without ceding the essential distinction on which the theory of the TMA is based. In "On Minimum and Maximum; on Bodies and Minds" of 1672–73 (to be discussed further below), Leibniz no longer identifies indivisibles with the infinitely small things contained in the continuum (Aiii5: 98) but instead equates them with minima and rejects them (97). This does involve a shift in Leibniz's position, as we shall see. Yet the arguments for beginnings of motions and lines survive essentially intact in this later piece, indicating that the distinction between the infinitely small and true minima proposed in the TMA is not the result of mere terminological confusion. In fact Leibniz is explicit there about the difference. By a minimum he has in mind such an entity as an Euclidean point, "that which has no part, or has no magnitude." Hobbes had already criticized this definition, suggesting that a point be defined instead as "that whose magnitude is not considered"; it would then be undivided rather than properly indivisible (see Appendix 2d). But in the TMA Leibniz takes this a stage further. Rejecting Hobbes's redefinition of points in favor of his own construal of them as unextended quantities, he denies that there exist any Euclidean minima in the continuum at all. The argument he gives—that if there are any, "the whole [will have] as many minima as the part, which implies a contradiction"—is expanded upon in his later reflections. If there is one indivisible in a line, he says in Aiii5 (where indivisibles are identified with minima), "there will be indivisibles in it everywhere" (97); "if there are minimum parts in the continuum, it follows that the continuum is composed of them" (Aiii58: 470). But this is absurd, because there will be as many in the whole as in the part, as he demonstrates in Aiii5 and later papers by the example of the one-to-one correspondence between the points in a rectangle's side and those in its diagonal.

The latter objection, Leibniz believes, does not apply to his "unextended" points, nor to instants and endeavours. The diagonal and the side may contain the same number of points without being the same length because the points in question will be unequal. Following Hobbes, this in-

equality of points is justified in two ways. First there is the appeal to angles of contact, or "horn angles." Each of these, being the place of contact between a straight line and a circle, is a point, as are rectilinear angles. It will be greater or smaller in proportion to the radius of the circle, "and yet any rectilinear angle, however small, is greater than any angle of contact whatsoever" (Aiii5: 99).[37]

But Leibniz gives a second justification of the inequality of his unextended points in kinematic terms, and this argument is ultimately to prove the more significant one. Applied to the case above of the diagonal and side, it goes as follows. Suppose the two lines are generated by the motion of two points in the same time, with the faster-moving point generating the diagonal; in any finite subinterval of this time, the line segments generated will be in the same ratio as the side to the diagonal, and so, by hypothesis, will be the infinitesimal lengths traversed at the very beginning of the motion and interval.[38]

This, Leibniz claims, is "the basis of the Cavalierian Method"—again following Hobbes's lead in assimilating these unequal points with Cavalieri's indivisibles. But his claim is not as fanciful as might be assumed. One can of course dwell on the fact that Cavalieri studiously refrained from defining his indivisibles as infinitesimals, i.e. as the "lines and figures smaller than any that can be given" that Leibniz imputed to him. Yet what is crucial to the above kinematic argument is that the indivisibles be comparable, that the lines be generated by their motion, and that the indivisibles be in the same ratio to one another as the lines so generated. Leibniz is quite correct to see this as the basis of Cavalieri's method, where only indivisibles generated by the *transitus* or passage of the same *regula* may be compared.

Now part of the allure of this identification of "unextended points" with indivisibles, as mentioned above, is the promise of a connection with the theory of substance. "For I will demonstrate," Leibniz writes in "On the Necessity of Demonstrations for the Immortality of the Soul" of 1670(?), "that the Mind consists in a point, that cognition is endeavour or a minimum motion, that there can be several endeavours in the same thing simultaneously, but not several motions" (A II.i: 114). This immediately yields one of the main properties of mind in Leibniz's view, its indestructibility. For a point, being indivisible, cannot be destroyed: so "it will follow that mind can no more be destroyed than a point" (114). These considerations also enable him, so he believes, to render "the true distinction between bodies and minds, till now explained by no one" (Appendix 1c; A VI.ii: 266). For any two different endeavours in a body are immediately composed into a new one, and no endeavour can last longer than a moment

in a body without becoming a motion, as successive preceding endeavours compose a body's present motion. But in the mind endeavours can be conserved, and thus compared, and from this comparison pleasure and pain and all more complicated psychic states can arise.[39] Thus "thought consists in endeavour, as body consists in motion; . . . as body consists in a stretch of motions, so mind consists in a harmony of endeavours" (A II.i: 173).

Here we are offered two ways of conceiving mind: that it consists in a point, and that it consists in a harmony of endeavours. I do not think Leibniz saw any opposition between these characteristics, and there is a sense in which both remain, subtly transformed, characteristics of the simple substances of his later thought. In the *New System* of 1695, for example, simple substances (which are of course unextended) are described as "metaphysical points" and *"real and animated points"*; and these are characterized not only as involving an "original activity" (elsewhere described as monadic *conatus,* i.e. endeavour), but by the harmony among their states. But even in these early stages minds are not identified with spatial indivisibles: it is the dynamic aspect that is basic. This becomes even more pronounced when Leibniz decides against the existence of indivisibles in "On Minimum and Maximum" in 1672–73, a change of mind that is worth some commentary in its own right.

In the TMA Leibniz argues for "indivisibles or unextended things" with an ingenious inversion of Zeno's dichotomy argument against motion. He assumes that any body, space, motion, and time must have a beginning. He then takes a line representing any one of these, whose beginning is on the left, and proceeds to cut off half the line from the right side, which leaves the beginning intact. But so will any subsequent trimming of the line by a part to the right that is extended. "Therefore," he concludes, "the beginning of a body, space, motion, or time (namely, a point, an endeavour, or an instant) is either nothing, which is absurd, or is unextended, which was to be demonstrated" (A VI.ii: 264).

In "On Minimum and Maximum," however, the argument is given a different conclusion. If the subtraction is continued to infinity he argues there, "it follows that the beginning of the line, i.e. that which is traversed in the beginning of the motion, is infinitely small" (Aiii5: 99). This supports the argument that "there are in the continuum infinitely small things, that is, things smaller than any given sensible thing." But these infinitely small things cannot be indivisibles, Leibniz recognizes, since "every indivisible point can be understood as the . . . boundary of a line" (97), and then the above argument against indivisibles based on the side and diagonal would apply. Rather, they must be understood as infinitely small lines standing in the same proportion as the "beginnings" of different motions.

Thus the true beginning of a body implied by the dichotomy argument must be defined "as the beginning of motion itself, i.e. endeavour, since otherwise the beginning of the body would turn out to be an indivisible" (100). This means that there are no infinitesimals in space and time where there is no motion, and therefore that "there is no matter in body distinct from motion." "Hence," Leibniz concludes in a rapturous crescendo, "it is finally understood that *to be a body* is nothing other than *to move*." But motion depends for its definition on body, so what in the end are body and motion, Leibniz asks, if we are to avoid a vicious circle? "What else, but being sensed by some mind," a mind that is "immune from body, and different than all the others we sense" (100).

Does this then constitute a shift in Leibniz's view from having motion founded in individual minds back to its being founded in God directly? Leibniz does not seem to have firmly decided on this; both views remain in evidence in his writings of 1676. But the denial that there are infinitely small parts in space (and implicitly, time) independently of bodies and motion does appear to stand fast: witness Leibniz's remark to Malebranche in 1675: "it is necessary to maintain that the parts of the continuum exist only insofar as they are effectively determined by matter and motion." He also remains committed to the constitution of bodies by motion, explored further in "Certain Physical Propositions" of 1672 and in "On Matter, Motion, Minima, and the Continuum" of December 1675. This is how things appear to stand right up until the collapse of the endeavour theory of motion in 1676, as I shall argue below.

### 4. Continuity and Cohesion

One of the most important problems Leibniz thought he had illuminated with this theory of the continuum was the problem of *cohesion:* that is, the problem of what it is that holds the parts of a body together so that it forms a continuous (or possibly contiguous) whole. In the latter half of the seventeenth century this was very much an open problem, and by 1668 Leibniz had already identified it as a crucial one for the mechanical philosophy. Gassendi, Magnen, and others had revived the classical atomist explanation that the cohesion of macroscopic bodies is due to the tangling together of the constituent atoms, which hold onto each other "by hooks, crooks, ringlets, projections" and so forth (A VI.i N13: 492). Thus, Gassendi explained, although macroscopic bodies whose fissures are insensible may be called continuous, the only truly continuous wholes are atoms (Appendix 2e). Galileo had also adopted an ancient cause, speculating in his *Two New Sciences* that materials were held together by nature's horror of the vacuum. Just as a column of water of a certain height could be sustained by

the aversion to an external vacuum, so the greater cohesiveness of solids could be explained by positing indivisible gaps between the infinite indivisible parts (*non quante*) of a solid, which would hold them together by suction, or aversion to the vacuum within. In the wake of Torricelli, Pascal, and Boyle, however, most natural philosophers explained the column of water in terms of a balance and the weight of the air, rejecting the idea of nature's abhorrence of an external vacuum. Atom-and-plenum physicists like Huygens then applied the same sort of explanation to the apparent force of suction within, attributing the excess cohesion of solids to the pressure of a hypothesized subtle matter.[40]

But all such accounts, Leibniz objects, take for granted the cohesiveness of the ultimate particles themselves. Thus whatever the success of each one in accounting for the phenomena, it has done no more with respect to the origin of cohesion than push the problem down another level, opening up the prospect of an infinite regress. This becomes one of Leibniz's favorite arguments, repeated by him in the TMC of 1671 (A VI.ii: 250–51, 365), in "On the Cohesiveness of Bodies" (Aiii4: 96), in "Motion Is Something Relative" of 1677 (Aiv360), and in the Note on Firmness and Fluidity tucked into his *Specimen of Discoveries* of around 1686. "If we wish to derive cohesion from the pressure of the surroundings, as in the case of tablets," he says in the latter (Aiv312: 1628), "we are stuck, in that the firmness of the tablets needs to be established first. . . . To explain the fact that bodies cohere by pressure, one must first establish firmness in the parts." When he first advances the argument in his *Confession of Nature Against the Atheists* in 1668, he urges it as demonstrating the existence of God, in reasoning parallel to Aristotle's argument for the prime mover. Without recourse to such a cause lying outside the regress, he claims, no account could be given for the cohesion or firmness of the "ultimate corpuscles" composing matter: "Thus in providing a reason for atoms, it is right that we should have recourse to God, who is responsible for the firmness in these ultimate foundations of things. And I'm surprised that neither *Gassendi* nor anyone else among the very acute philosophers of our age has noticed this splendid occasion for demonstrating Divine Existence" (A VI.i N13: 492). But by 1670 Leibniz had found a way to explain this "primary cohesion" without recourse to God, as an immediate corollary to his neo-Hobbesian solution to the problem of the composition of the continuum.

Leibniz presents this account of cohesion as a demonstration from his definitions in the TMA, but the same explanation is given in the canceled draft of "A Demonstration of Incorporeal Substances" (Aiii3₄) as well as in "On the Cohesiveness of Bodies" (Aiii4), both written ca. fall 1672 and reproduced below. If one body impels another, i.e. endeavours to move it,

it has already begun to penetrate it. This is because at the moment of contact, the boundary point of the impinging body occupies a space that is not a minimum, but proportional to the body's endeavour to move. Therefore the two bodies overlap at the point of impact (albeit inassignably), and consequently share an extremum, it being a place smaller than any determinable by us. But, as Leibniz also explained in letters to Hobbes and Oldenburg in 1670, according to the Aristotelian definition of continuity (discussed above, and given in Appendix 2a), this means that the bodies in question are "not only contiguous but continuous, and truly one body, movable in one motion." Thus "whatever things move in such a way that one endeavours to enter the other's place, cohere together while the endeavour lasts."[41]

Whilst the Hobbesian provenance of this theory is clear, especially with respect to the central role of endeavours, it may well also have been inspired by the dynamic theory of chemical composition of Julius Caesar Scaliger (1484–1558), championed also by Daniel Sennert (on whom more below), both of whom Leibniz had read by this time. Where Aristotle had defined mixtion (*mistio,* or the forming of a chemical compound) simply as "the union of the miscibles," Scaliger defined it as "the motion of minimum bodies towards mutual contact so that a union is made."[42] In the same Exercise he comments: "Our particles not only lie close together like the atoms of Epicurus, but do so in such a manner that a continuous body which forms a unit results. It becomes one through the continuity of its limits, and is common to all that has entered into the composition."[43]

One curious feature of this neo-Aristotelian way of looking at continuity, however, is that in explaining the continuity (i.e. holding together) of two bodies, it appears to presuppose the unit or cohesion of the constituent bodies themselves. For Scaliger this is no great problem, since the constituent particles—atoms or natural minima—are assumed as primitive. But Leibniz, as we saw, is trying to explain this primary cohesiveness without presupposing it in the "ultimate particles" themselves. This suggests that the same analysis is intended to apply within each body also: just as two bodies are continuous at their mutual boundary because one is impelling the other there, so any two parts of a continuous body are continuous at their mutual boundary because one has an endeavour to enter the place of the other there. So a continuous body is one strung together, as it were, by a spatially continuous series of endeavours. (This I take to be the gist of Proposition 3 in Aiii3$_4$; at any rate, it fits with Leibniz's composition of the continuum out of points whose magnitudes are determined by "beginnings of motions," or endeavours.)

Even so, this dynamic composition is still only a foundation, rather than

a complete explanation of cohesion. For a momentary endeavour will only hold the parts of a body together momentarily, as it propagates across their mutual boundaries. In order for the parts of a body to cohere together continuously through time, there needs to be a continuous sequence of endeavours propagated across it, in other words, *a continuous motion.* Leibniz rejects what he takes to be Hobbes's solution—that the cohesiveness of bodies would arise as a reaction (directed inwards) to the centrifugal action (directed outwards) of a rotating body—on the grounds that this would be "a reaction without an impact."[44] Nevertheless, Leibniz's own preferred solution, like Hobbes's, involves circular motion. The cohesiveness of the solar and terrestrial globes, he argues, presupposes a motion, and his "New Physical Hypothesis" is that they each possess "a motion around their own center," resulting in a cohesion in lines parallel to the equator. He then further supposes that the perpendicular action of light rays from the sun falling upon the earth (assumed as originally homogeneous), when combined with this rotatory motion, produces *bullae* (bubbles) like those of a glassmaker.[45] These bubbles, like the earth itself, are spheres spinning around their own centers, and thus are again cohesive along lines parallel to their equators. They are what the earth is now composed of, and that "by which everything is made solid and holds together."

On his arrival in Paris, Leibniz expands on this account of cohesion in the *Certain Physical Propositions* (hereafter PQP), written in the spring and summer of 1672 and probably intended for publication. Here in Proposition 24 he offers an account of cohesion along the meridians of his terrellas (his collective name for the hollow bubbles and solid globules).[46] This is needed because "the motion of a body simply around its own center does not give it cohesion and, so to speak, arching [*fornicatio*—a Latin pun?], except in the equator and parallel circles, which will not at all impede one parallel from being broken away from another" (Aiii2: 32). The basic idea of Proposition 24 is that each interposition of a heterogeneous body in a circulating fluid will cause a disturbance. Leibniz then applies a principle of the minimization of disturbance to prove that the effect of a general motion along a meridian will be to attract the disturbing bodies in towards the circulating matter. Thus, having explained the primary cohesion of his bubbles and globules in these terms, Leibniz could now avail himself of the standard explanations of what he called "secondary cohesion" in terms of the pression of the atmosphere (TMC, § 59, A VI.ii: 250). In the parts added later to the PQP, he proceeds to use it in explaining the results of Boyle's and Huygens's experiments with polished marble tablets in the exhausted chamber of a "Torricellian Tube."[47]

It is not clear how long Leibniz maintained this particular theory of the

cohesion of bodies. He explicitly advances it in "On the Cohesiveness of
Bodies" of the fall of 1672(?), but by early 1676 the explanation of cohesion in terms of endeavours has been abandoned. As I discuss further below, in February of that year Leibniz advocates a form of atomism in
which the atoms are as genuinely indissectible as Gassendi's. He appears
very uncertain, however, of how these ultimate particles are held together,
typically attributing their connection to "motion or some mind." In his
"Notes on Science and Metaphysics" of 18 March he says he "has shown
satisfactorily elsewhere" that "since connection cannot be explained in
terms of matter and motion alone," it follows that thought enters into the
formation of a portion of matter, which "becomes a single and indissectible body or atom . . . whenever it has a single mind" (Aiii36: 393).
But he has written "Error" over his claim to have shown this satisfactorily.
A little less than a month later, however, he writes confidently that "the solidity, or unity, of a body is due to mind, . . . there are as many minds as
vortices, and as many vortices as solid bodies" (Aiii71:509).

One probable factor contributing to Leibniz's abandonment at this time
of explanations of cohesion in terms of endeavours is that his theory of
motion enters a crisis at the beginning of April 1676, precipitated by a new
understanding of endeavour itself. According to his "On Motion and Matter" written then, he has "demonstrated elsewhere very recently that endeavours are true motions, not infinitely small ones" (Aiii68: 492). But
this spells the dénouement of the theory outlined above, which depends
critically on the conception of endeavour as an infinitesimal motion, "the
beginning of action," and thus the beginning of entering a place, the latter
being a part of it smaller than any given part. For if there are no infinitesimal motions, the two bodies, impinging and impelled, will no longer have
such an infinitesimal part or physical point in common; instead, as Leibniz
writes in "On Motion and Matter," their states will be incompatible, "and
incompatibility does not admit of more or less" (Aiii68: 493).

This change in Leibniz's theory of motion is shown up very clearly by a
comparison of "On the Cohesiveness of Bodies" (1672?) with the dialogue *Pacidius Philalethi,* written in October/November 1676, where he
makes good on his promise to himself to tackle the problem of the continuity of motion. In the former, Leibniz defines endeavour as "the beginning of motion at a given moment." Thus it is "the beginning . . . of a transition from place to place, and therefore is in both places at once, since it
cannot be in neither, i.e. nowhere" (Aiii4: 95–96). In the *Pacidius,* by contrast, Leibniz has Charinus say of a body in instantaneous motion that "it
will either be nowhere or in two places, the one it leaves and the one it acquires, which is perhaps no less absurd than what you have shown, that it

simultaneously is and is not in some state" (Aiii78: 545). This absurdity can only be avoided, he claims with the approval of the other interlocutors, if the instantaneous state of motion is analyzed as being "the aggregate of two momentaneous existences in two neighboring places" (546). This is characteristic of the dialogue: the word *endeavour* does not occur anywhere in its forty-two-page treatment of the continuity of motion.

Still, this does not spell the end of the entire theory of cohesion Leibniz had erected on that basis. For the first consequence he had drawn from the endeavour theory was that one of the two bodies "cannot be impelled without the other,"[48] and this gradually becomes transformed from being a consequence of the endeavour theory into being the principle of cohesion itself. Thus in the canceled manuscript Aiii3$_4$ of 1672, where Leibniz is trying to put his theory on an axiomatic basis, Proposition 4 is "Cohering bodies are sympathetic." For "cohering bodies are co-moving, i.e. one cannot be impelled without the other. . . . Therefore it is necessary that cohering bodies sympathize" (Aiii3$_4$: 80).[49] In support of this construal of cohesion as motion in common, Leibniz points out in "On the Cohesiveness of Bodies" that "even liquids, when they are vigorously disturbed by some motion, imitate the nature of a solid as long as they have the disturbed motion in common" (Aiii4: 96). One can also see Leibniz applying a principle of minimization of disturbance in the case of meridial motion discussed above; this exploits the same principle of harmony of motion.

This conception is made explicit fourteen years later in *A Specimen of Discoveries,* where the terminology of the doctrine of sympathy that occurred in the earlier piece (and even the allusion to Hippocrates in support of it) is echoed: "The principle of cohesion is harmonizing motion (*motus conspirans*). . . . Even in particular disturbances there is a general harmony (*conspiratio*) in certain laws of the system of the universe. . . . The principle of cohesion brings it about that nature opposes disturbances" (Aiv312: 1630). These statements come after a long digression on firmness and fluidity interpolated in the *Specimen,* in which Leibniz appears to have been trying to attain clarity on their nature. In a marginal note there he even claims experimental corroboration for this view:

> That cohesion arises from motion insofar as it is harmonious, we have from two experiments: that of plaster when poured, which forms bubbles; and that of iron filings, which, when a magnet is moved towards them, turn into threads—to say nothing of vitrification. (Aiv312: 1627)

The harmony of motion principle is also evident in Aiv267 of c. 1678–79, where it is equated with the minimization of disturbance:

The cohesiveness of a body, i.e. the cohesion of its parts, arises from the fact that they are agitated with so little motion that they hardly separate at all, and since they are endowed with a motion by the whole surrounding system, they cannot be pulled apart without force, that is without some disturbance of the system. (Aiv267: 1400)

Thus by the end of the 1670s Leibniz is once again explaining cohesion in terms of motion. But by then he has ceased to believe that a harmony of motion is sufficient to explain the real unity of a body. His thought seems to have progressed from bodies held together by endeavours, to atoms held together by minds, to divisible bodies held together by harmony of motion, but whose unity comes from a principle analogous to a mind. In fact, though, there may be a greater continuity of thought in this progression than first appears. For according to his theories of 1670–72, mind itself is a "harmony of endeavours"; according to the atomist phase in 1676, atoms are held together "by motion or a kind of mind"; and according to the *Specimen* of 1686, it is not so much bodies as systems that are "to be derived from harmonious motion" (Aiv312: 1630). Thus whatever differences there are in his thinking about cohesion at these three distinct phases of his thought, the root idea seems to be the same in all three: that all accounts of cohesion presuppose unities that are irreducibly coherent, on pain of an infinite regress; and that this irreducible or natural cohesion is to be explained in terms of a harmony of motions or endeavours, which Leibniz takes to be equivalent to positing something quasimental in bodies. If this is right, it certainly casts an interesting light on the otherwise mystifying idea that "mind" could be responsible for the cohesion of atoms. At one end of this development of thought is the Hobbesian construal of the mental in terms of endeavour, recast by Leibniz as a harmony of endeavours; at the other is the idea of a principle of action within body that provides not only for its degree of cohesiveness but also for the elastic deformations of the body itself.[50]

Before taking a look at the latter, however, we need to consider why Leibniz's first reaction to the failure of his endeavour theory of cohesion should have been a return to atoms. What were the attractions of atomism for him?

## 5. Atoms and the Void

Of all the tangled threads Leibniz wove through the continuum, his line on atoms and the vacuum is perhaps the hardest to unravel. To begin with, as noted above, he is an ardent advocate of Gassendi's atoms; and his criticism in 1668 that the cohesion of such ultimate particles can only be ex-

plained by recourse to God is a qualification rather than a withdrawal of this advocacy. But when in his TMC of 1670–71 Leibniz finds an explanation for primary cohesion in terms of his "new physical hypothesis," it is not atoms but the insensible *bullae* that he postulates as the ultimate cohesive units, dismissing atoms as "naïve" and "too remote from experiment."[51] This rejection of atoms, moreover, accords with his position in the TMA, that there are no minima in space, time, body, or motion: the extended is always further divisible, and only unextended things are indivisible. And here, one might think, Leibniz would have let the matter rest.

Surprisingly, though, this is far from the end of atoms and the void in Leibniz's consideration. In a piece written shortly after the TMA and TMC, the *Hypothesis of the System of the World* (hereafter HSM), Leibniz explicitly proposes atoms and the vacuum as the sole constitutive principles of bodies; and he claims that a vacuum must be supposed between the "globes" or "worlds" of "On the Nature of Corporeal Things," written in the second half of 1671. In several of the papers written in the spring of 1676, moreover, as Parkinson notes in his introduction to *De Summa Rerum* (DSR xxxix), Leibniz argues for or presupposes atoms and void with varying degrees of commitment: in Aiii36 and 76 of March, and in Aiii68 and 74 of April. By contrast, in the *Pacidius Philalethi* of early November of that year, he denies atoms on essentially the same grounds as he will in his mature writings. Yet barely a month later, in *A Chain of Wonderful Demonstrations About the Universe,* one may still find him maintaining that atoms can be proved to exist.[52]

Actually, the problem is not just the incompatibility of Leibniz's expressed statements concerning atoms, but why he should be advocating atoms at all. For if we take atoms in the orthodox sense of Democritus, Epicurus, and Gassendi—strictly indivisible elements of a fixed shape and finite extension—then Leibniz's thesis that matter is actually infinitely divided *directly precludes them.* As we have seen, he came by the latter thesis at least as early as the TMA of 1670–71, and he was not slow to recognize its incompatibility with atoms. In the fragment "On Primary Matter" of the same period (Appendix 1d) he wrote: *"Matter is actually divided into infinite parts. There are infinitely many creatures in any body whatever. . . . There are no Atoms,* i.e. bodies whose parts never separate."

This accords with his rejection of atoms in favor of *bullae* in the TMC, as noted above. Yet Leibniz continued to make positive allusions to atoms in this period, even in the TMC itself. For instance, he claims there that the divisibility of the continuum to infinity entails that "any atom will be of infinite species, like a sort of world, and there will be *worlds within worlds to infinity"* (A VI.ii: 241). Here he clearly cannot mean "atom" in the strict

sense of indivisible extended body, since he is claiming that any such atom is divisible into further worlds to infinity.

One potential explanation is that what Leibniz means by "atoms" here, and in his other favorable references to them in the papers of this time, is the "indivisibles" of the TMA, the points that are the foundations of bodies. But I do not find this persuasive. Although some of Leibniz's points are infinitely smaller than others, they are the boundaries or beginnings of bodies rather than extended bodies themselves.[53] They are *unextended,* whereas Leibniz equates atoms with "worlds," bodies that are extended, even if insensibly small. This is why it is necessary for him to give an account of the cohesiveness of his atomlike "bullae" in the TMC, the "concrete" part of the HPN. If indivisibles were atoms this would be unnecessary. Moreover, atoms remain in the forefront of Leibniz's physical thought long after he has rejected indivisibles in his mathematics.

The answer I suggest is that Leibniz uses the word "atom" in more than one sense. Sometimes it refers to the classical atoms revived by Gassendi and Magnen,[54] but often, I propose, (as in the above quotation) Leibniz uses it to refer to the insensibly small, very hard particles he hypothesized in their place, such as the *bullae* of the HPN and the terrellas of the PQP. In support of this we may note a similar ambiguity in Hobbes's usage. Hobbes, of course, had argued that "there is no minimum divisible thing," and therefore that "there is no tininess of a body that is impossible"[55]— both theses that Leibniz himself embraced. Yet Hobbes freely alludes to atoms, by which he appears to mean finite but insensibly small particles of matter that are neither infinitely hard nor strictly indivisible.[56]

This is not as idiosyncratic as it may sound to us now. For we must remember that Gassendism was not the only source of atomism available to Hobbes and Leibniz. There was also a flourishing tradition of chemical atomism, which Leibniz had imbibed in his teens and twenties from the writings of his fellow Germans Daniel Sennert and Joachim Junguis.[57] The atoms of this tradition, although sharing many of the properties of classical atoms, such as insensible smallness and indestructibility through natural process, differed in many other respects. Sennert's atoms, for example, were insensible corpuscles inferred from such phenomena as sublimation, solution of metals in acids, and putrefaction. In order to explain these reactions, he supposed the atoms to have active powers: they were "'units of formation' or of 'action (ἐνεργεία)'" (Partington, op. cit., p. 273), rather than the homogeneous and infinitely hard atoms of the philosophical tradition. As mentioned in the previous section, Sennert explicitly approved and adopted Scaliger's dynamic theory of mixtion (chemical combination). On Jungius's view, similarly, atoms of bodies of the same

kind have a mutual appetite for each other, allowing for a more intimate cohesion than could arise from mere juxtaposition.[58]

This makes it quite plausible that Leibniz could have regarded his *bullae* as atoms in this non-standard sense (suitably modified to accord with mechanism). The description of their origin in the HPN is laced with chemical terms, and the account of their cohesion is certainly analogous to the Scaligerian theory of mixtion. Like Hobbes's atoms, they are very hard (but not everlasting) cohesive particles that are insensibly small and spin about their own axes. Leibniz does not hesitate to call them "seeds of things" (A VI.ii: 226), the same expression Democritus, Lucretius, and Magnen had used for their atoms.

Whether a similar explanation can be given for the atoms in the HSM is not so clear. The atoms hypothesized in that piece are described as spinning "globes," and, as we saw above, in the PQP of 1672 Leibniz distinguishes whirls that are "solid," the "globules," from those that are "hollow," the "bubbles" (*bullae*). Yet even while claiming that atomic bodies are the only "integral" bodies in the world, lacking a vacuum within, Leibniz notes that "it suffices for a body to be integral on the surface; for inside it is again composed of infinitely many globes, and new worlds can be contained in it without end." So once again we have the "worlds within worlds" thesis, seemingly precluding a Gassendian interpretation of the atoms. At any rate, it seems safe to say that, like other mechanists of the period who eschewed classical atoms, Leibniz nevertheless felt constrained to posit atomic bodies of a kind, these being very hard, but insensibly small, spinning corpuscles, which, although not strictly indivisible, are nevertheless impossible to divide by natural means.[59]

These considerations, however, do not appear adequate to explain Leibniz's espousal of atomism in 1676. For in the papers of that year we find him committed to atoms that are not just very small bodies, each associated with its own vortex, like the *terrellae* of his earlier work: they are strictly *indestructible* too. Now, instead of their cohesion being explained in terms of their spinning on their own axes, each atom is assumed single and *indissectible,* and creates its associated vortex by its motion in the fluid.[60] Thus the above considerations about Sennertian and Hobbesian atoms are not adequate to this case, and something more needs to be said about why Leibniz should have reverted to a quasi-Gassendism at this time.

One set of motivations appears to arise from the status of *minds* in bodies, the minds that Leibniz had declared to be the foundations of bodies in his papers of 1670–71. As we saw at the end of Section 3 above, the status of these minds had been thrown into some doubt by Leibniz's concluding in "On Minimum and Maximum" of 1672–73 that there are in fact no in-

divisibles in body, space, or time. Minds can therefore no longer be located in indivisible points, because there aren't any; what then is their relation to bodies? At the end of that paper he had opted for a theo-mechanist conclusion, in which the existence of bodies consists in their "being sensed by some mind," namely God's. But this sidesteps the issue of whether there are minds everywhere, or even somewhere, in bodies. In 1676, however, this issue seems to have come again to the forefront of Leibniz's thought. In "Secrets of the Sublime," written in February, he declares in passing that "all solids seem . . . to be informed with a mind of some kind" (Aiii60: 473), the argument being that without such a principle holding them together they would be dissipated by the action of the plenum. But by the same argument, if such an atom should once subsist, "it will always subsist," since otherwise it would have been dissipated long ago by the endeavours of the surrounding liquid plenum (473; cf. Aiii76: 525).

These reflections are complemented by a very interesting argument in some notes written the following month (Aiii36: 393). Suppose two separate portions of matter floating in a vacuum, each containing its own mind, collide and coalesce: what then happens to the minds they contain? If the minds coalesce, the memories of the two will be intermingled, "which probably cannot happen." If, however, a new mind is formed to go with the new body, then the old minds will have to perish, contrary to the eternity of minds Leibniz assumes axiomatically. But if minds are conserved every time bodies perish by coalescing, then "there will in fact be as many minds in any body as there are assignable points in it" since every whole can be divided into parts in the same way. But this "is impossible, since there is no number of points." Therefore the portion of matter containing a mind must be "solid and unbreakable," and "it follows that thought enters into the formation of this portion, and that, whatever its size, it becomes a body that is single and indissectible, i.e. an atom, whenever it has a single mind." Conversely, "from this we can easily understand why no mind can be dissolved naturally; for if it could, it would have been dissolved long ago, since the whole nature of things is perpetually striving to dissolve any mind" (393).

A further motivation for these claims is revealed later in both of these papers. In "Secrets" Leibniz follows the claim that "there are inumerable minds everywhere" with the gloss: "there are minds in the human ovum even before conception, and they do not perish, even if conception never follows"; in Aiii36 he refers to "recent experiments concerning the already preformed fetus" (394). Both remarks are instances of his growing commitment at this time to the doctrine of *preformation,* pioneered by Gassendi

and popularized by Marcello Malpighi. In opposition to epigenesis, which held that living things are generated from an essentially homogeneous matter by the action of some vital force, preformationists believed that all generation of plants and animals is from seeds, and "the seed contains the thing itself, but contains it as rudiments not yet unfolded."[61] Thus the heterogeneity and complexity of organic matter is original, and is simply unfolded or developed as the organism is formed. This requires that the souls (and in the case of humans, minds) of as yet ungenerated animals be incorporated in some insensibly small part in organic bodies. Accordingly, in the papers of this period we find Leibniz experimenting with the idea of bodies as accretions around minds.[62] In "On the Seat of the Soul" Leibniz speculates that our body is a "flower of substance" persisting perpetually through all changes, analogous to the bone called a *Luz* by the Rabbis (Aiii61: 478; DSR 32–33). And in the passages written in late April that I have titled "On Body, Space, and the Continuum," Leibniz declares: "There seem to be elements, i.e. indestructible bodies, precisely because there is a mind in them" (Aiii74: 521), and "Body is as incorruptible as mind, but the various organs around it are changed in various ways" (Aiii71: 510).

But even in these reflections one can see elements that will eventually undermine atomism. If a body is a kind of accretion of matter around a kernel containing a soul or mind, whose organs may change in certain ways, and if the mind may withdraw within itself before returning to sensation of external things,[63] then there is no necessity for an indestructible core of the self-same matter, maintaining the same shape, size and extension. The combination of soul and its body, Leibniz will conclude in the next few years, is a "substantial atom" or corporeal substance, in that the soul itself is indivisible.[64] But this does not entail that the associated matter is indivisible, as Leibniz points out in his critical remarks on Cordemoy;[65] and also, much later, in the *Monadology* (70–71): "every living body has a dominant entelechy, which in animals is the soul. . . . But this does not mean . . . that each soul has a quantity or portion of matter appropriated to it or attached to itself forever. . . . The soul, therefore, changes its body only gradually and by degrees."

Equally nuanced is Leibniz's attitude towards the vacuum in the 1670s. His basic position is that *omnia esse plena,* "everything is a plenum." But this is conditioned by two major qualifications. The first is that a plenum everywhere at rest is effectively equivalent to a vacuum. This equivalence was already acknowledged in the TMC,[66] but the argument for it is spelled out in "On Primary Matter" written the same year. For in a plenum of this kind, full of aether or subtle matter at rest, there would be no variety. But

"that in which there is no variety is not sensed," and "whatever is not sensed is nothing." Therefore *everything is a plenum,* since primary matter and space are the same" (Appendix 1d, A VI.ii: 280). By the same principle, the parts of real, secondary matter, must be distinguished by circular motions within it, since a linear motion of the whole would be indiscernible. This argument is dear to Leibniz, and he reformulates the "no variety" principle—with a crucial change of modality from "is not sensed" to "cannot be sensed"—in December 1675 as "to be is nothing other than to be capable of being perceived" (Aiii58: 466); and again in Hanover a few years later as his "Herculean argument": "all those things which are such that it is impossible for anyone to perceive whether they exist or not, are nothing" (Aiv316). Again, this cuts both ways. On the one hand, it means that explanations given in terms of a perfect fluid and in terms of a space are equivalent: "For example, it cannot be said whether a place is empty, or full of perfectly fluid matter; for there is no difference between the two cases" (Aiv277; cf. also Aiii58: 466). On the other, it functions as an argument for the heterogeneity of matter: it implies that insofar as matter is anything real, there is no portion of it, however small, that does not move with a motion different from an infinity of others.

A second argument qualifying the *omnia esse plena* doctrine occurs more than once in the papers of 1676, although again Leibniz had discovered it before arriving in Paris. This concerns the "interspersed vacuum," i.e. one scattered about in the interstices between bodies. Such a vacuum is not precluded even if one supposes the world to be composed of "spheres smaller than spheres to infinity, or posits spheres smaller than any given spheres whatever," Leibniz notes in a piece dating from spring–fall of 1671 (A VI.ii: 284). An explanation for this surprising claim is given by him in Aiii60 of February 1676: for such vacua could be "metaphysical" (i.e. true and real), even though smaller than any that could be assigned; and this would still be consistent with a "physical plenum," i.e. one in which any assignable place is full. Thus perfectly fluid matter could be a discrete multiplicity of "perfect points," i.e. "all the parts into which it could be divided," and yet differ from a continuous space by an unassignable quantity. This argument is reiterated in "On the Plenitude of the World" (Aiii76: 525), probably written within a month of Aiii60, where it is concluded that "all the vacuities collected into one do not have a greater ratio to any assignable space than the angle of contact has to the straight line."

But it is at about this time (March/April 1676) that Leibniz proves to his own satisfaction that the unassignable is not "something true and real," but rather nothing at all, and this argument collapses. To say that the difference between a true plenum and one with arbitrarily small interstitial voids is

"unassignable," is to say that there is no discernible difference, and therefore that they are identical, and that such voids do not exist. Thus in December 1676 we find him arguing that there is no such thing as the interspersed vacuum, even while maintaining that matter could be divided into points (Aiii85: 585; DSR 109). This is reinforced in February 1677, as Leibniz turns his "Herculean argument" against the vacuum itself, by means of an argument concerning relative motion. If there is a vacuum, motion must be possible in it; now motion must be relative to some body or other, but in a vacuum "there is nothing by which it could be distinguished; but whatever cannot be distinguished, not even by someone omniscient, is nothing"; therefore "there is no such thing as a vacuum" (Aiv360).

Naturally, given the equivalence of the vacuum and perfectly fluid matter, the same principle entails the unreality of the latter, the "subtle matter" of Descartes: "There is no such thing as a perfectly fluid body. There is no such thing as a vacuum. Descartes, having introduced his subtle matter, did away with the vacuum in name only," he wrote in 1678–79 (Aiv365: 1988). Thus what began as an argument for the epistemological underdetermination of the problem of the vacuum and the plenum is gradually transformed into an argument for the imaginary nature of the matter presupposed in the hypotheses of physics. In the early 1670s Leibniz had been content to argue that, given that atoms are insensible, any divisions in them will be beyond the power of our senses to detect. Thus a variety of hypotheses are possible, provided they save the phenomena with no sensible error. "For," as he says in the TMA, "sensation cannot discriminate whether some body is a continuous or contiguous unit, or a heap of many discontiguous ones separated by gaps" (A VI.ii: 246).[67] By the early 1680s, however, he would claim that "from the fact that different and contradictory hypotheses can be made about [matter and motion], all of which nevertheless satisfy the phenomena perfectly," it follows that they are "only phenomena, or contain in themselves something imaginary" (Aiv277). From this point on in his work, any appeal to atoms and the vacuum would therefore be merely heuristic. Thus we find him saying in his "Note on Firmness and Fluidity" of 1686, some years after his final abandonment of atoms, that

> Even if there is nothing in the universe of the utmost fluidity, nor of the utmost firmness, one may still imagine for purposes of clarification that everything consists of globules of any desired smallness and infinite firmness, and of a fluid running between them of infinite fluidity, just as in geometry we imagine lines that are infinite and infinitely small. (Aiv312: 1628)

But there are other considerations of great relevance to Leibniz's change of mind in 1676 concerning the status of atoms and perfect fluidity, and it is to these that we should now turn.

## 6. Actually Infinite Division and the Infinitely Small

Leibniz's theory of the continuum depends crucially on his interpretation of actually infinite division, and this in turn is intimately bound up with the Cartesian philosophy, most specifically with "the argument from motion in a plenum," by which Descartes had concluded that matter is actually indefinitely divided. This argument is implicitly referred to by Leibniz in his TMA of 1671, as we saw in Section 3 above. But it continues to occupy a central role in his thinking, serving as a kind of touchstone for the success of his attempts on the continuum problem, undergoing constant reinterpretation as his views on the infinite develop. Consequently, if we follow the thread of Leibniz's changing interpretations of the argument's implications, we gain a particularly clear perspective on the development of his thought about the continuum.

The argument was originally given by Descartes in his *Principles of Philosophy,* §§ 33–35; it was also featured prominently by Spinoza in his geometrical exposition of Descartes's *Principles,* which Leibniz might conceivably have read. It is reproduced in Appendix 2c below. As can be seen, it occurs in the context of Descartes's attempt to show that, contrary to the claims of Lucretius, motion can occur in a plenum. This can happen, Descartes argues, if matter moves in a circle, with each contiguous body in the ring moving simultaneously. Moreover, matter can circulate with differing rates through spaces of differing sizes, as he demonstrates by means of his example of matter flowing between two circles, one set off-center inside the other. Matter will be able to flow between the circular spaces, he argues, provided it moves proportionately faster through the narrower space between them.[68] But in order for this to occur, at least some part of this matter must "adapt its own shape to the innumerable measures of those [progressively narrower] spaces." In other words, Descartes explains, although there may be undivided corpuscles of solid matter (i.e. parts not changing their shape, but only their speed), the parts of matter between them must be such that each of their constituent particles is moving with a different motion. But this requires "that all the imaginable particles of this part of matter—which are in fact beyond number—be to some degree mutually displaced from each other; and such a displacement, however slight, is a genuine division."[69]

Granted, Descartes qualifies the baldness of this assertion of the actual "division of certain particles of matter to infinity" with the claim that how

it occurs is incomprehensible to our finite minds. It is, therefore, "indefinite": the division is "into so many parts that we can distinguish in thought none so minute that we do not understand it to be actually divided into parts still smaller." But right from the outset Leibniz will have no truck with the indefinite, which he dismisses in the TMA as "not in the thing, but the thinker." Instead of Descartes's "indefinite particles," for him the division issues in actually infinitesimal parts. These are "unassignable," smaller than can be expressed by a ratio to another sensible magnitude unless the ratio is infinite, smaller than any ratio that can be given." That is, they are the unequal *points* that constitute the beginnings of bodies, and are traversed by bodies with different endeavours in the same moment.

This interpretation of Descartes's "indefinite particles" as actual infinitesimals informed Leibniz's first theory of the continuum, explored in Section 3 above. As I explain there, Leibniz had initially identified these unassignable points as *indivisibles;* but even after rejecting indivisibles in the winter of 1672–73, he continued to uphold the existence of "things infinitely smaller than any given sensible thing" (Aiii5: 98). Meanwhile, as I explain in Sections 4 and 5, the minds that he had earlier supposed to be located in indivisibles reappear in the papers of his last year in Paris, each one now associated with an indestructible atom and an accompanying vortex.

Now it might be thought that Leibniz's return to atomism would entail his abandonment of Descartes's plenistic metaphysics, and with it the argument from motion in a plenum for the actually infinite division of matter. Curiously, though, it is more nearly the other way around: Leibniz repeatedly uses the argument from motion in a plenum as an argument *for* atoms. In fact, from the moment he reexamines Descartes's actual wording of it in the *Principles* in December 1675, the argument seems to gain in importance in his thinking. In his reading notes he objects as before to Descartes's description of the fluid matter as "indefinitely divided," insisting that it is "really divided by motion into parts that are smaller than any assignable, and therefore actually infinite" (Aiii15: 214). That is, each part will be excited by a motion that is different from all the others, and given Leibniz's principle that "cohering bodies are co-moving," the fluid will therefore lack any cohesion whatever: it will be a perfect liquid. But what of the solid corpuscles that Descartes had supposed could be contained in his circulating fluid? Leibniz now appears to hold that, given the action on them by the surrounding fluid and the fact that in his view every endeavour is efficacious (Aiii4: 95; Aiv267: 1400), no solid will be able to remain cohering unless it is assumed indissectible: "if there were no atoms, everything would be dissolved, given the plenum" (Aiii76: 525); "for the liquid

matter of the surrounding plenum will immediately endeavour to dissipate [each atom], since it disturbs its motion, as can easily be shown" (Aiii60: 473).

Thus Leibniz is led by his own principles to an ontology in which there are only perfect fluids and perfect solids. Moreover, Descartes's argument implies that a perfect fluid is composed of points: "It seems to follow from a solid in a liquid," he writes in "On the Secrets of the Sublime" in February 1676 (Aiii60: 473), "that a perfectly fluid matter is nothing but a multiplicity of infinitely many points, i.e. bodies smaller than any that can be assigned." But if these points are interpreted as "perfect" or "metaphysical" points, i.e. minima, this means that "a perfect fluid is not a continuum, but discrete, i.e. a multiplicity of points." This in turn seems to entail that all matter is discrete: "for even if it is assumed solid, then, insofar as matter exists when it ceases to have a cement—motion, for example, or something else—it will be reduced to a state of liquidity, or divisibility, from which it follows that it is composed of points. This I prove as follows: every perfect fluid is composed of points, since it can be dissolved into points, which I prove by the motion of a solid in it. Therefore," Leibniz concludes, "matter is a discrete entity, not a continuous one; it is only contiguous, and is united by motion or by a mind of some sort."

This constitutes a significant revision of Leibniz's thinking about the continuum. Matter is an infinite aggregate of discrete contiguous points, or minima. "But it does not therefore follow from this that a continuum is composed of points, since liquid matter will not be a true continuum, even though space is a true continuum," thus distinguishing space from matter. In fact, there are no minima in space and time (as he had demonstrated again as recently as December 1675, in "On Matter, Motion, Minima, and the Continuum"). Thus whereas before Leibniz had identified the points resulting from the actually infinite division of matter not as minima, but as unassignable points composing a continuum, now they are minima, but do not compose a true continuum. As before, however, the understanding of the infinitely small is decidedly non-finitist. Just as he had previously interpreted the "infinitely small things" in the continuum as "infinitely smaller than any given sensible thing" (Aiii5: 98), so the doctrine of worlds within worlds does not just mean an indefinite containment of one finite world within another, but a division into infinite points: "if it is true that any part of matter, however small, contains an infinity of creatures, i.e. is a world, it follows also that matter is actually divided into an infinity of points" (Aiii60: 474).

But this interpretation of infinite division is never more than tentative. Even as Leibniz is trying to follow out all its implications, he is hedging

his bets. In "Secrets of the Sublime" he expresses three doubts, all of which will provoke him to further reflection. First, he argues, matter's being actually divided into an infinity of points implies that "any part of matter will be commensurable with any other" (474). This being so, it seems the actual division of matter into points will stand or fall with the possibility of squaring the circle. Leibniz will take up this issue in the seminal paper "Infinite Numbers," as we shall discuss further below. Second, it implies that "an infinite whole is one" (474), and that there is such a thing as an infinite number, contrary to his proofs in "On Minimum and Maximum." Conversely, given the argument from motion in a plenum, if infinite number is impossible, then "it will follow that a liquid [i.e. a perfect liquid] is also impossible" (475). Third, and not least, is Leibniz's discomfort with the perfectly fluid and perfectly solid themselves. According to the Hobbesian principles that have underpinned his physics from the start, bodies cannot be infinitely solid or fluid, but instead come in every degree of consistency. Thus at the beginning of this piece, Leibniz wonders whether he can prove that his atoms "are at least flexible," and also whether there are "bodies that are neither solid nor fluid, but by their very nature intermediate between the two" (473). Later in the paper he picks up this lead, and gives the first hint of what will become a new understanding of infinite division, when he wonders whether a liquid might not have "a subdivision that is now greater, now less, in accordance with the various motions of a solid in it," a division which would not be a "perfect" one issuing in metaphysical points or minima (474).

At first, though, these doubts only encourage him to experiment further with infinitesimals. Perhaps, after all, the perfect division of a liquid is only into "mathematical points" or "Cavalierian indivisibles" (474). Perhaps there are real things that are "infinitely small, yet not indivisible" (475), on the model of the differentials of his calculus; for the consistency and success of the hypothesis of infinites and the infinitely small in geometry "increases the likelihood that they really exist" (475). Now just as a line $l$ can be the sum of an infinity of differentials $dl,$ so $dl$ can be represented as a sum of second order differentials $ddl.$ Accordingly, the doctrine of worlds within worlds to infinity may now be interpreted as involving an increasing order of infinites: just as our world is bounded, but infinitely bigger than such infinitesimals, so in turn ours could be imagined to be infinitely small in comparison to another world "that is of infinite magnitude, and yet bounded" (475). This, Leibniz concludes, shows that the true infinite, or *immensum,* is different from the *unbounded.*

In the months that follow, Leibniz will amplify this notion of the unbounded as a "lower" species of infinite. But already in "Secrets" it begins

to have effect. At the end of this paper (477), Leibniz returns to the question of infinite number, and immediately recapitulates his Galilean-inspired proof of its impossibility from "On Minimum and Maximum." He also argues that in a series of integers increasing by finite differences, such as $1 + 3 + 5 + 7 + \ldots$, "the last number will always be greater than the number of all numbers," again proving the impossibility of the latter. But in a note to himself, he stresses that "this proves only that such a series is unbounded" (477). Leibniz expands on this when he returns to the subject in the postscript to "Infinite Numbers" (Aiii69) written about 10 April. "In fact," he says there, "there is no last number of the series, since it is unbounded" (503). One final possibility might be to suggest that "there exists no last finite number that can be written in, although there can exist an infinite one" (504). But to this he responds that "not even this can exist, if there is no last number."

This conclusion that there is no last number in an infinite series, not even an infinite one, is very much in keeping with the new interpretation of the calculus that Leibniz develops at this time, and it is worth digressing a little here to explain the latter. In his first comprehensive treatise on the calculus, written between the fall of 1675 and the summer of 1676, Leibniz writes that his readers "will sense how much the field has been opened up when they correctly perceive this one thing, that every curvilinear figure is nothing but a polygon with an infinite number of sides, of an infinitely small magnitude."[70] These infinitely small sides, of course, are the differentials of his calculus, and according to this conception the length of any curve can now be represented as an infinite "sum" of such differentials (what we now call an integral, after Bernoulli's suggestion to Leibniz). Similarly, the area can be represented as an infinite sum of the products of each ordinate and a differential. Are these differentials then actual infinitesimals? In Aiii52, Leibniz sketches a proof that they cannot be. If a curvilinear figure such as the circle is approximated by an inscribed regular polygon of $n$ sides of length $s$, and its length $L$ (say) is calculated by adding the sides of the polygon, it can be proved that the error $L - ns$ will always be less than $s$ for any integer $n$. Therefore, as $n$ goes to infinity and the side becomes a differential, if the differential is assumed to be infinitely small, "the error will be smaller." But this is impossible; therefore the differential is not infinitely small, but nothing.[71]

But how then is the calculus to be understood? If the differential is "nothing" how can any of the results obtained by the calculus be either true or meaningful? How can a circle, for instance, be "a polygon with an infinite number of sides, of an infinitely small magnitude" if these sides are "nothings"? Leibniz's answer is forthright, clear, and profound: The

circle, as a polygon greater than any assignable, is a *fictitious entity.* Thus "when something is said about the circle," he writes, "we understand it to be true of any polygon such that there is some polygon in which the error is less than any assigned amount *a,* and another polygon in which the error is less than any other definite assigned amount *b.* However, there is no polygon in which the error is less than all assignable amounts *a* and *b* at the same time, even if it can be said that polygons somehow approach such an entity in order" (498). Thus the circle is a kind of ideal limit to a sequence of polygons. If there is a law to the sequence, so that, for instance, as *n* increases the area of the polygon approaches more and more nearly to $\pi r^2$, "our mind imagines some ultimate polygon; and whatever it sees becoming more and more so in the individual polygons, it declares to be perfectly so in this ultimate one" (498). Thus, to say that the unit circle has an area of $\pi$ is to say that one can find a rational approximation of $\pi$ to any prescribed degree of accuracy, but not that one can express $\pi$ as a ratio. This, Leibniz notes, accords with the fact that no rational quadrature of the circle had by then been discovered, although formulae had been found for giving approximations for $\pi$ to any desired degree of accuracy. A case in point is the expression Leibniz himself had already obtained for $\pi/4$ as the sum of the infinite alternating series (now known as Leibniz's Series): $1 - \frac{1}{3} + \frac{1}{5} - \frac{1}{7} + \frac{1}{9} - \ldots$ . One can obtain a rational approximation of $\pi$ to any desired degree of accuracy by truncating the series after a (suitably large) finite number of terms. Moreover, the absolute value of the remainder is always less than the last term; therefore, by the same logic as in Aiii52, if the last term is supposed infinitely small, the remainder is smaller.

Of course, the proposal that infinitesimals are nothings contradicts everything Leibniz had written in favor of actual infinitesimals earlier. So one might expect that he would have a stronger argument than the rather laconic proof sketched in Aiii52.[72] And if he had such a strong argument against actual infinitesimals, one would expect to see (at least) echoes of it elsewhere in Leibniz's rejection of the infinitely small. One possible candidate is his "Herculean argument," which we already encountered in Section 5 above. As Leibniz writes in "A Body Is Not a Substance," probably composed in the late 1670s, according to this argument "all those things which are such that it is impossible for anyone to perceive whether they exist or not, are nothing" (Aiv316). But since things that are infinitely small "cannot be perceived," this will put an end to all controversy over their existence. For an infinitesimal or differential is by definition a difference that is smaller than any that can be assigned or perceived. Therefore it is nothing. A second possible reason for his abandoning actual infinites-

imals, suggested by his discussion at the beginning of "On Matter and Motion," is the collapse of the endeavour theory of motion. If "endeavours are true motions, not infinitely small ones" (Aiii68: 492), then a continuous motion cannot be composed from them in the way he had earlier described. As I discuss below, this seems to have persuaded Leibniz to abandon the continuity of motion altogether, and with it the theory of unequal points defined in terms of infinitesimal motions.[73] If points cannot be distinguished by the infinitesimal motions of bodies, then all points will be true Euclidean minima, things whose parts are nothing. This could explain Leibniz's remark in Aiii69 that he has "already shown" that nothing is unassignable save a point in the sense of "that whose part is nothing, an extremum" (498).

But what of Leibniz's earlier positive arguments in favor of infinitesimals? In "On Minimum and Maximum" he had argued that an angle remains intact even when the lines subtending it become infinitely small, so that the space intercepted becomes "infinitely smaller than any sensible space, and is consequently a point" (Aiii5: 99). Consequently, he reasoned, there is quantity in a point, namely, the quantity of the angle (99). After reiterating this argument in "Infinite Numbers," he now raises two objections to it. First he argues that there will be no angle unless there are lines; but even if these lines are infinitely small, they are still lines, and so long as they are lines it will be possible to cut them back further (Aiii69: 498).[74] Second, "an angle is not the quantity of a point," since, as we have seen, he has "already shown" that the only points are Euclidean points or mere extrema, i.e. things lacking quantity (498). "Therefore the quantity of the angle will be nothing but the quantity of the proportion of the sine, which is the same however far you might produce it, so that the angle itself, it seems, is a fictitious entity" (498). That is, an angle conceived as remaining even when the sides are infinitely cut back, or as being what is subtended by lines that are smaller than any assignable, is a fictitious entity.

Returning to infinite series, Leibniz must now account for how it is that a series with no last term can nevertheless have a finite sum. Reasoning in the same way as he had about angles and circles, he is led to propose a definition of the sum of a converging infinite series that is essentially the same as that in terms of partial sums which can be found in today's calculus textbooks: "Whenever it is said that a certain infinite series of numbers has a sum, I am of the opinion that all that is being said is that any finite series with the same rule has a sum, and that the error always diminishes as the series increases, so that it becomes as small as we would like" (503).

Naturally, this new understanding of infinite series and unbounded lines as possessing no last element has implications for infinite division too, and

in a paper written a few days after "Infinite Numbers" we see Leibniz's first recognition of this: "if we were to suppose that any body whatever is actually resolved into smaller bodies—i.e. if it is supposed that there are always some worlds within others—would the body thereby be divided into minimum parts? Accordingly, being divided without end is different from being divided into minima, in that [in such an unending division] there will be no last part, just as in an unbounded line there is no last point" (Aiii71: 513). Thus Leibniz has finally cast off the ambiguity that had hitherto afflicted his understanding of actually infinite division.[75] As we saw above, as recently as February he had understood the "worlds within worlds" thesis as committing him to the actual division of matter into points or minima (Aiii60: 474). But now he realizes that there are no minima: the only unassignable is an extremum, such as the endpoint of a line (Aiii69: 498). Accordingly, there is no last world within all the other worlds, and no last part of an actually infinite division. As he writes in November: "There is no portion of matter which is not actually divided into further parts, so that there is no body so small that there is not a world of infinitary creatures in it. . . . This does not mean, however, either that a body or space is divided into points, or time into moments, because indivisibles are not parts, but the extrema of parts; which is why, even though all things are subdivided, they are still not resolved all the way down into minima" (Aiii78: 565–66).

This trend of thought culminates in the view put forward in the *Pacidius Philalethi,* or "First Philosophy of Motion," of November 1676, from which the latter quotation is taken. There Pacidius (speaking for Leibniz) proposes an inspired analogy to explain his new conception of the division of the continuum:

> If a perfectly fluid body is assumed, a finest division, i.e. a division into minima, cannot be denied; however, even a body that is everywhere flexible, but not without a certain and everywhere unequal resistance, still has cohering parts, although these are opened up and folded together in various ways. Accordingly, the division of the continuum must not be considered to be like the division of sand into grains, but like that of a sheet of paper or tunic into folds. And so although there occur some folds smaller than others infinite in number, a body is never thereby dissolved into points, i.e. minima. On the contrary, every liquid has some tenacity, so that although it is torn into parts, not all the parts of the parts are so torn in their turn; instead they merely take shape for some time, and are transformed; and yet in this way there is no dissolution all the way down into points,

even though any point is distinguished from any other by its motion. (Aiii78: 555)

The parts of matter, on this view, are all inherently elastic. This is not in itself a new idea for Leibniz. It was forcefully promoted in the HPN, and he continued to find it attractive in Paris in 1676, even while promoting atoms (Aiii60: 473, 474).[76] But here it is combined with the new conception of an unending division into a dynamic conception of the continuum: at each instant the parts of matter are individuated by their own proper motions, but over time each part may maintain its shape or be transformed. Thus there is one infinite partition at one moment, another at the next, like a sheet of paper undergoing successive infinite enfoldings and refoldings. These infinite partitions could be conceived on the model of a converging infinite series, such as Zeno's series, $\frac{1}{2} + \frac{1}{4} + \frac{1}{8} + \ldots$, or on the model of a continued fraction. The image of the fold of matter (*plica materiae*), on the other hand, may well be of Baconian origin. Leibniz proposes it as a middle ground between the "perfectly solid body" of Gassendi and the "perfectly fluid body" of Descartes (Aiii78: 554). Similarly, in his *History of the Dense and Rare* (1658), Francis Bacon had written: "Between the bounds of denseness and rarity there is a fold of matter, through which matter folds and unfolds itself without creating a vacuum."[77] But if Bacon provides any further development of this conception beyond the aphorism itself, I have been unable to find it.

There is, however, a difficulty with this conception of infinite division. This is to see how, if "any point is distinguished from any other by its motion," matter is not after all divided into points. Leibniz appears to want it both ways: to have each part of matter infinitely subdivided by the differing motions within it, and yet to have "not all the parts of the parts so torn in their turn," but for them instead "merely [to] take shape for a time, and [be] transformed."[78]

A partial resolution of this difficulty can be found, I believe, in the notion of a "part of matter" itself. On the Cartesian view, a part is individuated by its own proper motion. Nevertheless, that does not rule out there being other differing motions within. As Descartes writes in his *Principles:* "By a 'body' or a 'part of matter' I understand everything that is transferred together, even though this may consist of many parts which have different motions relative to one another" (*Principles* II, §25; AT VIII.1 53–54). Leibniz's early theory of cohesion had given the same result: according to Proposition 14 of his PQP of 1672–73,

It is manifest that a body is constituted as definite, one, particular, distinct from others, by a certain motion or particular endeavour of its

own, and if it is lacking this it will not be a separate body, but [there will be] one continuous body cohering with it by whose motion alone it is moved. And this is what I have said elsewhere, that cohesion comes from endeavour or motion, that those things that move with one motion should be understood to cohere with one another. (Aiii2: 28)

As we have seen, the status of this theory of cohesion entered a kind of limbo in the spring of 1676, when Leibniz was toying with the idea that solids were instead united by a kind of mind. The "folds of matter" theory promoted here therefore seems to mark a return to the earlier view. Just as Leibniz had conceived the worlds or globules of his earlier papers as moving with one (rotatory) motion, and yet having a variety of motions inside, so here the parts of matter or bodies are those moving with a common motion, each containing a variety of motions within. In each case, it is the internal motions that account for the elasticity of the body, and thus its tenacity or cohesion. But the tenacity or cohesion is a matter of degree. As Leibniz explains in "On the Present World," every assignable point in the world is agitated somewhat differently from any other point however near to it, but on the other hand "no point can be assigned that does not have some motion in common with some other given point; under the former head, all bodies are fluid; under the latter, all are cohering. But to the extent that a common or proper motion is more or less observable, a body is called one solid, or a separate body, or perhaps even a fluid" (Aiv301: 1511).

Thus there is a sense in which, despite the discreteness of the parts into which matter is actually divided by its internal motions, "the parts of any body constitute one continuum," as Leibniz explains in "Metaphysical Definitions and Reflections" (Aiv267: 1401): "For a unity always lasts as long as it can without destroying multiplicity, and this happens if bodies are understood to be folded rather than divided." But this does not so much resolve the problem of how bodies constitute unities, as highlight it. For this conception of a body remaining one whilst folding and unfolding into multiple parts demands some account of the *unity* of body that can accommodate this multiplicity, and this the theory of cohesion is plainly unable to provide. What Leibniz needs is some principle internal to body that governs these divisions and motions. Matter, according to his formulations after 1678, is "the principle of passion," that is, the principle in each thing that governs how it is acted upon. Now all passion is by division; but unless there is some law followed by the divisions, internal to the body, there is nothing in it to make it one. "Anyone seeking the primary sources

of things," he writes, "must investigate how matter is divided into parts, and which of them is moving" (Aiv267: 1401). Leibniz's early efforts are well represented by Aiii58 and Aiii68, where he struggles to derive the conservation of motion from that of matter. But by the time he pens Aiv267 from about 1678 to 1680 he has discovered that the key to a body's being one despite the multiplicity of its divisions is the conservation, not of quantity of motion, but of power. According to his investigations, he writes, "A unity must always be joined to a multiplicity to the extent that it may. So I say that matter is divided not even into parts of equal bulk, as some have supposed, nor into parts of equal speed, but into parts of equal power, but with bulk and speed unequal in such a way that the speeds are in inverse ratios to the magnitudes" (1401).

Now the question of how there can be unities in matter despite the infinite diversity resulting from internal motions is a deep and complex one, which I cannot do justice to here. It is closely connected in Leibniz's mind with the need to revive the idea of substantial forms, or souls. For, as he says in connection with the multiplicity-in-unity principle quoted above, "Whoever understands this proposition well enough will laugh at the vain questions concerning the seat of the soul" (1401). But the reintroduction of substantial forms turns on Leibniz's arguments for the need to recognize immaterial "principles of unity" in matter, which is the subject of the next section.

## 7. Infinite Aggregates: Body, Space, and Substance

Leibniz's newfound interpretation of the continuum has profound implications not only for his understanding of matter, but for his whole metaphysics. From its inception in his "Paris spring" of 1676 and throughout most of the decade following, he devotes much effort to elaborating a theory of substance that can accommodate it. Some of his arguments are premised directly on his new conception of actually infinite division; but there is also a more subtle and profound line of argument drawn from his new analysis of continuous quantities, and the implications of this for the nature of magnitude and wholeness in general. As we unravel these threads in this section, the relevance of some of Leibniz's own remarks about the relevance of the continuum problem to the forming of his mature philosophy should begin to become apparent.

Concerning the actually infinite division of matter, three considerations seem particularly pertinent. First, there is the infinitude of the division itself. Given Leibniz's rejection of infinite (cardinal) number, this implies that there is no assignable number of parts. If every body or part of matter is further divided, then no body can be considered a completed collection

of its parts. Second, since the division is without a lower bound—i.e. there are no minima and no atoms—every body is an aggregate of parts that are themselves bodies. Thus every part is an aggregate, but no part is a unit, because what is divided is not truly one. Consequently, matter has a merely accidental unity. Third, because the divisions of matter are determined by the instantaneous motions of its parts, and because these are constantly changing due to the actions of the plenum, no part will remain exactly the same for longer than a moment, and the aggregate of parts will change from one instant to another. So matter has a merely accidental unity through time as well; and the same applies to universal space, or the aggregate of places. Therefore, Leibniz concludes, insofar as any given body has a real unity, whatever is responsible for this unity in space and self-identity and continuity through time must be something nonmaterial. Otherwise put, if body were merely material—if it consisted solely in extension or bulk, whose defining properties are magnitude, shape, and motion—this would be insufficient to constitute it as a true unity or substance, and it would be a mere phenomenon. As we shall see, this conclusion is then reinforced by arguments to the effect that magnitude, shape, and motion all "involve something imaginary."

The first line of reasoning can be seen at the close of the paper "Infinite Numbers," where, as noted above, Leibniz had concluded that there is no such thing as an infinite number. But this means an infinite aggregate cannot be considered one whole. For suppose an unbounded line is divided into parts, and to each point of division is assigned a number exceeding the previous one by unity. Then "the number of terms will be the last number of the series"; but there is no such number. Therefore, Leibniz concludes, either "there is no infinite multiplicity," in which case there will only be a finite number of things in the universe, in agreement with Aristotle—a conclusion that Leibniz is not inclined to embrace—or "it must be said that an infinity of things is not one whole, or that there is no aggregate of them" (Aiii69: 503).

Here we see the origins of Leibniz's distinctive interpretation of the actual infinite, which he upholds from here on. According to this subtle position, although there is no infinite number, there is nevertheless an actual infinity of created things. That is, things have a multiplicity exceeding all numbers, but the infinity in question is a distributive infinite, not a collective one.[79] There is no such thing as an infinite aggregate in the sense of a completed collection. As he writes to Bernoulli in 1699: "I concede the infinite multiplicity of terms, but this multiplicity does not constitute a number or a single whole. It signifies only that there are more terms than can be designated by a number. Just so, there is a multiplicity or complex

of all numbers, but this multiplicity is not a number or a single whole"
(GM.iii.575). Thus to say that there is an actual infinity of things in the
universe is to say that no matter how large a number one takes, the number
of things in the universe is greater.[80] Likewise, the number of material
parts (or bodies) in any body is greater than any given number. In "Created
Things Are Actually Infinite," Leibniz lays out the argument for this explicitly: "any body whatever is actually divided into several parts, since
any body whatever is acted upon by other bodies. And any part whatever
of a body is a body, by the very definition of body. So bodies are actually
infinite, i.e. more bodies can be found than there are unities in any given
number" (Aiv266). From this he concludes, as early as 1680, that "unless
there were a soul, i.e. a kind of form, a body would not be an entity, since
no part of it can be assigned which would not again consist of further parts,
and so nothing could be assigned in body which could be called *this something, or some one thing*" (Aiv365: 1988). This illustrates the second line
of argument against purely material wholes referred to above.

Leibniz's third line of argument—that a body will not be self-identical
through time because of the continuous changes it undergoes—is also alluded to in the paper "Infinite Numbers" (Aiii69) of 1676. There, at the
end of a long argument concerning incommensurability and the nature of
magnitude (to which we shall return below), he concludes that "a whole
exists when many things can come to be out of one. But to come to be out
of one is to remain something" (503). Matter, however, insofar as it is an
aggregate of parts defined by their individual motions, does not remain the
same thing. As he had written on 18 March: "it can easily be demonstrated
that matter itself is perpetually being extinguished, i.e. becomes one thing
after another" (Aiii36: 391). And the same applies to space, considered as
the totality of places, since its parts too are only individuated by the motions of the matter contained in it. For "so long as it is divided by bodies
into empty and full parts of various shapes, it follows that space itself is a
whole or entity accidentally, that it is continuously changing and becoming something different: namely, when its parts change, and are extinguished and supplanted by others" (391).

Let us pursue this argument as it applies to space first. Because of this
continual changing of its parts, Leibniz argues, there must exist something
in space which remains through these changes, otherwise it could not be
called the same space. In his notes of 18 March Leibniz explicitly identifies this something as "the immensity of God, namely, an attribute that is
one and indivisible, and at the same time immense" (Aiii36: 391). Ex-
panding on this a month or so later, Leibniz dubs it "the immensum," and
identifies it with "that which is extended in itself," which has modes but no

parts: "Space, by the very fact that it is divided into parts, is changeable, and variously dissected; indeed, it is continuously one thing after another. But the basis of space, the extended per se, is indivisible, and remains during changes; it does not change, since it pervades everything. . . . [I]t is the immensum which persists during continuous change of space" (Aiii74: 519). Places are not parts of it, but modifications of it arising from the addition of matter, i.e. "bulk, or mass." When this is added, "there result spaces, places, and intervals, whose aggregates give Universal Space" (519). Thus universal space is the aggregate of places, as the Republic of Minds is the aggregate of individual minds,[81] and the divine mind is to ours as the immensum, or "real space," is to universal space (519).

Now it might be thought that this commitment to "real space" is something that would evaporate as soon as Leibniz had formulated his relational theories of space and time, where space is the order of situations, and time the order of successives. In this regard, it is very interesting to compare Aiii74 with Aiv321. The latter is a piece from the late 1680s which begins by taking for granted the relational theory, time and space being "real relations, or orders of existing." As real relations, however, they must have a foundation in reality,[82] and Leibniz declares, just as he had in the paper of 1676, that this foundation of time and space is divine magnitude, that is, eternity and immensity, respectively.[83] Just as before, too, immensity or real space is characterized as "one, indivisible, immutable": it is only divided into parts by the addition of something substantial. Only now what has to be added is not matter directly, but endeavour, equated with appetite: when this is added to space, "it makes existing substances, and thus matter, i.e. the aggregate of infinite unities" (Aiv321). Space, considered in itself, "contains not only existences but possibilities"; it is only a particular order of existing things when it has been divided by the motions or endeavours within it.[84] This anticipates statements of Leibniz's mature position, such as in his *Remarques sur les objections de M. Foucher* (G.iv.490), and the letter to Pierre Bayle of 1702.[85]

Returning to Leibniz's reflections of March and April 1676 on the need for a "basis of space," we see him drawing analogous conclusions about matter. If universal space is an accidental entity rather than an eternal being because it continually changes, then so too is matter, which "is perpetually becoming one thing after another" (Aiii36: 392). But just as the immensum persists through the changing forms of space, so, analogously, there is something divine and eternal in body which is "not subject to variation like the forms of bodies," namely, God's omnipotence (392). Of course, even if every body must contain such an eternal component, not every body is eternal. In particular, there is nothing eternal about aggre-

gated bodies, which, like place and shape, can be destroyed. This, Leibniz argues, is because "whatever is acted upon and does not act can be destroyed." On the other hand, "whatever acts cannot be destroyed, for it at least endures as long as it acts, and therefore it will endure forever" (Aiii74: 521). What, then, does Leibniz conceive as acting and enduring forever? The context reveals that he means *minds*. "There seem to be elements or indestructible bodies [i.e. atoms]," he argues, "because there is a mind in them" (521). Similarly, in Aiii69 Leibniz explicitly argues that what endures through material changes need not be matter, but "can be mind itself, understanding a certain relation" (503). In short, without minds in bodies there would be no atoms, and therefore nothing indestructible in matter.

But according to this logic, one is not compelled to posit atoms: for so long as there are minds in bodies, there is something indestructible, even if bodies, considered as merely material, are just entities by aggregation, and thus not eternally enduring wholes. In the spring of 1676 Leibniz is committed to the idea that a corporeal unity must be a "perfect solid": the atom is held together "by motion or a kind of mind" as by a "cement." Thus since the mind is eternal and indestructible, the atom is too, and there are as many minds as there are perfect solids. Absent the mind from one of these solids, however, and it will immediately begin to disintegrate as a result of the actions of the surrounding plenum. In fact, there is nothing to prevent this disintegration anywhere, so that the atom's matter would dissolve all the way down into points, the infinity-dust of a perfect fluid.

Once Leibniz abandons the ontology of perfect solids and perfect fluids, however, another option opens up. If matter has varying degrees of resistance to division, a given body can respond to the actions of the plenum by differing internal divisions, manifested as elasticity. And once he has discovered the conservation of force (*vis viva*) in 1678, the unity of the body through such changes can be ascribed to a force within. These are the necessary ingredients for Leibniz's rehabilitation of substantial forms in about 1679. The forms, identified with the primitive active forces manifesting themselves as *vis viva,* perform the same functions that the minds in bodies did previously. They are eternally existing organizing principles of matter, responsible for the differing divisions of matter from one instant to another. Every body is either a real entity united by such a substantial form, or an aggregate of such entities, just as previously every body was either an atom united by a mind, or an aggregate of atoms. The difference is that it is not necessarily the same matter that is united by the substantial form from one moment to the next, so that now Leibniz is free to reject atoms. Every soul is immortal, and every soul is embodied, but not in a

portion of matter that is itself indestructible. The soul together with its current body is a corporeal substance, and these substantial atoms, just like Leibniz's erstwhile mind-containing atoms, participate in divine omniscience and omnipotence. And each corporeal substance, like each of the minds in the spring of 1676, is "confusedly omniscient": "omniscient" because it is acted on by every other body in the universe (it "senses all endeavours, and receives them through its own body" (Aiii36: 393)), "confusedly," because it receives these endeavours all composed (or "fused together") into one resultant endeavour. It is also "diffusedly omnipotent": "omnipotent" because it acts on all others, "diffusedly" because "its action is diffused by things acting in contrary ways" (Aiv267, Aiv279). But confusion of perceptions and diffusion of actions are matters of degree. Thus everything perceives and acts to some extent: there are no purely disembodied intelligences save God, and likewise there are no purely passive bodies: all sense and act, and are thus organic. But from this it follows that there cannot be atoms. For in order to sense, a body must be capable of being acted upon. But all cases of being acted upon are by division, and atoms are in principle indivisible.[86] But "it is absurd for there to be a body which cannot be acted upon or have sensation" (Aiv267: 1399). Thus "every body is organic, i.e. is actually divided into smaller parts endowed with their own particular motions, so that there are no atoms" (1398).

So the very reasons that had led Leibniz to introduce atoms, now, under his revised interpretation of actually infinite division, ineluctably lead to their rejection. The mind-analogs within every part of matter do not require an atomic casing, but, on the contrary, one that is quintessentially plastic. They need to be contained in an organic body that is capable of responding to every action upon it by undergoing different internal subdivisions and foldings. Consequently "there are no atoms, but every part again has parts actually divided from each other and excited by different motions, or what follows from this, every body however small has actually infinite parts, and in every grain of powder there is a world of innumerable creatures" (Aiv312: 1623).

Thus the argument from the difficulties of the continuum plays a crucial and constitutive role in leading Leibniz to his new theory of substance. It is encapsulated well in the following passage:

> I shall demonstrate that if we consider bulk as a substance, we will fall into contradiction as a result of the labyrinth of the continuum. In this context we must above all consider: first, that there cannot be atoms, since they conflict with divine wisdom; and second, that bodies are really divided into infinite parts, but not into points. Conse-

quently, there is no way one can designate one body, rather, any portion of matter whatever is an accidental entity, and, indeed, is in perpetual flux. (Aiv316)

To recapitulate: if matter consists only in bulk, then there is no unit of matter, but only an infinite regress of parts within parts, with no undivided wholes. Again, if matter consists only in bulk, then each of these parts will be ephemeral: the parts out of which it is in turn constituted last only for an instant, due to the changing motions that define them.

It is worth stressing the hypothetical character of this argument. For some commentators have seen Leibniz's claims that "Matter and motion are only phenomena" and that "Body is not a substance, but only a mode of being or coherent appearance" as indicating a commitment to phenomenalism at this time. Robert Merrihew Adams, in particular, has used this to argue that the fragment with the latter statement as title must have been written prior to Leibniz's revival of substantial forms in 1679.[87] But Leibniz is at pains to point out there that his conclusions only apply to body in the sense of what the "Democriteans elsewhere call bulk," not to body composed of "matter and a certain intelligible form" (Aiv316). Thus the logic of this fragment (and, I would argue, of Aiv277) is all of a piece with the reasoning he presents in manuscripts written after he has introduced substantial forms; indeed, it is part of the argument *for* introducing them! An example is this passage from Aiv267 (ca. 1678–80), where Leibniz justifies his assertion that "Substantial form or soul is the principle of unity and of duration, matter is that of multiplicity and change" in the following words:

> For since we have said that body is actually divided into parts, each of which is agitated with a different motion, and since for the same reason each part is again divided, then certainly if we consider matter alone, no point will be assignable that will remain together with another, nor a moment at which a body will remain identical with itself; and there will never be a reason for saying that a body is a unity over and above a point, and the same for longer than a moment. And since points and moments themselves are not things, but bounds, i.e., modes, of things, it follows that if there were only matter in body, there would be no reality or perfection in it. But if there were only form in body, there would be nothing changeable and imperfect in it. (Aiv267: 1399)

Here the asserted consequences are contrary to fact. Leibniz does not believe that matter does in fact evaporate into "a powder of points," nor does

he believe that there is no unity that lasts longer than a moment. The argument is a *modus tollens,* and the conclusion is that matter—contrary to the opinions of the Cartesians and Gassendists—does *not* consist only in bulk, that there must be something in body apart from extension, motion, shape, and magnitude. That is, unless one accepts that there is some other principle accounting for unity and duration in matter, then as a result of the labyrinth, matter—and space too—will be reduced to a powder of points, each lasting no longer than a moment. Body will have no spatial or temporal unity beyond that supplied by a perceiving mind and will therefore be merely phenomenal.

Complementing these considerations about the inadequacy of the usual conception of body, Leibniz also offers critiques of two other defining properties of the material, motion and shape. His argument for the phenomenality of motion will occupy us in the next section, where we will also consider the ramifications of the discontinuity of motion for his conception of mathematical figure. But Leibniz also derives the phenomenality of shape as a direct corollary of infinite division. "There is no precise and fixed shape in bodies," he writes in a piece in 1686, "because of the actual division of the parts to infinity." For although one can draw an imaginary line at each instant, "that line will endure in the same parts only for this instant, because each part has a motion different from every other. . . . Thus there is no body that has any shape for a definite time, however short it might be" (Aiv310). This argument recurs in *A Specimen of Discoveries* of the same year: "from the fact that no body is so very small that it is not actually divided into parts excited by different motions, it follows that no determinate shape can be assigned to any body, nor is a precisely straight line, or circle or any other assignable shape of any body, found in the nature of things" (Aiv312: 1622). Consequently "shape involves something imaginary, and no other sword can sever the knots we tie for ourselves by misunderstanding the composition of the continuum" (1622).

All this, of course, is premised on Leibniz's thesis of the actually infinite division of matter: if matter consists only in bulk, then—given that it is actually infinitely divided—it will be a mere phenomenon. But although he believed that the actual infinite division of matter was an inescapable conclusion of the Cartesian analysis of motion, Leibniz had another line of argument not premised on it, which still shows that extension is "not as transparent a notion as is commonly believed," especially by those like Cordemoy who take bulk as basic. This reasoning is based on his principle of individuation. It is alluded to in the paper of 18 March 1676, when he writes: "Matter too is perpetually becoming one thing after another, since it exists only in relation, as I have shown elsewhere from the

principle of the individuation of all things" (Aiii36: 392). On 1 April he returns to the principle of individuation to demonstrate the necessity of
minds in bodies. According to this principle, every individual thing must
contain within it something that marks it out as the same thing over time.
But if matter is purely homogeneous, two identical portions of matter
could be produced in different ways. For instance, one "square" atom
could be produced by the coalescing of two triangles, another identical
one by the combining of two rectangles. On the other hand, "if we admit
that two different things always differ in themselves in some way as well,
then it follows that in any matter there is something which retains the effect of its prior states, namely, mind" (Aiii67: 491; DSR 50–51). Leibniz
gives an almost identical argument in his critical notes on Cordemoy, concluding "Certainly no difference can be conceived in them as they are now,
unless we suppose something in bodies besides extension; rather they are
distinguished solely by memory of their former conditions, and there is
nothing of this kind in bodies." The difference is, of course, that in April
1676 Leibniz was arguing for mind-containing atoms on the grounds that
there cannot be an enduring body that does not contain a mind; in 1685 he
was arguing against Cordemoy's atoms (conceived as units of pure extension or bulk) on the grounds that there cannot be an enduring body that
does not contain (at least something analogous to) a mind, namely, something which acts, and retains a memory of its former conditions.

Both lines of attack—the argument from infinite division and the argument from the principle of individuation—are in evidence in a paper I surmise is from early in the Hanover period, "There Is No Such Thing as One
Body" (Aiv278; 1678–79). Interestingly, Leibniz appears to have realized
that these constitute two independent arguments halfway through writing
this piece. To prove the conclusion announced in the title he adduces three
axioms, of which the second is originally that "every body is actually divided into several parts, which are also bodies." From this premise, as we
have already seen, it will follow that matter is an infinite aggregate, and
thus not a true whole. And from this Leibniz will infer "that there is no
such thing as one body," and therefore that "either bodies are mere phenomena, and not real entities, or there is something other than extension in
bodies" (Aiv278). But as Leibniz constructs the proof he realizes that this
conclusion follows from the other two axioms alone (which he renumbers
(1) and (2)) "—provided it is conceded that contact alone does not make
one entity." Axiom (1) is that "what has no greater unity than the logs in a
bundle of firewood or logpile, or bricks placed one on top of another, is not
properly one entity, but rather entities, although one name can be supposed
for them all." Axiom (2) is that body consists only in "extension, i.e. what

has parts beyond parts." Here the argument is the same one Leibniz had leveled at Cordemoy: "if two equal triangular bodies (that are not further subdivided) are imagined to compose a cube, one new entity is no more made from them than if they were touching each other only through their vertices, i.e. at points." And this is so, Leibniz claims, whether the bodies are moving together or touch only for the instant at which they are being considered.

In fact, Leibniz writes in a sequence of definitions in 1685, it is not even necessary that the parts constituting a whole "exist at the same time, or at the same place; it suffices that they be considered at the same time. Thus from all the Roman emperors together, we construct one aggregate. But actually no being that is really one is composed of a plurality of parts, and every substance is indivisible, and those things that have parts are not be-ings, but merely phenomena" (Aiv147: 627). Similar remarks occur in other papers of the period. In order for the various parts to be said truly to belong to the same whole, to the same substance, it is necessary that there should be a substantial form, a principle that underlies the changing phe-nomena: "Certainly those things which lack these forms are no more one entity than a pile of wood, indeed they are not real entities any more than rainbows or mock-suns. Certainly they do not persevere the same for longer than a moment, whereas true substances persist through changes" (Aiv147: 627–68).

Of course, if everything that has parts is a mere phenomenon, Leibniz does not need the full battery of arguments from the actual infinitude of material aggregates. So in his mature work, beginning with his correspon-dence with Arnauld in 1686, the axiom that unity and entity are intercon-vertible—that "that which is not truly *one* entity is not truly one *entity* ei-ther"—gains precedence.[88] Now it might be thought that this whole line of argument that aggregates consist in our mode of considering things is quite distinct from the problem of the continuum. But there is in fact quite a deep connection in Leibniz's thought between this interpretation of ag-gregated wholes and the interpretation of magnitude and continuity. This is particularly evident in Leibniz's discussion of mathematical incommen-surables in the paper "Infinite Numbers" (Aiii69), and it is worth going back to that paper to follow out the argument.

In "Secrets of the Sublime" of February 1676, Leibniz had proposed that matter's being actually divided into points or actual infinitesimals en-tailed that any part would be commensurable with any other part; and that this in turn would appear to entail the squarability of the circle, "if it ex-ists" (Aiii60: 474). This is what he sets out to explore in "Infinite Num-bers" that April, where he appears to reason as follows. If a circle exists

and is squarable, this means it should be expressible as an infinite sum of infinitesimal areas $y_1dx$, whose ratio to the elements of area of the corresponding square $y_2dx$, $y_1{:}y_2$, must be rational—or, he corrects himself, must be "as infinite number to infinite number." By 'infinite number' he apparently means irrational roots such as $\sqrt[3]{2}$, which require an infinite expansion. Conversely, if it can be shown that the diameter of the circle and the side of the square have no common measure, not even an infinitely small one, then a quadrature of the circle of this kind is impossible, and it will follow "that the magnitude of a circle cannot be expressed by an equation of any degree" (Aiii69: 498); or as we would say, it would prove that $\pi$ is a transcendental number.

Leibniz has not proved this result. Even so he appears to take the lack of an infinitely small common measure for granted, thus entailing that the circle is a figure whose magnitude is not algebraically expressible. This seems to have encouraged him in his emerging conception of the circle as a fictitious entity. At any rate, without even pausing to begin a new paragraph, Leibniz plunges into the formulation of his new conception discussed above, where the circle is viewed as a kind of ideal limit of a sequence of polygons. Crucial to this conception is the idea of a law of progression through the sequence, with the circle as limiting case. The same insight, as we saw, allows him to redefine an angle by an implicit limiting process without assuming actually infinitely small lines, and to define the sum of a converging series (in so many words) as the limit of a sequence of partial sums of series with the same law. Accordingly, an infinite sum is not to be thought of as a completed aggregate of parts, nor is any geometric quantity an aggregate of actual infinitesimals.[89]

This has implications for the meaning of both 'magnitude' and 'whole,' as Leibniz proceeds to explore in the remainder of the paper. In 1671 he had still naively defined magnitude as "the multiplicity of parts"[90] of a thing, although he had "later considered that to be worthless, unless it were established that the parts are equal to one another, or in a given ratio" (Aiii64: 482; DSR 36–37). Now, however, he is confronted by the result that a continuous quantity must be something more than the sum of its infinitesimal parts. If a curve is regarded as made up of infinitely many infinitely small straight sides, then no matter how many sides are taken, they never add up to the whole; rather, as in the sum of a continuous series, the sum is a kind of limit to which their continuous aggregation attains. Thus, Leibniz concludes, "in the continuum the maximum is something, and the minimum is not; . . . in the continuum, the whole is prior to its parts, . . . There is no greatest number, and no least line" (Aiii69: 502).[91]

But what of other incommensurable lines—for instance, the diagonal

and side of a square? Even if one cannot express the magnitude of the circle by an equation of any degree, one can so express the ratio of these. Here Leibniz responds that if such a ratio is expressed by numbers, as in a decimal expansion, "there will also be a need for infinite numbers," since expansions of incommensurables never terminate or repeat. But in that case, there being no infinitieth number, what will the magnitude of the ratio consist in? Leibniz realizes he can give a similar solution to that of the angle: the ratio "in itself is nothing but the very agreement of the divisions; an agreement that always remains, as did the sine above." That is, just as the sine of an angle remains even when the two lines subtending it are reduced to zero, so here "the ratio always subsists" (503) even if its expansion is infinite. Ratio is not derived from two previously existing magnitudes; rather, "in two similar quantities it is the only thing with magnitude." It is "the quantity of one determined by relation to the other" (503). That is, continuous things of the same kind do not have any magnitude in themselves: their magnitude can be determined only by comparison. So we see that not only are shape and motion phenomenal, but continuous magnitude itself is not something absolute, but essentially consists in a relation of comparison.

All of this leads Leibniz to a redefinition of magnitude. It must not be defined as the multiplicity of parts of a thing, but rather as "the constitution of a thing by the recognition of which it can be regarded as a whole" (503). Given this intimate connection between the notions of 'magnitude' and 'whole', however, it follows that a whole, too must be redefined: "a whole is not what has parts, just what can have parts." And this leads Leibniz to doubt "whether what is really divided, that is, an aggregate, can be called one." It just "seems to be" one, he writes, "because names are invented for it." Here his argument connects back up with the argument from the Principle of Individuation discussed above. For "a whole exists when many things can come to be out of one"; yet in order for something to become something else, "something must remain which pertains to it rather than to the other thing." And this thing that remains need not be matter— in fact, as we have seen, it cannot be, since matter considered as the aggregate of its parts does not remain the same thing from one moment to the next. Rather, Leibniz argues, "it can be mind itself, understanding a certain relation" (503). In this way, Leibniz claims, provided there is a law underpinning these transitions from one aggregated whole to another new one produced from it, "continuous motion is imitated in a way, just as polygons imitate the circle. And hence one may be said to come out of the other, by a similar abuse, as it were, of the imagination."

From here it is only a short step to the characteristic themes of the ma-

ture Leibnizian philosophy of the continuum, which we can see beginning
to emerge in the Hanover period. A continuous whole is not one that is divided, just one that *can* be divided. Consequently it should be defined as
"that whose parts are indefinite" (Aiv132: 565); it connotes only possibility, not actuality. As Leibniz will write to de Volder thirty years after leaving Paris, "Continuous quantity is something ideal, which pertains to possibles and to actuals considered as possible" (to de Volder, January 1706;
G.ii.282). When we consider a body or a line as continuous, we are treating it as undivided; its parts are indeterminate, all the possible parts into
which it can be divided.[92] "In actuals," though, "there is nothing indefinite—indeed, in them any division that can be made is made. . . . The parts
are actual in the real whole, not in the ideal whole." The actuals referred to
here are not, of course, the simple substances (which are indivisible), but
the phenomena that actually occur: namely, existing bodies (and their situations and changes).[93] And not only are the parts of these "actually assigned in a certain way, as nature actually institutes the divisions and subdivisions according to the varieties of motion," but, as we have seen,
"these divisions proceed to infinity" (to de Volder, June 1704; G.ii.268).
Matter is an infinite aggregate and thus not a true whole; it is a phenomenon that presupposes true unities. Nevertheless, precisely because of this
unending internal division, matter corresponds arbitrarily closely to the
ideal of continuity, just as do the polygons to the circle. Thus "the science
of continua, i.e. of possibles, contains eternal truths that are never violated
by actual phenomena, since the difference is always less than any assignable given difference" (G.ii.282).

Finally, the idea of phenomenal bodies "imitating continuous motion"
in the same way as polygons imitate the circle brings to mind Leibniz's
Principle of Continuity, expounded in his "A Certain General Principle,
Useful not only in Mathematics but in Physics" of 1688: "When the cases
(or given quantities) continually approach one another, so that one finally
passes over into the other, the consequences or events (or what is sought)
must do so too"[94] (G.iii.52; Aiv371: 2032). But this mention of continuous
transition leads us to a consideration of the continuity of time and change,
the final thread through Leibniz's labyrinth that I wish to trace.

## 8. Motion, Change, and Substance

Leibniz's investigation of the continuity of motion is intimately connected
with his construal of geometric curves as infinite polygons. This can be
seen particularly clearly in the fragment "On Motion and Matter," written
at the beginning of April 1676. There, without any preamble, he launches
into a consideration of the question of whether perfect circles exist. In fa-

vor is the fact that perfect circles seem to be presupposed in the behavior of bodies, which undergo circular motion in certain ideal conditions. But against this "there is the great difficulty that endeavours are along tangents, so that motions will be too" (Aiii68: 492). That is, all motion at an instant is along the tangent to the curve at that point, so that a curvilinear motion is apparently reducible to a succession of straight line motions over vanishingly small times. Previously, of course, Leibniz had construed these "beginnings of motions" or endeavours as infinitely small entities that composed into a continuous motion. Now this is precluded by his "very recent" discovery that "endeavours are true motions, not infinitely small ones." Thus the whole foundation of his earlier theory of motion falls through, and he is compelled to consider that motion might after all be discontinuous.

How Leibniz goes about considering this is very revealing. The issue for him is whether perfect circles exist in nature. If they do, then there must be some method of establishing their functions directly, and not just as an ideal limit to a sequence. Thus "as long as there is no method for directly establishing the quadratures of curved lines, there will be a strong suspicion that none exist" (492), i.e. that no curves really exist in nature. What this implies is that a line appearing to be curved would in fact be the connected sequence of ever smaller finite straight lines that are presumed in the process of taking the limit to find the quadrature (i.e. the integral giving the area under the curve). Evidently Leibniz does not regard the process of approximating a curve by ever smaller straight lines (the justification of tangent and quadrature methods) as a purely mathematical technique, as we do today. If a truly continuous curved line is something fictitious, yet there is still an apparently curved line in nature, then this curve must be a mere appearance—an appearance produced by a succession of ever smaller straight lines in nature that approximate the continuous arbitrarily closely. In order for the alternative to hold, that a body in motion actually describe a perfect curve, it would have to be "possible for a new endeavour to be impressed at any moment whatever"; but this would require not only a perfect fluid, but also time's being divided into (and therefore composed of) instants, "which is impossible" (492).

One upshot of these reflections is that they embolden Leibniz to view all geometric figures as fictitious. "Assuming there are no curved lines," he writes (494), "what is said about them will be the properties of polygons. And some particular circle will be nothing but a general entity, i.e. what is demonstrated about it will have to be understood of any polygon inscribed in it, or of one whose number of sides is greater than we have employed." This sets the scene for his later and more extensive reflections

on the fictitious nature of mathematical figures in Aiii69, discussed in previous sections. Secondly, though, it entails that there is no truly continuous motion. Instead, the appearance of continuity is an effect of the ever more subtle buffeting of any body by all the endeavours impinging on it. For in Leibniz's physics "no endeavours die away, but all are in general *efficacious and perpetual*" (Aiii4: 95). Yet this property of being pushed from one place to another is not the only property of matter, he reasons in "On Motion and Matter" (Aiii68: 493). Indeed, the body undergoing the changes of motion could not even be said to be the same body unless it retains within itself some memory of its former states, i.e. contains a mind, as we saw above; that is, unless the changes themselves follow some law.

This prompts Leibniz to treat the question of how even rectilinear motion could be continued, given the demise of the endeavour theory (493). The treatment of curved motion as really discontinuous, but preserving the appearance of continuity, opens up the same possibility for all motion. If the same body is not actually conserved from one instant to the next, this will be equivalent to its being annihilated and re-created at another place, provided these changes happen according to a law, a process Leibniz dubs *transcreation* or *transproduction*. As we saw above, only a few days later in "Infinite Numbers" he will say that it is not necessarily matter that remains through a thing's changes: "It can be mind itself, understanding a certain relation: for instance, in *transproduction,* even though everything is new, still, by the very fact that this transproduction happens by a certain law, continuous motion is imitated in a way, just as polygons imitate the circle" (Aiii69: 503). Likewise, here he concludes that in the annihilation and re-creation of a body, "a mind always remains intact that assists it" (Aiii68: 494). That is, the appearance of continuity of motion is guaranteed by an enduring mind that "assists" the body by ensuring that its successive states follow one another in an orderly way.

This brings us close to the monads or simple substances of Leibniz's mature philosophy. But it doesn't quite bring us there yet. For the minds in individual bodies are inadequate to ground the law of conservation of quantity of motion, according to which "magnitude compensates for speed, as if they were homogeneous things"; and this, Leibniz argues in the same piece, "is an indication that matter itself is resolved into something into which motion is also resolved, namely, a certain universal intellect. For when two bodies collide, it is clear that it is not the mind of each one that makes it follow the law of compensation, but rather the universal mind assisting both, or rather all, equally" (Aiii68: 493). In fact, the conservation of the quantity of motion cannot be true of motion taken absolutely,[95] but "must be asserted of the action, i.e. relative motion, by which one body is

related to or acts on another" (493). That is, the minds of the bodies taken singly would not "know" to adjust their speeds so that the sum of the quantities *mv* ("bulk" times speed) is the same before and after collision. Thus the "assisting mind" that guarantees this is not the individual mind, but God, as Leibniz duly (and triumphantly) concludes.[96]

Therefore the individual minds in bodies—which it is necessary to posit in order to account for the self-identity of bodies through time, as we have seen—are inadequate to ground motion. It is also necessary to posit a universal mind to found the conservation of relative motion—the same mind, of course, that constitutes the immensum, the "basis of space" that remains during the changes of matter. This is of great significance for understanding the development of Leibniz's thought in this period. For it is not until a conservation of force can be ascribed to individual bodies that Leibniz can attribute to them an individual principle of activity, and therefore dispense with the divine mind as the direct cause of motion: it is his failure to derive any such principle for the continuation of motion from the nature of body itself that accounts for Leibniz's return in 1676 to something like the (dis)continuous creation view he had espoused in 1668.

This discontinuist view is subjected to a rigorous examination by Leibniz in his comprehensive treatment of the continuity of motion in the dialogue *Pacidius Philalethi*. There he begins by rehearsing some of the Ancients' arguments concerning the problematic nature of change. Chief among these is the old dilemma of the Sophists concerning the moment of death, made famous by Sextus Empiricus: did Socrates die while still living, or when he was already dead? Leibniz adroitly uses this to argue for a position with respect to time analogous to that for space. It will be remembered that he had long upheld Aristotle's distinction between contiguity and continuity: two bodies in contact do not have a point in common, otherwise they would form one continuous body. Rather their extrema are "together," i.e. they are "indistant" from one another, yet distinct points. Similarly, here he argues that there is no "moment of death": there cannot be a moment that is both the last moment of Socrates' living and the first moment of his being dead, on pain of contradiction. Rather, "the state of being alive and that of being dead are merely contiguous, and have no extrema in common" (Aiii78: 537). The state of change, "although it is usually called momentaneous, . . . in fact contains two moments: just as a place of contact, which is said to be at a point, contains an extremum of each of the bodies that are touching" (541).

This solution, however, presupposes that there are two temporally continuous states, one on either side of the change: in the case of Socrates, his state of living and his state of being dead. In the case of continuous mo-

tion, though, this is problematic. For if motion is a change of place, then at any moment a body is in motion, it must be changing place. On the above analysis of change, this means that there will be two contiguous moments, one on each side of the change, where the body will be in contiguous places. But if this is true for any moment of the body's motion, this immediately suggests that a continuous motion will be composed of "an aggregate of different existences through moments and points," and "time will be an aggregate of nothing but moments, and space an aggregate of nothing but points" (547). To admit this, however, is to be "swamped by the whole stream of difficulties that stem from the composition of the continuum" (548).

This gives Leibniz the opportunity for a lucid exposition of all the difficulties of the composition of the continuum out of points that we have already discussed above. First he proves the impossibility of a composition out of finitely many points (548–59); then he presents the argument from "On Minimum and Maximum" that, if lines are aggregates of points, then the number of points in the diagonal of a rectangle will be both equal to and greater than the number of points in the side (549–50). The analogy with Galileo's argument concerning roots and squares is noted, as is his solution, that "the attributes of equal, greater, and less have no place in infinities, but only in bounded quantities" (EN 79). But Leibniz does not follow Galileo (and Gregory of St. Vincent) here, as would Cantor two centuries later, for he is convinced that it is "no less true in the infinite than in the finite that the part is less than the whole" (551). Instead, he dissolves the paradox by denying there is a number of all numbers; so, by parity of reasoning, "there is no number of all assignable points either" (552). This invites a consideration of Descartes's argument for the actual division of matter (treated in Section 6 above), which again seems to suggest a resolution of matter into all assignable points (553–54); against which Pacidius responds with his "tunic" speech, quoted above: "although some folds are smaller than others to infinity, bodies are always extended and points never become parts, but always remain mere extrema" (555). Thus, Leibniz's interlocutors conclude, "the continuum can neither be dissolved into points nor composed of them, and there is no fixed and determinate number (either finite or infinite) of points assignable in it" (555). Therefore, given that change of place is an aggregate of existences of the body in two neighboring points at two neighboring times, "it must be conceded that a continuous motion, where a moving body uniformly traverses some place in some stretch of time successively and without any intervening rest, is impossible" (556).

But what are the alternatives? To Leibniz, abandoning the continuity of

motion immediately suggests the Gassendian analysis of motion he had subscribed to in his youth (see Appendix 2e, and Sections 1 and 3 above), according to which an apparently continuous motion is really an alternation of motions and rests. But in the *Pacidius,* as in "On Motion and Matter," this is regarded as a non-starter. This is because the same problem recurs for the motions between the rests—unless a body can be transferred from place to place without traversing the intervening spaces, a view Leibniz considers absurd. A second possibility seems to have suggested itself to Leibniz at this point, based on the distinction he had upheld in February between "metaphysical" and "geometrical" voids. In a canceled passage of the *Pacidius,* he speculates that a "geometrically continuous motion" could still be an alternation of leaps and rests if "the spaces through which these leaps occur are smaller than can be expounded by their ratio to magnitudes known by us" (Aiii78: 568). For "these kinds of spaces are taken in geometry to be points or null spaces, whence even a motion metaphysically interrupted by rests will be geometrically continuous" (569). This echoes his earlier speculation in "Secrets of the Sublime" that "a physical plenum is consistent with a metaphysical vacuum," where the latter is an empty space smaller than any assignable, yet "true and real" (Aiii60: 473). However, as we saw above, by April Leibniz had convinced himself that what is less than anything assignable is a fiction, resulting in his complete rejection of the interstitial vacuum the following December (in Aiii85) and February (in Aiv360). We see the hardening of this conviction occurring here, for no sooner has Leibniz given voice to this speculation about metaphysical gaps than he crosses it out, with the remark that "it is not in the least to be defended, lest geometry and mechanics be subverted by metaphysical speculations" (569).

In the text of the fair copy, the idea gets one last mention (although even this is set in parentheses). "Perhaps," Charinus offers, "leaps through infinitely small spaces are not absurd, and nor are little rests for infinitely small times inserted between these leaps. For assuming the spaces of the momentaneous leaps to be proportional to the times of the rests, they will all correspond together in the same way as the leaps and rests through ordinary times and lines" (564). Pacidius (speaking for Leibniz) replies that although he "would indeed admit these infinitely small spaces and times in geometry, for the sake of invention, even if they are imaginary," he doubts "whether they can be admitted in nature" (564). His first objection is that if infinitesimals are actual parts, then there will be an indefinite number in a definite integral, which he deems absurd;[97] and secondly, "since further infinitely small spaces and times can also be assumed, each smaller than the last to infinity, again no reason can be provided why some

should be assumed rather than others; but nothing happens without a reason" (565). This rejection of actual infinitesimals is reinforced in the argument of the fair copy by the comparison with atoms.

What, then, is Leibniz's conclusion about the continuity of motion? Motion cannot be continuous, because this would entail that space and time are composed of points and instants, and this leads to an absurdity. It cannot be a Gassendian alternation of motions and rests, since if there is "even a portion of continuous motion" between two rests, then "our previous difficulties will return concerning this" (556). Nor can it be a sequence of momentaneous creations of all bodies in consecutive locations (as some of the Occasionalists proposed), since this would be to compose time out of moments, and thus precipitate all the paradoxes of the continuum. Nor, finally, can it be an alternation of leaps through infinitely small spaces and rests for infinitely small times, for the reasons just stated. Instead, Leibniz opts for the conclusion that "the motion of a moving thing is actually divided into an infinity of other motions, each different from the other, and . . . does not persist the same and uniform for any stretch of time" (565).

Thus "there is no part of time in which some change or motion does not happen to any part or point of a body," and given that "no motion stays the same through any space or time however small," it follows that "both space and time will be actually subdivided to infinity, just as a body is" (566). Although individual states of phenomena will "endure for some time, i.e. be void of changes," still "during any state whatsoever some other things are changing" (559). Consequently there is "no moment of time that is not actually assigned, or at which change does not occur, that is, which is not the end of an old or beginning of a new state in some body" (566). Thus the analogy with space and matter is complete: however small a space one takes, there are divisions inside it corresponding to the divisions of matter, but never more than two consecutive assignable points; similarly, however small a time one takes, there will always be other assignable times within it corresponding to changes occurring in that time, but there will never be more than two assignable moments next to each other.

Now, as Leibniz has Pacidius observe, this analysis has a corollary that is of profound importance for the nature of body, namely, "that bodies do not act while they are in motion" (566). For "there is no moment of change common to each of two states, and thus no state of change either, but only an aggregate of two states, old and new." But this means that "there is no state of action in a body, that is to say, no moment can be assigned at which it acts." Nonetheless, there is action in a body, even if it "cannot be con-

ceived except through a kind of aversion"; therefore it does not belong to the body per se, but "to those things which by acting do not change" (566). The latter phrase presumably alludes to the true substances or minds contained in every body. But Leibniz is mute about these here beyond this single allusion. Nor does he follow his own suggestion in the margin of the first draft to demonstrate that bodies do not even exist between moments (since "things do not exist unless they act, and do not act except when they change" [558]). Instead he is concerned to prove that since a body does not act through its motion, what moves and transfers it "is not the body itself, but a superior cause which by acting does not change, which we call God" (567).

As noted earlier, Leibniz's return to God as the direct cause of bodies' continuance in motion is connected with the abandonment of the endeavour theory, and his inability to find a principle of activity specific to each individual body from which the conservation of its motion could be derived. For on the one hand, the discovery of Huygens, Christopher Wren, John Wallis, and Edme Mariotte that the quantity of motion is conserved only vectorially and not absolutely, as the Cartesians had maintained, means that without the direct action of God, the quantity of motion in the universe would gradually decrease, due to inelastic impacts. And on the other, if it is relative motion that is conserved, this is information that cannot be contained in the individual minds Leibniz had posited in bodies. Thus as Leibniz writes in a note later appended to the head of the dialogue, the two matters not treated in it are the problem of "the subject of motion, to make it clear which of two things changing their mutual situation motion should be ascribed to; and second, the cause of motion, i.e. motive force" (529).

The first of these themes is taken up in earnest by Leibniz as soon as he arrives in Hanover. In "Space and Motion Are Really Relations" (Early 1677?) Leibniz explicitly draws the consequence that, since space is not "a certain thing consisting in a supposed pure extension," "motion is not something absolute, but consists in relation" (Aiv359: 1968). In "Motion Is Something Relative" (February 1677) he explores the metaphysical consequences of this. From the fact that "motion is something relative, and we cannot distinguish just which of the bodies is moving," Leibniz infers that "if it is an affection, its subject will not be any one individual body, but the whole world" (Aiv360: 1970). Absolute motion, consequently, is a fiction. It is something we imagine to ourselves for the sake of representing everything in the universe with respect to one body taken as at rest. For example, as Leibniz had already considered in December 1675 in his notes on Descartes's *Principles,* one can consider two bodies mov-

ing away from each other on the surface of the earth, taken as immobile. "But also nothing prevents me from imagining in turn that I am on one of the smaller bodies, which will thus be regarded as being at rest" (Aiii15: 215). In a postscript to this piece, however, he instead provides a principle which encapsulates the greater simplicity of the Copernican hypothesis: "when things are mutually changing their situation and it is asked which of them should be said to be moving, motion should always be ascribed to a certain finite thing rather than to the rest of the entire world outside it" (217). Thus, strictly speaking, the Ptolemaic and Copernican hypotheses are equivalent descriptions of the motions of the heavenly bodies. But the Copernican assumes fewer motions on the part of the individual planets and stars, and it is therefore more intelligible to ascribe all the diurnal motions to the earth's rotation and to imagine the sun as at rest.[98] The same interpretation of the relativity of motion is expounded in *A Specimen of Discoveries* through the example of a solid moving in a liquid: one can understand the same things to occur whether the solid is supposed to stir up certain waves in the fluid, or whether the solid is supposed at rest, with the fluid undergoing "certain equivalent motions"—indeed, "the same phenomena can be explained in infinitely many ways" since "motion is really a relative thing" (Aiv312: 1620). Nonetheless, "that hypothesis which attributes motion to the solid, and from this deduces the waves in the liquid, is infinitely simpler than the others, and for this reason the solid is adjudged to be the cause of the motion."

This has important consequences for the question of the reality of space. If there are, strictly speaking, "no principles for determining the subject of motion," as Leibniz writes in a footnote to the *Specimen,* then "there is no absolute place or motion," with the result that "space and time are not things, but real relations." This is further elaborated in "Motion Is Not Something Absolute" (Aiv317). If what is in motion depends on the simplest hypothesis about what is at rest, then absolute space will be "no more a thing than time is, even though it is pleasing to the imagination." Both will be "merely relations of a mind trying to refer everything to intelligible hypotheses—that is, to uniform motions and immobile places—and to values deduced on this basis" (Aiv317).

Thus the phenomena of motion—which of the surrounding bodies appear to move, and how fast—will be different from the point of view of each body in relative motion, taking itself as at rest. Each body, insofar as it has the ability to represent, represents the universe from its own point of view. Moreover, there is a harmony among these points of view, encapsulated in the laws of motion. Yet if motion is merely relative, then there will be nothing more to bodies than this: a series of representations of the uni-

verse from their own point of view, with God ensuring consistency among the phenomena by imposing the conservation of relative motion on the universe as a whole.

But as we have seen, Leibniz is adamant that the solution to the labyrinth of the continuum requires there be more to body than this. As a foundation of extension there must be units of substance that are not themselves extended, and as a foundation for motion there must be temporal continuants that contain within themselves their law of progression. This statement explains Leibniz's sustained search in the late 1670s for a measure of force that would enable him to attribute an individual principle of activity to bodies, culminating in 1678 with his discovery of the law of conservation of motive, force, or, as he later called it, *vis viva*. And once he has discovered this law, as we shall see, he is able to attribute the reality of motion to the conservation of this force within each individual body (insofar as it is a temporal continuant). Thus whereas in the *Pacidius* "body cannot even continue motion of its own accord, but needs to be continuously propelled by God, who acts constantly and in accordance with certain laws" (Aiii78: 567), by 1683 these laws are derived from the constitution of individual things: in *Wonders Concerning the Nature of Corporeal Substance,* Leibniz claims that motion has its reality in "the force and power vested in things, that is to say, beyond their having such a constitution that from it there follows a change of phenomena constrained by certain rules" (Aiv279). But because he had already established through the arguments from the labyrinth of the continuum that this force or principle of activity could not be material, he found himself obliged to return to the scholastic idea of immaterial essences of bodies, *substantial forms.*

That these concerns about the reality of motion were instrumental in Leibniz's reintroduction of substantial forms is attested to by the Hanover writings of the late 1670s and early 1680s. In *The Origin of Souls and Minds* (Aiv275), Leibniz defines the substantial form of a body as resulting from God's "think[ing] of all the appearances or relations of things to this body considered as immobile" (1460). This relates directly to what he writes in the *Discourse on Metaphysics:* "For when God, so to speak, turns on all sides and in all ways the general system of phenomena, . . . and regards all aspects of the world in all possible manners, since there is no relation that escapes his omniscience, the result of each view of the universe, as seen from a certain place, is a substance which expresses the universe in conformity with this view, if God finds it good to render his thought effective and produce this substance" (§ 14: Aiv306; G.iv.439; PW 26). Thus, Leibniz writes in "Motion Is Not Something Absolute," "any substance whatever expresses the whole universe, according to its own point of

view," as is made particularly clear by the example of "the phenomena of motions": for there "every single body must be supposed to have a motion in common with any other, as if they were in the same ship, as well as its own motion, reciprocal to its bulk; how this could be so could not be imagined if motions were absolute and each body did not express all others" (Aiv317).

There is, however, more to the nature of substantial form than a mere series of such points of view. Once it is rendered actual, each form or soul has in addition a kind of sensation and appetite (Aiv275, Aiv267: 1400). The reason for this, Leibniz explains in his "Conspectus for a Little Book on the Elements of Physics," is that "souls result from God thinking of things, that is, they are imitations of his ideas" (Aiv365: 1988–89). "Every soul," he says in *Wonders,* "or rather every corporeal substance, is confusedly omniscient and diffusedly omnipotent" (Aiv279: 1466). Where God perceives all the relations of things to the body considered as immobile, the soul likewise perceives everything that happens in the whole world, albeit confusedly. Similarly, because "it has no endeavour that does not extend to infinity," every corporeal substance acts on everything else, albeit with its actions hugely diffused by things acting in contrary ways (1466).

But this talk of corporeal substance acting is merely metaphorical. If bodies acted on one another "in metaphysical rigor," then the cause of motion could be identified by determining which body acted on which, thus defeating the relativity of motion. In actual fact, however, in collisions "no impetus is transferred from one body to another, but each body moves by an innate force, which is determined only on the occasion of, i.e. with respect to, another" (Aiv312: 1620). That is, on a commonsense understanding of a perfectly elastic collision between two bodies, "the elasticity of one propels the other when they are in contact" (1628). In reality, though, the force of each body—measured by its power of producing its full effect (1629, 1630)—remains the same before and after impact.

This depends on Leibniz's understanding of his new law of force, some explanation of which is needed. On the conventional modified Cartesian view, in a collision between two bodies that are not perfectly elastic, some quantity of motion (as measured by the scalar quantity mv) is necessarily lost, since only directed motion (called by Leibniz "direction," and then in the *Specimen,* "progress") is conserved. On his account, however, the same quantity of force must always be present, on pain of the universe's coming to an eventual standstill. The problem is to determine the correct measure of this force; and the clue that leads Leibniz to it is what he calls his "metaphysical principle of the equality of cause and effect," where force is understood as a power that "is consumed in acting, that is, in pro-

ducing an effect" (1629). For if the effect were greater than the cause, then, as he explains in the *Discourse,* "the force of a machine (which is always diminished slightly by friction, and must soon come to an end) would restore itself" (G.iv.442; PW 30), and one would be able to get work from nothing or "mechanical perpetual motion"; but if less, then one would not get "physical perpetual motion" (Aiv365: 1989): that is, the total amount of motion in the universe would diminish through inelastic collisions, and all motion would eventually cease. In his seminal application of this principle to the case of a falling body, Leibniz reasoned that the entire cause of a four-pound body's fall through a fathom must equal the full effect of the raising of a one-pound body to four fathoms, so that, given the Galilean proportionality of height to the square of the speed, the force of a body acquired through fall must be proportional to the square of the speed (G.iv.442–43). Therefore the innate force of a body is proportional to $mv^2$.

This is now generalized to apply to all bodies. Thus in inelastic collisions, when the total quantity of *vis viva* of the two bodies is apparently less afterwards than before, the deficit is ascribed to the increase in motions of their internal parts due to friction. Hence each body, insofar as it continues the same, always conserves the same quantity of total force. What occurs in a collision is that each body (rather than rebounding instantaneously, as Descartes believed) is compressed and subsequently restituted in a continuous way, and the compression and restitution of the bodies is simply a redistribution of the motions of the internal parts in such a way that the entire force is conserved in each one.

So each body, insofar as it is a temporal continuant, conserves the same quantity of force overall, and this is merely redistributed among its parts on collision with another body, producing the effects of cohesion and elasticity. Consequently, whilst one may say, physically speaking, that "all bodies act on and are acted upon by all others" (Aiv312: 1626) and that "every effect is propagated indefinitely in time as well as in place, but is diminished" (1630); in fact, "rigorously speaking, no force is transferred from one body to another, but every body moves by an innate force" (1630). When another body collides with it, this provides a mere *occasion* for a body to undergo a redistribution of its internal motions, in keeping with the conservation of its total force. Thus everything acts spontaneously: its actions flow from its own nature. But such is the correspondence and harmony among points of view expressing the world at the same instant, that the illusion is created of action or influence of one substance on another.

This accords well with the analysis of action given in the *Pacidius.* As we saw there, action is not locatable in body "except by a kind of aver-

sion." There is no state of change in a body, "but only an aggregate of two states, old and new," with the result that "no moment can be assigned at which it acts." Leibniz valued this result, alluding to it in one of the analyses of concepts by division that he composed in 1679,[99] and again in a manuscript written in French in 1686.[100] But in the latter, he subjects it to an interesting reexamination in the course of arguing that the actual infinite division of matter implies that "there is no body that has any shape for a definite time, however small that might be." For although "it is true that it will always be possible to draw an imaginary line each instant . . . that line will endure in the same parts only for this instant, because each part has a movement different from every other, since it expresses the whole universe differently" (Aiv310). Yet "what exists only at a moment has no existence, since it starts and finishes at the same time." Alluding now to his proof in the *Pacidius* that "there is no middle moment, or moment of change, but only the last moment of the preceding state and the first moment of the following state," he objects that "this supposes an enduring state" and "all enduring states are vague; there is nothing precise about them."

Thus enduring states, like shape, are like those notions to which the Stoics' paradox of the heap applies—heat, cold, tepidness, and so forth—which, when "taken absolutely," says Leibniz in *Chrysippus's Heap,* "are vague imaginary notions" (Aiv23). Because of the infinite division of matter, one can never arrive at a precise shape, each surface and line being, on closer inspection, further divided; similarly, each state during which a body remains unchanged is, on closer inspection, divided by the changes occurring in each of its parts. Thus what shape something has, and what state it remains in, are notions depending on the precision of knowledge required. And the fact that such notions are imaginary, according to Leibniz, provides the solution to the paradox (which he had left unsolved in the *Pacidius*). For being notions "which are not in the things outside us, but whose essence it is to appear to us," they "indicate something with respect to our opinion, which varies" (Aiv23). In a word, they are phenomena, not essential qualities of things.

This cannot be so, however, of the force within bodies that grounds their motion, and thus their very reality. As Leibniz concludes in *There Is No Perfect Shape in Bodies,*

> *In an instant,* with motion not being considered, it is as if the mass were all one; and thus one can give it any such shapes one wants. But also all variety in bodies ceases; and, consequently, all bodies are destroyed. For motion or endeavour makes their essence or difference.

And in this moment everything reverts to chaos. Endeavour cannot be conceived in mass by itself. (Aiv310)

That is, to put it positively, the endeavour or momentaneous action that cannot be found in mass or bulk except by a sort of aversion must nevertheless exist, since motion is the very essence of body. Instantaneous actions or tendencies to change state must exist, or "all variety in bodies would cease"; indeed, all phenomena would cease, since whatever has no variety cannot be sensed, and whatever is in principle imperceptible does not exist. But "if to space or magnitude is added appetite, or, what comes to the same thing, endeavour, and consequently action too, already something substantial is introduced" (Aiv321). Thus it is *substance,* and by the above arguments not anything phenomenal, that consists in an endeavour or instantaneous tendency to change its relations to all other things according to certain laws contained in it. Indeed, "each substance is a kind of force of acting, or an endeavour to change itself with respect to all the others according to certain laws of its own nature" (Aiv317). Thus, even if continuity cannot be found in the phenomena of motions, all such motions presuppose a continuity of activity that is resolvable into instantaneous changes of state or endeavours or "appetitions."

This, then, is how Leibniz finally emerges from his labyrinth. Body is constituted by motion; but continued motion presupposes things which by acting do not change, and whose action consists in their tendency to change relations to all other such things, so that the continuity of their actions requires an endeavour or appetition at each instant. So one recoups the idea of a continuity of change and duration with the idea of a unity of substance which is continuously acting, and which therefore has a state and an action or endeavour to change this state at every instant.

In sum, Leibniz's solution to the problem of the composition of the continuum is as follows: The parts of the continuum are indefinite; they are the homogeneous parts that can be imagined in anything when one has abstracted away from the diversity really in it. Consequently, a continuous entity is not an actually existing thing, but something incomplete, an abstract entity. In existing things, by contrast, the parts are determinate, and are prior to any whole they compose. Thus matter, considered abstractly (i.e. as primary matter) is a continuous whole consisting in a pure potentiality for division. Taken concretely, however (i.e. as secondary matter), it is at any instant not only infinitely divisible, but actually infinitely divided by the diverse motions of its parts. Therefore no part of matter, however small, remains the same for longer than a moment; there are no motions that do not contain other motions, and no enduring states; even shape is

something evanescent, and a body with an enduring shape is something imaginary. Thus the perduring element in matter is not something material, i.e. explicable in terms of magnitude, shape, and motion. There must, however, be such a perduring element in any part of matter however small, which is the principle of all the changes occurring in it: for if there is no unity, there can be no multiplicity. Just as bodies presuppose units of substance, so changes presuppose things which by acting do not change. But action cannot be found in any phenomenal state, no matter how far it is divided, just as substance cannot be found in body by repeated division. Therefore all phenomenal action presupposes substantial action; the latter, however, cannot consist in a real influence of one substance on another, any more than one body can exert force on any other. For all motion is relative, so that what is real in it consists in mutual changes in relation of situation, together with some conserved power for maintaining these changes in each thing in such a way that they agree with the simultaneous states of all other things. Thus each thing represents all others from its point of view, and this representation of the other things in its own state is a kind of cognition; and this, together with an appetition or endeavour to change state, and to form a continuous series of states according to an internal law, constitutes the substantial form or primitive force of acting of the thing. Thus the substantial form provides for the unity of every thing that is a unity per se, and accounts not only for all its phenomena and their continuance according to the laws of physics, but also for the correspondence of its states and changes with the states and changes of all simultaneously existing substances.

But it doesn't seem fitting to emerge from an infinite labyrinth on such a note of finality, so let me end with one last stir of the pot, by returning to the comparison with Ts'ui Pên's labyrinth in Borges's story "The Garden of Forking Paths." This labyrinth, it will be remembered, turned out to exist after all, as a conceptual labyrinth contained in a great pile of manuscripts bequeathed to posterity. Similarly, I have suggested, Leibniz's references to the labyrinth of the continuum are not just to the problem conceived abstractly, but to his own tortuous mental labours contained in the manuscripts presented here. Now it seems to me not too outrageous to suggest a further analogy between them. Just as in Borges's story Stephen Albert found the clue to the riddle of the missing labyrinth in the fact that the one word that wasn't mentioned in the manuscripts was 'time', so here the one thing that Leibniz doesn't stress about his labyrinth is the special status of temporal continuity. For despite the emphasis on the discreteness of substance (and also the discreteness of body and phenomenal change), underlying this there is a real continuity of substantial activity in time,

within each discrete substance. And this continuous activity is, paradoxi-cally, at once both more real and more ideal than anything phenomenal. It is more real in that the states of a substance form a true continuum, unlike the shapes or notions of a body, which only approximate such a continuum arbitrarily closely. Yet it is more ideal in that the instantaneous states and endeavours on which this real continuity of activity is based are ideal or limiting concepts, modeled on the instantaneous states and changes of his differential calculus. Or, to put the point more succinctly: What exists only for an instant does not really exist; yet without an instantaneous endeavour or appetition, there would be no variety, no plurality, and in short, no phe-nomena at all.[101]

Now Leibniz might perhaps have resisted this charge of paradox by of-fering an analogous defense to the one he gave de Volder for monads themselves: continuous change is not composed of instantaneous states, but results from them; and these states are not existents, but foundations of existence.[102] I cannot go any further here into the adequacy of such a re-sponse. But even if the above consideration is thought to constitute a diffi-culty for his approach, it is no less a difficulty for contemporary meta-physics of science, which avoids it only by hypostatizing mathematical objects and inheriting therewith the notorious paradoxes of the infinite be-setting set theory. Indeed, I think there is much of great profundity in Leib-niz's thought on the continuum, and, as I have hinted here and there in my notes, more than a little contemporary appeal in an approach that eschews infinite sets.

# I Paris Writings, 1672–76

**74** *DEMONSTRATIO SUBSTANTIARUM INCORPOREARUM*

**79** *Quod impellit immediate conatur intrare locum impulsi.* Omnis enim impulsus actio est corporis in corpus. Omnis actio corporis in corpus est motus corporis agentis. Motus est loci mutatio. Corpus mutando locum suum non agit ideo immediate in aliud, nisi quia immediate seu statim conatur intrare in alienum. Ergo quicquid impellit conatur intrare in alterius locum.

**80** Quorum unum intrare conatur in alterius locum, eorum extrema iam in eodem loco sunt. Conatus enim est initium actionis. Ergo et initium effectus, licet quolibet dato effectu minus. Initium intrandi in locum est intrasse parte sui qualibet data minore, id est extremi.

*Impellere* est conari movere.

*Conatus* est pars actionis qualibet data minor, seu initium medium finisve actionis. Ut instans temporis, punctum lineae.

*Motus* est mutatio loci.

*Corpus* est cuius actio passioque est motus.

*Quae se impellunt* cohaerunt. Nam aut immediate se impellunt aut per interpositum interpositave. Si per interposita, saltem interposita immediate impelluntur et impellunt aut respectu extremorum aut inter se. Iam omnia se immediate impellentia cohaerent. Unum enim conatur intrare in alterius locum, *per prop. 1.* Ergo *per prop.*—cohaerent. Tota ergo series etiam mediate impellentium cohaeret, quia ex immediate impellentibus, ac proinde cohaerentibus componitur.

Corpora cohaerentia sympathica sunt.

Nam corpora cohaerentia sunt συγκίνητα, seu unum sine altero impelli non potest, *per def.*—. . . Si unum sine altero impelli non potest, etiam

## 1. A Demonstration of Incorporeal Substances[1]
### (4th Draft)

[Fall 1672?][2]

**74**          *A DEMONSTRATION OF INCORPOREAL SUBSTANCES*[3]

**79** | [Proposition 1:][4] *Whatever impels another thing, immediately endeavours to enter its place.* For every impulse is an action of one body on another. Every action of one body on another is a motion of the acting body. Motion is change of place. In changing its place, a body does not thereby act immediately on another body unless it immediately, i.e. at once, endeavours to enter the other one. Therefore whatever impels another thing, endeavours to enter its place.

**80** |          [Prop. 2:] If one body endeavours to enter the place of another, their extrema are already in the same place. For an endeavour is the beginning of an action. Therefore it is also the beginning of an effect, although this is smaller than any given effect. The beginning of entering a place is having entered by a part of it smaller than any given part, i.e. an extremum.[5]

[Definition 1:] To *impel* is to endeavour to move.

[Def. 2:] An *endeavour* is a part of an action smaller than any given part, or the beginning, middle, or end of an action—as an instant is of time, and a point of space.

[Def. 3:] *Motion* is change of place.

[Def. 4:] A *body* is that whose action and passion is motion.[6]

[Prop. 3:] *Things that impel one another* cohere. For either they impel one another immediately, or by means of some thing or things lying between them. If by means of things between, then the things between, at least, impel and are impelled immediately, either by each other or by their extremities. Now all things impelling one another immediately cohere. For one endeavours to enter the place of the other, *by Prop. 1.* Therefore *by Prop.—,*[7] they cohere. Therefore the whole series of mediately impelling things also coheres, because it is composed of immediately impelling, and thus cohering, things.

[Prop. 4:] Cohering bodies are sympathetic.
          For cohering bodies are co-moving, i.e. one cannot be impelled without the other, by definition—.[8] If one cannot be impelled without the other, then one cannot even be acted on without the other. For every passion of bodies

3

unum sine altero pati non potest. Omnis enim corporum passio est moveri ab alio seu impelli. Necesse est ergo corpora cohaerentia συμπαθεῖν.

Quicquid movetur momento motus est in duobus locis.

Nam momento Motus mutat locum. Momento mutationis non est extra locum.

**81** Spatium Continuum componitur ex partibus qualibet a nobis determinabili minoribus.

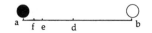

Esto spatium *ab,* in eo ferri intelligatur corpus *C* motu uniformi et horae spatio pervenire ex *a* in *b,* necesse est semihorae spatio pervenire in *d* et spatio quadrantis in *e* et semiquadrantis in *f* et sic perpetuo subdividendo in eadem ratione locum et tempus; necesse est ergo momento dato seu nunc pervenire aliquousque, nam si nunc non mutat locum seu non pervenit aliquousque quiescit ergo, at supponimus nunc moveri, id est momento dato incipere motum seu conari. Nunc ergo seu momento dato progredietur, sed per spatium minus quolibet a nobis determinabili. Componitur ergo spatium ex partibus qualibet a nobis determinabili minoribus. Vel brevius: tempus componitur ex momentis seu partibus qualibet a nobis determinabili minoribus nunquam enim existit nisi momentum; motus lineam dividit in partes partibus temporis proportionales, sunt ergo partes in linea momentis proportionales, seu qualibet a nobis determinabili minores. Ex his facile demonstratur harum partium alias esse aliis minores.[L1]

## Notes on Galileo's *Two New Sciences*

Aiii11$_2$

**167** Galilaeus putabat in *Dial. 1.* non assurgere aquam ultra 18 ulnas quia scilicet pondus eius ipsiusmet cohaesionem superaret. Aquam autem cohaerere ait, idque a se demonstratum, nullo alio vinculo, nisi vacui. Hinc calculari ait posse et reliquorum resistentiam an a fuga vacui, aut quantum ultra, quatenus scilicet maioris chordae pondus sustineat.

L1. IN THE MARGIN: *Omnia Mundi aspectabilis Corpora sensibilia sympathica sunt.*

is a being moved, i.e. impelled, by another. Therefore it is necessary that cohering bodies sympathize.[9]

[Prop. 5:] Whatever moves is in motion at two places in a moment.
For in a moment a thing in motion changes place. In a moment of change it is not outside a place.

**81**  [Prop. 6:] A continuous space is composed of parts smaller than any determinable by us.

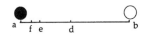

Let there be a space *ab* and let us understand a body *C* to be traveling in it with a uniform motion, so that it gets from *a* to *b* in the space of one hour. It is necessary that in the space of half an hour it gets to *d*, in a quarter of an hour to *e*, in an eighth of an hour to *f*, and so on, continually subdividing the space and time in the same ratio. Therefore it is necessary that at a given moment or 'now' it gets somewhere, for if now it is not changing place, i.e. not getting somewhere, then it is at rest; but we are supposing that it is moving now, i.e. that at a given moment it begins or endeavours to move. Therefore now, i.e. at a given moment, it will advance, but through a space smaller than any determinable by us. Therefore space is composed of parts smaller than any determinable by us. Or more briefly: time is composed of moments, or parts smaller than any determinable by us; for nothing of it ever exists but a moment; motion divides the line into parts proportional to the parts of time, therefore there are parts in the line proportional to moments, i.e. smaller than any determinable by us. From this it is easily demonstrated that some of these parts are smaller than others.[L1]

### 2. Notes on Galileo's *Two New Sciences* (First Dialogue)[1]                                    Aiii11₂

[Fall 1672?][2]

**167**  Galileo supposed in *Dialogue 1* [EN 64] that water does not rise up beyond 18 cubits[3] because its weight would exceed its cohesion. But he says that water coheres—and this he demonstrates—by no bond except that of a vacuum. Hence, he says, one can also calculate for other materials the resistance due to the avoidance of the vacuum, or how much the resistance is in excess of this by how much longer a column the weight will support.[4]

L1. IN THE MARGIN: *All sensible bodies in the visible world are sympathetic.*

Galilaeus ex principio indivisibilium suppositorum explicare conatur volutionem circulorum.

Gal. *dial* 1. p. 22. Edit. 1656. Ital. dicit definitiones Geometricas non esse nisi compendia loquendi. Adde quae Pascal. in *Triang. Arithm.* de variandis enunciandi modis.

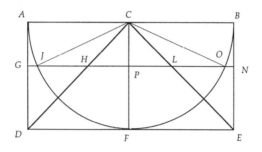

Galil. *dial 1.* p. 21. egregie demonstrat punctum quoddam cuidam lineae, nempe circumferentiae cujusdam circuli aequale esse. Si rectangulum *ABED,* semicirculus *AFB,* Triangulum *CDE* circumagantur circa *CF,* rectangulum generabit Cylindrum, semicirculus hemisphaerium, Triangulum conum. Auferatur Hemisphaerium ex cylindro, restabit locus hemisphaerii vacuus, inter conum et scutellam quandam ex cylindro residuam, quae erit cono aequalis, et eodem modo conus *HCL* plano utcunque alto *GN* abscissus, et idem est quantacunque sit linea *CA.* Iam si *GN* sit summae *ACB* ita propinqua, ut differentia sit minor quolibet dato, conus iste *CHL* evanescet in punctum, et scutella ex cylindro relicta evanescet in Circulum. Erit ergo ultimus conus aequalis ultimae scutellae, seu punctum circulo. Haec satis demonstrant, puncta nihil esse, nec utendum nisi corporibus minoribus quolibet dato, ex quibus infinitum latitudine, sed angustissimum instar scutellae, potest esse aequale, alteri et latitudine et longitudine minore quovis dato, infinitum aequale indivisibili. Hoc etiam esse demonstratum a Luca Valerio fatetur.

**168**    Gal. *Dial 1.* p. 23. Bologn. 1656, Lucae Valerii tract. *de centro gravitatis solidorum,* mire laudat, vocat alterum Archimedem seculi nostri.

P. 24. Indivisibile additum indivisibili nil efficere nisi addantur infinita indivisibilia. In infinito non esse nec maius nec minus ait p. 25. quod mihi

Galileo endeavours to explain the rotation of circles by means of the principle of supposed indivisibles.[5]

Galileo (*Dialogue 1*, p. 22, edition of 1656, Italy [EN 74]) says that geometrical definitions are nothing but abbreviations of speech.[6] One should also add what Pascal says in his *Triang. Arithm.* about the need to vary modes of expression.[7]

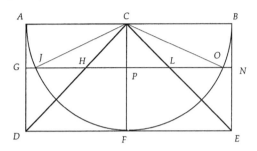

Galileo (*Dialogue 1*, p. 21 [EN 74–75]) demonstrates exceptionally well that a certain point is equal to a certain line, namely, to the circumference of a certain circle. If the rectangle *ABED*, the semicircle *AFB*, and the triangle *CDE* are rotated around *CF*, the rectangle will generate a cylinder, the semicircle a hemisphere, and the triangle a cone. Let the hemisphere be removed from the cylinder, and in place of the hemisphere there will be left a void between the cone and what is left of the cylinder, a sort of bowl. This bowl will be equal to the cone, and in the same way the cone *HCL* cut off by a plane *GN* of any height whatever is also the same [as the upper portion of the bowl cut off by the same plane] however big the line *CA* is. Now if *GN* is so close to the top *ACB* that the difference is smaller than any given quantity, this cone *CHL* vanishes into a point, and the bowl that remains of the cylinder vanishes into a circle. Therefore the ultimate cone will be equal to the ultimate bowl, or the point to the circle. These things demonstrate well enough that points are nothing, and that only bodies smaller than any given must be used. From among these one infinite in width, but of the utmost thinness, like the bowl, can be equal to another that is smaller than any given quantity in both width and length, so that the infinite is equal to the indivisible. This, he admits, has also been demonstrated by Luca Valerio.

**168**    Galileo (*Dialogue 1*, p. 23, Bologna 1656 [EN 76]) gives wonderful praise to Luca Valerio's ["On the Center of Gravity of Solids"] and calls him a second Archimedes of our age.[8]

P. 24 [EN 77]: One indivisible added to another makes nothing unless an infinity of indivisibles are added together.[9] In the infinite there is nei-

videtur contra ea esse, quae ait ipse Galilaeus. Putat infinitum non tantum
non esse maius alio infinito, sed nec finito. Et demonstratio est notanda: In
Numeris infinitae sunt radices, infinita quadrata, infiniti cubi. Porro tot
sunt radices quot numeri. Et tot sunt quadrata quot radices. Ergo tot sunt
quadrata quot numeri, seu tot numeri quadrati quot numeri in universum.
Quod est impossibile. Hinc sequitur aut totum non esse maius parte in infinito, quae est sententia Galilaei et Gregorii a S. Vincentio quam probare
non possum, aut ipsum infinitum esse nihil, seu non esse Unum nec totum.
An dicemus: distinguendo inter infinita, scilicet infinitissimum, seu Omnes
numeros esse quiddam implicans contradictionem, nam si totum sit, intelligi potest factus ex numeris omnibus continue in infinitum, qui erit longe
major omnibus numeris seu numero maximo. An dicemus non debere dici
aliquid de infinito, ut de toto, nisi ubi adest demonstratio. Galilaeus addit
nec infinitum esse maius finito, quia in millione numerus quadratorum
non est centesima pars millionis, at in denario numerus quadratorum (*1. 4.
9.*) est pene tertia, in novenario tertia pars; radicum, in unitate aequatur numerus radicum et quadratorum. Hinc millio magis abit ab infinito, quam
denarius, cum in infinito aequalis sit numerus radicum et quadratorum.
Ad quaestionem an partes continui sint finitae, an infinitae respondet
Galilaeus neutrum esse, sed tales ut respondeant cuilibet numero dato ( +
seu indefinitas + ).

## De minimo et maximo. De corporibus et mentibus          Aiii5

**97**  *Nullum datur Minimum, sive indivisibile in spatio et corpore.*
Nam si quod datur indivisibile in spatio vel corpore, dabitur et in linea *ab*
( *fig. 1.*). Si datur in linea *ab* dabitur in ea ubique. Porro omne punctum indivisibile, potest intelligi terminus lineae indivisibilis ergo ductae intelligantur lineae infinitae inter se parallelae, ad *ab* perpendiculares ex linea
*ab* in lineam *cd.* Iam nullum potest assignari punctum in linea transversali
vel diagonali *ad* quod non incidat in aliquam linearum infinitarum parallelarum ex *ab* perpendiculariter exeuntium. Esto enim aliquod, si fieri
potest, *g,* ex eo certe ducta intelligi potest recta *gh* ad [*ab*] perpendicularis,

ther greater nor smaller, he says on p. 25 [EN 78], which seems to me contrary to what Galileo himself says. He thinks that one infinity is not only not greater than another infinity, but not greater than a finite quantity [EN 80]. And the demonstration is worth noting: Among numbers there are infinite roots, infinite squares, infinite cubes. Moreover, there are as many roots as numbers. And there are as many squares as roots.[10] Therefore there are as many squares as numbers, that is to say, there are as many square numbers as there are numbers in the universe. Which is impossible. Hence it follows either that in the infinite the whole is not greater than the part, which is the opinion of Galileo and Gregory of St. Vincent,[11] and which I cannot accept; or that infinity itself is nothing, i.e. that it is not one and not a whole. Or perhaps we should say, distinguishing among infinities, that the most infinite, i.e. all the numbers, is something that implies a contradiction, for if it were a whole it could be understood as made up of all the numbers continuing to infinity, and would be much greater than all the numbers, that is, greater than the greatest number. Or perhaps we should say that one ought not to say anything about the infinite, as a whole, except when there is a demonstration of it. Galileo adds [EN 79] that the infinite is not greater than the finite, because in a million the number of squares is not a hundredth of a million, but in the first ten the number of squares (1, 4, and 9) is almost a third of the number of roots, and in the first nine it is a third; whereas in unity the number of roots and squares are equal. Hence a million is much farther from infinity than ten, since in infinity the number of roots and squares are equal. To the question whether the parts of the continuum are finite or infinite, Galileo replies [EN 80–81] that they are neither, but rather such as correspond to any given number you please (+ that is, indefinite +).

### 3. On Minimum and Maximum;
### On Bodies and Minds[1]                                          Aiii5

[Nov. 1672–Jan. 1673][2]

**97**    *There is no minimum, or indivisible,[3] in space and body.[4]*

For if there is an indivisible in space or body, there will also be one in the line *ab* ( *fig. 1*). If there is one in the line *ab,* there will be indivisibles in it everywhere. Moreover, every indivisible point can be understood as the indivisible boundary of a line. So let us understand infinitely many lines parallel to each other, and perpendicular to *ab,* to be drawn from *ab* to *cd.*[5] Now no point can be assigned in the transverse line or diagonal *ad* which does not fall on one of the infinitely many parallel lines extending perpendicularly from *ab.* For, if this is possible, let there exist some such point *g:*

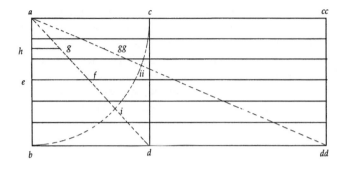

at hanc lineam *gh* unam ex omnibus illis parallelis ex *ab* perpendiculariter exeuntibus esse necesse est. Incidit ergo punctum *g*, id est assignabile quodcunque in aliquam earum linearum incidet. Porro idem punctum non potest incidere in plures parallelas nec una parallela in plura puncta, tot ergo erunt puncta indivisibilia lineae *ad*, quot lineae parallelae exeunt ex *ab*, id est quot sunt puncta indivisibilia in linea *ab*, tot ergo sunt puncta indivisibilia in *ad*, quot in *ab*. Sumatur ex *ad* linea *ai* aequalis *ah*, cum tot sint puncta in *ai*, quot in *ab* (sunt enim aequales) et tot in *ab*, quot in *ad* per os-
**98** tensa, tot erunt puncta indivisibilia in *ai*, quot in *ad*, nulla ergo erunt puncta in differentia inter *ai* et *ad*, nempe in *id*, quod est absurdum.

*Nullum datur minimum seu indivisibile in tempore et motu.*

Ponatur enim tempore *ab* percurri spatium *ad* motu uniformi, ergo dimidio temporis *ae* dimidium spatii *af* absolvetur, et millesima parte temporis, millesima spatii etc. ergo indivisibili temporis, indivisibilis spatii, cum tempus et spatium proportionaliter dividantur. Ponatur enim temporis minimo, percurri spatii non minimum, quantulocunque tempore, dummodo non minimo, infinita spatia divisibilia, et sensibili quodam tempore, percurretur spatium infinitum. Ratio enim indivisibilis, si quod esse intelligatur, ad divisibile est seu minimi in continuo ad quodcunque non minimum quae finiti ad infinitum.

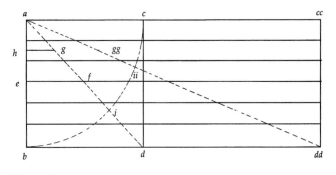

Figure 1

then a straight line *gh* may certainly be understood to be drawn from it perpendicular to *ab*. But this line *gh* must necessarily be one of all the parallels extending perpendicularly from *ab*. Therefore the point *g* falls—i.e.
any assignable point will fall—on one of these lines. Moreover, the same
point cannot fall on several parallel lines, nor can one parallel fall on several points. Therefore the line *ad* will have as many indivisible points as
there are parallel lines extending from *ab*, i.e. as many as there are indivisible points in the line *ab*. Therefore there are as many indivisible points in
*ad* as in *ab*. Let us assume in *ad* a line *ai* equal to *ab*. Now since there are
as many points in *ai* as in *ab* (since they are equal), and as many in *ab* as in
**98**  *ad,* as has been shown, there will be as many indivisible points in *ai* as in
*ad.* Therefore there will be no points in the difference between *ai* and *ad,*
namely, in *id,* which is absurd.

*There is no minimum or indivisible in time and motion.*

For let us suppose a space *ad* is traversed with a uniform motion in a
time *ab*. Then in half the time *ae* half the space *af* will be completed, and
in a thousandth of the time, a thousandth of the space, etc. Therefore in an
indivisible of time, an indivisible of space will be traversed, since time and
space are divided proportionately. For let us suppose that in a minimum of
time the amount of space traversed is not a minimum: then in a time however small, provided it is not a minimum, infinite divisible spaces would
be traversed, and in some perceptible time, an infinite space would be traversed. For the ratio of an indivisible—if such a thing is understood to exist—to the divisible, or the ratio of the minimum in the continuum to
whatever is not a minimum, is that of the finite to the infinite.

*Nullum datur Maximum in rebus, vel quod idem est Numerus infinitus omnium unitatum non est unum totum, sed nihilo aequiparatur.*

Nam si numerus infinitus omnium unitatum, seu quod idem est, Numerus infinitus omnium numerorum est aliquod totum, sequetur aliquam eius partem esse ipsi aequalem. Quod est absurdum. Consequentiae vim ita ostendo. Numerus omnium Numerorum Quadratorum est pars Numeri omnium Numerorum: at quilibet Numerus est radix alicuius Numeri quadrati, nam si in se ducatur, fiet aliquis numerus quadratus; nec idem numerus potest esse radix diversorum quadratorum, nec idem quadratus diversarum radicum, tot ergo sunt Numeri, quot Numeri quadrati, seu Numerus Quadratorum aequalis est Numero Numerorum, totum parti, quod est absurdum.

*Scholion.* Habemus ergo exclusa rebus intelligibilibus, duo: Minimum et Maximum; indivisibile, vel omnino *unum,* et *omne;* quod partibus careat, et quod pars alterius esse non possit.

*Sunt aliqua in continuo infinite parva, seu infinities minora, quovis sensibili dato.*

Id de spatio primum ita ostendo. Esto linea *ab,* percurrenda aliquo motu. Cum possit aliquod intelligi initium motus in illa linea, initium etiam lineae hoc initio motus percurri intelligetur, esto illud initium *ac.* **99** Sed manifestum est posse ab eo resecari *dc* salvo initio, et si initium credatur *ad* ab eo rursus *ed* resecabitur initio salvo, idque in infinitum. Etsi enim nec manus mea, possit, nec animus velit prosequi divisionem in infinitum; potest tamen semel in universum intelligi, id omne ad initium non pertinere, quod salvo initio abscindi potest, cumque in infinitum queat abscindi, continuum enim, ut alii demonstravere in infinitum divisibile est, sequitur initium lineae, seu quod initio motus percurritur esse infinite parvum.

Idem intelligitur ex angulis, et contactibus, quos si corpora perfecte elaborata intelligantur (quod possibile esse per rerum naturam nemo negaverit), necesse est fieri in puncto.

*There is no maximum in things, or what is the same thing, the infinite number of all unities is not one whole, but is comparable to nothing.*[6]

For if the infinite number of all unities, or what is the same thing, the infinite number of all numbers, is a whole, it will follow that one of its parts is equal to it; which is absurd. I will show the force of this consequence as follows. The number of all square numbers is a part of the number of all numbers: but any number is the root of some square number, for if it is multiplied into itself, it makes a square number. But the same number cannot be the root of different squares, nor can the same square have different roots. Therefore there are as many numbers as there are square numbers, that is, the number of numbers is equal to the number of squares, the whole to the part, which is absurd.

*Scholium.* We therefore hold that two things are excluded from the realm of intelligibles: minimum, and maximum; the indivisible, or what is entirely *one,* and *everything;* what lacks parts, and what cannot be part of another.

*There are in the continuum infinitely small things,*[7] *that is, things infinitely smaller than any given sensible thing.*

Figure 2

First I show this for the case of space as follows. Let there be a line *ab*, to be traversed by some motion. Since some beginning of motion is intelligible in that line, so also will be a beginning of the line traversed by this beginning of motion. Let this beginning of the line be *ac*. But it is evident that *dc* can be cut off from it without cutting off the beginning. And if *ad* is believed to be the beginning, from it again *ed* can be cut off without cutting off the beginning, and so on to infinity. For even if my hand is unable and my soul unwilling to pursue the division to infinity, it can nevertheless in general be understood at once that everything that can be cut off without cutting off the beginning does not involve the beginning. And since parts can be cut off to infinity (for the continuum, as others have demonstrated, is divisible to infinity), it follows that the beginning of the line, i.e. that which is traversed in the beginning of the motion, is infinitely small.

The same thing may also be understood of angles of contact, which, if the bodies are understood to be perfectly finished (which no one will deny to be possible in the nature of things), will necessarily occur at a point.

*Punctum* est longitudinis latitudinis et profunditatis; *Linea* est latitudinis et profunditatis, *Superficies* est profunditatis, infinities minoris quavis sensibili data.

Sequitur ex praemissis. Cum ostensum sit nulla esse indivisibilia, esse tamen infinite parva. Nolui autem definire punctum, lineam longitudinis quavis data minoris, quia Centrum intelligi debet non linea, sed figura minor quavis data, ut Centrum Circuli intelligi debet Circulus minor quovis dato, cuius portiones sunt anguli.

*Datur Punctum puncto minus.*

Ita punctum concursus anguli majoris maius est puncto concursus anguli minoris. Et Angulus quantitas puncti est, scilicet centri. Manifestum est enim etsi perpetuo lineae diminuantur, angulum tamen salvum manere. Ad angulum ergo non nisi lineas infinite minores quavis sensibili data, requiri, quibus interceptum spatium itidem quovis sensibili infinite minus ac proinde punctum est. Item, cum corpus unum alio celerius movetur, initia ipsa motuum inaequalia esse necesse est, quibus percurritur linea infinities minor quavis sensibili data, id est eas lineas esse inaequales. Eae autem lineae puncta sunt.

*Punctum unum alio potest esse infinities minus.*

Nam angulus contactus punctum est, et angulus rectilineus punctum est, et rectilineus tamen quantuluscunque major est angulo contactus quolibetcunque.

*Nullum est spatium sine corpore, et nullum corpus sine motu.*

Mira et a nemine observata haec demonstrandi ratio mihi patuit, ex interiore indivisibilium cognitione. Ostendam nimirum, si quod sit spatium in rerum natura, a corpore distinctum, si quod corpus a motu; indivisibilia esse admittenda quod est absurdum, et demonstratis adversum. Consequentia probatur: Pone punctum intelligi lineam infinite parvam, aliamque alia esse majorem, eamque in spatio aut corpore designatam cogitari; et de aliquo corporis aut spatii cujusdam initio, id est prima parte, quaeri, et illud pro initio non haberi, cui aliquid salvo initio abscindi potest; hoc posito in spatio corporeque ad indivisibilia necessario deveniemus. Nam nec linea ista utcunque infinite parva erit verum corporis initium, cum adhuc

A *point* is of a length, breadth, and depth infinitely smaller than any that can be sensed; a *line* is of a breadth and depth infinitely smaller than any that can be sensed; a *surface* is of a depth infinitely smaller than any that can be sensed.

This follows from the premisses, since it has been shown that there are no indivisibles, yet that there are infinitely small things. But I do not wish to define a point as a line of length smaller than any given length, since a center should be conceived not as a line, but as a figure smaller than any given figure, as, for example, the center of a circle should be conceived as a circle smaller than any given circle, the parts of which are angles.

*There is one point smaller than another.*

Thus the vertex of a larger angle is greater than the vertex of a smaller angle. And the angle is the quantity of a point, namely, of its center [i.e. its vertex]. For it is evident that even if the lines are perpetually diminished, the angle still remains intact. Therefore only lines infinitely smaller than any given sensible lines are required for an angle, and the space intercepted by them is in the same way infinitely smaller than any sensible space, and is consequently a point. Likewise, since one body moves faster than another, it is necessary that the very beginnings of the motions by which a line infinitely smaller than any given sensible line is traversed, be unequal—i.e. that these lines be unequal. But these lines are points.

*One point can be infinitely smaller than another.*

For an angle of contact is a point, and a rectilinear angle is a point, and yet any rectilinear angle, however small, is greater than any angle of contact whatsoever.[8]

*There is no space without body, and no body without motion.*

This wonderful method of demonstration, unnoticed by anyone else, became clear to me from a more intimate knowledge of indivisibles. For I 100 shall show that if there is some space in the nature of things distinct from body, and if there is some body distinct from motion, then indivisibles must be admitted. But this is absurd, and contrary to what has been demonstrated. The consequence is proved as follows. Suppose we understand a point as an infinitely small line, there being one such line greater than others, and this line is thought of as designated in a space or body; and suppose we seek the beginning of some body or of a certain space, i.e. its first part; and suppose also that anything from which we may cut off something without cutting off the beginning cannot be regarded as the beginning: with all this supposed, we shall necessarily arrive at indivisibles in

aliquid ab ea abscindi possit, differentia scilicet inter ipsam, et aliam lineam infinite parvam, adhuc minorem: nec quiescetur, donec ad rem parte carentem, seu qua minor fingi nulla possit, deveniatur, qualem ostendi impossibilem. At si corpus intelligatur, id quod movetur, tunc initium eius linea infinite parva definietur, etsi enim ea linea alia minor extet; huius tamen motus, nullum aliud Initium assumi potest, quam quod alterius motus tardioris Initio sit maius. Corporis autem initium ipso motus initio seu conatu definimus, cum alioquin initium corporis indivisibile sit futurum. Hinc sequitur nullam esse in corpore materiam a motu distinctam, ea enim necessario indivisibilia contineret. Quare multo minus spatium a materia distinctum est. Hinc intelligitur denique nihil aliud esse, *esse corpus* quam *moveri*.

*Si nullae essent mentes, omnia corpora essent nihil.*

Cum corpus esse sit moveri, quaerendum est quid sit moveri; si mutare locum; at quid locus? nonne a corporibus determinatur. Si transferri de vicinia corporis in corpus; redit quaestio quid corpus. Erit ergo corpus inexplicabile, seu impossibile, nisi motus explicari possit corpore eius definitionem non ingresso. Moveri esse spatium mutare, frustra dicetur, cum confecerimus nihil esse spatium a corpore distinctum. Quid ergo tandem revera corpus motusque, ut circulus evitetur. Quid nisi ab aliqua ⟨mente⟩ sentiri.

*Ad Corporum existentiam, requiri certum est mentem quandam a corpore immunem, aliam ab illis omnibus, quas sentimus.*

Eae enim mentes quas sentimus patet, ut in se quisque experitur, nihil conferre ad existentiam rerum. Experimento enim constat, omnia ab aliis **101** non ideo minus sentiri, quod ego abfui, idemque in singulis verum est. Ergo et in omnium aggregato, quod eas non nisi consideratione conjungit. Mentem autem illam a corpore liberam, seu corporis ad existendum non indigentem esse debere, per se patet. Alias huius Mentis proprietates ex aliis principiis derivamus.

En ergo quantas res in philosophia quam paucis lineis gesserimus! Exclusimus ex natura indivisibilia, seu Minima, quemadmodum et Maxima;

space and body. For that line, however infinitely small it is, will not be the true beginning of body, since something can still be cut off from it, namely, the difference between it and another infinitely small line that is still smaller; nor will this cease until it reaches a thing lacking a part, or one smaller than which cannot be imagined, which kind of thing has been shown to be impossible. But if a body is understood as that which moves,[9] then its beginning will be defined as an infinitely small line. For even if there exists another line smaller than it, the beginning of its motion can nonetheless be taken to be simply something that is greater than the beginning of some other slower motion. But the beginning of a body we define as the beginning of motion itself, i.e. endeavour, since otherwise the beginning of the body would turn out to be an indivisible. Hence it follows that there is no matter in body distinct from motion, since it would necessarily contain indivisibles, so that there is even less ground for a space distinct from matter. Hence it is finally understood that *to be a body* is nothing other than *to move*.

*If there were no minds, all bodies would be nothing.*

Since to be a body is to to move, it must be asked what it is to move. If it is to change place, then what is place? isn't this determined by reference to bodies? If to move is to be transferred from the vicinity of one body to another body, the question returns, what is body? Thus body will be inexplicable, that is, impossible, unless motion can be explained without body entering into its definition. It is no good saying that to move is to change space, when we have concluded that there is no distinction between space and body. So what in the end are body and motion really, if we are to avoid this circle? What else, but being sensed by some mind.

*For the existence of bodies, it is certain that some mind immune from body is required, different from all the others we sense.*

For it is clear that these minds we sense, such as anyone experiences in himself, confer nothing towards the existence of things. For it is known **101** from experience that everything is not sensed any the less by others because I am absent, and the same is true of every individual. Therefore this will also be the case in the aggregate of all things, which combines them only by considering them together. On the other hand, it is clear that that mind that is free from body, i.e. does not need a body in order to exist, must exist per se. We derive other properties of this mind by means of other principles.

So look how many things we have accomplished in philosophy in how few lines! We excluded indivisibles, i.e. minima, from nature, just as we

tum vero spatium a materia et materiam a motu distinctam, quibus indivisibilia nobis inferebantur: denique Mentium vindicavimus necessitatem,
sed ex mentibus non nisi Dei. Supersunt alia non minora, quae ex iisdem
principiis ducuntur; cogitationis modus et immortalitas animae et mundus
in parvo sine penetratione, ne dicam de Mentium ex mentibus propaga-
tione. Quae omnia indivisibilium cognitioni debentur.

### De consistentia corporum                                              Aiii4

**94**  *Consistentia* corporum est quantitas virium necessariarum ad solutio-nem
contiguitatis.
*Continua* sunt contigua cum aliqua consistentia. Contigua sunt inter
quae distantia nulla est.[L1]
*Si duo corpora ita contigua sint, ut nullo in diversa conatu cieantur, ea
corpora non ideo continua sunt,* seu conatui in diversa resistentia. Cum
enim omnia corpora omnes recipient conatus, qui ipsis imprimuntur, (etsi
**95**  ob aliorum conatuum concursum, conatus illi non semper effectum sor-
tiantur). Ideo non ideo minus corpora contigua conatus in diversa recipi-
unt, quod eos iam non habent; conatus autem in diversa, ne exitum nanciscantur aliis oppositis aequalibus conatibus opus est, ergo ad resistentiam
contra conatus novos in diversa euntes non sufficit eorum absentia praece-
dens, nec proinde ad continuitatem contiguitas.
Nemo mirari debet a summi viri Renati Cartesii sententia (quam nuper
etiam Illustri Hugenio suspectam fuisse video) nobis fuisse abeundum.
Nam ille suam quam affert causam continuitatis, a sententia de motu et

---

L1. In the margin: Hypothesis mea concursuum eventus per meras conatuum
compositiones, et hos per corporum diversorum superimpositiones explicandi
adeo necessaria est, ut sine ea intelligi non possit acceleratio, cum corpus impelli-
tur in plagam ad quam jam tendit. Ad hoc intelligitur, cum corpus intelligitur
moveri in corpore jam moto. Ego antequam hoc detexissem de ista acceleratione
ipse dubitabam.

also excluded maxima; then we excluded space distinct from matter, and matter distinct from motion, from which we had inferred indivisibles; finally we vindicated the necessity of minds, but from among minds, only God's. There are other things no less important that are deduced from these same principles: the mode of thought, the immortality of the soul, and a world in the small without penetration, not to speak of the propagation of minds by minds; all of which are due to a knowledge of indivisibles.[10]

### 4. On the Cohesiveness of Bodies[1]                Aiii4

[Fall 1672–Winter 1672–73][2]

**94** The *cohesiveness*[3] of bodies is the quantity of force needed to destroy their contiguity.[4]

*Continuous* things are contiguous ones with some cohesiveness. *Contiguous* things are those between which there is no distance.[L1]

*If*[6] *two bodies are contiguous in such a way that they are not incited in different directions by any endeavour, these bodies are not for that reason continuous,* that is, resistant to an endeavour to move in different direc-
**95** tions. For all bodies receive all endeavours which are impressed on them (even though, because of the running together of different endeavours, those endeavours do not always have a share in the effect); and it is for this reason, and not because contiguous bodies are less receptive to endeavours to move in different directions, that they do not have such endeavours now. Endeavours to move in different directions, however, need equal and opposite endeavours if they are not to escape. Therefore their previous absence does not suffice for a resistance against new endeavours going in different directions, nor, consequently, for the continuation of their contiguity.[7]

No one ought to be surprised that we have departed from the opinion of the great René Descartes (which I see was recently looked down upon by the illustrious Huygens).[8] For Descartes derived his own proposed account of continuity from an opinion about motion and rest that can hardly

L1. In the margin: My hypothesis of collisions coming about through compositions of endeavours alone, and of explaining the latter by the superposition of different bodies, is necessary precisely because without it we cannot understand the acceleration of a body when it is pushed in a direction in which it is already tending. If we do make this hypothesis we can understand it, as one body is understood to be moved on another already in motion. Before I unraveled this, I was unsure how to deal with acceleration.[5]

quiete minime probanda derivavit. Cum enim illi corpus quiescens simpliciter magis videatur resistere impingenti, quam si contrario motu cieretur, mirum non est [s]ufficere illi quoque corpus quiescens apud aliud corpus, ad motum ab eo sive discessum prohibendum. Sed cum omnis scientiae de Motu pariter ac Mente principium alibi demonstratum ponam, Conatus scilicet nullos perire, sed omnes in universum esse *efficaces, perpetuosque* etsi allis conatibus super additis mixti non sentiantur, motuum lineis ea compositione tam multiplici in immensum variatis; hinc sequitur, corpus quoque quiescens, si quod extat conatum impressum esse accepturum, eumque conatum perinde ut alios omnes esse efficacem, ac proinde si nullus alius in corpore extet, a quo compensetur aut temperetur, in motum prorupturum. Hoc me, si quis pergat dubitare, peculiari opera in clara luce positurum spero; interea ne alienis domestics huius argumenti differantur, Hypotheseos loco mihi admitti postulo. Apparebit nihil harmonicum magis concinnumque dici posse. Idem ita confirmatur: Si quies causa consistentiae est primum nulla consistentia erit separabilis, infinite enim distat quies a motu; nam si fortius resistet quies quam motus oppositus, infinite fortius resistet, deinde omnes consistentiae erunt inter se aequales; omnes enim quietes sunt aequales.

  *Si corpus unum conetur in alterius locum, ea duo corpora continua sunt.* Conatus est initium motus, momento aliquo dato, est ergo initium
**96** loci mutati, seu transitus de loco in locum, simul ergo in loco utroque est, cum in neutro id est nullibi esse non possit. Quod ut clarius pateat intelligatur punctum *A* ex *a* conari versus *b,* id est ex *a* incipere exire; momento ergo primo occupat lineam quandam, minorem quidem quavis assignabili, sed tamen modo majorem modo minorem, prout conatus ipse seu initium

fortius est [debiliusve]. Ponatur enim ea linea inassignabilis in conatu debili esse ut *ac,* erit in forti ut *ad.* Patet ergo quod conatur iam incipere effi-

be approved. For it seemed to him that a body simply at rest would resist a body impinging on it more than it would if it were moving with a contrary motion;[9] this being so, it is not surprising that for him a body's being at rest against another body is also sufficient to prevent it from moving away from it, or separating.[10] But I take as a principle of every science, not only of motion but equally of mind, something I have demonstrated elsewhere:[11] namely, that no endeavours die away, but all are in general *efficacious and perpetual,* even though they cannot be sensed, having been mixed up with the other endeavours added on top of them, with lines of motion varied beyond measure by such a manifold composition. From this principle it follows that a body at rest, too, will accept any extant endeavour that is impressed upon it, and that this endeavour is just as efficacious as all the others; and, consequently, that if there were no other endeavour extant in the body that would compensate for or moderate it, the body would break forth into motion. If anyone remains in doubt about this, I hope to put it in a clear light with a special work; meanwhile, to prevent disagreement between those at home with this argument and those who are strangers to it, I insist that it be allowed me as a hypothesis. It will be clear that nothing more harmonious and elegant can be said. The same thing is confirmed as follows: If rest is the cause of cohesiveness, first of all no cohesive thing will be separable, since rest is infinitely different from motion; for if rest were to resist more strongly than an opposite motion, it would resist infinitely more strongly. And secondly, all things will be equally cohesive, since all rests are equal.

*If one body endeavours to move into the place of another, these two bodies are continuous.* Endeavour[12] is the beginning of motion at a given moment. Therefore it is the beginning of a change of place, i.e. of a transition from place to place, and therefore is in both places at the same time, since it cannot be in neither, i.e. nowhere. To make this clearer, let us conceive a point $A$ to have an endeavour from $a$ towards $b$, i.e. to begin to move out of $a$; at the first moment, then, it occupies a certain line, one that is indeed smaller than any assignable, but nonetheless sometimes greater, sometimes smaller, accordingly as the endeavour, or beginning, is stronger [or weaker]. For let us suppose this unassignable line to be proportional to $ac$ in a weak endeavour, and proportional to $ad$ in a strong one. Then it is clear that any endeavour whatsoever already begins to have an effect, even if

**96**

the effect is smaller than any assignable. Hence it follows that whatever endeavours to move into another's place already at its boundary begins to

cere, etsi effectus minor sit quovis assignabili. Hinc sequitur quicquid in alterius locum conatur, iam extremo suo incipere in eius loco esse, id est extrema eorum esse unum, sive se penetrare; ac proinde alterum sine altero impelli non posse. Ac proinde ea corpora esse continua.

Magni momenti haec propositio est, hinc sequitur enim propagatio motuum in pleno, et corpus unum motum caetera omnia secum abripere conari et quantulacunque in Mundo sentiri a toto universo. Idem [experimentis] confirmatur, constat enim fortissime agitata etiam liquida, solidorum naturam imitari, dummodo communis sit ipsis agitatio.

Phaenomena Consistentiae sive cohaesionis nuper publicata quorum ratio a pressione aëris reddi non potest: ex Boylii Gerickii et Hugenii observatis sumta.

(1) Duo corpora polita in loco aëre exhausto, non minus quam in pleno, aegre divelluntur: sed et antliaeque ac siphonis bicruri officia exercentur non in Antlia minus exhausta quam aëre libero.

(2) Mercurius aëre purgatus majoris licet altitudinis, quam cui pressio aëris aequivaleat, non descendit e Tubo infra aperto.

His phaenomenis sensibile redditum est, quod antea sola ratione constabat, non omnem consistentiam ab aëris pressione oriri, ut quidam credebant. Nam Tabulis quibusdam solidis politisque iam praeformatis ad eam rem opus est; sed harum soliditas unde? Altius ergo repetenda consistentiae ratio est, propositione quadam mea ex alio opusculo huc translata.

## Notes on Descartes's *Principles of Philosophy*

**Aiii15**

. . .

**214** **[Cartes. princip. part 1.] n. 21.** *Ex eo quod nunc sumus non sequitur nos futuros in momento proxime sequente, nisi aliqua causa nos continue reproducat seu conservet.* Mihi videtur parum firma haec ratiocinatio. Neque enim mutationem nisi ab aliqua causa esse. Quod principium inter potissima mihi videtur ponendum philosophiae.

exist in the other's place, i.e. their boundaries are one, i.e. penetrate each other; and consequently one cannot be impelled without the other. And consequently these bodies are continuous.

This proposition is of great importance, for from it follows the propagation of motions in a plenum, and that when one body is moved it endeavours to carry away all the other bodies with it, and that things in the world of however small a size can be sensed by the whole universe. The same thing is confirmed by experiments,[13] since it is well known that even liquids, when they are vigorously disturbed by some motion, imitate the nature of a solid as long as they have the disturbed motion in common.

Recently published phenomena of cohesiveness, or cohesion, which cannot be accounted for by the pressure of the air: taken from the observations of Boyle, Guericke, and Huygens.[14]

(1) Two polished bodies in a place exhausted of air are no less difficult to separate than they are in a plenum; but also both the air pump and the bipedal siphon do not perform their functions any less in an exhausted air pump than in free air.[15]

(2) Mercury purged of air, although of a greater height than that to which the pressure of the air would balance it, does not descend from the tube below the aperture.

These phenomena have rendered sensible a fact that was known beforehand by reason alone: that not all cohesiveness arises from the pressure of the air, as some people used to believe. For in this case there would be a need for certain solid and polished tablets to be already preformed: but where does the solidity of these come from?[16] The reason for cohesiveness, then, must be investigated again more deeply, by transposing here a certain proposition of mine from another little work.[17]

### 5. Notes on Descartes's *Principles of Philosophy* (Selections)[1]                                    Aiii15

[Fall—Dec. 1675?][2]

On Part 1:

. . .

**214**  **§21:** "From the fact that we exist now it does not follow that we will exist in the next following moment, unless some cause continually reproduces us, i.e. conserves us."[3] This reasoning does not seem very sound to me. For there is no change except as a result of some cause—a principle that seems to me to be among the most powerful that are to be supposed in philosophy.

**n. 26. et n. 27.** pro infinito indefinitum adhibere suadet, id est cuius limites a nobis inveniri non possunt, atque veri infiniti nomen servandum Deo solo. At contra **n. 36. part. 2.** fatetur materiam reapse dividi motu in partes qualibet assignabili minores, ac proinde actu infinitas.

. . .

215     **n. 51.** nomen substantiae non convenire Deo et creaturis univoce, hoc est nullam eius nominis significationem intelligi posse Deo et creaturis communem.

**Part. 2. num. 4. et 11.** naturam corporis in extensione ait consistere, caetera enim ex corpore tolli posse salva, ut sic dicam corporalitate. Mihi videtur esse qualitatem quandam praeter extensionem quae a corpore tolli nequeat nempe impenetrabilitatem, seu quae facit, ut corpus corpori cedat; nec video quomodo ea possit ab extensione derivari.

**num. 20.** nullas atomos dari posse, quia a Deo saltem dividi possint, hoc nec Gassendus negaverit.

**num. 21.** *Mundum nullos extensionis suae fines habere.* Eodem opinor argumento quo illic utitur, quod semper spatium ultra intelligere liceat, probaverit, etiam esse aeternum.

**num. 25.** Motum definit per corporum translationem ex vicinia corporum, sed mihi videtur corporis naturam per motum explicandam.

**n. 30. fig. 1.** duobus corporibus in globo Terrae motis, altero ab oriente versus occidentem, altero ab occidente versus orientem, intelligi potest terra immobilis. Sed et vicissim nil prohibet, me fingere: esse me in aliquo corporum minorum, quod proinde ut quiescens spectabitur. Patet ergo cuilibet corpori affingi posse quietem, modo intelligatur sentiens in ipso esse. Sed nec rejectio per tangentem realem arguit motum circumacti; cum idem futurum sit si omnia circa ipsum agantur. Nimirum solemus homines quietem corporibus majoribus tribuere, idque compendii seu ordinatae cogitationis causa; uti duas fractiones utile reducere ad communem denominatorem; diversos angulorum sinus ad eundem radium; ita utile est id ut immobile suppone quod perenne et late fusum est.

**Cartes. princip. part 1. n. 36.** Deum eandem semper quantitatem motus in universo servare. Mihi videtur eandem semper quantitatem conatus,

**§§26 and 27:** Instead of 'infinite', he recommends that we use the term 'indefinite', i.e. that whose limits cannot be found by us, and that the term 'true infinity' be reserved for God alone. But contrary to this, in **Part 2, §36,**[4] matter is admitted to be really divided by motion into parts that are smaller than any assignable, and therefore actually infinite.[5]

. . .

215 **§51:** The term 'substance' is not univocally applicable to God and to creatures, that is, no meaning can be understood for this name that is common to God and creatures.

On Part 2:

**§§4 and 11:** He says the nature of body consists in extension, for everything else can be taken away from body except, so to speak, corporeality. To me it seems that there is a certain quality besides extension that cannot be taken away from body, namely, impenetrability, i.e. what makes one body yield to another; and I do not see how this could be derived from extension.

**§20:** There cannot be atoms, since they could at least be divided by God; this Gassendi would not have denied.

**§21:** "The world has no limits to its extension." I believe that by the same argument he uses there that one may always conceive another space beyond [any supposed limit]; he will have proved that it is eternal too.[6]

**§25:** He defines motion by the translation of bodies from the vicinity of other bodies, but it seems to me that the nature of body should be explained through motion.

**§30, fig. 1:**[7] When two bodies are moving on the surface of the Earth, the one from east to west, the other from west to east, the Earth can be understood to be immobile. But also nothing prevents me from imagining in turn that I am on one of the smaller bodies, which will thus be regarded as being at rest. Therefore it is clear that any body can be imagined to be at rest, if only a sentient being is understood to be on it. But being thrown off along the tangent does not argue the real motion of the rotating thing, since it would be the same if everything moved around it.[8] Of course, we humans are accustomed to attribute rest to larger bodies, and this for the sake of the abbreviation or ordering of thought. Just as it is useful to reduce two fractions to a common denominator, or the sines of two angles to the same radius; so it is useful to suppose as immobile that which is of a broad and enduring cast.

**§36:** God always conserves the same quantity of motion in the universe. It seems to me that he conserves the same quantity of endeavour, impetus, or

impetus sive actioni servare. Quia scilicet conatus nunquam destruuntur, sed componuntur inter se, ac fieri potest, ut ex duobus conatibus oppositis
**216**  aequalibus sequatur quies vel saltem motus tardior, si non sint aequales. Servata nihilominus quantitate actionum sive conatum.

**n. 39.** Refert Cartesius inter naturae leges, ut omnis sua natura sit rectus. Hoc a me demonstratur ex definitione; mutatione scilicet situs: Et pone esse curvam, mutatio seu distantiae variatio, semper in linea recta est. Nam et distantia semper linea est recta.

**n. 40.** *Tertia naturae lex* est quod corpus alteri occurrens cuius major est resistentia quam vis pergendi prioris, amissa tantum determinatione, servato motu alio deflecti. Si minor resistentia sit, tantum perderet quantum ei de motu suo tribuit. Demonstrat partem priorem ex eo quod determinatio a motu differat et altera destructa alter superesse possit: posteriorem ex eo quod Deus eandem motus quantitatem servet, sed mihi lex haec falsa videtur. Fateor partem motus servari quae servari potest, sed hoc non sufficere (sine Elaterio), infra ex reflexionibus patebit. Alterum jam ostendi falsum esse. Illud tamen ex alio principio dicendum est, posito pleno non facile corpus ab alio corpore impelli, atque ideo corpori impellenti aliquid decedere, sed sine Elaterio non utique tantundem. Vim autem resistendi ait in eo consistere, quod omnia conantur in priore statu perseverare, et quantitatem aestimandam ab ipsa magnitudine superficiei, et celeritate motus corporum v. g. quae disjungi debent. Sed videtur nullum esse corporibus conatum perseverandi in eodem statu, neque resistentiam contra mutationem; alioquin resistentia quiescentium foret infinita. Adde quod nihil referret quae sit vis agentium, nam eo ipso quod major esset impellentis celeritas, major quoque resistentia quiescentis, ob majorem secuturam mutationem.

**[n. 46–52. ]**  Caeterum ex hac naturae lege, septem regulae motus Cartesianae ducuntur. Ex quibus *prima, B* et *C* aequalia et aequivelocia directe occurentia redire eadem via et celeritate. Verum posito Elaterio. 2$^{\text{da}}$, si *B* esset majus, celeritas eadem, abripere *C* eadem quae est ipsius *B* celeritate. Hoc omnibus modis falsum est. 3$^{\text{tia}}$, si *B* esset aequale, sed velocius,

action; for endeavours are never destroyed, but are instead compounded with each other. And in fact it can happen that from two equal and opposite
**216** endeavours rest will follow, or at least a slower motion, if they are not equal; but with the quantity of actions, i.e. endeavours, nevertheless conserved.

**§39:** Descartes reckons among the laws of nature that every motion is by its own nature straight. This I have demonstrated from the definition, by defining motion as change of situation. And supposing a curve to be a change or variation of distance, it is always in a straight line. For distance too is always a straight line.

**§40:** The *third law of nature* is that a body colliding with another whose resistance is greater than the first's force of continuing is deflected in another direction with its motion conserved, losing only its determination. If the resistance is smaller, it would lose only as much motion as it contributes to it of its own motion. He demonstrates the first part from the fact that determination differs from motion, and that when one is destroyed the other can be left intact; and demonstrates the second part from the fact that God conserves the same quantity of motion; but to me this law seems false. To the first I reply that if motion ceases when a determination is taken away, it will be impossible to provide a reason for a new determination. I admit that the part of a motion that can be conserved is conserved, but this is insufficient (without elasticity), as will be clear from the reflections below. The second I have already shown to be false. However, it must be said to be so according to another principle: namely, that, supposing a plenum, one body is not easily impelled by another body, and therefore something is given up by the impelling body, but—without elasticity— certainly not very much. Yet he says that the force of resistance consists in this, that everything endeavours to persevere in its prior state, and the quantity is to be calculated from the size of the surface, and the speed of motion of the bodies, e.g. those which have to be separated. But it seems that bodies have no endeavour for persevering in the same state, nor do they have a resistance to change; otherwise bodies at rest would have an infinite resistance.[9] Add that it does not matter what the force of the acting body is, for however much greater the speed of the impelling body was, the resistance of the body at rest would also be that much greater, on account of the greater change that would follow.

**[§§46–52]:** As for the rest, the seven Cartesian rules of motion are derived from this law of nature.[10] Of these the *first* is that if *B* and *C* were the same size and had equal [and opposite] velocities, and collided along a straight line, they would rebound along the same path and with the same speed. This is true, if elasticity is supposed. The *second* is, if *B* were larger but had

differentiae medietas in minus velox transferretur, et proinde $C$ abripere-
tur a $B$, motu ipsius $B$ dimidio ipsius differentiae qua motum $C$ excessit,
minuto. Ideo ($4^{ta}$) si $C$ quiesceret et esset majus, nunquam moveretur; ($5^{ta}$)

**217**  si minus, moveretur quantulocunque impellentis motu, sed tantum ab eo
reciperet, ut ambo moverentur aequaliter. Et ideo inquit si $B$ esset duplo
maius quam $C$ daret ei motus tertiam partem (quia ipsa scilicet est tertia
pars totius ex utroque composit), quia tertia illa pars tam celeriter moveret
corpus $C$, quam duae tertiae eius duplum. Obscur[a] ista, et contradic-
tori[a]. Quomodo potest in uno tantum una tertia motus, si eadem celeritas. Sed hoc intelligendum est de quantitate motus, non celeritatis, cum
posita eadem celeritate, motus quantitas est ut corporum. ($6^{ta}$) si corpus $C$
quiescens esset aequale ipsi $B$ moto, 4 graduum celeritatis exempli causa,
tunc cum $3^{bus}$ gradibus celeritatis reflectetur, et ipsum $C$ cum uno gradu in
oppositum ibit. Non capio unde hic ratio 1 ad 3 in supposita aequalitate.
An forte error ex negligentia. ($7^{ma}$ regula) si $B$ et $C$ versus eandem partem
moveantur, $C$ tardius $B$ insequens celerius, ita ut attingat; tunc si excessus
celeritatis major excessu magnitudinis, tunc $B$ transferret tantum motus in
$C$, ut moveantur aeque celeriter, si excessus celeritatis minor, in contrariam partem reflecteretur $B$ retento motu utriusque. Haec Cartesius
adeo manifesta ait, ut non egeant probatione; mihi aliter visum.

N.B. Hoc superioribus adjicendum, cum quaeritur utrum ex iis quae situm ad se invicem mutant, dici debeat moveri. Tunc semper corpori cuidam finito, potius, quam reliquo toti mundo extra ipsum tribuendum esse
motum. Ideo si quaeritur ex duobus particularibus ad se invicem acceden-
tibus utrum moveatur, tantum alia praeterea intuenda sunt, quae si situm
cum utroque mutant, putandum est utrumque moveri; sin cum uno tantum
ei tribuetur motus; sed haec conclusio probabilis, cum corpora quae pro
mensura assumimus particularia sunt; forte enim et ipsa moventur.

the same speed as *C* [after the collision], *B* would carry *C* away with it at the same speed as itself. This is false in every way. The *third,* if *B* were equal to *C* but faster, half of the difference in velocity would be transferred to the slower body, and consequently *C* would be carried away by *B* with *B*'s motion diminished by half of the difference by which its speed exceeds *C*'s. Therefore, *fourth,* if *C* were at rest and larger, it would never be

**217**  moved [by *B*]; if *fifth,* it were smaller, it would be moved by however small a motion of the impinging body, but would only receive from it such an amount that both bodies would move with the same speed. And thus, he says, if *B* were twice as large as *C,* it would give it a third of its motion (since this is a third of the total of the two combined), because that third of the motion would move body *C* with the same speed as two-thirds would move twice *C*. These things are obscure and contradictory. How can there be only one-third in one if they have the same speed? But this is to be understood of the quantity of motion, not that of speed, since, assuming they have the same speed, the quantity of motion is as the quantity of the bodies. *Sixth,* if body *C* were at rest and equal in size to *B,* and the latter were moving with, for example, four degrees of speed, then it would be reflected with three degrees of speed, and *C* would go with one degree of speed in the opposite direction. I do not get where this ratio of 1 to 3 comes from in the supposed equality. Perhaps it is an error of negligence. The *seventh* rule: if *B* and *C* were moving in the same direction, with *C* moving more slowly and *B,* following behind more quickly so as to strike it: then if the excess of speed [of *B* over *C*] is greater than the excess of size [of *C* over *B*], then *B* would transfer as much motion to *C* as would make them move equally fast; and if the excess of speed is smaller, then *B* would be reflected in the opposite direction retaining all its motion. These things, Descartes says, are so evident as not to be in need of proof; to me it seems otherwise.

N.B. This needs to be added to the above considerations: when things are mutually changing their situation and it is asked which of them should be said to be moving, motion should always be ascribed to a certain finite thing rather than to the rest of the entire world outside it. So if it is asked which of two particular bodies approaching one another is moving, then one only has to consider other bodies besides these: if these others change situation with respect to both, then both of them should be thought of as moving; but if they change situation with respect to one only, motion is to be attributed to it. But this conclusion is a probable one when the bodies we assume as measures are particular, for they themselves may well be moving too.

**466**　Decembr. 1675

Esse nihil aliud esse quam percipi posse, sequitur ex quibusdam ratiocinandi modis. Ut si dicam omnia in certain quandam plagam moveri; idem
est ac si dicam omnia quiescere. Si dicam omnia majori quam nunc celeritate proportione moveri, nihil reapse immutatum erit. Si in Spatio loco
extensi imaginer fluidum quiescens perfectum, quod corpore alto in [eo]
natante moveatur ad locum replendum, nihil aliud quam spatium vacuum
dico. Esset Materia, si eius motu corporis motus retardaretur.

Subtilissimae Geometriae res est exquirere quomodo flat, quibus lineis
circulationum, ut liquidum anterius redeat ad locum corporis posterioris.
Examinandum qua quodlibet punctum linea feratur, ut demonstretur quodlibet punctum alia atque alia linea ferri, quo posito sequetur absurdum
scilicet continuum componi ex minimis. Unde rursus sequetur liquidum
perfectum esse impossibile, quod omnia repleat, sive spatium vacuum intelligi debere. Examinanda tamen prius illa demonstratio est eiusque absurditas; antequam dicatur perfectam fluiditatem implicare, vel ideo quia
non videtur intelligi posse differentia inter modum explicandi per fluidum
et per spatium.

Eandem motus quantitatem servari, sive si corporis movendi magnitudo augeatur celeritatem diminui, quae a Galilaeo et Cartesio et Hobbe-
sio, imo et Archimede observata sunt, res est ex phaenomenis ducta, sed
cuius originem in ipsa natura ostendit nemo. Hoc scilicet praejudicio quasi
quodam sumimus, maius corpus difficilius moveri, quasi ipsa materia motui resistat. Quod repugnat, indifferens est enim materia ad quemlibet
locum, adeoque et ad mutationem loci, sive motum. Cartesius confugit ad
immutabilitatem Dei; debebat appellate harmoniam rerum Dei, simplicissima enim eligere ad maxima praestanda sapientissimi est. Sed difficile
erit ostendere consentaneum esse harmoniae rerum, ut servetur eadem

**467**　quantitas motus in toto mundo. Forte enim intererat harmoniae rerum.
Quoniam contra videtur consentaneum varietati rerum, ut in aliis atque
aliis systematis, aliae atque aliae leges motus habeantur. Quod si vero ostendatur necessariam esse quantitatem motus ex ipsa materiae et pleni facilius concedetur, quod desidero. Nam plenitudinem mundi esse consen-
taneam harmoniae rerum utique concedetur. Aliquam enim partem loci
inutilem sine necessitate relictam esse intelligi non potest. Plena autem

## 6. On Matter, Motion, Minima, and the Continuum[1]

**466**   December 1675

According to certain ways of reasoning, it follows that to be is nothing other than to be capable of being perceived.[2] For instance, if I say that everything is moving in some specific direction, this is the same as saying that everything is at rest.[3] If I say that everything is moving with a speed proportionally greater than its speed now, nothing will really be changed. If I imagine in space, instead of the extended, a perfect fluid which is at rest, but which, when another body is floating in it, moves to keep the place filled, then I mean nothing other than empty space. It would be matter if the motion of the body were retarded by its motion.

It is something for the subtlest geometry to find out how—by what lines of circulation—it happens that the liquid in front of a body flows back to its rear. It must be examined along what line any point would move, so that it may be demonstrated that any point moves first along one line, then another; granted which, an absurdity will follow: namely, that the continuum is composed of minima. From this in turn it will follow that a perfect liquid which fills everything is impossible, i.e. that space must be understood as a vacuum. But the former demonstration and its absurdity must be examined first, before it is said that a perfect fluidity implies a contradiction on the grounds that there seems to be no intelligible difference between an explanation given in terms of a fluid and one given in terms of space.[4]

That the same quantity of motion is conserved, i.e. that if the magnitude of a moving body is increased, its speed is diminished, has been observed by Galileo, Descartes, and Hobbes, and even by Archimedes.[5] This fact has been derived from the phenomena, but no one has shown its origin in nature itself. We have assumed by a kind of prejudice that a greater body is harder to move, as if matter itself resisted motion. But this is unreasonable, for matter is indifferent to any place whatever, and thus also to change of place, or motion. Descartes took refuge in the immutability of God;[6] he ought to have appealed to the harmony of things for God, since it is apt for the wisest being to choose the simplest means to achieve the greatest results. But it will be difficult to show that it is consonant with the harmony of things for the same quantity of motion to be conserved in the whole

**467**   world. For perhaps the harmony of things played a role; yet, on the other hand, it seems consonant with the variety of things that in different systems different laws of motion should hold. But if the quantity of motion is shown to be necessary as a result of that[7] of matter and the plenum, then what I want will be granted more readily. For it will at least be granted that the plenitude of the world is consonant with the harmony of things, since it is not intelligible that some part of a place should have been needlessly left

esse omnia intelligo, id est materia varie mota, nam si tota quaedam massa
infinita intelligatur universali quodam motu ferri, is motus poterit haberi
pro nullo. Posita ergo plenitudine rerum, seu posito nullam esse spatii
partem, in qua non sit materia quae feratur motu ab infinitis aliis diverso;
ita ostendo eandem motus quantitatem servari.

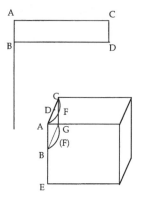

Fingamus aliquamdiu eandem servari quantitatem, et tempus vocemus
AB, spatium autem quod eo tempore materia percurrit ABCD, intelli-
gendo scilicet unumquodque punctum materiae assignabile eo tempore
durante certam spatii partem percurrisse. Unde ut rectius dicam fiat quasi
solidum. Sit tempus licet portio abscissa ex latere cubi, AE, nempe ipsa
AB. Recta autem AC, aliud cubi latus perpendiculare priori repraesentet
materiam. Ipsi AC perpendiculariter insistent rectae DF, quae repraesen-
tent celeritates cuiuslibet materiae partis, seu infinitesimas spatiorum, a
quolibet determinate tempore percurrendorum. Et spatium totum a materia percursum erit quasi cylindrica portio AFCG(F)BGCA. Quod si jam
una materiae pars celerius quam ante moveri incipiat, sequetur eam durante tempore AB plus spatii occupasse, quam alioqui occupasset. Definitum autem est spatium mundi, sive certum ac determinatum, etiamsi infinitum ponatur, et si omnia sint plena, non poterit aliquod maius occupasse
spatium quam ante, nisi aliud minus occupet spatium quam ante, alioquin
corpora se penetrate intelligentur. Quare non poterit aliquid moverl celerius

useless. Now, I conceive everything to be a plenum, i.e. to be matter with various motions, for if some whole infinite mass were understood to be moving with a certain universal motion, this motion could be considered nonexistent. Therefore, supposing the plenitude of things—in other words, supposing there is no part of space that does not contain matter moving with a motion different from an infinity of others—I show that the same quantity of motion is conserved as follows.

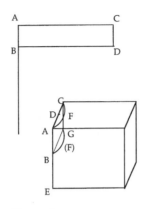

Figure 1

Let us imagine that the same quantity [of matter] is conserved for a while, and let us call the time AB, and the space which the matter traverses in this time ABCD—understanding each assignable point of matter to have traversed a specific part of space during this time. To be more precise, let there be a kind of solid. Let the time be a portion cut from the side AE of the cube, namely, AB. Now let the straight line AC, another side of the cube perpendicular to the latter, represent matter. Extending perpendicularly from AC, let there be straight lines DF, which represent the speeds of any part of matter, i.e. the infinitesimals of the spaces that will be traversed by each in a determinate time. And the total space traversed by the matter will be the portion of a kind of cylinder AFCG(F)BGCA. Now, if a part of matter should begin to move faster than before, it follows that it will have occupied more space during the time AB than it would otherwise have occupied. But the [amount of] space in the world is definite, that is, certain and determinate, even if it is assumed to be infinite; and if everything is a plenum, something could not occupy more space than before unless something else occupied less space than before, otherwise bodies would be understood to penetrate each other. And therefore something could not move more quickly than before unless something else moved

quam ante, nisi aliud moveatur tardius quam ante, quantum satis est, ut
eodem tempore tota materia tantundem spatii occupasse intelligatur. Id
**468**    est, eadem servabitur quantitas motus in summa, cum quantitas motus in
summa eadem sit cum quantitate spatii determinato tempore successive
occupati a determinate materiae quantitate. Nimirum in eo consistit natura
motus, ut nulla sit temporis pars tam parva, quin in ea corpus in pluribus sit
locis successive. Necesse est ergo si omnia sint plena, alia etiam ei cedere
successive. Si quid plura successive loca occupavit, et aliud etiam plura
successive loca occupavit, denique si summa omnium locorum successive
a singulis corporis partibus occupatorum in unum colligatur, prodibit
spatium totum repetitum eo saepius, quo maius sumtum est tempus; neque
vero fieri potest ut maior minorve aequalibus temporibus oriatur spatiorum occupatorum summa, quia tunc distributione facta necesse fuisset,
plus materiae pro eo quod superest spatio implendo accersi, aut aliquid
materiae ejici, quae omnia fieri non posse supponimus.

Illud hic notabile est ad reddendam demonstrationem exactiorem, quod
aliunde ostendi potest, summam motus non posse diminui, vel ideo quod
omnia necessario flexilia sunt. Consideranda hic res, quomodo possibile
sit perfecte rectilinea se flectere, nulla est enim ratio, cur in hanc quam illam se potius partem flectant. Itaque posito concursu duorum perfecte rec-

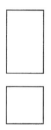

tilineorum homogeneorum, sequetur tunc motum perditum iri, adeoque
turbari totam harmoniam rerum. Responderi potest quidem talia corpora
nec fuisse nec esse nec fore, sed hoc nondum satisfacit menti. Certe enim
adhuc possibile manet tale corpus. Fingamus enim id existere, sequetur
inde impossibile, ut nos supponimus, scilicet mutatio quantitates motus.
Ergo non Elaterium, sed haec conservatio quantitatis est vera causa gener-

more slowly—by an amount sufficient for matter as a whole to be understood as having occupied precisely the same amount of space in the same

**468** time. That is, the same quantity of motion will be conserved in the whole, since the total quantity of motion is the same as the quantity of space successively occupied by a determinate quantity of matter in a determinate time. For the nature of motion surely consists in this, that there is no part of time so small that in it a body is not in several places successively. Therefore, if everything is a plenum, it is necessary that other things should yield to the body successively. If something has occupied several places successively, and something else has also occupied several places successively, and finally if the sum of all the places successively occupied by the individual parts of the body is collected into one, this will result in the whole space being repeated the more often the greater the time taken. And in fact it is not possible that the sum of the spaces occupied in equal times should turn out to be greater or smaller; because then, when the distribution was made, it would have been necessary either for more matter to have been added to fill the space that remains, or for some matter to have been ejected, both of which we have supposed to be impossible.

To provide a more precise demonstration, it is worth noting here that there is another way to show that the sum of motion cannot be diminished, on the basis of the fact that all bodies are necessarily flexible. The thing to be considered is how it is possible for perfectly rectilinear bodies to bend, since there is no reason why they should bend in this direction rather than

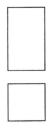

Figure 2

that. Thus, assuming a collision between two perfectly homogeneous rectilinear bodies, it will then follow that some motion will be lost, so that the overall harmony of things is disturbed. Of course, it may be replied that such bodies neither have existed, nor do exist, nor will exist; but this does not yet satisfy the mind. For such a body certainly still remains possible. Let us then imagine that it exists; from this there will follow something we have supposed impossible, namely, a change in the quantity of motion.

alis. Quoniam haec causa generalis, etiam ipsius Elaterii est. Duo in hac consideratione notabilia, unum, quomodo differant impossibilia, ab iis quae nec sunt nec erunt nec fuerunt; alterum, quomodo plures ejusdem rei causae.

Ut res profundius explicetur de relations inter motum et impletionem spatii, videtur ex iis quae dixi sequi non tantum in tota massa non posse plus minusve motus esse, quia tunc tota massa plus spatii occuparet, sed videtur eodem jure dici posse, quod etiam quaelibet corporis pars celerius quam nunc moveri non possit, quin alternetur, fiatque proinde minus levis, quod experientiae repugnat. Certum est idem corpus plus minusve spatii in dato aliquo tempore occupare posse, quia celerius tardiusve moveri

**469** potest. At si omnia sint plena, et corpus aliquod moveatur celerius quam ante; necesse erit aliud corpus moveri tardius quam ante. Nam alioqui corpus unum occupans maius spatium quam ante, et alterum tantundem quantum ante, sequitur utrumque magis quam ante in eodem spatio fuisse; quod est contra ideam impenetrabilitatis qualem corpori dare debemus. Quod si ponamus diminui quantitatem motus, diminuetur et quantitas spatii a materia dato tempore occupati; atqui ea non diminuta est, supererit ergo spatium non occupatum. Illud ergo sufficit pro principio sumi, Naturam materiae sive corporis talem esse, ut iisdem temporibus tantundem spatii occupet.

Motus corporis expansio est, nam quo quid celerius movetur hoc plus spatii occupat tempore aliquo definito. Supposito ergo non posse in pleno corpus unum expandi, quin aliud contrahatur, neque unum contrahi quin aliud expandatur: item non posse expansionem aliam intelligi nisi per motum: Sequitur eandem semper motus quantitatem servari, idem esse quod eandem semper materiae servari quantitatem.

Per idem spatium intra datum tempus plus materiae transire, est materiam moveri celerius, ut scilicet morae parvitate, moles pensetur. Punctum velocitate infinita motum lineam momento implet. Si quid velocitate aliqua moveatur, qua nequeat intelligi major, simul erit ubique.

Minimum tempus (Minimum spatium) est majoris temporis (spatii) lntra cuius terminos est, pars. Ex notione quam habemus de toto et parte. Ergo Minimum tempus est minima temporis pars; et minimum spatium est minima spatii pars. Non datur minima spatii pars. Quia alioqui tot essent

Therefore not elasticity, but this conservation of quantity, is the true general cause. Since it is the general cause, it is also the cause of elasticity itself. There are two things to be noted in this consideration: first, how impossibles differ from things which neither exist, nor will exist, nor have existed; second, how there are many causes of the same thing.

To give a more profound explanation of the relation between motion and the filling of space, it seems to follow from what I have said not only that there cannot be more or less motion in the whole mass—since then the whole mass would occupy more space—but (as it seems can be said with equal justice) that not even a part of a body could move faster than it does now without alternating, and so becoming less light, which is contrary to experience.[8] It is certain that the same body can occupy more or less space in some given time, since it can move more quickly or more slowly. But if everything is a plenum, and some body moves more quickly than before, **469** then it will be necessary for some other body to move more slowly than before. For otherwise, with one body occupying more space than before, and the other just as much as before, it follows that each of them will have been in the same space more than before; which is contrary to the idea of impenetrability that we must attribute to body. On the other hand, if we assume the quantity of motion to be diminished, the quantity of space occupied by matter in a given time will also be diminished; this, however, is not diminished, therefore there will be space left unoccupied. Therefore it is enough to assume this as a principle: that the nature of matter or body is such that it occupies the same amount of space in equal times.[9]

The motion of a body is an expansion, since the faster anything moves the more space it occupies in some definite time. Supposing, then, that in a plenum one body cannot be expanded without another one being contracted, nor be contracted without another being expanded, and also that another expansion can only be understood in terms of motion: assuming all this, it follows that for the same quantity of motion always to be conserved is the same thing as for the same quantity of matter always to be conserved.

For more matter to pass through the same space within a given time is for the matter to be moved faster, so that the bulk is compensated by the smallness of the period of time.[10] A point moving with infinite velocity fills a line in a moment. If something were to move with a velocity greater than which cannot be conceived, it would be everywhere at once.

A minimum time (minimum space) is a part of a greater time (space) between whose boundaries it lies—from the notion that we have of whole and part. Therefore a minimum time is a minimum part of time, and a minimum space is a minimum part of space. There is no such thing as a mini-

minimae in diagonali, quam in latere, adeoque diagonalis aequalis lateri, nam quorum omnes partes aequales, ea aequalia. Eodem modo facile demonstratur, nec temporis minimum dari. Si Minimum est alicuius minimum est, minimum erit ergo eorum quae sunt in spatio, vel partium potius spatii, ut a corporibus distinguas. Nec aliter de re poterimus loqui. Posito ergo Minimum, ideoque et momentum et tempus implicare. Omne maius componitur ex aliquo minore. Ergo omne minimum est pars elus majoris intra cuius terminos est.

**470**    Si continuum aliud est quam summa minimorum (si in eo minima) positorum; sequitur esse partem quae supersit ablata summa minimorum; ergo ea pars est major minimo, cum nec minor sit nec aequalis, ergo et in ipsa sunt minima. Quod est absurdum, cum omnia jam minima abstulerimus. Ergo: Si sunt in continuo partes minimae, sequitur continuum ex ipsis componi. Absurdum est autem continuum componi ex minimis, ut demonstravi, ergo et esse Minima in continuo, seu Minima esse continui partes. Esse in aliquo (id est intra terminos) et aliquid sine alio intelligi non posse, est esse partem. Ergo non datur. Hinc si instantia in tempore, non nisi instantia erunt, nec tempus nisi instantium summa.

Ex his jam praeclare demonstrantur: (1) Continuum omne infinitum esse. Nempe supposito corpore moto usque ad extremitates Mundi, incipiet egredi, adeoque spatium ultra est contra hypothesin. (2) Mutationem cessare non posse, seu quicquid movetur, motum iri. Eandem nec incipere posse. (3) Omne corpus moveri. Nam omne corpus mobile est. Quicquid mobile est motum est. (4) Esse in loco est per locum transire, quia momentum nullum; et omne corpus movetur. (5) Materia non potest eodem tempore idem cum allo spatium occupasse. (6) In pleno et spatio certo, si corpus impellat corpus, minuetur eius celeritas. Potius scilicet huic non datur plus motus, quam ut totius massae motus diminuatur. Et hic jam locum habet illud memorabile: quod potius mutatio fiat in magno quam parvo. Hoc scilicet pro principio ponendum est. Si in alterutro fieri muta-

mum part of space. Because otherwise there would be as many minima in
the diagonal as in the side, and thus the diagonal would equal the side,
since two things all of whose parts are equal, are equal.[11] In the same way
it is easily demonstrated that there is no such thing as a minimum of time.
If a minimum is a minimum of anything, then it will be a minimum of
those things that are in space, or rather of the parts of space, seeing as you
distinguish them from bodies. Nor can we speak otherwise about the matter. If, then, we suppose a minimum, both a moment and time will entail a
contradiction. Everything greater is composed out of something smaller.
Therefore every minimum is a part of the greater thing within whose
boundaries it lies.

**470**    If the continuum is something other than the sum of supposed minima
(if there are minima in it), it follows that there is a part that is left over
when the sum of the minima has been taken away; therefore this part is
greater than a minimum, since it is neither smaller nor equal, therefore
there are also minima in it. But this is absurd, since we have already taken
away all the minima. Therefore if there are minimum parts in the continuum, it follows that the continuum is composed of them. But it is absurd
for the continuum to be composed out of minima, as I have demonstrated;
therefore it is also absurd for there to be minima in the continuum, or for
minima to be parts of the continuum. To be in something (i.e. to be within
its boundaries) and to be something which cannot be understood without
something else, is to be a part. Therefore there is no such thing [as a minimum in the continuum]. Hence if there are instants in time, there will be
nothing but instants, and time will be nothing but the sum of instants.

From these things the following are now very clearly demonstrated: (1)
Every continuum is infinite. For if we suppose that a body is moved all the
way out to the extremities of the world, it would begin to exceed them, so
that there would be a space beyond, contrary to hypothesis.[12] (2) Change
cannot cease, or whatever is moved will go on moving. And by the same
token, it cannot begin. (3) Every body is in motion. For every body is movable, and whatever is movable has been moved. (4) To be in a place is to
traverse a place, because a moment is nothing; and every body is in motion. (5) Matter cannot have occupied the same space as other matter at the
same time. (6) In a full and determinate space, if one body impels another,
its speed is diminished. That is to say, it is preferable for no more motion
to be given it, than that the motion of the whole mass should be diminished. And now here is the place for something memorable: that change
takes place in the large rather than the small. That is to say, this should be
supposed as a principle. If it is necessary for a change to occur in one of
two ways, as a small change in many things, or as a large change in a few

tionem necesse sit, in multis exigua, et in paucis multa, potius mutatio fiet in paucis. Et hoc est principium detrusionis gravium. Quia multiplicatio subjectorum inutilis, rescindatur, et reuniatur potius mutatio in unum.

**Linea infinita est immobilis** Aiii59

**471** 3 Ianuar. 1676.

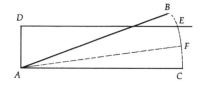

*LINEA INFINITA EST IMMOBILIS.*

Sit linea *AB* infinita a parte *B* quae motu transferenda sit in *AC*. Sit inter *B* et *C* ipsa parallela *AC*. Quando perveniet in *AC*, erit tota infra *DE*, et in quocunque puncto ponatur, ut in *AF*, erit pars ejus infinita supra *DE*. Unde si *AC* ponatur perfecte interminata, seu si nullum sit punctum ultimum, necesse est, ut tandem simul tota illa linea interminata infra *DE* descendat, totaque spatium interjectum simul conficiat, id est ut sit in pluribus locis. Ἄτοπον. Hinc videtur probari interminatum corpus esse immobile. Etiamsi angulum *FC* facias infinite parvum, tamen idem semper locum habebit, proportionaliter quod in his magnis. Similis enim figura duci potest, supponendo ipsam *BC* infinite parvam.

**On Spinoza's *Ethics*; and On the Infinite**

**On Spinoza's *Ethics*** Aiii33$_4$

**384** Mons. Tschirnhaus m'a conté beaucoup de choses du livre Ms. de Spinosa. Il y a un marchand à Amsterdam (nommé Gilles Gerrit, puto), qui entretient Spinosa. Le livre de Spinosa sera de Deo, mente, beatitudine seu perfecti hominis idea, de Medicina Mentis, de medicina corporis. Il pretend de demonstrer de Deo des choses. Quod sit solus liber. Libertatem in eo

things, the change will occur rather in the few things. And this is the principle of the downward thrust of heavy objects. Since a multiplication of subjects is to no avail, it is rescinded, and the change is instead reunited in one subject.[13]

### 7. An Infinite Line Is Immovable[1]                    Aiii59
**471**   3 January 1676

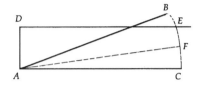

*AN INFINITE LINE IS IMMOVABLE*[2]

Let there be a line *AB,* infinite in the direction *B,* which is to be translated by a motion to *AC.* Between *B* and *C* let there be a line *DE* parallel to *AC.* When it reaches *AC,* it will be completely below *DE;* and at whatever [intermediate] point is assumed, for example at *AF,* there will be an infinite part of it above *DE.* Whence if *AC* is assumed to be perfectly unbounded, i.e. if there is no last point, it is necessary that the whole of that unbounded line should finally descend below *DE* at the same time, and the whole of it would complete the intervening space simultaneously, i.e. be in several places at the same time—an absurdity. Hence it seems to be proved that an unbounded body is immovable. Even if you make the angle *FC* infinitely small, the same thing will hold, in proportion to what holds in the large. For a similar figure can be drawn, by supposing the line *BC* infinitely small.

### 8. On Spinoza's *Ethics;* and On the Infinite[1]

(i) On Spinoza's *Ethics*                              Aiii33$_4$

[February 1676?][2]

**384**   M. Tschirnhaus has given me an account of many things from M. de Spinoza's book. There is a shopkeeper in Amsterdam (named Gilles Gerrit, I think), who has conversed with Spinoza. Spinoza's book will be about God, mind, blessedness, or the idea of the perfect man, therapy for the mind, and medicine for the body. He claims to demonstrate things about

consistere putat, cum actio seu determinatio non ex extrinseci impulsu, sed sola agentis natura resultat. Hoc sensu recte ait solum Deum esse liberum. Mens secundum ipsum est quodammodo pars Dei, putat sensum quendam in omnibus esse rebus pro gradibus existendi. Deum definit Ens absolute infinitum, item Ens, quod omnes continet perfectiones, id est affirmationes, seu realitates, seu quae concipi possunt. Item Deum solum **385** esse substantiam, sive Ens per se subsistens seu quod per se concipi potest, creaturas omnes non nisi modos esse; hominem eatenus liberum esse, quatenus a nullis externis determinatur. Sed cum hoc sit in nullo actu hinc hominem nullo modo esse liberum. Etsi plus participet de libertate quam corpora. Mentem esse ipsam corporis ideam. Putat etiam oriri unionem corporum a pressione quadam. Vulgus philosophiam incipere a creaturis. Cartesium incepisse a mente, se incipere a Deo. Extensionem non inferre divisibilitatem inque eo lapsum esse Cartesium, lapsum item esse Cartesium cum clare se videre credidit ac distincte, quod mens agat in corpus vel a corpore patitur. Putat nos morientes plerorumque oblivisci et ea tantum retinere, quae habemus cognitione, quam ille vocat intuitivam, quam pauci norint. Nam aliam esse sensualem, aliam imaginativam, aliam intuitivam. Credit quandam transmigrationis Pythagoricae speciem, nimirum mentes ire de corpore in corpus. Christum ait fuisse summum philosophum. Putat infinita alia esse attributa affirmativa praeter cogitationem et extensionem, sed in omnibus esse cogitationem ut hic in extensione; qualia autem sint illa a nobis concipi non posse, unumquodque in suo genere esse infinitum, ut hic spatium.

( + Ego soleo dicere: tres infiniti gradus, infimum *v.g.* ut exempli causa asymptoti hyperbolae; et hoc ego soleo tantum vocare infinitum. Id est majus quolibet assignabili; quod et de caeteris omnibus dici potest; alterum est maximum in suo scilicet genere, ut maximum omnium extensorum est totum spatium, maximum omnium successivorum est aeternitas. Tertius infiniti, isque summus gradus est ipsum, *omnia,* quale infinitum est in Deo, is enim est unus omnia; in eo enim caeterorum omnium ad existendum requisita continentur. Haec obiter annoto. + )

God; that He alone is free. He thinks freedom consists in this, that an action or determination results not from an extrinsic impulse, but solely from the nature of the agent. In this sense he is right to say that God alone is free. Mind, according to him, is in a way a part of God; he thinks there is some sensation in all things in proportion to their degree of existing. He defines God as an absolutely infinite being, likewise as a being that contains all perfections, i.e. affirmations, or realities, or things that can be conceived.

**385**  Likewise God alone is substance, or, a being subsisting through itself, or, that which can be conceived through itself, and all creatures are nothing but modes. Man is free to the extent that he is not determined by anything external. But since this is not the case in any of his acts, man is in no way free—even if he participates in freedom more than bodies do. [He thinks] mind is the very idea of the body. He also thinks that the union of the body arises from a kind of pressure. The vulgar begin philosophy with created things, Descartes began with the mind, he begins with God. Extension does not entail divisibility, and in this Descartes was mistaken. Descartes was likewise mistaken in believing he could see clearly and distinctly that the mind acts on the body, and that the mind is acted upon by the body. He thinks that when we die we forget almost everything, and retain only those things that we have through a knowledge that he calls intuitive, and which few people are aware of. For sensual knowledge is one thing, imaginative knowledge another, and intuitive another again. He believes in a kind of Pythagorean transmigration, at least that minds go from body to body. He says Christ was the greatest philosopher. He thinks that there are infinitely many other affirmative attributes besides thought and extension, but that there is thought in all of them, as there is here in extension; but that we cannot conceive what they are like, each one being infinite in its own kind, as, here, is space.

(+ I usually say that there are three degrees of infinity.[3] The lowest is, for the sake of example, like that of the asymptote of a hyperbola;[4] and this I usually call the mere infinite. It is greater than any assignable, as can also be said of all the other degrees. The second is that which is greatest in its own kind, as for example the greatest of all extended things is the whole of space, the greatest of all successives is eternity. The third degree of infinity, and this is the highest degree, is *everything,* and this kind of infinite is in God, since he is all one; for in him are contained the requisites for existing of all the others. I make these comments in passing. +)

## De infinito observatio notabilis                              Aiii63

**481**    De infinito ecce observationem notabilem: cum sit infinitum infinito
majus dabiturne aliquid alio aeternius. Ut potest res esse ante quodlibet
tempus imaginabile et tamen ab aeterno, quia tempus ejus non absolute
sed nostra tantum relatione erit infinitum. Fuit ergo tempus cum non esset,
sed id tempus abest abhinc infinite. Quemadmodum est linea infinite
parva relatione puncti.

## De arcanis sublimium vel De summa rerum                      Aiii60

**472**  11. Febr. 1676
Recte expensis rebus, pro principio statuo, Harmoniam rerum, id est ut
quantum plurimum essentiae potest existat. Sequitur plus rationis esse ad
existendum, quam non existendum. Et omnia extitura si id fieri posset.
Cum enim aliquid existat, nec possint omnia possibilia existere, sequitur
ea existere, quae plurimum essentiae continent, cum nulla sit alia ratio,
eligendi caeteraque excludendi: Itaque ante omnia existet Ens omnium
possibilium perfectissimum. Ratio autem cur perfectissima ante omnia
existant manifesta est, quia dum simplicia simul et perfecta sunt, seu plurimum includunt, plurimis aliis locum relinquunt. Unde unum perfectum
praeferendum multis imperfectis aequipollentibus, quia haec aliorum existentiam impediunt, dum occupant locum et tempus.[L1]

**473**    Ex hoc principio jam sequitur, nullum esse vacuum in formis; item nullus esse vacuum in loco et tempore, quoad ejus fieri potest. Unde sequitur
nec tempus ullum assignabile esse, in quo non fuerit aliquid, nec locum
esse, qui non sit plenus. Quoad eius fieri potest. Videndum ergo quid sequatur ex plenitudine Mundi.

L1. Ex eo quod aliquid existit, sequitur eius rei esse aliquam necessitatem,
⟨adeoque⟩ aut omnes res esse necessarias per se, quod falsum, aut certe earum
causas ultimas. Unde sequitur Ens absolute necessarium esse possibile, seu non implicare contradictionem. Unde sequitur ipsum existere: Unde videndum jam ⟨an⟩
de eo demonstrari possit esse unicum, etc. Porro quoniam aliqua existunt, et
quaedam non existunt, hinc sequitur ⟨existere⟩ perfectissima.
*Elementa philosophiae arcanae, de summa rerum,* Geometrice demonstrata.

(ii) A Noteworthy Observation Concerning the Infinite    **Aiii63**

[February 1676?][5]

481    Here is a noteworthy observation concerning the infinite. Since there is
one infinity greater than another, will there be something more eternal
than something else? For instance, a thing can exist before any time imaginable, and yet [not][6] from eternity, because its time [in existence] will not
be absolutely infinite, but infinite only in relation to us. Therefore there
was a time when it did not exist, but that time is infinitely remote from
now. This is just as an infinitely small line is in relation to a point.

### 9. On the Secrets of the Sublime, or
### On the Supreme Being (Selections)[1]                         **Aiii60**

472    11 February 1676[2]

After due consideration, I lay down as a principle the harmony of things:
that is, that there exists the greatest quantity of essence possible. It follows
that there is more reason for existing than not existing, and that all things
would exist if that were possible. For since something exists, and not all
possibles can exist, it follows that those things exist which contain the
most essence, since there is no other reason for choosing some and ex-
cluding the rest. So there exists first of all the most perfect of all possible
beings. Moreover, the reason why the most perfect beings should exist
first of all is manifest: for since they are simple and at the same time perfect, i.e. include the most, they leave room for the greatest number of others. Whence one perfect being is to be preferred to many imperfect ones
equivalent to it, since the latter, while they occupy place and time, prevent
the existence of others.[L1]

473      From this principle it now follows that there is no vacuum in forms;
likewise that there is no vacuum in place and time, so far as this is possible.
Whence it follows that there is no assignable time at which something will
not have existed, nor any place which is not full, so far as this is possible.
It must be seen, therefore, what follows from the plenitude of the world.

L1. From the fact that something exists, it follows that there is some necessity
for that thing, and so either that all things are necessary per se, which is false, or at
any rate that their ultimate causes are. From which it follows that an absolutely necessary being is possible, that is, does not imply a contradiction; from which it follows that it exists. Whence it must now be seen whether it can be demonstrated of it
that it is unique, etc. Moreover, since some things exist, and certain things do not, it
follows from this that the most perfect things do.
   *The elements of a secret philosophy, concerning the supreme being,* geometrically demonstrated.

Ante omnia autem probabimus necessario praeter fluida etiam existere solida. Sunt enim fluidis perfectiora, quia plus essentiae continent, non tamen omnia possunt esse solida, tunc enim se mutuo impedirent, sunt ergo solida immixta fluidis. Origo solidorum, ex solo fluidorum motu, non videtur explicari posse. Videntur, ut id obiter dicam, omnia solida esse quadam mente informata. Videndum an solida illa saltem flexilia sint, etsi separari non possint, videndum item an non sint corpora, neque solida neque fluida, sed media ex ipsa natura sua. Quod tamen videtur paulo difficilis explicatu.

An videtur rationi consentaneum Atomos? Si Atomus aliqua semel substiterit semper subsistet. Statim enim materia liquida circumjacens plena, ipsam dissipare conabitur, quia ejus motum turbat, ut facile ostendi potest. Si quod corpus magnum dissipationi nonnihil resistens, moveatur in liquido, statim formabit speciem terrellae, et vorticem.

Videtur sequi ex solido in liquido, quod materia perfecte fluida sit nihil nisi multitudino infinitorum punctorum, seu corporum minorum quam quae assignari possint, seu quod necessario detur vacuum interspersum, Metaphysicum; quod non pugnat pleno physico. Vacuum Metaphysicum est locus vacuus quantuluscunque modo verus et realis. Plenum Physicum stat cum vacuo metaphysico inassignabili. Forte ex his sequitur materiam divisam esse in puncta perfecta, seu in omnes partes in quas dividi potest. Unde non sequitur absurdum. Sequetur enim perfecte fluidum non esse continuum, sed discretum, seu punctorum multitudinem. Quare non hinc sequitur continuum componi ex punctis, materia cum liquida non foret verum continuum, etsi spatium sit verum continuum, unde rursus patet, quantum intersit inter spatium et materiam. Materia sola explicari potest multitudine sine continuitate. Et revera Materia videtur esse Ens discretum, nam ⟨etiam⟩ si solida sumatur, tamen quatenus materia est cessante caemento, motu verbi gratia aliove, reducta erit ad statum liquiditatis, seu

**474** divisibilitatis, unde sequitur ipsam ex punctis componi. Quod sic probo: omne perfecte liquidum ex punctis componitur. Quia in puncta dissolve potest. Probo, motu solidi in ipso. Materia ergo est End discretum, non continuum, contiguum tantum est, et unitur motu vel a mente quadam.

[Videtur] esse quoddam totius universi centrum, et quendam vorticem generalem infinitum; et quandam Mentem perfectissimam sive Deum. Hanc ut animam totam in toto esse corpore Mundi; huic menti etiam exis-

First of all we will prove that besides fluids there necessarily also exist solids. For they are more perfect than fluids, since they contain more essence. However, not all things can be solids, for then they would impede each other. So there are solids mixed in with fluids. The origin of solids does not seem explicable from the motion of fluids alone. All solids seem, I might say in passing, to be informed with a mind of some kind. It must be seen whether these solids, even if they cannot be separated, are at least flexible; it must also be seen whether there are not bodies that are neither solid nor fluid, but by their very nature intermediate between the two; this, however, seems a little difficult to explain.

Does it seem in accord with reason for there to be atoms? If an atom once subsists, it will always subsist. For the liquid matter of the surrounding plenum will immediately endeavour to dissipate it, since it disturbs its motion, as can easily be shown. If some large body that to some extent resists dissipation moves in a liquid, it will at once form a kind of terrella,[3] and a vortex.

It seems to follow from a solid in a liquid that a perfectly fluid matter is nothing but a multiplicity of infinitely many points, i.e. bodies smaller than any that can be assigned,[4] or, that there must be such a thing as an interspersed vacuum—a metaphysical one, which is not contrary to a physical plenum. A metaphysical vacuum is an empty place however small, only true and real. A physical plenum is consistent with an unassignable metaphysical vacuum. Perhaps it follows from this that matter is divided into perfect points, that is, into all parts into which it can be divided.[5] Nothing absurd follows from this. For it will follow that a perfect fluid is not a continuum, but discrete, i.e. is a multiplicity of points. But it does not therefore follow from this that a continuum is composed of points, since liquid matter will not be a true continuum, even if space is a true continuum; from which it is again clear how great a difference there is between space and matter. Matter alone is explicable by a multiplicity without continuity. And matter does in fact seem to be a discrete entity; for even if it is assumed solid, still, insofar as it is matter, when its cement—motion, for example, or something else—ceases to exist, it will be reduced to a state of liquidity, i.e. of divisibility, from which it follows that it is composed of 474  points. This I prove as follows: every perfect liquid is composed of points, since it can be dissolved into points, which I prove by the motion of a solid in it. Therefore matter is a discrete entity, not a continuous one; it is only contiguous, and is united by motion or by a mind of some sort.

There seems to be a sort of center of the whole universe,[6] and an infinite general vortex;[7] as well as some kind of most perfect mind, or God. This mind exists as a whole soul in the whole body of the world;[8] to this mind

tentiam deberi rerum. Ipsam esse causam sui. Nihil aliud esse existentiam, quam id quod causa est sensum conformium. Ratio rerum, aggregatum requisitorum omnium rerum. Deum de Deo. Totum infinitum esse unum. Mentes particulares existere summa, ideo tantum, quod summa Ens harmonicum judicat, alicubi esse quod intelligat, sive esse quoddam speculum intellectuale, sive replicationem Mundi. Existere nihil aliud esse quam Harmonicum esse: notam existentiae esse sensus conformes.

Si verum est quamlibet partem materiae, utcunque exiguam continere infinitas creaturas, sive esse Mundum, sequitur etiam materam esse reapse in infinita puncta divisam. Verum autem hoc es, modo sit possibile, nam auget multitudinem existentium et harmoniam rerum, sive admirationem sapientae divinae. Hinc porro sequitur quamlibet materiae partem esse cuilibet commensurabilem, qui rursus est admirabilis effectus harmoniae rerum. Videndum an hoc vere sequatur. Ubi examinanda illa alibi usus sum ratiocinatio qua videbatur sequi, quod circulus si sit rationem habeat ad diametrum ut numerus ad numerum. Videndum an haec consequentia sit bona. Videndum tamen an non in liquido nunc major nunc minor sequatur subdivisio, pro variis in eo solidi motibus; adeoque examinandum rigorose, an perfecta divisioi liquidi in puncta metaphysica, an vero tantum in puncta mathematica sequatur. Nam puncta mathematica possent appellari indivisibilia Cavaleriana, etsi non sint metaphysica seu minima. Quod si ostendi posset plus minusve dividi liquidum, sequetur non resolvi liquidum in indivisibilia. Posset tamen defendi liquidum componi ex punctis perfectis, etsi numquam in illa prorsus resolvatur, vel ideo quia omnium est resolutionum capax, et caemento cessante, mente scilicet et motu, cessabit.

. . .

**475**    Evolvendus est quam rigorissime omnis ille de compositione continui labyrinthus, videatur liber Fromondi, agendum de angulo contactus, nam ad Geometras non pertinet illa disputatio sed ad Metaphysicos. Tentandum an demonstrari possit esse aliquod infinite parvum, nec tamen indivisibile. Quo existente sequuntur mira de infinito. Nempe si [fingantur] creaturae alterius Mundi, infinite parvi, nos ipsorum comparatione fore infinitos. Unde patet vicissim nos fingi posse infinite parvos comparatione alterius Mundi, qui infinitae magnitudinis et tamen terminatus sit. Unde

the existence of things is also due. It is the cause of itself. Existence is nothing but that which causes conforming sensations. The reason for things is the aggregate of all the requisites of things. The reason for God is God. An infinite whole is one.[9] In sum, particular minds exist only because the supreme being judges it harmonious that there should somewhere be something that understands, that is, that there should be a kind of intellectual mirror, or replication of the world. To exist is nothing other than to be harmonious; conforming sensations are the mark of existence.[10]

If it is true that any part of matter, however small, contains an infinity of creatures, i.e. is a world, it follows also that matter is actually divided into an infinity of points. But this is true, provided it is possible, for it increases the multiplicity of existents and the harmony of things, or admiration of divine wisdom. Hence it follows further that any part of matter is commensurable with any other, which again is an admirable effect of the harmony of things. It must be seen whether this truly follows. In that connection, I should examine the line of reasoning I have used elsewhere, according to which it seems to follow that a circle, if it exists, has a ratio to the diameter as one number to another.[11] It must be seen whether this inference is a good one. It must be seen, on the other hand, whether there does not follow in a liquid a subdivision that is now greater, now less, in accordance with the various motions of a solid in it; accordingly it must be rigorously examined whether there follows a perfect division of a liquid into metaphysical points, or only one into mathematical points. For mathematical points could be called Cavalierian indivisibles, even if they are not metaphysical points, i.e. minima. But if a liquid can be shown to be divided to a greater or lesser degree, it will follow that a liquid is not resolved into indivisibles. Yet one could defend the composition of a liquid out of perfect points, even if it is never absolutely resolved into them, on the grounds that it is capable of all resolutions, and will cease to exist when its cement—namely, mind and motion—ceases to exist.

. . .

**475**    The whole labyrinth of the composition of the continuum (see Froidmont's book)[12] must be unraveled as rigorously as possible, and the angle of contact must also be treated, for that dispute is of concern not to geometers, but to metaphysicians.[13] We must try to see if it can be demonstrated that there is something infinitely small, yet not indivisible. If such a thing exists, there follow some wonderful consequences concerning the infinite: namely, if we imagine creatures of another world that is infinitely small, we will be infinite in comparison with them. Whence it is clear in turn that we could be imagined as being infinitely small in comparison with another world that is of infinite magnitude, and yet bounded. Whence it is clear

patet infinitum aliud esse, ut certe vulgo sumimus, quam interminatum. Rectius hoc infinitum appellaretur Immensum. Mirum illud quoque, qui ab infinitis vixerit annis, posse incepisse, et qui numero annorum majore quam quilibet numerus finitus vivat, aliquando mori posse. Unde sequetur esse numerum infinitum. Aliunde constat necessario numerum esse infinitum, quando liquidum reapse dividitur in partes numero infinitas, quod si impossibile est, sequetur et liquidum esse impossibile. Cum videamus Hypothesian infinitorum et infinite parvorum praeclare consentire ac succedere in Geometria, hoc etiam auget probabilitatem esse revera.

. . .

**476**    Mentem omnem esse durationis interminatae. Mentem omnem etiam Materiae cuidam indissolubiter implantatam; Materiam illam esse certae
**477**    magnitudinis. Omnem mentem habere vorticem circa se. Omnes globos Mundanos forte Mente praeditor esse; nec absurdas videri intelligentias. Obstat quidem quod liberum non satis habeant motum, sed cum intelligant officium suum, et cum Deo communicent, per influentias illas mutuas corporum quas sentiunt; non affectabunt motus varietatum. Innumeras ubique esse mentes, Mentes in ovo humano esse etiam ante conceptionem nec perire, etsi nunquam sequatur conceptio. Nescire nos miros rerum usu quibus a providentia destinantur.

. . . Ego mentes singularibus guadiis, et insigni felicitati destinatas considero, ut in magno infinitorum numerorum numero eos, qui insignia praebent theoremata. Et disquisitionis foret egregiae, an ex tota numerorum finitorum universitate aliquis definiri possit, omnium pulcherrimus, nisi is forte unitas, quae simul omnes potentia refert.

Numerorum finitorum numerus non potest esse infinitus. Unde sequitur non posse infinitos numero Quadratos finitos, deinceps ab unitate ordine sumtos. Unde videtur sequi Numerum infinitum esse impossibilem. Tantum videtur probandum quod Numerorum finitorum numerus non potest esse infinitus. Si numeri ponantur se excedere unitate continue, numerus numerorum talium finitorum non potest esse infinitus, qui tunc numerus numerorum aequatur numero maximo, qui supponitur esse finitus. Respondendum est nullum dare maximum. Etsi autem aliter quam per uni-

that the infinite is—as, of course, we commonly take for granted—something other than the unbounded. This infinite should more properly be called the Immensum.[14] This is a wonder, too: that someone who has lived for infinitely many years can have begun to live, and that someone who lives for a number of years that is greater than any finite number can at some time die. From which it will follow that there is an infinite number.[15] Another way of establishing that there is necessarily an infinite number is from the fact that a liquid is actually divided into parts infinite in number: if this is impossible, it will follow that a liquid is also impossible.[16] Since we see the hypothesis of infinites and the infinitely small is splendidly consistent and successful in geometry, this also increases the likelihood that they really exist.[17]

. . .

**476**  Every mind is of unbounded duration. Every mind is also indissolubly
**477**  implanted in some matter; this matter is of a definite magnitude. Every mind has a vortex around it. All the mundane globes are perhaps endowed with a mind; nor do intelligences seem absurd. Of course it might be objected that they do not have a free enough motion, but since they understand their duty, and since they communicate with God through the mutual influences of the bodies they sense, they will not assume a variety of motion. There are innumerable minds everywhere; there are minds in the human ovum even before conception, and they do not perish, even if conception never follows. We do not know the wonderful uses for which things are destined by providence.

. . . I consider minds to be destined for unparalleled joys and extraordinary happiness, just as there are in the great number of infinite numbers those which yield extraordinary theorems. And it would be something for an exceptional inquiry to find out whether, out of the whole totality of finite numbers, some one number could be defined as the most beautiful of all—unless this is perhaps the number one, which represents all powers at once.[18]

The number of finite numbers cannot be infinite. Whence it follows that the number of finite squares, taken one after another in order from the number one, cannot be infinite. Whence it seems to follow that an infinite number is impossible. It seems that all that needs to be proved is that the number of finite numbers cannot be infinite. If numbers can be assumed as continually exceeding each other by one, the number of such finite numbers cannot be infinite, since in that case the number of numbers is equal to the greatest number, which is supposed to be finite. It must be responded that there is no such thing as the greatest number. But even if they increase otherwise than by ones, nevertheless, provided only that they al-

tates crescunt, attamen si modo crescant semper per finitas differentias, necesse est semper numerum omnium numerorum ad numerum ultimum rationem habere finitam, [imo] amplius, numerus ultimus semper erit major numero omnium numerorum. Unde sequitur numerum numerorum non esse infinitum.[L2] Ergo nec numerum [uni]tatum. Ergo non datur numerus infinitus seu non est ⟨possibilis⟩.

## Extensio interminata                                   Aiii66

**489**  *Extensio interminata* non debet implicare, quia videntur aliqua de ea demonstrari posse, ut duas rectas interminatas in eodem plano quae non sint parallelae, unum habere punctum commune. Quod de terminatis dici
**490**  non potest. Sed hoc tamen de terminatis dici potest, produci posse dum concurrant. Videtur vero intelligi recta jam producta; imo rectae per se interminatae a nobis aut corporibus terminantur.

## Notes on Science and Metaphysics                       Aiii36$_1$

**389**  18. Martii 1676.
. . .
**391**  Si on prouve que la plus grande étendue possible est immobile, comme je croy; il s'en suit qu'il y a une étendue immobile.

Nunc tandem video possibilium non existentium sive quae nec sunt nec fuere nec erunt, nullum esse numerum, sive multitudinem, quia ipsamet positione sive per accidens impossibilia sunt.

Posito spatium habere partes, dum scilicet in partes vacuas et plenas, variarum figurarum, a corporibus dividitur, sequitur spatium esse totum sive Ens per accidens: continuo mutari, et aliud atque aliud fieri: mutatis scilicet partibus, et extinctis, aliisque subnatis. Sed est aliquid in spatio, quod manet inter mutationes, id vero aeternum est, neque aliud est, quam ipsa immensitas Dei, attributum scilicet unum atque indivisibile simul et

L2. Imo NB. hinc fantum probatur quod talis series sit interminata.

ways increase by finite differences, it is necessary that the number of all
numbers always has a finite ratio to the last number; and furthermore, the
last number will always be greater than the number of all numbers.
Whence it follows that the number of numbers is not infinite.[L2] Neither,
therefore, is the number of unities. Therefore there is no such thing as infinite number, that is, it is not ⟨possible⟩.

## 10. Unbounded Extension[1]                                            Aiii66

[Feb. 1676?][2]

**489**  An *unbounded extension* ought not to entail a contradiction, since it seems
that some things can be demonstrated about it, for instance, that two unbounded straight lines in the same plane that are not parallel have one
**490**  point in common. And this cannot be said of bounded ones. What can be
said about bounded lines, however, is that it is possible for them to be further produced until they meet. Indeed, it seems, a straight line is understood as being already produced; or rather, straight lines, unbounded in
themselves, are bounded by us or by bodies.[3]

## 11. Notes on Science and Metaphysics (Selections)

First Entry[1]                                                           Aiii36$_1$

**389**  18 March 1676

. . .

**391**     If one proves that the greatest possible extended thing is immovable, as
I believe; then it follows that there is an immovable extended thing.[2]

Now I finally see that there is no number or multiplicity of nonexistent
possibles, that is, things which neither are, nor were, nor will be, because
by their very position, that is, accidentally, they are impossible.[3]

Supposing space to have parts—that is to say, so long as it is divided by
bodies into empty and full parts of various shapes—it follows that space
itself is a whole or entity accidentally, that it is continuously changing and
becoming something different: namely, when its parts change, and are extinguished and supplanted by others. But there is something in space
which remains through the changes, and this is eternal: it is nothing other
than the immensity of God, namely, an attribute that is one and indivisible,

L2. No, N.B. this only proves that such a series is unbounded.

immensum. Cuius spatium est consequentia tantum, ut proprietas Essentiae. Demonstrari facile potest materiam ipsam perpetuo extingui sive aliam atque aliam fieri. Eodem modo ostendi potest, et mentem continue mutari, excepto eo quod Divinum est in nobis seu quod extrinsecus advenit, prorsus ut in spatio est aliquid divinum, ipsa immensitas Dei, ita in mente est divinum quiddam, quod Aristoteles vocabat intellectum agentem, et hoc idem est cum omniscientia Dei; quemadmodum id quod in spatio divinum atque aeternum est, idem est cum Dei immensitate et id quod in corpore sive ente mobile divinum atque aeternum est, idem est cum Dei

**392** omnipotentia; et id quod in tempore est divinum idem est cum aeternitate. Unum attributum mire servit ad alterum declarandum; nam aeternitas quiddam indivisibile est, est enim existendi necessitas, quae non exprimit successionem, durationem, divisibilitatem. Eodem modo, omnipraesentia seu ubiquitas non est divisibilis, quemadmodum spatium; et omnipotentia non est subjecta variationi, quemadmodum corporum formae.

Valde notabilia sunt ista, ad ostendum, quod solus Deus sit aeternus, nam si spatium non est aeternum multo minus materia erit. Nimirum et materia perpetuo alia atque alia fit. Quoniam ipsa non nisi in relatione existit, ut alibi vel ex individuationis principio omnium rerum ostendi.

Quicquid divisibile est, quicquid dividitur, id alteratur, imo extinguitur. Materia est divisibilis, ergo est destruibilis, nam quicquid dividitur, destruitur. Quicquid in minima dividitur annihilatur; sed hoc impossibile. Alius annihilandi modus possibilis. Materia quodammodo esse habet a forma.

Est in materia, ut et in spatio quiddam aeternum; et indivisibile, quod illi intellexisse videntur, qui Deum ipsum esse credidere materiam rerum. Quod tamen non dicitur proprie, quia Deus non facit partem rerum: sed principium. Perfectio est attributum affirmativum absolutum; continetque semper omnia sui generis, cum nihil sit, quod ipsum limitet: nam cui aliquid dandum est, et ratio non est cur certum quiddam des, ei omnia dedisti.

Liquida agitantur in omnes partes, eo ipso quia liquida sunt, id est seperationi partium non resistunt, adeoque quolibet impulsu externo undulantur. Non est ergo in eo sita natura Liquidi, sed ex ea sequitur posito externo motore.

and at the same time immense. Space is only a consequence of this, as a property is of an essence.[4] It can easily be demonstrated that matter itself is perpetually being extinguished, or becomes one thing after another. In the same way it can be demonstrated that mind also continuously changes, excepting that which is divine in us, or which comes from without. In a word, just as in space there is something divine, the immensity of God itself, so in mind there is something divine, which Aristotle used to call the active intellect,[5] and this is the same as God's ominiscience; just as what is divine and eternal in space is the same as God's immensity, and what is divine and eternal in body, i.e. in a movable entity, is the same as God's om-

**392** nipotence; and what is divine in time is the same as eternity. One attribute serves admirably to disclose another; for eternity is something indivisible, since it is the necessity of existing, which does not express succession, duration, or divisibility. In the same way, omnipresence or ubiquity is not divisible, as space is; and omnipotence is not subject to variation like the forms of bodies.

These things are well worth noting for showing that God alone is eternal. For if space is not eternal, much less will matter be. For matter too is perpetually becoming one thing after another, since it exists only in relation, as I have shown elsewhere from the principle of the individuation of all things.[6]

Whatever is divisible, whatever is divided, is altered, or rather is extinguished. Matter is divisible, and is therefore destructible, for whatever is divided is destroyed. Whatever is divided into minima is annihilated; but this is impossible. Another way of being annihilated is possible. In some way matter has its being from form.

There is in matter, as also in space, something eternal and indivisible; which seems to have been understood by those who believed God himself to be the matter of things. But it is improper to call him this, since God does not constitute a part of things, but a principle. Perfection is an absolute affirmative attribute; and it always contains everything of its own kind,[7] since there is nothing which limits it: for if there is a thing to which something must be attributed, and there is no reason why you should attribute some particular thing to it, you will have attributed everything to it.

Liquids are agitated in all directions, because of the very fact that they are liquids, i.e. because they do not resist a separation into parts, and so are set undulating by any external impulse whatever. The nature of liquid does not therefore lie in this [nonresistance to separation], but it follows from it if an external mover is supposed.[8]

Conatus penduli circa centrum immobile agitati sunt ut sinus situum.

Cum Mens sit aliquid certam habens relationem ad aliquam materiae portionem, tunc dicendum est cur in hanc et non adjacentes omnes se extendat, seu cur aliquod corpus, non omne ad eam pertineat eodem modo. **393** Ponamus certam aliquam portionem esse materiae non interruptam, vacuo undique cinctam: dicamus ad eam pertinere, ut habeat suam quandam mentem; vel ideo quia haec portio ab omni alia sejuncta est. Ponamus jam ab alia Materiae portione ac velut insula in Vacuo natante attingi: sequetur ex solo attactu coalescere in unum has duas mentes, quia vacuum nullum interjectum est, unde sequetur utriusque cogitationes confundi, et utramque simul et hanc et illam se meminisse, quod fortasse nec fieri potest. Sin putas hoc contactu fieri novam mentem, ob novum factum corpus, dicendum erit priores duas interiisse, quia et duo corpora illa interiere; sin dicas servari, extincto licet corpore, profecto tot erunt mentes in quolibet corpore, quot in eo assignabilia sunt puncta, quod est impossibile, quia punctorum numerus nullus. Consequentia facile patet. Quod enim de hoc modo dividendi novum totum in partes scilicet, dici potest, dici poterit de omnibus. Itaque necesse est novam fieri mentem, prioribus extinctis; scilicet quae non habeat sensum identitatis, cum priore. Quod ego esse puto contra cogitationis naturam. Praeterquam quod hoc modo nullo negotio minimisque de causis mutarentur mentes, et alias planeque prioribus incohaerentes nanciscerentur cogitationes, quod toto vitae temporis minime experimur. Cum ergo aliunde mihi constet esse aliquam materiae portionem solidam, et infrangibilem, neque enim ulla tenax in primis originibus admitti potest, ut facile demonstrari posse arbitror, cumque praeterea connexio ex sola materia et motu explicari nequeat, ut satis alibi ostensum arbitror;[L1] sequitur accedere cogitationem ad eam formandam, et unum fieri corpus atque insecabile, sive ἄτομον, cuiuscunque sit magnitudinis, quandocunque aliquam unam habet mentem. Porro quot sunt cor-

---

L1. Above this: error.

The endeavours of a pendulum about an immovable center are as the sines of their situations.

Given that a mind is something having a certain relation to some portion of matter, what then needs to be said is why it extends itself into this portion of matter and not all the adjacent ones; that is to say, why it is that **393** some body, and not every body, belongs to it in the same way. Let us suppose there is some portion of matter that is not broken up, and is surrounded on all sides by a vacuum; let us say that it has the property of having a kind of mind of its own, on the grounds that this portion is separated from every other. Let us suppose now that it comes into contact with another portion of matter, like an island floating in the vacuum: it will follow by virtue of this contact alone that these two minds will coalesce into one, because there is no vacuum between them; whence it will follow that the thoughts of the two will be fused together, and each of them will simultaneously remember both one of them and the other, which probably cannot happen. If, on the other hand, you think that a new mind will be made by this contact, because of the new body that has been made, it will have to be said that the two former minds have perished, because the two bodies will also have perished; whereas if you think they are conserved even though the bodies have been extinguished, there will in fact be as many minds in any body as there are assignable points in it, which is impossible, because there is no number of points. It is easy to see how this follows. For what can be said of this way of dividing a new whole into parts can be said of all. So it is necessary for a new mind to come into being when the former ones have ceased to exist, namely, one that does not have a sense of identity with the former one. And this I think to be contrary to the nature of thought. Besides, in this way minds would be changed with no difficulty and by the slightest of causes, and different thoughts would arise that were obviously incoherent with preceding ones, which we do not at all experience in a whole lifetime. Since, therefore, I have established on other grounds that there is some portion of matter that is solid and unbreakable—for no adhesive can be allowed in the primary origins of things, as I judge to be easily demonstrable—and since, moreover, connection cannot be explained in terms of matter and motion alone, as I believe I have shown satisfactorily elsewhere,[L1] it follows that thought enters into the formation of this portion, and that, whatever its size, it becomes a body that is single and indissectible, i.e. an atom, whenever it has a single mind.

L1. ABOVE THIS: error.

pora firma in natura, tot necessario excitantur vortices, solo corporum firmorum motu. Et quot sunt vortices in Mundo, tot sunt Mentes, sive
Munduli, sive perceptiones. Hinc facile intelligitur cur nulla mens naturaliter dissolvi possit, si posset enim, dissoluta fuisset dudum. Cum perpetuo ad quamlibet solvendum tota rerum natura connitatur. Hinc porro
sequitur etsi non dissolvatur, sentire tamen mentem conatus omnes, et
corpore suo excipere. Porro conatus nullus perditur in natura rerum, com-
ponunturque in mente, non destruuntur. Mens ad cognitionem veritatis
pervenit, et ad faciendas propositiones, tum ad constantes quasdam et
**394** similiter recurrentes passiones pervenit. Neque enim nisi ab experientia incipimus ratiocinari. Omnem Mentem esse Organicam, et discere
aliquid, sed vix longissimo tempore, scilicet pro periodis rerum quas sentiunt. Si nostrae sensiones diu essent incohaerentes et perturbatae, velut
aegri somnia, nec quaedam recurrerent, certa lege, diu futuri essemus in-
fantes. Transmigratio animarum satis refuta est novis experimentis, de
foetu jam praeformato. An memoria unice ab organis dependeat, atque an
et quatenus ad cogitationem necessaria signa et imagines. Negari non
potest, mentem aliam, ad aliam materiae portionem specialorem obtinere
relationem, quod quomodo fiat explicandum est.

## De plenitudine mundi                                                    Aiii76

**524** 1676

Mihi videtur Omnem mentem esse omnisciam, confuse. Et quamlibet
Mentem simul percipere quicquid fit in toto mundo; et has confusas infinitarum simul varietatum perceptiones dare sensationes illas quas de colo-
ribus, gustibus, tactibusque habemus. Tales enim perceptiones non uno
constat actu intellectus, sed aggregato infinitorum; praesertim cum ad sensum alicuius coloris alteriusve rei perceptibilis, sit opus quodam temporis
tractu. Tempus autem in infinitum divisibile, et certum est quolibet momento percipere animam, alia atque alia, sed ex omnibus perceptionibus

Furthermore, it is necessary that as many vortices are stirred up as there are firm bodies in nature, solely by the motion of the firm bodies. And there are as many minds, or little worlds, or perceptions, as there are vortices in the world. From this we can easily understand why no mind can be dissolved naturally; for if it could, it would have been dissolved long ago, since the whole nature of things is perpetually striving to dissolve any mind. From this it follows further that even though it is not destroyed, mind nevertheless senses all endeavours, and receives them through its own body. Further, no endeavour is lost in the nature of things, and they are composed together in the mind, not destroyed.[9] Mind attains to a knowledge of truth and the making of propositions when it attains to cer-

**394**   tain constant and similarly recurring passions. For we do not begin to reason except from experience. Every mind is organic and learns something, but with difficulty and over a very long time, in proportion to the periods [of repetition] of the things it senses. If our sensations were incoherent and disturbed for a long time, like the dreams of someone sick, and no particular thing recurred in a lawlike manner, we would be infants for a long time. The transmigration of souls is sufficiently refuted by new experiments concerning the already preformed fetus.[10] [It must be seen] whether memory depends on the organs alone, and whether and to what extent signs and images are necessary for thought. It cannot be denied that one mind obtains a more special relation to one portion of matter, and another mind to another, and it must be explained how this comes about.

### 12. On the Plenitude of the World[1]                         Aiii76

**524**   [March?] 1676[2]

It seems to me that every mind is omniscient, confusedly; and that any mind perceives simultaneously whatever happens in the whole world; and that these perceptions, of infinite varieties fused together[3] at the same time, give rise to those sensations we have of colors, tastes, touches. For such perceptions do not consist in one act of the intellect, but in an aggregate of infinitely many acts; especially since some stretch of time is necessary for the sensation of a color or some other perceptible thing. Time, though, is infinitely divisible, and it is certain that at any moment the soul perceives many different things, but that out of all the infinitely many per-

infinitis in unum confusis oriri rerum sensibilium perceptiones. Sed existentiae, cogitationis ipsius, aliorumque id genus perceptio fit momento.
Porro mirum non est quandam mentem percipere quae aguntur in toto
mundo, quia nullum est corpus tam exiguum, quin posita Mundi plenitudine alia omnia sentiat. Itaque hoc modo mira oritur varietas, quot enim
mentes, tot diversae universi relationes; quemadmodum si urbs eadem e
diversis locis spectetur, itaque plurium Mentium creatione Deus efficere
voluit de universo, quod pictor aliquis de magna urbe, qui varias eius
species sive projectiones delineatas exhibere vellet, pictor in tabula, ut
Deus in mente.

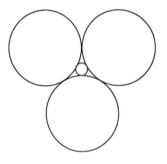

Ego magis magisque persuasus sum de corporibus insecabilibus, quae
cum non sint orta per motum, ideo simplicissima esse debent ac proinde
sphaerica, omnes enim aliae figurae subjectae varietati. Non ergo videtur
**525**  dubitandum esse Atomos sphaericas infinitas. Si nullae essent Atomi omnia dissolverentur posito pleno. Rationale est plenum mirabile quale explico, quanquam meris ex sphaeris. Nullus enim locus est tam parvus quin
fingi possit esse in eo sphaeram ipso minorem. Ponamus hoc ita esse, nullus erit locus assignabilis vacuus. Et tamen Mundus erit plenus, unde intelligitur quantitatem inassignabilem esse aliquid. Diversi resistentiae
gradus non possunt esse in primis et simplicissimus, explicanda enim
causa varietas. Est tamen ubi demonstrari potest varietas, ut globorum,
nam posita plenitudine Mundi, necesse est globulos esse alios aliis minores in infinitum. Videndum an globulis tribuendus motus circa proprium centrum. Ex globulis solis explicari potest connexio corporum, sine
ullis hamis, uncisque, qui inepti et a rerum simplicitate et pulc[h]ritudine
alieni. Causa autem connexionis, cum pilae majores separari non possunt
facile quin motum mediocrium circumfusarum turbent, quae in earum
locum succedere non possunt, ob interstitia non satis magna, inter globos
majores, ita fit, ut globi valde parvi tantum transire possint, mediocrium

ceptions fused together into one arise the perceptions of sensible things.[4] But the perception of existence, of thought itself, and of other things of that kind, occurs in a moment. Moreover it is no wonder that a mind perceives what is going on in the whole world, since there is no body so minute that it will not, given the plenitude of the world, sense all others. And so there arises in this way a wonderful variety, for there are as many different relations in the universe as there are minds—just as when the same town is looked at from different locations. So, by creating a plurality of minds, God wanted to bring about for the universe what some painter does for a large town, when he wants to display delineations of its various aspects or projections: the painter does on canvas what God does in the mind.

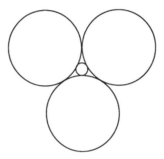

I am more and more persuaded about indissectible bodies; and since these did not originate through motion, they must be the simplest, and therefore spherical, for all other shapes are subject to variety.[5] So it seems 525  indubitable that there are infinitely many spherical atoms. If there were no atoms, everything would be dissolved, given the plenum. It is reasonable for there to be a wonderful plenum of the kind I am expounding, even though it consists only of spheres. For there is no place so small that we cannot imagine a smaller sphere to exist in it. If we suppose this to be so, there will be no assignable place that is empty. And yet the world will be a plenum, from which it is understood that an unassignable quantity is something. There cannot be different degrees of resistance in the primary and simplest things, for the cause of variety would have to be explained. Still, there is a case in which variety can be demonstrated, for instance that of the globes: for given the plenitude of the world, it is necessary that there exist some globules smaller than others to infinity.

We must see whether globules should be ascribed a motion around their own center. The connection of bodies can be explained solely in terms of globules, without any hooks or crooks, which are inept as well as foreign to the simplicity and beauty of things.[6] Rather, the cause of the connection

vero circumfusorum turbetur motus, et omnia quasi removeantur, totaque horum mediocrium atmosphaera elevetur, quod non fieret si mediocria circumfusa in locum majorum se separantium succedere et inter eorum loca vacua transire possent. An difficilis explicationis, unde oriatur gyratio corporum mundanorum circa sua centra? nisi putemus id fieri ut in turbine quem pueri impellunt aliisque, omnia scilicet talia a caeteris non moveri tantum, sed et rotari. Mirum vero unde fiant periodi translatae, in motu circa suum centrum.

Quot sunt corpora insecabilia, tot sunt vortices, seu motus circumsectorum relatione ad unum quoddam variati. Discrimen est tamen inter corpus insecabile quietum per se, et motum tantum motu aliorum et inter id quod sponte sua in linea recta motum, caeteris motum imprimit. Nisi probabilis putemus quodlibet insecabile moveri in linea recta, alia atque alia, nimirum nullam duci posse rectam quin alicuius insecabilis directioni sit parallela. Ubi porro discutiendum, an omnes directiones debeant esse aequiveloces. An forte mirabilis quaedam observabitur proportio, ut sint directionum velocitates in reciproca ratione magnitudinis, adeoque unaquaeque Atomus aequali vi aget in universum. Hoc mihi pulcherrimum et summae rationi consentaneum videtur. Itaque parvae celerrime movebuntur.

526

Non assumo initio plenitudinem mundi, sed hoc tantum, quod facile quivis concedere se posse videt, ut scilicet in loco quolibet intelligi posse natare sive includi corpus aliquod loco ipso minus. Hoc jam uno posito, quod nullus sit locus in quo non existat aliquod corpus ipsi aequali vel ipso minus, sequitur nullam assignabilem Mundi partem esse vacuam, non tamen ideo dico spatium et corpus esse coextensa; imo contra sequitur non esse coextensa, quia sphaerae quotcunque non replent totum. Omnes tamen vacuitates in unum collectae non majorem haberet rationem ad spatium quoddam assignabile, quam angulus contactus ad rectilineum.

is this: the larger balls cannot easily be separated without disturbing the motion of the middle-sized ones clustered around them, which cannot move into the larger globes' place because the gaps between them are not big enough; for this reason, it happens that only very small globes can pass through; the motion of the surrounding middle-sized globes, however, is disturbed, and it is as if they are all moved away and the whole atmosphere of these middle-sized globes is lifted up, which would not happen if the surrounding middle-sized globes could move into the place of the large ones separating them and could pass among their empty places.[7] Is it difficult to explain the origin of the rotation of mundane bodies around their centers?—unless we suppose it to happen in the same way as in the spinning top that boys push along, and other things of this sort: for all such things are not only moved by the others, but also rotated. But in the motion of a thing around its own center, it is a wonder where the periods of revolution of the translated body might come from.

There are as many vortices, i.e. motions of surrounding sectors that are varied in relation to some one thing, as there are indissectible bodies. But there is a difference between an indissectible body in itself at rest and which is moved only by the motion of others, and one that is moving of its own accord in a straight line and which impresses its motion on others—unless we think it probable that any indissectible body whatever moves in one straight line after another: then, of course, no straight line could be drawn that would not be parallel to the direction of some indissectible body. In this connection, moreover, it should be discussed whether tendencies in all directions ought to be of equal velocity; or whether perhaps some remarkable proportion is observed, so that the velocities of bodies tending in different directions are inversely proportional to their magnitude, so that every single atom will act with an equal force overall.[8] This seems to me the most beautiful, and it is consonant with the highest reason. So small atoms will move the fastest.

I do not assume the plenitude of the world at the outset, but only this, which anyone will easily see himself able to concede: namely, that one can understand there to be floating in, or enclosed in, any place whatever a body that is smaller than that place. Now granted this one thing—that there is no place in which there does not exist some body equal to or smaller than it—it follows that no assignable part of the world is empty. But I do not for this reason say that body and space are coextended; on the contrary, it follows that they are not coextended, because however many spheres we take, they will not fill the whole. But all the vacuities collected into one do not have a greater ratio to any assignable space than the angle of contact has to the straight line.

**434** 26. mars. 1676

Videndum exacte an demonstrari possit in quadraturis, quod differentia
non *tamen* sit infinite parva, sed quod omnino nulla, quod ostendetur, si
constet eousque inflecti semper posse polygonum, ut differentia assumta
etiam infinite parva minor fiat error. Quo posito sequitur non tantum errorem non esse infinite parvum, sed omnino esse nullum. Quippe cum nullus assumi possit.

*Indesignabilem* voco quantitatem, cuius magnitudo nullis signis characteribus sensibilibus exprimi potest. Omnis enim magnitudo designabilis
**435** quantacunque poterit semper scribi in aliquo libro satis parvo ope com-
pendiorum et repraesentationum. Quod ut ostenderat Archimedes suscepit
disquisitionem de *Numero arenae.*

**485** April. 1676.

Linea interminata ut *CB etc.* est aliquid. Linea interminata *EB* est aliquid.
Linea interminata *CB etc.* constat ex linea interminata *EB etc.* et recta *CE*
terminata in directum jacentibus, communeque punctum habentibus *E.*
Recta *CB etc.* totum, partes *CE, EB etc.* Recta *CB* major est, quam recta

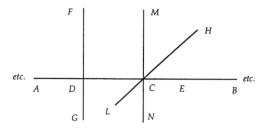

*EB,* etsi utraque sit interminata. Interminatam voco lineam rectam *EB etc.*
versus *B,* maximam omnium ab *E* ductarum per *B.* Item illam, in qua nullum est punctum extremum. Extremum autem punctum voco in recta quod
a puncto aliquo in eadem recta sumto magis quam alia omnia distat. Vel interminata est, in qua puncto quolibet aliud remotius a dato sumi potest.
Videtur a data recta ex dato puncto alia, data minor, abscindi posse.
Ideoque rectae *EB etc.,* quae minor est recta *CB etc.,* aequalis recta poterit

## 13. On the Infinitely Small[1]

**434**   26 March 1676[2]

*difference*   We need to see exactly whether it can be demonstrated in quadratures that a differential is nonetheless not infinitely small, but that which is nothing at all.[3] And this will be shown if it is established that a polygon can always be bent inwards to such a degree that even when the differential is assumed infinitely small, the error will be smaller.[4] Granting this, it follows not only that the error is not infinitely small, but that it is nothing at all—since, of course, none can be assumed.[5] ✕

I call that quantity *undesignatable* whose magnitude cannot be expressed by any character signs detectable by the senses. For every desig-
**435**   natable magnitude whatsoever will always be writable in a sufficiently small book with the aid of abbreviations and representations. It was in order to show this that Archimedes undertook his investigation in *The Sand-Reckoner*.[6]

## 14. Unbounded Lines[1]

**485**   April 1676[2]

An unbounded line such as *CB* . . . is something. The unbounded line *EB* . . . is something. The unbounded line *CB* . . . consists of the unbounded line *EB* . . . and the bounded line *CE* lying in a straight line, and having the point *E* in common. The straight line *CB* . . . is the whole, *CE, EB* . . . are

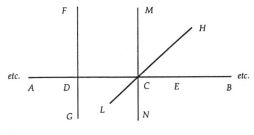

Figure 1

the parts. The straight line *CB* is greater than *EB,* even though each of them is unbounded. I call a straight line *EB* . . . "unbounded" in the direction of *B* if it is the greatest of all straight lines drawn from *E* through *B*. I also call it that line in which there is no endpoint. I call the endpoint of a line, on the other hand, that which is farther than all other points from any point that is taken in the same line. Or, an unbounded line is that in which, for any point whatever, another point can be taken that is farther away from the given point. It seems possible to subtract from a given line at a given point an-

assumi incipiens a *C* et tendens versus *E*. Itaque ex dato puncto *C,* duae versus *E* vel *B* sumi poterunt rectae interminatae, una *CB etc.,* altera aequalis ipsi *EB [etc.],* minor priore. Quod est absurdum, ita enim ipsa *CB*

**486**  *etc.,* ipsa ex *C* versus *E* sumta, ipsi *EB etc.* aequali erit longior, adeoque punctum habebit, remotius quam aliquod prioris; adeoque minor non poterit esse interminata. Ergo si Linea aliqua interminata intelligi potest, non potest in qualibet recta majore assumi quaelibet ipsa minor, incipiens ab aliquo eius extremo; vel contra; si hoc potest semper fieri, linea interminata intelligi non potest. Recta interminata etiam utrinque minor est tribus ab una licet parte tantum interminatis. Sive recta utrinque interminata non nisi in duas ab una parte interminatas dividi potest.

Linea *etc. AB etc.* divisa sit in duas partes *etc. AE,* et *EB etc.* Hae duae lineae vel sunt aequales vel inaequales, si aequales punctum *E* erit medium; si inaequales, erit altera altera major, esto major *etc. AE,* minor *EB etc.* Iam ajo duarum interminatarum ab una parte differentiam esse terminatam. Quod sic ostendam. Si *etc. AE* majori *EB etc.,* erit eius pars aliqua ut *etc. AD* aequalis ipsi *EB etc.,* et differentia earum erit *DE,* quae erit terminata, nam si esset interminata, tunc tota utrinque interminata componeretur ex tribus interminatis, [ex] duabus scilicet una minore, altera parte majoris minori aequali, tertia differentia majoris a minori, ex tribus autem interminatis componi unam est absurdum, ergo differentia haec necessario terminata, *DE.* Haec bisecetur in puncto *C,* quod fieri utique potest si terminata est, eritque *C* necessario punctum rectae totius utrinque interminatae medium, seu recta *CA etc.* aequalis rectae *CB etc.,* quia *CD ∩ CE,* et *DA etc. ∩ EB etc.* Invenimus ergo punctum medium in utrinque interminata. In recta ab una parte tantum terminata, punctum medium inveniri impossibile est; semper enim ab una pars interminata, altera terminata erit, impossibile est autem terminatam aequari interminatae. Recta terminata bisecari potest, quia si duo puncta ab utroque termino aequali celeritate ad se invicem ferantur, alicubi occurrent, et punctum occursus medium erit.

Duae rectae interminatae ab una parte, unum habentes terminum communem, aliquando sunt inaequales, ut *EA etc.* et *EB etc.*; sunto enim ae-

other line smaller than the given one. Accordingly, a straight line equal to
*EB* . . . , which is smaller than the line *CB* . . . , could be assumed beginning from *C* and tending towards *E.* Thus from the given point *C,* two unbounded straight lines towards *E* or *B* could be taken, one being *CB* . . . ,
the other equal to *EB* . . . , smaller than the first. But this is absurd, for in
this way *CB* . . . , the line taken from *C* towards *E,* will be longer than the
**486**   equal line *EB* . . . ; so that it will have a point farther away than some point
in the former line; so that it will be impossible for the smaller line to be unbounded. Therefore if some line is understood to be unbounded, one cannot assume in any greater such straight line any smaller one starting from
one of its endpoints; and conversely: if the latter can always be done, then
the line cannot be understood to be unbounded. Also a straight line that is
unbounded on both sides is smaller than three straight lines each unbounded on only one side. In other words, a straight line unbounded on
both sides can only be divided into two lines unbounded on one side.

   Let a line . . . *AB* . . . be divided into two parts . . . *AE* and *EB* . . . .
These two lines are either equal or unequal. If equal, *E* will be the midpoint; if unequal, one will be bigger than the other: let . . . *AE* be the bigger, *EB* . . . the smaller. Now I say that the difference of two lines unbounded on one side is a bounded line. This I will show as follows. If . . .
*AE* [is] greater than *EB* . . . , there will be some part of it, such as . . . *AD,*
equal to *EB* . . . , and their difference will be *DE,* which will be bounded.
For if it were unbounded, then a whole line unbounded on both sides
would be composed of three unbounded lines, one of them being the
smaller of two unbounded lines, the second being a part of the greater line
equal to the smaller one, and the third the difference between the greater
and the smaller. But it is absurd for one unbounded line to be composed of
three. Therefore this difference *DE* is necessarily bounded. Let this be bisected at the point *C,* which is certainly possible if it is bounded, and *C* will
necessarily be the midpoint of the whole line unbounded on both sides: in
other words, the straight line *CA* . . . [will be] equal to *CB* . . . , because
*CD* $-$ *CE,* and *DA* . . . $=$ *EB* . . . . We have therefore found the midpoint in
a line unbounded on both sides. In a straight line bounded only on one
side, it is impossible to find the midpoint; for with one side always unbounded, the other will be bounded, yet it is impossible for a bounded line
to equal an unbounded one. A bounded straight line can be bisected, because if two points are moved towards each other from both ends with
equal speeds, they will meet somewhere, and the meeting point will be the
midpoint.

   Two straight lines unbounded on one side, having one bound in common, are sometimes unequal, for instance *EA* . . . and *EB* . . . ; for assum-

quales, tunc utique DB *etc. DA etc.* erunt inaequales; et habemus duas inaequales termini communes [*D*]. Error ergo est, quod aliquando ratio-cinabamur esse aequales, quia scilicet una semper ut *EB etc.,* alteri *EA etc.* imposita intelligi seu in ea sumi possit, quod paulo ante impossibile os-tendi. Porro ex his sequitur non posse rectam utrinque interminatam moveri circa centrum *E,* quod medium in ea non sit, ita enim poterit conti-nuato motu pervenire *EB etc.* in locum *EA etc.* quod impossibile esse os-tendimus.

**487**     Diversa puncta media esse possunt in spatio interminato, ob diversas scilicet rectas utrinque interminatas. Sit scilicet recta *FDG* utrinque inter-minata, datam *AB* interminatam secans in puncto*D,* alio a puncto datae medio *C,* ajo punctum ipsius medium aliud esse a puncto datae medio *C,* nam punctum eius medium est vel *D,* vel aliud. Si *D,* utique est aliud a *C,* sin est aliud a *D,* utique erit extra rectam AB, duae enim rectae licet inter-minatae non nisi unum habent punctum commune; si autem hoc punctum est extra rectam *AB,* utique erit aliud a *C,* quod in ea est. Quodsi rectam sumamus in alio plano, quae ipsam *AB* ne secet quidem, adhuc mani-festius est, punctum eius medium aliud esse a *C,* quia recta illa utrinque in-terminata, nullum cum ipsa *AB* habet punctum commune, adeoque nec punctum *C.*

Illud tamen quaerendum est, an punctum *C,* medium unius intermi-natae, medium sit omnium aliarum interminatarum *MCN, HCL* ipsam in puncto *C* secantium. Sed hoc ita refutatur: possibile est unam rectam per duarum rectarum media puncta transire, recta enim per duo quaelibet data puncta transire potest, ergo alterutram (si non utramque) secat puncto sui non medio, non ergo necesse est rectam quae aliam secat, aliam in puncto sui medio secare. Hinc sequitur porro interminatam ne circa medium qui-dem suum moveri posse, quandocunque contingit, ut aliae in quarum locum motu transferri deberet, eam in mediis suis punctis non secent.

Videndum an necesse sit omnium Parallelarum ejusdem plani media puncta esse in una recta (eaque ipsis normali). Hoc posito omnium datae parallelarum in aliis planis omnibus sumtarum puncta media cadent in planum ipsis normale. Unde sequitur planum aliquod dari quod bisecet universum. At vero planum aliquod dari quod bisecet universum aliunde facile probari potest, eadem plane methodo qua ostendimus rectam inter-minatam posse bisecari. Sed ut a lineis ad plana ascendamus nec per saltus ad solidum eamus videndum est an recta inveniri possit quae planum

ing they are equal, then *DB* . . . and *DA* . . . will certainly be unequal; and we will have two unequal lines with a common bound *D*. Therefore we were in error when we once[3] reckoned them to be equal, because one, e.g. *EB* . . . , can always be understood to be superimposed on the other *EA* . . . , i.e. can be assumed to be contained in it, which I showed to be impossible just now. Moreover, from these considerations it follows that it is not possible for a straight line unbounded on both sides to move around a center *E* that is not its midpoint; for in this way by a continuous motion *EB* . . . could reach the place *EA* . . . , which we have shown to be impossible.

**487**     There can be different midpoints in an unbounded space, because of the different straight lines unbounded on both sides. Let there be, namely, a straight line *FDG* unbounded on both sides, cutting the given unbounded line *AB* at the point *D*, different from the midpoint *C* of the given line: I say the midpoint of this line is different from the midpoint *C* of the given line. For its midpoint is either *D* or another point. If *D*, it is certainly different from *C;* but if other than *D*, it will certainly lie outside the straight line *AB*, since two lines, even if unbounded, only have one point in common; if however this point is outside the straight line *AB*, it will certainly be different from *C*, which is in it. But if we take a straight line in another plane, which *AB* does not even intersect, still it is clear enough that its midpoint is different from *C*, because that straight line unbounded on both sides has no point in common with *AB*, and so no point *C* either.

Still, we must inquire whether the point *C*, the midpoint of one unbounded line, is the midpoint of all other unbounded lines *MCN*, *HCL* cutting it at the point *C*. But this can be refuted as follows: it is possible for one straight line to pass through the midpoints of two straight lines, for a straight line can pass through any two given points whatever. Therefore one of them (if not both) cuts it at a point not its midpoint. Therefore it is not necessary for the straight line which cuts one, to cut the other at its midpoint. Hence it follows, moreover, that an unbounded line cannot even move about its midpoint, whenever it happens that the other lines into whose place it is supposed to be transferred by a motion do not cut it at their midpoints.

We must see whether it is necessary for the midpoints of all the parallels in the same plane to be in one line (and for this to be normal to them). Supposing this is so, the midpoints of all the lines parallel to the given one assumed in all the different planes fall in a plane normal to them. Whence it follows that there is some plane that bisects the universe. Actually, that there is a plane which bisects the universe can easily be proved in another way, by using the same method by which we showed that an unbounded line can be bisected. But in order for us to ascend from lines to the plane,

ubique interminatum quodlibet bisecet. Ubi quidem manifestum est, si
concedimus interminatam suis vestigiis parallelam moveri posse, posse
planum quodlibet bisecari. Cum nunc citra nunc ultra sit majus tandem eo
pervenietur, ut cum paulo ante citra esset maius spatium, nunc fiat ultra, et
ubi incipit, ibi bisecabitur. Quae ratiocinatio et divisioni rectae intermi-
**488**  natae, per motum puncti accommodari potest, item et ista, si recta vel
punctum assumitur, ab uno latere, similiter se per omnia habens ab alio latere assumi potest; nulla enim differentia inter formam, utrobique. Quae
duo puncta, lineaeve ad se tendendo aliquando convenient, et ibi erit
medium. Sed sine motu assumto idem evincetur, si scilicet cogitemus tantum alias atque alias duci posse parallelas, alias plus citra alias plus ultra
relinquere, et semper accedendo ad se invicem, seu propiores semper parallelas ducendo, aliquo tempore futurum esse, ut sibi tam prope accedant
quam velis, adeoque spatium interceptum longitudine licet, non tamen latitudine infinitum, fiat latitudinis quavis data minoris.

Sed probandum adhuc restat planum inter duas parallelas interminatas
interceptum, interminatae longitudinis sed terminatae latitudinis, esse
bisecabile per allquam rectam extremes parallelam. Equidem ubi maius et
minus et omnia utrinque paria, videtur et aequale, sed sine assumto motu,
probatio minus manifesta. Ex quo motu illud sequitur in plano cuilibet rectae aliam duci posse parallelam planum bisecantem, eamque non nisi
unam. Hinc sequitur duas rectas idem planum bisecantes se secare. Haec
de terminatis et interminatis vera, et in terminatis et de trisecantibus. Interminata quantitas in plures duabus partes aequales secari non potest.

Videndum jam an non necesse sit, omnes planum bisecantes in eodem
puncto se secare, adeoque aliquod totius plani medium esse punctum. Hoc
videtur eodem probari argumento, quo centrum gravitatis in finitis. Videndum et an hoc punctum ita sit medium, ut omnes rectae ab ipso in omnes
partes in plano ductae sint aequales. Et tale quidem punctum videtur esse
unicum tantum in uno plano; quod scilicet omnes rectas per ipsum transeuntes bisecet. Porro planum interminatum si incedat parallelum sibi, bise-

and for us not to go to the solid by a leap, we must see whether a straight line can be found which bisects any unbounded plane everywhere. Indeed, in this connection it is obvious that, if we concede that an unbounded line can be moved parallel to itself, it is possible for any plane to be bisected. When there is more first on this side, then on that, it will eventually reach it—as for example, when a bigger space that was on this side a little while ago, now comes to be on that—and when this begins to happen it will be bisected at that point. This reasoning can also be accommodated to the di-

**488** vision of an unbounded line by the motion of a point: if in the same way this straight line or point is also assumed to proceed from one side, it can be assumed as conducting itself similarly through all those from the other side; for there is no difference in form on either side. And these two points or lines tending towards each other will meet at some time, and the mid-point will be there. But the same thing will be evinced without assuming motion if we consider only that parallels can be drawn one after another, leaving some on the nearer side, others on the farther one, and by making them always nearer to each other, i.e. by drawing ever nearer parallels, at some time it will be the case that they are as near together as you wish, so that even though the intercepted space is infinite in length, it is not, how-ever, infinite in breadth, and becomes of a breadth smaller than any given.

But it still remains for us to prove that the plane intercepted between two parallel unbounded lines, having an unbounded length and a bounded breadth, is bisectible by some straight line parallel to the outermost ones. For my part it seems that, whenever greater and less and everything on each side are alike, they are also equal, but without the assumption of mo-tion the proof is less evident. With the assumption of motion, it follows that to any straight line in a plane another can be drawn parallel to it bi-secting the plane, and only one such parallel can be drawn. Hence it fol-lows that two straight lines bisecting the same plane intersect. These things are true about both bounded and unbounded things, and in bounded ones they are also true about lines trisecting the plane. An unbounded quantity cannot be cut into more than two equal parts.

Now we must see whether it is not necessary that all lines bisecting a plane at the same point intersect, so that some point will be the midpoint of the whole plane. It seems this can be proved by the same argument as for the center of gravity in finite things. We must also see whether this is a midpoint in the sense that all straight lines drawn from it in all directions are equal. And it seems that indeed there is only one such point in one plane; namely, that which bisects all the straight lines passing through it. Moreover an unbounded plane, if it proceeds parallel to itself, will finally bisect the universe, and if several planes of this sort intersect in the same

cabit denique universum, et plura plana ejusmodi si in eodem se puncto secent, communis omnium sectio erit medium universi. Sed bisectio plani
atque universi, et multo magis media eorum puncta non aeque certa.

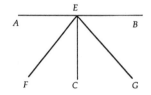

Videtur probari posse quod interminata *AB* parallela sibi normaliterque
per *EC* moveri non possit. Posset enim eius motus *EC* intelligi compositus
ex *EF, EG,* ita scilicet, ut unum movens rectum *AB* sibi parallelam ferens
moveatur per *EF,* aliud per *EG,* motusque uterque sit aequalis. Ita enim
**489**  reapse movebitur per *EC.* Quomodo autem poterit motus possibilis componi ex duobus impossibilibus? Hoc accurate examinandum. Ratio tamen
cur *LH* interminata non possit ire in locum *MN* interminatae ex eo sumta

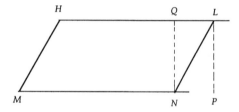

quod ille motus compositus ex uno impossibili, ipsius *LH* per sua vestigia,
et altero, per *LP,* videtur aliter enuntiari posse, scilicet punctum *L,* ab *LP*
venisse in *NQ,* itemque de caeteris lineae *LH* punctis, adeoque totam versus aliquam sui partem vel plagam processisse, quod de *AB* non ita dici
potest. Re exacte expensa, talium compositionum impossibilitas forte sic
probatur, si scilicet in duos motus resolvi possit datus, unum possibilem,
alterum impossibilem, erit datus impossibilis, ponamus enim uno ferri,
ergo si simul et dato fertur, eo ipso et altero impossibili aliorsum feretur;

point, the section common to them all will be the middle of the universe. But the bisection of the plane and of the universe, and much more so their midpoints, are not equally certain.

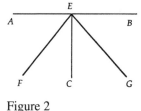

Figure 2

It seems possible to prove that an unbounded line *AB* cannot be moved parallel to itself and normally along *EC*. For its motion [along] *EC* could be understood to be composed of [those along] *EF* and *EG* in such a way that one moving straight line *AB* carried parallel to itself would move **489** along *EF*, the other along *EG*, the two motions being equal. For in this way it would really move along *EC*. But how could a possible motion be composed out of two impossible ones? This needs to be examined carefully.

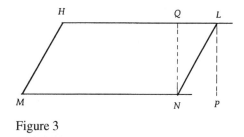

Figure 3

Nevertheless, the reason why the unbounded line *LH* could not pass into the place of the unbounded line *MN* is derived from the fact that the aforesaid motion would be composed out of one impossible motion, that of *LH* along its own path, and another along *LP*. It seems that we can express this in another way: the point *L* would have come from *LP* into *NQ*, and likewise for all the other points of the line *LH*, so that the whole line would have proceeded to another of its parts or regions, and such a thing cannot be said of *AB*. On considering the matter precisely, the impossibility of such compositions should perhaps be proved as follows: If a given motion can be resolved into two motions, one of them possible, the other impossible, the given motion will be impossible. For let us suppose it to be moved with one of the motions, then if it is also moved simultaneously with the

sed si uterque sit impossibilis, videtur neuter necessario evenire, modo res aliter describi possit.

Videndum, an angulus contingentiae possit per aliquam curvam bisecari. Examinandum quid per talem quaestionem intelligatur.

## De motu et materia                                     Aiii68

**492**     Non video quomodo circulus aliquis perfectus describi possit, nisi jam aliquis supponatur. Imo vero videtur, si corpori *AB* occurrant corpora duo

motu contrario *CB,* motum quendam circularem inde oriturum. Item ex motu in pleno (etsi vacuum interspersum admittatur) videtur probari, quod fiant lineae curvae. Sed contra magna est difficultas. Quod conatus sunt in tangentibus. Ergo et motus, alibi enim demonstravi, nuperrime, conatus esse veros motus, non infinite parvos. Unde sequetur nullum esse motum revera curvilineum eorum quae per tangentes cona[n]tur. Ergo alterutrum verum est, aut esse quae non conentur per tangentes; aut nullum esse motum curvilineum. Quamdiu nulla dabitur ratio probandi directe Quadraturas curvilineorum, magna suspicio erit, nulla extare. Nam alioqui possit directe aliquid de illis probari. Examinanda est Lunulae Hippocratis quadratio; quae supponit Circulos esse ut quadrata diametrorum, quod posterius si absolute probari potest, concludere licet aliquam quadraturam directe probari posse. Et cessabit haec difficultas.

Videndum an possibile sit in quovis momento novum imprimi conatum. Posset, si daretur fluidum perfectum. Sed hoc concesso tempus actu divisum foret in instantia. Quod fieri non potest. Quare nec dabitur motus uniformiter ubique acceleratus, quare nec hoc modo describi poterit Parabola. Quare satis credibile est, Circulos, et Parabolas, aliaque id genus omnia esse Entia fictitia. Videndum an non argumentum quod concludit aliquem modum Parabolam producendi esse impossibilem. Ostendas ipsam para-

given motion, by this very fact it will be moved in another direction with the second motion; but if either of the motions is impossible, it seems that necessarily neither of them will occur, unless the matter can be described in another way.

It must be seen whether an angle of contact can be bisected by a curved line. We must examine what is understood by such a question.

### 15. On Motion and Matter[1]                                    Aiii68

[1?–10 April 1676][2]

**492**  I do not see how a perfect circle can be described unless one is already pre-supposed. Indeed, it seems that if two bodies with contrary motions, *DA* and *CB,* run into a body *AB,* a certain circular motion will arise from this.

Figure 1

Likewise it seems to be proved that curved lines would arise from motion in a plenum (even if one admits an interspersed vacuum). But on the other hand there is the great difficulty that endeavours are along tangents, so that motions will be too. For I have demonstrated elsewhere very recently that endeavours are true motions, not infinitely small ones.[3] From this it will follow that there is no really curvilinear motion in things which endeavour along tangents. Therefore one of two things is true: either there are things which do not endeavour along tangents; or there is no curvilinear motion. As long as there is no method for directly establishing the quadratures of curved lines, there will be a strong suspicion that none exist. For otherwise something could be established about them directly. The squaring of Hippocrates' lunule[4] must be examined; it supposes circles to be as the squares of their diameters, which latter, if it can be established absolutely, allows one to conclude that some quadrature can be established directly. And this difficulty will cease.

We must see whether it is possible for a new endeavour to be impressed at any moment whatever. It could, if there were such a thing as a perfect fluid. But if this is conceded, time will be actually divided into instants, which is not possible. So there will be no uniformly accelerated motion anywhere, and so the parabola will not be describable in this way. And so it is quite credible that circles and parabolas, and other things of that kind, are all fictitious entities. We must see whether there is not an argument

bolam esse impossibilem; ponamus enim punctum aliquod ferri in linea parabolica, utique de eo verum erit id in quandam plagam ferri motu uniformi, in aliam motu uniformiter accelerato in quovis instanti, quod impossibile est. Quodsi ergo parabola impossibilis, satis intelligi poterit eandem fore Circuli fortunam. Discere hinc debemus quam saepe fallamur, cum nos res clare et distincte percipere putamus, quis enim Geometrarum non putet Circulum a se perfecte intelligi. Addendae huc Hobbii ratiocinationes.[L1]

**493**    Videndum [an] omnis motus semper quandam contineat directionem. Caeterum posito omnem motum esse rectilineum, impossible est Mundum esse plenum, ita ut vacuum sit tantum interspersum, sed necesse est esse magnas quasdam insulas, aut saltem interruptiones. Certum est enim lineam quandam interminatam per sua vestigia moveri non posse (sed hoc etiam supponit corpus certum occupare locum) ideoque plenum, sine interruptionibus sive insulis, seu vacuum interspersum, postulat motum in se redeuntem. Nos vero posuimus, eum semper esse directum. Quoniam vero ista supponunt, certum corporis esse locum, ut vim habeat nostra de vacuo demonstratio. Ideo id superest examinandum.

Experientia docet corpus a corpore pelli, id est uno in locum tendente, alterum excedere conari. Hoc autem non videtur aliter explicari posse, quam quod incompatibilia. Nec incompatibilitas fert plus et minus. Sed hoc exactius et subtilius excutiendum. Natura Corporis seu Materiae, ultra hoc ut unum ab altero loco pellatur, hoc continet arcanum adhuc mirabile, quod scilicet magnitudo celeritatem compensat, quasi essent res homogeneae. Quod indicio est materiam ipsam resolvi in aliquid, in quod et motus resolvatur, scilicet intellectionem quandam generalem, nam cum duo corpora colliduntur, patet non singulorum mentes efficere, ut sequatur lex compensationis, sed generalem illam, utrique, imo omnibus aeque assistentem. Caeterum ob id non est necesse eandem semper motus quantitatem servari in mundo, quoniam si unum corpus ab alio feratur, in certam plagam, sua sponte autem in contrariam, aequaliter, utique quiescet, id est non exibit loco. Unde de actione, sive motu respectivo, quo scilicet corpus

L1.—Qui ista tractavere, difficultates collegere, non selegere convincenter, ut definirent quid de reliquis statuendum esset.

which concludes that some way of producing a parabola is impossible: by this you would show that the parabola itself is impossible. For supposing a point moves in a parabolic line, it will by all means be true of it that at any instant it is moving with a uniform motion in one direction, and with a uniformly accelerated motion in another, which is impossible. But if the parabola is therefore impossible, it will be quite understandable for the same fortune to befall the circle. We should learn from this how often we are deceived when we think we perceive things clearly and distinctly, for what geometer will not regard the circle as perfectly understood in itself? To this we should add the reasonings of Hobbes.[L1]

**493**     It must be seen whether every motion always includes a direction. Otherwise, supposing every motion is rectilinear, it is impossible for the world to be a plenum, with the vacuum only interspersed; instead there will have to be some large islands, or at least some interruptions. For it is certain that an unbounded line cannot move along its own path[6] (but this also supposes that a body occupies a definite place), and for this reason a plenum with no interruptions or islands, that is, an interspersed vacuum, requires a motion that comes back on itself. Indeed we have ourselves assumed that motion is always directed, since, in order for our demonstration concerning the vacuum to be valid, those considerations suppose that the body has a definite place.[7] Therefore this remains to be examined.

Experience teaches that one body is pushed by another, i.e. that if one body tends towards a place, the other endeavours to leave it. But this does not seem explicable in any other way except that they are incompatible. And incompatibility does not admit of more or less. But we must examine this more exactly and more subtly. The nature of body or matter, over and above the fact that it is pushed from one place to another, contains a secret marveled at until now: namely, that magnitude compensates for speed, as if they were homogeneous things.[8] And this is an indication that matter itself is resolved into something into which motion is also resolved, namely, a certain universal intellect. For when two bodies collide, it is clear that it is not the mind of each one that makes it follow the law of compensation, but rather the universal mind assisting both, or rather all, equally. On the other hand, it is not necessary for the same quantity of motion always to be conserved in the world, since if one body is carried by another in a certain direction, but is moving of its own accord equally in the contrary direction, it will certainly come to rest, i.e. it will not leave its place. From this

---

L1. —Who has treated these matters, and collected together the difficulties, but has not selected them convincingly enough to determine what should be established concerning the rest.[5]

ad aliud refertur, aut in aliud agit, enuntianda quantitatis motus conservatio.

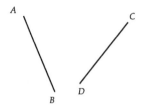

Unum adhuc examinandum reliquimus: certe motum rectilineum, eumque continuum. Nam etsi interruptus poneretur quietulis (quod aliunde
constat esse ineptum) tamen portiones aliquae erunt continuae, aut sequeretur, corpus a loco in locum transferri, ita, ut non eat per intermedia.
Quod absurdum esse pono, et alias ostendi debet, quanquam id videatur
satis difficile. Sed talis positio induceret nobis aliud semper corpus recrea-
**494**  tum, nunc hic nunc illic. Sed hoc nunc relicto videamus quid sequatur.
Corpus *A* moveatur recta *AB*, corpus *C* recta *CD,* quae rectae non sunt parallelae, patet quovis momento mutari distantiam, adeoque infinitae numero mutationes fient, imo tot quot sunt possibiles, seu quot puncta in
recta, adeoque recta in omnia puncta dividetur, quod est impossibile. Et
caetera omnia evenient absurda. Quid ergo? concludere cogar Motum non
esse continuum, sed fieri per saltus, seu corpus aliquandiu durans in uno
loco, immediate post fore in alio licet dissito, id est materiam hic extinc-
tam, alibi reproduci. Mens vero salva semper manet, quae ipsi assistit. Et
idem ex aliis confirmari potest, quod scilicet posito motu continuo, demonstrari potest eum non cessaturum; ut conclusit Hobbes. Sed hoc ferri
posset, nisi hinc sequeretur, nec certas eius species seu modos cessaturos,
quod contra est. Imo absolute loquendo probari poterit, fieri posse, ut corpus quiescat. Si aequali celeritate huc illuc feratur. Cum tamen demonstrari possit, quod movetur motum iri, adeoque nullum esse terminum mo-

it follows that the conservation of the quantity of motion must be asserted of the action,[9] i.e. relative motion, by which one body is related to or acts on another.[10]

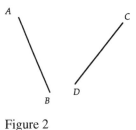

Figure 2

One thing we have left out that must still be examined is, of course, rectilinear motion and its[11] continuity. For even if it is supposed to be interrupted by little intervals of rest (which is known to be inept on other grounds), some portions will still be continuous, or else it will follow that a body is transferred from one place to another in such a way that it does not go through the intermediate places—and this I consider to be absurd, **494** as must be shown at another time, although this would seem to be quite difficult.[12] But such a position would induce us to believe that a different body is always being recreated, now here, now there. But leaving this aside for now, let us see what would follow. Supposing body *A* moves in the straight line *AB,* body *C* in the straight line *CD,* where these straight lines are not parallel, it is clear that at any moment the distance between them changes, and so an infinity of changes will occur, or rather as many as there are possibles, that is, as many as there are points in the line, and so the line will be divided into all points, which is impossible. And all the rest will become absurd. What, then? I am forced to conclude that motion is not continuous, but happens by a leap: that is to say that a body, staying for some time in one place, may immediately afterwards be found to be in another place; i.e. that matter is extinguished here, and reproduced elsewhere. Yet a mind always remains intact that assists it. And the same thing can be confirmed on other grounds: for if motion is assumed continuous, it can be demonstrated that it will never stop; as Hobbes concluded.[13] But that could be tolerated, if it did not follow from this that certain specific motions or modes of motion would also never stop, which is contrary to reason. Indeed, absolutely speaking, it can be proved that it is possible for a body to come to a stop, namely, if it is moved with equal speed in opposite directions. Since it can be demonstrated, however, that what is moved will go on moving, there is accordingly no bound to motion. Whence again

tus. Unde rursus conficitur Motum non esse continuum: quae videtur Empedoclis sententia.

Sed nec explicari potest, quomodo possibile sit motum unum alio esse celeriorem, et locum habebunt difficultates complures, si motus continuus supponatur. Motum unum alio celeriorem esse cum probant motu radii circa aliquod centrum, in quo varia puncta designantur; facile nunc respondemus, nullum esse motum circularem. Posito curvas esse nullas, erunt quae de ipsis dicuntur, polygonorum proprietates. Et certus quidam circulus non erit ens nisi generale, id est, quod de ipso demonstrabitur, intelligendum erit de quolibet polygono ipsi inscripto, aut majoris quam quo utimur laterum numeri.

Caeterum ex his quae diximus etiam illud sequitur omnes atomos esse planilateras. Posito Motum esse reproductionem de distantia in distantiam, jam illud praeclare patet, multo magis, quomodo Deus sit immediate omnium causa, quomodo conservatio continua productio, quomodo nulla alia Lex naturae, quam natura ipsius, cum alioqui posito Motu continuo res se producant, seu quaedam ex ipsis necessario sequantur. Hinc demum patet admirabiliter causa rerum, et productio ex nihilo. Mens tamen semper persistit.

**495**  *10. April.* Quaedam jam mutare sum in his coactus. Nempe ratiocinationem quod motus non sit continuus, quia tunc in quolibet puncto fieret mutatio distantiae, adeoque essent tot distantiae quot puncta; eodem argumento probaretur nec corpus esse continuum, quia si sic disponeretur unum *AB,* alterum *CD,* rursus in quolibet puncto alia atque alia esset distantia; adeoque tot sunt distantiae, quot puncta. Quod si quis crederet mederi, ponendo corpus non esse continuum, sed constare ex punctis meris disgregatis, huic obstaret, tum quod compressa non componerent corpus; tum, quod maneret eadem difficultas, quoad eorum intervalla. Videtur

it follows that motion is not continuous[14]: which, it seems, was the opinion of Empedocles.[15]

But if motion is supposed continuous, it is also inexplicable how it is possible for one motion to be faster than another, and a great many difficulties will occur. One proves that there is one motion faster than another by the motion of a radius about some center, in which radius various points are designated; now we may easily reply that there is no circular motion. Assuming there are no curved lines, what is said about them will be the properties of polygons. And some particular circle will be nothing but a general entity, i.e. what is demonstrated about it will have to be understood of any polygon inscribed in it, or of one whose number of sides is greater than we have employed.

On the other hand, from what we have said it also follows that all atoms will be plane-sided.[16] Assuming motion is a reproduction of distance into distance, then it is now exceedingly clear, very much more so, how God is the immediate cause of all things, how conservation is continuous production, how there is no other law of nature than his nature itself, since otherwise, assuming continuous motion, things would produce themselves, that is, things would necessarily ensue from themselves.[17] Hence the cause of things is at last made clear in an admirable way, as well as production out of nothing. Yet mind always persists.

**495**            10. April

Already I am compelled to change something in this, namely, the reasoning that motion is not continuous because then at any point whatever there would be a change of distance, so that there would be as many distances as points. By the same argument it could also be proved that body is not continuous; because if we arrange one body AB and another CD in this way, again at any point there would be varying distances, and so there would be as many distances as points. If someone believed that this could be remedied by supposing that body is not continuous, but composed out of mere detached points, to this we could object first that when compressed together they would not compose a body; and second that the same difficulty would remain with respect to their intervals.

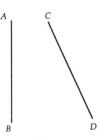

ergo dicendum: Relationum, quae sunt Entia, tum vera, cum a nobis cogitantur, ut sunt numeri, lineae seu distantiae, aliaque id genus; non esse numerum, nam perpetuis semper reflexionibus possunt multiplicari, adeoque nec sunt Entia realia, possibiliave nisi cum cogitantur. Quaeritur an
ullus sit numerus, qui desit in mundo, videtur id non posse fieri, ubi enim
obsecro subsisteremus, dicendum scil. id intelligendum ita tamen, ut eaedem res in diversos aliquando numeros intrent. Nam alioqui si semper id
fieri posset ope novarum rerum, tunc tot essent res [quot] numeri, quod
impossibile, quia aliqua certa est multitudo rerum, nulla est Numerorum.

Modificationes existentes sunt illae, quae possibiles; idem [—BREAKS
OFF.]

## Numeri infiniti                                        Aiii69

496     Si duo Numeri infiniti, sint homogenei, id est ut unus certo numero
finito multiplicatus alterum superet; sive qui sint inter se, ut duae lineae
designabiles; tunc si sint commensurabiles, erunt, ut numerus finitus[L1] ad
numerum finitum.[L2] Sint duae lineae infinitae *AB etc. CD etc.* Utraque dividi posse intelligatur exacte in pedes *AI, IF etc.* vel *CG, GH etc.* sive intelligatur utramque ex multitudine pedum conflari ita, ut nulla pedis frac-
tio supersit, tunc manifestum est has duas lineas, licet infinitas, esse
commensurabiles, sive habere communem mensuram, pedem scilicet *AI.*

L1. ABOVE numerus finitus LEIBNIZ WROTE: Error.
L2. ABOVE numerus finitus: error.

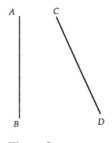

Figure 3

Therefore it seems that what should be said is this: there is no number of relations, which are true entities only when they are thought about by us: for example, numbers, lines, or distances, and other things of that kind; for they can always be multiplied by perpetually reflecting on them, and so they are not real entities, or possibles, except when they are thought about. Supposing it is asked whether there is any number which ceases to exist in the world, it seems that this is impossible: for as long as (pray) we subsist, it must be said that the number would have to be understood, but in such a way that the same things would sometimes enter into different numbers. For otherwise, if it could happen that there were always a need for new things, then there would be as many things as numbers; but this is impossible, because the multiplicity of things is something determinate, that of numbers is not.[18]

Modifications that exist are those which are possible; likewise (—BREAKS OFF).

## 16. Infinite Numbers[1]                                   Aiii69

[c. 10 April 1676][2]

**496**  If two infinite numbers are homogeneous, i.e. such that one multiplied by a certain finite number exceeds the other; or, are to each other as two designatable lines; then if they are commensurable, they will be as finite[L1] number to finite[L2] number. Let there be two infinite lines $AB$ . . . and $CD$. . . . Let both be understood to be divisible exactly into feet, $AI, IF, etc.$ and $CG, GH, etc.$; that is, let both be understood to be made up of a multiplicity of feet in such a way that no fraction of a foot is left over. Then it is evident that these two lines, though infinite, are commensurable, i.e. have

L1. ABOVE THIS: Error.
L2. AGAIN, ABOVE THIS: error.

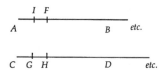

Intelligatur jam has ipsas duas lineas, licet infinitas, esse finitae inter se invicem rationis, seu ut lineae finitae *LM* et *NP* sive homogeneas, id est tales, ut aliquoties repetita minor (aliquoties, finito scilicet repetitionum numero) majorem excedat; tunc manifestum est has duas lineas fore inter

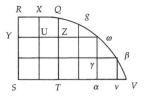

se, ut numerus finitus ad numerum finitum. Sunt enim ut duae lineae *LM* et *NP,* et ipsae sunt commensurabiles. Ergo hae duae lineae *LM* et *NP* sunt commensurabiles; duae autem lineae finitae commensurabiles sunt ut numerus finitus[L3] ad numerum finitum.[L4] Ergo et duae lineae propositae *AB* etc. et *CD etc.*

Sint jam duae figurae, una rectilinea *QRST,* altera curvilinea mixta *QTVQ,* eiusdem altitudinis *QT.* Ponatur curvilinea esse polygonum *QTvβγω*

seu figura gradiformis, divisa in infinita Quadrata infinite exigua qualia
**497** *αvβ[γ]* eodem modo figura rectilinea in quadrata aequalia prioribus qualia

L3. Above numerus finitus: error.
L4. Above numerus finitus: error.

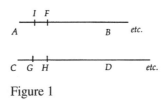

Figure 1

a common measure, namely, the foot *AI*. Now let it be understood that these same two lines, though infinite, have a finite ratio to each other, i.e. are as the finite lines *LM* and *NP*. In other words, let them be *homogeneous,* i.e. such that the smaller, when repeated several times ('several times' meaning 'by a finite number of repetitions'), exceeds the greater;

Figure 2

then it is evident that these two lines will be to each other as finite number to finite number. For they are as the two lines *LM* and *NP,* and they are commensurable. Therefore these two lines *LM* and *NP* are commensurable; but two commensurable finite lines are as finite[L3] number to finite[L4] number. Therefore so are the two lines proposed, *AB* . . . and *CD* . . . .

Now let there be two figures, one rectilinear *QRST,* the other a mixed curvilinear one *QTVQ,* of the same height *QT.* Let us suppose that the curvilinear one is a polygon *QT*νβγω, that is, a gradiform figure divided into an infinity of infinitely small squares, such as ανβ[γ].[3] In the same

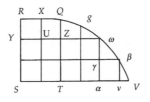

Figure 3

way, let the rectilinear figure be understood to be divided into squares equal to these, such as *XQZ[U].* In this way, the height *QT* is understood to
**497** be divided into an infinity of parts, and however many ordinates the recti-

L3. AGAIN, ABOVE THIS: error.
L4. AGAIN, ABOVE THIS: error.

*XQZ[U]* divisa intelligatur; hoc modo et altitudo *QT* divisa intelligetur in partes infinitas; et quaelibet ordinata tam figurae rectilineae, ut *ZY,* quam curvilineae, ut *Zω.* Ponatur autem quaelibet ordinata curvilineae, ut *Zω,* esse rationalis ad ordinatam respondentem rectilineae, ut *ZY,* quod fieri poterit, si ita ferat aequatio curvae; erit et numerus quadratorum infinitorum unius commensurabilis, numero quadratorum alterius, si una exhauritur, exhaurietur et altera repetitione quadratorum; cumque singulae ordinatae singulis hoc modo habeant communem figuram, etiam totae figurae habent communem mensuram, quadratum scilicet assumtum; si ordinatae hae omnes in rectum extendantur, seu quadrata in directum ponantur, erit eorum numerus ex figura rectilinear ad numerum e curvilinea, ut linea quaedam infinita, commensurabilis, ad infinitam commensurabilem, adeoque ut supra ostendimus, ut numerus finitus ad numerum finitum. At ejusmodi curvilinea est circulari σύλλογος, ut alibi ostendi, ergo circulus ad quadratum, ut numerus finitus ad numerum finitum, quod est absurdum. Et jam video rationem erroris. Negandum duas lineas commensurabiles finitas esse ut numerus finitus ad numerum finitum. Possunt esse, ut numerus infinitus ad infinitum. Duo numeri infiniti commensurabiles possunt esse qui non sint ut duo numeri finiti; si scilicet maxima eorum communis mensura sit numerus finitus. Ut si ambo sint primi. Illud interea hic certum est, has duas figuras circulum et quadratum esse commensurabiles, seu habere mensuram communem, sive finitam et ordinariam (quo casu essent, ut numerus finitus ad numerum finitum, quod minime conciliabile arbitror cum appropinquationibus), sive infinite parvam; quod necessarium arbitror.

Hinc jam tandem videtur aditus apertus ad mirabilem demonstrationem, quod quadratura circuli sit impossibilis, qualis quaeritur; quae scilicet aequatione aequabili exprimat relationem. Quod ut fiat ostendendum est, quod Diameter et latus, ne infinite quidem parvam habeant communem mensuram, et in genere linea quae sit ut radix irrationalis, sive **498** quadratica, sive cubica; ut exempli causa, latus cubi dupli; alteriusve. Ecce hinc praeclarum usum demonstrationum, de incommensurabilibus linearium, possunt enim et ad infinite parva transferri, quod non possunt arithmeticae. Hoc posito, sequitur circuli magnitudinem non posse aequatione quadam ullius gradus exprimi. Eodem argumento evincitur ne ullam quidem circuli portionem hoc modo quadrari posse; idemque est de Logarithmis et Hyperbola.[L5] Circulus aliaque id genus, Entia ficta sunt; ut

L5 IN THE MARGIN: Huic ratiocinationi, quae probare videtur, Circulum non esse quadrabilem, tamdiu non est fidendum, quamdiu non est evictum, Diagonalem non

linear figure has, e.g. *ZY,* so does the curvilinear one, e.g. *Z*ω.[4] Now let us assume any arbitrary curvilinear ordinate, such as *Z*ω, to be in rational proportion to the corresponding rectilinear ordinate, *ZY,* which will be possible if the equation of the curve allows it; then the number of infinite[simal] squares of one will also be commensurable with the number of squares of the other, and if one is exhausted by a repetition of squares, then so will the other be. And since in this way the individual ordinates taken one by one have a common figure, so the whole figures will also have a common measure, namely, the assumed square. If all these ordinates are extended in a straight line, i.e. the squares are taken directly, the number of them in the rectilinear figure will be to the number in the curvilinear one as one commensurable infinite line to another, and so as we showed above, as finite number to finite number. But a curvilinear figure of the above kind is congruent with the circle, as I have shown elsewhere. Therefore the circle is to the square as finite number to finite number, which is absurd.

And now I see the reason for the error. It must be denied that two commensurable finite lines are as finite number to finite number. It is possible for them to be as infinite number to infinite.[5] Two infinite numbers which are not as two finite numbers can be commensurable, namely, if their greatest common measure is a finite number—for instance, if both are prime.[6] Meanwhile, this much is certain here, that these two figures, the circle and the square, are commensurable, i.e. have a common measure, whether (i) finite and ordinary (in which case they would be as finite number to finite number, which I believe to be completely irreconcilable with approximations); or (ii) infinitely small, which I believe to be necessary.[7]

Hence now at last there seems to be a way open for a marvelous demonstration that it is impossible for there to be a quadrature of the circle of the kind we are seeking: namely, one which would express the relation by an equable equation. And in order for this to be done, it must be shown that the diameter and the side do not have even an infinitely small common measure, even in the kind of line which is as an irrational root, whether quadratic or cubic—c.g. the side of a double cube [$^3\sqrt{2}$]—or of some higher power. Hence here we have a splendid use for demonstrations about incommensurables using lines, for they can also be carried over to the infinitely small, which those of arithmetic cannot. Supposing this, it follows that the magnitude of a circle cannot be expressed by an equation of any degree.[8] By the same argument it is proved that not even a portion of a circle can be squared by this means; and it is the same with the logarithm and the hyperbola.[L5]

**498**

L5. IN THE MARGIN: This reasoning, which seems to prove that a circle is not squarable, should not be relied on as long as it has not been proved that the diago-

Polygonum, quolibet assignabili maius, quasi hoc esset possibile. Itaque cum aliquid de Circulo dicitur, intelligimus id verum esse de quolibet polygono, ita, ut aliquod sit polygonum, in quo error minor sit quovis assignato *a,* et aliud polygonum in quo error minor alio quolibet certo assignato *b.* Non vero erit polygonum, in quo is sit minor omnibus simul assignabilibus, *a* et *b,* etsi dici possit, ad tale ens quodammodo accedere polygona ordine; itaque si polygona certa quadam lege crescere possint; et de iis aliquid verum sit quo magis crescunt, mens nostra quiddam ultimum fingit; deque eo id quod in singulis magis magisque evenire videt, perfecte pronuntiat, quod etsi non sit in rerum natura, ferri tamen eius expressio potest; compendiosarum enuntiationum causa.

Caeterum videndum est an non sint adhuc alia, infinite parva, ut anguli. Ecce enim angulus, nonne in puncto est. Nihil enim ad eum pertinet laterum longitudo, et manet etsi semper abscindas. Ergo quantitas in puncto, nam anguli quantitas est. Respondendum primum angulum in solo puncto nullum esse, nisi accedant lineae. Si jam eae lineae sint infinite parvae, lineae tamen, manebit difficultas, eodem enim modo ab illis resecabo. Porro non est angulus quantitas puncti. Posuimus enim punctum cuius pars nulla est, extremum scilicet; aliud enim inassignabile, nullum esse, jam ostendimus. Erit ergo anguli quantitas nihil aliud quam quantitas sinus proportionalis, quae utcunque producas eadem, ita ut ipse angulus videatur esse Ens fictitium. Si pro aliqua re in ipso puncto existente sumatur, scilicet si ponamus, Angulus est in puncto, seu linea quavis assignabili resecta subsistit, datur quantitas anguli. Idem est angulus, lateribus productis. His positis erit angulus, id quod est in lineis qualibet intersecta minoribus, seu spatium comprehensum duabus lineis concurrentibus, qualibet assignabili minoribus. At tale Ens fictitium est, quoniam lineae eiusmodi fictitiae.

**499**

Etsi Entia ista sint fictitia, Geometria tamen reales exhibet veritates, quae aliter, et sine ipsis enuntiari possunt, sed Entia ilia fictitia praeclara

---

posse, detracta saltem quantitate infinite parva, tunc reddi commensurabilem lateri, sumta mensura infinite parva. Idemque esse de caeteris radicibus.

The circle—as a polygon greater than any assignable, as if that were possible—is a fictive entity, and so are other things of that kind. So when something is said about the circle we understand it to be true of any polygon such that there is some polygon in which the error is less than any assigned amount $a$, and another polygon in which the error is less than any other definite assigned amount $b$.[9] However, there will not be a polygon in which this error is less than all assignable amounts $a$ and $b$ at once, even if it can be said that polygons somehow approach such an entity in order. And so if certain polygons are able to increase according to some law, and something is true of them the more they increase, our mind imagines some ultimate polygon; and whatever it sees becoming more and more so in the individual polygons, it declares to be perfectly so in this ultimate one.[10] And even though this ultimate polygon does not exist in the nature of things, one can still give an expression for it, for the sake of abbreviation of expressions.

For the rest, it must be seen whether there are not still other things that are infinitely small, such as angles. Here, for instance, is an angle; is it not in a point? For the length of the sides is irrelevant to it, and it remains even if they are shortened forever. Therefore there is a quantity in a point, for it is the quantity of an angle.[11] First it should be replied that there is no angle in a point by itself unless lines are added. Now if these lines are infinitely small, but are lines, the difficulty will remain, for I will cut them back in the same way. Moreover, an angle is not the quantity of a point. For we have supposed a point to be that whose part is nothing, an extremum; for we have already shown that there is nothing else unassignable. Therefore the quantity of the angle will be nothing but the quantity of the proportion of the sine, which is the same however far you might produce it, so that the angle itself, it seems, is a fictitious entity. If we take it for some thing existing in the point itself, that is, if we suppose that the angle is in the point, i.e. that it subsists when any assignable line has been cut back, the quantity of the angle is given. It is the same as the angle with the sides produced. If these things are assumed, an angle will be that which is in lines smaller than any that intersect, i.e. the space comprised by two intersecting lines that are smaller than any assignable. But such an entity is fictitious, since lines of this kind are fictitious.

Even though these entities are fictitious, geometry nevertheless exhibits real truths which can also be expressed in other ways without them. But

---

nal cannot—at least, by subtracting an infinitely small quantity—be rendered commensurable to the side, assuming an infinitely small measure. And the same holds for the other roots.

sunt enuntiationum compendia, vel ideo admodum utilia, quia imaginatio
nobis Entia eiusmodi apparere facit id est polygona quorum latera non distincte apparent, unde nobis suspicio oritur postea Entis nulla latera haben-
tis. Quid vero an non imago illa saltem nulla exprimit polygona? Ergo
imago illa menti perfectum exprimit Circulum. Est hic quaedam difficultas mira et subtilis. Etsi enim falsa sit imago, in se tamen Ens est verum;
adeoque sequitur in mente esse circulum perfectum, vel potius esse imaginem realem. Erunt ergo in mente et caetera omnia: et in ea omnia jam
fient, fieri quae posse negabam. Sed dicendum est in mente esse cogitationem uniformitatis, nullam autem circuli perfecti imaginem, sed a nobis
applicari uniformitatem postea ad hanc imaginem, quod nos sensisse inaequalitates, obliviscimur; consciine aliquando fuimus nos sensisse? hoc
enim necesse ad oblivionem. Sed hoc non est. Dicendum ergo potius, cum
circulum sentimus, vel polygonum, nunquam nos in eo sentire uniformitatem, sed saltem non sentire difformitatem, seu meminisse nos nihil in eo
difforme sensisse; quoniam inaequalitas non statim percellebat oculos. Et
ob hanc memoriam ipsi jam uniformitatis nomen tribuimus. Videndum an
non multorum per exigua temporis intervalla conscii simus, quorum non
meminimus, seu de quibus non possumus loqui, scribere, quae non possumus characteribus exprimere, ob eorum exiguitatem, cum parvam habeant ad talia relationem. Non ideo tamen minus sentiuntur a nobis con-
sciis. Sed eorum, quemadmodum eorum quae somniamus, obliviscimur.

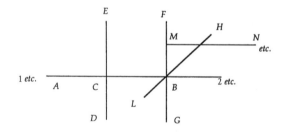

Examinandum adhuc restat nonnihil de Lineis interminatis. Primum in
linea interminata necesse est esse punctum medium. Sit in ea punctum *C*
**500**   alicubi, jam sunt aut aequales aut inaequales lineae *Cl etc.* et *C2 etc.* Si ae-

these fictitious entities are excellent abbreviations for expressions, and for this reason extremely useful. For entities of this kind, i.e. polygons whose sides do not appear distinctly, are made apparent to us by the imagination, whence there arises in us afterwards the suspicion of an entity having no sides. But what if that image does not represent any polygons at all? Then the image presented to the mind is a perfect circle. Here there is a surprising and subtle difficulty. For even if the image is false, the entity in it is nevertheless true; and so it follows that in the mind there is a perfect circle, or rather, there is a real image. Therefore everything else will also exist in the mind: and in it everything that I denied to be possible will now be possible. Instead, what must be said is that in the mind there is a thought of uniformity, yet no image of a perfect circle: instead we apply uniformity to this image afterwards, a uniformity we forget we have applied after sensing the irregularities. Were we then conscious at some time that we had sensed them? for consciousness is necessary for forgetting. But this is not the case. Therefore it must be said, rather, that when we sense a circle or polygon, we never sense uniformity in it, but neither do we even sense a nonuniformity, that is to say, we do not remember having sensed anything nonuniform in it, since the inequality did not immediately strike us. And because of this memory we now ascribe the name of uniformity to it. It must be seen whether we might not be conscious for very small intervals of time of many things we do not remember, or about which we are unable to speak or write, which we cannot express in characters on account of their extremely small size, since they would have little relation to such things. But they are not on this account any less sensed by our consciousness. Rather, we forget about these things, just as we forget about the things we dream about.[12]

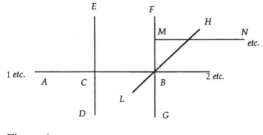

Figure 4

Something still remains to be examined concerning unbounded lines.[13] First, in an unbounded line there is necessarily a midpoint. Let there be a

**500**   point $C$ somewhere in it. Now the lines $C1$ . . . and $C2$ . . . will either be

quales, punctum *C* erit medium. Si inaequales, alterutra earum erit major. Equidem posse videor statim assumere, ita licere lineam *1 etc. 2 etc.* interminatam utrinque secare, ut partes duae sint aequales, in *B* scilicet, et tunc *B* erit medium, sed videndum an hoc amplius probari possit. Sit ergo major *[2] etc.*, minor *1 etc.:* ajo primum non posse esse unam alterius triplam. Quoniam in tres interminatas ab uno latere non resolvi potest interminata utrinque, sed in duas tantum; eademque ratione ostendi potest, nec rationem posse exprimi fractione numeris finitis assignabili media, inter *2* et *3* eandem ob causam. Itaque fractionis illius numerus infinite parva quantitate excedet *2*. Sin linea interminata una *C2 etc.* alteram *CA1 etc.* finita excedet quantitate, qualis e. g. *CB,* ipsa ergo assignata et definita, erit *B* punctum medium. Hinc jam lineae *ED* per *C* transeuntes, non erunt in medio universi, sed *FBG* erit. Ponatur eodem modo et *B* punctum esse medium ipsius *FG* interminatae, et ipsius *LH* interminatae, aliarumque omnium inde ductarum, erit ergo punctum *B* medium universi. Videndum autem an necesse sit inveniri eiusmodi medium posse. Sed hinc videtur sequi difficultas; ducatur recta *MN etc.* interminata versus *N;* erit illa aequalis ipsi *B2 etc.*, cum sit parallela, certum est enim illam infinitam sibi parallelam ferri posse angulo ad se ipsam recto seu in recta *BF.* Videndum jam an ipsi *BH* sit aequalis an inaequalis; major an minor. Si *BH* aequalis, seu si aliquod Medium universi, uti aliunde videtur judicari posse, dicendum erit *BH* aequari *MN.* Hinc jam patet, quomodo moveri possit linea infinita, seu transferri *BH* in *MN,* non continuo motu, id enim impossibile est, sed per saltus, si scilicet *transcreetur.* Est enim motus nihil aliud, quam transcreatio.[L6]

Sed una restat magna *difficultas.* Sit linea infinita, vel utrinque, vel ut lubet, ab una parte, quae actu resoluta ponatur in suas partes; *etc. AB, BC, CD, DE, etc.* Potest enim intelligi innumera eiusmodi esse Entia. Unumquodque eorum moveri potest, unum ex *AB* in [αβ,] alterum ex *BC* in βγ, tertium *CD* in γδ, quartum ex *DE* in δε, quot cum in singulis sit possibile, singula translata intelligamus; dici poterit totam lineam paralleliter sibi et

**501**

L6. IN THE MARGIN: Forte hinc probari potest, omnem conatum esse in rectis perpendicularibus aut coincentibus. Idque experientia confirmat, ut in Tangentibus. Mirum arcana illa interiora experimentis comprobari.

equal or unequal.[14] If they are equal, point $C$ will be the midpoint; if unequal, one or the other of them will be greater. It seems to me I can assume straightaway that the line . . . *1 2* . . . , unbounded on both sides, can be divided in such a way that the two parts are equal, by dividing it at $B$. Then $B$ will be the midpoint. But it must be seen whether this can be proved more fully. Therefore let the greater part be $C2$ . . . , and the smaller $C1$ . . . . I say, first, that it is not possible for one to be the triple of the other, since a line unbounded on both sides cannot be resolved into three unbounded lines, but only into two. And by the same method it can be shown that the ratio cannot be expressed by an assignable fraction of a finite number intermediate between 2 and 3, for the same reason. So the number of that fraction exceeds 2 by an infinitely small quantity. If, on the other hand, one unbounded line $C2$ . . . exceeds the other $CA1$ . . . by a finite quantity, such as, for example, $CB$, with this therefore assigned and definite, $B$ will then be the midpoint. Hence now the lines $ED$ passing through $C$ will not be in the middle of the universe, but $FBG$ will. In the same way, let us suppose that $B$ is also the midpoint of the unbounded line $FG$, and also of the unbounded line $LH$, and of all others drawn through it. Then the point $B$ will be the middle of the universe. It must be seen, however, whether it is necessary for us to be able to find a midpoint of this kind. But a difficulty seems to follow from this; let a straight line $MN$ . . . be drawn unbounded towards $N$; this will be equal to $B2$ . . . , since it is parallel, for it is certain that that infinite line can be carried parallel to itself in a line at right angles to itself, that is, in the line $BF$. Now it must be seen whether $BH$ is equal to $B2$ . . . , or unequal to it, greater or less. If $BH$ is equal to it, that is, if it is the middle of the universe, as it seems possible to judge on other grounds, it must be said that $BH$ will equal $MN$. Hence it is now clear how an infinite line can be moved, that is, how $BH$ can be translated into $MN$: not by a continuous motion, for this is impossible, but by a leap—in other words, if it is *transcreated.*[15] For motion is nothing but transcreation.[L6]

But there remains one great *difficulty.*[16] Let there be an infinite line—infinite either on both sides, or if you prefer, on one side—which we suppose to be actually resolved into its parts, . . . $AB$, $BC$, $CD$, $DE$, . . . . For there can be understood to be innumerable entities of this kind. Each of **501** these can be moved, one from $AB$ into $\alpha\beta$, a second from $BC$ into $\beta\gamma$, a third from $CD$ into $\gamma\delta$, a fourth from $DE$ into $\delta\varepsilon$. Let us understand as many of

L6. IN THE MARGIN: Perhaps it can be proved from this that every endeavour is in either perpendicular straight lines or coincident ones. And experience confirms this, as in tangents. It is surprising that these inner secrets are confirmed empirically.

$$\text{etc.} \quad \alpha \ldots \beta \ldots \chi \ldots \delta \ldots \varepsilon \quad \text{etc.}$$

$$\text{etc.} \quad A\text{——}B\text{——}C\text{——}D\text{——}E \quad \text{etc.}$$

$$\text{etc.} \quad a \ldots b \ldots c \ldots d \ldots e \quad \text{etc.}$$

perpendiculariter promotam. Nec hic absurdum. Jam ponatur oblique *AB, BC, CD, DE, etc.* transferri in *ab, bc, cd, de, etc.*, nonne dici poterit eodem modo totam lineam adhuc promotam. Unde sequitur magis progressam totam lineam in plagam *DE;* nam et motus eiusmodi obliquus, compositus ex perpendiculari et per sua vestigia eunte qui est si *AB* moveatur in *BC,* et *BC* in *CD.* quod fieri utique impossible est, posito corpus eundem semper occupare locum; et certe nulla erit penetratio, semper enim unum excedit altero succedente. Hinc sequitur, vel lineam interminatam esse impossibilem, vel non posse sic moveri oblique, vel non posse appellari unum totum. Sed illud hinc conclude optime posse arbitror lineam eiusmodi materialem interminatam *noninterruptam* implicare. Sed non video an interruptio nos salvet. Non enim ideo ad se propius accedent, quia uno accedente, alterum porro procedit. Revera ergo fatendum erit, Mundum esse finitum, si quantitas interminata totum sive unum est. Ita vicisset Aristoteles, et foret creaturarum quoque corporearum, numerus finitus; sed non incorporearum, ob memoriam mentium. Infinitas autem competeret Deo, ob aeternitatem, item ob alia creaturarum genera.

Una responsio adhuc supererit, scilicet quod translatio ejusmodi obliqua etiam in singulis sit impossibilis, neque a nobis perfecte intelligi, quia possibilia non possunt intelligi in singulis, nisi intellecto ordine universi, quod hic rursus illustri admodum exemplo patet. Nam alioquin ut infinitum esse posse creaturarum numerum probem, fingam similiter inde ab aeternitate, quavis hora novum positum fuisse corpus, in eadem semper recta; manifestum est, cum in singulis possibile ponam, fore tunc eius-

*etc.*   $\alpha \ldots \beta \ldots \chi \ldots \delta \ldots \varepsilon$   *etc.*

*etc.*   A——B——C——D——E   *etc.*

*etc.*   $a \ldots b \ldots c \ldots d \ldots e$   *etc.*

## Figure 5

them as possible, taken one at a time, to have been translated one at a time. It could be said that the whole line has been moved parallel to itself and in a perpendicular direction; and this is not absurd. Now let us suppose *AB*, *BC*, *CD*, *DE*, . . . to be obliquely translated into *ab*, *bc*, *cd*, *de*, . . . : couldn't it be said that the whole line has been moved here in the same way? But from this it follows that the whole line has advanced in the direction *DE;* for an oblique motion of this kind is also one composed of a perpendicular motion and one going along its own path, i.e. one where *AB* moves into *BC*, and *BC* into *CD;* and this is not at all possible, assuming that the body always occupies the same place; and certainly there will be no penetration, for one always moves on when another comes into its place.

Hence it follows either that an unbounded line is impossible, or that it cannot be moved obliquely in this way, or that it cannot be called one whole. But I believe that what can best be concluded from this is that for an unbounded material line of this kind to be *uninterrupted by gaps* implies a contradiction. But I cannot see if an interruption of the line will save us. For the parts will not thereby get any closer together, because when one approaches, the other proceeds further ahead. Therefore it really will have to be admitted that the world is finite, if an unbounded quantity is a whole or one. In this case Aristotle would have been vindicated, and there would be a finite number of corporeal creatures too; but not of incorporeal creatures, because of the memory of minds. And yet infinity would be applicable to God, on account of eternity, as well as on account of created things of other kinds.

One response will still remain: this is that this kind of translation, oblique and also one at a time, is impossible, and not perfectly understood by us, because possibles cannot be understood one at a time without understanding the order of the universe. Again this can be made clear by a very splendid example. For otherwise, to prove that the number of created things can be infinite, I imagine similarly that at each hour from eternity onwards a new body be supposed to have come into existence, always in the same straight line; it is evident that, since it is possible to suppose them one at a time, there will then be an infinity of bodies of this kind. And so no

modi infinitum. Itaque non aliter quis respondere poterit, quam negando in singulis possibile. Et si ita fingi posse videatur, quidni ergo idem respondeam statim ab initio.

**502**     Unum adhuc considerandum, etsi quis neget interminatam quandam esse lineam, tamen non videtur concedi posse (posito nullam esse finem materiae seu ad lineam productam semper materiam [inveniri]), quod *AB* in locum *BC,* et *BC* in locum *CD,* etc. semper simui moveri possint. Ponamus enim id fieri, et nova adhuc addatur, aliunde assumta, quae in locum ipsius *AB* primae succedat; reddita quiete, omnia erunt ut ante, et tamen facta mutatio est. Certe locum aliquem deseri, pluribus motis, successive, nec novum acquiri, impossibile. Breviter, quae sunt multa, eorum multitude, et totum et pars etc. Ergo vel negandum est infinitum actu esse possible, vel recurrendum ad nostra, quod impossibilis sit dicendus singulorum motus, etsi in ipsis per se consideratis non appareat absurditas, quia ut perfecte considerentur, Mens consideranda, quae in ipsis, et relatio facienda ad totum universum. Et ita habendum est, si in omnibus eodem modo cuncta referre possemus ad universum, appariturum nobis, quomodo revera certus tantum determinatusque rerum status sit possibilis et multa excludantur a possibilium numero in quibus nos nullam impossibilitatem invenimus, quoniam fallimur notione materiae, eamque ut extensam tantum consideramus, quod non est.

Ratio cur interminatum, seu quolibet finito maius sit aliquid, non vero infinite parvum, haec est, quod Maximum in continuo est aliquid, non vero Minimum; perfectissimum est quiddam, non vero Minimum, Deus est aliquid, nihilum non est aliquid. Totum in continuo est prius partibus. Absolutum prius limitato. Adeoque interminatum, habente terminum, cum terminus sit accessio quaedam. Nullus est numerus maximus, et nulla est linea minima.

Excutiendum adhuc, an et quatenus vera haec, v. g. quadratum est ad circulum, ut 1 ad $\frac{1}{1} - \frac{1}{3} + \frac{1}{5} - \frac{1}{7} + \frac{1}{9} - \frac{1}{11}$ *etc.* Nam cum dicitur *etc. in infinitum,* intelligitur ultimus numerus non esse quidem numerorum maximus, is enim nullus, sed esse tamen infinitus. Sed quoniam non determinatur quomodo? Adjiciendum enim aliquid, etiamsi numerus infinitus sumatur, ideo dicendum id non esse rigorose verum. Et quoniam circulus est nihil; utique et series ista nihil erit.

one will be able to reply in any other way than by denying it possible to suppose them one at a time. And if it seems imaginable in this way, why then should I not make the same reply at once from the start?

**502**      One thing still to be considered is that, even if someone should deny that a certain unbounded line exists, it still doesn't seem possible to concede (assuming there to be no end of matter, i.e. that matter can always be found for extending the line) that $AB$ could always be moved into the place $BC$, and $BC$ into $CD$, etc., simultaneously. For let us suppose this happens, and a new one taken from elsewhere is added, which takes the place of the first one, $AB$; when they have returned to rest, all will be as before, and yet a change will have occurred. Certainly, when many things are moved in succession, it is impossible for some place to be vacated and no new one to be acquired. And there are, in a word, many, a multiplicity of them, both whole and part, etc. Therefore either it must be denied that it is possible for an infinity to exist actually, or we must return to our previous conclusion, that the motion of the individual parts must be said to be impossible, even if there does not appear any absurdity in them considered in themselves—since in order for them to be considered perfectly, the mind which is in them must be considered, and relation must be made to the whole universe. And so it must be maintained that if in all things we could in the same way relate everything to the universe, it would be clear to us how in fact only a certain and determinate state of things is possible, and how it is that many things in which we find no impossibility are excluded from the number of possibles, since we lack a notion of matter, and consider it merely as the extended, which it is not.

The reason why the unbounded, i.e. that which is greater than anything finite, is something, and the infinitely small is not, is that in the continuum the maximum is something, and the minimum is not; the most perfect is something, the least is not, God is something, nothing is not. In the continuum, the whole is prior to its parts; the absolute is prior to the limited; and so is the unbounded prior to that which has a bound, since a bound is a kind of addition. There is no greatest number, and no least line.

We must still investigate whether and to what extent the following is true, namely, that the square is to the circle as 1 to $\frac{1}{1} - \frac{1}{3} + \frac{1}{5} - \frac{1}{7} + \frac{1}{9} - \frac{1}{11} + \ldots$.[17] For when we say 'etc.', ' . . . ', or 'to infinity', the last number is not really understood to be the greatest number, for there isn't one, but it is still understood to be infinite. But seeing as the series is not bounded, how can this be the case? For something must be added, even if it is assumed to be an infinite number, so that it must be said that this is not rigorously true. And seeing as the circle is nothing, this series will of course also be nothing.

Interea superest haec difficultas. Diagonalis ad Quadratum est ratio quaedam, est enim diagonalis linea, quantitas realis, et latus itidem. Quae si numeris explicanda sit, opus etiam erit numeris infinitis. Imo in universum numeris omnibus. Dicere autem numeros omnes est nihil dicere; quare et ratio illa nihil dicit, nisi aliquid quantumvis propinquum. Non **503** ideo tamen tollitur ratio harum duarum linearum, etiamsi nulla assignetur mensura. Nisi dicas (sine Mensura), quod de angulo, id et de ratione, ipsam per se nihil esse, sed ipsum consensum divisionum; semper manentem, ut supra sinus. Imo videtur ratio semper subsistere, est enim ea ratio, per quam duae figurae sunt similes. Itaque in duabus quantitatibus similibus, id est sola magnitudine, non vero modis magnitudinis differentibus; si scilicet ipsa[e] in se sine aliis considerentur; ratio est quantitas unius determinate per relationem ad aliud. Sine similitudine non possemus intelligere rationem.

Magnitudo est rei constitution qua cognita, ipsa tota haberi potest. Videtur Totum esse etiam quod non habet partes modo habere possit. Totum est, cum ex uno fieri possunt plura. Ex uno autem fieri, est aliquid manere. Quod reapse divisum est seu Aggregatum, nescio an dici possit unum. Videtur tamen, cum sint nomina ad hoc inventa. Sed haec omnia accuratissime excutienda. Ex aliquo fieri aliud, est aliquid restare, quod ad ipsa potius quam ad aliud pertinet. Sed hoc non semper est materia. Potest esse ipsa Mens relationem quandam intelligens, ut in *transproductione,* etsi omnia nova, tamen hoc ipso quod certa lege fit haec transproductio, imitatur quodammodo motum continuum, ut polygona circulum. Et hinc dicitur unum ex alio fieri, simile quasi abusu imaginationis.

Quandocunque dicitur seriei cuiusdam infinitae numerorum dari summam, nihil aliud dici arbitror, quam seriei finitae cuiuslibet eadem regula summam dari, et semper decrescere errorem, crescente serie, ut fiat tam parvus quam velimus. Nam ipsi *per se* absolute numeri in infinitum non eunt, daretur enim numerus maximus. Sed in infinitum eunt applicati certo spatio, seu lineae interminatae in partes divisae. Hic jam ecce nova difficultas. Estne ultimus eiusmodi seriei ultimus, quae scilicet ascriberetur divisionibus lineae interminatae? non est, alioqui et ultimum in serie interminata daretur. Imo videtur dari, quia scilicet Numerus terminorum seriei, utique erit numerus ultimus, pone puncto divisionis ascribi numerum uni-

Meanwhile there remains this difficulty. Diagonal to square is a certain ratio, since the diagonal is a line, a real quantity, and the side is too. If this is to be expounded by means of numbers, there will also be a need for infinite numbers—indeed, for all numbers in general. But to say all numbers is to say nothing; and for this reason that ratio also means nothing, unless **503** it is something as close as desired. Still the ratio of these two lines is not thereby eliminated, even if no measure is assigned. Unless (there being no measure) you also say of the ratio what you said of the angle, that in itself it is nothing but the very agreement of the divisions; an agreement that always remains, as did the sine above. Indeed it seems that the ratio always subsists, since it is through this ratio that two figures are similar. And so in two similar quantities it is the only thing with magnitude, but not with different modes of magnitude—that is, if they are considered in themselves without others, the ratio is the quantity of one determined by relation to the other. Without similarity, we would not be able to understand ratio.

Magnitude is that constitution of a thing by the recognition of which it can be regarded as a whole.[18] It also seems that a whole is not what has parts, just what can have parts. A whole exists when many things can come to be out of one. But to come to be out of one is to remain something. I doubt whether what is really divided, that is, an aggregate, can be called one. It seems to be, though, because names are invented for it. But all these matters must be investigated very carefully. For something to become another thing is for something to remain which pertains to it rather than to the other thing. But this is not always matter. It can be mind itself, understanding a certain relation: for instance, in *transproduction,* even though everything is new, still, by the very fact that this transproduction happens by a certain law, continuous motion is imitated in a way, just as polygons imitate the circle. And hence one may be said to come out of the other, by a similar abuse, as it were, of the imagination.

Whenever it is said that a certain infinite series of numbers has a sum, I am of the opinion that all that is being said is that any finite series with the same rule has a sum, and that the error always diminishes as the series increases, so that it becomes as small as we would like.[19] For numbers do not *in themselves* go absolutely to infinity, since then there would be a greatest number. But they do go to infinity when applied to a certain space or unbounded line divided into parts. Now here there is a new difficulty. Is the last number of a series of this kind the last one that would be ascribed to the divisions of an unbounded line? It is not, otherwise there would also be a last number in the unbounded series. Yet there does seem to be, because the number of terms of the series will be the last number. Suppose to the point of division we ascribe a number always greater by unity than the

tate majorem semper praecedente, utique Numerus terminorum erit ultimus seriei, at vero non datur seriei ultimus, quia est interminata; inprimis si series sit utrinque interminata; ergo concludemus tandem quod nulla sit multitudo infinita. Unde sequeretur nec infinitas res esse. Vel dicendum infinitas res non esse unum totum, seu non esse earum aggregatum. Si res

**504** infinitae esse non possent, foret mundus necessario tempore et loco finitus, sed mundum tempore finitum esse, non videtur possibile. imo sequeretur, et aliquando res cessaturas, omniaque in nihilum reditura, nam alioqui omnia futura essent infinita. Itaque si dicas in [serie] interminata non dari ultimum finitum numerum inscriptibilem, posse tamen infinitum dari: Respondeo, ne hunc quidem dari posse, si nullum sit ultimum. Ad hanc ratiocinationem non aliud habeo quod respondeam, quam numerum Terminorum non semper esse ultimum seriei. Patet scilicet etsi in infinitum augeantur numeri finiti, nunquam nisi finita aeternitate, id est nunquam, pervenire ad infinitos. Subtilis admodum haec consideratio est.

## Communicata ex literis Domini Schulleri     Aiii19

**275**     *COMMUNICATA EX LITERIS D. SCHULL.*

(1) *Demonstrat quod omnis substantia sit infinita, indivisibilis et unica.*
Per substantiam intelligit id quod in se est, et per se concipitur, hoc est id cuius Idea vel conceptus ex Idea vel conceptu alterius rei non oritur.[L1]

L1. Videntur a nobis *per se concipi,* quorum termini sive Voces sunt indefinibiles, seu quorum ideae irresolubiles, ut Existentia, Ego, perceptio idem, mutatio; tum qualitates sensibiles; ut calor, frigus, lumen, etc. *Per se vero intelligi* non nisi id cuius omnia requisita concipimus, sine alterius rei conceptu, sive id quod sibi ipsi existendi ratio est. *Intelligere* enim nos vulgo res dicimus cum eorum generationem concipimus, sive modum quo producuntur. Unde per se intelligitur, id tantum quod causa sui est, sive quod necessarium est, sive Ens a se. Adeoque id hinc concludi potest, nos, si Ens necessarium intelligamus, id per se intellecturos. Dubitari vero potest, an Ens necessarium a nobis intelligatur, imo an possit intelligi, etsi possit sciri sive cognosci.

Conceptus distinguit in claros tantum, et claros distinctosque simul. Omnis con-

preceding one, then of course the number of terms will be the last number of the series. But in fact there is no last number of the series, since it is un-bounded; especially if the series is unbounded at both ends. Therefore we conclude finally that there is no infinite multiplicity, from which it will follow that there is not an infinity of things, either. Or it must be said that an infinity of things is not one whole, i.e. that there is no aggregate of them. If an infinity of things could not exist, the world would be necessar-ily finite in time and place, but for the world to be finite in time does not seem possible. Indeed, it would then follow also that at some time things will come to an end, and everything will be reduced to nothing, for other-wise [the number of] all future things would be infinite. Thus if you say that in an unbounded [series][20] there exists no last finite number that can be written in, although there can exist an infinite one: I reply, not even this can exist, if there is no last number. The only other thing I would consider replying to this reasoning is that the number of terms is not always the last number of the series. That is, it is clear that even if finite numbers are in-creased to infinity, they never—unless eternity is finite, i.e. never—reach infinity. This consideration is extremely subtle.

## 17. Annotated Excerpts from Spinoza[1]          Aiii19
[2nd half of April 1676?][2]

*Items Communicated in Mr. Schuller's Letter*[3]

(1) *He demonstrates that every substance is infinite, indivisible, and unique.*[4]

By substance he understands that which is in itself, and is conceived through itself,[L1] that is, that whose idea or concept does not arise from the idea or concept of another thing.[5]

L1. It seems that we *conceive through themselves* those things whose terms or expressions are undefinable, i.e. whose ideas are irresolvable, such as existence, the ego, perception, the same, change; as well as sensible qualities, such as heat, cold, light, etc. But something is *understood through itself* only if we conceive all its requisites without having conceived another thing, i.e. only if it is the reason for its own existence. For we commonly say that we *understand* things when we can *conceive* their generation, i.e. the way in which they were produced. Hence we un-derstand through itself only that which is its own cause, i.e. that which is necessary, i.e. is a being in itself. And so it can be concluded from this that if we understood a necessary being, we would understand it through itself. But it can be doubted whether we do understand a necessary being, or, indeed, whether it could be under-stood even if it were known or recognized.

He distinguishes concepts into the merely clear, and the clear and distinct to-

**276**     (2) *Deum sic definit*. Quod sit Ens *absolute* infinitum, hoc est substantia constans infinitis attributis, quorum unumquodque infinitam et aeternam essentiam exprimit adeoque immensum est.

N.B. Dicit *absolute,* et non in suo genere, infinitum, cum de eo, quod in suo solum genere infinitum est infinita attribute possint negari, hoc est infinita attributa possint concipi, quae ad eius naturam non pertinent.

(3) *Quaestio de infinito.* Quaestio de infinito omnibus difficillima, imo inexplicabilis visa fuit, propterea quod non distinxerunt, inter id quod sua natura, sive ex vi definitionis suae, sequitur esse infinitum, et id quod nullos fines habet, non quidem ex vi suae essentiae, sed ex vi causae. Et etiam, quia non distinxerunt inter id quod infinitum dicitur, quia nullos habet fines, et id quod quamvis eius maximum et minimum habeamus, sive determinatum sit, eius tamen partes nullo numero explicare vel adaequare possumus. Denique non distinxerunt inter id quod tantum intelligere, non vero imaginari, et inter id quod etiam imaginari possumus. Ad haec si attendissent, nunquam tam ingenti difficultatum turba obruti fuissent; nam tum clare intelligerent, quale infinitum in nullas partes dividi, seu nullas partes habere potest; quale vero contra, idque sine contradictione. Porro

---

ceptus est clarus, quoniam semper homo unum ab alio discernit, exempli gratia, calorem a frigore. Sed non est semper distinctus, hoc est ut sciam quae causa sit diversitatis. Idea, conceptus, cognitio, conscientia, perceptio etc. eodem redeunt.

*Volitio* apud Cartesium est affirmandi vel negandi facultas.

*Per se concipitur* cuius conceptus [non] ex atterius conceptu oritur. Distincte aliquid de aliquo concipitur, cum eius aliqua affectio intelligitur.

Essentialis rei proprietas est quae reciproca est.

Lumen, calor concipiuntur, non intelliguntur. Proprietates Luminis, Caloris notae nobis sed experientia tantum adeoque a nobis non intelliguntur vel demonstatur, etsi percipiuntur. Ita fieri potest mea sententia, ut et proprietas quaedam circa existentiam, circa nos ipsos, seu ipsum Ego, aliaque observentur seu sentiantur, quae non possint demonstrari.

Omne indemonstrabile est vel propositio identica, vel experimentum.

Si de aliquo plura attributa seu plures propositiones invicem aut a priore independentes enuntientur, tum eae propositiones experimenta sunt, aut ex experimentis sequuntur.

**276**    (2) *He defines God as follows:* that which is an *absolutely* infinite being, i.e. a substance consisting of infinite attributes, each of which expresses an infinite and eternal essence and is thus immense.[6]

N.B. He says *absolutely* infinite, and not infinite in its own kind, because if something is infinite only in its own kind, infinite attributes can be *denied* of it, i.e. infinite attributes can be conceived which do not pertain to its nature.[7]

(3) *[Spinoza's Letter on] the Problem of the Infinite.*

To everyone the problem of the infinite has seemed very difficult, if not insoluble, precisely because they have not distinguished between that which is infinite as a consequence of its own nature, or by the force of its definition, and that which has no limits not by the force of its own essence, but by the force of its cause. And also because they have not distinguished between that which is called infinite because it has no limits, and that whose parts cannot be expounded by or equated with any number, even though we know its maximum and minimum, i.e. that it is bounded. Finally, they have not distinguished between that which can only be understood but not imagined, and that which can also be imagined. Had they paid attention to these distinctions, they would never have been overwhelmed by such a huge multitude of difficulties. For then they would have clearly understood what kind of infinity cannot be divided into any

---

gether. Every concept is clear, since a man always discerns one concept from another, for example, heat from cold. But it is not always distinct, that is, such that I know what the cause of the difference is. Idea, concept, cognition, consciousness, perception, etc., come down to the same thing.

*Volition,* according to Descartes, is the faculty of affirming or denying.

That is *conceived through itself* whose concept does not arise from the concept of another thing. Something is conceived *distinctly* from something else when one of its affections is understood.

An essential property of a thing is that which is reciprocal.

Light and heat are conceived, not understood. The properties of light and heat are known by us, but only experienced, and so are not understood or demonstrated by us even though they are perceived. Thus in my opinion it is possible that certain properties concerning existence, concerning us ourselves—the ego itself, and so forth—are also observed or sensed, but cannot be demonstrated.

Everything that cannot be demonstrated is either an identical property or an empirical fact, or both.

If several attributes of some thing, or several mutually independent or a priori propositions about it, are expressed, then these propositions are either empirical facts or follow from empirical facts.

intelligerent, quale infinitum maius alio infinito sine ulla implicantia, quale vero non item concipi potest, quod ex mox dicendis clare apparebit.

**277** Verum ante omnia haec quatuor paucis exponam, videlicet *Substantiam, modum, aeternitatem,* et *durationem.* Quae circa *Substantiam* considerata velim, sunt: (1) quod ad eius Essentiam pertinet existentia,[L2] hoc est quod [ex] sola eius essentia et definitions sequatur, eam existere, quod ni fallor antehac viva voce absque ope aliarum propositionum tibi demonstravi. (2) et (quod ex hoc primo sequitur) substantiam non multiplicem, sed unicam tantum eiusdem naturae existere. (3) denique omnem substantiam non nisi infinitam posse intelligi.

Substantiae vero af fectiones *modos* voco, quorum definitio, *quatenus* non est ipsa substantiae definitio,[L3] nullam existentiam involvere potest, quapropter quamvis existant, eos, ut non existentes concipere possumus, ex quo iterum sequitur, nos, ubi ad solam modorum essentiam, non vero ad ordinem totius materiae attendimus, non posse concludere ex eo quod jam existant, ipsos postea extituros aut non extituros, aut antea extitisse, aut non extitisse; ex quo clare apparet nos existentiam substantiae toto genere ab existentia modorum diversam concipere.[L4]

---

L2. Ostendendum est, id sequi ex eo quod per se concipitur. Conceptus distinctus est propositionis cuius ratio reddi potest. Omnes conceptus simplices sunt clari et distincti. Sunt conceptus qui non sunt puri, sed in quibus imagines aut signa loco conceptuum intercedunt et hi ne sunt clari quidem. Et eatenus confusi dici possent. Sunt quidam conceptus tales, ut in iis resolutio sufficiat ad solutionem alicuius problematis aut [ostendendam] impossibilitatem, ut fere in geometricis. Sed hoc non est necessarium in omnibus. Nam si resolutio desinat in qualitates sensibiles, quorum scilicet ratio quaeri potest, sunt de quorum causa quaeri non potest, ut in extensione et duratione cum omnia sunt resoluta. De Motu et materia quaeri potest causa: item de soliditate; itaque in his ultima resolutio non sufficit ad solutionem et impossibilitatem. Si tamen Leges quasdam sufficientes ex certa quadam hypothesi demonstremus; e.g. sumendo Materiae naturam esse, ut certum una spatium impleat, hincque assumto pleno satisfiat experimentis, poterit nobis imposterum haec ratiocinatio sufficere. Interea nondum nota absoluta soliditatis natura, aliaque. Si omnis soliditas aequalis et summa esset I [—BREAKS OFF]

L3. Ergone certa ratione definitio modi definitio substantiae esse potest?

L4. Hoc ipsum est, quod vulgo contingens appellant.

parts, i.e. cannot have any parts; and what kind can be so divided without contradiction. Again, they would have understood what kind of infinity can be conceived to be greater than another infinity without implying any contradiction, and what kind cannot be so conceived. This will be made clear by what I am about to say presently.

**277**     But first of all let me briefly explain these four [terms]: *Substance, mode, eternity, and duration.* What I should like you to consider about *substance* are: (1) that existence pertains to its essence,[L2] i.e. that from its essence and definition alone, it follows that it exists (if I am not mistaken, I have demonstrated this to you before in conversation, without the aid of other propositions); and (2) (which follows from (1)) that substance is not manifold; rather, there exists only one unique substance of the same nature; and finally, (3) that every substance can be understood only as infinite.

The affections of substance I call *modes.* Their definition, *insofar as* it is not the definition of substance itself,[L3] cannot involve existence. So even though they exist, we may conceive them as not existing. Again it follows from this that when we attend only to the essence of modes, but not to the order of the whole of matter, we cannot infer from the fact that they exist now that they will or will not exist later, or that they did or did not exist earlier. From this it is clear that we conceive the existence of a substance to be of a wholly different kind than the existence of modes.[L4]

L2. It should be shown that this follows from that which is conceived through itself. A distinct concept is a proposition whose reason can be provided. All simple concepts are clear and distinct. There are concepts which are not pure, but in which images or signs act as intermediaries for concepts, and these are not even clear. And to this extent they might be said to be confused. There are certain concepts such that there is sufficient resolution in them for solving some other problem or for [proving] its impossibility, as is usually the case in geometry. But this is not necessarily the case for all concepts. For if the resolution of those things whose cause is sought ends in sensible qualities, there are concepts whose cause cannot be sought, as when everything is resolved into extension and duration. A cause can be sought for motion and matter: likewise for solidity; and so in these things an ultimate resolution is not sufficient for a solution or [proving] an impossibility. If, however, we should demonstrate certain laws to be sufficient on the basis of some particular hyothesis—e.g. if we assume the nature of matter to be such that one [portion of matter] fills a certain space, and as a result, when the space is assumed full, this agrees with experiments—this reasoning could suffice for us in the future. Meanwhile, the absolute nature of solidity, and other such things, are not yet known. If every solidity were equal and as great as possible [—BREAKS OFF].

L3. So can the definition of a mode be the definition of substance in some manner?

L4. This is exactly what is commonly called contingent.

Ex quo oritur Differentia inter aeternitatem et Durationem. Per Durationem enim modorum tantum existentiam explicate possumus; substantiae vero per aeternitatem, hoc est infinitam existendi, sive invita Latinitate, essendi fruitionem.[L5]

**278**     Ex quibus clare constat, nos modorum existentiam et durationem, ubi, ut saepissime fit, ad solam eorum essentiam non vero ordinem naturae attendimus, ad libitum, quin ideo,[L6] quem eorum habemus conceptum destruamus, determinare, majorem minoremque concipere, atque in partes dividere posse. Aeternitatem vero et substantiam, quandoquidem non nisi infinita concipi possunt,[L7] nihil horum pati posse, quin simul eorum conceptum destruamus.

Quare ii prorsus garriunt, ne dicam insaniunt,[L8] qui substantiam extensam ex partibus sive corporibus ab invicem realiter distinctis conflari putant. Idem enim est, ac si quis ex sola additione aut coalitione circulorum, quadratum aut Triangulum, aut quid aliud tota essentia diversum conflare studeat. Quare omnis illa farrago argumentorum, quibus substantiam corpoream finitam esse ostendere moliuntur, sua sponte ruunt. Omnia enim illa argumenta substantiam corpoream ex partibus conflatam supponunt.[L9] Ut etiam alii, qui postquam sibi persuaserunt, lineam ex punctis componi, multa invenire potuerunt argumenta, quibus ostenderent, lineam [non] esse in infinitum divisibilem.

Si autem quaeras cur nos naturae impulsu adeo propensi sumus ad dividendam substantiam extensam? Ad id respondeo, quod quantitas duobus modis a nobis concipitur; abstracte scilicet sive superficialiter, prout ope sensuum eam in imaginatione habemus, vel ut substantia quod a solo intellectu fit. Itaque si ad quantitatem prout est in imaginatione attendimus, quod saepissime et facilius fit, ea finita, divisibilis, ex partibus composita, et multiplex reperitur; si vero ad solum intellectum attendamus, et res ut in se est percipiatur, quod difficillime fit, tum ut satis antehac Tibi demonstravi, infinita, indivisibilis et unica reperietur.

---

L5. Satis congruat cum definitones aeternitatis Boëtiana.

L6. *Sans que pour cela,* quanquam non ideo

L7. Nondum hic probatum Substantiam non nisi infinitam concipi posse.

L8. Paulo durius, cum haec et in veteres et Cartesium torqueri possint | [— CROSSED OUT]

L9. Partes non existere in totis fuse probare conati sunt Digbaeus et Thom. Anglus.

This is the source of the difference between *eternity* and *duration*. For it is only the existence of modes that we may explain by means of duration; but the existence of substance is explained by means of eternity, i.e., the infinite enjoyment of existing, or, in bad Latin, of being.[L5]

**278** From these considerations it is clear that whenever (as is most often the case) we attend only to the essence of modes and not to the order of nature, we can limit their existence and duration as we please, conceive them as greater or smaller, and divide them into parts, without thereby[L6] destroying whatever concept we have of them. But eternity and substance, inasmuch as they can only be conceived as infinite,[L7] cannot be treated by us in any of these ways without at the same time destroying the concept we have of them.

So those who hold extended substance to be made up of parts or bodies really distinct from each other are, in a word, talking nonsense, bordering on insanity.[L8] For this is the same as if someone should try, simply by adding circles or piling them one on top of another, to make up a square or triangle or anything else whose whole essence is different. So that whole hodgepodge of arguments by which they struggle to show that corporeal substance is finite falls apart of its own accord. For all these arguments suppose corporeal substance to be made up of parts.[L9] In the same way there are others who, having persuaded themselves that a line is composed of points, have been able to find many arguments by which they would show that a line is [not][10] divisible to infinity.

But if you ask why we are so inclined, by a natural impulse, to divide extended substance, I reply that we conceive quantity in two ways: abstractly, i.e. superficially, as we have it in the imagination with the aid of the senses; or as a substance, which occurs by the intellect alone. So if we attend to quantity as it is in the imagination, which is what we do most often and quite easily, we find it to be finite, divisible, and composed of parts, and manifold; but if we attend to it as it is in the intellect alone, and perceive the thing as it is in itself, which is very difficult, then, as I demonstrated to you well enough before, we find it to be infinite, indivisible, and unique.

L5. This agrees well enough with Boethius's definition of eternity.[8]

L6. "*Sans que pour cela* [were it not for this]," although not "thereby."

L7. It has not yet been proved here that substance can only be conceived as infinite.

L8. A bit too harsh, since these [insults] could be hurled at both the ancients and Descartes. [—CROSSED OUT]

L9. That parts do not exist in wholes was something that Digby and Thomas White endeavoured to prove in great detail.[9]

Porro ex eo quod Durationem et Quantitatem pro lubitu determinate possumus, ubi scilicet hanc a substantia abstractam concipimus, et illam a modo quo a rebus aeternis fluit separamus, oritur tempus et mensura. Tem-

**279** pus nempe ad durationem, mensura vero ad quantitatem tali modo determinandam, ut quoad fieri possit, eas facile imaginemur.

Deinde ex eo quod affectiones substantiae ab ipsa substantia separamus, et ad classes, ut eas quoad fieri potest, facile imaginemur, redigimus, oritur numerus, quo ipsas determinamus, ex quibus clare videre est, mensuram, tempus, et numerum nihil esse nisi cogitandi seu potius imaginandi modos. Quare non mirum est, quod omnes qui similibus notionibus, et quidem male intellectis progressum naturae intelligere conati sunt, adeo mirifice se intricarint, ut tandem se extricare nequiverint, nisi omnia perrumpendo, et a nullo absurdo, quantumvis turpissimo cavendo.

Nam cum multa sint, quae nulla imaginatione, sed solo intellectu assequi possumus, uti sunt substantial aeternitas et alia, si quis talia similibus notionibus, quae tantum auxilia imaginationis sunt, explicate conatur, nihilo plus agit, quam si det operam, ut sua imaginatione insaniat.

Porro ipsi substantiae modi, si cum similibus rationis Entibus seu imaginationis auxiliis confundantur, nunquam recte intelligi poterunt. Nam cum id facimus, ipsos a substantia et modo, quo ab aeternitate fluunt, separamus, sine quibus tamen non possunt recte intelligi; quod ut adhuc clarius videas, cape hoc exemplum: nempe ubi quis durationem abstracte$^{L10}$ conceperit, eamque cum tempore confundendo in partes dividere incepit, nunquam poterit scire, quomodo hora, e.g. transire potest. Nam ut hora transeat, necesse erit ejus dimidium prius transire, postea dimidium reliqui, et deinde dimidium, quod huius reliqui relinquebatur, et sic porro indefinite dimidium a reliquo substrahat, nunquam ad finem horae pervenire poterit,$^{L11}$ quare multi qui entia rationis a realibus non distinguere

L10. Id est, ut puto concipiendo Durationem ut Ens per se a suo subjecto abstractum, quo modo fit, ut ait, imaginarium seu Ens rationis. Quae Hobbianis forte consentiunt. Hobbius enim Locum vocat phantasma existentiae et Tempus phantasma motus.

L11. Hinc illud tantum sequitur neminem posse absolvere enumerationem partium in quas hora proportionaliter continue dividi potest. Quod idem est ac si dicerem, nullum posse librum inveniri, in quo scribere liceat omnes numeros progressionis Geometricae duplae. Non vero hinc sequitur horam non transire, sed horam non nisi hora transire.

Time and measure, moreover, arise from the fact that when we conceive quantity abstracted from substance, and separate duration from the way it flows from things eternal, we can limit duration and quantity as we please. **279** Time is for limiting duration,[11] measure for limiting quantity, so that we may as far as possible imagine them easily.

Next, from the fact that we separate the affections of substance from substance itself, and reduce them to classes so that we may as far as possible imagine them easily, there arises number, by which we limit them. From these considerations you can see clearly that measure, time, and number are nothing but modes of thinking, or rather, of imagining. So it is no wonder that all those who have endeavoured to understand the process of nature by similar notions, and badly understood ones at that, should have tangled themselves up so marvelously that in the end they have been unable to untangle themselves again except by forcing their way through everything, oblivious to any absurdity, no matter how gross.

For since there are many things which we cannot at all grasp with the imagination, but only with the intellect—such as substance, eternity etc.— anyone who tries to explain such things using similar notions, which are merely aids to the imagination, does nothing more than if he were to engage himself in running wild with his imagination.

Moreover, the modes of substance themselves can never be correctly understood if they are confused with similar entities of reason or aids for the imagination. For when we do this, we separate them from substance and from the way they flow from eternity, without which they cannot be correctly understood. To see this more clearly still, take this example: Whenever someone conceives duration abstractly[L10] and by confusing it with time begins to divide it into parts, he will never be able to understand how an hour, for example, can pass. For in order for the hour to pass, it will be necessary for half of it to pass first, and then half of the remainder, and then half of what remains of this remainder. And if he goes on in this way subtracting half from the remainder indefinitely, he will never be able to reach the end of the hour.[L11] Hence many people who are not accustomed

L10. That is, I suppose, by conceiving duration as an entity through itself, abstracted from its own subject, in which case it would be, as he says, imaginary or a being of reason. Which considerations strongly agree with Hobbes's. For Hobbes calls place the phantasm of existence and time the phantasm of motion.[12]

L11. From this it only follows that nobody can complete the enumeration of parts into which an hour can be divided in continuous proportion. And this is the same thing as saying that no book can be found in which one could write all the numbers of a double geometrical progression.[13] It does not follow from this, however, that an hour cannot pass, but that an hour can only pass in an hour.

consueverunt, durationem ex momentis componere ausi sunt asseverare. **280** Inciderunt scilicet in Scyllam, cupientes vitare Charybdin. Idem enim est durationem ex momentis, quam numerum ex sola nullitatum additione oriri.[L12]

Porro cum ex modo dictis satis pateat, nec numerum, nec mensuram, nec tempus, quandoquidem non nisi auxilia imaginationis sunt[L13] posse esse infinitos, nam alias numerus non esset numerus, nec mensura, mensura, nec tempus esset tempus. Inde clare videre est, cur multi, qui haec tria cum rebus confundebant, propterea quod veram rerum naturam ignorarunt, infinitum actu negarunt; sed quam misere ratiocinate sint, judicent Mathematici, quibus huiusmodi farinae argumenta nullam moram injicere potuerunt, circa res ab iis distincte perceptas.

Nam praeterquam quod multa invenerunt, quae nullo numero *explicari* possunt,[L14] quod satis numerorum ad omnia determinanda defectum patefacit; multa etiam sunt, quae nullo numero *adaequari* possunt, sed omnem numerum, qui dari possit, superant,[L15] nec tamen concludunt talia omnem numerum superare ex partium multitudine, sed ex eo quod rei natura non sine manifesta contradictione numerum pati potest.[L16] Ut e.g. omnes inaequalitates spatii duobus circulis *ab cd* interpositi, omnesque variationes, quas materia in eo mota pati debet, omnem numerum superant, idque non

L12. Hanc rationem qua et alii probare conantur continuum in infinitum dividi posse, nondum satis accurate deductam, vidi, ut convincat. Aliunde autem idem rigide demonstrari potest.

L13. An ergo tempus et mensura ex punctis componuntur? Hoc innui videtur, quoniam paulo ante dicebatur, ideo eos errasse, qui durationem ex punctis composuere, quod eam, quae realis est, a tempore, quod est ens imaginarium, non distinxere. Vix tamen crediderim hoc ab autore asseri, quod continuum ullum componatur ex punctis.

L14. Finito scilicet. Nam etiam irrationalia, si infinitos (id est assignabili quantitate plures) adhibeas numeros, possunt explicari ratione numerorum ad numeros.

L15. Finitum scilicet. Nam de reliquo, si tanta eorum multitudo est, ut quemlibet numerum, assignabilem scilicet a nobis, superent; poterit haec ipsa Multitudo appellari Numerus, major scilicet assignabili quovis.

L16. Quid ni ex partium multitudine, id ostendatur; si scilicet pateat plures esse, quam ut numerum assignabilem ferant?

**280** to distinguishing entities of reason from real things have ventured to declare that duration is composed of moments, thus running into Scylla in their eagerness to avoid Charybdis. For generating duration from moments is the same as generating number simply by adding noughts.[L12]

Moreover, from what has just been said it is clear enough that neither number, nor measure, nor time, inasmuch as they are only aids for the imagination,[L13] can be infinite. For otherwise number would not be number, nor measure measure, nor time time. Hence it is easy to see why many people who have confused these three for real things, because they were ignorant of the true nature of things, have denied the actually infinite. But let the mathematicians judge how miserably these people have reasoned; for arguments of such poor quality have never caused them any hesitation about things they perceived distinctly.

For apart from the fact that they have discovered many things which cannot be *expounded* by any number[L14]—which reveals well enough the inability of numbers to limit everything—there are also many things which cannot be *equated* with any number[L15] but exceed every number that can be given. Yet they do not conclude that such things exceed every number because of the multiplicity of their parts, but because the nature of the thing cannot admit a number without a manifest contradiction.[L16] For example, all the inequalities *ab* and *cd* of the space lying between two circles, and all the variations which the matter moving in it must undergo, exceed every number. And this is not concluded from the excessive magni-

L12. This reason, by means of which other people also endeavour to prove that the continuum can be divided to infinity, does not yet seem to have been deduced carefully enough to be convincing. But the same thing can be strictly demonstrated on other grounds.

L13. Are then time and measure composed of points? This seems to be given the nod, since it was said a little while ago that those who composed duration of points were in error because they had not distinguished duration, which is real, from time, which is an imaginary entity. But I would scarcely believe that this author is asserting that any continuum is composed of points.

L14. That is, any finite number. For, if you employ infinite numbers (i.e. more than an assignable quantity of them), even irrationals can be expounded by a ratio of numbers to numbers.

L15. That is, any finite number. For concerning the rest, if their multiplicity is so great that they exceed any number, that is, any number assignable by us, this multiplicity itself could be called a number, to wit, one that is greater than any assignable number whatever.

L16. Why they do not exceed every number because of this multiplicity of parts is yet to be shown; why shouldn't they, if indeed it is obvious that they are more numerous than can bear an assignable number?

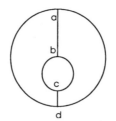

**281** concluditur ex nimia spatii interpositi magnitudine,[L17] nam quantumvis parvam eius portionem capiamus, eius tamen parvae portionis inaequalitates omnem numerum superabunt. Neque etiam ideo concluditur, ut circa alia contingit, quod eius maximum et minimum non habeamus. Utrumque enim in hoc nostro exemplo habemus, maximum nempe *ab,* et minimum *cd;* sed ex eo tantum concluditur, quod natura spatii inter duos circulos diversa centra habentes interpositi, nihil tale pati potest; ideoque si quis omnes illas inaequalitates certo numero aliquo terminare velit, simul curare debebit, ut circulus non sit circulus. Sic etiam, ut ad nostrum propositum revertar, si quis omnes motus materiae qui huc usque fuerunt determinare velit, eos scilicet eorumque durationem ad certum numerum et tempus redigendo, is certe nihil aliud quaerit, quam substantiam corpoream, quam non nisi existentem concipere possumus,[L18] suis affectionibus privare et efficere, ut naturam quam habet, non habeat. Quod clare demonstrare possem, ut et alia quae in hac Epistola attigi, nisi id superfluum judicarem.

Ex omnibus jam dictis clare videre est, quaedam sua natura esse infinita, nec ullo modo finita concipi posse;[L19] quaedam vero vi causae cui inhaerent,[L20] quae tamen, ubi abstracte concipiuntur, in partes possunt dividi, et finita considerari,[L21] quaedam denique infinita, vel si mavis indefinite dici, propterea quod nullo numero, adaequari possint, quae tamen

---

L17. Probare susceperat hoc non concludi ex partium multitudine; hic vero ostendit tantum id non concludi ex totius magnitudine, quod longe aliud est. Manifestum autem id revera ex eo concludi, quod materia in infinitum divisibilis, reapse in omnes partes sic dividitur, in quas dividi potest. Eadem consideratio locum habet in omni motu solidi, in liquido perfecto, pleno. Emergunt vero difficultates, quarum resolutio exhibet praeclara quaedam theoremata, in quae si incidisset Cartesius, quasdam sententias suas correxisset.

L18. eo ipso scilicet, ex phraseologia autoris nostri, quia substantia est.

L19. ut substantia, aeternitas ex sententia autoris.

L20. ut duration extensio.

L21. ut mensura, tempus.

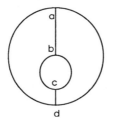

**281**  tude of the intervening space,[L17] for however small a portion of it we take, the inequalities of this small portion will still exceed every number. Neither is it concluded from the fact that, as happens in other cases, we do not know its maximum and minimum. For we know both in this example of ours: *ab* is the maximum, and *cd* is the minimum. Instead it is concluded simply from the fact that the nature of the space lying between two non-concentric circles can admit no such thing. So if anyone should wish to determine all those inequalities by some definite number, he will have to see to it at the same time that a circle not be a circle. In the same way, to return to our purpose, if anyone should wish to determine all the motions of matter there have been up till now by reducing them and their duration to a definite number and time, he will of course only be asking for corporeal substance (which we can conceive only as existing)[L18] to be deprived of its affections, and made not to have the nature that it does have. I could give a clear demonstration of this, as well as other things which I have touched on in this letter, if I did not regard it as superfluous.

From everything already said it seems clear that some things are infinite by their nature, and cannot in any way be conceived to be finite;[L19] others are infinite by the force of the cause in which they inhere,[L20] although when they are conceived abstractly they can be divided into parts and regarded as finite;[L21] and others, finally, are called infinite, or if you prefer, indefinite, because they cannot be equated with any number, although they

L17. He had undertaken to prove that this is not concluded from the multiplicity of the parts; but here he has shown only that it cannot be concluded from the magnitude of the whole, which is far different.[14] Now it is evident that what is really to be concluded from this is that matter, which is divisible to infinity, is in fact so divided into all the parts into which it can be divided. The same consideration applies in every case of a solid moving in a perfect liquid plenum. Indeed, there emerge difficulties whose resolution occasions certain splendid theorems, and if Descartes had happened to discover them, he would have corrected certain of his opinions.

L18. —for the very reason that, in the phraseology of our author, it is substance.

L19. —such as substance and eternity, according to the author's opinion.

L20. —such as duration and extension.

L21. —such as measure and time.

majora et minora possunt concipi,[L22] quia non sequitur illa necessario esse aequalia debere, quae nullo numero adaequari possunt,[L23] ut ex allato exemplo et aliis multis, fit manifestum.

Denique causas errorum et confusionum, quae circa quaestionem infiniti ortae sunt breviter indicavi,[L24] easque ni fallor deposui adeo, ut non **282** putem ullam manere quaestionem de infinito, quam hic non attigi, aut quae non ex dictis facillime solvi queat, quare circa haec te diutius detinere, non operae pretium judico.

Verum hic obiter notare velim, quod Peripatetici, ut puto, male intellexerunt, demonstrationem Veterum, qua ostendere nitebantur, *Dei* existentiam. Nam ut ipsam apud Iudaeum quendam, Rab. Jaçdai vocatum reperio, sic sonat: Si datur progressus Causarum in infinitum, sunt ergo omnia quae sunt, etiam causata, atqui ad nullum, quod causatum est, pertinet ex vi eius naturae necessario existere, ergo nihil est in natura ad cuius essentiam pertinet necessario existere, sed hoc est absurdum, ergo et illud; quare vis argumenti non in eo sita est, quod impossibile sit dari actu infinitum, sed tantum in eo, quod supponant scilicet quae sua natura non neces-

L22. ut motuum variationes.

L23. hoc Mathematicis plerisque agnitum, nominatim Cardano, egregie autem, ut video observatum et diligenter inculcatum ab autore nostro.

L24. Ego semper distinxi Immensum ab Interminato, seu terminum non habente. Et id cui nihil addi potest, ab eo quod numerum assignabilem superat. Breviter gradus constituo: Omnia, Maximum, Infinitum. Quicquid *omnia* continet, est maximum in entitate; quemadmodum spatium in omnes dimensiones interminatum est maximum in extensione. Item quod omnia continet, infinitissimum, ut vocare soleo, sive absolute infinitum est. *Maximum,* est *omnia* sui generis, seu cui nil apponi potest, ut linea recta utrinque interminata, quam et infinitam esse patet; nam omnem continet longitudinem. *Infinita* denique *infimi gradus* sunt quorum magnitude major est, quam ut a nobis ratione assignabili ad sensibilia, possit explicari. Quanquam aliquid detur ipsis majus. Quemadmodum spatium infinitum inter asymptoton et Hyperbolam Apollonii comprehensum quod ex moderatissimis infinitis unum est, cui respondet quodammodo in numeris summa huius spatii; $\frac{1}{1}$ $\frac{1}{2}$ $\frac{1}{3}$ $\frac{1}{4}$ etc. quae est $\frac{1}{0}$. Modo scilicet intelligamus ipsum 0, seu Nullitatem, aut potius hoc loco quantitatem infinite seu inassignabiliter parvam, majorem esse minoremve, prout ultimum seriei huius fractionum, infinitae, Nominatorem, qui infinitus et ipse est, minorem majoremve assumserimus. Maximus enim in numeros non cadit.

can be conceived as being greater or smaller.[L22] For it does not follow that things which cannot be made equal to any number must necessarily be equal,[L23] as is evident from the example adduced, and from many others.

In sum, I have briefly indicated the causes of the errors and confusions which have arisen concerning the problem of the infinite,[L24] and unless I am mistaken, I have so disposed of them that I do not think there remains any problem about the infinite which I have not touched upon here, or which cannot be very easily solved from what I have said. So I do not regard it as worthwhile to detain you any longer with these matters.

**282**

But I would like to note here in passing that the Peripatetics have, I think, misunderstood the demonstration by which the Ancients tried to show the existence of *God*. For as I find it according to a certain Jew called Rabbi Jaçdai,[18] the demonstration goes as follows: Supposing there is an infinite progression of causes, then everything that exists has also been caused; however, it does not pertain to anything that has been caused that it should exist necessarily by the force of its own nature; therefore there is nothing in nature to whose essence it pertains to exist necessarily; but this is absurd, therefore the supposition is too. Hence the force of this argument does not lie in the assertion that it is impossible for the infinite to exist actually, but only in the supposition that things which do not exist nec-

L22. —such as the variations of motions.

L23. This is acknowledged by most mathematicians, expressly by Cardano, but above all, as I see it, observed and carefully elaborated by our author.[15]

L24. I have always distinguished the Immensum from the Unbounded, i.e. that which has no bound. And that to which nothing can be added from that which exceeds an assignable number. Briefly, I set in order of degree: Everything, Maximum, Infinity.[16] Whatever contains *everything* is maximum in entity; just as a space unbounded in every dimension is maximum in extension. Likewise, that which contains everything is the most infinite, as I am accustomed to call it, or the absolutely infinite. The *maximum* is *everything* of its kind, i.e. that to which nothing can be added, for instance a line unbounded on both sides, which is obviously also infinite; for it contains every length.[17] Finally those things are *infinite in the lowest degree* whose magnitude is greater than we can expound by an assignable ratio to sensible things, even though there exists something greater than these things. In just this way, there is the infinite space comprised between Apollonius's Hyperbola and its asymptote, which is one of the most moderate of infinities, to which there somehow corresponds in numbers the sum of this space: $\frac{1}{1} + \frac{1}{2} + \frac{1}{3} + \frac{1}{4} + \ldots$, which is $\frac{1}{0}$. Only let us understand this 0, or nought, or rather instead a quantity infinitely or inassignably small, to be greater or smaller according as we have assumed the last denominator of this infinite series of fractions, which is itself also infinite, smaller or greater. For a maximum does not apply in the case of numbers.

sario existunt, non determinari ad existendum$^{L25}$ [nisi] a re sua natura necessario existente.


## On Body, Space, and the Continuum

## De veritatibus, de mente, de deo, de universo                 Aiii71


**508**   15 April. 1676
           . . .

**509**   . . . Ergo ita sentio, soliditatem seu unitatem corporis esse a mente, tot
esse mentes, quot vortices, tot vortices, quot corpora solida, corpus re-


L25. Hoc recte observatum est, et convenit cum eo quod dicere soleo, nihil existere, nisi cuius reddi possit ratio existentiae sufficiens; quam in serie causarum non
esse facile demonstratur; nam nec in singulis utcunque regrediamur, inveniamus,
ubi subsisti possit; et si totam seriem in infinitum retro sumtam intelligamus esse
sequentibus singularibus rationem existendi sufficientem, quod unum dissentien-
tibus effugium superesse potest, contrarium facile evincitur quod singulaquaelibet
ab hac serie rescindi possent, ut tamen quod superest ratio adhuc sequentibus esse
debeat; unde sequitur totam tandem seriem, id est summam omnium rescindibi-
lium, detrahi posse, sibi, salva illa Existendi ratione, quam in ipsa supposuimus,
quod absurdum est; vel potius, quod contrarium ei quod suppositum erat, *directe*
evincit; rationem scilicet existendi extra seriem esse. Quod argumentum etiam sic
enuntiare possis, non posse dici, ubi series illa in infinitum retro, quae sequentibus
ratio esse debet, quaeque ab una parte interminata, ab altera terminata est; a terminata sui parte incipere debeat; unde quaevis singularia ei detrahi possunt, adeoque
ut dixi, ipsa sibi. Item hinc patet, quod, quoniam hoc modo determinatae certaeque
magnitudinis series quae sequentium Rationem contineat, non est, nulla erit. Sed
haec subtiliora, etsi certa. Aliud autem manifestissimum in promptu argumentum
est, cur tota series non contineat sufficientem existendi rationem, quia tota series
alia fingi sive intelligi potest, unde reddenda extra ipsam ratio, cur sic sit. Ex his illud quoque sane memorabile sequitur, in serie causarum, id quod est prius non esse
Rationi rerum, seu Enti primo, propius, quam id quod est posterius, nec Ens primum posteriorum, mediantibus prioribus, sed omnium aeque immediate rationem
esse.

essarily by their own nature are not determined to exist[L25] [unless][19] by a
thing existing necessarily by its own nature.

## 18. On Body, Space, and the Continuum
## (Selections)

### (i) On Truths, the Mind, God, and the Universe[1]                    **Aiii71**

**508**   15 April 1676[2]

. . .

**509**   . . . So what I believe is this: that the solidity, or unity, of body is due to
mind, that there are as many minds as vortices, and as many vortices as
**510**   solid bodies;[3] that body resists (that is, it resists what endeavours to divide

---

L25. This is rightly observed, and agrees with what I am accustomed to saying,
that nothing exists but that for whose existence a sufficient reason can be provided.
It is easily demonstrated that this sufficient reason cannot be in the series of causes.
For we cannot discover where it might subsist in the individual causes, however far
we regress; and if we understand the whole series taken back to infinity to be a sufficient reason for the existence of every single succeeding cause—which remains
the one escape for those dissenting—it is easy to prove the contrary of this. For any
single cause whatever could be rescinded from this series, seeing as what remains
must still be a reason for those following it. Hence it follows that in the end the
whole series, i.e. the sum of all the rescindible causes, could be subtracted from itself, while leaving intact the reason for existence we assumed in it, which is absurd.
Or rather, the contrary of what was supposed is proved *directly:* namely, that the
reason for its existence lies outside the series. You could also express this argument
as follows: it cannot be said where that reverse series to infinity—which has to be
the reason for the succeeding causes, and which is unbounded at one end—is
bounded at the other end. It would have to begin bounded at its own end; whence
any individuals whatsoever can be subtracted from it, and so, as I said, it can be
subtracted from itself. It is likewise evident from this that, since by this argument a
series which contains the reason for those following does not have a determinate and
definite magnitude, there will be no such series. But these considerations are rather
too subtle, even though certain. Yet there is another much more obvious argument at
hand why the whole series does not contain a sufficient reason for existing. This is
that since the whole series can be imagined or understood by other means, a reason
must be provided from outside it why this should be so. From these considerations
a truly memorable thing also follows, that what is earlier in the series of causes is
not nearer to the Reason for the universe, i.e. to the First Being, than what is later,
nor is the First Being the reason for the later ones as a result of the mediation of the
earlier ones; rather it is the reason for all of them equally immediately.

**510** sistere, hanc resistentiam esse sensum. Resistit scilicet diverdere conanti. Sensus quaedam reactio est. Corpus incorruptibile pariter ac mens, varia circa ipsum organa varie mutantur.

. . .

**512** . . . Caeterum satis hinc patet spatium differre a Deo, quia plura spatia esse possent, Deus Unus, eadem tamen in omnibus Dei immensitas. Sed quoniam spatium in continua est mutatione unumquodque scilicet et in utroque aliquid persistit, an haec duo persistentia a se invicem differunt;
**513** an vero eadem in utroque velut idea seu natura universalis? Ita puto. Et haec natura facit ut Deus illi pariter ac huic mundo sit praesens, posset enim in illo Mundo alia esse Lex naturae. Valde considerandum; si poneremus quodlibet corpus rursus in minora actu resolutum esse; seu si ponantur semper alii in aliis Mundi, an ideo divisum sit in Minimas partes. Itaque aliud est sine fine divisum et in minima divisum esse. Scilicet pars ultima erit nulla. Quemadmodum in linea interminata punctum ultimum est nullum. Ut si corpus ponamus in tot esse partes divisum quot pedes in linea interminata, non ideo erit in minimas divisum, nam in plures divideretur, si in tot quot sunt digiti in eadem. At si inciperet motus in liquido homgeneo, absolute in minimas divideretur, quia ratio nulla foret cur non in minores.

Unum per se corpus facere ⟨dur⟩item, forte nec a Cartesii sententia abhorruit.

## De origine rerum ex formis                                        Aiii74

. . .

**519** Mens nostra differt a Deo, ut Extensum absolutum, quod maximum, et indivisibile est a spatio, seu loco; sive ut ipsum per se extensum, a loco. Spatium totus locus est. Spatii sunt partes, ipsius extensi per se nullae sunt partes; sed aliqui sunt eius modi. Spatium eo ipso quia in partes dissecatur, mutabile est, et varie dissecatur; imo continue aliud atque aliud est, at basis spatii, ipsum per se extensum, indivisibile est, manetque durantibus mutationibus, neque immutatur, quia omnia penetrat. Non ergo locus es eius pars, sed eius modificatio, ex accedente materia, seu aliquid ex ipsa et materia resultans. Eodem plane modo Mens divina est as nostram, ut spatium quod vocant imaginarium (cum sit maxime reale, est enim ipse

it), and that this resistance is sensation. Sensation is a kind of reaction. Body is as incorruptible as mind, but the various organs around it are changed in various ways . . . .

512      . . . Still, it is clear enough from this[4] that space differs from God, in that there could be many spaces and yet one God, the immensity of God being the same in all of them.[5] But since each space is in continuous change, and since in each of two spaces something persists, do these two persisting

513  things differ from each other? or is it really the same idea, as it were, i.e. universal nature, in each space? I think it is. And this nature brings it about that God is just as present to that world as to this, since there could be another law of nature in that world.

This especially needs to be considered: if we suppose that any body we please is actually resolved into still smaller bodies—i.e. if some worlds are always supposed within others—would it thereby be divided into minimum parts? Thus being divided without end is different from being divided into minima, in that [in such an unending division] there will be no last part, just as in an unbounded line there is no last point. For instance, if we suppose a body to be divided into as many parts as there are feet in an unbounded line, it will not thereby be divided into minima: for it would be divided into more parts if it were divided into as many parts as there are inches in the same unbounded line. But if motion were to begin in a homogeneous liquid, it would be divided absolutely into minima, since there would be no reason why it should not be divided into smaller parts.[6]

That a body's being a unity in itself constitutes hardness was perhaps not incompatible with Descartes's view.[7]

### (ii) On the Origin of Things from Forms[8]                **Aiii74**

[2nd half? of April 1676][9]

. . .

519      Our mind differs from God as the absolute extended, which is a maximum and indivisible, differs from space or place; that is, as that which is extended in itself differs from place. Space is the whole of place. Space has parts, but that which is extended in itself has no parts, although it does have some modes. Space, by the very fact that it is dissected into parts, is changeable, and variously dissected; indeed, it is continuously one thing after another. But the basis of space, that which is extended in itself, is indivisible, and remains during changes; it does not change, since it pervades everything. Therefore place is not a part of it, but a modification of it arising from the addition of matter, i.e. something resulting from it and matter. Plainly in the same way the divine mind is to ours as the space they

Deus, quatenus consideratur ubique seu immensus) est ad locum, et varias in ipso immenso natas figuras. Perplacet itaque, ut hoc ut a spatio distinguam, vocem ipsum *Immensum*. Immensum itaque est, quod in continua spatii mutatione perstat, hoc ergo terminos nec habet nec habere potest, estque unum et indivisibile. Posses et appellare ipsum Expansum. Satis ex his patet ipsum hoc immensum non esse intervallum, nec esse locum, nec esse mutabile; modificationes autem fieri nulla eius mutatione, sed superadditione alterius, nempe Molis, sive Massae; ex additione molis et massae resultant spatia, loca, intervalla, quorum aggregata dant Spatium Universum, sed hoc spatium universum est Ens per aggregationem, continue variabile; compositum scilicet ex spatiis vacuis plenis, ut rete, quod rete continuo aliam accipit formam, adeoque mutatur; sed quod in illa mutatione perstat, est ipsum immensum. Ipsum autem immensum est Deus quatenus cogitatur esse ubique, seu quatenus eam perfectionem, sive formam absolutam affirmitivam quae tribuitur rebus, quando dicitur eas esse alicubi, continet.

. . .

**520**   Non potest dari Motus celerrimus, nec Numerus maximus, nam numerus est quiddam discretum, ubi non totum prius partibus sed contra. Motus celerrimus, esse non potest, quia motus est modificatio. Estque certae rei translatio; in certo tempore. Prorsus quemadmodum figura maxima dari non potest. Non potest unus motus esse totius; et potest cogitatio quaedam esse omnium. Quandocunque Totum prius partibus, tunc maximum est, ut in spatio, in continuo. Si materia est quemadmodum figura, id quod facit modificationem, tunc videtur nec materiae quoddam esse totum.

. . .

**521**   . . . Porro Spatium Universale tam est Ens per aggregationem, quam Respublica universalis, sive Societas omnium Mentium. In eo uno differentia est, quod Locus sive intervallum destruitur, sublato enim locato tollitur locus, at Anima quae illi proportione respondet, destrui non potest. Quicquid agit, illud destrui non potest, saltem enim durat dum agit, ergo durabit semper. Quicquid patitur neque agit, id destrui potest, ut locus, figure. Corpus omne aggregatum destrui potest. Videntur esse Elementa sive corpora indestruibilia, quia scilicet Mens in illis. Ut figura jam est in Intelligentia prima. Ut figura est in spatio; ita scilicet idea in mente nostra.

call imaginary (when it is most assuredly real, for it is God himself insofar as he is considered to be everywhere, i.e. immense) is to place, and to the various shapes that are produced in that immense thing. Accordingly, it is best that I should call it 'the Immensum',[10] in order to distinguish it from space. And so it is the immensum which persists during continuous change of space; therefore it does not have and cannot have bounds, and is one and indivisible. You might also call it 'the expanded'.[11] From this it is sufficiently clear that the immensum is not an interval, nor is it a place, nor is it changeable; its modifications occur not by any change in it, but by the superaddition of something else, namely, of bulk, i.e. mass; from the addition of bulk and mass, there result spaces, places, and intervals, whose aggregates give Universal Space. But this universal space is an entity by aggregation, and is continuously variable; in other words, it is a composite of spaces empty and full, like a net, and this net continuously receives another form, and thus changes; but what persists through this change is the immensum itself.[12] But the immensum itself is God insofar as he is thought to be everywhere, i.e. insofar as he contains that perfection or absolute affirmative form which is attributed to things when they are said to be somewhere.

. . .

**520**     There can be no such thing as a fastest motion, nor a greatest number. For number is something discrete, where the whole is not prior to the parts, but the converse. There cannot be a fastest motion, since motion is a modification, and is the translation of a certain thing in a certain time—in short, just as there cannot be a greatest shape. There cannot be one motion of the whole; but there can be a kind of thought of everything. Whenever the whole is prior to the parts, then it is a maximum, as for example in space and in the continuum. If matter, like shape, is that which makes a modification, then it seems that there is not a whole of matter, either.

. . .

**521**     . . . Moreover, Universal Space is as much an entity by aggregation as the Universal Republic, or Society of all Minds. There is one difference between them, that place or interval is destroyed—for when that which has a place is eliminated, so is its place—but the soul which proportionally corresponds to it cannot be destroyed. Whatever acts cannot be destroyed, for it at least endures as long as it acts, and therefore it will endure forever. Whatever is acted upon and does not act can be destroyed, as, for example, can place and shape. Every aggregated body can be destroyed. There seem to be elements, i.e. indestructible bodies, precisely because there is a mind in them. As there is already a shape in the Immensum before it is designated, so there is already an idea, i.e. a differentia of

Anima Mundi nulla est, quia non potest continuum quoddam componi ex mentibus, ut ex spatiis componi potest. Dices imo certo etiam modo, quatenus sese sentiunt. Respondeo et dico Animam non esse ens per aggregationem, Spatium autem universum esse Ens per aggregationem. Unde mirum non est nullam esse Animam universi. . . .

thoughts, in the primary Intelligence. As the shape is in space; so the idea is in our mind. There is no World Soul because a continuum cannot be composed of minds, as it can of spaces. No, you will say, it can too, in a certain way, insofar as minds perceive one another. I say in reply that the soul is not an entity by aggregation, but that universal space is an entity by aggregation. Hence it is no wonder that there is no soul of the universe. . . .

# II    Dialogue on Continuity and Motion

## 19. Pacidius to Philalethes: A First Philosophy of Motion[1]

[29 October–10 November 1676]

### Editorial Preface

Leibniz wrote this dialogue at the end of his second trip to England, on board a ship in the Thames estuary in London. He was bound for Holland, where he would meet with various celebrated intellectuals—the mathematician Hudde in Amsterdam, the microscopists Swammerdam and Leeuwenhoek in Amsterdam and Delft, and Spinoza in The Hague—before traveling on from there to take up his court appointment at Hanover. He had been offered passage on a yacht that Prince Ruprecht von der Pfalz was sending to Germany via Rotterdam for a cargo of wine, and having boarded ship on 29 October 1676, he sailed two days later only to have to wait four days for the loading of cargo in Gravesend, and six days more at Sheerness in the mouth of the Thames for good weather.[2]

It is not known exactly why or for whom the dialogue was written, although it appears to be connected with a plan that Leibniz had drawn up earlier in the year, for an encyclopedia entitled "Guilielmus Pacidius's *On the Secrets of Things.*"[3] The sixth and seventh articles of this plan are the two labyrinths later mentioned in the preface to the *Theodicy:* "(6) The first labyrinth, or, on fate, fortune, and freedom. (7) The second labyrinth, or, on the composition of the continuum, time, place, motion, atoms, the indivisible, and the infinite." After this description of the second labyrinth, Leibniz had written, then crossed out, "in a word, concerning the Metaphysics of Motion."[4] This suggests that the *Pacidius Philalethi* might have been a partial execution of article 7. For on the rough draft $L^1$ of the dialogue was the subheading *S. Dial. Mot.* ("or, A Dialogue on Motion"), and in the margin of the fair copy *l* was *Prima de Motu Philosophia* ("A First Philosophy of Motion"), which I have taken to be the intended subtitle.

In the draft Leibniz had initially named the interlocutors Pacidius, Polybius, Terentius and Gallutius; he first changed Polybius to Charinus and Terentius to Theophilus towards the end of the dialogue (from p. 558, line 5), and subsequently altered the names throughout.

*Pacidius* is a pseudonym that Leibniz used for himself on occasion. It probably derives from *pax, pacis* (peace), and *dius/divus* (divine), making it a rendering of his first name *Gottfried* into Latin.[5] *Charinus* is introduced as "a young man from a distinguished family, who was nonetheless inquisitive and keen to learn, who had enlisted in the army at a tender age, and had become famous for his outstanding successes." But an earlier version of this description is more revealing: "Now it happened that there had

**Pacidius Philalethi**                                                    Aiii78

**529**     *PACIDIUS PHILALETHI*<sup>L1</sup>
            *Prima de motu philosophia*<sup>L2</sup>

Cum nuper apud illustres viros asseruissem, Socraticam disserendi
methodum, qualis in Platonicis Dialogis expressa est, mihi praestantem
videri: nam et veritatem animis familiari sermone instillari, et ipsum me-
ditandi ordinem, qui a cognitis ad incognita procedit, apparere dum quisque
per se nemine suggerente vera respondet, modo apte interrogetur, rogatus
sum ab illis, ut specimine edito rem tantae utilitatis resuscitare conarer,

L1. IN THE MARGIN OF THE DRAFT $L^1$: Scripta in navi qua ex Anglia in Hollan-
diam trajeci. 1676. Octob.

L2. IN THE MARGIN OF THE FAIR COPY $l$ BENEATH THIS SUBTITLE: Consideratur
hic natura mutationis et continui, quatenus motui insunt. Supersunt adhuc trac-
tanda tum subjectum motus, ut appareat cuinam ex duobus situm inter se mutan-
tibus ascribendus sit motus: tum vero motus causa seu vis motrix.

arrived in Paris a young German, intelligent and eager to learn, who, having served in the army with honors and success, being skilled in both tactics and the art of siegecraft, had touched upon the first elements of Arithmetic and Geometry." In this connection it is worth noting that Leibniz's friend and younger compatriot in Paris, Ehrenfried Walther von Tschirnhaus (1651–1708), was a young nobleman from Saxony, who arrived in Paris in August 1675 after having served as a volunteer in the Dutch army for a short time during 1672–73; previously he had attained great skill in algebraic analysis in Leiden, where he had become a notoriously avid Cartesian. If the character is modeled on him, "Charinus" could be a play on Tschirnhaus's name. The third character, *Theophilus,* is described as an older gentleman and a close friend of Pacidius's, a wealthy retired businessman. Conceivably, Leibniz might have modeled this character on his host in Paris, Johann Friedrich Sinold (called Schütz, d. 1692);[6] but too little is known about his private life in Paris for this to be suggested with any confidence. Lastly, the description of *Gallutius,* the medical expert who was not a professional physician, conforms to what we know about Günther Christoph Schelhammer, 1649–1716, another of Leibniz's circle in Paris, and a lifelong friend whose controversy with Sturm prompted Leibniz to intervene on his side with *De ipsa natura* ("Concerning Nature Itself") in 1698, and whose publications included a book on hearing (*De auditu, Liber 1,* Leipzig 1684), and a manuscript "Novae institutiones medicae" ("New Principles of Medical Instruction");[7] but again, the identification is pure conjecture.

**529**           *PACIDIUS TO PHILALETHES*[L1]

*A First Philosophy of Motion*[L2,8]

When I was with some distinguished men recently, I asserted that the Socratic method of discussion, as expressed in the Platonic dialogues, seemed to me outstanding. For not only are souls imbued with the truth through familiar conversation, but one can even see the order of meditation itself, which proceeds from the known to the unknown, provided each person replies for himself when asked an appropriate question, with no

L1. IN THE MARGIN OF THE DRAFT $L^1$: Written on board the ship by which I crossed from England to Holland. October 1676 [OS].

L2. IN THE MARGIN OF THE FAIR COPY *1* BENEATH THIS SUBTITLE: Here are considered the nature of change and the continuum, insofar as they are involved in motion. Still to be treated are, first, the subject of motion, to make it clear which of two things changing their mutual situation motion should be ascribed to; and second, the cause of motion, i.e. motive force.

quae ipso experimento ostendit indita mentibus scientiarum omnium semina esse. Excusavi me diu, fassus difficultatem rei majorem quam credi
possit; facile enim esse dialogos scribere, quemadmodum facile est te-
mere ac sine ordine loqui; sed oratione efficere, ut ipsa paulatim e tenebris
eniteat veritas, et sponte in animis nascatur scientia, id vero non nisi illum
posse, qui secum ipse accuratissime rationes inierit, antequam alios do-
cere aggrediatur. Ita resistentem me hortationibus, arte circumvenerunt
amici: sciebant diu me de motu cogitasse, atque illud argumentum habere

**530** paratum. Forte advenerat juvenis familia illustris caeterum curiosus ac
discendi avidus, qui cum in tenera aetate nomen militiae dedisset, succes-
sibusque egregiis inclaruisset, maturescente cum annis judicio elementa
Geometriae attigerat, ut vigori animi artem atque doctrinam jungeret. Is
Mechanicam Scientiam sibi deesse quotidie sentiebat, et in scriptoribus
hujus artis plerisque, nonnisi pauca et vulgaria de elevandis ponderibus et
quinque potentiis, quas vocant, tradi; at fundamenta scientiae generalioris
non constitui, sed nec de ictu ac concursu, de virium incrementis ac detri-
mentis, de medii resistentia, de frictu, de arcubus tensis et vi quam Elasti-
cam vocant, de cursu ac undulationibus liquidorum, de solidorum resistentia, aliisque hujusmodi quotidianis argumentis, certa satis praecepta
tradi querebatur. Hunc mihi adduxere amici, atque ita instruxere, ut paulatim irretitus in colloquii genus laberer, quale toties laudaveram, quod illis
ita successit, ut consumtis frustra tergiversationibus accenso omnium studio tandem obsequi decreverim.

*Charinum* (hoc advenae nomen erat) adduxit mihi *Theophilus,* senex
egregio judicio ad omne argumentum paratus, qui consumto in negotiis
flore aetatis, opibus atque honoribus partis, quod reliquum vitae quieti
animi atque cultui Numinis dare decreverat, vir pietatis solidae interiore
quodam sensu, et communis boni studio accensus, cujus augendi, quoties
spes affulgebat, neque opibus ille neque laboribus parcebat. Arcta mihi
cum eo familiaritas, et non injucunda consuetudo erat: multus tunc forte
de Republica sermo, et infidis historiarum monumentis, quae rerum ges-

one suggesting the right answers. When I had made this claim, they asked me to try to revive so very useful a thing by producing a specimen, which, by that very experiment, would show minds to be endowed with the seeds of all knowledge. I excused myself at length, confessing that this matter was more difficult than might be believed. For it is easy to write dialogues, just as it is easy to speak rashly and in no particular order; but to compose a speech in such a way that truth itself might gradually shine out of the darkness, and knowledge might grow spontaneously in the soul, this is really only possible for someone who has himself gone into the reasons very carefully on his own, before taking it on himself to teach others.

My friends cleverly got around me resisting in this way by encouraging me: they knew I had been thinking about motion for a long time, and that I had come prepared with that argument. Now it happened that there had arrived a young man from a distinguished family, who was nonetheless inquisitive and keen to learn, who had enlisted in the army at a tender age, and had become famous for his outstanding successes. As his judgment matured with the years, he had touched upon the elements of geometry, in order to marry some learning to the vigor of his soul. Every day he sensed that Mechanical Science was failing him, and that in the majority of writings on this subject nothing was related but a few commonplaces about the lifting of weights and the five powers, as they are called, whereas the foundations of a more general science were not established. Nor, he complained, were sufficiently accurate precepts laid down concerning impact and collision, increases and decreases of force, the resistance of a medium, friction, stretched bows and the so-called elastic force, the flow and undulations of liquids, the resistance of solids, and other everyday matters of this kind. My friends brought this young man to me, and set things up so that I gradually became ensnared in a conversation of the kind I had so often praised. This succeeded for them in such a way that, having used up all my excuses in vain, I finally decided to give in to their excited enthusiasm for everything.

*Charinus* (this was the name of the new arrival) was brought to me by *Theophilus,* an older gentleman ready with an outstanding judgment for every argument. Having spent the flower of his youth in business, where he had procured wealth and honors, he had decided to dedicate the rest of his life to peace of mind and worship of the Divine. A man with a kind of inner sense of solid piety, he was consumed with the study of the common good, on whose increase he had often pinned his hope, and on which he had stinted neither wealth nor labor. I had a close friendship with him, and enjoyed his company. At that time, by chance, we were having a long conversation about the State, and the unreliable records of histories, which

tarum simplicitatem fictis causarum narrationibus corrupere, quod ille in negotiis quibus ipse interfuerat, accidisse luculenter ostendebat. Ego cum viderem cum Theophilo ac Charino advenisse *Gallutium* virum insignem, in experimentis exercitatissimum, et singulares corporum proprietates doctum, rei vero medicae peritia inprimis admirabilem, et successibus **531** clarum, quoties flagitantibus amicis, quanquam a medici nomine ac professione et omni lucro alienus, remedia dederat; hujus causa a Republica ad Philosophiam, non invito Theophilo, sermonem ita flexi:

PACIDIUS: Quod de historian, civili ais, Theophile, corrumpi ab illis, qui ex conjectura causas occultas eventuum conspicuorum fingunt, id in historia naturali etiam periculosius fieri Gallutius noster saepe questus est.

GALLUTIUS: Ego certe saepe optavi, ut observationes naturales, et inprimis historiae morborum nobis exhiberentur nudae et ab opinionibus liberae, quales Hippocraticae sunt, non Aristotelis, non Galeni, non recentioris alicujus sententiis accommodatae: tum demum enim resuscitari poterit philosophia, cum fundamenta solida jacta erunt.

THEOPHILUS: Non dubito quin regia sit via per experimenta, sed nisi ratiocinatio eam complanaverit, tarde proficiemus et post multa secula in initiis haerebimus. Quam multas enim observationes praeclaras apud Medicos congestas habemus, quot elegantia Chymicorum experimento feruntur, quanta rerum sylva a Botanicis aut Anatomicis suppeditatur, quibus miror philosophos non uti, nec ducere ab ipsis, quicquid inde duci potest: quod si facerent, forte haberent in potestate multa quae sibi deesse queruntur.

PACIDIUS.: Sed nondum extat ars illa, per quam in naturalibus ducatur ex datis quicquid ex illis duci potest, quemadmodum id ordine certo in Arithmetica atque Geometria praestatur. Geometrae enim proposito problemate vident an sufficientia habeant data ad eius solutionem, ac viae cuidam tritae atque determinatae insistentes, omnes problematis conditiones tamdiu evolvunt, donec ex ipsis quaesitum

corrupt the simplicity of deeds with fictitious accounts of their causes, as he was brilliantly showing to have happened in business transactions he had been involved in.

Now, I saw that along with Theophilus and Charinus there had come that most distinguished of men, *Gallutius*, who, being very accomplished in experimental work, was an expert on the individual properties of bodies. In fact he was especially admired for his skill in medicine, and, famous **531** for his successes, he used to give out remedies whenever friends demanded them, although he was a stranger to the name and profession of medical doctor, and to all profit. So, on his account, there being no objection from Theophilus, I changed the topic of conversation from the State to Philosophy:

PACIDIUS: What you say, Theophilus, about civil history being corrupted by people who think up hidden causes for conspicuous events, is something that becomes even more dangerous in natural history, as Gallutius here has often complained.

GALLUTIUS: I have certainly often wished that observations of nature, especially histories of diseases, could be presented to us unadorned and free from opinions, as are those of Hippocrates, and not accommodated to the opinions of Aristotle or Galen or somebody more recent.[9] For we will only be able to revive philosophy when we have laid solid foundations for it.

THEOPHILUS: I do not doubt that the royal road is through experiments, but unless it is leveled out by reasoning we will make slow progress, and will still be stuck at the beginning after many generations. For I am amazed at how many excellent observations we have that the doctors have accumulated, at how many elegant experiments the chemists have performed, at what an abundance of things the botanists or anatomists have provided, which philosophers have not made use of, nor deduced from them whatever can be deduced. But if they were to do so, perhaps they would have in their power many of the things they complain they are lacking.

PACIDIUS: But there does not yet exist a technique in natural philosophy for deducing whatever can be deduced from the data, as is done according to a definite order in Arithmetic and Geometry. For geometers, when a problem is proposed, see whether they have enough data for its solution, and pursuing a certain well-tried and definite course, spend a long time unfolding all the conditions of the problem until from among these the one they were looking for drops out of its own

sponte prodeat sua. Hoc ubi in naturali philosophia praestare didicerint homines, (discent autem ubi meditari volent) mirabuntur forte multa a se tamdiu ignorata, quod non ignaviae aut caecitati antecessorum, sed methodi verae defectui tribui debet, quae sola lucifera est.

CHARINUS: Si mihi talium inexperto sententiam dicere permittitis, asseverarim a Geometria ad Physicam difficilem transitum esse, et desiderari scientiam de motu, quae materiam formis, speculationem praxi connectat, quod experimentis qualibuscunque tyrocinii castrensis didici: Saepe enim mihi machinas novas et jucunda quaedam artificia tentanti successus defuit, quod motus ac vires non perinde ac

**532** figurae et corpora delineari atque imaginationi subjici possint. Quoties enim structuram aedificii aut munimenti formam animo conceperam, initio quidem exiguis modulis ligneis aliave ex materia confectis cogitationi fluctuanti subveniebam; postea provectior delineationibus in plano factis ad solida repraesentanda contentus eram; denique eam imaginandi facilitatem paulatim nactus sum, ut rem totam omnibus numeris absolutam, omnesque eius partes ad vivum expressas animo formarem, et velut oculis subjectas contemplarer. Sed cum de motu agebatur, omnis mea cura atque diligentia irrita fuit, neque unquam assequi potui, ut virium rationes atque causas imaginatione comprehendere, ac de machinarum successu judicare liceret, semper enim in ipso motus inchoandi initio haesi, nam quod toto reliquo tempore evenire debebat, jam momento primo fieri quodammodo debere animadvertebam. Circa momenta autem atque puncta ratiocinari, id quidem supra meum captum esse fatebar. Quare a rationibus depulsus ad experientiam meam atque alienam redactus sum, sed quae nos saepe fefellit, quoties eorum, quae experti eramus, falsas causas pro veris sumseramus, atque inde argumentum ad ea quae nobis similia videbantur porrexeramus.

PA.: Praeclara nobis narras, Charine, et unde mihi ingeniis aestimandis sueto quid a te expectari possit si recte ducaris, judicare facile est. Gaudeo enim impense, quod tua experientia didicisti vires ac motus

accord. Once people have learnt to do this in natural philosophy
(which will only be when they have learned to meditate), they will
perhaps be surprised that many things were unknown to them for so
long—which should not be put down to the laziness or blindness of
their predecessors, but to their desertion of the true method, which
alone sheds light.

CHARINUS: If I may be allowed to offer an inexpert opinion on such
matters, I would declare that the transition from Geometry to Physics
is difficult, and that we need a science of motion that would connect
matter to forms and speculation to practice—something I learned
from experiments of various kinds in my early military training. For
I was often unsuccessful in trying out new machines and other de-
lightful tricks of the trade, because the motions and forces involved
could not be drawn and subjected to the imagination in the same way
as figures and bodies could. For whenever I conceived in my soul the
structure of a building or the form of a fortification, to begin with I
would reinforce my wavering thought with tiny models made of
wood or some other material. Afterwards when I was more advanced
I was content to represent solids by plane drawings; and finally I
gradually evolved such a facility of imagining that I could picture in
my mind the whole thing complete with all its numbers, and could
form vivid expressions of all its parts, and contemplate them as if
they were in front of my eyes. But when it came to motion, all my
care and diligence were of no use, and I could never reach the point
where one might comprehend the reasons and causes of forces by the
imagination, and form an opinion about the success of machines. For
I always became stuck at the very beginning of an incipient motion,
since I had noticed that what must come about in the whole of the remaining time must somehow already happen at the first moment. But
to reason about moments and points, I had to admit, was indeed beyond my grasp. This is why, let down by my reasonings, I was reduced to relying on my own and other people's experience. But this
experience often deceived us, as often as we had assumed false
causes for the things we had experienced instead of the true ones, and
had extended the argument from them to things which to us seemed
similar.

PA.: You relate this very clearly, Charinus, and being accustomed to
judging abilities, it is easy for me to tell from this what can be expected of you if you get the right guidance.[10] For I am glad that you
have learnt with great effort from your experience that forces and

**532**

non esse rem subjectam imaginationi, quod magni momenti est in philosophia vera. Quod autem de necessitate doctrinae motuum ad naturalem philosophiam ais, verissimum est, sed iis non adversatur, quae supra dixi de Logica ante omnia constituenda. Nam Scientia rationum generalium, immersa naturis mediis, ut veteres vocabant, id est figuris (quae per se incorruptibiles atque aeternae sunt) velut corpore assumto, Geometriam facit. Eadem caducis atque corruptibilibus sociata ipsam constituit scientiam mutationum sive motuum de

**533** tempore, vi, actione. Itaque quemadmodum recte Geometriam esse Logicam Mathematicam egregius nostri seculi philosophus[L3] dixit, ita Phoronomiam esse Logicam Physicam audacter asseverabo.

CH.: Magno me beneficio affeceris, Pacidi, si aliquam in hoc argumento mihi lucem accenderis.

GA.: Diu est, quod nobis meditationes tuas de motu promittis: tempus est ut satisfacias expectationi nostrae, nisi arculae tuae, qua chartas recondis, vim a nobis adhiberi mavis.

PA.: Reperietis in ea pro thesauro, quod ajunt, carbones; pro elaborates operibus schedas sparsas, et subitanearum meditationum vestigia male expressa, et memoriae tantum causa nonnunquam servata. Quare si quid a me desiderabatur dignum vobis, dies mihi dicendus erat.

TH.: Post tot interpellationes paratum esse oportet debitorem, nisi malum nomen audire velit.

GA.: Veritatis assequendae causa societas inter nos contracta est, actionem autem pro socio scis, Pacidi, non ultra esse quam in id quod facere possis. Quantum autem possis, tuae fidei committimus, ut agnoscas liberalitatem nostram. Scilicet contenti erimus solutione per partes; fac tantum ne Charinum studio ardentem frustra ad te adduxerimus.

CH.: Ego amicorum postulationibus preces meas jungo, nec absolutum opus, aut continuum sermonem flagito, sed instructiones fortuito nascentes, ut sermonis occasio tulerit.

L3. IN THE MARGIN OF *l:* Galilaeus

motions are not subject to the imagination, something which is of great importance in true philosophy. What you say, on the other hand, about the need for a doctrine of motion in natural philosophy is very true, but it is not opposed to the things I said above about establishing Logic before everything else. For the science of general reasons, immersed in "intermediate natures," as the ancients called them[11]—i.e. immersed in figures (which are incorruptible and eternal per se), as if they have assumed a body—constitutes Geometry. If the same science is taken together with the perishable and corruptible it constitutes the science of changes or motions, concerning time, force, and action. And so just as an outstanding philosopher of our time[L3] rightly said that Geometry is Mathematical Logic,[12] so I will boldly declare that Phoronomy is Physical Logic.

533

CH.: You would do me a great favor, Pacidius, if you could throw some light on this matter for me.

GA.: It has been ages since you promised us your meditations on motion: it is time for you to satisfy our expectation, unless you would prefer us to force open the chest where you keep your papers!

PA.: Instead of the treasure they say is in it, you will find only ashes; instead of elaborate works, a few sheets of paper and some poorly expressed vestiges of hasty reflections, which were only ever saved for the sake of my memory. So if what you wanted from me was worthy of your consideration, it was up to me to name the day.

TH.: After so many interruptions, the debtor had better be ready, unless he wants to get himself a bad name.

GA.: We struck up this friendship for the sake of getting at the truth, but you know, Pacidius, that in doing something for a friend you cannot go beyond what it is in your power to do. But just how much this is, we will leave to your discretion, so that you can see how generous we are. That is to say, we shall be content with a partial solution; only make sure it isn't in vain that we've brought you Charinus burning with enthusiasm.

CH.: Allow me to add my own entreaty to the demands of my friends: I do not insist on a completed work or continuous discussion, but I do insist that instructions be given me in the course of the discussion as the occasion requires.[13]

L3. IN THE MARGIN OF *1:* Galileo

TH.: Meministi, Pacidi, quid nobis saepe de Socraticis Dialogis praedicaveris: quid obstat quominus nunc tandem earum utilitatem exemplo discamus, nisi forte Charinum infra Phaedonem aut Alcibiadem ponis, quibus ille neque ingenio neque animis neque fortuna cedit.

PA.: Video vos meditatos atque instructos venisse ad me circumveniendum: quid agam? dum alius mecum lege agit, alius precibus non minus valituris tarditatem meam expugnat. Fiat, ut jubetis; permitto me voluntati vestrae; sed qualiscunque successus erit, periculo vestro erit, neque enim illum aut sententiis meis (quarum in ea festinatione ne meminisse quidem satis possum) aut Socraticae methodo (quae meditatione opus habet) praejudicare volo. Caeterum res omnis ad te redit, Charine.

CH.: Quid ita?

**534**     PA.: Quia tute te docebis, haec enim Socratica methodus est.

CH.: Qui possim discere ab ignaro.

PA.: Disces a te, nec ab ignaro, plura enim scis, quam quorum meministi. Ego tantum reminiscendi eorum quae scis, et inde ducendi quae nescis occasionem dabo, et ut Socrates ajebat, gravido tibi atque parturienti obstetricio munere adero.

CH.: Grave est, quod a me postulas, ut ignorantiam meam utcunque silendo tectam, prodam sermone.

GA.: Si Pacidio credimus, scientiam tuam ipse mirabere.

CH.: Quanquam magnus mihi sit autor Pacidius, praesentior tamen est conscientia mei.

PA.: Nondum expertus es, Charine, quid per te possis; tentanda aliquando fortuna est, ut scias ipse quanti tibi esse debeas.

TH.: Age, Chari ne, permitte te nobis, neque intercede diutius utilitati tuae ac voluptati nostrae.

CH.: Pareo vobis, quanquam periculo opinionis, quam de me habere potuistis, quantulacunque enim fuerit certe experimento adhuc am-

TH.: Remember, Pacidius, what you have often preached to us about the Socratic Dialogues: what is stopping us now from finally learning their utility by example, unless perhaps you rate Charinus below Phaedo or Alcibiades,[14] to whom he is inferior neither in ability, nor spirit, nor fortune.

PA.: I see that you have come prepared and equipped to get around me. What am I to do when some of you are threatening me with the law, while others are attacking my slowness with imprecations that are no less powerful? Let it be done as you decide; I surrender myself to your will. But whatever follows will be at your risk, since I do not want to prejudice this either with my own opinions (which I cannot even remember enough of in such a hurry) or with the Socratic method (which requires careful thought); everything else redounds to you, Charinus.

CH.: Why is that?

**534**   PA.: Because you will teach yourself, since this is the Socratic method.

CH.: How can I learn from someone who doesn't know?

PA.: You will learn from yourself, and not from someone who doesn't know, for you know more things than you can remember. I shall merely provide you with the occasion for recalling what you know, and then for inferring from this what you do not know. As Socrates said, when you are heavy with child and in labor, I shall be there in the role of midwife.[15]

CH.: It's a heavy thing you are demanding of me, that whenever I would have concealed my ignorance by remaining silent, I should instead betray it in the discussion.

GA.: If we are to believe Pacidius, you will be surprised at your knowledge.

CH.: Important though my teacher Pacidius is to me, my consciousness of myself is more immediate.

PA.: Charinus, you have not yet experienced what you can do by yourself; sometimes you have to try your luck in order to know how highly you ought to rate yourself.

TH.: Come on, Charinus, put yourself in our hands, and stop coming between your usefulness and our desire.

CH.: I give in—although at the risk of losing the opinion you may have had of me. For however low this may have been, it will certainly

plius minuetur. Sed ingenui est fallere nolle. Itaque facile patiar, ut de me sentiatis, ut res est, dummodo haerenti subveniatis et proficiendi occasionem detis.

PA.: Id faciemus, quantum in nobis erit. Tantum mihi si placet responde interroganti. Quoniam de motu tractare nobis propositum est, quaeso, Charine, dic nobis quid motum esse putes.

CH.: Qui possum ab initio dicere, quod vix in progressu multa industria erui posse arbitrabar.

PA.: Nonne motum aliquando cogitasti?

CH.: Perinde est ac si quaeras an sensibus ac ratione usus sim.

PA.: Dic ergo nobis quid animo obversatum sit cum de motu cogitares.

CH.: Difficile est id statim colligere atque ex tempore explicare.

PA.: At tenta tamen, neque enim periculum est errandi, quicquid enim per motum a te intelligi dicas, perinde erit; dummodo non in progressu aliquid assuas, quod in ea notione quam sumsisti non contineatur.

CH.: Id cavere vestrum est, ego *motum* esse arbitror: *mutationem loci,* et motum in eo corpore esse ajo, quod locum mutat.

PA.: Euge Charine, liberaliter et ingenue facis, quod nobis statim exhibes, quae vix multis interrogationibus extorquere sperabam: fac modo ut integrum sit beneficium tuum.

CH.: An aliquid amplius adjiciendum putas?

PA.: Non utique, ubi quae dixisti intellexerimus.

CH.: Quid vero clarius quam mutatio, quam corpus, quam locus, quam inesse.

**535**   PA.: Ignosce tarditati meae, quae facit, ut nec ea intelligam, quae aliis clarissima videntur.

CH.: Ne illude quaeso.

PA.: Obsecro te Charine, ut persuadeas tibi nihil alienius esse ab ingenio meo, et sinceram esse professionem haesitationis meae.

fall even lower as a result of this experiment. But it is only natural not to want to fail. Therefore I will readily comply, so that you may judge me according to how things go, provided that you come to my assistance when I get stuck and give me the opportunity to make progress.

PA.: This we shall do, as far as we are able. Only please answer when I ask my questions. Since it has been proposed that we should treat the subject of motion, please tell us, Charinus, what you think motion is.

CH.: How can I tell you at the outset what I thought we would hardly be able to root out in the process of a great deal of hard work?

PA.: Haven't you ever thought about motion?

CH.: That's exactly the same as asking whether I've used my senses and reason.

PA.: So tell us what you see in your mind's eye when you think about motion.

CH.: It is difficult to recollect it all at once and explain it on the spur of the moment.

PA.: But try anyway: there is no risk of making an error, for whatever you say you understand motion to be, it will be precisely that; provided that in the process you do not tag on something that is not contained in the notion you assumed.

CH.: That is for you to look out for. I believe *motion* to be *change of place,* and I say that there is motion in that body which changes place.[16]

PA.: Well done, Charinus, you have been generous and open in displaying for us straightaway what I was scarcely hoping to wrest out of many lines of questioning. Only make sure that your service is complete.

CH.: Do you then think something further should be added?

PA.: Not at all, when we have understood what you have said.

CH.: What on earth could be clearer than 'change', 'body', 'place', or 'being in' something?[17]

535    PA.: Pardon my slow-wittedness, which prevents me from understanding things that seem very clear to other people.

CH.: Please don't make fun of me.

PA.: Charinus, I implore you to persuade yourself that nothing could be further from my intentions, and that in professing to be at a loss I am quite sincere.

CH.: Tentabo explicare sententiam, si interrogaveris.

PA.: Recte. Statum mutationis nonne statum quendam rei esse putas?

CH.: Puto.

PA.: Differentem a priore rei statu ante mutationem, cum omnia adhuc integra essent?

CH.: Differentem.

PA.: Sed et ab eo qui erit post mutationem?

CH.: Haud dubie.

PA.: Vereor, ne id nos conjiciat in difficultates.

CH.: Quas obsecro?

PA.: Permittisne mihi exempli electionem?

CH.: Non habes opus permissione.

PA.: Mors nonne mutatio est?

CH.: Haud dubie.

PA.: Actum ipsum moriendi intelligo.

CH.: Et ego eundem.

PA.: Qui moritur vivitne?

CH.: Perplexa est quaestio.

PA.: An qui moritur mortuus est?

CH.: Hoc impossibile esse video. Mortuum enim esse significat mortem alicujus esse praeteritam.

PA.: Si mors mortuo praeterita est, viventi erit futura, quemadmodum nascens nec nasciturus est nec natus.

CH.: Videtur.

PA.: Non ergo qui moritur vivit.

CH.: Fateor.

PA.: Moriens ergo nec mortuus est, nec vivus.

CH.: Concedo.

PA.: At videris concessisse absurdum.

CH.: Nondum absurditatem animadverto.

PA.: Nonne vita in certo aliquo consistit statu?

CH.: Haud dubie.

CH.: I'll try to explain my opinion if you will put the questions.

PA.: All right. Do you not think that a state of change is a sort of state of a thing? |9 2

CH.: Yes, I do.

PA.: Different from the earlier state of the thing before the change, when everything was still intact?[18]

CH.: Yes.

PA.: But also different from what it would be after the change?

CH.: Undoubtedly.

PA.: I am afraid this throws us into some difficulties.

CH.: May I ask what they are?

PA.: Will you permit me the choice of an example?

CH.: You do not need to ask permission.

PA.: Isn't death a change?[19]                     *death*

CH.: Undoubtedly.

PA.: I understand it to be the act of dying.

CH.: And so do I.

PA.: Is someone who is dying alive?

CH.: That's a puzzling question.

PA.: Or is someone who is dying dead?

CH.: This I see to be impossible. For to be dead means for one's death to be past.

PA.: If death is past for the dead, then it will be in the future for the living, just as someone who is being born is neither about to be born nor already born.

CH.: So it seems.

PA.: Therefore it is not the case that someone who is dying is alive.

CH.: Agreed.

PA.: So someone who is dying is neither dead nor alive.

CH.: I concede this.

PA.: But you seem to have conceded something absurd.

CH.: I do not see the absurdity yet.

PA.: Doesn't life consist in some particular state?

CH.: Undoubtedly.

PA.: Hic status aut existit aut non existit.

CH.: Tertium nullum est.

PA.: In quo non est hic status id vita carere dicimus.

CH.: Esto.

PA.: Nonne mortis momentum illud est, quo quis incipit vita carere.

CH.: Quidni.

PA.: Aut quo desinit vitam habere.

CH.: Perinde est.

PA.: Quaero an hoc momento absit an adsit vita.

CH.: Video difficultatem, neque enim ratio est cur alterum prae altero dicam.

PA.: Opus est ergo, ut neutrum dicas aut utrumque.

CH.: Sed tute mihi exitum hunc interclusisti. Nam satis video, statum aliquem necessario adesse aut abesse, neque simul adesse et abesse, vel nec adesse nec abesse.

PA.: Quid ergo.

CH.: Quid? nisi me haerere.

PA.: Quid si ego quoque?

**536**   GA.: Siccine nos deseris Pacidi.

PA.: Saepe fassus sum magnas esse circa principia difficultates.

GA.: Cur nos in locum tam lubricum duxisti, si labantes sustentare non posses.

PA.: Sed tanti erat agnoscere difficultatem.

TH.: Si te novi, Pacidi, non utique quievisti antequam tibi satisfaceres, neque enim in haec hodie primum incidisti; quare tempus est ut sententiam tuam nobis edisseras.

PA.: Si vobis obsequar, amici, in portu naufragium fecero nondum provectus in plenum mare.

TH.: Quid ita.

PA.: Quia methodi Socraticae leges violavero, qua primum die eam vobis hortantibus attentavi.

PA.: This state either exists or it doesn't exist.

CH.: There is no third alternative.[20]

PA.: We say that anything in which this state does not exist is lacking life.

CH.: Yes.

PA.: Isn't the moment of death the moment at which someone begins to lack life?

CH.: Why not?

PA.: Or is it the moment at which he ceases to have life?

CH.: Precisely.

PA.: I am asking whether life is absent or present at that moment.

CH.: I see the difficulty, for there is no reason why I should say one rather than the other.

PA.: Therefore you must either say neither or both.

CH.: But you have blocked this way out for me. For I see well enough that a given state is necessarily present or absent, and cannot at the same time be both present and absent, nor neither present nor absent.

PA.: What, then?

CH.: Yes, what?, otherwise I am stuck.

PA.: What if I am too?

**536**    GA.: Is this how you desert us, Pacidius?

PA.: I have often admitted that there are great difficulties concerning principles.

GA.: Why have you led us onto such slippery ground if you cannot support us when we fall?

PA.: But it was important to acknowledge the difficulty.

TH.: If I know you, Pacidius, you did not remain the least bit calm before you satisfied yourself, for today is not the first time you've come across this difficulty: so it is high time you aired your own opinion to us.

PA.: If I were to oblige you, my friends, I would be shipwrecked in port before I even made it to the open sea.

TH.: Why is that?

PA.: Because I would have violated the laws of the Socratic method, which I am attempting today for the first time with your encouragement.

TH.: Id nolim equidem.

PA.: Quare sententiam meam desiderare non debes, Charini est hortante me invenire veritatem, non a me quaerere inventam, neque enim illi fructum methodi, aut successus voluptatem invidere debemus.

GA.: Fac obsecro ut gustare incipiamus, quos narras fructus.

PA.: Tentabo, atque ita porro quaeram; dic mihi Charine, putasne aliquos esse mortuos, qui vixerant.

CH.: Certum hoc est, quicquid argutemur.

PA.: Desiitne aliquando vita?

CH.: Desiit.

PA.: Ergone aliquod ultimum vitae momentum fuit.

CH.: Fuit.

PA.: Rursus Charine, putasne aliquos vixisse qui nunc mortui sunt.

CH.: Certum est hoc quoque, imo idem priori est.

PA.: Sufficit certum esse. Ergone status mortui coepit.

CH.: Coepit.

PA.: Et primum aliquod hujus status momentum sive initium fuit.

CH.: Fuit.

PA.: Superest hoc unum mihi respondeas, idemne sit ultimum momentum vivendi, et primum momentum non vivendi.

CH.: Si nihil asserendum est quam quod certo comprehendimus, id quidem asseverare non ausim.

**537**   PA.: Gratulor tibi Charine, quod artem dubitandi, sane non exiguam, didicisti. Hic enim (fatebor tibi) aliquod judicii tui experimentum capere volui. Sed dic mihi quaeso quid te hic tam cautum fecerit.

CH.: Videbam inferre te velle, communi vivendi ac non vivendi momento eundem simul vivere ac non vivere. Quod absurdum esse agnosco.

PA.: An rectam futuram fuisse putas illationem.

CH.: Non puto ei resisti posse.

PA.: Quid ergo de sententia sentis ex qua absurdum necessario sequitur.

TH.: I, for one, would not want that to happen.

PA.: In that case you should not wish for my opinion. It is for Charinus to discover the truth with my encouragement, not to ask me what I have discovered. For we ought not to begrudge him the fruit of this method, or the pleasure of success.

GA.: Please go on, so we can begin to taste the fruits you mention.

PA.: I shall try, by asking next: tell me, Charinus, do you think that some people are dead who used to be alive?

CH.: This is certainly the case, however we may keep on arguing.

PA.: Did life end for them at some time?

CH.: Yes.

PA.: So was there some last moment of life?

CH.: Yes, there was.

PA.: Again, Charinus, do you think that some people used to be alive, who are now dead?

CH.: This is certain, too, but it is the same case as before.

PA.: Suffice for it to be certain. So did a state of death begin for them?

CH.: Yes.

PA.: And there was some first moment or beginning of this state?

CH.: Yes.

PA.: There remains this one thing for you to answer me: is the last moment of living the same as the first moment of not living?

CH.: If nothing is to be asserted but what we understand for certain, then I definitely would not dare to seriously maintain this.

**537**     PA.: Congratulations, Charinus, on having learnt the by no means inconsiderable art of doubting. For here (I must confess) I wanted to make a test of your judgment. But tell me, please, what made you so wary at this point?

CH.: I saw that you wanted to infer that if there was a moment in common to the living and the nonliving, then the same person would be simultaneously living and not living, which I acknowledge to be absurd.

PA.: Do you think my inference would have been right?

CH.: I do not think it can be resisted.

PA.: What, therefore, do you feel about an opinion from which an absurdity necessarily follows?

CH.: Absurdam esse.

PA.: Ergo duo momenta se immediate sequi possunt, unum vivendi, alterum non-vivendi.

CH.: Quidni, cum possint et duo puncta. Quod mihi opportune admodum in mentem venit, cum rem quodammodo oculis subjiciat. Super tabula perfecte plana AB feratur sphaera prorsus rotunda C; manifestum est non cohaerere sphaeram plano, neque extrema habere communia, alioqui unum sine altero non moveretur; manifestum est tamen contactum non nisi in puncto esse, et extremum aliquod sive punctum sphaerae *d* ab extremo sive puncto tabulae *e* non distare. Duo ergo puncta *d* et *e* simul sunt, etsi unum non sint.

PA.: Nihil planius aptiusque potuit dici.

TH.: Memini Aristotelem quoque Contiguum a Continuo ita discernere, ut *Continua* sint quorum extrema unum sunt, *Contigua* quorum extrema simul sunt.

PA.: Eodem ergo modo dicemus cum Charino statum vivi mortuique tantum contigua esse, nec communia extrema habere.

CH.: Urbane admodum me autorem citas, eorum quae tu in animo meo nasci fecisti.

PA.: Jam dixi te sententias tuas tibi debere, occasiones mihi. Sed hoc in majoribus comprobabitur, quanquam eundum sit per gradus.

GA.: Patere ergo ut quaeram, an ex his aliquid momenti cujusdam putes duci posse.

PA.: Mirarer hoc te non jam dudum quaesiisse nisi te Gallutium esse nossem. Scio enim alioqui viris in naturae inquisitione et experimentorum luce versatis, haec aut inepta aut certe inutilia videri. Sed acquiesces opinor, ubi consideraveris, cum de principiis agitur nihil parvum debere videri.

538

CH.: That it is absurd.

PA.: Therefore it is possible for two moments, one of living and the other of nonliving, to follow one immediately after the other?

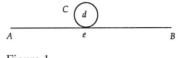

Figure 1

CH.: Why not, when this is also possible for two points? I find this comes to mind most conveniently when I can set the thing before my eyes in some fashion. So let a perfectly rounded sphere *C* be placed on a perfectly flat table *AB*. It is clear that the sphere does not cohere with the plane, and that they have no extrema in common, otherwise one would not be able to move without the other. On the other hand, it is clear that there is no contact unless it is at a point, and there is some extremum or point *d* in the sphere that is no distance from the extremum or point *e* of the table. So the two points, *d* and *e,* are together, although they are not one point.

PA.: Nothing plainer or more appropriate could be said.

TH.: I remember that Aristotle, too, distinguishes the contiguous from the continuous in such a way that those things are *continuous* whose extrema are one, and *contiguous* whose extrema are together.[21]

PA.: In the same way, therefore, we will say with Charinus that the state of being alive and that of being dead are merely contiguous, and have no extrema in common.

CH.: It is very polite of you to cite me as the author of what you have brought into being in my soul.

PA.: I have already told you that you owe your opinions to yourself, and the occasions for them to me. But this will be confirmed in the larger view, although it is the same through the stages.

GA.: To be clear, then, I would like to know whether you think anything of particular moment can be deduced from this.

PA.: If I didn't know who you were, Gallutius, I would have been surprised you hadn't asked me this long ago. For I know that otherwise, to men who are versed in the investigation of nature and the light of
**538** experiments, these things seem either foolish or at any rate useless. But you will acquiesce, I believe, upon considering that when principles are at stake nothing ought to be regarded as insignificant.

GA.: Non sum adeo a rebus abstractis alienus, ut non agnoscam, tenuia omnium scientiarum initia esse velut stamina prima telae majoris. Sed cum sciam solere te paulatim viam ad majora moliri, praegustum aliquem expectabam qui dictis dicendisque luci esset.

PA.: Non possum hic, Galluti, satisfacere desiderio tuo, nec si possem deberem. Non possum, quia ut venatores non certam semper ac designatam sequuntur feram, sed obvia saepe praeda contenti sunt; ita nos aliquando cogimur arripere veritates, ut quaeque primum occurrit, certi nunquam non lucrosam hanc esse capturam, et magno satis numero collecto, tum demum subductis rationibus recognitisque opibus nostris atque digestis majorem spe thesaurum reperiri. Adde quod non meo tantum arbitrio colloquium connectitur, sed Charini: responsionibus accommodandae sunt interrogationes meae. Si vero possem tibi jam tum ante oculos ponere futuri sermonis oeconomiam, etiam te judice, ubi me audieris, non deberem: nonnunquam enim gaudemus falli, et major eventus gratia est, cum non expectatur. Scis circulatores tum maxime oblectare, cum versis aliorsum oculis spectatorum, inopinatum aliquid e pera velut e nihilo educunt.

GA.: Hac spe non amplius interpellabere.

PA.: Ad te igitur redeo Charine; conclusimus impossibilem esse statum mutationis.

CH.: Ita certe si momentum mutationis pro momento status medii seu communis sumatur.

PA.: At nonne res mutantur?

CH.: Quis neget.

PA.: Mutatio ergo est aliquid.

CH.: Certe.

PA.: Aliud ab eo quod impossibile ostendimus, momentaneo scilicet statu.

CH.:Aliud.

Pa.: An ergo status mutationis aliquem temporis tractum postulat.

CH.: Videtur.

GA.: Actually, I am not such a stranger to abstract matters that I do not recognize that the elements of all the sciences are tenuous things, like the first threads of a larger warp. It is just that since I know you usually build a road to larger concerns gradually, I was expecting to get a foretaste of this which would throw light on the things you have said and are about to say.

PA.: I cannot satisfy your desire at this point, Gallutius, and nor ought I to if I could. I cannot do so because, just as hunters do not always chase a certain designated wild animal, but are often content with whatever prey they come upon, so we should force ourselves to snatch up truths as they come. It will never be unprofitable for a certain truth to be caught, and when we have collected a large enough number of them, and have drawn up reasons for them and have reviewed and digested our work, then at last we may hope to obtain a greater treasure. Besides, it is not just by my judgment that this conversation is connected together, but Charinus's too: my lines of questioning are to be met with appropriate replies. If, then, I really could already set before your eyes a précis of the future course of this discussion, even with you judging it when you have heard me, I ought not to: for sometimes we are glad to be disappointed, and an event has greater charm when it is not anticipated. You know that pedlars delight the most when, with the eyes of the onlookers turned the other way, they pull something unexpected out of the bag as if out of nothing.

GA.: With this hope we shall not interrupt any further.

PA.: I therefore return to you, Charinus. We concluded that a state of change is impossible.[22]

CH.: Yes, we did, if the moment of change is assumed to be the moment of a mediate or common state.

PA.: But don't things change?

CH.: Who would deny it?

PA.: Then change is something.

CH.: Of course.

PA.: Something other than what we have shown to be impossible, namely, a momentaneous state.

CH.: Yes.

PA.: Then does a state of change require some stretch of time?

CH.: So it would seem.

PA.: Potestne aliquid pro parte existere aut non existere.

CH.: Hoc clarius explicandum est.

PA.: Potestne crescere aut decrescere veritas alicujus propositionis certo temporis tractu, quemadmodum aqua incalescit aut refrigeratur per gradus.

**539**

CH.: Minime quidem. Puto enim totam statim falsam aut totam veram esse propositionem: nunc enim intelligo quaestionem. Ut cum aqua calida sit etsi magis magisque incalescat, uno tamen momento opus est, ut ex non-calida fiat calida vel contra, quemadmodum momento fit ex recto obliquum.

*calida*

PA.: Rursus ergo rediimus ad momentaneum mutationis statum, quem impossibilem esse apparuit.

CH.: Nescio quomodo reciderimus in difficultates quibus exieramus.

PA.: Si duorum hominum facultates non nisi uno obolo different, poteritne unus dives censeri, quin idem et de altero judicium fiat.

CH.: Non poterit credo.

PA.: Ergo unius oboli differentia divitem vel pauperem non facit.

CH.: Non opinor.

PA.: Neque unius oboli additio vel detractio divitem faciet non-divitem, aut pauperem non-pauperem.

CH.: Non utique.

PA.: Nemo ergo unquam fieri potest ex paupere dives vel ex divite pauper; quotcumque obolis datis vel ademtis.

CH.: Quid ita obsecro?

PA.: Pone pauperi obolum dari, an desiit pauper esse?

CH.: Minime.

PA.: Detur iterum obolus, an tum desiit?

CH.: Non magis.

PA.: Ergo nec tertio obolo dato desinet pauper esse.

CH.: Fateor.

PA.: Can something partly exist or not exist?

CH.: You should explain what you mean by this more clearly.

PA.: Can the truth of some proposition increase or decrease over a certain stretch of time, in the same way as water gets hotter or colder by degrees?

**539** CH.: Certainly not. I think a proposition is either at once wholly true or wholly false—for now I understand your question. For example, whilst water is hot even if it is getting hotter and hotter, there must still be one moment when it changes from being not-hot to hot, or vice versa, just as there must be a moment when a line changes from being straight to oblique.

PA.: Therefore we have again come back to the momentaneous state of change, which appeared to be impossible.

CH.: I don't know how we have fallen back into the difficulties we had escaped.[23]

PA.: If the wealth of two people differs by only one penny, could one of them be regarded as rich without the same judgment being made about the other?

CH.: No, I do not believe so.

PA.: Therefore a difference of one penny does not make one rich or poor.

CH.: Not in my opinion.

PA.: Nor would the gain or loss of one penny make a rich person not rich, or a pauper not poor.

CH.: Not at all.

PA.: Therefore no one can ever become rich from being poor, nor become poor from being rich, however many pennies are given to or taken from him.

CII.: Why is that, may I ask?

PA.: Suppose a penny is given to a pauper. Does he cease to be poor?

CH.: No.

PA.: If another penny is given him, does he cease to be poor then?

CH.: No more than before.

PA.: Therefore he does not cease to be poor if a third penny is give him?

CH.: No.

PA.: Par est ratio de alio quocunque: aut enim nunquam aut unius oboli adjectione desinet pauper esse. Pone millesimo pauperem esse desinere, nongentesimo

nonagesimo nono adhuc fuisse; utique unus obolus depulit paupertatem.

CH.: Agnosco vim argumenti, et me ita delusum miror.

PA.: Faterisne igitur aut nunquam aliquem divitem vel pauperem fieri aut fieri posse uno obolo addito vel detracto.

CH.: Cogor fateri.

**540** PA.: A discreta ad continuam quantitatem argumentum transferamus, ut si punctum *A* ad punctum *H* accedat fiet aliquando ex non-propinquo propinquum ut in *B*. Nonne eodem argumento quo paulo ante colligemus aut nunquam propinquum fieri, aut fieri unius pollicis ut *FB* accessione.

CH.: Colligemus.

PA.: At nonne pro pollice substituere poterimus pollicis centesimam aut millesimam aut aliam partem quantumlibet parvam?

CH.: Poterimus salva vi argumenti.

PA.: Poterimus ergo minorem substituere quavis a nobis nominata.

CH.: Certe.

PA.: Si pollicis *FB* centesima pars *CB* facit ex propinquo non propinquum, totus pollex non facit.

CH.: Non utique: nam priores nonaginta novem partes *FC* nondum fecere propinquum.

PA.: Patet ergo pollicis accessionem non facere ex non propinquo propinquum, nisi quia continet ultimam centesimam.

CH.: Et ultima centesima *CB* pari jure non facit propinquum, nisi ob novissimum sui *B*.

PA.: Novissimum autem nonne minimum est?

CH.: Minimum utique, nam si non esset minimum aliquid ab eo rescindi posset, salvo eo quod propinquitatem facit.

PA.: The same applies to any other one: for either he never ceases to be poor, or he does so by the gain of one penny. Suppose he ceases to be poor when he gets a thousandth penny, having already got nine hundred and ninety-nine; it is still one penny that removed his poverty.

CH.: I can see the force of the argument, and I'm surprised I was deluded like this.

PA.: Do you admit, then, that either nobody ever becomes rich or poor, or one can become so by the gain or loss of one penny?

CH.: I am forced to admit this.

**540** PA.: Let us transpose the argument from discrete to continuous quantity:[24] for example, if a point *A* approaches a point *H,* then at a certain time it will turn from not being near to being near, as at *B,* for instance. Shall we not conclude by the same argument as a little while ago that either it never gets near to *H,* or it does so by the gaining of one inch, such as *FB*?

CH.: Yes.

PA.: But couldn't we have substituted for the inch a hundredth or thousandth of an inch, or any other part, however small?

CH.: We could, without affecting the force of the argument.

PA.: Therefore we could have substituted a part smaller than any named by us?

Figure 2

CH.: Of course.

PA.: If it is the hundredth part *CB* of the inch *FB* that makes the near into the not-near, then it is not the whole inch which does this.

CH.: Of course not: for the first ninety-nine parts *FC* have not yet made the point near.

PA.: Then it is clear that the gaining of an inch only makes the not-near into the near because it contains the last hundredth of an inch.

CH.: And by the same token, the last hundredth *CB* does not make it near except by virtue of its last part *B*.

PA.: But isn't the last part a minimum?

CH.: Yes it is, for if it were not a minimum, then something could be removed from it, leaving intact whatever produces the nearness.

Pone enim novissimum illud ipsius *CB* non esse minimum *B* sed rectam [*DB*] non per se sed ob aliam sui partem adhuc minorem *EB* faciet ex propinquo non propinquum.

PA.: Habemus ergo vel nihil esse per quod quid proprie ac per se fiat propinquum, vel minimi adjectione aut detractione aliquid fieri ex propinquo non propinquum, adeoque minima esse in rebus. Jam minimum in loco potestne alio quam minimo temporis absolvi?

CH.: Non potest, alioquin pars ejus temporis partem loci absolveret, minimi autem pars nulla est.

**541**  PA.: Rursus ergo patet statum mutationis in praesenti exemplo (a longinquitate ad propinquitatem) momentaneum esse.

CH.: Esto.

PA.: Redit ergo difficultas prior, ultimone momento status prioris an primo posterioris ascribi debeat status mutationis.

CH.: Videor tandem mihi exitum reperisse. Dicam enim componi ex utroque et licet momentaneus dici soleat, duo tamen momenta continere, quemadmodum locus contactus qui in puncto esse dicitur utrumque corporum se tangentium extremum continet.

PA.: Recte dixisti, et superioribus tuis congruenter neque ita habeo quod objiciam huic sententiae tuae.

CH.: Mutationem ergo nuper proscriptam velut postliminio reduximus in naturam.

PA.: Modo teneamus esse contactum vel aggregatum duorum statuum oppositorum, non vero esse entis genus a qualitate sive statu ipso distinctum, neque adeo esse statum medium sive transitum a potentia ad actum vel a privatione ad formam quemadmodum vulgo philosophi mutationem et motum concipere videntur.

CH.: Jam ergo mihi permissum erit, Motum definire Mutationem.

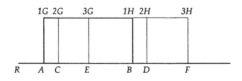

For suppose that the last part of *CB* is not the minimum *B* but a straight line [*DB*]:[25] this line would not make the near into the not-near of its own accord, but by virtue of some other still smaller part of itself, *EB*.

PA.: Therefore we hold that either there is no way for something to become near properly and of its own accord, or something turns from being near to being not-near by the addition or subtraction of a minimum, so that there are minima in reality. Now can a minimum in place be completed in anything other than a minimum of time?

CH.: No, otherwise in part of this time part of the place would be completed, but a minimum has no part.

**541** PA.: Therefore, again, it is clear that the state of change in the present example (from remoteness to nearness) is momentaneous.

CH.: Yes.

PA.: Therefore our former difficulty has returned, whether the state of change should be ascribed to the last moment of the earlier state or the first moment of the later state.

CH.: I think I have finally found a way out. For I would say that it is composed from both, and that although it is usually called momentaneous, it in fact contains two moments: just as a place of contact, which is said to be at a point, contains an extremum of each of the bodies that are touching.

PA.: You have spoken correctly, and consistently with what you said above, so that I have no objection to this opinion of yours.

CH.: So we have reinstated in nature the change we recently proscribed, as if by postliminy.[26]

PA.: Provided only that we maintain it to be the point of contact or aggregate of two opposite states, and not a kind of entity distinct from the quality or state itself, nor indeed a mediate state or transition from potential to act or from privation to form, as the philosophers commonly seem to conceive change and motion.

CH.: So now I shall be allowed to define motion as a change.

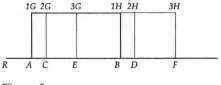

Figure 3

PA.: Ergo fateri debes motum corporis ut *GH* ex *AB* vel *1G1H* versus *EF* vel *3G3H* esse compositum ex novissimo momento existentiae in loco *AB* a quo fit motus, et primo momento existentiae in loco proximo ad quem fit motus corporis. Quaeso jam, Charine, designa mihi locum proximum in quem fit.

CH.: Designabo tibi quemlibet *CD* vel *2G2H*.

PA.: At ego non quemlibet, sed proximum quaero.

CH.: Satis video ut proximus sit, intervallum *AC* debere minimum esse.

PA.: Aut necesse est mobile de loco *AB* in locum *EF* ire per saltum, ita ut non eat per locos intermedios (verbi gratia *CD*) omnes.

**542**   CH.: Quod impossibile est.

PA.: Ita sane videtur, sed quaero: motus nonne continuum est?

CH.: Quid hoc loco continuum vocas?

PA.: Hoc volo, aliquando nulla quiete interrumpi, sive ita durare posse, ut corpus *GH* nullo in loco (aequali sibi) *AB, CD, EF* vel intermediis existat ultra momentum.

CH.: Quid si hoc tibi negem?

PA.: Poteris non sine exemplo. Nam et ex veteribus Empedocles, et ex recentioribus docti quidam Viri quietulas quasdam intersperses asseruere.

CH.: Hac fiducia nego, alioqui vix ausurus.

PA.: Non habes ad negandum aut certe ad dubitandum alia opus autoritate, Charine, quam tua. Sed hoc mihi responde, interspersa quies nonne est existentia corporis in eodem loco per aliquem temporis tractum?

CH.: Certe.

PA.: Sunto ergo quietes interspersae, quaero an inter duas quietes motui intersperses aliquis intercedat motus.

CH.: Utique, nisi pro quietibus intersperses, continuam quietem velimus.

PA.: Then you must admit that the motion of a body such as *GH* from *AB* or *1G1H* towards *EF* or *3G3H* is composed of the last moment of its existence in the place *AB* from which it is moved, together with the first moment of its existence in the next place it is moved to. Now, Charinus, please specify for me the next place it goes to.

CH.: I will designate any place *CD* or *2G2H* for you.

PA.: But I did not ask for just any place, but the next one.

CH.: I see well enough that in order for it to be the next one, the interval *AC* would have to be a minimum.

PA.: Or else the moving body must get from the place *AB* to the place *EF* by a leap, so that it does not go through all the intermediate places (e.g. *CD*).

**542**   CH.: And this is impossible.

PA.: It certainly seems so. But please tell me, isn't the motion continuous?

CH.: What do you call continuous in this context?

PA.: By this I mean that the motion is not interrupted by a rest at any time, that is to say, that it is able to last in such a way that the body *GH* does not exist in any place (equal to itself), such as *AB, CD, EF,* or the places between these, for longer than a moment.

CH.: What if I deny you this?

PA.: You will not be able to do so without precedent, since both Empedocles among the ancients and certain learned men of more recent times have claimed that there are certain little rests interspersed.[27]

CH.: With this assurance I do deny it, otherwise I would hardly have dared.

PA.: You need no authority for denying things, Charinus, and certainly none for doubting them, besides your own. But answer me this: isn't an interspersed rest just the existence of a body in the same place for some stretch of time?

CH.: Of course.

PA.: Then, assuming interspersed rests, I ask you whether there is some intervening motion between two rests interspersed in the motion.

CH.: Of course, unless we want a continuous rest instead of interspersed rests.

PA.: Motus intercedens aut momentaneus est, aut aliquo temporis tractu durans.

CH.: Non utique momentaneus, alioqui corpus momento uno iret per spatium quoddam quod perinde est ac si ad saltus, supra vitatos, reverteremur. Esto enim tempus *NP,* quo corpus *GH* transit ex loco *AB* in locum *EF.* Sit tempus quietis *MN,* quo durante corpus haeret in loco *AB,* et sic *OP* tempus quo haeret in loco *CD,* erit utique *NO* tempus motus quo corpus transibit ex *AB* in *CD,* et *PQ* tempus motus quo transibit ex *CD* in [*EF*]. Pono autem *AC,* [*CE*], intervalla esse non minima sed alia quaecunque, exempli gratia, centesimam pollicis partem aliamve minorem aut majorem: utique tempora motuum quoque non momentanea sive minima, sed designabilia esse deberent; alioqui vel nullus foret progressus, vel tempore aliquo minimo *NO* sive momento inter duas quietes posito, fieret saltus corporis *GH* ex loco *AB* in locum *CD* distantem, adeoque vel non foret medio tempore (quippe quod in minimo nullum est) in loco medio ut *L* inter *A* et *C* vel simul uno momento foret in omnibus locis intermediis. Quae omnia absurda videntur.

PA.: Optima est ratiocinatio tua sed in rem meam.

CH.: Quid ita.

PA.: Saltem enim motum durante tempore *NO* per spatium *LC* continuum nullisque amplius quietulis interruptum fatebere. Atque ita redisti ad id quod declinaveras.

CH.: Non possum id diffiteri, nam si alias rursus quietulas introducerem, rediret tantum quaestio eadem; et tametsi indefinite progred-

PA.: Now the intervening motion is either momentaneous, or lasts for some stretch of time?

Figure 4

CH.: It is certainly not momentaneous, otherwise the body will traverse some space in one moment, which is tantamount to reverting to the leaps we rejected above. For let there be a time *NP* in which the body *GH* travels from *AB* to the place *EF.* Let the time of the interval of rest be *MN,* during which the body stays in the place *AB,* and *OP* the time for which it stays in the place *CD.* Then of course *NO* will be the time of the motion in which the body travels from *AB* to *CD,* and *PQ* the time of the motion in which it travels from *CD* to [*EF*].[28] I assume, however, that the intervals *AC* and [*CE*][29] are not minima but something else, e.g. a hundredth of an inch, or some smaller or larger fraction. Of course, the times of the motion should also not be momentaneous or minima, but designatable times; otherwise either there will be no progress, or, assuming there to be some minimum time or moment *NO* between the two intervals of rest, there will be a leap of the body *GH* from the place *AB* to the distant place *CD;* and so either it will not be at a place intermediate between *A* and *C* (such as *L*) at an intermediate time (since in a minimum there is none), or it will be in all the intermediate places at once at one moment—all of which seems absurd.

PA.: Your reasoning is very good, but to my advantage.

CH.: Why is that?

PA.: Because it acknowledges that at least the motion through the space *LC* during the time *NO* is a continuous motion that is not interrupted by any further little rests. And so you have come back to the very thing you had rejected.

CH.: I cannot disavow this, since if I were to introduce other little rests in their turn, the same problem would only recur; and even if I

543

erer subdividendo ac quietulas indefinite exiguas atque indesignabiles, motulis ejusdem naturae miscerem, opus tamen et tempusculis atque lineolis foret, restarentque eaedem semper ratiocinationes. Nam quies semper plus quam momentanea foret, alioqui quies non foret; ergo et motus non momentanei, alioqui eorum aggregatum ad aggregatum quictularum collatum nullam haberet rationem designabilem, ac proinde aut nullus foret corporis progressus, aut, quales vitavimus, saltus.

PA.: Gaudeo, Charine, me sagacitate ingenii tui magna laboris parte levari, haec enim omnia mihi probanda erant. Unum addo, admisso semel aliquo motu continuo quietes intersperses ei usui non servire, cui eas destinarant autores sui, nam illi capere non potuerunt, quo-

**544** modo motus unus alio celerior esse possit, sine quiete intersperse. Si enim corpus *A* feratur motu continuo per tempus non minimum utcunque exiguum, ostendam motus inaequalitatem oriri sine quiete intersperse. Si enim corpus *A* feratur motu continuo ex *d* in *e,* utique radium *cfd* aget in *cge,* motu etiam continuo, *ac* proinde celerior erit motus radii in puncto *d* percurrente arcum *dhe,* quam in puncto *f* percurrente arcum *flg.*

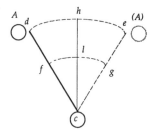

CH.: Manifestum id quidem.

PA.: Motu jam continuo admisso vide quae consequantur.

CH.: Quaenam obsecro.

PA.: Quod nunc movetur estne adhuc in loco, a quo movetur.

CH.: Non opinor, alioqui pari jure foret et in loco ad quem tendit ac proinde in duobus locis simul.

were to proceed by subdividing indefinitely, and were to mix together indefinitely small and undesignatable little intervals of rest
with little motions of the same nature, there would still be a need for
timelets and linelets as well, and the same reasoning would always
apply. Now a rest will always last longer than a moment, otherwise
there will be no rest; therefore motions are not momentaneous either,
otherwise an aggregate of them will have no designatable ratio to an
aggregate made up of little rests; and accordingly either the body will
make no progress, or there will be leaps of the kind we rejected.

PA.: I am pleased to say, Charinus, that the sharpness of your wits has
saved me most of my work, since it was my job to prove all these
things. I have only this to add, that once some continuous motion is
admitted, the interspersed rests do not serve the purpose which their
authors intended for them; for these people were unable to grasp how
**544**    one motion could be faster than another without supposing an interspersed rest. But I will show that if a body is carried by a continuous
motion through a time which, however small, is not a minimum, then
another motion arises which is unequal to it, without supposing an interspersed rest. For if a body *A* is carried by a continuous motion from
*d* to *e,* then the radius *cfd* goes to *cge,* also by continuous motion. Accordingly, the motion of the radius at point *d* running through the arc
*dhe* will be faster than its motion at the point *f* running through the arc
*flg.*

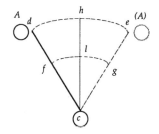

Figure 5

CH.: This is indeed obvious.

PA.: Now see what follows if continuous motion is admitted.

CH.: What does, may I ask?

PA.: Is what is now moving still in the place it is moving from?

CH.: I do not believe so, otherwise by the same right it would be in the
place it is tending towards: and therefore in two places at once.

PA.: Jam ergo locum aliquem deseruit.

CH.: Eum scilicet a quo venit.

PA.: Deserere autem non potuit sine motu.

CH.: Fateor.

PA.: Ergo quicquid movetur jam ante motum est.

CH.: Mira conclusio.

PA.: Eodem argumento concludetur et quod movetur, adhuc motum iri.

CH.: Fateor, nam quod movetur nondum est in loco in quo erit. Non potest autem ad eum venire nisi adhuc moveatur. Ergo quicquid movetur adhuc movebitur.

PA.: Sed inde sequitur motum esse aeternum, ac neque incipere neque finiri.

GA.: Hoc Aristoteles tibi concedet, et qui hoc argumentum tractavit Proclus.

TH.: Vitanda haec conclusio est.

PA.: Utique vitanda; sed si quis eam vere absurdam non putet, eum simili argumento ad absurdum evidens adigemus, si pro motu indefinito, adhibeamus aliquam speciem motus aut gradum, ut si corpus corpori continue appropinquet, demonstrabitur eodem argumento semper appropinquasse, et semper appropinquaturum esse. Quod absurdum est. Nam corpus *A* motu ab *1* ad *2* appropinquat puncto *B,* sed si ultra procedat a *2* ad *3,* tunc non amplius ei propinquius reddetur sed ab eo recedet.

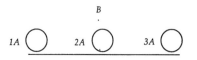

CH.: Videtur et mihi idem argumentum adhiberi posse. Nam quod appropinquat non amplius est in loco remotiore ex quo appropinquat; ergo jam eum deseruit, deserere autem locum remotiorem (nec tendere ad aeque vel magis remotum) est appropinquare. Idem nondum adhuc est in loco propiore versus quem appropinquando tendit; ergo adhuc in eum veniet; venire autem in locum propiorem est appropin-

545

PA.: Therefore it has already left some place.

CH.: Yes, the place it came from.

PA.: But it couldn't have left it without moving.

CH.: Agreed.

PA.: Therefore whatever is moving was already in motion before. *19 v*

CH.: A remarkable conclusion!

PA.: By the same argument one may also conclude that what is moving will keep on moving.

CH.: I agree. For what is moving is not yet in the place it is going to; but it cannot get there unless it keeps on moving. Therefore whatever is moving will keep on moving.

PA.: But from this it follows that motion is eternal, and neither begins nor ends.

GA.: Aristotle will grant you this, and so will Proclus, who discussed this argument.[30]    *Proclus*

TH.: We must avoid this conclusion.

PA.: We certainly must. But in case someone does not consider it truly absurd, we will force him to an obvious absurdity by a similar argument. If instead of an indefinite motion we use some specific kind or stage of motion, such as when one body continuously approaches another, the same argument will demonstrate that it has always approached it and will always keep approaching it. This is absurd, because body $A$ approaches point $B$ by moving from *1* to *2*, but if it proceeds further from *2* to *3* then it will no longer be getting nearer to point $B$ but will be receding from it.

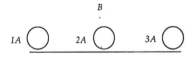

Figure 6

CH.: It seems to me too that the same argument can be applied to this case. For what is approaching is no longer in the more distant place from which it is approaching; therefore it has already left it. But to **545** leave a more distant place (and not to tend towards a place that is equally distant or farther away) is to approach. Likewise, it is still not yet in the nearer place it is tending towards while approaching; therefore it is still coming into it. But to come into a nearer place is to ap-

quare. Ergo adhuc appropinquabit. Ergo appropinquatio quoque aeterna sive initii atque finis expers erit, quod absurdum esse in confesso est.

PA.: Sed quid respondemus. Haec enim ratiocinatio videtur omnem nobis evertere motum.

CH.: Confugiam ex hac tempestate ad portum jam aliquoties salutarem.

PA.: Nactus aliquid mihi videris, Charine, quo confidas argumenti vim eludi posse.

CH.: Judicium penes vos esto. Si vera superius constituimus, negandum est veram atque admittendam esse propositionem hanc: *Corpus aliquod nunc movetur,* si quidem ipsum *nunc* sumitur pro momento, quoniam nullum est momentum transitus sive medii status, in quo dici possit corpus moveri, sive locum mutare. Nam eo momento *neque* foret in loco quem mutat, *neque* non foret, quemadmodum ostendisti; praeterea aut in nullo foret loco, aut in duobus, eo scilicet, quem deserit, et quem acquirit. Quod forte non minus absurdum quam quod tu ostendisti simul esse et non esse aliquo in statu. Evitantur ista, si ut te probante coepimus, motum esse dicamus statum compositum ex ultimo momento existendi in loco aliquo et primo momento non existendi in eodem sed in alio proximo. Non ergo aliud erit motus praesens quam aggregatum duarum existentiarum momentanearum in duobus locis proximis, nec dici poterit: *nunc aliquid moveri,* nisi ipsum *nunc* duorum proximorum momentorum summam, sive duorum temporum differentes status habentium, contactum interpretemur.

PA.: Fateor me quoque nullum alium videre portum, in quem nos recipiamus, sed vereor tamen ut tuta satis statio sit quo loco anchoram tu jecisti.

GA.: Ubi tandem consistemus, si hinc quoque pellimur.

PA.: Natura rerum viam inveniet; nemo unquam a recta ratione deceptus est.

**546** TH.: Multa hodie audivi praeter opinionem meam, et res quas arbitrabar clarissimas tam subito tenebris involutas sum miratus. Sed facile agnosco nostram hanc esse culpam, non tuam, neque a philosophia res certas dubias reddi, sed a nobis incerta pro certis arrepta esse,

proach. Therefore it will keep approaching. Therefore the approach will also be eternal, i.e. devoid of beginning and end, which is acknowledged to be absurd.

PA.: But what should we reply? For this reasoning seems to have destroyed all motion for us.

CH.: I will take refuge from this storm in the port I have already called upon a number of times.

PA.: It seems to me, Charinus, that you have come up with something by means of which you are confident you can avoid the force of the argument.

CH.: Let that be for all of you to judge. If what we established above is true, then we must deny the following proposition to be true or admissible: *Some body is moving now;* we must, that is, if the *now* is assumed to be a moment, seeing as there is no moment of transition, or of a mediate state, in which the body can be said to move, i.e. change place. For at that moment it will *neither* be in the place where it is changing, *nor* will it not be, as you have shown. Moreover it will either be nowhere or in two places, the one it leaves and the one it acquires, which is perhaps no less absurd than what you have shown, that it simultaneously is and is not in some state. These difficulties of yours can be avoided if we say, as we began to do with your approval, that motion is a state composed of the last moment of existing in some place and the first moment of existing, not in the same place, but in the next different place. Therefore the present motion will be nothing but the aggregate of two momentaneous existences in two neighboring places. So it cannot be said that: *something is moving now,* unless this *now* is interpreted as the sum of two neighboring moments or the point of contact of two times characterizing different states.[31]

PA.: I confess that I too can see no other port of refuge we can withdraw to, but I am afraid the place where you have cast anchor is still not safe enough.

GA.: Where will we finally stand firm if we are driven from here too?

PA.: The nature of things will find a way: no one is ever deceived by a correct reason.

**546**  TH.; I have heard many things today which are contrary to my expectations, and I have been surprised that things which I thought were very clear have so suddenly become shrouded in obscurity. But I readily acknowledge that this is our fault, not yours, and that it is not

quod agnoscere primus utique gradus est ad scientiam solidam atque imposterum inconcussam.

PA.: Gaudeo cum viris prudentibus mihi negotium esse, nam vulgus nos otio abuti diceret. Sed tanti est arceri profanos a philosophiae sacris. Nunc sumtam a nobis notionem motus excutiamus ut pateat an in ea quiescere liceat. Ais Charine nihil aliud esse motum quam aggregatum existentiarum momentanearum alicujus rei in locis proximis duobus.

CH.: Ita certe ajo.

PA.: Redeamus ad figuram supra sit mobile $G$ cujus loca duo proxima $A$ et $C$ quorum intervallum debet esse nullum; sive minimum; sive quod idem est, talia esse debent puncta, $A$, $C$ ut nullum inter ipsa sumi possit punctum, sive ut si duo adessent Corpora $RA$, $BC$, ea se tangerent extremis, $A$, $C$. Motus ergo nunc est aggregatum duarum existentiarum rei $G$ in duobus punctis $A$, $C$ proximis, duobus momentis etiam proximis.

CH.: Ita conclusum est.

PA.: Si jam continuum est aliquamdiu motus, sine intercedente quiete, per aliquod spatium tempusque, tunc sequitur id spatium componi non nisi ex punctis, et tempus non nisi ex momentis.

CH.: Velim id clarius ostendas.

PA.: Si motus praesens est aggregatum duarum existentiarum, erit continuatus plurium. Nam continuum sumsimus atque uniformem. Existentiae autem diversae diversorum sunt momentorum atque punctorum. Et toto tempore atque loco durantibus non nisi aliae atque aliae existentiae sunt sese immediate sequentes, ergo non nisi **547** momenta atque puncta se immediate sequentia in tempore ac loco erunt.

CH.: Etsi quia motuum continuum posuimus, vim argumenti subagnoscam, penitius tamen intelligam ex figura.

philosophy that renders certainties doubtful, but we who mistake uncertain things for certain ones. Recognizing this is at least a first step
towards a science that is solid and unshakable for posterity.

PA.: I am glad to be doing business with such prudent men, for the
common people would tell us we were wasting our time. But it is very
important to keep the uninitiated away from the sacred matters of
philosophy. Now let us scrutinize the notion of motion we have assumed in order to see whether rest be allowed in it. You say, Charinus,
that motion is nothing other than an aggregate of momentaneous existences of some thing in two neighboring places.

CH.: I certainly do.

PA.: Let us return to the above figure [*Figure 3*]. Let there be a moving body $G$ for which there are two neighboring places $A$ and $C$
whose interval must be null, i.e. a minimum; or, what is the same
thing, the points $A$ and $C$ must be such that no point[32] can be assumed
between them, or such that if two bodies $RA$ and $BC$ were there, they
would touch each other in the extrema $A$ and $C$. So the motion is now
the aggregate of the existences of the thing $G$ in the two neighboring
points $A$ and $C$ at two neighboring moments.

CH.: So we concluded.

PA.: If now a motion is continuous for a while, without any rest intervening through a certain space and time, then it follows that this
space is composed only of points and time only of moments.

CH.: I would like you to show this more clearly.

PA.: If the present motion is an aggregate of two existences, it will be
continued out of more existences, for we assumed it to be continuous
and uniform. But different existences belong to different moments
and points. And with nothing but different existences immediately
following each other during the whole time and place, there will
therefore be nothing but moments and points immediately following
each other in time and place.

547

CH.: Even though I appreciate the force of this argument, since we
did assume a continuous motion, I would understand it completely
from a figure.

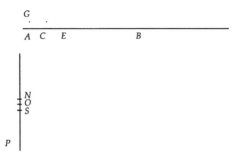

PA.: Sit mobile punctum *G*, id nunc movetur ex *A* in *C* sive duobus momentis proximis *N*, O, est in duobus spatii punctis proximis *A*, *C*, nempe primo momento *N* in primo puncto *A*, secundo momento *O* in secundo puncto *C* ex concessis. Quemadmodum autem puncto *A* proximum in spatio sumsimus punctum *C*, et momento *N* proximum momentum *O*, ita puncto *C* proximum sumi poterit punctum *E* et momento *O* proximum S.

CH.: Haud dubie neque enim ob motus, loci, temporis, *uniformitatem* ulla ratio pro uno potius quam pro alio inveniri potest, cum corpus de puncto non nisi in punctum proximum momento etiam proxime semper sequente, progredi possit.

PA.: Quoniam ergo motus non nisi diversarum existentiarum per momenta punctaque aggregatum est et aeque continuus est ac spatium tempusque, ideo etiam ubique in spatio puncta, et in tempore momenta sese immediate sequentur, ea ipsa scilicet in qua motus continua successione incidit, ideo tempus non nisi momentorum et spatium non nisi punctorum aggregatum erit.[L4]

CH.: Fateor.

PA.: Et si quid aliud in tempore aut spatio occurreret, id a mobili transmitti non posset. Pone enim *C* ab *E* intervallo aliquo abesse *DF*, quomodo id a mobili transibitur, nisi aut in puncta resolvatur proxima sibi aut saltus recipiamus a vobis declinatos, quo mobile spatium

**548**

L4. IN THE MARGIN OF *l*: | NB. Hic aliquid reponi potest; negandum scilicet motum esse uniformem per ullum temporis tractum; adeoque negandum est punctis binis *A*, *C* rursus alia bina proxima sumi posse. | —CROSSED OUT.

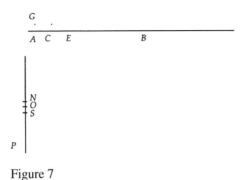

Figure 7

PA.: Let there be a moving point *G* that is moving now from *A* to *C*, i.e. at two neighboring moments *N* and *O* it is at two neighboring points of space *A* and *C*, being at the first point *A* at the first moment *N* and at the second point *C* at the second moment *O*, as agreed. But just as we assumed point *C* to be next to point *A* in space, and moment *O* to be next to moment *N*, so a point *E* could be assumed next to the point *C*, and a moment *S* next to the moment *O*.

CH.: No doubt, for because of the *uniformity* of motion, place, and time, no reason can be found for one rather than the other, since from a point a body can proceed only to the next point, and this always at the next moment following.

PA.: Therefore, since motion is nothing but an aggregate of different existences through moments and points, and is just as continuous as space and time, it also follows that points immediately succeed one another everywhere in space, and moments everywhere in time, these being the points and moments in which motion occurs by continuous succession. Therefore time will be an aggregate of nothing but moments, and space an aggregate of nothing but points.[L4]

CH.: I agree.

PA.: And if anything else were to occur in space or time, it could not be traversed by a moving body. For suppose *C* is some interval *DF* away from *E*, how will this interval be crossed by the moving body **548**     unless either it is resolved into neighboring points, or we readmit the

L4. IN THE MARGIN OF *1:* | N.B. Here something can be set aside: namely, it must be denied that motion is uniform for any stretch of time; and so it must be denied that one can assume another pair of points next to the pair *A* and *C*. | —CROSSED OUT.

aliquod momento transmittit, ita ut non successive per omnia media transeat; nam dicere intervallum *CB* transmitti tempore *OP,* nihil est dicere, cum distincte explicare necesse sit, quod momento quolibet, ut *S* ac puncto quolibet ut *E* inter duo extrema *O* et *P* vel *C* et *B* assignabili fiat, quoniam constat aliud semper atque aliud fieri; aliudque momentum ad aliud referri punctum, aut quietes intersperses (quas inutiles supra ostendi) et saltus admittendos esse, quibus fiat, ut mobile pluribus momentis haereat in uno puncto; et vicissim plura puncta absolvat uno momento.

CH.: Concedamus tibi spatium non nisi punctorum, ac tempus non nisi momentorum esse aggregatum, quid inde mali times.

PA.: Si haec admittitis, omnes in vos uno agmine incurrent difficultates, quae de continui compositione feruntur, famoso labyrinthi nomine insignes.

CH.: Haec praefatio etiam eminus terrorem incutere potest.

TH.: Non poteramus ergo penetrare in naturam motus, nisi in hunc labyrinthum introduceremur.

PA.: Non certe, quia motus ipse ex continuorum numero fertur.

GA.: Neque Aristoteles, neque Galilaeus neque Cartesius vitare nodum potuere, tametsi alius dissimularit alius pro desperato reliquerit, alius abruperit.

CH.: Excipiamus age, quicquid hoc ictuum est: tanti erit multis difficultatibus simul defungi.

PA.: Omnia huc transferre non est institute mei; suffecerit adduxisse quae totam ostendant difficultatem intellecta, totam exhauriant depulsa atque discussa. Quaerendum ante omnia est, lineam seu longitudinem finitam ex finito an infinito punctorum numero componas.

CH.: Tentemus an ex finito.

PA.: Hanc arcem non diu tenebis: dudum enim demonstratum est a Geometris lineam quamlibet in datum numerum partium aequalium dividi posse. Sit recta *AB,* ajo eam in tot dividi posse partes aequales, in quot dividi potest alia quaelibet major. Sumatur major aliqua *CD,*

**549**

leaps you rejected, by means of which the body could traverse some space in a moment in such a way that it does not go through all the intermediate points successively? For to say that the interval *CB* is traversed in the time *OP* is to say nothing, since it is necessary to explain distinctly what would happen at any assignable moment, say *S,* between the two extrema *O* and *P*, and at any assignable point, say *E,* between the extrema *C* and *B,* seeing as it has been established that there is always one after another; and that each different moment is referred to a different point. Or else we must admit interspersed rests (which were shown above to be useless) and leaps, by means of which it would be possible for the moving body to stay at one point for many moments; and, in turn, to cover many points in one moment.

CH.: Supposing we concede you that space is an aggregate of nothing but points and time an aggregate of nothing but moments, what do you fear so much from this?

PA.: If you admit this, you will be swamped by the whole stream of difficulties that stem from the composition of the continuum, and that are dignified by the famous name of the labyrinth.

CH.: This preface is capable of inspiring terror even from a distance!

TH.: So we shall not be able to penetrate into the nature of motion unless we are led into this labyrinth?

PA.: Certainly not, because motion itself is made up of a number of continua.

GA.: Neither Aristotle nor Galileo nor Descartes was able to avoid this knot, although one of them pretended not to see it, one abandoned it as hopeless, and the other severed it.[33]

CH.: Do let us take note of anything they said that is to the point; it will be worth a great deal to get rid of many difficulties at the same time.

PA.: It's not part of my undertaking to transfer here everything they said: it will be enough to adduce those things which reveal the whole difficulty when understood, and which completely dispose of it when they have been removed and dispelled. What we must ask first of all is, do you compose a line, or finite magnitude, from a finite or from an infinite number of points?

CH.: Let us try composing it from a finite number.

PA.: You will not hold this fortress for very long: for it was demonstrated by the geometers some time ago that any line whatsoever can be divided into a given number of equal parts. Let there be a straight line *AB*. I say that it can be divided into as many equal parts as any

ipsique *AB* constituatur parallela. Jam jungantur *CA, DB,* producanturque donec sibi occurrent in *E.* Sit *CF* una ex partibus aequalibus ipsius *CD,* exempli causa centesima, ducaturque recta *EF* quae secabit *AB* in puncto *G* eritque (ex *Elementis* Euclidis) ob triangula *AEB* et *CED* inter se similia, itemque ob triangula *AEG* et *CEF* similia, erit, inquam, *AG* ad *AB* ut *CF* ad *CD* ac proinde cum *CF* sit ad *CD* ut 1 ad 100, seu cum *CF* una centesima sit ipsius *CD* erit et *AG* una centesima ipsius *AB.*

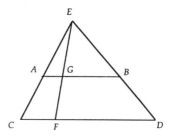

CH.: Non est cur pergas, jam enim hinc video impossibile esse, ut linea ex finito punctorum numero componatur, nam hoc posito aliqua utique intelligi poterit linea ex 99 punctis, cuius certe pars centesima sine fractione sive aliquota puncti parte intelligi non potest. Dicendum est, ergo Lineas ex punctis quidem constare, sed numero infinitis.

PA.: Videtur ejusdem argumenti vis contra omnem punctorum multitudinem valere. Sed alio diagrammate utamur ad eam rem aptiore: in parallelogrammo rectangulo *LNPM* ducatur diagonalis *NM.* Nonne idem est numerus punctorum in *LM,* qui in *NP*?

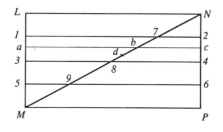

**549**   other line greater than it can be divided into. Let us take some greater
line *CD*, and position it parallel to *AB*. Now join up the lines *CA* and
*DB* and produce them until they meet at *E*. Let *CF* be one of the equal
parts of *CD*, for example a hundredth part, and let us draw a straight
line *EF* that cuts *AB* at the point *G*. Now (by Euclid's *Elements*)[34]—
because of the similarity of triangles *AEB* and *CED*, and likewise that
of triangles *AEG* and *CEF*—it follows that *AG* will be to *AB* as *CF* is
to *CD*. And therefore since *CF* is to *CD* as 1 to 100, or since *CF* is one
hundredth of *CD*, *AG* will also be one hundredth of *AB*.

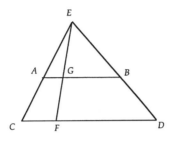

Figure 8

CH.: There is no need for you to go on, for from this I can already see
that it is impossible for a line to be composed of a finite number of
points. For on this supposition there will be some line, at any rate,
that can be conceived to consist of ninety-nine points, a hundredth
part of which certainly cannot be conceived without some fraction or
aliquot part of a point. Therefore it must be said that lines do indeed
consist of points, but of an infinite number of them.

PA.: The force of this same argument seems effective against every
multiplicity of points. But let us use another diagram more suited to
this case. In the rectangular parallelogram *LNPM*, let the diagonal
*NM* be drawn. Isn't the number of points in *LM* the same as the number in *NP*?

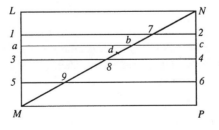

Figure 9

CH.: Haud dubie, nam ob *LN, MP* parallelas ipsae *LM, NP* aequales sunt.

[PA.:] Jam a quolibet puncto ipsius *LM* ut *1, 3, 5* ad quodlibet punctum ipsius *NP* ut *2, 4, 6* ductae intelligantur rectae, ut *12, 34, 56*, parallelae ipsi *LN* quae secabunt diagonalem *NM* in punctis *7, 8, 9* etc. ajo tot esse puncta intelligibilia in *NM*, quot in *LM*, adeoque si lineae sunt aggregata punctorum esse *LM* et [*NM*]l aequales, quod est absurdum cum assumi possint rationem habentes qualemcunque.

**550**   CH.: Consequentiam quam nexurus es, agnoscere mihi videor. Nam si plura sunt puncta in *NM* quam *LM*, aliquod erit punctum in *NM*, per quod nulla transit ex rectis *12, 34; 56* etc. Id punctum sit *b*, per ipsum ducatur recta ipsi *LN* parallela occurrens ipsi *LM* alicubi in *a*, et ipsi *NP* alicubi in *c;* at *a* non est ex numero punctorum *1, 3, 5*, alioqui enim et *b* foret ex numero punctorum *7, 8, 9* contra hypothesin. Ergo *1, 3, 5* etc. non sunt omnia puncta ipsius *LM*. Quod est absurdum nam posuimus esse. Idem est de puncto *c*. Patet ergo tot necessario intelligi puncta in *LM*, et *NP* quot in *NM*, adeoque si hae lineae mera sunt aggregata punctorum, esse lineam minorem aequalem majori.

[PA.:] Jam sumatur *Md* pars ipsius *MN*, aequalis ipsi *ML*, utique cum *ML* et *Md* sint aequales eundem habebunt numerum punctorum, jam si *ML* et *MN* eundem habent numerum punctorum (ut ex aggregatione punctorum sequi ostendimus) etiam *MN* et *Md* eundem numerum punctorum habebunt, pars er totum, quod est absurdum. Unde constat lineas ex punctis non componi.

CH.: Redegisti me ad summam perplexitatem.

GA.: Venit hic in mentem ratiocinationis similis quae extat apud Galilaeum. Numerus omnium quadratorum [minor] est quam omnium numerorum: sunt enim aliqui numeri non-quadrati: vicissim numerus omnium quadratorum aequalis est numero omnium nu-

**551**   merorum, quod sic ostendo: nam nullus est numerus cui non respondeat suus quadratus, non est ergo major numerus numerorum quam quadratorum; vicissim omnis numerus quadratus habet latus numerum: non est ergo major numerus quadratorum quam numerorum: neque major ergo neque minor, sed aequalis erit numerus numerorum omnium (quadratorum et non-quadratorum) et numerus omnium quadratorum: totum parti. Quod est absurdum.

CH.: Without doubt. For, since *NL* and *MP* are parallel, *LM* and *NP* are equal.

[PA.]:[35] Now from any point of *LM*, such as *1, 3,* or *5,* to any point of *NP,* such as *2, 4,* or *6,* let us conceive straight lines *1–2, 3–4,* and *5–6* to be drawn parallel to *LN,* which cut the diagonal *NM* at the points *7, 8,* and *9,* etc. I say there are as many conceivable points in *NM* as in *LM,* so that if lines are aggregates of points, *LM* and [*NM*][36] are equal, which is absurd, since they could be taken as having any ratio whatsoever.

**550**      CH.: I think I can see how you are going to draw this consequence. For if there are more points in *NM* than *LM,* there will be some point in *NM* through which none of the lines *1–2, 3–4, 5–6,* etc. passes. Let this point be *b.* Through it let a straight line be drawn parallel to *LN,* meeting *LM* at some point *a* and *NP* at some point *c.* But *a* is not one of the points *1, 3, 5,* for otherwise *b* will also be one of the points *7, 8, 9,* contrary to hypothesis. So *1, 3, 5,* etc. are not all the points of *LM,* which is absurd, since we have assumed they are. The same goes for point *c.* It is therefore clear that we must understand there to be just as many points in *LM* and *NP* as in *NM,* so that if these lines are mere aggregates of points, the smaller line will be equal to the greater.

[PA.:][37] Now let us take a part *Md* of *MN* that is equal to *ML,* so that since *ML* and *Md* are equal they, at least, will have the same number of points. Now if *ML* and *MN* have the same number of points (as we have shown to follow from the aggregation of their points), *MN* and *Md* will also have the same number of points, part and whole alike, which is absurd. Whence it is established that lines are not composed of points.[38]

CH.: You have brought me back to the height of perplexity.

GA.: There comes to mind here a similar line of reasoning conspicuous in Galileo's writings.[39] The number of all squares is less than the number of all numbers, since there are some numbers which are non-square. On the other hand, the number of all squares is equal to the

**551**      number of all numbers, which I show as follows: there is no number which does not have its own corresponding square, therefore the number of numbers is not greater than the number of squares; on the other hand, every square number has a number as its side: therefore the number of squares is not greater than the number of numbers. Therefore the number of all numbers (square and non-square) will be neither greater than nor less than, but equal to the number of all squares: the whole will be equal to the part, which is absurd.

TH.: Quid obsecro respondes Pacidi.

PA.: Ego Charinum interrogandum censeo.

CH.: Jocaris.

PA.: Minime vero arbitror enim te per te exire posse ex labyrintho.

CH.: Permitte quaeso ut prius ex Gallutio audiam quid dixerit Galilaeus.

GA.: Dixit: majoris, aequalis, minoris, nomina non habere locum in infinito.

CH.: Difficile est acquiescere, nam quis neget numero numerorum omnium contineri numerum numerorum quadratorum, qui inter omnes numeros reperiuntur. Contineri autem utique est partem esse, et partem toto minorem esse in infinito non minus quam in finito arbitror verum.

GA.: An alius tibi exitus patet Charine.

CH.: Quid si audeam dicere nullum omnino esse numerum omnium numerorum, talemque notionem implicare contradictionem?

TH.: Mirum aliquid et audax dixisti, Charine.

PA.: Imo rem dixit praeclaram et si quid judico veram. Nam quod contradictorias habet consequentias, utique impossibile sit necesse est.

CH.: Gaudeo me tam feliciter divinasse.

PA.: Vides quid per se possit animus si propositis recte difficultatibus interrogando excitetur.

GA.: Ergone assentiris Charino, Pacidi.

PA.: Ego multa et magna habeo argumenta cur ejus sententiam probem. Arbitror enim eam esse quarundam notionum naturam, ut sint incapaces perfectionis, atque absoluti et in suo quoque genere summi. Talis res est numerus, item motus: celerrimum enim motum intelligi non posse arbitror: pone rotam aliquam motu celerrimo agitari, jam si aliquis ejus radius produci intelligatur, punctum aliquod extra rotam in radio producto sumtum, motu agetur celeriore quam rota, id est **552** celeriore quam celerrimus: Eodem modo ut velocitas maxima, ita et numerus maximus quiddam impossibile est, numerus autem omnium numerorum idem est cum numero omnium unitatum (semper enim nova unitas addita prioribus novum numerum facit) et numerus omnium unitatum a numero maximo non differt.

TH.: What, may I ask, do you reply to this, Pacidius?

PA.: I think you should ask Charinus.

CH.: You're joking!

PA.: Not in the least, for I believe you are capable of getting out of the labyrinth by yourself.

CH.: Please allow me first to hear from Gallutius what Galileo said.

GA.: He said: the appellations of greater, equal, and less have no place in the infinite.[40]

CH.: It is difficult to agree with this. For who would deny that the number of square numbers is contained in the number of all numbers, when squares are found among all numbers? But to be contained in something is certainly to be a part of it, and I believe it to be no less true in the infinite than in the finite that the part is less than the whole.[41]

GA.: Do you see any other way out, Charinus?

CH.: What if I should dare to say that there is no number of all numbers at all, and that such a notion implies a contradiction?

TH.: That's a surprising and audacious thing to have said, Charinus!

PA.: No, what he's said is very clear, and, if I am any judge, true. For it is necessary that what has contradictory consequences is by all means impossible.

CH.: I am glad to have had such a fortunate inspiration.

PA.: You see what the soul can do by itself if, when difficulties are proposed, it is stimulated by being questioned correctly?

GA.: So you agree with Charinus, Pacidius?

PA.: I have many good reasons for approving his opinion. For I believe it to be the nature of certain notions that they are incapable of perfection and completion, and also of having a greatest of their kind. Number is such a thing, and so is motion: for I do not believe a fastest motion is intelligible.[42] Suppose some wheel is set spinning with the fastest motion; now if we conceive one of its radii to be produced, then any point we take on the produced radius outside the wheel will

552  be spinning with a motion faster than the wheel, that is, faster than the fastest. And just as this maximum velocity is something impossible, so also is the greatest number. But the number of all numbers is the same as the number of all unities (since a new unity added to the preceding ones always makes a new number), and the number of all unities is nothing other than the greatest number.

TH.: Ergo ne Deus quidem intelliget numerum omnium unitatum?

PA.: Quomodo eum intelligere putas quod impossibile est? an totum comprehendet quod parti suae aequatur. Eodem modo facile ostendemus etiam numerum omnium curvarum implicare impossibilitatem; neque id vero mirum videri debet admissa semel numeri maximi impossibilitate. Nam et in quolibet gradu finitus est curvarum analyticarum numerus, gradus autem dimensionum tot sunt quot numeri, ergo numerus omnium graduum impossibilis est, idem scilicet cum numero omnium numerorum: multo magis ergo et numerus ex summis omnium numerorum qui in singulis gradibus continentur.

TH.: Sed tempus est ut difficultati circa puncta quoque satisfaciatis.

CH.: Audebo dicere nec punctorum omnium assignabilium numerum esse.

TH.: At nonne puncta sunt in linea, etiam antequam assignentur. Determinata ergo est multitudo eorum atque certa.

**553** CH.: Si probas, Pacidi, dicemus puncta nulla esse, antequam designentur; Si sphaera planum tangat punctum esse locum contactus; si: corpus ab alio corpore vel superficies a superficie secetur, tunc superficiem vel lineam esse locum intersectionis. Sed alibi non esse et puncta, lineas, superficies, et in universum extrema non alia esse, quam quae fiunt dividendo: et partes quoque non esse in Continuo antequam divisione producantur. Nunquam autem fiunt omnes divisiones quae fieri possunt. Possibilium autem divisionum non magis est numerus quam possibilium Entium, qui coincidit cum numero omnium numerorum.

PA.: Mire profecisti Charine in hoc genere ratiocinandi: neque enim quod aliud dicerem ipse habebam. Una superest magna difficultas in qua ipse Cartesius haesit, cujus admoneor verbis tuis.

CH.: Postquam Galilaeo satisfecimus, cur de Cartesio desperemus.

PA.: Tantum his duobus viris tribuo, ut credam quidvis praestare potuisse, ubi animum applicuissent, sed ut sumus homines, varie distracti, et impetum potius cogitandi quam methodum constantem ac definitam sequentes, quandam etiam in cogitando fortunam experimur. In vase circulari *ABCD* sit liquidum *e, f, g,* liquidum inquam

TH.: So doesn't even God understand the number of all unities?

PA.: How do you suppose he understands what is impossible? does he comprehend a whole which is equal to its part?[43] In the same way we shall easily show that the number of all curves also implies an impossibility; nor should this seem very surprising, once we have admitted the impossibility of a greatest number. For the number of analytic curves in any degree whatever is finite, yet there are as many degrees of dimensions as there are numbers. Therefore the number of all degrees is impossible, since it is the same as the number of all numbers; much more so, then, is the number of sums of all the numbers which are contained in each degree.

TH.: But it is time you two resolved the difficulty about points as well.

CH.: I will be so bold as to say that there is no number of all assignable points either.

TH.: But aren't there points in the line even before they are assigned? Therefore their multiplicity is determinate and certain.

**553**   CH.: If you approve, Pacidius, we will say that there are no points before they are designated. If a sphere touches a plane, the locus of contact is a point; if a body is intersected by another body, or a surface by another surface, then the locus of intersection is a surface or a line, respectively. But there are no points, lines, or surfaces anywhere else, and in general the only extrema are those made by an act of dividing: nor are there any parts in the continuum before they are produced by a division. But all the divisions that can be made are never in fact made. Rather, the number of possible divisions is no more than the number of possible entities, which coincides with the number of all numbers.

PA.: Charinus, you have made amazing progress in this kind of reasoning, for I was not considering saying anything different myself. There remains one considerable difficulty at which Descartes himself became stuck, which I am reminded of by your words.

CH.: Now that we have satisfied Galileo, why should we despair of Descartes?

PA.: These are the only two men I would credit with having been able to excel at anything they applied themselves to. But as for us, being people who are distracted in various ways, and who follow the impetus of our thought rather than a constant and definite method, we experience a kind of luck even in our thinking. Let there be a liquid *e, f,*

perfectum cuius scilicet pars quaelibet utcunque exigua, a qualibet alia data separari possit. Sit in eo corpus circulare non liquidum, sed solidum *H*, fixum extra vasis centrum: jamque materia liquida agitetur seu fluat: erit motus ejus celerior in *g* quam in *e*, et, in *e* quam in *f*, tantundem enim materiae transit per *g* quantum per *e*, vel per *f*, minor autem est locus *g* quam *e*, et *e* quam *f*, necesse est ergo loci parvitas celeritate motus pensetur.

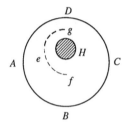

CH.: Haec manifesta sunt: nccesse est enim quod per *e* transit supplere debere id quod per *f* transit, quia vas plenum esse posuimus: et vicissim debere suppleri ab eo quod a *g* venit.

PA.: Hinc sequitur cum pro punctis *g*, *e*, *f* alia ubilibet puncta assumi queant, et par ubique ratio sit, materiam liquidam actu divisam esse **554** ubique neque in linea *gef* ullum assumi posse punctum, quin motus gradu proprio agitetur, a velocitate cuiuslibet alterius differente, ac proinde a quolibet alio assignabili erit actu separatum.

CH.: Fatendum hoc est posito materiam esse perfecte liquidam et vas plenum.

PA.: Hinc videtur sequi materiam divisam esse in puncta: divisa est enim in omnes partes possibiles, ac pro inde in minimas. Ergo corpus et spatium ex punctis componentur.

CH.: Quid hic Cartesius?

PA.: Contentus dixisse materiam actu dividi in partes minores omnibus quae a nobis intelligi possunt, monet non esse neganda quae demonstrata putat, tam etsi finita mens nostra non capiat quomodo fi-

*g* in a circular vessel *ABCD,* and let it be a perfect liquid, by which I mean that any part of it, however tiny, could be separated from any other given part. Let there be in it a circular body, not a liquid body but a solid one *H,* fixed on one side of the center of the vessel. And now let the liquid matter be set in motion, or flow: its motion will be faster at *g* than at *e,* and faster at *e* than at *f.* For just as much matter will pass through *g* as through *e* or *f;* but the place *g* is smaller than *e* or *f,* so the smallness of the place is necessarily compensated by the speed of the motion.[44]

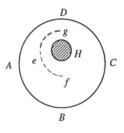

Figure 10

CH.: These things are obvious: for what goes through *e* must necessarily supply what goes through *f,* since we have assumed the vessel to be full: and it, in its turn, must be supplied by what comes from *g.*

PA.: Hence, since instead of the points *g, e,* and *f* we could have taken any other points anywhere we liked and the same reasoning would apply everywhere, it follows that the liquid matter is actually divided everywhere; nor can any point be taken in the line *gef* that is not excited with its own degree of motion, different from the velocity of any other, so that it will be actually separated from any other point assignable.

CH.: This must be conceded, assuming the matter to be perfectly liquid and the vessel full.

PA.: Hence it seems to follow that matter is divided into points: for it is divided into all possible parts, and thus into minima. Therefore body and space will be composed of points.

CH.: What did Descartes say to this?

PA.: Having contented himself with saying that matter is actually divided into parts smaller than all those we can possibly conceive, he warns that the things he thinks he has demonstrated ought not to be denied to exist, even if our finite minds cannot grasp how they oc-

554

ant. Sed aliud est explicare quomodo quid fiat, aliud satisfacere objectioni et evitare absurditatem.

CH.: Debuisset utique explicare quomodo sic materia non resolvatur in pulverem ut ita dicam ex punctis constantem: cum nullum punctum nulli cohaerens relinqui pateat, singula enim per se movebuntur motu differente a motu alterius cujuscunque.

PA.: Si huc usque produxisset ratiocinationem, fortasse recognovisset sententiam suam difficultatibus illis premi quibus laborat compositio continui ex punctis coactusque fuisset utique respondere difficultati.

GA.: Sed quid nos dicemus.

CH.: Poterimus negare liquidum perfectum seu corpus ubique flexile dari.

PA.: Multum interest inter liquidum perfectum et corpus ubique flexile; ego neque atomos Gassendi admitto seu corpus perfecte solidum, neque materiam subtilem Cartesii seu corpus perfecte fluidum, corpus tamen ubique flexile adeo non nego, ut putem omne corpus tale esse. Quae alias demonstrabo. Posito corpore perfecte fluido negari non potest, divisio summa sive in minima; at corpus ubique quidem flexile sed non sine resistentia quadam eaque inaequali, habet partes cohaerentes adhuc, licet varie diductas et complicatas, ac proinde divisio continui non consideranda ut arenae in grana, sed ut chartae vel tunicae in plicas; itaque licet plicae numero infinitae aliae aliis minores fiant, non ideo corpus unquam in puncta seu minima dissolvetur. Habet autem omne liquidum aliquid tenacitatis, itaque licet in partes divellatur, tamen non omnes partes partium iterum divelluntur, sed aliquando tantum figurantur, et transformantur; atque ita non fit dissolutio in puncta usque, licet quodlibet punctum a quolibet motu differat. Quemadmodum si tunicam plicis in infinitum multiplicatis ita signari ponamus ut nulla sit plica tam parva, quin nova plica subdividatur: atque ita nullum punctum in tunica assignabile erit, quin diverso a vicinis motu cieatur, non tamen ab iis divelletur; neque dici poterit tunicam in puncta usque resolutam esse, sed plicae licet aliae

**555**

cur.[45] But it is one thing to explain how something occurs, and an-        *Descartes*
other to satisfy the objection and avoid absurdity.

CH.: He ought to have at least explained how in this case matter is not
resolved into a powder, so to speak, consisting of points, when it is
clear that no point will be left cohering to any of the others, since each
one will move in its own right with a motion different from that of
any other.

PA.: If he had extended his reasoning this far, perhaps he would have
recognized that his own opinion was subject to the difficulties that af-
flict the composition of the continuum from points,[46] and he would at
least have been forced to respond to the difficulty.

GA.: But what shall we ourselves say?

CH.: We could deny that there is such a thing as a perfect liquid, or a
body that is everywhere flexible.

PA.: There's a big difference between a perfect liquid and a body that
is everywhere flexible. I myself admit neither Gassendi's atoms, i.e.
a body that is perfectly solid, nor Descartes' subtle matter, i.e. a body
that is perfectly fluid. But I do not deny the existence of a body that is
everywhere flexible, to the extent that I consider every body to be so,
as I will demonstrate at another time. If a perfectly fluid body is assumed, a finest division, i.e. a division into minima, cannot be denied; but even a body that is everywhere flexible, but not without a
certain and everywhere unequal resistance, still has cohering parts,
although these are opened up and folded together in various ways.
Accordingly the division of the continuum must not be considered to
be like the division of sand into grains, but like that of a sheet of paper or tunic into folds.[47] And so although there occur some folds
smaller than others infinite in number, a body is never thereby dissolved into points or minima. On the contrary, every liquid has some
tenacity, so that although it is torn into parts, not all the parts of the
parts are so torn in their turn; instead they merely take shape for some
time, and are transformed; and yet in this way there is no dissolution
all the way down into points, even though any point is distinguished
from any other by motion. It is just as if we suppose a tunic to be
scored with folds multiplied to infinity in such a way that there is no
fold so small that it is not subdivided by a new fold: and yet in this
way no point in the tunic will be assignable without its being moved
in different directions by its neighbors, although it will not be torn
apart by them. And the tunic cannot be said to be resolved all the way
down into points; instead, although some folds are smaller than oth-

555

aliis in infinitum minores, semper extensa sunt corpora, et puncta nunquam partes fiunt, sed semper extrema tantum manent.

TH.: Divine ista mihi dicta videntur, et mirifica haec a plicis comparatio est.

PA.: Gaudeo vobis sententiam meam probari, quam alias uberius exponam, nam a controversia de liquido et solido, vacuo et pleno verae et certae de natura rerum Hypotheseos constitutio pendet, quas ego quaestiones demonstratione dirimere mihi posse videor. Quod alterius loci temporisque est.

GA.: Speramus te nobis tam praeclaras cogitationes non negaturum: eaque conditione tibi praesentem eius materiae tractationem remittimus.

PA.: Vestra ergo venia in viam redeo. Scis, Charine, non frustra nos huc digressos.

CH.: Scilicet conclusimus continuum neque in puncta dissolvi posse, neque ex ipsis constare, neque certum ac determinatum (finitum vel infinitum) esse numerum assignabilium in eo punctorum.

PA.: Ergo mi Charine motus quoque continuum uniformis nullus est, quo scilicet corpus spatium aliquod utcunque exiguum tempore aliquo transmittat. Demonstravimus enim mutationem loci esse duarum existentiarum quibus corpus duobus proximis momentis in duobus proximis punctis est, aggregatum, adeoque continuando motum multiplicabimus tantum haec aggregata, ergo si continuata hac mutatione spatium tempore absolvitur, spatium ex punctis, tempus ex momentis componi.

**556**

CH.: Non possum negare posito motu continuo uniformi, et stabilita quam dixisti, mutationis notione, componi continuum ex punctis. Nam durante motu, ut uni puncto atque uno momento aliud proximum sumsimus, ita nulla ratio est cur non et huic secundo aliud tertium proximum assumamus; cumque hoc modo pergendo tandem spatium tempusque absolvantur, utique ex punctis momentisve sibi immediatis constabunt.

PA.: At constare ex illis non posse est credo a nobis demonstratum.

CH.: Concedendum est ergo quicquid tergiversemur, motum continuum quo mobile aliquo temporis tractu aliquem locum successive sine quiete intercedente uniformiter transmittat impossibilem esse.

ers to infinity, bodies are always extended and points never become parts, but always remain mere extrema.

TH.: To me what you have said seems divinely inspired, and the analogy with folds is marvelous.

PA.: I am glad you approve of my opinion, which I will expound more fully at another time. For the establishing of a true and certain hypothesis about the nature of things depends on the controversy about liquid and solid, and vacuum and plenum. These are questions which I think I can resolve with a demonstration; but this is something for another place and time.

GA.: We hope you won't deny us such brilliant thoughts; and on this condition we will forgive you a treatment of this matter now.

PA.: With your permission, then, I'll get back under way. You are aware, Charinus, that we have not digressed here in vain?

CH.: Of course. We have concluded that the continuum can neither be dissolved into points nor composed of them, and that there is no fixed and determinate number (either finite or infinite) of points assignable in it.

PA.: Then, my dear Charinus, there is also no continuous uniform motion, that is to say, one where a body passes over some space however small in a certain time. For we have demonstrated change of place to be the aggregate of two existences by which the body is at two neighboring points at two neighboring moments, so that by continuing the motion we will simply multiply these aggregates. Therefore if a space is completed by continuing this change for a time, then space will be composed of points and time of moments.

**556**

CH.: Assuming a uniform continuous motion, and taking the notion of change you spoke of as established, I cannot deny that the continuum is composed of points. For so long as the motion lasts, just as we assumed that next to one point or one moment there would be another, so there is no reason why we should not assume there to be a third next to this second. And since, continuing in this way, space and time will finally be completed, they will certainly consist of points or moments immediately next to each other.

PA.: But we have, I believe, demonstrated that they cannot consist of these.

CH.: Therefore, however we may keep changing our minds, it must be conceded that a continuous motion, in which a moving body uniformly traverses some place in some stretch of time successively and without any intervening rest, is impossible.

PA.: Constat tamen locum a mobili transmitti, sive aliquem esse motum.

CH.: Hoc utique experimur, neque enim nostrum est, sensuum fidem in dubium vocare et de veritate motus dubitare.

PA.: Atqui mobile locum durante quiete non transmittit.

CH.: Non certe.

PA.: Et inter duas quietes ne ulla quidem motus continue portio quantulocunque tempore intercedit alioqui de eo redirent priores difficultates. Ergo vel nil nisi quies erit, nec corpus omnino progredietur, sublatusque erit motus e natura; vel inter quietes interponetur motus instantaneus per saltum, ita ut corpus quod aliquamdiu quievit in hoc loco usque ad hoc momentum, proximo momento existere et quiescere incipiat in loco aliquo dissito, ita ut non transierit per loca intermedia.

CH.: Jam agnosco quo me adigas, et vix tandem praecipitio vicinus periculum video. Effecisti praestigiis tuis, unum, ut reliquum sit corpus scilicet a loco in locum per saltum transire, quemadmodum si ego uno statim momento Romam transferrer: quoniam enim nullum est tempus quo motus continuum duret, sequitur punctum mobile *E*, ubi fuerit in loco *A*, per tempus *MN*, transferri in locum *B* momento *N*, **557** ibique permanere tempore *NP*, quo finito rursus momento *P* transsiliat in *C*. Unde sequi videtur uno momento *N* punctum mobile *E* esse simul in toto loco *AB*, quemadmodum idem punctum E vicissim toto tempore [*MN*] est in uno puncto *A*. Sed vide an non absurdum sit idem corpus simul in pluribus locis esse.

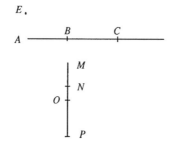

PA.: Still, we know that a place is traversed by a moving body, that is, that there is some motion.

CH.: This is what we experience, certainly, and it is not our place to call into question the reliability of the senses and to doubt the reality of motion.

PA.: And yet a moving body does not traverse a place while it remains at rest.

CH.: Certainly not.

PA.: And between two rests not even a portion of continuous motion intervenes for however short a time, otherwise our previous difficulties will return concerning this. Therefore either there will be nothing but rest, the body will make no progress at all, and motion will be eliminated from nature; or else there will be interposed between the rests an instantaneous motion by a leap, so that a body which was at rest in this place for some time till this moment, should at the next moment begin to exist and be at rest in some separate place, in such a way that it did not pass through the intermediate places.

CH.: Now I recognize where you would drive me, and close to the precipice I can finally just see the danger. With your sleights of hand you've brought it about that it only remains for a body to pass from place to place by a leap, just as if I were immediately transferred to Rome in a single moment. For since a continuous motion does not last for any time, it follows that when a moving point $E$ has been in place $A$ for a time $MN$, it will be transferred to place $B$ at moment $N$, and will remain there for a time $NP$, and at the end of this time, at moment $P$, it will again jump over into $C$. Whence it seems to follow that at one moment $N$ the moving point $E$ is in the whole place $AB$ simultaneously, just as the same point $E$ in its turn is at one point $A$ for the whole time $[MN]$.[48] But see if it isn't absurd for the same body to be in several places at once.

**557**

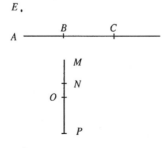

Figure 11

PA.: Qui saltum hunc admittent, non illud volent momento utriusque temporis communi *N* corpus esse in pluribus locis; reciderent enim in difficultates superiores; si aliquod momentum commune duorum statuum quietis scilicet in *A,* et quietis in *B* extra *A* assignarent. Sed dicent *N* ultimum (ipsius *MN*) temporis momentum existendi in *A* immediate excipi ab *O* primo momento (ipsius *OP*) temporis existendi non in *A,* sed in *B,* tempora autem *MN* et *OP* immediate esse atque habere sua extrema *N, O* indistantia sive contigua habere.

GA.: Obsecro te Pacidi jocarisne an serio nobis haec narras.

CH.: Dicis, Pacidi, punctum mobile *E* cum tempore *MN* extiterit ac quieverit in spatii puncto *A,* tempore proximo *OP* existere atque quiescere in spatii puncto B. Quomodo autem illuc venerit non dicis.

❖❖❖❖❖❖❖❖❖❖❖❖❖❖❖❖❖❖❖❖❖❖❖❖❖❖❖❖❖❖❖❖❖❖❖

PA.: Non possum aliter dicere quam excludendo sententias falsas. Jam enim ostendi non esse unquam in intermediis punctis; sed statim cum prius hic fuerit, mox illic esse.

558    CH.: Obsecro, dic nobis aliquid quo sententia tua saltem illustretur.

PA.: Expugnatis tarditatem meam: itaque igitur sentio, mobile E, cum aliquandiu in A fuerit, ibi extingui atque annihilari, et in B emergere atque recreari, motumque aliter explicare, impossibile esse facileque a vobis judicari, omnes illas machinas ratiocinationum eum in usum a me admotas, ut paulatim vos adigerem ad tanti momenti veritatem etiam praemonitos et invitos et renitentes.[L5] Agite nunc excutite omnes angulos, et si quid habetis, demonstrationi respondete.

TH.: Tam solicite semper attendi ad omnes ratiocinationum vestrarum articulos, ut vero putem aliquid a me reperiri posse, quo dissolvantur.

---

L5. IN THE MARGIN: Quidni potius momento tantum existere, medio tempore non existere, sequetur si poneretur res nisi agant non esse, nec agere nisi mutentur.

PA.: Those who would admit this leap would not maintain that the body is in several places at the moment $N$ common to the two times; for they would fall back into the above difficulties if they were to assign some moment that was common to the two states of rest, that in $A$ and that in $B$ apart from $A$. On the contrary, they would say that $N$, the last moment of the time $MN$ of its existence at $A$, is immediately succeeded by $O$, the first moment of the time $OP$ of its existence not at $A$, but at $B$. The times $MN$ and $OP$, though, are immediately next to each other, and in fact they have indistant or contiguous extrema $N$ and $O$.

GA.: I implore you, Pacidius, are you joking or are you telling us these things in all seriousness?

CH.: You say, Pacidius, that after the moving point $E$ has existed and been at rest at the point of space $A$ for the time $MN$, it will exist and be at rest for the next period of time $OP$ at the point of space $B$. But how this could happen you do not say.[49]

❖❖❖❖❖❖❖❖❖❖❖❖❖❖❖❖❖❖❖❖❖❖❖❖❖❖❖❖❖❖❖❖❖❖❖

PA.: I cannot say anything except by ruling out false opinions.[50] For now I have shown that it is never at the intermediate points; instead, immediately after first being here, it is next there.

**558**  CH.: Please tell us something by means of which your view could at least be illustrated.

PA.: You are attacking me for my slowness. Well, then, I am of the opinion that the moving point $E$, after it has been at $A$ for a while, is then extinguished and annihilated, and emerges and is recreated at $B$; and that it is impossible for motion to be explained in any other way. And you may easily judge that I have deployed all these logical stratagems so as to gradually drive you all, even unwilling and struggling as predicted, towards a truth of such importance.[L5] Come on, now, cut all the corners, and if any of you have a reply to this demonstration, then give it.

TH.: All this time I have listened so attentively[51] to all the twists and turns of your arguments that I should think I can find something by which to refute them.

L5. IN THE MARGIN: Why not rather say that the conclusion that things exist only for a moment, and do not exist at an intermediate time, will follow if it is supposed that things do not exist unless they act, and do not act unless they change?

GA.: Utile tamen erit omnia in unum recollecta exhibere, ut fides illis constet magis.

PA.: Hoc Charinum optime facturum confido.

CH.: Tentabo. Quicquid movetur mutat locum, sive mutatur quoad locum.[L6] Quicquid mutatur id duobus momentis sibi proximis in duobus est statibus oppositis, uno in priore altero in posteriore. Ergo Quicquid continue mutatur per aliquod tempus eius momento cuilibet existendi in statu uno, succedit eo tempore durante momentum proximum existendi in alio statu. Quoniam ergo toto illo tempore durante momentum momento immediate succedit. Ergo tempus hoc totum componitur ex aggregato momentorum quod est impossibile. Continua ergo per aliquod tempus mutatio impossibilis, ergo et motus continuum impossibilis. Sit jam mobile punctum *E* transferendum ex puncto *A*, in punctum *C*, tempore *MP*. Quod fiet aut motu continuo aut quiete continua, aut mixtura motus et quietis. Non motu continuo, quia is impossibilis, non quiete continua, ea enim motui opponitur, ergo mixtura motus et quietis. Ergo partim quiescit partim movetur mobile tempore *NP* durante.[L7]

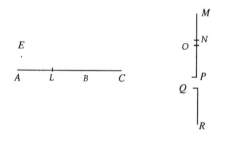

**559**     Ponamus exhiberi hanc mixturam et quiescere in puncto *A* tempore *MN*, inde transferendum in *B* tempore *NO*. Quiescere autem in *B* tempore *OP*, donec inde transferatur in *C* tempore *PQ*, ubi rursus quiescat tempore *QR*, donec rursus progrediatur et ita porro. His positis ajo

L6. IN THE MARGIN: (NB. Sine relatione ad motum videndum an generaliter demonstrari possit continuum non componi ex minimis et ita nec tempus).

L7. IN THE MARGIN: Durante statu nulla fit creatio, alioqui si quolibet momento fieret actus, continuum esset ex momentis.

GA.: Nevertheless, it would be useful to display all of them collected together into one, so that more faith can be had in them.

PA.: I am sure Charinus would do this best.

CH.: I will try. Whatever moves changes place, i.e. changes with respect to place.[L6] Whatever changes is in two opposite states at two
neighboring moments, one in the earlier moment, the other in the later
one. Therefore: If anything changes continuously for some time, then
any moment of its existing in one state during this time is followed by a
next moment of existing in another state. Since, therefore, one moment follows immediately upon another during the whole of that time,
it follows that this whole time is composed of an aggregate of moments. But this is impossible. Therefore a continuous change through
some time is impossible, therefore continuous motion is impossible
too. Now let there be a moving point E, which is to be transferred from
the point C in the time MP. This will happen either by continuous motion, or by continuous rest, or by a mixture of motion and rest. Not by
continuous motion, since this is impossible, not by continuous rest,
since this is the opposite of motion, therefore by a mixture of motion
and rest. Therefore the moving point is partly at rest and partly in motion during the time NP.[L7]

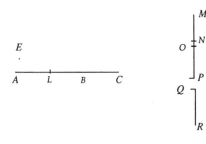

Figure 12

**559**     Suppose we give a representation of this mixture, and the moving
point is at rest at the point A for the time MN, to be transferred from
there to B during the time NO. At B it rests for the time OP, until it is
transferred from there to C during the time PQ, where it again rests for

L6. IN THE MARGIN: (N.B. Without relation to motion, it must be seen whether it
can be demonstrated generally that the continuum is not composed of minima, and
thus neither is time.)

L7. IN THE MARGIN: During a state no creation occurs, otherwise if [such] an act
occurred at any moment, the continuum would consist of moments.

tempus *NO* necessario esse minimum, sive momenta *N* et *O* (idem est de *P* et *Q*) sibi contigua atque proxima esse, neque ullum inter ipsa assumi posse aliud momentum, alioqui enim haberetur motus continuus ex *A* in *B* per aliquem temporis tractum *NO,* quod impossibile ostendimus. Quoniam autem mobile momento *N* est in *A,* momento *O* in *B,* nullum erit momentum quo sit in puncto intermedio *L,* adeoque mobile *E* saltum faciet sive transcreabitur ex *A* in *B,* id est evanescens in *A,* resuscitabitur statum in *B,* neque enim aliter explicari potest, quomodo corpus de loco in locum nec tamen per intermedia transferatur.

PA.: Mirifica brevitate totam demonstrationis vim complexus es.[L8] Unum addo non esse quod vos transcreatio turbet. (Nam dicere rem hic existere cessare, illic autem existere incipere, sublato transitu intermedio idem est ac dicere hic annihilari, illic resuscitari. Idem generaliter in omni mutatione dici potest, postquam momentum transitus sive status medii sustulimus.)[L9] Nam si unus simpliciter dicat rem esse desinere in statu priore, et nunc esse incipere in alio, alius vero dicat annihilari in statu priore, resuscitari in posteriore; utrumlicet admittas nullum in ipsa re discrimen notari potest, sed tantum in eo, quod prior causam dissimulat, alius eam exprimit: Nulla autem causa intelligi potest, cur res quae in aliquo statu esse cessavit, in alio esse incipiat (sublato quippe intermedio statu) nisi substantia quaedam permanens, quae et destruxit primum et produxit novum, quoniam sequens status ex praecedente utique necessario non sequitur.

❖❖❖❖❖❖❖❖❖❖❖❖❖❖❖❖❖❖❖❖❖❖❖❖❖❖❖❖❖❖❖❖❖❖❖❖

L8. IN THE MARGIN: (+ nonnihil hic erratum nimio contrahendi demonstrationem studio, tantum enim supra ostensum spatium non componi ex punctis, minime vero tempus non componi ex instantibus. Facile autem ex superioribus suppleri potest. Illud praesertim considerando, quod posito spatio continuo, et motu quoque etiam tempus necessario continuum est. +)

L9. IN THE MARGIN: (NB. uti corpora in spatio sunt indissoluta, et intra haec alia rursus interponuntur minora, nec ita ullus est locus vacuus corporibus; ita in tem-

the time $QR$, until it again moves on, and so forth. Assuming these things to be so, I say that the time $NO$ is necessarily a minimum, i.e. that the moments $N$ and $O$ (the same goes for $P$ and $Q$) are contiguous and next to each other. And no other moment can be assumed between them, for otherwise we would have a continuous motion from $A$ to $B$ through some stretch of time $NO$, which we have shown to be impossible. But since the moving point is at $A$ at the moment $N$, and at $B$ at the moment $O$, there will be no moment when it is at the intermediate point $L$. And so the moving point $E$ will make a leap, i.e. be trans-created[52] from $A$ to $B$, i.e. vanishing at $A$, the state will be resuscitated at $B$. For there is no other way to explain how a body may be transferred from one place to another and yet not through the ones in between.

PA.: You have made a wonderfully concise abbreviation of the whole force of the demonstration.[L8] I add only that transcreation is not what disturbs you. (For to say that a thing ceases to exist here, but begins to exist there, with the transition between them eliminated, is the same as saying that it is here annihilated, there resuscitated. The same can be said in general about every change, when we have eliminated the moment of transition, i.e. of the middle state.)[L9] For if one person were simply to say that a thing ceases to be in its earlier state, and now begins to exist in another one, someone else might say that it was annihilated in the earlier state and resuscitated in the later one. Whichever of the two you accept, no distinction can be observed in the thing itself, but only in the fact that the first way of putting it conceals the cause, whilst the second brings this out. But no cause can be conceived for why a thing that has ceased to exist in one state should begin to exist in another (inasmuch as the intermediate state has been eliminated), except a kind of permanent substance that has both destroyed the first thing and produced the new one, since the succeeding state does not necessarily follow from the preceding one.

❖ ❖ ❖ ❖ ❖ ❖ ❖ ❖ ❖ ❖ ❖ ❖ ❖ ❖ ❖ ❖ ❖ ❖ ❖ ❖ ❖ ❖ ❖ ❖ ❖ ❖ ❖ ❖ ❖ ❖ ❖ ❖ ❖ ❖ ❖ ❖

L8. IN THE MARGIN: (+ Here there is some mistake caused by too much eagerness in abridging the demonstration, for it is only shown above that space is not composed of points, but not that time is not composed of instants. However, this demonstration can easily be supplied from the above, especially by considering that if space is supposed continuous, and motion too, then time is also necessarily continuous. +)

L9. IN THE MARGIN: (N.B. Just as bodies in space form an unbroken connection, and other smaller bodies are interposed inside them in their turn, so that there is no

**560**   PA.: Qui saltus illos statuet, nihil aliud habet quam ut dicat, mobile *E*
cum aliquandiu in loco *A* fuerit, extingui et annihilari, et in *B* momento post iterum emergere ac recreari; quod motus genus possimus
dicere *transcreationem.*

GA.: Si hoc pro demonstrato haberi posset, rem profecto magnam
egissemus. Haberemus enim demonstratum creatorem rerum.

PA.: An ergo huic sententiae acquiescis Charine.

CH.: Ego vero ita hic quiesco, ut avis laqueo deprehensa ac diu sese
effugiendi spe nequicquam agitans, quae tandem lassata concidit.

PA.: Hoc est potius non habes quod respondeas quam ut assentiaris.

CH.: Fateor nam me valde mordent isti saltus; cum enim magnitudo
aut parvitas nihil ad rem faciat, aeque mihi absurdum videtur corpus-
culum aliquod exiguum ab uno extremo lineolae quantulaecunque ad
aliud pervenire, non tamen per puncta intermedia, quam me Romam
momento transferri intermediis omnibus perinde omissis, ac si in
natura non essent. Pone enim illi corpusculo rationem ac sensum
dari, eam profecto inconcinnitatem deprehenderet in saltu suo qui
nobis exiguus, at ipsi satis magnus est, quam nos in nostro. Ponamus
in corpore nostro esse animalcula tanto minora nobis, quanto caput
humanum minus est orbe terrarum; horum animalculorum unum si
ab una auricula ad alteram pervenerit, dicent socii eius, si ratione uti
fingantur, ab uno polo ad alterum pervenisse. Itaque omnia proportione sibi respondent et inconcinnitas aliqua atque violentia, sive
quod eodem redit, miraculum ordinarium, quale est saltus iste, tam in
parvis, quam in magnis vitari debet.

---

pore dum quaedam post momentaneum saltum durant, interim alia quorum subtil-
iores sunt mutationes in tempore aliquo intermedio et inter haec rursus alia. Et in
his velut ictibus seu vibrationibus mira videtur esse harmonia utique necesse est
per aliquod tempus durare statuum seu esse mutationum vacuum. Uti puncta extrema corporum seu contactus; ita mutationes statuum. Corpora minora celerius
moventur, majora tardius in pleno. Nec tempus ullum nec locus vacuus. Durante
quolibet statu aliqua alia mutantur.)

**560**   PA.: Anyone advocating these leaps would only mean to say that after the moving point $E$ has been in place $A$ for a while, it is extinguished and annihilated, and at the moment afterwards emerges again and is recreated at $B$; a kind of motion that we may call *transcreation*.

GA.: If this could be taken as demonstrated, then we would have done something really important. For we would have demonstrated the creator of the universe.

PA.: Don't you agree with this opinion, then, Charinus?

CH.: I am keeping very quiet here, just like a bird caught in a snare, which, after fruitlessly struggling for a long time in the hope of escape, finally collapses from exhaustion.

PA.: That is to say that you have nothing to respond, rather than that you agree.

CH.: Yes, for I find these leaps of yours very excruciating. For given that size has nothing to do with the matter, it seems to me just as absurd that some very small corpuscle should get from one end to the other of an arbitrarily small linelet without going through the intermediate points, as that I should be transferred to Rome in a moment, leaving out all the intermediate places in the same way, as if there weren't any in nature. For supposing this corpuscle were given reason and sensation, it would certainly find a lack of proportion in its own leap—which, although tiny to us, is big enough for it—just as we would in ours. Let us suppose that there are in our bodies animalcules that are as small compared to us as a human head is to the terrestrial sphere. If one of these animalcules were to pass through from one ear to the other, then its friends would say, if we imagine them using reason, that it had passed from one pole to the other. Thus everything would be in corresponding proportion for them, and a lack or violation of proportion—or what amounts to the same thing, an ordinary miracle—such as this leap of yours is, ought to be avoided just as much in the small as in the large.

---

place void of bodies; so in time, while some things last through a momentaneous leap, others meanwhile undergo more subtle changes at some intermediate time, and others between them in their turn. And in these (as it were) blows or vibrations there seems to be a wonderful harmony. At any rate, it is necessary for states to endure for some time or be void of changes. As the endpoints of bodies, or points of contact, so the changes of states. Smaller bodies move more quickly in a plenum, larger ones more slowly. Nor is any time or place empty. During any state whatsoever some other things are changing.)

PA.: Recte facis Charine, quod huic sententiae resistis, quae pugnat cum pulchritudine rerum, et sapientia Dei. Alioqui perinde esset ac si Deus incongruitates quasdam, quas in natura scilicet evitare non poterat, tegere tantum nobis ac dissimulare voluisset, transferendo scilicet illas in minutiora rerum, ubi animadverti non possint. Sed vides ipse, ut fortius adhuc stringam, ubicunque ponamus hunc saltum fieri, ibi eodem modo cum potuisse declinari; nam co jure quo nos contendimus, saltum illum contingere non apud nos, sed apud minutiora quaedam corpora, eodem jure eadem minutiora corpora, si ratiocinari de his rebus fingerentur, eandem inconcinnitatem ad minora adhuc alia relegarent. Quod rationi etiam consentaneum est, nam cum eligendi potestas est, utique sapiens minorem potius inconcinnitatem eliget; itaque jure dicent aiiimalcula illa, in minoribus potius hunc saltum debuisse evenire quam apud se. Sed cum minora alia quaecunque eodem argumento uti possint, patet saltus istos semper

**561**   ad minora ac minora propelli et nusquam consistere posse in natura rerum. Nec refert quod corpuscula illa forte non sint ratione praedita, neque enim hic quaeritur quid corpora pro se dicere possint, sed quid Deus omnium rerum Curator, dicere possit pro ipsis, non enim tam aliis quaerit satisfacere quam sibi. Denique, quod rem omnem conficit, nihil sine ratione facit sapientissimus rerum autor; nulla autem ratio est, cur huic potius quam illi corpusculorum gradui saltus illi miraculosi ascribantur, nisi atomos scilicet admittamus, seu corpora ita firma ut nullam subdivisionem nullumve flexum patiantur, his enim praeter summae soliditatis miraculum (nam sine extraordinario quodam Dei concursu explicari non potest), hoc novum miraculum saliendi de loco in locum omissis intermediis non incommode tribuemus. Sed talia ego corpora in natura rerum esse non puto; eo ipso plane argumento, quo hos saltus excludo, nulla enim ratio est, cur Deus hic stiterit opificem manum, harumque solarum creaturarum interiora sine aliarum creaturarum varietate velut torpentia et mortua reliquerit. Et profecto si corpuscula atoma ipsa aut atomis vicina sensu ac ratione praedita fingerentur, non nisi inconcinnitates ac quotidiana miracula sese offerrent. Legesque naturae sapientis, quas ali-

PA.: You do well to resist this opinion, Charinus, which is offensive to
the beauty of things and the wisdom of God. Otherwise it would be
exactly as if God had wanted to hide from us alone certain incon-
gruities that he evidently could not avoid in nature, and to disguise
them by transferring them to the realm of much smaller things, where
we wouldn't be able to notice them. But you yourself see, if I might
draw this together more tightly still, that wherever we might suppose
this leap to occur, we could have avoided it in the same way. For just
as we contended that the leap would not occur among us but only
among certain much smaller bodies, by the same right these same
more minute bodies, if we imagined them reasoning about these
things, would relegate this same disproportion to other still smaller
things. And this is also consistent with reason, for given the power of
choosing, a wise one, at least, would prefer to choose a smaller disproportion. So those animalcules are justified in saying that this leap
should have occurred in smaller things rather than among them. But
since any other smaller beings whatsoever could use the same argument, it is obvious that the leaps in question could always be driven
**561**     down into the realms of smaller and smaller things and could not remain in existence anywhere in the nature of things. Nor does it matter
that the corpuscles are not as it happens endowed with reason, for we
are not inquiring here what these bodies could say on their own behalf, but what God the Keeper of All Things could say for them; for
he does not so much seek to satisfy others as himself. Finally, because
He creates every thing, the supremely wise author of things does
nothing without a reason; yet there is no reason why these miraculous
leaps should be ascribed to this rather than that grade of corpuscles—
unless, of course, we admit atoms, i.e. bodies so firm that they do not
suffer any subdivision or bending. But to these atoms, in addition to
the miracle of their utmost solidity (which is a miracle because it
cannot be explained without a kind of extraordinary concurrence of
God),[53] we must, without undue inconvenience, attribute this new
miracle of jumping from place to place whilst omitting the places in
between. But I do not think that there are such bodies in the nature of
things; plainly, by the very same argument I use to exclude these
leaps, since there is no reason why God should have put a stop to his
handiwork at this point and left only these creatures without a variety
of other creatures inside them, as if they were paralyzed or dead. And
indeed, if we were to imagine atomic corpuscles, or corpuscles close
to atoms, to be endowed with reason and sensation, they would en-
counter nothing but disproportions and everyday miracles, and the

quando exponemus, minime observarentur. Sed de Atomis alias accuratius dicemus, nunc satis sit saltus utcunque ita refutasse; ut appareat declinandos esse, si quidem vitari possint.

TH.: Sed hoc opus hic labor est, ita enim tute nos implicuisti, ut exitum non videam, quin et denique ingratum videtur evertere totam aedificii nostri structuram, aut si mavis Penelopes telam retexere.

PA.: Videtis amici nos circa ipsa rerum primordia ac velut summas versari, ubi profecto patientia opus est, neque ulla mora longa videri debet. Quodsi relegenda nobis vestigia sunt culpare debemus festinationem nostram, atque cavendi artem discere ab exemplis. Denique neminem vestrum esse puto, cui non hi saltus aegre faciant; itaque necessitate quadam ad retexenda nostra argumenta compellimur.

GA.: Resumamus ergo quam primum, ac totam ratiocinationum praecedentium seriem breviter recollectam exhibeamus, ut uno obtutu lustrari possit faciliusque appareat, ubi sit hiatus.

**562**

PA.: Hoc Charinum optime facturum confido.

CH.: Tentabo:

Quicquid movetur, mutat locum, sive mutatur quoad locum. Quicquid mutatur id duobus momentis sibi proximis in duobus est statibus oppositis.

Quicquid continue mutatur eius cuilibet momento existendi in statu uno succedit momentum existendi in statu opposito. Itaque speciatim:

Si aliquod corpus continue movetur, ejus cuilibet momento existendi in puncto spatii uno, succedit momentum existendi in puncto spatii alio.

Haec duo puncta spatii vel sibi sunt immediate, vel mediata.

Si immediate, sequitur lineam componi ex punctis, tota enim linea transmittitur hoc transitu a puncto ad aliud punctum immediatum.

Lineam autem componi ex punctis est absurdum.

Si mediata sint duo puncta tunc corpus ab uno ad alterum momento transiens vel simul in intermediis et extremis erit, adeoque in pluribus locis, quod absurdum.

Vel faciet saltum, seu transibit ab uno extremo ad alterum omissis intermediis. Quod etiam est absurdum.

laws of wise Nature, which we will expound at another time, would not be observed at all. But we will discuss atoms more thoroughly elsewhere; for now it is enough one way or another to have refuted leaps in such a way that it is obvious that they must be avoided, if indeed they can be.

TH.: But this is a hard thing to require here, for you have so tangled us up that I see no way out that does not in the end also seem unwelcome, overturning our entire construction, or if you prefer, unraveling Penelope's yarn.

PA.: You see, my friends, we are concerned with the first and as it were highest principles of things, where there is certainly a need for patience, and no delay ought to seem long. But if we have to retrace our footsteps, we should blame our haste, and learn from these examples the art of exercising caution. Finally, I do not think you will find anyone for whom these leaps would not cause difficulty; and so it is a necessity of sorts that compels us to unravel our arguments.

GA.: Then let us go back to the very beginning and give a précis of the whole series of preceding arguments collected together, so it can be reviewed in a single glance, making it easier to see where there might be a gap.

**562**

PA.: I am sure Charinus would do this best.

CH.: I will try:

Whatever moves changes place, i.e. changes with respect to place. Whatever changes is in two opposite states at two neighboring moments.

If anything changes continuously, then any moment of its existence in one state is followed by a moment of existence in an opposite state. Thus in particular:

If any body moves continuously, then any moment of its existence at one point of space is followed by a moment of existence at another point of space.

These two points of space are either immediately next to each other, or mediately.

If immediately, it follows that a line is composed of points, for the whole line will be traversed by this passage from one point to the other immediately next to it.

But for a line to be composed of points is absurd.

If the two points are mediately next to each other, then a body passing from one to the other in a moment will either be simultaneously at

Ergo corpus non continue movetur, sed quietes et motus sunt sibi interspersi.

Sed motus ille interspersus rursus est vel continuus, vel alia quiete interspersus; et sic in infinitum.

Ergo vel alicubi incidemus in motum continuum purum, quem jam ostendimus esse absurdum.

Vel fateri debemus, nullum omnino superesse motum nisi momentaneum, sed omnia in quietes resolvi.

Rursus ergo incidimus in motum momentaneum, seu saltum, quem vitare volebamus.

PA.: Eleganter profecto Charine summam collationis nostrae complexus es. Videamus ergo an uspiam resisti possit.

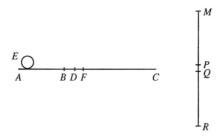

CH.: Quo rectius omnia expendam, figuras adhibebo, et superiores positiones nostras ad eas exigam. Sit mobile punctum *E,* quod momento *M* sit in loco *A,* et momento *R* in loco *C,* nec ullum assumi punctum possit ut *B* in quo non aliquo medii temporis momento ut *P* fuerit, ut scilicet saltus vitetur. Pro certo etiam habeo, quod a te demonstratum est Pacidi in ipso momento ut *P* nullam fieri mutationem, alioqui simul contradictoria essent vera. Itaque si momento *P* ipsum mobile est in loco *B,* et contingere debet mutatio utique, nihil aliud asseri potest, quam momento proximo Q fore in puncto proximo *D* ac duas lineas *AB, CD* se attingere in punctis diversis illam puncto *B,* hanc puncto *D;* eodemque modo duo tempora *MP, RQ* se attingere instantibus duobus illud instanti *P,* hoc instanti *Q.* Que-

**563**

the intermediate points and at the endpoints, which is absurd; or it will make a leap, and will pass from one endpoint to the other by omitting the ones in between. Which is also absurd.

Therefore the body does not move continuously, but rests and motions are mutually interspersed.

But the interspersed motion is again either continuous, or interspersed with another rest; and so on to infinity.

Therefore either somewhere we will come across a pure continuous motion, which we have already shown to be absurd, or we must admit that no motion is left at all except momentaneous motion, and that everything is resolved into rests.

So again we come across momentaneous motion, i.e. a leap, which we wanted to avoid.

PA.: You have summed up the gist of our discussion really elegantly, Charinus. So let us see whether it can be resisted at any point.

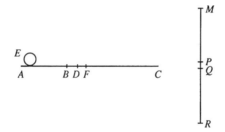

Figure 13

CH.: In order to weigh everything more exactly, I shall make use of some figures, and examine our above positions in terms of them. Let there be a moving point *E* which is at place *A* at moment *M* and place *C* at moment *R,* and let it be the case that no point, such as *B,* can be assumed without *E*'s being there at some moment of the intervening time, such as *P*—this, in order that a leap be avoided. I also hold for certain what you demonstrated, Pacidius, that no change could occur in the moment *P* itself, otherwise contradictories would be true at the same time. Accordingly, if at the moment *P* this moving point is at place *B,* and a change must in any case occur, then all that can be asserted is that at the next moment *Q* it will be at the next point *D,* and that the two lines *AB* and *CD* will touch at different points, the former at point *B,* the latter at point *D;* and in the same way the two times *MP* and *RQ* will touch at two instants, the former at instant *P,* the latter at

563

madmodum duae sphaerae se tangunt duobus diversis punctis, quae simul quidem sunt, unum tamen non sunt. Si jam in loco tempore et motu uniformitatem admittamus, necessario, quod de uno puncto *B* et uno instanti *P* diximus dicendum erit de quolibet alio puncto, et quolibet alio instanti. Itaque quod diximus de puncto *B* dicendum erit et de puncto *D,* adeoque uti punctum *B* excipitur immediato puncto *D,* ita punctum *D* excipietur alio immediato puncto, et hoc rursus alio, usque ad *C,* adeoque linea componetur ex punctis, quoniam mobile singula haec puncta sibi continue immediata transeundo lineam percurret. Lineam autem ex punctis componi absurdum esse demonstratum est. Quoniam autem negari non potest uniformitas in loco et tempore per se consideratis, superest ergo ut negetur in ipso motu. Et in primis negandum est uti puncto *B* sumtum est punctum immediatum *D,* ita puncto *D* sumi posse aliud punctum immediatum.

PA.: Sed quo jure id negas? cum nulla sit in linea uniformi continua praerogativa unius puncti prae altero.

CH.: At nobis hic sermo est non de linea aliqua uniformi continua, in qua duo eiusmodi puncta sibi immediata *B* et *D* ne sumi quidem potuissent, sed de linea *AC* jam actu in partes secta, a natura, quia ponimus mutationem ita factam, ut uno momento existeret mobile in unius ejus partis *AB* extremo *B,* et altero in alterius partis *DC* extremo *D.* Estque discrimen inter has lineas duas actu a se divisas contiguas, et unam indivisam seu continuam manifestum, quod ut jam Aristoteles notavit, extrema *B, D* in duobus contiguis lineis differunt, in una continua coincidunt, quemadmodum et supra notavimus. Nego igitur aliud punctum ipsi *D* immediatum in linea *DC* sumi posse, neque enim aliud punctum in rerum natura admittendum censo, quam quod sit alicuius extensi extremum.

PA.: Recte ratiocinaris, posito naturam sic actu lineam *AC* divisisse in partes *AB* et DC. Sed haec divisio fuit arbitraria. Quid si ergo sic divisionem instituisset ut *D* referretur ad lineam *AB,* et fieret linea *AD.*

**564**

instant $Q$—just as two spheres are tangent to each other at two different points, these points being together, but not one. If now we admit uniformity in place, time, and motion, then what we have said about one point $B$ and one instant $P$ will necessarily have to be said about any other point and any other instant whatsoever. Thus what we said about point $B$ will also have to be said about point $D$. And so just as point $B$ is immediately succeeded by point $D$, so point $D$ will be succeeded by another point immediately next to it, and this again by another, and so on right up to $C$. And so the line will be composed of points, since the moving point traverses the line by passing through every single one of these points that are continuously immediately next to each other. But for a line to be composed of points has been demonstrated to be absurd. Since, on the other hand, uniformity cannot be denied in place and time considered in themselves, it therefore remains for it to be denied in motion itself. And in particular it must be denied that another point can be assumed immediately next to the point $D$, in the same way that the point $D$ was assumed immediately next to point $B$.

PA.: But by what right do you deny this, since there is no prerogative in a continuous uniform line for one point over another?

CH.: But our discussion is not about a continuous uniform line, in which two such points $B$ and $D$ immediately next to each other could not even be assumed, but about the line $AC$ which has already been actually cut into parts by nature; because we suppose change to happen in such a way that at one moment the moving point will exist at the endpoint $B$ of one of its parts $AB$, and at another moment at the endpoint $D$ of the other part $DC$. And the distinction between these two contiguous lines actually divided from each other, and the one undivided or continuous line, is clear: it is, as Aristotle has already noted,[54] that the endpoints $B$ and $D$ in the two contiguous lines are different, while in the one continuous line they coincide, just as we also noted above. I deny, therefore, that another point could be assumed in the line $DC$ immediately next to $D$, for I believe that no point should be admitted in the nature of things unless it is the endpoint of something extended.

PA.: Your reasoning is correct, supposing that nature has actually divided the line like this into the parts $AB$ and $DC$. But this division was arbitrary. What, then, if the division had been arranged in such a way that $D$ was carried back to the line $AB$ to make the line $AD$? Wouldn't there have been another line $CF$, and wouldn't we have had a point $F$

564

Nonne utique altera linea fuisset *CF* ct habuissemus ipsi *D* immediatum punctum *F* adeoque tria puncta sibi immediata *B, D, F.*

CH.: Non video quid aliud responderi possit, quam hypothesin istam
impossibilem esse?

PA.: Quid ita, nonne punctum *D* eodem jure potuisset esse terminus
lineae *AB* quo punctum *B*?

CH.: Re satis expensa videtur mihi, quemadmodum et supra alia occasione te probante dixi, puncta ista non praeexistere ante divisionem
actualem, sed nasci divisione. Itaque si divisio facta sit uno modo, alterius divisionis puncta in rerum natura non extabunt neque ergo haec
tria *B, D, F* ex diversis divisionibus sumta in unum addi possunt. Imo
quia lineae *AB* et *AD* aequales similes et congruae sunt *B* unius divisionis et *D* alterius ne different quidem.

PA.: Acute quidem ista, sed quae nondum absolvant difficultatem.
Explicanda est enim difformitas illa quam in motu statuisti, quoniam
ab ea difformitas in divisione lineae repetenda est. Explosimus vero
saltus supra explicatos. Itaque nec quietes temporariae cuilibet motui
interponi possunt alioqui necessario veniemus ad saltus.

(CH.: Fortasse saltus per spatia infinite parva non sunt absurdi quemadmodum et quietulae per tempora infinite parva, his saltibus inter-
positae. Posito enim spatia saltuum momentaneorum temporibus
quietum esse proportionalia, cuncta respondebunt eo modo quo
supra saltus et quietes per tempora et lineas ordinaries explicuimus.

PA.: Ego spatia haec et tempora infinite parva in Geometria quidem
admitterem, inventionis causa, licet essent imaginaria. Sed an possint
**565**  admitti in natura delibero. Videntur enim inde oriri lineae rectae infinitae utrinque terminatae, ut alias ostendam; quod absurdum est.
Praeterea cum infinitae parvae quoque aliae aliis minores assumi
possint in infinitum, rursus non potest ratio reddi, cur aliae prae aliis
assumantur; nihil autem fit sine ratione.)

CH.: Quid si ergo dicemus Motum mobilis actu esse divisum in infinitos alios motus inter se diversos, neque per ullum temporis tractum eundem perseverare atque uniformem.

immediately next to *D,* and thus three points immediately next to each other, *B, D,* and *F?*

CH.: I do not see what else could be replied except that this hypothesis of yours is impossible.

PA.: Why? Couldn't the point *D* be the bound of the line *AB* with the same right as the point *B?*

CH.: When the matter is adequately weighed, it seems to me that—as I also said with your approval on another occasion above—these points of yours do not pre-exist before an actual division, but are brought about by division. Thus if the division is made in one way, the points of the other division will not exist in the nature of things; and so these three points taken from different divisions, *B, D,* and *F,* cannot be added into one whole. Rather, since the lines *AB* and *AD* are equal, similar and congruent, *B* from the one division and *D* from the other would not even differ.

PA.: That's very acute, but it does not yet completely dispose of the difficulty. For this nonuniformity which you have established in motion must be explained, since it is from this that the nonuniformity in the division of the line is to be derived. We have certainly rejected the leaps discussed above. Consequently temporary rests cannot be inserted in any motion, otherwise we will necessarily end up with leaps.

(CH.: Perhaps leaps through infinitely small spaces are not absurd, and nor are little rests for infinitely small times inserted between these leaps. For assuming the spaces of the momentaneous leaps to be proportional to the times of the rests, they will all correspond together in the same way as the leaps and rests through ordinary times and lines that we expounded above.

PA.: I would indeed admit these infinitely small spaces and times in geometry, for the sake of invention, even if they are imaginary. But I am

**565** not sure whether they can be admitted in nature. For there seem to arise from them infinite straight lines bounded at both ends, as I will show at another time; which is absurd.[55] Besides, since further infinitely small spaces and times can also be assumed, each smaller than the last to infinity, again no reason can be provided why some should be assumed rather than others; but nothing happens without a reason.)[56]

CH.: Then what if we say that the motion of a moving thing is actually divided into an infinity of other motions, each different from the other, and that it does not persist the same and uniform for any stretch of time?

PA.: Recte profecto, et vides ipse hoc unum superesse, sed et rationi consentaneum id est, nullum enim corpus est, quod non quolibet momento aliquam passionem subeat a vicinis.

CH.: Itaque jam divisionis ac difformitatis causam habemus, et quomodo hoc potius quam illo modo instituatur divisio, punctaque assignentur, explicare possumus. Tota res ergo eo redit: quolibet momento quod actu assignatur dicemus mobile in novo puncto esse. Et momenta quidem atque puncta assignari infinita sed nunquam in eadem linea immediata sibi plura duobus, neque enim indivisibilia aliud quam terminos esse.

PA.: Euge: nunc demum mihi spem exitus facis. Illud tamen vide: si indivisibilia sunt termini tantum, erunt et momenta tantum termini temporis.

CH.: Ita sane.

PA.: Est ergo aliud quiddam in tempore quam momentum, id vero cum nullo momento sit, non erit. Nunquam enim aliud quam momentum existit.

CH.: Tempus ipsum aliquando esse aut non esse dici non debet, alioqui tempore temporis opus esset. Neque dico aliud in tempore esse quam partes temporis, quae etiam tempora sunt, et earum terminos.

PA.: Omnem mihi objiciendi materiam ademisti.

CH.: Quam gaudeo.

PA.: Sed operae pretium erit considerare materiae temporis et motus harmoniam. Itaque sic sentio: nullam esse portionem materiae quae non in plures partes actu sit divisa, itaque nullum corpus esse tam exiguum in quo non sit infinitarum creaturarum mundus. Similiter nullam esse temporis partem in qua non cuilibet corporis parti vel puncto aliqua obtingat mutatio vel motus. Nullum itaque motum eundem durare, per spatium tempusve utcunque exiguum; itaque ut **566** corpus ita et spatium et tempus actu in infinitum subdivisa erunt. Neque ullum est momentum temporis quod non actu assignetur, aut quo mutatio non contingat, id est quod non sit finis veteris aut initium novi status in corpore quovis; non ideo tamen admittetur aut corpus vel spatium in puncta dividi, aut tempus in momenta, quia indivisi-

PA.: Absolutely right, and you yourself see that this is the only thing left for us to say. But it is also consistent with reason, for there is no body which is not acted upon by those around it at every single moment.

CH.: So now we have the cause of the division and the nonuniformity, and can explain how it is that the division is arranged and the points assigned in this way rather than that. The whole thing therefore reduces to this: at any moment which is actually assigned we will say that the moving thing is at a new point. And although the moments and points that are assigned are indeed infinite, there are never more than two immediately next to each other in the same line, since indivisibles are nothing but bounds.

PA.: Well done! Now at last you give me hope of finding a way out. Consider this, however: if indivisibles are merely bounds, then moments will also be merely bounds of time.

CH.: Yes, of course.

PA.: Therefore if there is something in time other than the moment, since it is not at a moment, it will not really exist. For nothing but a moment ever exists.

CH.: Time itself ought not to be said to exist or not to exist at some time, otherwise time would be needed for time. Nor, I say, is there anything in time but the parts of time—which are also times—and their bounds.

PA.: You have deprived me of the whole point of my objection.

CH.: I am very glad.

PA.: But it will be worthwhile to consider the harmony of matter, time, and motion. Accordingly I am of the following opinion: there is no portion of matter that is not actually divided into further parts, so that there is no body so small that there is not a world of infinitary creatures in it. Similarly there is no part of time in which some change or motion does not happen to any part or point of a body. And so no motion stays the same through any space or time however small; thus both space and time will be actually subdivided to infinity, just as a body is. Nor is there any moment of time that is not actually assigned, or at which change does not occur, that is, which is not the end of an old or beginning of a new state in some body. This does not mean, however, either that a body or space is divided into points, or time into moments, because indivisibles are not parts, but the ex-

**566**

bilia non partes, sed partium extrema sunt; quare etsi omnia subdividantur, non tamen in minima usque resolvuntur.

GA.: Admirandam nobis exhibes ideam rerum, tantum enim aberit, ut sint atomi, ut contra potius in quolibet corpusculo quidam mundus sit rerum infinitarum quod hactenus nescio an satis sit consideratum. Itaque neque in loco, neque in tempore quicquam vacuum admittis, neque in materia torpidum atque ut ita dicam expers vitae.

PA.: Ita est Galluti, eamque ego sententiam solam dignam puto maximo rerum autore qui nihil sterile, nihil incultum, nihil inornatum reliquit.

TH.: Profecto facis ut obstupescam. Magnam rem dixisse visi sunt, qui infinitos in spatio hoc Mundano stellarum globos, et in unoquoque globo esse mundum asseruere, tu in qualibet arenula non mundum tantum, sed et infinitos ostendis mundos, quo nescio an dici possit aliquid splendidius, ac magnitudini divinae convenientius.

PA.: Sed aliud velim a vobis animadverti, quod hic demonstratur corpora cum in motu sunt non agere.

TH.: Cur ita?

PA.: Quia nullum est momentum mutationis commune utrique statui, itaque nec ullus status est mutationis; sed aggregatum tantum duorum statuum veteris et novi; itaque nec status actionis est in corpore; seu nullum potest assignari momentum quo agat, nam corpus movendo ageret et agendo mutaretur seu pateretur, at nullum est momentum passionis seu mutationis vel motus in corpore. Itaque actio in corpore non nisi per aversionem quandam intelligi potest. Si vero ad vivum reseces, seu si momentum unumquodque inspicias nulla est. Hinc sequitur Actiones proprias et momentaneas, earum esse rerum quae agendo non mutantur. Ac proinde illa actio qua mobile ex una sphaera in aliam contiguam transfertur, seu qua efficitur, ut mobile *e* quod uno momento fuit in una sphaera, proxime sequenti sit in alia contigua, non ipsius est corporis transferendi *e*. Id enim quo mo-

**567**

trema of parts. And this is why, even though all things are subdivided, they are still not resolved all the way down into minima.

GA.: This is an admirable idea of reality you are presenting us with, since so much would be missing in order for there to be atoms; whereas the idea that there should rather be a kind of world of infinitary things in any corpuscle you please is something which, as far as I know, has not been adequately considered before now. So you admit no vacuum in either place or time, nor anything torpid or lacking in life, so to speak, in matter?

PA.: That's right, Gallutius, and I think that this is the only opinion worthy of the supreme creator of things, who has bequeathed us nothing sterile, nothing fallow, nothing unadorned.[57]

TH.: Well, you've really astounded me. Those who claimed that are infinite spheres of stars in this mundane space, and that there is a world in every sphere, seem to have said something of importance; whereas you show that in any grain of sand whatever there is not just a world, but even an infinity of worlds. I doubt if anything could be said that is more splendid than this, and more in keeping with divine greatness.

PA.: But I would like you to notice something else, that this demonstrates that bodies do not act while they are in motion.

TH.: Why is that?

PA.: Because there is no moment of change common to each of two states, and thus no state of change either, but only an aggregate of two states, old and new; and so there is no state of action in a body, that is to say, no moment can be assigned at which it acts. For by moving the body would act, and by acting it would change or be acted upon; but there is no moment of being acted upon, that is, of change or motion, in the body. Thus action in a body cannot be conceived except through a kind of aversion. If you really cut to the quick and inspect every single moment, there is no action. Hence it follows that proper and momentaneous actions belong to those things which by acting do not change. And therefore the action by which a moving point is transferred from one sphere into another one contiguous to it—that is, the action by which a moving body $e$ which was in one sphere at one moment is caused to be in another contiguous sphere at the next moment afterward—does not belong to the very body $e$ which is to

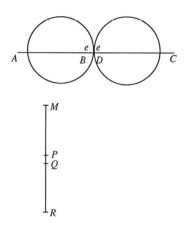

mento est in puncto *B* non est in motu, per supra ostensa, ergo nec agit motu; similiter non agit cum jam est in momento *D.* Id ergo a quo movetur corpus, et transfertur, non est ipsum corpus, sed causa superior quae agendo non mutatur, quam dicimus Deum. Unde patet corpus ne continuare quidem sponte motum posse; sed continue indigere impulsu Dei, qui tamen constanter et pro sua summa sapientia certis legibus agit.

CH.: At quomodo quaeso corpus ex puncto *B,* in corpus *D,* postquam momentum transitionis seu status, medii sustulimus.

PA.: Hoc non puto explicari posse melius quam si dicamus corpus *e* extingui quodammodo et annihilari in *B,* creari vero denuo ac resuscitari in *D.* Quod posses novo sed pulcherrimo vocabulo appellare *transcreationem.* Et hic sane est quasi saltus quidam ex sphaera una *B* in alteram *D,* non tamen qualem supra refutavimus quia hae duae sphaerac non distant. Atque hoc est illud denique cuius causa tot machinas rationum admovi, ut scilicet vos adigerem denique ad agnoscendam tanti momenti veritatem. Unum addo, non esse quod vos turbet transcreatio, nam dicere rem hic existere cessare, illic autem existere incipere, sublato transitu seu statu intermedio est idem dicere, ac illic annihilari illic resuscitari. Ac si unus simpliciter dicat rem esse desinere in statu priori, et nunc incipere esse in alio, alius

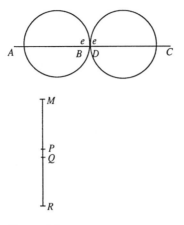

Figure 14

**567**    be transferred. For at the moment when it is at point *B* it is not in motion, as shown above, and therefore it does not act by motion; similarly it does not act when it is already at point *D*. Therefore what
moves and transfers the body is not the body itself, but a superior
cause which by acting does not change, which we call God. Whence
it is clear that a body cannot even continue its motion of its own accord, but stands in continual need of the impulse of God, who, however, acts constantly and by certain laws in keeping with his supreme
wisdom.

CH.: But how, please, is the body transferred from point *B* to point *D*
now that we have eliminated the moment of transition, i.e. of the intermediate state?

PA.: I do not think that we can explain this better than by saying that
the body *E* is somehow extinguished and annihilated at *B,* and is actually created anew and resuscitated at *D,* which you may call by the
new but very beautiful name *transcreation.*[58] Moreover, although
this is indeed a sort of leap from one sphere *B* into the other *D,* it is not
the kind of leap we refuted above, since these two spheres are not distant. And this is the thing, finally, for whose sake I have indulged in
so many logical stratagems, namely, to force you all into finally acknowledging so momentous a truth. I add only that transcreation is
not what disturbs you: for to say that a thing ceases to exist here, but
begins to exist there, with the transition or intermediate state eliminated, is the same thing as saying that it is there annihilated, there resuscitated. And if one person were simply to say that the thing ceases

vero dicat annihilari in statu priori resuscitari in posteriore, utrumlibet admittas, nullum in ipsa re discrimen notari potest, sed tantum in eo quod prior causam dissimulat, posterior exprimit. Nulla autem causa intelligi potest cur res quae in aliquo statu esse cessavit, in alio esse incipiat (sublato quippe transitu) nisi substantia quaedam permanens quae et destruxit primum et produxit novum, quoniam sequens status ex praecedente utique necessario non sequitur. ❖❖❖❖❖❖❖❖❖❖❖

**568**   TH.: Hinc mirifice confirmatur quod praeclare olim a Theologis dictum est conservationem esse perpetuam creationem, huic enim sententiae affine est quod a te demonstratur mutationem omnem quandam esse transcreationem.

GA.: Imo vero videtur ex solo statu praecedente status sequentis ratio reddi posse. Exempli causa, celebre est axioma philosophorum jam Aristoteli adhibitum *Quicquid semel movetur semper moveri eodem modo nisi superveniat impedimentum.* Hoc axioma demonstrari potest ex eo quod nulla ratio reddi potest cur praesente cesset momento, non vero jam cessaverit aliquo paulo priore.

PA.: Gaudeo haec a te objici, hinc enim praeclara doctrinae nostrae utilitas inprimis elucebit. Video enim aliquos ex hoc theoremate voluisse ducere materiam aliquando a Deo motam non amplius eius ope indigere, sed acceptum semel impetum sponte naturae suae retinere, alios qui de aeternitate motus persuasi non poterant capere quomodo aliquando impellere incipere potuerit, Deum plane sublatum credidisse. Id vero nostra de motu doctrina huc usque explicata plane evertit. Omnino enim cessat motus, neque per ullum tempus quantumcunque durat, sed quovis momento ope superioris causae intermortuus resuscitatur. Quoniam vero Deus perfectissimo modo operatur, hinc usus axiomatis, *quod nihil sit sine ratione* velut postliminio redit. Nam quas semel elegit Deus in aliquo temporis tractu mutationum formas, eas sine ratione non immutabit. Unde fiet ut in natura stabile maneat axioma, *motum eodem modo continuari quamdiu nullum supervenit impedimentum.* Si vero esset aliquis Mo-

to be in its earlier state and now begins to be in another one, someone else might say that it was annihilated in the earlier state and resuscitated in the later one. Whichever of the two you accept, no distinction can be observed in the thing itself, but only in the fact that the former way of putting it conceals the cause, and the latter brings it out. But no cause can be conceived for why a thing that has ceased to exist in one state should begin to exist in another (inasmuch as the transition has been eliminated), except a kind of permanent substance that has both destroyed the first state and produced the new one, since the succeeding state does not necessarily follow from the preceding one. ❖❖❖❖❖❖❖❖❖❖

**568**    TH.: This gives a wonderful confirmation of what the theologians said some time ago, that conservation is perpetual creation; for this opinion is related to the one you have demonstrated, that all change is a kind of transcreation.

GA.: Yes, but it seems that a reason for the following state can be provided from the preceding state alone. For example, there is the celebrated axiom of the philosophers, already employed by Aristotle: *Whatever is once set in motion will always move in the same way unless it meets with an obstruction.*[59] This axiom can be demonstrated from the fact that no reason can be provided why it should stop at the present moment given that it has not already stopped a short time before.

PA.: I am glad you have offered this objection, since the enormous advantage of our doctrine will become especially clear from it. For I see that some people have wanted to infer from this theorem that matter, once it has been set in motion by God, is no longer in need of his aid, but having once received an impetus, retains it spontaneously by its own nature;[60] whilst others who, convinced of the eternity of motion, have been unable to grasp how he could ever have begun to set things moving, have believed that God is thereby completely eliminated.[61] This axiom, however, is completely overturned by the doctrine of motion we have developed up to this point. For motion stops altogether, and does not last for any time however small, but at any moment you please the lifeless is resuscitated by the aid of a superior cause. In fact, since God acts in the most perfect way, from this a use for the axiom *that nothing is without a reason* returns as if by postliminy. For once God has chosen the forms of changes in some stretch of time, he will not change them without a reason. Whence it happens that the axiom that *motion continues in the same way as long*

tus continuum statusque medius in mutatione sive transitus momentum, fatendum esset, vim esse in argumento Gallutii: imo Deo careri nunc posse, ubi materia semel motum recepisset, quoniam status sequens ex ipsa motus ac materiae natura sponte consequeretur, non accedente naturae divinae consideratione. Habetis ergo quod hic **569** minime expectabatis Dei et creationis assertionem operationemque eius specialem mutationi rerum necessariam.[L10]

GA.: Quis unquam tantas res credidisset ex tantulis nasci posse.

TH.: Ego non possum satis explicare verbis quantopere admirer exitum tam inexpectatum.

CH.: Me vero maxime admiratione teneri par est, militem et non nisi rebus sensibilibus suetum, qui nunquam hactenus tota mea vita aut expertus aut etiam suspicatus sum, in rebus abstractis et ab imaginatione remotis, claras usque adeo atque firmas demonstrationes fieri posse. Equidem longe alia ab hoc congressu expectabam. Scilicet motuum leges, et mechanicas potentiarum rationes: non contemtu talium, quae nunc audivi, sed ignoratione. Nunc vero nollem ista tota cum Algebra atque Mechanica commutare, nec toto anno metaphysicae auditor esse recusarem, Pacidio interrogante. Usque adeo ille taedium sustulit, et arte tractandi, et ipsarum magnitudine rerum. Ad Mechanica autem non nisi cum illi tempus videbitur descendemus.

L10. NB. ratio cur aliqua res existat non est in ipsa et momento, nec est in alia praecedente, quia ea nunc aut non est amplius, aut non est ratio in ipsa cur sit amplius. Nec quod res paulo ante existit, ratio est cur nunc existat quoque, sed indicat tantum aliquam rationem esse cur nunc quoque existat seu rationem quae fecit eam esse paulo ante adhuc existere.—Quo majora sunt corpora, eo moventur tardius; ac proinde eo [minores] faciunt saltus, alioqui saltum eorum exigua circumjecta perciperent. Examinandum saltus potius [pauci], ac magni, an multi et exigui. Res ita explicanda, ut corpora non percipient unquam hos saltus. Itaque quando corpus magnum salit minora circumjecta etiam salient, sed tempore longiore indigent.

*as it meets with no obstruction* remains upheld in nature. If there really were some continuous motion and an intermediate state in change, or moment of transition, then we would have to admit that Gallutius' argument would have some force: indeed, in that case it would be possible to do without God once matter had received motion, since the following state would follow spontaneously from the very nature of motion and matter, without bringing in a consideration of divine nature. So you have what you least expected here, the assertion of God and creation, and that his special operation is necessary[62] for change among things.[L10]

**569**

GA.: Who would have ever believed that such great things could emerge from such slender beginnings?

TH.: As for me, I cannot adequately convey in words just how much I admire such an unexpected conclusion.

CH.: It is right for it to be held in the greatest admiration by me, however. For, as a military man accustomed only to sensible things, I have never till now in my entire life either experienced or even suspected that such clear and firm demonstrations as these could be achieved in matters that are abstract and remote from the imagination. I myself was for a long time expecting different things from this meeting, namely, laws of motion, and mechanical explanations of powers: not out of disregard for the things I have now heard, but out of ignorance. In fact now I would not be willing to exchange everything you have said for Algebra and Mechanics, nor would I be disinclined to listen to metaphysics for a whole year, if Pacidius were asking the questions. Up till now he has eliminated tedium, both by means of the art of discussion and by the sheer magnitude of the issues themselves. Mechanics, on the other hand, we will come back to only when there seems time for it.

L10. N.B. The reason why a thing exists is not in it at the moment, nor is it in another thing preceding it, because now this thing either no longer exists, or there is no reason in it why it should exist any longer. And the fact that the thing existed a little while before is not the reason why it should also exist now, but indicates only that there is some reason why it should also exist now, that is, that the reason that made it exist a little while before still exists.—The larger bodies are, the slower they move; and therefore, the [smaller] are the leaps they make, otherwise the tiny things around them would perceive their leap. It must be investigated whether the leaps are [few] and big, or rather many and very small. Matters are to be explained in such a way that bodies never perceive these leaps. So when a large body leaps smaller bodies will also leap, but they need a longer time.[63]

TH.: Agite amici fructus huius Meditationis bona fide gustemus. Ego quidem ex quo me ex mundo reducem, ad me recepi, nihil prius habui

**570**   cultu Dei et cura salutis, et consideratione aeternitatis. Nam si immortalis nobis anima est, exigui momenti nobis videri debet haec paucorum annorum vita, nisi quatenus effectus suos in futurum porrigere credibile est. Itaque virtutibus ac sapientiae operam demus, veris ac duraturis animae bonis. Sapientia autem inprimis consistit in perfectissima naturae cognitione, quam non esse tantum atque operari, sed et specialem omnium curam habere, nec res tantum creasse ex nihilo, sed et creare quotidie atque resuscitare, quisquamne unquam tam luculenter demonstravit. Equidem fateor exultasse me intellecta vi harum ratiocinationum, atque philosophiae gratulari quae tandem in gratiam reditura videtur cum pietate, cum qua ei non culpa sua, sed hominum opinione et judiciis temerariis, aut etiam expressionibus male consultis parum convenire videbatur. Desinant itaque viri pii ac gloriae divinae zelo accensi metuere aliquid a ratione; modo dent operam ut rectam nanciscantur. Quin potius ita habeant ut quisque in vera philosophia provectior est, ita divinam potentiam atque bonitatem magis agnoscere, neque aut a revelatione aut ab iis quae miracula aut mysteria vocantur alienum esse, cum demonstrare possit, vera quaedam ac propria miracula quotidie in natura evenire. Nullum enim ex revelatis magis mirum ac sensibus pugnans videatur, quam rem annihilari atque creari aut in re finita partes actu infinitas esse. Philosophi vicissim cessent omnia ad imaginationem et figuras referre, et nugarum atque imposturae postulare, quicquid cum notionibus quibusdam crassis ac materialibus pugnat quibus aliqui totam rerum naturam circumscribi putant: cum agnituri sint, ubi recte meditati fuerint, motum ipsum minime imaginationi subjici, et mysteria quaedam metaphysica ex spiritali natura profecta in eo contineri: arcanam quoque nobis vim intus assistere qua frui possit animus, amore atque caritate accensus, et meditatione attenta elevatus.

Haec cum pietate insignis et studio ardens dixisset senex, omnes, Alethophile, ignem quendam concepimus, ac certatim in divinas laudes effusi ad studium tam sanctum nos cohortati sumus, prae quo alia

TH.: Come, my friends, let us taste the fruits of this meditation in good faith. For my part I have taken it upon myself as a result of this to rescue myself from the world, holding nothing above the worship of God and the care of my health, and the contemplation of eternity. For if the soul in us is immortal, the few years of life we have ought to seem of very little importance to us, except in so far as we may believe that the effects of our actions extend into the future. So let us pay heed to the virtues and wisdom, the true and everlasting benefits for the soul. But wisdom consists especially in the most perfect knowledge of nature, and has anyone ever demonstrated more lucidly not only how it exists and operates, but also how it has a special care for all things, and has not only created things from nothing, but also creates and resuscitates them all the time? For my part I confess that understanding the force of these reasonings has given me great joy, and I congratulate philosophy, which finally looks as though it will return to grace with piety; with which it used to be in all too little agreement, not through any fault of its own, but as a result of the opinion of men and their rash judgments, or even their ill-considered expressions. So let pious men, inflamed with zeal for the divine glory, stop fearing something from reason; if only they would pay it attention, they would find out what is right. Why do they not rather maintain this, that the more progress anyone makes in true philosophy, the more he acknowledges divine power and goodness; and that that person is no stranger to revelation or to the things we call miracles or mysteries, since he can demonstrate that certain things that are near enough miracles happen every day in nature. For no revelation would seem more extraordinary and in conflict with the senses than for a thing to be annihilated and created, or for there to be an actual infinity of parts in a finite thing. And let philosophers, in their turn, stop referring everything to the imagination and figures, and stop declaiming as trifles and fraud anything that conflicts with those crass and materialistic notions by which some people think the whole nature of things is circumscribed. As they will recognize when they reflect on these matters properly, motion itself is not at all subject to the imagination, and certain metaphysical mysteries of a truly spiritual nature will be found contained in it: and they will recognize that the arcane force inside us assists us as much as the soul, inflamed with love and affection, and elevated by its careful meditation, can enjoy.

When the old man said these things with such remarkable piety and ardent enthusiasm, Alethophilus,[64] we all caught some of his fire, and competing with each other in pouring forth divine praise, we

omnia nihili videantur, cum non aliter aestimanda sint, quam prout conferre possint ad hunc animi statum in quo felicitas omnis ponenda est. Sed et consensus apparuit sapientum, et multa ex Theologorum mysteriis Theophilus, multa ex Hermeticorum atque Pythagoraeorum arcanis Gallutius attulit confirmandae veritati. Charinus autem talium novus in alium pene hominem mutatus videbatur. Ego cum unum adhuc demonstrationis huius fructum adjecissem, quod scilicet hinc appareat aliud longe esse actionem, aliud mutationem, et posse aliquid agere sine repassione, id magni rursus usus esse in divinis omnes agnovere cum applausu. Tandem cum sermo in multam noctem protractus esset, nec tantum in alium colloquii diem, sed et in certas quasdam communis studii leges consensissemus, data acceptaque arcani fide (quaedam enim dicta erant ultro citroque quae huc transferri non possunt, quod non omnes iis digni, aut certe pauci maturi atque praeparati videantur), colloquium sane diutissimum finivimus. Ego postero mane sumto calamo dum caleret animus recente memoria haec tibi pariter ac mihi Alethophile exaravi, tametsi animam illis infundere non potuerim quae loquentium vultu ac motu habent collationes, alioquin argumenti siccitate languentes. [His si placet fruere ac] vale.

571

excited ourselves into such a pitch of religious zeal, that compared to it all others seemed as nothing, since the only way they could be estimated would be by comparing them with that state of the soul in which all happiness is ordained. But also a consensus of wisdom appeared, and Theophilus introduced many of the mysteries of the theologians,[65] and Gallutius many of the secrets of the Hermeticists and Pythagoreans, in confirmation of its truth. Charinus, on the other hand, a novice in such matters, seemed to have been transformed almost into another man. Whereas I added one more fruit of this demonstration, which was that from this it would appear that action is something very different from change, and that it is possible for something to act without undergoing reaction, a fact that is in turn of great utility in divinity, as everyone acknowledged with applause.

Finally when this discussion had drawn on long into the night, and we had agreed not only on another day's discussion, but also on some definite rules of communal study, we gave and received a secret trust (for certain words were said back and forth which cannot be repeated here, because not everyone seems worthy of them, or certainly there are few who seem mature and ready), and finished our truly very long discussion. The next morning, while my soul was glowing with the recent memory, I took up my pen and—for you as much as for myself, Alethophilus—wrote these things down, even though I could not communicate the things that were contributed by the looks and gestures of those speaking, when they were otherwise languishing from a dearth of argument. [Please enjoy this and][66] farewell.

**571**

# III Hanover Writings, 1677–86

**1968** Si *Spatium* sit res quaedam in pura extensione posita, *materiae* autem natura sit spatium implere; et *Motus* est spatii mutatio, tunc motus erit absolutum quoddam, et duobus corporibus sibi invicem appropinquantibus dici poterit utrum moveatur aut quiescat; vel, si ambo moventur, quanam moveantur celeritate. Atque inde sequentur eae conclusiones, quas olim ostendi in *Theoria motus abstracte considerati*. Sed revera Spatium illud non est, neque motus est aliquid absolutum, sed consistit in relatione. Et proinde si duo corpora sibi concurrant, celeritas inter ipsa ita animo partienda est, ut sibi occurrere intelligantur eadem vi. Itaque si duo corpora concurrentia intelligantur aequalia, statim omnia phaenomena experimentis consentanea ex hoc solo deducentur. Assumo igitur corpora alia esse dura quae post concursum reflectantur, alia mollia quae simul maneant. Et assero: duo corpora [mollia] aequalia et similia eadem celeritate concurrentia, post concursum simul manere; dura vero ea qua venere celeritate reflecti.

**1969** His positis sit navis *LMN* in qua duo corpora aequalia et similia eadem celeritate concurrant; eodem tempore uno veniente ab *L* per *LM* altero ab *N* per *NM* ipsi *LM* aequalem, itaque eadem celeritate reflectentur contraria autem directione, ut eodem tempore quo ante concursum venerant ab *L* et *N* ad *M*, post concursum redeant ad *L* et *N*, si quidem perfecte elastica sunt, vel simul maneant, in *M* si mollia. Interea ponatur navis progredi ab $_1L_1M_1N$ in $_2L_2M_2N$, quae secum feret globis in ipsa decurrentes. Sit jam ripa immota *PT* in qua punctis $_1L_1M_1N$ respondeant puncta *P.R.Q.* et punctis $_2L_2M_2N$ puncta *S.V.T.*

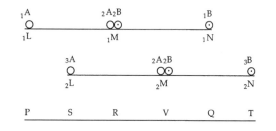

[Early 1677?][2]

**1968**  If *space* is a certain thing consisting in a supposed pure extension, whilst the nature of *matter* is to fill space, and *motion* is change of space, then motion will be something absolute; and so when two bodies are approaching one another, it will be possible to tell which of them is in motion and which at rest; or, if both are moving, with what speed they are moving. And from this will follow those conclusions which I once showed in the *Theory of Motion Abstractly Considered*.[3] But in reality space is not such a thing, and motion is not something absolute, but consists in relation. And therefore if two bodies collide, the speed must be understood to be distributed between them in such a way that each runs into the other with the same force. Thus if two colliding bodies are understood to be equal, then all the phenomena consistent with experiments will at once be deduced from this fact alone. I assume, then, that hard bodies that are reflected after collision are one thing, and soft ones that remain together another. And I assert that when two equal and similar soft bodies with the same speed collide, they remain together after the collision; whereas hard ones are reflected with the speed with which they came.

With[4] these things supposed, let there be a ship *LMN* in which two equal and similar bodies with the same speed collide. Then in the same time in which one comes from *L* through *LM* the other will come from *N* through *NM* equal to *LM,* and so they will be reflected with the same speed but in opposite directions, so that in the same time which before the collision they had come from *L* and *N* to *M,* after the collision they will go back to *L* and *N.* This, of course, is if they are perfectly elastic; otherwise, if they are soft, they will

**1969**  remain together at *M.* Meanwhile we suppose the ship to progress from $_1L_1M_1N$ to $_2L_2M_2N$, carrying with it the balls running along it. Let there now be an unmoving bank *PT* in which the points P.R.Q. correspond to the points $_1L_1M_1N$, and S.V.T. correspond to $_2L_2M_2N$.

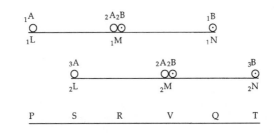

Figure 1

His positis sit navis *LMN,* in qua duo globi aequales et similes *A, B,* concurrant uno *A* veniente a prora *L* ad medium *M,* altero *B* eodem tempore a puppi *N* ad idem medium *M,* celeritate proinde aequali, et motu uniformi seu aequabili. In *M* autem concurrentia haec duo corpora *A* et *B,* si Elastri perfecte capacia sint reflectantur, et aequali tempore ac celeritate redibunt *A* quidem ex *M* in *L,* at *B* ex *M* in *N.*

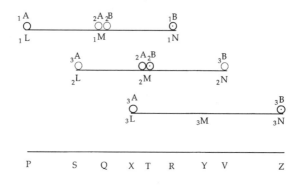

Haec dum in navi perinde fiunt, ac si quiesceret, ipsa navi interim motu aequabili secundo flumine recta deferatur, ita ut navis initio motus globulorum sit in loco $_1L_1M_1N$, momento autem concursus sit in loco $_2L_2M_2N$, et denique momento absoluti recursus, seu cum corpora *A* et *B* post concursum ad priora loca sunt reversa, sit in loco $_3L_3M_3N$. In ripa autem immota *PY* sint puncta respondentia, nempe *PQR* ipsis $_1L_1M_1N$, et *STV* ipsis $_2L_2M_2N$, et *XYZ* ipsis $_3L_3M_3N$. Patet absolute loquendo et respectu ripae immotae perinde esse ac si dicamus corpora *A* et *B* celeritatibus *PT* et *RT* concurrentia in *T* post concursumreflecti celeritatibus *TX* et *TZ,* ubi quidem (si corpora sint aequalia) manifestum est celeritates et directiones corporum concurrentium permutari, seu *TX* aequari ipsi *RT* et *TZ* ipsi *PT.* Est enim *TX* aequal. $_2M_2L$ seu *ML,* minus $_2L_3L$ seu *XS,* seu *PS.* Et *RT,* est $_1N_1M$ seu *NM* seu *ML,* minus $_1M_2M$ seu $_1L_2L$ seu *PS.* Si vero corpora sint mollia post concursum simul manebunt et cum navi deferentur, ex $_2M$ in $_3M$. Itaque si duo corpora mollia concurrant celeritatibus *PT* et *RT* post **1970** concursum simul ibunt celeritate et directione *TY,* directione quidem celerioris, celeritas autem *TY* seu $_2M_3M$ seu *XS* erit dimidia differentia celeritatum *PT* et *RT.* Est autem *PS* aequ. *XS* seu dimidia *PX* et *PX* est *PT* minus *TX* seu *PT* minus *TR.*

With these things supposed, let there be a ship *LMN* in which two equal
and similar balls *A* and *B* collide, the one, *A*, coming from the prow *L* to the
midpoint *M* in the same time as the other one, *B*, from the stern *N* to the
same midpoint *M*, with a speed accordingly equal, and by a uniform, i.e.
equable, motion. Now on colliding at *M* these two bodies *A* and *B* will be
reflected, provided they are perfectly elastic, and will recoil in equal times
with the same speed, *A* from *M* to *L*, and *B* from *M* to *N*.

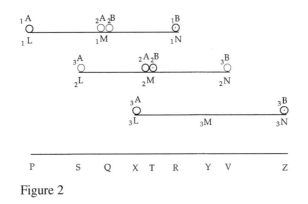

Figure 2

Meanwhile, as these things are happening in the ship exactly as if it
were at rest, the ship itself is being borne off straight downstream by an
equable motion, in such a way that when the balls begin to move the ship
is at the place $_1L_1M_1N$, but at the moment of collision it is at $_2L_2M_2N$, and
finally at the moment of their absolute return, i.e. when the bodies *A* and *B*
have returned to their former places after the collision, it is at place
$_3L_3M_3N$. Now in the unmoving bank *PY* there are corresponding points,
namely, *PQR* corresponding to $_1L_1M_1N$, *STV* to $_2L_2M_2N$, and *XYZ* to
$_3L_3M_3N$. It is clear that absolutely speaking, and with respect to the unmoving bank, it is exactly as if we said that the bodies *A* and *B*, colliding at
*T* with speeds *PT* and *RT*, are reflected after the collision with speeds *TX*
and *TZ*, from which, indeed, it is evident that (if the bodies are equal) the
speeds and directions of the colliding bodies will be interchanged, i.e. *TX*
is equal to *RT* and *TZ* to *PT*. For *TX* is equal to $_2M_2L$ or *ML*, minus $_2L_3L$ or
*XS*, i.e. *PS*. And *RT* is $_1N_1M$ or *NM* or *ML*, minus $_1M_2M$ or $_1L_2L$, i.e. *PS*. If,
however, the bodies are soft they will remain together after the collision
and be carried away by the ship, from $_2M$ to $_3M$. Thus if two soft bodies
collide with speeds *PT* and *RT*, after the collision they will go with a speed
and direction *TY*, that is, in the direction of the faster body. But the speed
*TY* or $_2M_3M$ or *XS* will be half the difference of the speeds *PT* and *RT*. For
*PS* equals *XS*, or half *PX*, and *PX* is *PT* minus *TX*, or *PT* minus *TR*.

**1970**

**1970** Febr. 1677

Mira res: motum esse quiddam respectivum, nec distingui posse quodnam ex corporibus moveatur. Ideoque si affectio est, subjectum eius erit non corpus ullum singulare, sed totus Mundus. Hinc etiam omnes effectus ejus respectivos esse necesse est. Motus autem absolutus quem nobis fingimus non nisi animi nostri affectio est, dum nos ipsi vel alias res velut immobiles spectamus, quando ipsis velut immobilibus spectatis cuncta facilius intelligere possumus. Ex eo quod motus non unius corporis sed totius Mundi affectio est, patet causam primam rerum omnium totiusque Mundi unicam esse, nec alias esse intelligentias astrorum diversorum motrices.

Notandum tamen motum non in se formaliter, sed ratione causae considerando, posse attribui eius corpori a cuius contactu provenit mutatio. Si quaerenti cur hic ignis urit, respondeam quia is ussit a quo accensus est, vel ita de quolibet, vel cur hic canis latrat, quia eius pater latravit, nihil explicuere etiamsi enim eam hoc modo in infinitum, non ideo explicuero cur canes latrent, seu quae sit eorum latratus causa.

**1971** Melius exemplum praebet consistentia. Quam aliqui per Tabulas sibi incumbentes explicant, sed rursus explicare debent unde ipsae tabulae sint consistentes: aut fateri se nihil perfecte explicuisse, nec rationem firmitatis intelligere, nisi supposita alia firmitate. Itaque firmitatem absolute non explicuere. Unde sequeretur firmitatem corpori competere per se, quod absurdum est.

Ex eo quod motus sit Ens respectivum, sequitur non dari vacuum, nam hinc tollitur motus in vacuo, quia nihil est quo dignosci possit. Quod autem dignosci non potest, ne ab omniscio quidem, id nihil est.

**Acervus Chrysippi** **Aiv23**

**69** *ACERVUS CHRYSIPPI*

Martii 1678

Tandem aliquando:

*Inventus Chrysippe tui finitor acervi.* Nimirum omnes illae notiones, in quibus locum habet acervus sive sorites Stoicorum, ut *divitiae, paupertas,*

**1970**  February 1677

A remarkable fact: motion is something relative, and one cannot distinguish exactly which of the bodies is moving. Thus if motion is an affection, its subject will not be any one individual body, but the whole world.[2] Hence all its effects must also necessarily be relative. The absolute motion we imagine to ourselves, however, is nothing but an affection of our soul while we consider ourselves or other things as immobile, since we are able to understand everything more easily when these things are considered as immobile. From the fact that motion is an affection not of one body but of the whole world, it is evident that the first cause of all things and of the whole world is unique, and that the motive intelligences in the various stars are nothing else.[3]

It should be noted, however, that when we consider motion not formally as it is in itself, but with respect to cause, it can be attributed to the body of that thing by whose contact change is brought about. If when someone asks why this fire is burning, I answer, because what lit it was burning, or if I answer in this way about anything, for instance, to why this dog is barking, because its father barked, I should have explained nothing. For even if I answer in this way to infinity, I shall not thereby have explained why dogs bark, or what the cause of their barking is.

**1971**  A better example is provided by cohesiveness, which some people explain by tablets lying one on top of another.[4] But they ought to explain in turn where the cohesiveness of these tablets comes from, or else admit that they have not completely explained anything, and that they understand the reason for firmness only by supposing some other firmness. So they have not explained firmness absolutely, and from this it would follow that firmness belongs to body through itself, which is absurd.

From the fact that motion is a relative entity, it follows that there is no such thing as a vacuum. For motion's being relative rules out motion in a vacuum, since there is nothing by which it could be distinguished; but whatever cannot be distinguished, not even by someone omniscient, is nothing.[5]

## 22. Chrysippus's Heap[1]     Aiv23

**69**      *CHRYSIPPUS'S HEAP*[2]

March 1678

Now at last: "The surveyor of your heap, Chrysippus, has been found."[3]

For all those notions to which the heap or Sorites of the Stoics applies,

*calvities, calor, frigus; tepor, album nigrum, magnum parvum,* absolute
sumtae sunt notiones vagae imaginariae, imo falsae, seu nullam ideam
habentes. Eae demum notiones, quibus objectio ista fieri non potest, a nobis pure ac liquide intelliguntur. Scilicet priores respectum dicunt ad nostram opinionem, quae variat, ex. g. quod uni frigidum id alteri calidem
videtur, utrumque vere, imo et eidem diverso tempore. Idem est de pau-
pertate. Nam quem certo respectu pauperem dicemus, alio respectu esse
negabimus. Si *pauperies* absolute sumta esset vera notio, deberet certo
obolorum numero definiri, quia necesse est aliquem uno abolo [abjecto]
fieri ex non paupere pauperem; aut nunquam. Hinc defectui isti succurunt
leges, et pauperem definiunt qui certum solidorum numerum non habet. Et
70   aetate majorem, qui 25 annos egressus est. De notionibus imaginariis verae saltem manent propositiones comparativae, neque illis potest objici
Sorites.

  Notiones imaginarias voco, quae non sunt in rebus extra nos, sed quarum essentia est nobis apparere. Hinc ubi dubitare incipmus, ut uno obolo
detracto, cessat quaestio, et is de quo agitur, mihi nec pauper est nec dives.
Si definiamus rem effectu quodam certo aliud est, ut pauper est, qui certum aliquid emere non potest. Calida res est, quae thermometrum ascen-
dere facit, tunc enim res reducitur ad sensum aliquem certum. Cum dubia-
mus res sit calida an frigida, tepidam dicimus, tepor ergo non certa idea
extra nos, sed nostra dubitatione constat.


### Conspectus libelli elementorum physicae                   Aiv365


1986   Elementorum Physicae conscribendus erit libellus. Cui adjiciatur De-
scriptio Pyropi, id est noctilucae constantis simulque ignis non consumen-
tis neque alimento indigentis.

  Physica nostra non aget de observationibus atque Historia naturae, sed
de rationibus; sive qualitatibus, et quae ex illis vel necessario vel certe per
se (si nil impediat scilicet), sequuntur. Nam tantum postea opus erit, has
ratiocinationes observationibus applicare. Erit ergo prima pars de Quali-

such as *wealth, poverty, baldness, heat, cold, tepidness, white* and *black, big* and *small,* taken absolutely, are vague imaginary notions, indeed false ones, that is, ones having no corresponding idea. Precisely those notions to which the Stoics' objection cannot be made are understood purely and transparently by us. That is to say, the above notions indicate something with respect to our opinion, which varies. For example, what is cold to one person seems hot to another, truly in each case, and this is even so for the same person at different times. It is the same with poverty. For someone we call poor in a certain respect, we deny to be so in some other respect. If *poverty,* taken absolutely, were a true notion, it ought to be defined by a certain number of pennies, because it is necessary for someone who is not poor to become poor on the removal of one penny;[4] or he will never become poor at all. Hence the laws come to the aid of this defect, and define a pauper as someone who does not possess some particular number of 70    shillings; and a major as someone who has reached the age of twenty-five. Concerning imaginary notions, comparative propositions, at any rate, remain true, and to these the Sorites cannot be raised as an objection.

I call those notions imaginary which are not in the things outside us, but whose essence it is to appear to us. Hence whenever we begin to be in doubt, as [when we doubt whether someone becomes poor] on the removal of one penny, there ceases to be a problem, and the person in question is neither poor nor rich to me. It is different if we define the matter by some particular effect: for instance, a pauper is someone who cannot buy some particular thing, a hot thing is one which makes the thermometer rise; for then the matter is restored to a definite sense. When we are in doubt whether a thing is hot or cold, we call it tepid, therefore tepid is not a definite idea outside of us, but consists in our doubt.

### 23. Conspectus for a Little Book on the Elements of Physics (Selections)[1]                                        Aiv365

[Summer 1678–Winter 1678–79?][2]

1986   We shall have to write a little book on the "Elements of Physics"; to which may be added "A Description of Phosphorus," i.e. of the noctiluca,[3] a constant nightlight that is at the same time a fire that neither consumes nor needs any fuel.

Our physics will not deal with observations and natural history, but with reasons; that is, qualities, and what follows from them either necessarily or certainly per se (to wit, if nothing impedes them). For only afterwards will there be a need to apply these reasonings to observations. Therefore

tatibus; altera pars vero aget de Subjectis qualitatum, sive de Corporibus quae in mundo extant, ubi Historia cum ratiocinatione jungetur.

Agemus igitur de Corpore et eius qualitatibus tum intelligibilibus, quae distincte concipimus, tum sensibilibus quae confuse percipimus.

**1987**     Corpus est extensum, mobile, resistens. Id est quod agere et pati potest quatenus extensum est; agere si sit in motu, pati si motui resistat. Consideranda itaque primum Extensio, deinde Motus, tertio Resistentia seu concursus.

Extensum est quod habet magnitudinem et situm. Est autem magnitudino modus determinandi omnes rei partes seu cum quibus res intelligi possit; *Situs* est modus determinandi cum quibus res percipi possit.

. . .

**1988**     Hinc jam demonstrandum est: Spatium esse indefinite extensum,[L1] nam nulla ratio esse potest cur alibi finiatur, quia de quocunque aliquid concludi potest, id de eius simili concludi potest. Itaque idem magis adhuc de circulo majore concludetur, quod conclusum est de minore. Itaque impossibile est assignari posse certam aliquam sphaeram, ultra quam ne spatium quidem extet. Nam si ratio esset aliqua pro ista, eadem ratio proportionaliter pro aliis omnibus valeret. Deus autem nihil agit sine ratione.

Demonstrandum est etiam omne corpus esse actu divisum in partes minores seu non dari atomos, ac nullum in corpore assignari posee accurate continuum. Ex huius divisionis modo oritur fluidum et firmum; spatium vacuum et corpus perfect fluidum nullo modo discerni posse. Non dari corpus perfect fluidum. Non dari vacuum. Cartesius introducta sua materia subtili, vacuum solummodo nominetenus sustulit.

Sequitur jam de incorporeis. Fiunt quaedam in corpore quae ex sola necessitate materiae explicari non possunt; qualia sunt leges motus; quae pendent ex principio Metaphysico de aequalitate causae atque effectus. Hic ergo agendum de anima, et ostendendum omnia esse animata. Nisi anima esset, seu forma quaedam, corpus non esset ens aliquod, quia nulla eius pars asignari potest, quae non iterum ex pluribus constet, itaque nihil

L1. ABOVE THIS: Hoc potius omittetur.

the first part will be on qualities; the second part will deal with the subjects of the qualities, i.e. with the bodies which exist in the world, where history will be combined with reasoning.

In treating body and its qualities, then, we shall deal first with its intelligible qualities, which we perceive distinctly, then its sensible qualities, which we perceive confusedly.

**1987** Body is extended, mobile, resistant. It is that which can act and be acted upon insofar as it is extended. It acts if it is in motion, is acted upon if it resists motion. So we should consider: first, extension; next, motion; and third, resistance or collision.

The extended is what has magnitude and situation.[4] Magnitude, on the other hand, is a mode for determining all the parts of a thing, i.e. those [entities] by means of which the thing can be understood;[5] *situation* is a mode for determining those [entities] by means of which a thing can be perceived.[6]

. . .

**1988** Now this must be demonstrated: that space is indefinitely extended,[L1] for there can be no reason why it should end somewhere, since something that can be concluded about whatever place it should end can likewise be concluded about any place similar to it. Thus the same thing that has been concluded about a smaller circle will be concluded all the more about a greater one. Thus it is impossible that a certain kind of sphere can be assigned beyond which there would be no space. For if there were some reason for this, then the same reason would hold for all other spheres in proportion. But God does nothing without a reason.[7]

It must also be demonstrated that every body is actually divided into smaller parts, i.e. that there are no such things as atoms, and that no continuum can be accurately assigned in body. The fluid and the firm have their origin in this division alone; empty space and perfectly fluid body can in no way be distinguished. There is no such thing as a perfectly fluid body. There is no such thing as a vacuum. Descartes, having introduced his subtle matter, did away with the vacuum in name only.

Now there follows the subject of incorporeals. There turn out to be certain things in body which cannot be explained by the necessity of matter alone. Such are the laws of motion, which depend on the metaphysical principle of the equality of cause and effect. Here therefore the soul must be treated, and it must be shown that all things are animated. Unless there were a soul, i.e. a kind of form, a body would not be an entity, since no part of it can be assigned which would not again consist of further parts, and so

L1. ABOVE THIS: Better this should be omitted.

assignari posset in corpore, quod dici posset *hoc aliquid,* sive *unum quid-dam.* De natura animae seu formae esse perceptionem aliquam et appeti-tum, quae sunt animae passiones et actiones et cur; nimirum quia resultant

**1989** animae ex Deo res cogitante, seu sunt imitationes idearum. Omnes animae sunt inextinguibiles, sed eae demum immortales sunt, quae cives in Re-publica universi, seu quibus Deus non solum autor sed et Rex est, his enim peculiari quadam ratione conjungitur, hae animae dicuntur Mentes, hae nunquam obliviscuntur sui, hae solae cogitant Deum; distinctasque habent de rebus conceptiones. Ineptum est perceptionem soli homini tribuere velle; cum tamen omnia corpora perceptionem aliquam pro modulo perfectionis suae habere possunt, adeoque et habeant, nam quicquid fieri potest, nullo aliorum detrimento, id utique fit, quia omnia perfectissime fiunt. Expli-canda hic natura voluptatis et doloris quae est nihil aliud quam perceptio successus, seu perfectionis suae; itaque cum conatui satisfit, successus est, cum ei resistitur oritur dolor. Tot sunt specula universi quot mentes; omnis enim mens totum universum percipit, sed confuse.

De vi seu potentia nunc agendum est; ubi sciendum est, eam aestiman-dum esse a quantitate effectus. Esse autem potentiam effectus et causae in-ter se aequalis, nam si major esset effectus, haberemus motum perpetuum mechanicum, si minor, non haberemus motum perpetuum physicum. Hic operae pretium ostendere non posse eandem servari quantitatem motus, sed servari tamen eandem quantitatem potentiae. In universo tamen viden-dum est an non servetur et eadem quantitas motus. . . .

**1392**          **Actu infinitae sunt creaturae**          **Aiv266**

**1393**     Actu infinitae sunt creaturae.
Nam quodlibet corpus actu subdivisum est in plures partes
    quia quodlibet corpus ab aliis corporibus patitur.
Et quaelibet pars corporis est corpus
    ex ipsa corporis definitione.
Itaque actu infinita sunt corpora
    seu plura reperiuntur corpora, quam sunt unitates in numero
    quocunque dato.

nothing could be assigned in body which could be called *this something,* or *some one thing.*[8] That it is the nature of a soul or form to have some perception and appetite, which are passions and actions of the soul, and why;

**1989** namely, because souls result from God thinking of things, that is, they are imitations of his ideas. All souls are inextinguishable, but precisely those are immortal which are citizens in the Republic of the Universe, i.e. those of which God is not only Author, but King. For joined to these is a particular kind of reason, these souls are called minds, these never forget themselves,[9] these alone think of God; and they have distinct conceptions of things. It is foolish to want to attribute perception to man alone; for all things can have some perception in proportion to the measure of their perfection; and thus they do have it, for whatever can happen without detriment to others, does indeed happen, since all things happen as perfectly as possible. To be explained here is the nature of pleasure and pain, which is nothing but the perception of success, i.e. of one's own perfection; and so when one satisfies an endeavour, there is success, when one resists it, there arises pain. There are as many universal mirrors as minds, for every mind perceives the whole universe, but confusedly.[10]

Force or power should now be treated; when it is to be known, it must be estimated from the quantity of the effect. But the power of the effect and of the cause are equal to each other, for if that of the effect were greater, we would have a mechanical perpetual motion, if less, we would not have physical perpetual motion. Here it is worth showing that the same quantity of motion cannot be conserved, but that on the other hand the same quantity of power is conserved.[11] It must be seen, however, whether the same quantity of motion is not even conserved in the universe as a whole. . . .

**1392**          **24. Created Things Are Actually Infinite[1]**          **Aiv266**
[Summer 1678–Winter 1680–81][2]

**1393** Created things are actually infinite.
For any body whatever is actually divided into several parts,
    since any body whatever is acted upon by other bodies.
And any part whatever of a body is a body,
    by the very definition of body.
So bodies are actually infinite,
    i.e. more bodies can be found than there are unities in any given number.

Consequentia patet; quia si quaelibet divisio poneretur facta in duas tantum partes, neglectis reliquis; et ex his duabus partibus altera tantum subdivisa poneretur, subdivisione alterius tot minimum prodirent partes, quot fiunt divisiones, ut $A = L + B, B = M + C, C = N + D,$ patet ex tribus divisionibus prodire minimum tria diversa, $L, M, N.$

| 1393 | **Definitiones cogitationesque metaphysicae** | Aiv267 |

*Corpus* est extensum resistens.

Eo enim solo discerni potest a spatio, quod concipimus ut extensum, absolute, sine alio addito.

1394   *Extensum* est quod habet magnitudinem et situm.

*Resistens* est quod agit in id a quo patitur.

*Vacuum* est extensum sine resistentia.

Physica est Arithmeticae sive Algebrae subordinata quatenus agit de magnitudine; Geometriae quatenus agit de situ; Metaphysicae quatenus de resistentia sive actione et passione.

Si duo corpora sibi resistant, et nos actionem passionemque unius velut ad nos pertinentem, alterius velut alienam, illud corpus dicetur *organon,* hoc dicetur *objectum;* ipsa autem perceptio dicetur *sensus.*

*Imago* est continuatio passionis in organo cessante licet actione objecti.

*Imaginatio* est imaginis perceptio.

*Memoria* est perceptionis suae perceptio.

*Judicium* est affirmatio vel negatio, eaque vera vel falsa.

Judicia de sensibilibus ex sequentibus principiis sumenda sunt.

*Prima principia intellectualia* de rerum *essentia*

Omne judicium vel verum vel falsum est.

Nullum judicium simul verum et falsum est.

Aut affirmatio aut negatio vera est.

Aut affirmatio aut negatio falsa est.

The inference is obvious; for if we suppose any division to be made into only two parts, neglecting the others; and we suppose only the second of these two parts to be subdivided, at least as many parts will be produced by this subdivision as there are divisions made: for example, if $A = L + B$, $B = M + C$, $C = N + D$, it is obvious that from the three divisions at least three different things are produced, $L$, $M$, and $N$.

**1393**       **25. Metaphysical Definitions and Reflections** [1]       Aiv267

[Summer 1678–Winter 1680–81][2]

**I**

*Body* is a resisting extended thing.[3]

For from this alone it can be distinguished from space, which we conceive as that which is extended, absolutely, without the addition of anything else.

**1394**       The *extended* is that which has magnitude and situation.

A *resisting* thing is that which acts on that by which it is acted upon.

A *vacuum* is an extended thing without resistance. Whether there is one, or whether it is even possible, is another question.

Physics is subordinated to Arithmetic, or Algebra, insofar as it concerns magnitude; to Geometry insofar as it concerns situation; to Metaphysics insofar as it concerns resistance, i.e. action and passion.

If two bodies resist one another, and we perceive the action and passion of one as pertaining to us, and those of the other as foreign to us, the former body is called an *organ,* the latter is called an *object;* but the perception itself is called a *sensation.*

An *image* is the continuation of a passion in an organ despite the cessation of the action of the object.

*Imagination* is the perception of an image.

*Memory* is the perception of one's perception.

*Judgment* is affirmation or negation, and it is either true or false.

Judgments about sensible things are derived from the following principles:

*Intellectual First Principles* of the Essence of Things

Every judgment is either true or false.

No judgment is simultaneously true and false.

Either the affirmation or the negation is true.

Either the affirmation or the negation is false.

Omnis veritatis ratio reddi potest, exceptis illis primis, in quibus idem afirmatur de se ipso aut negatur de opposito, *A est A. A non est non A.*

**1395** Omnis falsitas refutari potest exceptis primis, in quibus idem negatur de seipso, vel affirmatur de opposito, *A non est A. A est non A.*

Scilicet connexio praedicati et subjecti quae fundamentum est veritatis, vel immediata est, vel mediata, ac proinde ad immediatam reducibilis per resolutionem, quod ipsum est *probare a priori,* seu *rationem reddere.*

Principium intellectuale de rerum existentia.

Ex pluribus possibilibus incompatibilibus existit perfectius.

*Perfectius* voco quod plus essentiae involvit. Est enim perfectio nihil aliud quam essentiae gradus. Et ideo ante omnia existit Ens quod omnes perfectiones continet seu Deus, mundus etiam a Deo fit perfectissimo modo; et quam maxima praestantur quam minima loci temporis materiae impensa. Et ex variis modis formandi res, praeferuntur illi, qui pauciores ab existendo secludunt, uti sapiens Architectus lapides ita junget, ne plus spatii occupent quam impleant, ne locum aliis auferant. Hinc etiam si quid existentia sua nullius existentiam impedit, id existit. Denique operationes Dei sunt tanquam excellentissimi Geometrae qui optimas problematum constructiones exhibere novit.

*Prima principia sensualia* seu primae perceptiones

I. Ego sum qui percipio.
II. Varia sunt quae percipio.

Sunt nonnulli qui prius tantum inculcant, *cogito ergo sum.* Sed omittunt alterum quod longe est foecundius. Duo enim ante omnia experienti occurrunt, varias esse perceptiones, et unum eundemque esse se qui percipit. Unde non tantum infertur esse percipientem, sed etaim rationem tam variae perceptionis esse debere extra percipientem; ac proinde alia esse praeter me. Ex priori pervenio in cognitionem mei, ex posteriori in cognitionem mundi.

For every truth a reason can be provided, excepting those first truths in which the same thing is affirmed of the thing itself or is denied of its opposite. *A is A. A is not not-A.*

**1395**     Every falsehood can be proved false, excepting first falsehoods, in which the same thing is denied of the thing itself, or affirmed of its opposite. *A is not A. A is not-A.*

That is to say, the connection of predicate and subject that is the foundation of truth is either immediate; or it is mediate, and is accordingly reducible to an immediate connection through resolution, which is *to prove a priori*, i.e. *to provide a reason.*

### Intellectual Principles of the Existence of Things

Of several incompatible possibles, the more perfect exists.

I call *more perfect* what involves more essence. For perfection is nothing but degree of essence. And therefore above all there exists a Being that contains all perfections, that is, God. Also the world is made by God in the most perfect way; and a maximum outlay is achieved with minimum expenditure of place, time, and matter. And of the various ways of forming things, those are preferred which exclude the fewest things from existing, in the same way that a wise architect joins stones in such a way that they take up no more space than they fill, lest they take away space for others. Hence also if something by its existence does not impede the existence of any other thing, it exists. Finally the workings of God are like those of a most excellent geometer who knows how to produce the best constructions for his problems.[4]

### *First Principles of Sensation* or of First Perceptions

(i) I, who perceive, exist.
(ii) The things I perceive are various.

There are some who inculcate only the first of these, which they express as *cogito ergo sum* (I think therefore I am). But they leave out the second, which is much more fruitful. For two things above all occur to someone experiencing, that the perceptions are various, and that it is one and the same person who is perceiving. From this it is not only inferred that there is a percipient, but also that the reason that perceptions are so various must be outside the percipient; and therefore that there are other things besides me. From the first I arrive at a knowledge of myself, from the second at a knowledge of the world.

**1396**          Principia opinionum

Quod est facilius id est probabilius.

Facilius autem intelligo, quod pauciora habet requisita seu cujus gratia pauciores faciendae sunt suppositiones.

Mutatio non praesumitur.

Sive unumquodque credendum est manere statu in quo fuit, donec appareat ratio credendi quod ab eo discesserit.

Principium certitudinis physicae

Phaenomena caeteris consentientia *vera* habentur, ubi etiam adumbratur, quod *Corpus, Spatium, Tempus, Mundus, Individuum.*

Ex hoc principio somnia discernimus ab his quae nobis vigilantibus obveniunt. Nam si quod somnium perfecte cum statu vitae praecendentis ac sequentis cohaeret, aut si diu duraret sine ulla solita somniis incongruitate nemo suspicari posset se somniare. Ac si quis Platonicus diceret vitam praesentem totam somnium esse bene cohaerens, animamque morte evigilaturam; is fortasse nonnisi a priori refutari potest ex cognita ratione universi quae nulla hujusmodi interludia patitur, omnia enim ad tempus locumque generalem revocantur, et ex caeteris secundum certas quasdam leges exurgunt. Idemque de eo est, qui negaret ulla existere corpora ullasve alias substantias praeter ipsum cogitantem. Licet enim per se possibile esset mentem tuam ita esse constitutam ut cogitanti tibi soli existenti eaedem imagines objicerentur immidate, quae nunc coexistentibus aut mediantibus aliis rebus offerentur, hoc tamen non est consentaneum primis rationibus rerum; quia nulla causa est, cur in universo tui unius ratio habeatur, cum tot aliae possint dum non est, homines qui tecum quotidie loqui videntur, aeque veros homines esse ac te, cum par ipsis ratio esse possit dubitandi de te. Causae quoque phaenomenorum extra te esse debent, atque extra alios quoque cogitantes, cum consentientia pluribus **1397** appareant, et ex natura tua adeo limitata ratio tot novarum inter se cohaerentium apparitionum reddi non possit. Hinc jam or[itur consideratio *spatii cujusdam generalis*] dum phaenomenis situs quidam certi assignantur dis-

**1396**          Principles of Opinions

That which is easier is more probable.

By the easier I mean that which has fewer requisites, i.e. that for whose sake fewer suppositions must be made.

There is no presumption that change will occur.

That is to say, every single thing must be believed to remain in the state it was in, until one sees a reason for believing that it has abandoned this state.

Principles of Physical Certitude

Phenomena which agree with the rest are held to be *true*, whereby *Body, Space, Time, World, Individual* are also adumbrated.

By means of this principle we distinguish dreams from the things that happen when we are awake. For if some dream is perfectly coherent with the state of life preceding and following it, or if it lasts for a long time without the usual incongruity of dreams, no one could suspect himself of dreaming. And if some Platonist were to say that the whole of his present life is a well-cohering dream, and that his soul will awaken at death; perhaps he could not be refuted a priori without knowing the reason for a universe which underwent no interlude of this sort. For all things are referred to a generic time and place, and are extruded from the rest according to certain particular laws. And the same would apply to someone who denied that any bodies or any other substances exist apart from the person that thinks. For although it would in itself be possible for your mind to be so constituted that, with only you the thinker existing, the same images would be immediately presented as are now produced by coexisting or other thinking things; nevertheless, this is not consistent with the primary reasons of things; because there is no explanation why there would be reason for one of you in the universe, when there could be so many other thinking substances more perfect than you, or certainly no less perfect. So it is beyond doubt that people who seem to be speaking with you today are people just as real as you, since there is just as much reason for them to be in doubt about you. The causes of the phenomena, too, must be outside you, and also outside other thinking beings, since they appear to be in

**1397**   agreement with many things; and, with your nature being limited in this way, no reason can be provided for so many new appearances cohering among themselves.

Hence now there arises the consideration of a certain generic *space*[5] whenever certain particular situations are assigned to the phenomena, and

tantiaeque rerum observantur atque anguli, qui sine causa non immutantur. Ita si quid loco fixo clausoque reponimus, id eo loco iterum reperire non dubitamus, nisi vis quaedam aut alius casus supervenerit. Atque hoc spatium omnibus commune est, et ea ipsa phaenomena vocamus *corpora* quibus situm assignare possumus, ut stellas: nullumque est corpus quod non in spatio illo generale esse, et a dato alio corpore distare cogitetur. Quae vero situm hujusmodi certum non habent, ut iris, ut imago in aqua, ea ideo emphatica appellamus sive simpliciter apparitiones, quarum tamen rationes ex corporum actionibus reddimus. Cum autem contingant mutationes, quae situm assignatum perturbant, hinc evitandae confusionis causa, excogitatus est modus distinguendi quae quibus sint priora aut posteriora, aut simul, referendo omnia ad mutationes illas quae deprehensa sunt uniformes, quales sunt motus stellarum; atque hic rerum inter se respectus dicitur *tempus,* quod etiam generale est, cunctaque complectitur, nihil enim contingere potest, quod non sit prius vel posterius vel simul alteri cuilibet dato.

Ope jam temporis et loci etiam *individua* distinguimus et quae eadem quae diversa sint dijudicamus; exempli gratia si duo ova per omnia similia et aequalia ob oculos habeam, velimque ea distinguere, vel aliqua nota in ipsis facienda est, quo reddantur dissimilia, vel collocanda sunt in loco aliquo fixo, unum verbi gratia supra, alterum infra; veldenique si libera reliquenda sunt, aut etiam si motus eis permittendus est, verbi gratia si in aqu natant, tunc id unum superest ut motus eorum oculis persequar, quo appareat scilicet quomodo successione temporis situm mutent, neque enim idem corpus simul in diversis locis reperitur, neque a loco in locum nisi per intermedia transit.

Porro omnium corporum quae in spatio esse intelliguntur sive quae situm invicem habent collectio dicitur *Mundus,* et pro variis temporibus varii sunt Mundi status; quorum tamen unus ex alio nascitur, secundum **1398** certas quasdam Leges, quas tradere physici est, ut ex praesentibus praeterita ac futura in usum vitae colligamus. Nam ille demum in natura satis profecisse dicendus est, qui praedictiones cum successu facere potest. Itaque quae Sceptici contra observationes objiciunt, inania sunt. Dubitent sane de rerum veritate, ac si placet, quae nobis obveniunt, somnia vocent, sufficit haec somnia inter se consentanea esse, certasque leges servare ac

one observes the distances and angles of things, which do not change without cause. Thus if we put something in a fixed and enclosed place, we do not doubt that it will be found in this place unless some force or some other occurrence supervenes. And this space is common to everything, and those very phenomena to which we can assign a situation, for example, stars, we call *bodies;* and there is no body which cannot be thought to exist in this generic space, and to be at a distance from some other given body. But those bodies which do not have a definite situation of this kind, such as a rainbow or an image in water, we therefore call *emphatica* or simply apparitions, for which we can nevertheless provide reasons from the actions of bodies.

But since changes occur which disturb the assigned situation, for the sake of avoiding confusion a way is devised for distinguishing which are before or after which, and which are simultaneous, by referring everything to those changes which are discovered to be uniform, such as are the motions of the stars. And this relation of things with each other is called *time,* which is also generic, and comprises the whole of everything, for nothing can occur which is not either before or after or simultaneous with any other given thing.

Now with the aid of time and place we can also distinguish *individuals,* and decide which are the same and which are different; for example, if I have two eggs in front of me that are similar and equal throughout, and I want to distinguish them, we must either make some mark on them by which they will be rendered dissimilar, or collect them together in some fixed place, for example, with one above and the other below; or finally, if they are to be left free, or even if motion is allowed them, for example, if they are floating in water, then this one thing suffices, that their motions be followed by the eyes. By this means it may appear, that is to say, how they change situation by a succession of time, for the same body is not found in different places at the same time, nor can it pass from one place to another except through intermediary ones.

Furthermore, the collection of all bodies that are understood to be in space, i.e. those that have mutual situation, is called the *world,* and there are various states of the world at various times. Of these, however, one **1398** comes out of another according to certain laws, which it is for physics to treat, so that from present things we may infer past and future ones to life's advantage. For he who can finally make predictions with success must be said to have become sufficiently proficient in nature. And so the objections the Sceptics make against observations are inane. Certainly, they may doubt the truth of things, and if it pleases them to call the things that occur to us dreams, it suffices for these dreams to be in agreement with

proinde prudentiae humanae ac praedictionibus relinqui locum. Quo posito sola de nomine quaestio est, hujusmodi enim apparitiones a nobis verae appellantur neque video quomodo veriores vel reddi vel optari possint.

Corpus est Extensum mobile, vel corpus est substantia extensa.

Demonstrari potest has definitiones coincidere, substantia enim a me definitur, quod agere potest; actio autem extensi cum motu est, scilicet locali.

Omne corpus actu ipso movetur.

Nam omnis substantia actu ipso operatur, quod in Metaphysicis demonstratur.

Omne corpus organicum est, sive actu ipso divisum est in partes minores peculiari motu praeditas adeoque non dantur atomi.

Nam omnis substantia finita actu ipso patitur (cum enim actu ipso agat et finita sive imperfecta sit, semper refringitur actio ejus sive nonnihil impeditur), omnis autem passio corporis est cum divisione.

Omne corpus animatum est sive sentit et appetit.

Omnis enim substantia tam perfecta est quam per caeteras esse potest. Per caetera autem corpora non stat quin unoquoque anima sit, sive appetitus tantus quanta est in eo vis agendi, tantusque sensus quanta est in eo vis patiendi. Soli autem homini aliisque paucis corporibus animam tribuere, tam ineptum est, quam credere omnia solius hominis causa facta est.

**1399**

Forma substantialis seu Anima est principium unitatis et durationis, materia vero multitudinis et mutationis.

Cum enim corpus dixerimus divisum esse in partes actu, quae diverso singulae motu cientur, et ob eandem rationem quaelibet pars rursus divisa sit, sane si solam materiam spectemus nec punctum assignari poterit quod cum altero maneat, nec momentum quo idem corpus maneat secum ipso; et nunquam ratio erit dicendi aliquod corpus esse unum ultra punctum, et idem ultra momentum. Cumque ipsa puncta ipsaque momenta, non sint res, sed termini sive modi rerum, itaque si sola in corpore materia esset, nihil in eo realitatis sive perfectionis. Si vero sola in corpore forma esset, nihil in eo mutabile esset atque imperfectum.

Nullus est locus sine corpore, et nullum tempus sine mutatione.

Qui non satis intelligunt principia metaphysica facile vacuum et atomos, sive corpora infrangibilia credunt cum tamen absurdum sit esse cor-

each other, and to obey certain laws, and accordingly to leave room for human prudence and predictions. And granting this, it is only a question of names. For apparitions of this kind we call *true,* and I do not see how they could be either rendered or chosen truer.

## II

Body is a movable extended thing, or body is extended substance.[6]

It can be demonstrated that these definitions coincide,[7] for I define substance as that which can act; but the action of an extended thing is by motion, namely, local motion.

Every body is actually in motion.

For every substance is actually operating, as is demonstrated in Metaphysics.

Every body is organic, i.e. is actually divided into smaller parts endowed with their own particular motions, so that there are no atoms.

For every finite substance is actually acted upon (for, since it is actually acting, and is finite, i.e. imperfect, its action is always diffused, or to some extent impeded); every passion of a body, on the other hand, is by division.

Every body is animate, i.e. has sensation and appetite.[8]

For every substance is as perfect as it can be through all the others. But it cannot depend on all the other bodies without there being in each one a
**1399** soul, i.e. as much appetite as there is in it a force of acting, and as much sensation as there is in it a force of being acted upon. But to attribute a soul only to man and to a few other bodies is as inept as believing that everything is made for the sake of man alone.

Substantial form, or soul, is the principle of unity and of duration, matter is that of multiplicity and change.[9]

For since we have said that body is actually divided into parts, each of which is agitated with a different motion, and since for the same reason each part is again divided, then certainly if we consider matter alone, no point will be assignable that will remain together with another, nor a moment at which a body will remain identical with itself; and there will never be a reason for saying that a body is a unity over and above a point, and the same for longer than a moment. And since points and moments themselves are not things, but bounds, i.e. modes, of things, it follows that if there were only matter in body, there would be no reality or perfection in it. But if there were only form in body, there would be nothing changeable and imperfect in it.

There is no place without body, and no time without change.[10]

Those who do not well enough understand the principles of metaphysics easily believe in the vacuum and atoms, i.e. unbreakable bodies, when in fact it is absurd for there to be a body which cannot be acted

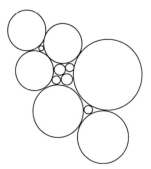

pus quod pati non possit aut sentire. Si jam ponamus omne corpus actu divisum esse in partes, facile resolvuntur objectiones contra plenum. Et vero
manifestum est si omnia globis plena ponantur, inter interstitia novos
iterum globos interponi posse in infinitum salvo motu, tantum enim
necesse est minores globos celerius moveri. Jam si possibile est omnia
esse plena, etiam omnia plena erunt, absurdum est enim locum relinqui inutilem, in quo infinitae creaturae esse possunt. Eadem est ratio cur nullum
tempus sit sine mutatione. Erit enim perinde ac si non esset.

*Corpus* est substantia quae agere et pati potest.

*Materia* est principium passionis,

*Forma* principium actionis.

Intelligentiae purae agere possunt pati non possunt. Itaque solus Deus
est intelligentia pura, caeterae omnes in materia sunt, quemadmodum
mens nostra, ita Angeli quoque.

**1400**     Quia principium passionis multitudinem in se potestate continere necesse est, ideo materia continuum est plura simul continens, sive *extensum*.

Omnis forma quodammodo *Anima* est sive sensus atque appetitus capax.

Tametsi omnia sint animata, nihilo minus omnia agunt secundum leges
Mechanicas, nam sensus atque appetitus organis (id est partibus corporis)
et objectis (sive circumstantibus corporibus) determinantur.

Omne corpus actu ipso agit et patitur.

Omne corpus in omnia alia agit et ab omnibus aliis patitur, sive omnia
alia percipit.

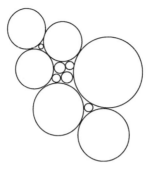

Figure 1

upon[11] or have sensation. Now if we suppose that every body is actually divided into parts, the objections against the plenum are easily resolved.[12] And truly it is evident that if everything is supposed full of globes, then between the interstices new globes can again be placed to infinity without violating motion, for it is only necessary for the smaller globes to move more swiftly. Now if it is possible for everything to be a plenum, then everything will be a plenum, for it is absurd for any place to be left useless in which there could be an infinity of creatures.[13] This is the same reason why there is no time without change. For it would be exactly as if it did not exist.

## III

*Body* is a substance that can act and be acted upon.

*Matter* is the principle of passion, i.e. of being acted upon;

*Form* is the principle of action.

Pure intelligences can act, but cannot be acted upon. Thus only God is a pure intelligence; all the rest are in matter, as is our mind, and so also an angel's.

**1400**      Because a principle of passion must effectually contain within itself a multiplicity, matter is a continuum containing a plurality of things at the same time, i.e. an *extended thing.*

Every form is in a way a *soul,* i.e. capable of sensation and appetite.

Even though all things are animate, nonetheless they all act according to the laws of mechanics, for sensation and appetite are determined by organs (i.e. parts of a body) and objects (i.e. by surrounding bodies).[14]

Every body is actually acting and being acted upon.

Every body acts on all others and is acted upon by all others, i.e. perceives all others.

Itaque omnis substantia quandam in se habet omniscientiae atque omnipotentiae divinae participationem, etsi confusa ejus cognitio sit, et actio a contrariis agentibus refracta.

Illae solae Animae verae immortales sunt, quae sese easdem esse agnoscere possunt; hae enim solae praemii poenaeque adeoque et legum sunt capaces. Et his Deus non solum principium est sed et princeps. Sunt enim cives in Republica Universi cujus rex Deus est. Quae cum optima sit, nullum bonum opus in ea neglectum erit, nullum peccatum impune.

Omnis materiae portio utcunque parva actu divisa est in partes minores, quae diverso motu cientur.

Consistentia corporis seu cohaesio partium ejus ex eo oritur, quod eo cientur motu, quo parum admodum sejunguntur, cumque cum motu a toto circumstanti systemate nacta sint, sine vi divelli non possunt, id est sine aliqua systematis perturbatione.

Nullum corpus perfecte quiescit.

Quando duo corpora ad se invicem accedunt ex sola causa motus dijudicari potest, non ex ipso motu, utrum quiescat aut moveatur, aut an ambo moveantur. Idem est de pluribus.

Omne corpus agit in omne aliud corpus, et ab eo patitur. Nam quia omnia plena sunt omnis conatus propagatur in infinitum. Omnis autem conatus aliquid efficit, etsi debilioris effectus sit minor.

**1401**  Omnis corporis potentia infinita est; unum autem corpus voco, cujus partium actio omnis ipsius illius corporis unius actio est cujusque autem corporis infinitae sunt partes, adeoque infinita vis, quae cum a circumstantibus pari aut etiam majori nisu pollentibus contineatur, ne scilicet extra agere, aut imposita corpora a se rejicere possit, intra seipsam exercetur. Hoc similitudine declarari potest aëris naturalis, qui incumbente remoto sponte se dilatat in spatium majus quam credi possit.

Si omnia corpora juxta se quiescerent, tanta foret unius potentia, quanta singulorum ejusdem molis.

Nam unumquodque omnium aliorum vim sustineret. Declarari potest similitudine Elastri aëris, nulla enim tam exigua aeris portio est, quae non toti ponderi atque Elastro aëris incumbentis et circumstantis sustinendo par sit.

Cujuslibet corporis partes unum continuum consituunt.

Thus every substance has in itself a certain participation in divine omniscience and omnipotence, even though its knowledge is confused, and its action is diffused by things acting in contrary ways.

Only those true souls are immortal which can recognize themselves to be the same; for these alone are capable of reward and punishment and therefore also receptive of laws. And for these God is not only the principle, but also the prince. For they are citizens of the Republic of the Universe, whose king is God. And since this republic is the best, there will be no good deed in it unheeded, and no sin unpunished.

Every portion of matter however small is actually divided into smaller parts, which are agitated by different motions.

The cohesiveness of a body, i.e. the cohesion of its parts, arises from the fact that they are agitated with so little motion that they hardly separate at all, and since they are endowed with a motion by the whole surrounding system, they cannot be pulled apart without force, that is, without some disturbance of the system.

No body is perfectly at rest.

When two bodies approach each other, it can only be decided from the cause of motion, not from the motion itself, which of the two is at rest or moves, or whether both are moving. It is the same with several bodies.

**IV**

Every body acts on every other body, and is acted upon by it. For since everything is a plenum, every endeavour is propagated to infinity. But every endeavour has some effect, even though the effect of a weaker endeavour is smaller.

**1401**  The power of every body is infinite. Now I call a body one if every action of its parts is an action of that one body and if the parts of this body are infinite. And so the infinite force, which is contained by an equal or even greater striving from the powerful surrounding bodies, is consequently exerted inwards so as to prevent it from acting outwards, or repelling bodies that are placed on it. This can be clarified by analogy with the natural air, which, on the removal of whatever was holding it in, spontaneously expands into space more than might be believed.

If all bodies were at rest against each other, each one would have as much power as every other one of the same bulk.

For each would sustain the force of all the others. This can be clarified by analogy with the elasticity of air, for no portion of air is so small that it is not equal to the sustaining of the whole weight and elasticity of the surrounding air pressing down on it.

The parts of any body constitute one continuum.[15]

Nam unitas semper manet quanta maxima potest, salva multitudine, quod fit si corpora plicari potius quam dividi intelligantur. Ut chorda tremens una est, etsi nulla sit pars ejus quae non peculiarem habeat motum. Qui hanc propositionem satis intelliget, vanas quaestiones de sede animae ridebit.

Primos rerum fontes quarenti investigandum est quomodo materia in partes divisa sit, et quis earum motus.

Hoc ita mihi investigasse videor. Semper unitas multitudini jungenda est quantum licet. Itaque divisam ajo materiam non quidem in partes mole aequales, ut aliqui posuere, neque in partes celeritate aequales, sed in partes potentia aequales, mole autem et celeritate inaequales, ita ut essent **1402** siclicet celeritates in reciproca magnitudinum ratione. Ita enim omnia turbata quidem erunt, sed summa cum ratione. Nam si turbata non essent, non viverent, si non certa ratione turbata essent, non cognoscerentur.

*Universum est animarum causa et finis rerum est summa Dei gloria, cujus effectus est maxima felicitas possibilis animarum.*

Haec propositio altioribus quibusdam contemplationibus nititur de natura Dei.

*Eae demum animae immortales sunt, quae sunt Leges capaces.*

Hae solae habendae pro civibus universi, id est ejus Reipublicae cujus Rex Deus est. His poenae; his praemia destinantur: hi soli cogitant quid universo debeant, aut potius quid Deo. Caeterarum animarum principium est Deus, princeps non est: neque enim illis notus esse potest velut una quaedam substantia quae cuncta regit. Unde sequiur quanto quisque magis noscit autorem suum eo esse vera vita digniorem.

*Etsi omnia animata sint et cum sensu atque appetitu agant, attamen secundum leges Mechanicae agunt.*

Video plerosque in hoc negotio in extrema ire. Nam nonnulli qui cuncta mechanicis legibus geri putant, omnes substantias incorporeas causasque finales tollunt. Contra qui has admittunt, jam sibi solo instinctu quidvis efficere posse videntur, nec quaerunt quomodo res gerantur. Ego arbitror utramque efficientem et finalem conjugendas, omnia enim fieri voluptatis animarum causa, adeoque animas volendo agere, sed vicissim vim earum in infinitum ituram mechanicis legibus determinari. Eas autem ex pari nisu contrario corporum oriri. Itaque anima hominis efficere non potest, ut corpus altius exiliat, quam pro impetu, quem ei motus partium interiorum

For a unity always lasts as long as it can without destroying multiplicity, and this happens if bodies are understood to be folded rather than divided.[16] As, for example, a chord is one vibration, even though there is no part of it that does not have its own particular motion. Whoever understands this proposition well enough will laugh at the vain questions concerning the seat of the soul.

Anyone seeking the primary sources of things must investigate how matter is divided into parts, and which of them is moving.

This, so it seems to me, I have investigated. A unity must always be joined to a multiplicity to the extent that it may. So I say that matter is divided not even into parts of equal bulk, as some have supposed, nor into parts of equal speed, but into parts of equal power, but with bulk and speed unequal in such a way that the speeds are in inverse ratios to the magnitudes. For in this way all things will indeed be disturbed, but with the utmost reason. For if they were not disturbed, they would not be alive, and if they were not disturbed in a certain ratio, they would not become known.

**1402**

*The overall cause of souls and purpose of things is the greatest glory of God, the effect of which is the maximum possible happiness of souls.*

This proposition depends on certain rather profound contemplations about the nature of God.

*Those souls, finally, are immortal which are receptive of laws.*

These alone are to be considered citizens of the universe, i.e. of the Republic of which God is King. To these are destined punishments, to these rewards.[17] These alone think about what they owe to the universe, or rather what they owe to God. God is the principle of the other souls, not their prince; for he cannot be known by them as a certain unique substance who rules everything. Whence it follows that the better someone knows his author, the more worthy he is of a true life.

*Even though all things are animated and act with sense and appetite, they nevertheless act according to the Laws of Mechanics.*

I see that in this matter most people go to extremes. For some who think that everything is governed by the laws of mechanics, do away with all incorporeal substances and final causes. On the other hand, those who admit them see them as being able to bring anything about by instinct alone, and do not try to find out how things are governed. I believe that both efficient and final cause should be conjoined, for everything happens because of the will of souls, so that souls act by willing, but again, each of their forces going to infinity is determined by the laws of mechanics. These forces, however, have their origin in an equal contrary striving of other bodies. And so a man's soul cannot make his body jump to any greater height than one proportional to the impetus which the motion of his interior parts col-

in eum usum collectus inprimere potest. Neque est cur illi sibi prae aliis sapere videantur, qui omnibus corporibus praeterquam humanis animas ridicula dissimulatoris fortasse magistri imitatione adimunt Nam quemadmodum non ideo minus homo secundum leges motuum agit patiturque, etsi sentiat atque appetat, ita in caeteris animatis idem proportione quadam intelligetur. Caeterum animarum quae Deum noscere possunt, rectaque vi-

**1403** tam ratione dirigere ad generale bonum in Republica universi infinitum a caeteris discrimen erit. Ideo non est quod animas brutorum hominumque ejusdem conditionis fore metuamus.

*Omnia naturae phaenomena explicari possent per solas causas finales, perinde ac si nulla esset causa efficiens; et omnia naturae phaenomena explicari possent per solas causas efficientes, quasi nulla esset finalis.*

Prior Methodus Platonis fuisse videtur, de qua ille eleganter disseruit in *Phaedone* ubi Anaxagorae corpuscula irridet, altera fuit Democriti, quam suo quodam modo nostra quaedam egregii quidam viri resuscitavere. Potest enim Deus considerari tum ut principium rerum corporearum, tum ut Rector animarum, ut enim partes materiae motu semel impresso, ita animas sensu boni excitat. Illi demum utramque methodum conjungiunt, qui cogitant Deum autorem rerum et summe potentem et summe sapientem esse eumque et magnitudinem suam et pulchritudinem in mundo quadam ratione expressisse. Caeterum haec et in usu vitae et in ipsis scientiis utilia sunt, prodest enim fines rerum ususque ex ipsis effectibus rimari, cum ut providentiam gubernatricem adoremus, tum etiam aliquando ut occulta naturae opera divinemus. Quod saepe fit ab anatomicis, ex usus partium consideratione. Atque ut exemplo utar etiam in alio rerum genere, facilius demonstrantur leges reflexionis et refractionis radiorum ex contempla-

**1404** tione finalis quam efficientis causae.

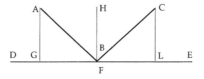

Nam exempli causa quod radius incidens *AB,* et reflexus *BC* faciunt angulos incidentiae *ABD* et reflexionis *CBE* aequales, dupliciter demonstrari

lected for this use can impress upon it. And isn't this why those who do away with souls for all bodies other than human ones—in a laughable imitation of the master dissembler, perhaps[18]—seem to know themselves better than others? For just as a man neither acts nor is acted upon any the less in accordance with the laws of motion even though he has sensation and appetite, so the same thing will be understood in a certain proportion in the other animated beings. Still, those souls that can know God and direct their life with sound reason towards the general good in the universal Republic will be infinitely distinguished from the rest. There is therefore no reason to fear that the souls of the lower animals and those of people will be in the same condition.

1403

*All the phenomena of nature can be explained solely by final causes, exactly as if there were no efficient cause; and all the phenomena of nature can be explained solely by efficient causes, as if there were no final cause.*

The former seems to have been the method of Plato, concerning which he discoursed elegantly in the *Phaedo* when he made fun of Anaxagoras's corpuscles; the latter was that of Democritus, which certain distinguished men have revived in their own way in our times.[19] For God can be considered not only as a principle of corporeal things, but also as the director of souls. For as he once excited the parts of matter with an impressed motion, so he excited souls with good sense. Finally, those conjoin both methods who think God is the author of things and is supremely powerful and supremely wise, and has expressed his magnitude and beauty in the world by a certain reason. For the rest, these things are useful both in life and in the sciences themselves, for it is an advance for the limits and uses of things to be examined by their effects, not only that we should adore a governing providence, but also that we should divine the hidden works of nature. This often happens in anatomy, from a consideration of the uses of the parts. And in order to use an example in things of another kind too, the laws of reflection and refraction of rays are more easily demonstrated by the contemplation of final than efficient causes.[20]

1404

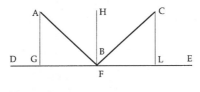

Figure 2

For example, the fact that the incident ray *AB* and the reflected ray *BC* make equal angles of incidence *ABD* and reflection *CBE* can be demon-

potest, per causam efficientem quidem considerando rectam *DE* inciden-
tis descensu flecti in arcum *DFE,* seque restituentem repercutere incidens
in perpendiculi *BH.* Hinc jam ratio habetur ejus quod alias sine ratione assumitur cur motus incidentiae adeoque et reflexionis hic dividendus sit in
compositum ex directione perpendiculari *AG* (quae sola et arcum, in tantum scilicet cedere coactum, in quantum ab incidente descenditur, flectit,
et restitutione ejus in contrariam aequivelocem vertitur) et horizontali *GB,*
qui nihil passus eadem ad perpendicularem proportione celeritatis
residuus manet. Ideo quo tempore ille pervenit ex *B* in *H,* hoc iste ex *B* in
*L,* si *BL* ad *BH* ut *BG* ad *AG* vel si *BL* aeq. *BG* et si *HB* aequal. *CL,* motus
autem compositus ex directionibus *BH* et *BL* est in *FC.*

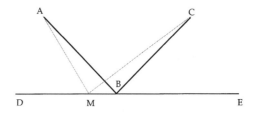

Sed idem veteres demonstravere argumento petito a causa finali, hoc
modo: Sit punctum *A* et aliud *C* posito jam quod illi assumunt, a quolibet
puncto *A* ad quodlibet ob easdem superficie reflectentis *DE* partes positum
*C* aliquem radium pervenire. Quis sit ille radius, sive sitne *AMC* an *ABC.*
Hoc ut inveniant utuntur principio sumto a causa finali, quod scilicet
natura aliquem sibi finem proponens optima media eligit. Itaque cum hic
ob diaphanum uniforme sola longi vel brevis itineris ratio haberi habeat,
sequitur eam a puncto *A* per reflexionem tendentem ad punctum *C* ituram
per punctum *B,* si *ABC* sit via omnium brevissima, seu si aggregatum rectarum *AB* + *BC,* sit minus quam aliarum quarumcunque ut *AM* + *MC.*
Constat autem ex Geometria si anguli *ABD* et *CBE* sint aequales aggregatum *ABC* fore omnium hujusmodi aggregatorum possibilium minimum.
Huic argumentationi recentiores quidam objicere solent, radium ex *A*
egredientem cognitione praeditum non esse nec quaerere an ad *C* iturus

1405

strated in two ways. It can be demonstrated by efficient causes by considering that a straight line *DE* is bent into an arc *DFE* by the fall of the incident body, and in restituting itself, pushes back the incident body along the
perpendicular *BH*. Hence now we obtain the reason for that which is elsewhere assumed without a reason[21]: why the motion of the incident body
and thus of the reflected body should here be divided into a composite of a
tendency in the perpendicular direction *AG* (in which direction alone the
arc both bends, having been forced to yield to exactly the degree that the
incident body descends, and returns, by recoiling with an equal velocity in
the opposite direction) and one in the horizontal direction *GB*, which, having not suffered change, is left with the same proportion of speed to the
perpendicular. Therefore in the time the former goes from *B* to *H*, the latter goes from *B* to *L*, so that if *BL* to *BH* is as *BG* to *AG*, or if *BL = BG* and
if *HB = CL*, then the motion composed from the tendencies in the directions *BH* and *BL* is along *FC*.

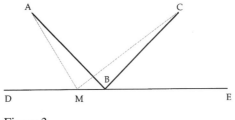

Figure 3

But the ancients demonstrated the same thing by an appeal to final
causes in this way[22]: Let there be a point *A* and another *C*, having supposed already what they assume: from any point *A*, because of the same
parts of the reflecting surface *DE*, some ray travels to any supposed point
*C*. Which is that ray, is it *AMC* or *ABC*? In order to discover this they use a
principle taken from final causes, namely, that nature, proposing some end
**1405** to itself, chooses the optimal means. And so since here, because of the uniform diaphanum, there ought to be a reason only for a long or a short journey, it follows that, tending from the point *A* to the the point *C* by reflection, it will go through the point *B* if *ABC* is the shortest path of all, or
if the sum of the straight lines *AB + BC* is smaller than that of each of the
others, e.g. *AM + MC*. But it is known from Geometry that if the angles
*ABD* and *CBE* are equal the sum *ABC* will be the minimum of all possible
sums of this kind. To this line of argument certain people of more recent
times have been wont to object that the ray coming from *A* is not endowed
with cognition, nor does it inquire whether it will go to *C* and which is the

sit, et quanam optima via eo sit perventurus, sed caeco impetu incurrere in
superficie refringentis punctum, ad quod concepta jam directione feretur;
atque inde secundum Mechanicas leges repercuti. Sed his non cogitant argumentum veterum esse sumtam a causa finale, et non radium quidem,
sed naturam tamen legum opticarum fundatricem cognitione praeditum
esse. quidque optimum et commodissimum futurum sit, praevidere.

### Materiam et motum esse phaenomena tantum          Aiv277

1463  Materiam et Motum esse phaenomena tantum, seu continere in se aliquid
imaginarii, ex eo intelligi potest, quod de iis diversae hypotheses contra-
dictoriae fieri possunt, quae tamen omnes perfecte satisfaciunt phaenomenis, ita ut nulla possit ratio excogitari definiendi utra sit praeferenda. Cum
tamen in realibus, omnis veritas accurate invenire et demonstrari possit.
Ita de motu alibi ostendi, non posse definiri in quo sit subjecto; et de materia non potest dici, utrum sit sublata. Exempli causa dici non potest an locus sit vacuus an materia perfecte fluida plenus; nihil enim interest. Item si
quis fingat materiae partem esse sublatam, reliquae in ejus locum succe-
dent; ab omnibus partibus universi, quod cum sit indefinitum, in extremis
ejus quae nulla sunt non potest intelligi aliquod vacuari in locum spatii re-
pleti quod corpus destructum deseruit. Itaque omnia erunt ut ante. Si quis
fingat Deum conservare locum illum vacuum, perinde est ac si fingamus
non corpus in eo esse destructum, sed infinita celeritate moveri, ut resitat
iis quae ab omni parte ingredi conantur, nec tamen in ipsa agere aliter seu
ea repellere, Deo eum effectum destruente.

### [Nullum datur unum corpus]          Aiv278

1464      (1) Pono id quod non majorem habet Unionem, quam ligna in fasce seu
strue lignorum, vel lateres sibi impositi, non esse proprie unum Ens sed
potius Entia, licet unum pro omnibus nomen ponatur.
       Idque verum esse sive parva sive magna sit eorum distantia item sive
lateres illi aut ligna in strue sint bene coordinata, sive non, id enim

best route for it to get there, but with blind impetus comes down on a point of the reflecting surface, to which it is carried in the direction already conceived, and from there rebounds according to mechanical laws. But these people do not think that the ancients' argument is derived from final causes; and it is not the ray itself, but the founding nature of optical laws that is endowed with cognition, and foresees what will be best and most fitting.

### 26. Matter and Motion Are Only Phenomena[1]     Aiv277
[c. 1678–79?][2]

**1463**   That matter and motion are only phenomena, or contain in themselves something imaginary, can be understood from the fact that different and contradictory hypotheses can be made about them, all of which nevertheless satisfy the phenomena perfectly, so that no reason can be devised for determining which of them should be preferred. In real things, on the other hand, every truth can be accurately discovered and demonstrated. Thus concerning motion I have shown elsewhere that it is not possible to determine which subject it is in;[3] and concerning matter, that it cannot be said whether it has been destroyed. For example, it cannot be said whether a place is empty, or full of perfectly fluid matter; for there is no difference between the two cases.[4] Likewise if anyone imagines that a part of matter is destroyed, the remaining matter will come into its place from all parts of the universe. For since the universe is indefinite, it has no extremities, so that it is unintelligible for something in them to be emptied into the place of the full space that the destroyed body abandoned. So everything will remain as before. And if anyone imagines that God keeps that place empty, this is exactly the same as imagining not that the body in it is destroyed, but that it moves with infinite swiftness to resist those things which are endeavouring to enter it from all sides, without, however, acting on them in any other way, or repelling them, God having destroyed this effect.

### 27. There Is No Such Thing as One Body[1]     Aiv278
[c. 1678–79][2]

**1464**   (1) I suppose that what has no greater unity than the logs in a bundle of firewood or logpile, or bricks placed one on top of the other, is not properly one entity, but rather entities, although one name can be supposed for them all.

And this is true whether they are close together or far apart, and likewise whether those bricks or logs in the pile are arranged together in an orderly

Unionem eorum non facit majorem; item licet singulae partes quendam motum communem habeant, vel aliud quiddam quod de omnibus praedicari possit.

(2) Pono item in corpore nihil aliud quam extensionem intelligi seu quod habeat partes extra partes.

(3) Pono denique omne corpus esse actu divisum in plures partes, quae sint etiam corpora.

Hinc sequitur

*Primo* nullum dari unum corpus.

*Secundo* imo nec ulla dari corpora, quae nihil aliud sunt quam corpus et corpus.

Hinc sequitur aut corpora esse mera phaenomena, non vero Entia realia, aut in corporibus aliud esse quam extensionem.

Argumentum hoc procedit, etiamsi positio tertia non concedatur. Modo concedatur, solum contactum non facere unum Ens, et proinde si duo fingantur corpora triangularia aequalia (non amplius subdivisa) quae componunt cubum, non magis ex iis fieri unum novum Ens, quam si ita se tangant tantum per apices seu in punctis. Item non magis fieri ex iis unum Ens, si

1465   alterum apud alterum in illa compositione cubi quiescat, quam si moveantur aut si momento aliquo tantum sint in illa situatione cubi, unde sequeretur cubum simul nasci et interire.

Item non magis fieri inde unum novum Ens, sive moveantur ita ut se tangant, sed motu in aequali, aut in diversa; sive moveantur ut comites cubum componentes.

## [Corpus non est substantia]                                               Aiv316

1637            *CORPUS NON EST SUBSTANTIA*
                *sed modus tantum Entis sive apparentia cohaerens*

Intelligo autem per corpus non id quod Scholastici ex materia et forma quadam intelligibili componunt sed quod molem alias Democritici vocant. Hoc ajo non esse substantiam. Demonstrabo enim si molem consideramus ut substantiam incidere nos in implicantia contradictionem, ex ipso continui labyrintho: ubi illud inprimis considerandum est, primum Atomos esse non posse, nam cum divina sapientia pugnant. Deinde corpora reipsa divisa esse in partes infinitas, nec tamen in puncta, ideoque

way or not, for this does not give them greater unity; likewise the individual parts may have some motion in common, or anything else that can be predicated of them all.

(2) I also suppose that nothing is intelligible in a body other than extension, i.e. what has parts beyond parts.

(3) Finally, I suppose that every body is actually divided into several parts, which are also bodies.[3]

From this it follows:

*First,* that there is no such thing as one body.

*Second,* that there are no such things as bodies either, these being nothing but one body after another.

Hence it follows that either bodies are mere phenomena, and not real entities, or there is something other than extension in bodies.

This argument succeeds even if the third supposition is not conceded, provided it is conceded that contact alone does not make one entity. Accordingly, if two equal triangular bodies (that are not further subdivided) are imagined to compose a cube, one new entity is no more made from them than if they were touching each other only through their vertices, i.e. at points.[4] Likewise one entity is no more made from them if one is at rest on top of the other in that composition of the cube, than if they are moving, or if they are in that situation of the cube only for a moment, in which case it would follow that the cube would come into being and perish simultaneously.

Likewise one new entity is no more made from them whether they move so that they are touching each other, but with a motion in the same or in different directions; or whether they move as companion pieces composing the cube.

**28. A Body Is Not a Substance[1]**                                              Aiv316

[c. 1678–79?][2]

1637                        *A BODY IS NOT A SUBSTANCE*
                          *but only a mode of being or coherent appearance*[3]

By 'body', however, I do not mean what the Scholastics compose out of matter and a certain intelligible form, but what the Democriteans elsewhere call bulk.[4] This, I say, is not a substance. For I shall demonstrate that if we consider bulk[5] as a substance, we will fall into contradiction as a result of the labyrinth of the continuum. In this context we must above all consider: first, that there cannot be atoms, since they conflict with divine wisdom; and second, that bodies are really divided into infinite parts, but

non posse ullo modo assignari corpus unum sed materiae portionem quamlibet esse ens per accidens, imo et in perpetuo fluxu: Si vero hoc tantum dicamus: corpora esse apparentias cohaerens, cessat omnis inquisitio de infinite parvis, quae percipi non possunt. Sed et hic locum habet, Herculeum illud argumentum, meum, quod ea omnia quae sintne an non sint a nemine percipi potest, nihil sunt. Jam ea est corporum natura, nam si Deus ipse vellet creare substantias corporeas quales fingunt homines, nihil ageret, neque ipse percipere posset, se aliquid egisse, quoniam nihil denique quam apparentiae percipiuntur. Signum veritatis itaque cohaerentia est, causa autem est voluntas Dei, formalis ratio est quod Deus percipit aliquid optimum esse seu hamonicwtaton, sive quod aliquid Deo placet. Itaque ipsa ut ita dicam voluntas divina est rerum existentia.


### Origo animarum et mentium                                              Aiv275


**1460**       *ORIGO ANIMARUM ET MENTIUM*

Quatenus Deus universum refert ad certum quoddam corpus, ipsumque totum velut ex hoc corpore spectat sive quod idem est omnes apparentias seu rerum relationes ad hoc corpus velut immobile consideratum cogitat, eo ipso corporis huius forma substantialis sive anima inde resultat quae sensu quodam atque appetitu absolvitur. Inest enim rebus omnibus quidam sensus atque appetitus naturalis qui legibus Mechanismi nihil derogat; neque enim ille tam causa quam occasio agendi est Deo.

**1461**       Mentes autem oriuntur, cum Deus totum universum considerat non tantum, ut Systema rerum sed et ut Civitatem cuius ipse Rex est. Itaque Mentes non tantum perfectione differunt ab Animabus aliis, sed et toto genere sive natura. Dedit enim Deus mentibus, ut cogitent de seipsis, unde oritur reminiscientia quae facit ut mens semper meminerit se eandem illam esse quae prius. Hinc sequitur etiam immortalitas, neque enim, vel incipere potest sui oblivisci, semperque cogitatio alia aliam trahit. At in animabus nulla est causa cur easdem manere dicamus, tametsi a corpore sint distinctae. Vera enim conservatio, consistit in conservationis suae sensu, qui si absit perinde est ac si extinctus sim, et alius creatus loco mei; neque enim unum ab altero discerni potest; adeoque pro eodem habendum est.

not into points. Consequently, there is no way one can designate one body,[6] rather, any portion of matter whatever is an accidental entity, and, indeed, is in perpetual flux. But if we say only this, that bodies are coherent appearances, this puts an end to all inquiry about the infinitely small, which cannot be perceived. But this is also a good place for that Herculean argument of mine, that all those things which are such that it is impossible for anyone to perceive whether they exist or not, are nothing.[7] Now this is the nature of bodies, for if God himself wished to create corporeal substances of the kind people imagine, he would have done nothing, nor could he perceive himself to have done anything, since in the last analysis nothing but appearances are perceived. So coherence is the sign of truth,[8] but its cause is the will of God, and its formal reason is that God perceives something to be the best or most harmonious, i.e. that something is pleasing to God. So divine will itself, so to speak, is the existence of things.

### 29. The Origin of Souls and Minds[1]                           Aiv275
[March–June 1681?][2]

**1460**        THE ORIGIN OF SOULS AND MINDS[3]

Insofar as God relates the universe to some particular body, and regards the whole of it as if from this body or, what is the same thing, thinks of all the appearances or relations of things to this body considered as immobile, there results from this the substantial form or soul of this body, which is completed by a certain sensation and appetite. For there is in all things a certain sensation and a natural appetite which does not at all detract from the laws of mechanism; for the latter is not so much a cause as an occasion for God's acting.

**1461**    Minds, on the other hand, arise when God considers the whole universe not merely as a system of things but as a community of which he is king. So minds differ from other souls not merely in perfection, but also in their whole genus or nature. For God granted minds that they should think about themselves, which gives rise to memory, which brings it about that the mind always remembers itself to be the same thing as before. From this, immortality also follows, for the mind cannot begin to forget itself, and one thought always attracts another. But in souls there is no cause for us to say that they remain the same, although they are distinct from body. For true conservation consists in a sense of one's conservation, and if this is absent, it is exactly as if I were extinguished, and another person created instead of me; for one cannot be discerned from the other; and so it would have to be regarded as the same.

Brutis est sensus, decretumque, sed non animadversio. In Deo solo est intelligere velle posse. In nobis est intellectus et voluntas, sed potentia nulla.

Realitatem differe ab existentia rei in certo aliquo momento vel ex eo intelligi potest, quod tempus ipsum quandam realitatem habet, neque tamen unquam dici potest, ipsum nunc existere, persona intelligens et intellecta certo quodam modo duae sunt, etsi alio quodam modo sint una eademque. Sunt enim una eademque ex Hypothesi. Ponitur enim Mens seipsam intelligere. Duae sunt tamen, eo ipso quod duo sunt quodammodo diversa inter quae relatio est quaedam. Est itaque in Mente Binitas quaedam, sed cum in Deo ipsa intellectio sit perpetuum quiddam et subsistens, ideo veram Trinitatis ideam habere non possumus; possumus tamen non minus, accurate demonstrare Trinitatem in Deo sed binitatem in nobis. Contradictio in his nulla, quia non satis considerant homines quid sit idem et diversum.

## Mira de natura substantiae corporeae                     Aiv279

**1465**      *MIRA DE NATURA SUBSTANTIAE CORPOREAE*

Etsi extensio et motus prae aliis qualitatibus distinctius intelligantur, caeterae enim ipsis adhibitis sunt explicandae, revera tamen fatendum est, neque extensionem, neque motum a nobis omnino distincte intelligi tum quia semper involvimur difficultatibus de compositione continui atque infinito, tum quia revera nullae certae figurae extant in natura rerum ac proinde nec certi motus. Et quemadmodum color et sonus, ita etiam extensio et motus sunt phaenomena potius quam vera rerum attributa quae sine respectu ad nos absolutam quandam naturam contineant. Revera enim dici non potest cuinam subjecto insit motus, et proinde nihil in motu reale est, praeter vim et potentiam in rebus inditam, seu talem earum constitutionem, ut inde sequatur phaenomenorum mutatio certis regulis alligata.

With the lower animals there is sensation and discrimination, but not observation. In God alone there is understanding, willing, having power. In us there is intellect and will, but no power.[4]

That reality differs from the existence of a thing at a certain moment can perhaps be understood from the fact that time itself has a certain reality, yet it cannot ever be said that it exists now. A person understanding and a person understood in a particular sort of way are two things, even though in another way they are one and the same. For they are one and the same by hypothesis. For it is supposed that the mind understands itself. Yet there are two things, by the very fact that two things between which there is a certain relation are different in some way. There is for this reason a certain duality in the mind, but since in God understanding itself is something perpetual and subsisting, we are therefore unable to have a true idea of the Trinity; yet we can no less accurately demonstrate the trinity in God, but a duality in ourselves. There is no contradiction in these considerations, because people do not sufficiently consider what identity and difference are.

### 30. Wonders Concerning the Nature of Corporeal Substance[1]                    Aiv279
[29 March 1683][2]

**1465**        *WONDERS CONCERNING THE NATURE OF CORPOREAL SUBSTANCE*[3]

Even though extension and motion are more distinctly understood than other qualities, since all the rest have to be explained using them, it really must still be acknowledged that neither extension nor motion can be understood distinctly by us at all. This is because on the one hand we are always embroiled in the difficulties concerning the composition of the continuum and the infinite, and on the other, because there are in fact no precise shapes in the nature of things, and consequently no precise motions.[4] And just as color and sound are phenomena, rather than true attributes of things containing a certain absolute nature without relation to us, so too are extension and motion. For it cannot really be said just which subject the motion is in. Consequently, nothing in motion is real besides the force and power vested in things, that is to say, beyond their having such a constitution that from it there follows a change of phenomena constrained by certain rules.[5]

Extensio non pertinet ad substantiam corporis, ut nec motus sed tantum
*materia* seu principium passionis, sive limitatae naturae, et *forma* seu
principium actionis sive naturae illimitatae. Nam est in omni creatura et
limitatum et illimitatum. Limitatum respectu cognitionis distinctae, et po-

**1466**   tentiae irresistibilis, illimitatum vero respectu cognitionis confusae, et actionis refractae. Est enim omnis Anima aut potius omnis substantia corporea omniscia confuse et omnipotens refracte. Nihil enim in toto mundo
fit, quod non percipiat, et nihil ipsa conatur, quod non in infinitum pertin-
gat. Forma non male dicetur actus primus. Omnis creatura habet materiam
et formam sive corporea est. Omnis substantia est immortalis. Omnis substantia corporea habet animam. Omnis anima est immortalis. Probabile est
omnem animam imo omnem substantiam corpoream, semper ab initio rerum extitisse. Strues aliqua seu ens per aggregationem ut lapidum congeries non dicetur substantia corporea sed est phaenomenon tantum. Substantia corporea nullam habet extensionem definitam.

Quot sunt animae, tot sunt Atomi substantiales seu substantiae corporeae.

Si moles est de essentia humanae substantiae explicari non potest quomodo homo idem maneat.

Difficultates inextricabiles de origine rerum et formarum cessant, quia
nulla earum origo aut substantiarum generatio.

**558**         **Divisio terminorum ac**
             **enumeratio attributorum**                                **Aiv132**

      . . .

**559**   Suppositum est aut *Substantia Singularis* quae est Ens completum unum
per se, ut Deus, Mens aliqua, ego; aut *Phaenomenon reale,* ut aliquod corpus, Mundus, Iris, Strues lignorum; quae ad instar Substantiae unius com-
pletae a nobis concipiuntur, cum tamen corpus, nisi animatum sit, vel
Unam quandam Substantiam in se contineat, animae respondentem, quam
Formam Substantialem, vel primam Entelechiam vocant, non magis una
substantia sit, quam strues lignorum; et si rursus nulla ejus pars sit, quae
pro uno per se haberi possit (si quidem corpus actu subdivisum aut certe
subdividuum est in partes), consequens est corpus omne fore tantum
phaenomenon reale, quale est Iris. Similiter Res Mathematicae, ut

**560**   spatium, tempus, sphaera, Hora, tantum phaenomena sunt, quae a nobis ad
instar substantiarum concipiuntur. Et proinde nulla est Substantia Realis,

Extension does not belong to the substance of a body, and neither does motion, but only *matter,* i.e. the principle of passion or of limited nature, and *form,* i.e. the principle of action or of unlimited nature. For every created thing contains both the limited and the unlimited:[6] the limited in re-

**1466** spect of distinct cognition, and of irresistible power, and the unlimited in respect of confused cognition and of diffused action. For every soul, or rather every corporeal substance, is confusedly omniscient and diffusedly omnipotent.[7] For nothing happens in the whole world which it does not perceive, and it has no endeavour that does not extend to infinity. Form is not improperly said to be the primary act. Every created thing has matter and form, i.e. is corporeal. Every substance is immortal. Every corporeal substance has a soul. Every soul is immortal. It is probable that every soul, indeed every corporeal substance, has always existed from the beginning of things. A pile or entity by aggregation such as a heap of stones should not be called a corporeal substance, but only a phenomenon.[8] Corporeal substance has no definite extension.

There are as many souls as there are substantial atoms or corporeal substances.

If bulk is of the essence of human substance it is inexplicable how a person might remain the same.

This puts an end to the inextricable difficulties concerning the origin of things and forms, because they have no origin and there is no generation of substances.


### 31. On Substance, Change, Time, and Extension (Selections)[1]                                Aiv132

[Summer 1683–Early 1685?][2]

. . .

**559**    A *suppositum* is either an *individual substance,* which is a complete entity, one in itself, such as God, a mind, the ego; or it is a *real phenomenon,* such as a body, the world, a rainbow, a woodpile. We conceive the latter on the model of one complete substance, but since body—unless it is animated, or contains within it a certain single substance, corresponding to the soul, which they call a substantial form or primary entelechy—is no more one substance than a woodpile; and since again there is no part of it which can be regarded as a unity in itself (since body is actually subdivided, or certainly subdivisible, into parts), it is a consequence that every body will be only a real phenomenon, like a rainbow. Similarly mathemat-

**560** ical things, such as space, time, a sphere, an hour, are merely phenomena, which we conceive on the model of substances. And accordingly there is

quae non sit individua. Et vero demonstrari posset, ea quae dividua sunt, et magnitudine constant, ut spatium, tempus, moles, non esse Res completas, sed aliquid superaddi debere, quod ea omnia involvat, quae huic spatio, huic tempore, huic mole, tribui possunt.

. . .

**561** Ante omnia Menti ocurrere videtur materia conceptus alicujus positivi sive realitas vel essentia; in quo conveniunt omnia quaecunque a nobis percipiuntur. Et ideo aliquid vocamus Ens vel *Rem* sive Subjectum, postea concipimus *Substantiam* seu Subjectum ultimum, deinde videtur a nobis concipi praesentia, seu *quod nunc est* quanquam quicquid Menti observatur revera nunc esse credituri eramus, nisi experimentis nudas apparentias imaginationes et somnia a phaenomenis realibus distinguere didicissemus.

In his autem quae nunc sunt, aliquam observamus varietatem. Itaque hic notamus diversum, et plura, et *simul.* Ut cum percipio equum et bovem, noto bovem non *idem* esse sed *diversa,* cum tamen in aliquo conveniant *plura* erunt scilicet animalia vel entia. *Idem* autem est, quod alteri substitui potest salva veritate. Quod si *A* sit *D,* et *B* sit *D,* et *C* sit *D,* sintque *A,* et *B* et *C* idem, Unum erit *D.* Sin *A* et *B* et *C* singula a singulis sint diversa, erunt *plura,* unde Numeri.

Observamus deinde et Novitatem seu *Mutationem,* hoc est contradictoria attributa ejusdem. Exempli causa quae contigua sunt, a se invicem se-
**562** parari, ubi omnia alia manent, praeterquam contactus, ac proinde nos concipimus potius easdem res ex contiguis fieri separatas, quam prioribus quae continguae erant abolitis, alias separatas substitui. Cum vero duo penitus contradictoria de eodem dici sit impossibile, itaque discrimen illud quod solum caeteris manentibus intercedit, facitque ut omnimoda contradictio non sit, cum res eadem et contigua alteri, et separata dicitur, est discrimen *temporis.* An autem revera semper eadem sint quae a nobis talia esse ponuntur, altioris est discussionis. Sufficit, aliqua esse quae maneant eadem cum mutantur ut Ego. Quodsi quis ne me quidem durare contendat ultra momentum, is scire nequit an ipse existat. Hoc enim non aliter novit, quam quod semet experitur atque percipit. Omnis autem perceptio tempore indiget, itaque aut toto durante tempore hujus perceptionis permanet quod nobis sufficit, aut semet ipse non percipit, alioqui tantum momento perciperet, eo scilicet quo solo existit.

no real substance which is not an indivisible one. And indeed, it may be demonstrated that those things that are divisible and consist in magnitude, such as space, time, and bulk, are not complete things, but must have something superadded to them, which involves all those things that can be attributed to this space, this time, this bulk.

. . .

**561**    Above all there seems to occur to the mind the matter of a concept of something positive, that is to say, reality or essence; in which everything whatsoever that is perceived by us combines. And therefore we call something an entity or *thing,* i.e. a subject, then we conceive a *substance,* i.e. ultimate subject, and then it seems that we conceive the present, i.e. *what is now,* although we would have believed that whatever is observed by the mind is really now, unless by experience we had learnt to distinguish bare apparent imaginations and dreams from real phenomena.

In those things which exist now, we observe some variety. And so here we note the different, and the many, and the *simultaneous.* For example, when I perceive a horse and an ox, I note that the ox is not *the same,* but *different.* But since they combine in something there will be *many* things, to wit, animals or beings. But that which can be substituted for another without altering the truth is *the same.* But if A is D, and B is D, and C is D, and A, B, and C are the same, D will be *one* thing. If, on the other hand, A, B, and C are each different from the other, they will be *many,* whence numbers.

Next we observe also novelty or *change,* that is, contradictory attributes of the same thing. For example, things that are contiguous are separated

**562**    from each other when everything else remains the same except for contact. And consequently we conceive that the same things that were contiguous have become separated, rather than that the things that were previously contiguous have been destroyed, and other separate ones have been substituted for them. But since it is impossible for two completely contradictory things to be said about the same thing, it follows that the only difference that occurs when everything else remains the same, and that brings it about that there is no contradiction of any kind when the same things are said to be both contiguous and separate, is the difference of *time.* But whether those things are always really the same that we think to be so, is a matter for a more profound discussion. It is enough that there are some things which stay the same while they change, such as the Ego. But if someone contended that not even I endure beyond a moment, he cannot know whether he himself exists. For this he knows only by experiencing and perceiving himself. But every perception needs time, and so either he persists during the whole time of his perception, which suffices for us, or he himself does not perceive, otherwise he would perceive only for a moment, namely, for that moment alone at which he exists.

Et cum conscientia suae perceptionis, memoriam involvat, adeoque praeteritum, neque is qui perceptus, ille est qui nunc loquitur vel cogitat. Et in universum si omnia quae in tempore sunt momentanea sunt, necesse est tempus componi ex momentis sane si omnia mutabilia continue abolentur aliis surrogatis necesse est dari aliquid immutabile, quod sit causa et surrogans, si enim semel sit nihil, in aeternum nihil erit; sed hoc ipsum Ens permanens necessario contradictioria habebit attributa, nunc enim hujus nunc illius est causa. Quod si neges de eo dici posse *nunc* et *tunc;* neque in tempore erit, manetque. Proinde tempus ex meris componi momentis, neque enim tempus intelligi potest extra res. Tempus autem ex momentis componi aeque absurdum est quam lineam componi ex punctis. Qui vero dicunt res easdem continue reproduci a Deo, non laborant eadem difficultate, neque enim dividere debent tempus ad momenta, sed ita tantum dicere debent, nullum as |

**563**    Et cum conscientia meae perceptionis, memoriam involvat, adeoque praeteritum, neque enim eodem momento et cogito et meam cogitationem percipio, falso dicemus nosmet experiri, si neque is qui percepit, neque is qui perceptus est, ille est qui nunc cogitat seu meminit.

Sublato autem hoc experimento sui, quod omnium primum est, alia cessant omnia, nam si incertum est an sim, incertum est an percipiam; itaque incertum quoque est an sint ali de quibus non aliunde judico, quam ex his quae percipio. Itaque aut nihil scimus, aut scimus nos durare etsi mutemur.

Porro ex duobus statibus contradictoribus ejusdem rei, is prior tempore est, qui natura prior est, seu qui alterius rationem involvit, vel quo eodem redit, qui facilius intelligitur. Ut in horologio, ut perfecte intelligamus statum praesentem rotarum, requiritur ut intelligamus rationem ejus, quae continetur in statu praecedente; atque ita porro. Idemque est in alia quavis serie rerum, semper enim certa connexio est, etsi necessaria non sit.

*Simul* autem sunt, quae connexa sunt; sive necessitate, sive certitudine cujus ratio reddi potest. Quae autem vel omnino simul esse non possunt,

And[3] since consciousness of one's perception involves memory, and thus the past, neither the person perceiving nor the person perceived is the one who is now speaking or thinking. And in general, if all things that are in time are momentaneous, it is necessary for time to be composed of moments. But certainly, if all things mutable are continually annihilated while others are substituted for them, it is necessary for there to be something immutable that is their cause and that does the substituting, since if once there were nothing, there would be nothing for eternity. But this permanent entity itself will have contradictory attributes, since it is the cause now of the former thing, now of the latter. But if you deny that it can be said to be *now* and *then,* then it will not be in time either, or endure. Consequently time is composed of mere moments, for time cannot be understood apart from things. But it is just as absurd for time to be composed of moments as for a line to be composed of points. However, those who say that the same things are continually reproduced by God are not troubled by the same difficulty, for they do not have to divide time into moments, but have to say only that nothing |

**563**     And since consciousness of my perception involves memory, and thus the past, for I do not both think and perceive my thought at the same moment, we are in error when we say that we experience ourselves, if neither he who perceives nor he who is perceived is he who is thinking or remembering now.

But without this experience of oneself, which is the first experience of all, everything else ceases. For if it is uncertain whether I am, it is uncertain whether I perceive; and so it is also uncertain whether the other things exist that I judge to have their source only in the things I perceive. And so either we know nothing, or we know ourselves to endure even though we change.

Next, from two contradictory states of the same thing, that is *earlier in time* which is prior by nature, i.e. which involves the reason for the other, or what amounts to the same thing, which is more easily understood. For example in a clock, in order to understand completely the present state of its hands, it is required that we understand its reason, which is contained in the preceding state; and so on. And it is the same in any other series of things, for there is always a certain connection, even though it is not always a necessary one.

*Simultaneous* things are those that are connected; either by necessity, or if a reason for the connection can be given with certainty. But those things which cannot be simultaneous either absolutely or according to reason,

vel cum ratione, et tamen existunt, ea diverso tempore existere; estque illud prius tempore, quod rationem alterius simplicius involvit, ut dixi.
. . .

**565** *Extensionem* vocamus quicquid omnibus simul perceptis commune observamus; et *extensum* vocamus cujus perceptione plura percipere possumus simul; idque indefinita quadam ratione, unde extensum est totum continuum cujus partes sunt simul et habent situm inter se, ipsumque totum rursus eodem modo se habet tanquam pars respectu alterius. Totum continuum est cujus partes sunt indefinitae, tale est ipsum spatium abstrahendo animum ab his quae sunt in ipso. Hinc tale continuum est infinitum, ut tempus et spatium. Cum enim ubique sibi simile sit, quodlibet totum erit pars. In extenso consideramus esse divisibile in partes, esse partem alterius, esse terminatum; situm habere ad aliud. Punctum quod situm habet, extensionem non habet.

Post extensionem sequitur Mutatio circa extensionem seu Motus. Sed antequam huc veniremus, dicendum erat de Mutatione in universum, Actione scilicet et passione; potentia, conatu, aliisque id genus. . . .

**624** **Definitiones notionum metaphysicarum**
**atque logicarum** **Aiv147**

. . .

**627** *Requisitum* est Conditio simplicior, seu ut vulgo vocant natura prior.
*Conditio* est, quo remoto aliquid tollitur.

Requisita rerum alia sunt mediata, quae per ratiocinationem investiganda sunt, ut causae; alia sunt immediata ut partes, extrema, et generaliter quae rei insunt.

Si pluribus positis, eo ipso unum aliquod poni immediate intelligatur, illa dicuntur *partes,* hoc *totum.* Nec vero necesse est eodem tempore existere aut eodem loco, sufficit, ut eodem tempore considerentur. Ita ex omnibus imperatoribus Romanis simul Unum aggregatum conficimus. Revera autem nullum ex partibus pluribus componitur Ens vere Unum, et omnis substantia est indivisibilis et quae partes habent non sunt Entia, sed phaenomena tantum. Unde recte philosophi veteres his rebus, quas Unum per se facere dixerunt, tribuerunt formas substantiales, ut Mentes, Animas seu primas Entelechias, et negarunt Materiam per se aliquod Unum Ens

and still exist, exist at different times; and that is earlier in time which involves a reason simpler than the other, as I have said.

. . .

**565**     We call *extension* whatever we observe as common to all simultaneous perceptions; and we call *extended* that by the perception of which we can perceive several things simultaneously; and this for some indefinite reason. Whence the extended is a continuous whole whose parts are simultaneous and have a situation among themselves, and in the same way this whole behaves as a part with respect to another whole. A continuous whole is that whose parts are indefinite;[4] space itself is such a thing, abstracting the soul from those things that are in it. Hence such a continuum is infinite, as are time and space. For since it is everywhere similar to itself, any whole whatsoever will be a part. Under "extended" we consider being divisible into parts, being part of another, being bounded; having situation to another. A point is what has situation and does not have extension.

After extension comes change with respect to extension, i.e. motion. But before we come to this, something must be said about change in general, that is, about action and passion; about power, endeavour, and other things of that kind.[5] . . .

### 32. On Part, Whole, Transformation, and Change (Selections)[1]                          Aiv147

[Mid-1685][2]

. . .

**627**     A *requisite* is a simpler condition, or, as it is commonly called, a prior nature.

A *condition* is that whose removal would eliminate something.

Some requisites of things are mediate, and must be investigated by reasoning, such as causes; others are immediate, such as parts, extremes, and generally whatever is contained in things.

If when several things are posited, by that very fact some unity is immediately understood to be posited, then the former are called *parts,* the latter a *whole.* Nor is it even necessary that they exist at the same time, or at the same place; it suffices that they be considered at the same time. Thus from all the Roman emperors together, we construct one aggregate. But actually no entity that is really one is composed of a plurality of parts, and every substance is indivisible, and those things that have parts are not entities, but merely phenomena. For which reason the ancient philosophers rightly attributed substantial forms, such as minds, and souls or primary entelechies, to those things which they said make a unity per se, and denied that

esse. Certe quae his carent, non magis unum Ens sunt quam strues lignorum, imo non magis Entia realia sunt, quam irides aut parhelia. Certe nec
**628**  momento amplius eadem perseverant, cum tamen verae substantiae maneant sub mutationibus; id enim in nobis experimur, alioqui enim ne nosmet ipsos quidem percipere liceret, cum omnis nostri perceptio memoriam
aliquam involva. Sed haec obiter.

Libenter definirem Homogenea quae transformatione possunt reddi similia, quemadmodum definio Aequalia quae transformatione reddi possunt congrua, sed in transformatione explicanda occurrit difficultas. Nam
ea satis quidem intelligitur, cum non fit analysis ad minima usque, sed
manent partes, tantumque transponantur, verum quando v.g. ex recta fit
curva, unde cognoscemus idem manere quod ante, cum tamen revera nihil
remaneat; nulla enim pars rectae in curva est superstes, quod si quis dicat
omnia superesse puncta, rem valde obscuram dicet, nam non est in continuo certus definitusque punctorum numerus, imo puncta sunt modi tantum. Itaque nisi in rebus extensis aliquid admittatur praeter materiam non
apparet quomodo maneant. Possumus tamen transformationem nostram
saltem aliquo indicio definire, ut scilicet Transformatio a nobis dicetur,
cum ex uno fit aliud nulla parte addita vel ademta; quamvis enim partes
priores destruantur in omnimoda transformatione, nulla tamen earum
aufertur, id est separatur, ut nempe vel permaneat vel ipsamet transformatione sua aliquid constituat, hoc est (ne transformatio definitionem trans-
formationis ingrediatur) ut licet mutetur, tamen mutatione sua ad rem nostram nihil amplius conferat.

Si transformationem nolimus adhibere in definiendo, aliter *Homogenea*
erunt definienda, ea scilicet quae vel mensuram habent communem, vel
exactam, vel utcunque exactam, ut scilicet residuum sit data quantitate minus.

*Aequalia* autem erunt quae congruis similiter determinantur.

*Majus* est cujus pars alteri toti aequalis est, quod *minus* dicitur.

Quod nec majus est, nec minus, et tamen homogeneum, id est aequale.

*Simul* sunt quorum unum absolute alterius conditio est. Sin unum alterius conditio est interveniente mutatione, tunc unum est *prius,* alterum
*posterius.* Illud autem intelligitur prius quod simul est cum causa, posterius quod simul est cum effectu. Vel prius intelligitur quod est simplicius

matter per se is one entity. Certainly those things which lack these forms are no more one entity than a woodpile, indeed they are not real entities any more than rainbows or mock-suns. Certainly they do not persevere the **628** same for longer than a moment, whereas true substances persist through changes; for we experience this in ourselves, for otherwise we would not be able to perceive even ourselves, since each of our perceptions involves a memory. But these things are by the way.

I would willingly define Homogeneous things as those which can be rendered similar by a transformation, just as I define equals as those which can be rendered congruent by a transformation: but there is a difficulty in explaining by transformation. For it is easily enough understood when an analysis is not made all the way down to minima, and instead the parts persist and are merely transposed. Yet when, for example, a curve is made from a straight line, we recognize that the same thing persists as before, when nothing really does remain: for no part of the straight line survives in the curve; and if someone says that all the points survive, he says something very obscure, for there is no certain and definite number of points in the continuum, indeed points are merely modes. Thus unless it is admitted that there is something else apart from matter in extended things, it is not evident how they persist. Nevertheless we can define our transformation at least by some indication, so that we may call it a Transformation when one thing becomes another without any part being added or taken away. For although the previously existing parts are destroyed in every type of transformation, none of them is removed, i.e. separated in such a way that it either persists or constitutes something else by its very transformation; that is (lest transformation enter into its own definition), in such a way that even though it changes, nevertheless by its change it contributes nothing further to our thing.

If we do not wish to use transformation in defining them, *Homogeneous* things will have to be defined in another way, namely, as those which have a common measure, either an exact one, or one as exact as desired, namely, such that the remainder is less than any given quantity.

Now *equals* will be those which are determined similarly by congruents.

The *greater* is that whose part is equal to the whole of another, which is called the *smaller.*

What is neither greater nor smaller than something else, yet homogeneous with it, is equal to it.

Those things are *simultaneous* one of which is the condition of the other absolutely. Whereas, if the first is the condition of the second by an intervening change, then the first is *earlier,* the second *later.* Now the earlier is understood to be that which is simultaneous with the cause, the later that

vel quod est alterius requisitum. Requisitum autem definivi conditionem natura simpliciorem eo cujus conditio est.

**629**  Si *A* sit *B*, et *A* non sit *B*, dicitur *A* esse *mutatum,* seu verum esse de diverso tempore: Metimur autem tempus uniformi quadam mutatione ad partes rei permanentis applicata ita ut prius sit quod applicatur parti minus distanti a termino assumto.

Illud est fundamentum mensurandae rerum durationis, quod assumtis diversis motibus uniformibus (tanquam diversis horologiis exactis) habetur consensus; adeoque quaecunque fiunt aut sunt simul, aut aliquo priora aut posteriora.

*Tempore prius* est quod cum aliquo positione incompatibile est, et eo simplicius est. Alterum autem dicitur *posterius. Simul* sunt, quae suppositione connecessaria sunt, suppositione inquam id est posita serie rerum.

*Tempus* est Ens imaginarium, quemadmodum, locus, qualitates, aliaque multa.

Cognoscimus uniformi aliqua mutatione, utrum aliquod sit prius, an posterius, sed quia diversae uniformes mutationes sunt simul, est aliqua causa hujus simultaneitatis et prioritatis; nam horologia non efficiunt sed indicant tantum prioritatem et posteritatem. Idem est de motu coeli neque enim a motu horologii differt, quam ut majus et minus. Radix autem temporis est in causa prima, successiones rerum virtute in se continente, quae facit, ut omnia sint simul, aut priora vel posteria. Idem est de Loco nam efficit causa prima ut omnia distantem quandam habeant. Quicquid ergo reale est in spatio et tempore, id est in Deo omnia complectente.

Sed haec omnia difficilioris explicationis sunt, coguntque nos venire ad divinae naturae considerationem. . . .

**1797**      **Ex Cordemoii tractatu *De corporis***
              ***et mentis distinctione***                          **Aiv346**

**1798**      *Ex Cordemoii tractatu* De corporis
              et mentis distinctione                              **Aiv346$_1$**

Ex eo quod natura atque distinctione corporis et materiae non satis clare noscuntur, fere omnes vulgaris physicae errores oriuntur.

which is simultaneous with the effect. Or the earlier is understood to be that which is simpler than or what is the requisite of the second. A requisite I have defined as a condition simpler by nature than that whose condition it is.

**629**     If A is B and A is not B, A is said to have *changed,* i.e. to be true at a different time. Now we measure time by some uniform change to the parts of a permanent thing, applied so that the earlier is that which is applied to a part less distant from the assumed starting point.

The basis for measuring the duration of things is the agreement that is obtained between several motions that are assumed uniform (like those of several precise clocks); so that whatever things happen are either simultaneous, or earlier than something, or later.

That is *earlier in time* which is incompatible with some position, and is simpler than it. The other position is called *later.* Those things are *simultaneous* which are by supposition co-necessary; I say, by supposition, i.e. with the series of things posited.

*Time* is an imaginary entity, just like place, qualities, and many other things.

We recognize by some uniform change whether something is earlier or later, but because several different uniform changes are simultaneous, there is a cause of this simultaneity and earliness; for clocks do not make earliness and lateness, but merely indicate it. It is the same with the motion of the heavens, for it only differs from the motion of a clock as greater and less. Now the root of time is in the first cause, potentially containing in itself the successions of things, which makes everything either simultaneous, earlier or later. It is the same with place, for the first cause makes everything have some distance. Therefore whatever is real in space and time consists in God comprising everything.

But all these latter things are rather difficult to explain, and force us to come to a consideration of divine nature.[3] . . .

---

**1797**          **33. Annotated Excerpts from
                   Cordemoy's *Treatise*[1]**                    **Aiv346**

[1685][2]

**1798**
                 *FROM CORDEMOY'S TREATISE* ON THE DISTINCTION
                 BETWEEN BODY AND MIND[3]

                 *I. On the First Discourse*                    **Aiv346₁**

Almost all the errors of common physics arise from the fact that the nature of body and mind and the distinction between them are not known sufficiently clearly.

Corpus est substantia extensa, et proinde (cum multa talia sint) limitata seu figura praedita; et cum unumquodque corpus sit unica eademque substantia, ideo nec dividi nec ejus figura mutari potest, neque penetrari. *Materia* est multorum corporum compages; si plura corpora considerentur ut inter se unita dicentur *portio materiae,* si unio absit *cumulus,* si inter se invicem fluunt *liquor,* si [partes] connexae inter se, quasi uncinis quibusdam, vel parvo adeo motu ut facile separari non possint, *massa.* Corpus partes habere nequit, sed materia. *Clarissima interim substantiae extensae [idea] est,* sed male cum materiae perceptionibus confunditur, non omne extensum divisibile est. Res considerandae non ut apparent, sed ut sunt, nulla in materia extensio est, nisi quia unumquodque corpus ex [quo] constat, ea praeditum est, et massa ideo est divisibilis quia componitur ex partibus quae sunt diversae substantiae. (+ Notabile est tum Cartesianos vulgares, qui omne extensum divisibile vocant, tum Cordemoium semi Gassendistam qui omnem substantiam indivisibilem judicat, et vere unam, ad ideas provocare. Forsan ambo recte ex mea sententia, si enim omnia corpora organica sunt animata et omnia corpora vel organica vel inorganicorum corporum collectanea sunt, consequens est, omnem quidem molem divisibilem esse, sed substantiam ipsam nec dividi nec extingui posse. +) Absque his physicae principia nosci non possunt.

Magna est consuetudo materiam cum corporibus (+ substantiis extensis +) confundendi. Verum est corpus esse substantiam extensam, sed falsum est materiam esse substantiam. Nam unaquaeque substantia in semet ipsam dividi non potest (+ vir clarissimus confuse et per nebulam vidit veritatem, accurate demonstrare non potuit +) et si ejus natura in extensione sita est statim ac extensa concipitur, cum eadem in omnibus suis extremitatibus sit, nullam ejus extremitatem ab alia separabilem esse fatendum est. (+ Eodem argumento probaret nec corpus humanum posse dividi, quia anima una eademque in toto corpore existit. Scilicet in eo lapsus est, quod non agnovit, aliud in corpore substantia dari praeter extensionem a quo scilicet ipsa substantiae notio oriatur, quam solo extensio dare non potest. Id vero est potentia seu virtus agendi patiendique, secundum axioma receptissimum quod actiones sunt suppositorum. +) In nullum incidere potui, quem de materia et corpore tanquam de una eademque

**1799**

*Body* is extended substance, and accordingly (since there are many such bodies), they are limited, i.e. endowed with shape; and since each body is a unique and self-same substance, for this reason it can neither be divided, nor can its shape be changed, nor can it be penetrated.

*Matter* is an assembly of many bodies; if several bodies are considered as united together, they are called a *portion of matter;* if there is no union among them, a *heap;* if they flow among themselves changing places with each other, a *liquid;* if they are connected together by little hooks of some kind, or move so little that they cannot easily be separated, a *mass.*

A body cannot have parts, but matter can. *The idea of extended substance, however, is very clear;* but it is wrongly confused with the perceptions we have of matter. Not everything that is extended is divisible.

Considering things not as they appear, but as they are, there is extension in matter only because each of the bodies it consists of is endowed with it; and a mass is therefore divisible because it is composed of parts which are different substances. (+ It is noteworthy that not only the common Cartesians, who call everything that is extended divisible, but even the semi-Gassendist Cordemoy, who deems every substance indivisible and truly one, appeal to ideas. According to my opinion it turns out they are both right: for if all organic bodies are animate, and all bodies are either organic or collections of organic bodies, it follows that indeed every extended mass[4] is divisible, but that substance itself can neither be divided nor destroyed. +). Without these considerations, the principles of physics cannot be recognized.

There is a widespread custom of confounding matter with bodies (+ extended substances +). It is true that a body is an extended substance, but false that matter is a substance. For every single substance is in its very self indivisible (+ the most distinguished gentleman has confused and seen through a cloud a truth he could not accurately demonstrate +), and if its nature is founded in extension as soon as it is conceived as extended, then it must be admitted that since it is the same thing in all its extremities, none of its extremities is separable from another.[5] (+ By the same argument he would prove that the human body cannot be divided either, because the soul exists one and the same in the whole body. That is to say, he has made the mistake of not acknowledging that there is something in corporeal substance besides extension; something, to wit, from which the very notion of substance might arise, which extension alone cannot give: this being the power of or potential for acting and being acted upon, in compliance with the widely received axiom that actions belong to subjects.[6] +).

Of those I have heard discussing matter and body as if they are one and the same thing,[7] I have not been able to find anyone who could explain to

**1799**

re verba facientem audivi, qui super hac re mentem suam mihi explicare potuerit, etiam quando cum ipsis supponere volui substantiam esse divisibilem quod [lumini] naturali repugnat. Cum quaesivi an substantia esset divisibilis in infinitum, negabant, et indefinite divisibilem dicebant, sed hanc indefinitam divisibilitatem eodem modo explicabant, ut infinitam, et cum tandem candide faterentur esse in ea re quae captum hominum superent, necesse tamen ajebant, ut res se ita haberet. In nostra autem sententia eadem obscuritas non esse videtur. Alterum in contraria opinione incommodum est, quod corporis separati non concepto motu conceptum formare non possunt, nec secundum eorum doctrinam concipi possit corpus quiescens inter alia corpora, nam si ab aliis tangitur, eo ipso in unum idemque corpus cum ipsis conflatur (+ nisi contactus sit in puncto. Sunt quae ipsum Cordemoium premant, ponamus duo atomos triangulares se tangere et componere quadratum perfectum, et ita juxta se quiescere, detur alia substantia corporea seu Atomus quadrata aequalis composito ex his duabus, quaero in quo differant haec duo extensa; certe nulla in ipsis ut nunc sunt concipi potest diversitas nisi ponamus aliquid in corporibus praeter extensionem, sed sola memoria pristinorum discernuntur qualis in corporibus nulla est, quomodo diversa in ipsis deinde evenire possunt, si et tertio aliquo impellantur, ut unum dissiliat in partes, aliud secus. Hoc premit omnes Atomistas, et cogit fateri dari in materia aliquid aliud ab extensione. +). Interim habemus perfectam ideam corporis inter alia corpora quiescentis. (+ Imaginem habemus, fingamus corpus creare substantiam extensam de cujus natura sit moveri, eadem erunt phaenomena quae nunc et tamen nos fingere poterimus eam quiescere, prorsus haec imaginatio est, qualis dicentium se concipere vacuum. +) Tertium incommodum est, quod hinc sequetur, nullum concipi posse momentum quo corpus eandem magnitudinem et figuram conservare possit, cum scilicet corpus a variis corporibus ex diversis partibus pellitur, dividetur enim tot modis quod pelletur, et partes separatae adversus eas quae supersunt repulsae eas ita divident, ut nullus divisionis limes concipi possit. Et si corpus quadratum **1800** circa proprium centrum moveri supponatur et licet dicant tot partes uniri rursus quot pereant, facile est redire incommodum, ut idem corpus non

me his own mind on this subject, even when I was willing to suppose with them that substance is divisible, which is repugnant to the natural light.[8] When I asked whether substance was divisible to infinity, they would deny this, and say that it was indefinitely divisible; but this indefinite divisibility they explained in the same way as infinite divisibility. And although in the end they would candidly admit that in this subject there are things which exceed the grasp of men, they would still say that it was necessary for it to happen this way.[9] However, there does not seem to be the same obscurity in what I propose.

A second inconvenience in this contrary opinion [of the Cartesians] is that they cannot form a concept of a separate body without conceiving motion. Nor, according to their doctrine, can one conceive a body to be at rest among other bodies, for if it is in contact with the other bodies, then by this very fact it is forged into one and the same body with them (+ unless the contact is at a point. But these are difficulties for Cordemoy himself: let us suppose two triangular atoms come into contact and compose a perfect square, and that they rest next to each other in this way, and let there be another corporeal substance or atom, a square one equal to the composite of the latter two. I ask, in what respect do these two extended things differ? Certainly no difference can be conceived in them as they are now, unless we suppose something in bodies besides extension; rather they are distinguished solely by memory of their former conditions, and there is nothing of this kind in bodies.[10] How can they become different in themselves afterwards, as in the case where they are struck by some third body in such a way that that one breaks into parts and the other does not? This is a difficulty for all atomists, and obliges one to admit that there is something else in matter apart from extension +). Meanwhile, we do have a perfect idea of a body at rest among other bodies.[11] (+ We have an *image* [of it as at rest]; suppose we imagine body to consist in[12] an extended substance whose nature it is to be moved, the phenomena will be the same as now, and we will still be able to imagine it at rest; in short this is an imagination, of the sort people have when they say they can conceive a vacuum +).

A third inconvenience is that it will follow from this that no moment can be conceived at which a body could conserve the same magnitude and shape. This is because a body is pushed by various bodies in different directions, and is divided in as many ways as it is pushed, and the parts that have separated from it, being pushed back against those which remain, so divide them that no limit of the division can be conceived. And if a square body be supposed to turn around its own center, even though they say that **1800** as many parts join back together as are destroyed, one easily falls back into the inconvenience that the body will not remain the same. The same peo-

permaneat. Coguntur ipsi inter philosophandum supponere multa per aliquod tempus actualiter non dividi. (+ Imo nil tale coguntur asserere. +) Natura autem ferimur ad corpus indivisibile concipiendum et corpus ipsum nostrum ex innumeris compositum, ut unum concipimus, quia omnes partes ita ad finem unum concurrunt ut dividi nequeant, nisi violata oeconomia, et Jurisconsulti corpus vocant, quicquid sine interitu dividi nequit (+ imo vocant non corpora, sed species +), quantitatem vero rerum congeriem quae a se invicem independenter subsistunt, ut triticum vinum oleum. +) Scilicet naturali idea corpus rem indivisibilem materia divisibilem repraesentat. Corpus autem non ideo divisibile est, quia de una extremitate missis aliis cogitare possumus, sed necesse est corpus eo ipso quia extensum est plures extremitates habere; et potius inde concludes esse inseparabiles, quia ejusdem sunt extremitates. Ut autem Extensio competit corpori, ita quantitas materiae. (+ Quidni detur et quantitas extensionis. [+)]

Non est necesse omnia intervalla esse corporibus plena. Non assentior illis qui putant sublato contento vasis latera uniri, neque enim intelligo quid unum corpus ad alterius subsistentiam conferat. (+ Imo omnes substantiae sibi sunt correquisitae. [+)] Distantia non erit substantiae, sed situs. [(+] Necesse est situm seu relationem in aliquo fundari, si dicis in possibili interpositione, dico debere hanc possibilem rursus fundari in aliquo jam tum actuali. +)

## De machina animata          Aiv346$_2$

Axioma hoc: *dispositionem habenti non denegatur forma,* adeo quidam certum esse estimant, ut sibi persuadeant, si massam eodem disponere possint, ut corpus humanus dispositum est, animam ei non defuturam, dicturique sint non se facturos corpus simile nostro, sed homine nobis similem. Tali philosopho si in animum sibi induxerit horologium esse animatum, difficile erit persuadere contrarium. Sed quia entia multiplicanda non sunt, sufficit omnia in horologio per figuram et motum posse explicari.

1801

ple are forced to suppose, while philosophizing, that many bodies are not actually divided for some time (+ No, they are forced to maintain no such thing +).[13]

On the other hand, we are driven by nature to conceive body as indivisible, and to conceive our own body, itself composed of innumerable bodies, as one, since all its parts so cooperate towards one end that they cannot be divided without doing violence to their system of operation. And legal experts call *body* whatever cannot be divided without being destroyed[14] (+ No, they do not call them bodies, but species. +), whereas they call *quantity* a collection of things which subsist independently of each other, such as wheat, wine, or oil.[15]

Evidently it is by a natural idea that one represents body as an indivisible thing and matter as a divisible one. However, a body is not divisible just because we can think of one of its extremities without the others; instead, it is necessary for a body, by the very fact that it is extended, to have several extremities; and from this it is rather to be concluded that they are inseparable because they are extremities of the same thing.

Moreover, as extension is properly applicable to body, so is quantity to matter (+ Why shouldn't there also be quantity of extension? [+)].

It is not necessary for all intervals to be full of bodies. I do not agree with those who maintain that if the contents of a vessel were destroyed, the sides would join back together,[16] for I do not understand what one body contributes to the subsistence of another (+ On the contrary, all substances are co-requisites of each other [+)]. Substances will not have distance, but situation. (+ It is necessary that situation or relation be founded in something; if you say, on a possible interposition,[17] then I say this possible interposition must in turn be founded on something already then actual +).[18]

## II. On Animated Machines[19] Aiv346$_2$

*Form cannot be denied to something having an orderly arrangement:* This is an axiom some people deem to be so certain that they persuade themselves that if they could give a mass the same orderly arrangement
**1801** that the human body has, a soul would not be lacking in it; and they would say not that they had made a body similar to ours, but a man similar to us. With such a philosopher, if it entered his mind that a clock was animate, it would be difficult to persuade him to the contrary. But, since entities must not be multiplied, it suffices that everything in a clock can be explained by shape and motion.

Haec Cordemoy *distinctio corporis et animae* diss.3.

Mihi videtur axioma verissimum, sed a nemine posse fabricari corpus humano perfecte simile, nisi qui possit servare Ordinem dividendo in infinitum. Itaque nulli angelo possibile est hominem vel ullum animal verum formare, nisi ex semine, ubi jam aliquo modo praeexistit. Facere posset machinam, quae forte externa specie non satis examinanti hominem mentiretur, revera homo vel animal non esset.

**1505**               **De mundo praesenti**                **Aiv301**

**1506**  Omne Cogitabile est vel Ens vel Non Ens.

*Ens* est de quo aliquid affirmari potest.

*Non ens* cujus nulla sunt attributa nisi negativa. Scilicet si *A* neque est *B* neque *C* neque *D,* et ita porro in infinitum, erit *Nihil.*

Omne Ens vel est Reale vel Imaginarium. *Ens reale,* quod est citra mentis operationem ut sol de quo judiciamus ex consensu plurium perceptionum. *Ens imaginarium* quod secundum unum percipiendi modum percipitur ad instar Entis realis, ut iris, parhelius, Somnium, sed secundum alios modos non percipitur neque examina sustinet, quod tamen fieri deberet, si esset Ens reale, unde sequitur a dispositione nostri et medii fieri quod percipitur, ipsum autem perceptionis causam non esse. Et saepe intellecta origine phaenomeni etiam causa deceptionis cognoscitur.

Omne Ens reale est unum per se aut Ens per Accidens. *Ens (unum) per se* ut Homo, *Ens (unum) per accidens,* ut strues lignorum, machina, quod scilicet non est unum nisi per aggregationem, nec alia in eo realis unio est, quam connexio vel contactus aut etiam concursus ad idem vel saltem convenientia a mente in unum colligente animadversa. At in Ente per se, realis quaedam unio requiritur consistens non in partium situ et motu ut in catena, domo, navi sed in unico quodam individuo principio et subjecto attributorum et operationum, quod in nobis dicitur anima, in omni corpore forma substantia modo id sit unum per se.

Omne Ens est vel *Substantia* vel *Accidens* seu Modus. Substantia ut Mens, corpus. Modus ut calor, motus. Nimirum ex Accidente vel modo formari potest concretum, quod de substantia praedicatur vel etiam de alio accidente. Substantiae autem jam tum concretus est conceptus, nec praedi-

Thus Cordemoy, *Distinctio corporis et animae,* Third Discourse.

It seems to me that the axiom is very true, but that no one can build a body perfectly similar to the human one, unless someone can conserve the Order by dividing to infinity. So it is not possible for an angel to fashion a man or any genuine animal, except from a seed, where it already preexists in some way. He could make a machine which would perhaps remind you of a man by its outward appearance if you did not examine it well enough, but it would not really be a man or an animal.

**1505**              **34. On the Present World[1]**              **Aiv301**

[March 1684–Spring 1686][2]

**1506**   Every *thinkable* is either an entity or a non-entity.

An *entity* is that about which something can be affirmed.

A *non-entity* is that which has only negative attributes. In other words, if *A* is neither *B* nor *C* nor *D,* and so on to infinity, it will be *nothing*.

Every entity is either real or imaginary. A *real entity*—for instance, the sun—is what is on this side of the mind's operation, concerning which we judge from the agreement among several perceptions. An *imaginary entity*—for instance, a rainbow, a mock-sun, a dream—is what is perceived on the model of a real entity according to one mode of perception, but which is not perceived according to other modes of perception, and does not withstand examination, as it ought to if it were a real entity. Hence, as a result of how we and the medium are disposed, it comes to be what is perceived, although it is not itself the cause of the perception. And often when the origin of the phenomenon is understood, we come to know the cause of the deception as well.

Every real entity is either a unity in itself, or an accidental entity. An *entity (unity)[3] in itself* is, for instance, a man; an *accidental entity (unity)*— for instance, a woodpile, a machine—is what is only a unity by aggregation, and there is no real union in it other than a connection: perhaps a contact or even a running together into the same thing, or at least an agreement observed by a mind gathering it into a unity. But in an entity per se some real union is required, consisting not in the situation and motion of parts, as in a chain, a house, or a ship, but in some unique individual principle and subject of its attributes and operations, which in us is called a soul, and in every body a substantial form, provided the body is a unity in itself.

Every entity is either a *substance,* or an *accident* or *mode.* A substance is, for instance, a mind, a body; a mode, for instance, heat, motion. Now from an accident or mode one can form a concrete term, which is predicated of a substance or even of another accident. But whereas the concept

**1507**  cari potest nisi de substantia, et substantia singularis nulli alii rei singulari
inest, cum tamen Accidens singulare substantiae singulari insit, plura ac-
cidentia substantiae uni. Et quidem substantiae singularis conceptus est
quiddam completum, qui omnia jam virtute continet, quaecunque de ipso
possunt intelligi. Ita ut Deus eo ipso dum hujus Petri substantiam concipit,
omnia concipiat quae ei contigere aut contingent. Quod de accidente singulari dici non potest, nisi quatenus substantiae singulari inesse concipitur. Ex Alphonsi regia potestate non concipio ejus Astronomiam, nisi re-
deam ad ipsius Alphonsi naturam singularem. Porro substantia universalis
nihil aliud quam omnis substantia singularis talis cum autem substantia
singularis involvat relationes ad totum universum patet eam semper esse
infinitam.

Substantia est vel perfecta seu absoluta nempe *Deus,* vel limitata quae
dicitur *creatura.* Necesse est autem limitatam dependere ab absoluta, alioqui haec ipsa limitata esset. Est etiam unica, eo ipso quia conceptus ejus
est completus, ex vi essentiae ipsius. Conceptus autem completus est nota
substantiae singularis.

Substantia omnis habet intra se operationem quandam, eaque vel est
ejusdem in se ipsum, quae dicitur Reflexio sive Cogitatio, et talis substantia est spiritualis, sive *Mens,* vel est diversarum partium, et talis *Substantia*
dicitur *Corporea.*

Cum Deus sit Mens et se ipsum intelligat atque amet, hinc oritur mira
quaedam diversitas ejusdem a se ipso, sive compositio rei indivisibilis,
quam in *Sacrosanctae Trinitatis personis* agnoscimus; et cujus in mente
nostra semel cogitante aliquod indicium habemus.

Mens est, aut secreta aut corpori unita. Secreta ut Deus; unita, ut *anima
nostra.* Sunt et aliae *mentes,* quae *Angelicae* dicuntur, nostris perfectiores,
quas tamen corporibus quibusdam sed longe subtilioribus unitas esse veteres credidere, quod si verum esset, videri posset anima quoque nostra
licet in se incorporea tamen non nisi crassum corpus morte deponere. Nec
ulla esset creatura corporis adjuncti expers.

Substantia corporea habet partes et species. Partes sunt Materia et
Forma. Materia est principium passionis, seu vis resistendi primitiva,
**1508**  quam vulgo vocant molem seu ἀντιτυπίαν, ex qua fluit corporis impene-
trabilis. *Forma substantialis* est principium actionis seu vis agendi primi-

**1507**  'substance' is already a concrete concept, and cannot be predicated of anything but a substance, and an individual substance is not contained in any
other individual thing, an individual accident, on the other hand, is contained in an individual substance, with several accidents in one substance.
And indeed the concept of an individual substance is something complete,
which already potentially contains everything, whatever can be understood of it. Thus, for example, God, in conceiving the substance of this Peter, by that very fact conceives everything that has happened or will happen to him. And this cannot be said of an individual accident, except
insofar as it is conceived to be contained in an individual substance. From
the sovereign power of Alphonso I cannot conceive his Astronomy, unless
I have recourse to the individual nature of Alphonso himself.[4] Moreover,
universal substance is nothing but every such individual substance,
though since an individual substance involves relations to the whole universe, it is clear that it is always infinite.

A substance is either perfect, i.e. absolute, namely, *God,* or limited, in
which case it is called a *created thing.* A limited substance, though, necessarily depends on the absolute one, otherwise the latter would itself be limited. It is also unique, because of the fact that its concept is complete, by
dint of its very essence.[5] But a complete concept is the mark of an individual substance.

Every substance has within it a kind of operation, and this operation is
either of the same thing on itself, in which case it is called reflection or
thought, and such a substance is spiritual, i.e. a *mind;* or it is the operation
of its various parts, and such a substance is called a *corporeal substance.*

Since God is a mind, and understands and loves himself, this is the
source of a kind of wonderful difference of the same person from himself,
or composition of an indivisible thing, which we acknowledge in the *per-
sons of the Holy Trinity;* and of which we also have some indication in our
mind once it is thinking.[6]

Mind is either separate from or united to a body: separate, as is God;
united to a body, as is *our soul.* There are also other minds more perfect
than ours, called *angelic minds.* These the ancients believed to be united to
certain bodies, but ones far more subtle than ours. But if this were true, our
soul too, even though it is in itself incorporeal, could be seen as only giving up its gross body at death. And there would be no created thing without
a body attached.

Corporeal substances have *parts* and *species.* The parts are matter and
form. *Matter* is the principle of passion, or primitive force of resisting,
**1508**  which is commonly called bulk or antitypy, from which flows the impenetrability of body. *Substantial form* is the principle of action, or primitive

tiva. Est autem in omni forma substantiali quaedam cognitio hoc est expressio seu repraesentatio externorum in re quaedam individua, secundum quam corpus est unum per se, nempe in ipsa forma substantiali, quae reprasentatio conjuncta est cum reactione seu conatu sive appetitu secundum hanc cognitionem agendi.

Hanc formam substantialem necesse est reperiri in omnibus substantiis corporeis, quae sunt unum per se. Itaque si bestiae non sunt purae machinae, necesse est formas substantias habere quae dicuntur *animae*. Caetera autem corpora quae forma substantiali carent sunt tantum aggregata corporum ut strues lignorum, congeries lapidum, neque proinde cognitionem aut appetitum habent. Omnis substantia quae unum per se est, sua natura perpetua est, et quomodo Mens, Anima, forma substantialis, seu principium unitatis in Entibus per se, aliter quam creatione et annihilatione produci aut extingui possit, non apparet, cum determinatae partes materiae ad essentiam ejus non pertineant. Itaque credibile est saepe animal oriri ex jam praeexistente in semine animalculo quodam invisibili in ovarium delato et ibi crescente; et vicissim saepe non extinctionem sed transformationem contingere, ut erucae in papilionem eadem utrobique anima manente, licet vetus aut novum animal plerumque non aeque ut eruca aut papilio sensibus nostris pateat. Et somniorum indicio discimus ad percipiendum non semper opus esse sensibus, nec in summa refert major an minor fiat materiae mutatio, nisi ad hoc ut perceptiones priores a posterioribus plus minusve differant. Mentes autem omnes, quia cum Deo rempublicam constituunt prioris vitae memoriam conservant.

Quantum ad Species corporis, negligamus nunc considerationem formae substantialis, et an corpus sit unum per se, tantumque *Materiae* differentias consideremus, quoniam plerumque dubitari potest an corpus sit Machina tantum et partium congeries, an vero sit forma substantiali vel anima praeditum. Hoc de ipsis animalibus controvertitur, multo magis adhuc de plantis et lapidibus et metallis, maxime autem de sideribus ac de Mundo universo.

**1509**    Corporum omnium Aggregatum dicitur *Mundus,* qui si infinitus est ne unum quidem Ens est non magis quam linea recta infinita aut numerus maximus. Itaque Deus non potest intelligi *anima Mundi,* non finiti, quia ipse Deus infinitus est, non infiniti quia corpus infinitum non potest unum Ens intelligi, quod autem non est unum per se id nec formam substantialem adeoque nec animam habet. Itaque recte Deus a Martiano Capella appellatur intelligentia extramundana.

force of acting. But in every substantial form there is a kind of cognition, that is, an expression or representation of external things in a certain individual thing,[7] according to which the body is a unity in itself, namely, in the substantial form itself. This representation is conjoined with a reaction, i.e. endeavour or appetite, according to this cognition of its acting.

This substantial form is necessarily found in all corporeal substances, which are one in themselves. So if beasts are not mere machines, it is necessary for them to have substantial forms, and these are called *souls.* Other bodies that lack a substantial form, on the other hand, are merely aggregates of bodies, like a woodpile or a heap of stones, and consequently do not possess cognition or appetite. Every substance which is a unity in itself is by its own nature perpetual, and it is not evident how mind, soul, substantial form, i.e. the principle of unity in entities per se, could be produced or extinguished except by creation and annihilation, since the determinate parts of matter do not belong to its essence. So it is easy to believe that an animal should often originate in some invisible animalcule already preexisting in the semen that has been carried down into the ovary, where it begins to grow; and also that there should often occur not an extinction but a transformation, as for example when a caterpillar turns into a butterfly, with the same soul remaining on both sides of the transformation, even though the old and new animals are not for the most part as obvious to our senses as the caterpillar and butterfly are. And from the evidence of dreams we learn that the senses are not always needed for perceiving, nor does it matter in the end whether the change occurring in matter is greater or less, except to the extent that the earlier perceptions would differ more or less from the later ones. All minds, on the other hand, since they constitute a republic with God, preserve a memory of their preceding life.

As for the species of body, we may now neglect the consideration of substantial form, and whether a body is a unity in itself, and shall consider only the differentiae of *matter.* For in most cases it is debatable whether a body is only a machine and conglomeration of parts, or whether it is really endowed with a substantial form or soul. This is a matter of controversy concerning animals themselves, and much more so still concerning plants and stones and metals, but most of all concerning stars and the world as a whole.

**1509**     The aggregate of all bodies is called the *world,* which, if it is infinite, is not even one entity, any more than an infinite straight line or the greatest number are. So God cannot be understood as the *World Soul:* not the soul of a finite world because God himself is infinite, and not of an infinite world because an infinite body cannot be understood as one entity, but that which is not a unity in itself has no substantial form, and therefore no soul.[8] So Martianus Capella is right to call God an extramundane intelligence.[9]

Nullum datur in Mundo *Vacuum* neque in materia neque in forma hoc est neque plura corpora in hoc mundano spatio creari possent, neque perfectioria. Possunt in rebus distingui receptacula a receptis. Receptacula sunt *Tempus* et *Locus* seu spatium. Recepta sunt corpora quae in his existunt.

Mundus praesens respectu nostri et loci in duas partes dividi potest in *Mundum Trans-Sidereum* de quo nihil a nobis percipitur, et in *Mundum Sidereum seu aspectabilem,* cujus quicquid extra Tellurem est dicitur *coelum,* et corpus sive sidus rotundum quod incolimus dicitur terra seu *Tellus.*

Mundus aspectabilis constat ex corporibus magnis solidis aut saltem cohaerentibus, ex longinquo nobus lucentibus, quae *Sidera* vocamus, et ex fluidis motum quendam periodicum habentibus, cum quibus aliqua sidera deferuntur, unde haec fluida quidam non inepte *vortices* appellant.

Sidera sunt vel per se lucentia, quae dicuntur *Soles,* vel sunt illustrata quae dici possunt *Terrae.*

Sunt et sidera vel fixa vel libera. Et fixa quidem unum locum servant aut certe hactenus non mutant satis notabiliter, libera vel periodos absolvunt quae dicuntur *Planetae,* vel nondum cognita lege et propemodum recta linea per mundana spatia trajiciunt quae *Cometas* dicimus.

**1510**      Et quidem hactenus observatum est Fixas esse soles, planetas vero esse terras et moveri circa suum solem, itaque fixa aliqua cum suis planteas dicitur componere *orbem Magnum,* et creditur tot esse forsan orbes magnos seu systemata planetaria quot sunt fixae. Interim nihil prohibet et erraticos soles dari et fixas Tellures.

Sunt et planetae qui circa alios planetas majores feruntur, qui dicuntur *Satellites.* Ita Galilaeus quatuor deprehendit satellites circa Jovem, Hugenius unum circa Saturnum, cui postea plures addidit Cassinus. Ipsa Luna est satelles Telluris nostrae. Tellus autem nostra intra planetes circa solem nobis lucentem motos computatur, quae omnia veteribus parum cognita nostro demum seculo in clara luce collocata sunt.

Cometas notabile est radios longe emittere interdum instar crinis sed plerumque instar caudae, quae in partem a sole aversam porrigitur.

Sed antequam longius progrediamur explicandum est discrimen inter *Corpora Fluida* et inter *firma* vel saltem connexionem habentia, seu quo-

There is no *vacuum* in the world, either in matter or in form: that is, neither a greater number of bodies, nor bodies that are more perfect, can be
created in this mundane space. One can distinguish things into those that
are receptacles, and those that occupy them, their recepts. *Time* and *place,*
or space, are receptacles. The bodies which exist in them are recepts.

With respect to us and our location, the present world can be divided
into two parts: the world beyond the stars or *trans-sidereal world,* of
which nothing is perceived by us; and the *sidereal or visible world,* of
which what is outside the Earth is called the *heavens,* and the body or
round star on which we live is called the *Earth.*

The visible world consists of large solid bodies, or at any rate cohering
ones, shining down on us from far away, which we call *stars;* and also of
fluids having a kind of periodic motion by which some stars are borne
along. For this reason people call these fluids, not inappropriately, *vortices.*

Stars either shine by themselves, in which case they are called *suns,* or
they are illuminated, in which case they may be called *earths.*

Stars are also either fixed or free. And the fixed stars do indeed stay in
one place, or at least they have not till now changed place enough for this
to be noted; the free ones either complete periodic orbits, in which case
they are called *planets,* or they follow trajectories in the mundane space
according to an as yet unknown law and along lines that are practically
straight, in which case we call them *comets.*

**1510**    Indeed, so far it has been observed that the fixed stars are suns, whereas
the planets are earths which move around their own sun, so that a fixed star
with its planets is said to compose a *great orb.* It is also believed that there
are perhaps as many great orbs or planetary systems as there are fixed
stars. Meanwhile, there is nothing to prevent there being both wandering
suns and fixed earths.

There are also planets which are carried around other bigger planets,
and these are called *Satellites.* Thus Galileo discovered four satellites
around Jupiter, Huygens one around Saturn, to which Cassini afterwards
added more.[10] The moon itself is a satellite of our Earth. Our Earth, on the
other hand, is counted among the planets moving around the sun that
shines on us. All these things, little known by the ancients, have in our day
finally been set in a clear light.

It is worth noting that comets sometimes emit long rays like hair, but
more usually like a tail, which stretch out away from them in the direction
of the sun.

But before we proceed too far we must explain the distinction between
*fluid bodies* and *firm* ones, or ones having at least some connection, that is,

rum partes cohaerent. Et quidem sciendum est, revera omne corpus habere aliquem gradum firmitatis, nec quicquam tam fluidum esse, quin vi aliqua opus sit ad partes flectendas vel omnino divellendas, et omne corpus habere aliquem gradum fluiditatis, ut non tantum satis magna vi partes ejus separari, sed et quacunque minima vi nonnihil inflecti possint. Nulla autem flexio sine aliquorum se prius contingentium divulsione est. Itaque nullae sunt *Atomi* in rebus, quae scilicet infinitae sint duritiei. Horum autem causa est, quod Creator nihil sterile reliquit, sed in qualibet particula materiae utcunque exigua innumerabil[ium] creaturarum velut mundum condidit. Nam quoniam continuum in infinitum divisibile est, relictam esset Vacuum formarum, si in aliqua parte materiae nulla actualis facta esset subdivisio, quod cum perfectione Dei pugnat. Itaque nulli dantur in mundo globi perfecti quos Cartesius longo temporis tractu tornatos credidit, neque ulla sunt in Mundo Elementa seu corpora prima ex quibus

**1511**  caetera componantur, itaque nec datur materia subtilis summae fluiditatis, neque Globuli secundi Elementi, et tam absurdum est corpus summe fluidum, quam summe durum. Et corpora quae nostrorum respectu Elementaria censeri possunt, possunt aliorum minorum respectu tam magna rursus intelligi ac sol est respectu scintillae. Dicendum est ergo in Mundo nullum posse assignari punctum, quod non diverso nonnihil ab alio quovis utcunque vicino puncto motu cieatur, sed rursus nullum posse assignari punctum, quod non cum alio dato mundi puncto communem quendam motum habeat, ex priori capite omnia sunt fluida, ex posteriori omnia sunt cohaerentia. Sed prout motus communis aut proprius plus minusve notabilis est, corpus unum solidum, aut separatum, vel etiam fluidum dicitur.

Notatur autem hoc ex resistentia quam sentimus, vel non sentimus in separando. Cujus ratio est, quod magnam mutationem in rebus procurare sine magna vi non licet. Itaque quae secundum praesentem rerum statum motumque universi et fluidorum in eo decurrentium sive visibilium sive invisibilium, partes habent quae ad se invicem compelluntur, et ab ambientibus comprimuntur, ea sine vi separari non possunt, ut grave a fundamento cui innititur, apprehensum corpus a forcipe quo tenetur, quin et si non comprimantur, attamen secundum aliquem divellendi modum sine turbatione notabili circumjacentium separari non possunt, ad ea divellenda vi opus est, ut experimento duarum tabularum politarum discimus.

whose parts cohere. And indeed it must be realized that truly every body has some degree of firmness, and there is nothing so fluid that some force is not needed to bend its parts or pull them apart completely; and that every body has some degree of fluidity, so that its parts may not only be separated by a sufficiently strong force, but may also be bent inwards somewhat by however minimal a force. But no bending can occur without some things that were previously touching being pulled apart. So there are no *atoms* in things, that is, no things having an infinite degree of hardness.

Now the cause of these things is that the Creator left nothing sterile, but instead fashioned a kind of world of innumerable[11] creatures in any particle of matter whatever, however minute. For since the continuum is divisible to infinity, a vacuum of forms would be left if in some part of matter no actual subdivision were made, which is contrary to God's perfection. So there are no perfect globes in the world, such as Descartes believed to have been turning on their axes for a long period of time,[12] nor are there any elements in the world, i.e. primary bodies from which the rest are 1511 composed. So, too, there is no such thing as subtle matter of the utmost fluidity, nor globules of the second element, and it is as absurd for a body to be of the utterly fluid as it is for it to be utterly hard. And bodies which can be judged elementary with respect to us, can with respect to other smaller bodies be understood to be as big again as the sun is with respect to a spark. Therefore it must be said that no point can be assigned in the world which is not set in motion somewhat differently from any other point however near to it, but, on the other hand, that no point can be assigned that does not have some motion in common with some other given point in the world; under the former head, all bodies are fluid; under the latter, all are cohering. But to the extent that a common or proper motion is more or less observable, a body is called one solid, or a separate body, or perhaps even a fluid.

But this is observed from the resistance we either feel or do not feel in separating them. The reason for this is that one may not administer a big change in things without great force. So according to the present state of things and motion of the universe, and of the fluids (whether visible or invisible) running through it, those things which have parts that are mutually forced together, and are pressed together by their surroundings, cannot be separated without force: as, for example, a heavy body cannot be separated from the base on which it rests without force, nor can a body that has been picked up be so separated from the forceps holding it. So that, even if they are not pressed together, they still cannot be separated, however one pulls them apart, without some observable disturbance in the surrounding bodies; and for this pulling apart a force is necessary, as we learn from the

Contra vero quae neque comprimuntur, neque cum aliqua circumjacentium turbatione dimoventur, in his nulla notatur cohaerentia. Et credibile
est, quae constant particulis planas superficies aut congruas multas et ma-
jusculas habentibus, non facile divelli, quia plurimus in ipsis est contactus,
unde divulsio non fit sine ambientum turbatione. In quibus autem exiguus
contactus est, in iis divellendis parum resistentiae sentiri. Et in universum
dicendum est nullam esse in Mundo quietam perfectam, nec absolute, nec
respectu corporum vicinorum, minorem tamen motum pro quiete habendum esse. Et quae prope se invicem quiescunt hoc est quae communi motu
cientur aut ad se invicem propius accedere conantur, hoc ipso sine aliqua
vi, hoc est sine ambientum mutatione, non posse separari. Quatenus autem
corpora varios motus exercent, et jam a se invicem discedere conantur, eo
facilius separari. Est ergo firmitatis origo, pressio ambientium, seu motus,
**1512**     qui separatione turbatur; quies ipsa per se neque ulla est, neque si esset,
causa firmitatis intelligi posset. Firmitate autem semel constituta, jam ex
firmorum corporum implicatione in se invicem rursus nova corpora cohaerentia formari possunt.

Interdum corpus cedens ubi sibi relictum est se restituit, quale corpus
dicitur *Elasticum,* restituit autem sese eandem ob causam, ob quam initio
flectenti restitit, quod scilicet hoc modo ambientum fluidorum invisibilium motus minus turbatur, sed quando tamen alius inter divellendum ipsis
exitus aeque commodus datus est, cessat restitutio. Unde raro fit ut partes
avulsae se reconjungant toti, fieri tamen aliquando discimus exemplo
Magnetis. Sciendum est autem in omnibus esse aliquem et Elastri gradum.
Exempli causa quid vitro durius et fragilius, et tamen tenuissima vitri fila
elastica sunt, contra, quid molius atque flexilius tenuissimo filo, et tamen
si aliquoties filum filo addatur, fiatque filum paulo crassius non tantum re-
sisitit nonnihil sed et [fragile] se restituit. Hinc etiam nihil tam molle est
quin percussum aliquem edat sonum, quem a restitutione aliqua tremula
elastici corporis oriri constat.

Haec ideo affecere placuit ut attollere animum a sensibus et universi oeconomiam admirabilem, et in summa varietate summam connexionem

experiment with the two polished tablets. On the other hand, in things which are neither pressed together nor moved apart by any disturbance of the surrounding bodies, no coherence is observed. And it is easy to believe that those things which consist of particles having flat surfaces or many fairly extensive congruent surfaces are not easy to pull apart, because they have the most contact in them, and hence they cannot be pulled apart without disturbing the bodies around them. But in those bodies in which there is hardly any contact, very little resistance is felt upon pulling them apart. And in general it must be said that there is no perfect rest in the world, neither absolutely, nor with respect to neighboring bodies, although if a motion is too small it is taken for rest. And those things which are at rest near to each other, that is, those either moving with a common motion or endeavouring to approach each other, cannot for this very reason be separated without some force, that is, without a change in the bodies around them. On the other hand, the more bodies are performing various motions, and are already endeavouring to pull apart from each other, the more easily they are separated. Therefore the origin of firmness is the pressure of the surrounding bodies, i.e. a motion which is disturbed by their separa-

**1512**   tion. Rest is nothing in itself, and if it were, the cause of firmness could not be understood. But once firmness has been established, further new cohering bodies can be formed by the entanglement of firm bodies with one another.

Sometimes a body that yields where it is standing restitutes itself, and this kind of body is called *elastic*. Now it restitutes itself for the same reason that it resisted at the beginning of the bending, namely, that in this way the motion of the invisible surrounding fluids is disturbed less. But when there is another equally convenient way for these fluids to escape as the body is being pulled apart, the restitution stops. Hence it rarely happens that parts that have been pulled out from a whole join back together, although we learn from the example of the magnet that this sometimes happens. It should be realized, though, that there is some degree of elasticity in everything. For example, what could be harder and more brittle than glass? And yet the slenderest threads of glass are elastic. And conversely, what could be softer and more pliable than the slenderest thread? And yet if the threads are added together one by one to make a slightly thicker thread, it not only resists a little, but its brittleness[13] is also restituted. Hence also nothing is so soft that it does not produce some sound when beaten, which sound is well known to arise from a kind of quivering restitution of the elastic body.

It seemed appropriate to relate these things so that we should become used to turning our soul away from the senses, to consider both the ad-

considerare assuescamus; et terminos Creatori non tantum in extensione, sed et in subdivisione rerum nullos praescriberamus, omniaque motu, vita creaturis plena esse intelligamus; et ineptam spem deponamus universum Mundi Systema animo concipiendi, et analysin ad usque prima corporum velut stamina atque Elementa, sive principia quae nulla sunt, producendi. Sed quemadmodum Magister scientiae muniendi, cum de terris disserit, satis habet de arenis, lapillis, calce, argilla dicere, at vero de minoribus corporibus, in terra latentibus, tanquam ad institutum suum non pertinentibus solicitus non est, ita nos satis felices erimus, si ea corpora insensibilia explicare possimus, quorum effectus notabiliter ad nos usque pervenit, cum ultra progredi nec possibile mortalibus, nec utile sit.

1513     Porro cum tanta sit varietas in Mundo, mirum non est Deo sapientissima voluntate sua omnia in motus aptissimos concitante alicubi factum esse aliquid simile coagulo in lacte moto, ut scilicet ingens aliqua respectu nostri massa abiret partim in partes caeteris firmiores, partim in alias notabiliter tenuiores, hoc est in sidera et vortices, sidere motum vicinae fluidi partis servante. An alia sit Mundi portio, ubi nec sidera sint nec vortices, sed major consistentiae aequabilitas, qualis est lactis ante coagulum, dicere non habemus. Rotunda autem sidera esse mirum non est, cum instar guttarum initio fuerint.

An vero planetae prodierint ex solibus seu fixis crusta paulatim obductis, an contra soles ex planetis inflammatis, et an in his ipsis aliqua sit vicissitudo, an vero ab initio statim vel exiguo tempore in praesentem formam omnia abierint, ex solo rationis iudicio dicere non habemus. Illud tamen multis argumentis agnoscere mihi videor, totam globi nostrae telluris superficiem aliquando inflammatam fuisse, quod nec a Scriptura Sancta abhorret, initio enim Deus dixit ut lux fieret, quam cum a tenebris separaret, hoc est lucida ab opacis secreverit, prius commixta fuisse, et ignem omnia pervasisse consentaneum est.

Post discrimen fluidi et firmi quod tactu percipimus, proximum est lucidi et opaci quod visu. Et quidem necesse est inter nos et rem lucentem commeare fluidum aliquod, quod motum ab illo ad nos deferat. Simplex tamen conatus ad motum sufficere non videtur. Videntur in lucente fieri in-

mirable economy of the universe and the greatest connection in the widest variety; so that we should not prescribe any bounds to the Creator, either in extension or even in the subdivision of things, and should understand everything to be filled with motion, life, and creatures; and so that we should lay aside the false hope of forming a conception of a universal System of the World, and of extending our analysis down to the first rudiments, as it were, and elements of bodies, i.e. to principles that do not exist. But just as a teacher of the science of fortification, when he lectures about earths, has plenty to say about sands, pebbles, limestone, and clay, but does not trouble with the smaller bodies hidden in the earth, regarding them as irrelevant to his purpose, so we shall be happy enough if we can explain those insensible bodies whose effect observably reaches us, since it is neither useful nor possible for us mortals to proceed any further.

**1513**     Moreover, since there is so much variety in the world, it is no wonder that when God, by his own supremely wise volition, roused everything into the most appropriate motions, he somewhere made something similar to the curd in coagulated milk: so that, in other words, some mass, huge with respect to us, changed partly into parts that were firmer than the rest, and partly into other ones that were observably finer, i.e. into stars and vortices, with each star maintaining the motion of the neighboring part of the fluid. Whether there is another region of the world where there are neither stars nor vortices, but which has a more equable consistency, like milk before coagulation, we do not presume to say. But it is no wonder that stars are round, since in the beginning they would have been like drops.

Whether in fact the planets came from suns or fixed stars that had been gradually enveloped with crust, or whether, conversely, suns came out of planets that had burst into flames, and whether these things are subject to any change, or whether they all turned into their present form immediately at the beginning or a very short time afterwards, we do not presume to say solely on the basis of reason. However, it seems to me to be acknowledged by many arguments that the whole surface of our earthly globe was once in flames. This does not conflict with the Holy Scripture. For in the beginning God said "Let there be light,"[14] and this is consistent with his separating it from the darkness, i.e. separating out the bright things from the dark ones with which they had previously been mixed together, after they had all been permeated with fire.

The next distinction after that between fluid and firm, which we perceive by touch, is that between light and dark, which we perceive by sight. And, indeed, it is necessary that between us and the shining thing something fluid should pass back and forth, conveying a motion from it to us. A simple endeavour to move, on the other hand, does not seem to suffice.[15]

numerabiles ictus validi seu subitae explosiones, sive a crasso ad tenue transitus, ut fit in sclopeto ventaneo vel pyrio exploso, unde pressio valida rectilinea in omnes partes exercetur[. P]erspicuum est, quod satis aequabiliter porosum est, ad pressionem sensibilem ubique recta transmittendam.

## Dans les corps il n'y a point de figure parfaite          Aiv310

**1613**   Il n'y a point de figure precise et arrestée dans le corps à cause de la division actuelle des parties à l'infini.

A          B          C

Soit par exemple une droite *ABC* je dis qu'elle n'est pas exacte. Car chaque partie de l'univers sympathisant avec toutes les autres il faut necessairement que si le point *A* tend dans la droite *AB,* le point *B* ait une autre direction. Car chaque partie *A* tachant d'entrainer avec elle toute autre, mais particulierement la plus voisine *B,* la direction de *B* sera composée de celle d'*A,* et de quelques autres: et il ne se peut point que *B* indefiniment voisine de *A* soit precisement exposée de la même facon à tout l'univers que *A,* en sorte que *AB* composent un tout, qui n'ait aucune sousdivision.

Il est vray que qu'on pourra tousjours mener une ligne imaginaire chaque instant, mais cette ligne dans les mêmes parties ne durera que cet instant, parce que chaque partie a un mouvement different de toute autre puisque elle exprime autrement tout l'univers. Ainsi il n'y a point de corps qui ait aucune figure durant un certain temps quelque petit qu'il puisse estre. Or je crois que ce qui n'est que dans un moment n'a aucune existence, puisqu'il commence et finit en meme temps. J'ay prouvé ailleurs qu'il n'y a point de moment moyen, ou moment du changement. Mais seulement le dernier moment de l'estat precedant et le premier moment de l'estat suivant. Mais cela suppose un estat durable. Or tous les estats durables, sont
**1614**   vagues; et il n'y [a] aucun de precis. Par exemple, on peut dire qu'un corps ne sortira pas d'une telle place plus grande que luy durant un certain temps, mais il n'y a aucune place precise ou egale au corps, où il dure.

On peut donc conclure, qu'il n'y a aucun mobile d'une certaine figure, par exemple il n'est pas possible qu'il se trouve dans la nature une sphere parfaite qui fasse un corps mobile, en sorte que cette sphere puisse estre mue par le moindre espace. On pourra bien concevoir une sphere imagi-

In a shining body there seem to occur countless powerful collisions or sudden explosions, or transitions from dense to rare—as happens in a hunting musket or in blasting powder—from which a powerful rectilinear pressure is exerted on all sides. A transparent body[16] is one that is uniformly porous enough for the transmitting of a sensible pressure in straight lines in all directions.


### 35. There Is No Perfect Shape in Bodies[1]                    Aiv310

[April–October 1686?][2]

**1613**  There is no precise and fixed shape in bodies, because of the actual division of the parts to infinity.

A          B          C

Let there be, for example, a straight line *ABC:* I say that it is not exactly straight. For with each part of the universe sympathizing with all the others, it is necessarily the case that if the point *A* tends along the straight line *AB,* the point *B* should have a tendency in another direction. For with each part *A* striving to carry with it every other, but particularly the nearest *B,* the direction of *B* will be composed of that of *A* and some others; and it is not at all possible that *B,* which is indefinitely near to *A,* should be exposed to the whole universe in precisely the same fashion as *A,* in such a way that *AB* composes one whole which has no subdivision.

It is true that it will always be possible to draw an imaginary line at each instant; but that line will endure in the same parts only for this instant, because each part has a motion different from every other, since it expresses the whole universe differently. Thus there is no body that has any shape for a definite time, however short it might be. Now I believe that what exists only at a moment has no existence, since it starts and finishes at the same time. I have proved elsewhere that there is no middle moment, or moment of change, but only the last moment of the preceding state and the first moment of the following state.[3] But that supposes an enduring state. Now all enduring states are vague; and there is nothing precise about them. For ex-

**1614**  ample, one can say that a body will not leave some place greater than itself for a definite time, but there is no place where the body may endure that is precise or equal to it.

One can thus conclude that there is no moving thing of a definite shape. For example, it is impossible for there to be found in nature a perfect sphere which would compose a moving body in such a way that this sphere could be moved through the least space. In a pile of stones, one

naire qui dans un tas de pierres passe à travers de toutes ces pierres, mais on ne trouvera jamais aucun corps, dont la surface soit precisement spherique.

*In instanti* le mouvement n'estant pas consideré, c'est comme si la masse estoit toute unie; et alors on peut luy donner telles figures qu'on veut. Mais aussi toute la varieté dans le corps cesse; et par consequent tous les corps sont detruits. Car le mouvement ou l'effort fait leur essence ou difference. Et dans ce moment tout revient en caos. L'effort ne sçauroit estre concû dans la masse seule.

### Infiniti possunt gradus esse inter animas                Aiv304

1524  Infiniti possunt gradus esse inter animas, idque similtudine petita a nostra Geometria sublimiore videtur illustrari posse. Animae est connectere inter se differentes corporis status, ut ejus ope praeterita et futura simul existant,
1525  praeterita per quandam reminiscentiam, futura per praesensionem. Et licet verum sit corpus etiam praeteritos et praesentes suos status referre; hoc tamen interest, quod in corpore non est nisi praesens status, etsi is sit effectus praeteriti referens causam; et idem sit causa futuri referens effectum. Sed in anima omnis status per se repraesentatur, praeteritus ut praeteritus, futurus ut futurus, praesens ut praesens; unusquisque non solum exprimitur per consequentiam, sed et repraesentatur.

Repraesentandi tamen modus plus minusve est clarus plenusque pro animae perfectione; ut transitus in lineis suos gradus habent. Nempe in omni linea curva transitus est a puncto ad punctum. Quod si jam linea concipiatur ut polygonum infinitorum laterum; utique pro transitu seu progressu in linea considerare oportet puncta plura. Nam unum punctum praesentem quidem statum designat, non tamen mutationem. Si conjungamus tantum duo puncta, exprimetur directio motus seu quae sit tangens lineae; si tria puncta conjungamus, habetur non tantum directio, sed et flexus, seu mutatio directionis; adeoque habetur circulus osculans. Si conjungamus puncta quatuor, habebitur osculum secundi gradus; et ita porro. Sed his omnibus nondum exprimitur plena linea curvedo, quae omnia possibilia oscula simul involvit; exprimitque quaenam sit linea osculans cujuscunque gradus. Corpus respondet situi puncti seu statui praesenti; sed animae respondent gradui mutationis in motu puncti. Et Anima infimi gradus respondet directioni, anima secundi gradus osculo primo, anima tertii gradus osculo secundo; et ita porro. Sed mens respondet osculo infiniti

could easily conceive an imaginary sphere which passes through all these stones, but one could never find any body whose surface would be precisely spherical.[4]

*In an instant,* with motion not being considered, it is as if the mass were all united; and thus one can give it any such shapes as one wants. But also all variety in bodies ceases; and, consequently, all bodies are destroyed. For motion or endeavour makes their essence or difference. And in this moment everything reverts to chaos. Endeavour cannot be conceived in mass by itself.

### 36. There Can Be Infinite Degrees of Souls[1]                    Aiv304

[c. 1686?][2]

**1524** There can be infinite degrees of souls, and it seems this can be illustrated by drawing from a rather sublime similarity with our Geometry. The soul has the ability to connect together different states of the body, so that past

**1525** and future exist together by its help, the past by a kind of reminiscence, the future by presentiment. And although it is true that a body also relates its past and present states, there is, however, this difference: In a body there is nothing but a present state, even if it is an effect relating a cause of the past, and likewise, a cause relating an effect of the future. But in the soul every state is represented per se, past as past, future as future, present as present; each state not only is expressed as a consequence, but is also represented.

The mode of representing, however, is more or less clear and full in proportion to the perfection of the soul, just as transitions in lines have their degrees. Of course, in every curved line the transition is from point to point. But if now the line is conceived as a polygon of infinite sides, for the transition or progression in the line it is proper to consider many points. Now one point designates a particular present state, but not a change. If we connect only two points, the direction of motion or the tangent to the line will be expressed; if we connect three points, we have not only the direction but also the bending, or change of direction; and so we have the osculating circle. If we connect four points, we will have an osculation of the second degree; and so on. But these things do not yet express the full curvature, which involves all possible osculations at once; and expresses just which osculating line belongs to each degree. A body corresponds to the situation of a point or present state; but souls correspond to the degree of change in the motion of the point. And the soul of lowest degree corresponds to tendency in a given direction, a soul of second degree to the first osculation, a soul of the third degree to the second osculation; and so on. But mind corresponds to an osculation of infinitieth degree; and expresses

gradus; et exprimit integram lineae curvedinem in puncto dato, seu quicquid a puncto dato non abest assignabiliter. Unde patet Mentes esse ad
simplices animas ut infinitum ad finitum, seu ut finitum ad infinite
parvum. Sed mens infinita respondet toti progressui motus per lineam,
transitui a puncto dato ad aliud punctum assignabiliter distans quodcunque, seu saltum.

**1526**    Quod si quis putet distingui hic rursus posse inter Mentes saltum fa-
cientes per distantias finitas diversas, quae omnes Mentem saltu carentem
infinite excedant; et tamen ipsae sint infinite depressae infra mentem cujus
saltus est in distantias omnes, dicendum tamen ubi mera est continuitas
seu sola differentia per majus et minus non posse diversas species assignari, adeoque mentem quae saltum faciat, facere in quantamcumque distantiam cum oscul[a] numeris seu discreta differe sit manifestum.

Habemus ergo

Punctum seu statum          Progressum

directionem          flexum

Habemus ergo

Punctum seu statum     Progressum

elementarem          plenum

directionem          flexum
tangentis            osculantis
                     pro gradu

primo,  secundo,  tertio, etc.

**1527**          Habemus ergo

Punctum seu statum          Progressum

elementarem          absolutum
seu inchoatum

partialem          totalem lineae
secundum           speciem exprimentum

the entire curvature of a line in a given point, in other words, whatever is not assignably missing from the given point. Whence it is clear that minds are to simple souls as the infinite is to the finite, or as the finite is to the infinitely small. But an infinite mind corresponds to the whole progression of motion through the line, to the transition from the given point to any other point assignably distant from it, that is to say, a leap.

**1526**     Now it might be thought possible here to make a further distinction among minds making a leap through different finite distances, which all infinitely exceed a mind lacking a leap, and yet are still infinitely inferior to a mind whose leap is to all distances: but to this it must be said that whenever it is a mere continuity, or only a difference through greater or less, it is not possible for different species of mind to be assigned. And so a mind that makes a leap makes it to however great a distance, since it is evident that osculations differ numerically, i.e. are discrete.[3]

Therefore we have

| a point or state | progress |
|---|---|
| | direction — bending |

Therefore we have

| a point or state | progress |
|---|---|
| | elementary — full |

| in the direction of the tangent | along the osculating curve of |
|---|---|
| | first, second, third, etc. degree |

**1527**     Therefore we have

| a point or state | progress |
|---|---|
| | elementary or inchoate — absolute |

| partial, along the | total, expressing a species of line |

directionem tangentem  flexum osculi
in gradu

primo,  secundo,  tertio, etc.

| Status | Directio | Osculum | | | Lineatio | Linea |
|--------|----------|---------|---|---|----------|-------|
| | | primi, | secundi, | tertii gradus | | utcunque producta |

Respondent his:

| Corpus | Anima ima seu vita | sensus primi, | secundi, | tertii gradus | Anima intelligens | Deus |
|--------|--------------------|---------------|----------|---------------|-------------------|------|

seu

rationis expers  rationalis

finitum. Anima  infinitum

aggregatum, quod per se torpet  una substantia, seu vivum

Substans

---

**1615**    **Specimen inventorum de admirandis
naturae generalis arcanis**    **Aiv312**

**1616**    *SPECIMEN INVENTORUM DE ADMIRANDIS
NATURAE GENERALIS ARCANIS*

In omni veritate universali affirmativa praedicatum inest subjecto, expresse quidem in veritatibus primitivis, sive identicis, quae solae sunt per se notae; implicite autem in caeteris omnibus, quod analysi terminorum ostenditur, substituendo sibi definita et definitiones.

Itaque duo sunt prima principia omnium ratiocinationum: Principium nempe contradictionis, quod scilicet omnis propositio identica vera, et

| | direction of the tangent | | curve of osculation in | | | |
|---|---|---|---|---|---|---|
| | | | first, | second, | third, etc. degree | | |
| State | Direction | Osculation of the first, | second, | third degree | Lineation | Line however extended |

Corresponding to:

| | | | | | | |
|---|---|---|---|---|---|---|
| Body | Lowest Soul or Life | Sensation of the first, | second, | third degree | Intelligent Soul | God |

or

non-rational soul                   rational soul

the finite. Soul                    infinite

an aggregate, in itself lifeless          one substance, or living thing

Substance

---

**1615**      **37. A Specimen of Discoveries of the Admirable**
              **Secrets of Nature in General[1]**                    **Aiv312**

[c. 1686?][2]

**1616**      *A SPECIMEN OF DISCOVERIES OF THE ADMIRABLE*
              *SECRETS OF NATURE IN GENERAL*[3]

In every universal affirmative truth the predicate is in the subject: explicitly so in primitive or identical truths, which are the only ones known through themselves; implicitly so in every other truth, which is shown by an analysis of terms, substituting for one another defined terms and definitions.[4]

Thus there are two first principles of all reasoning: the Principle of Contradiction, which is that every identical proposition is true, and its contradictory false; and the Principle of Providing a Reason,[5] which is that every

contradictoria ejus falsa est; et principium reddendae rationis, quod scilicet omnis propositio vera quae per se nota non est, probationem recipit a
priori, sive quod omnis veritatis reddi ratio potest, vel ut vulgo ajunt, quod
nihil fit sine causa. Hoc principio non indiget Arithmetic et Geometria, sed
indiget Physica et Mechanica, eoque usus est Archimedes.

Essentiale est discrimen inter Veritates necessarias sive aeternitas, et
veritas facti sive contingentes differuntque inter se propemodum ut numeri rationales et surdi. Nam veritates necessariae resolvi possunt in iden-
ticas, ut quantitates commensurabiles in communem mensuram, sed in
veritatibus contingentibus, ut in numeris surdis, resolutio procedit in infinitum, nec unquam terminatur, itaque certitudo et perfecta ratio veritatum contingentium soli Deo nota est, qui infinitum uno intuitu complectitur. Atque hoc arcano cognito tollitur difficultas de absoluta omnium
rerum necessitate: et apparet quid inter infallibile et necessarium intersit.

Vera causa cur haec potius quam illa existant sumenda est a liberis divinae voluntatis decretis, quorum primarium est, velle omnia agere quam
optime, ut sapientissimum decet. Itaque licet interdum perfectius exclu-
datur ab imperfectiore, in summa tamen electus est ille modus creandi
mundum, qui plus realitatis sive perfectionis involvit, et Deus agit instar
**1617**    summi Geometrae, qui optimas problematum constructiones praefert.
Itaque omnia Entia quatenus involvuntur in primo Ente, praeter nudam
possibilitatem habent aliquam ad existendum propensionem, proportione
bonitatis suae existuntque volente Deo nisi sint incompatibilia perfec-
toribus, vel pluribus quod posterius fit si nimium voluminis habeant proportione virtutis, ita ut plus spatii occupent, quam impleant, ut angulosa
aut sinuosa. Exemplo res erit clarior. Hinc etiam determinata praeferuntur
indeterminatis, in quibus ratio electionis nulla intelligi potest. Itaque si
sapiens decreverit tria assignare puncta in aliquo spatio, nec ulla sit ratio
pro una potius quam alia specie trianguli, eligetur aequilaterum in quo
puncta tria similiter se habent. Et si tres globi aequales et similes sint col-
locandi inter se, nec alia praeterea detur conditio, collocabuntur ut se tangant.

Definitio realis est, ex qua constat definitum esse possibile, nec implicare contradictionem. Nam de quo id non constat, de eo nulla ratiocinatio
tuto institui potest, quoniam si contradictionem involvit, oppositum for-

true proposition which is not known through itself receives an a priori proof, i.e. that a reason can be provided for every truth, or as is commonly said, that nothing happens without a cause. Arithmetic and Geometry do not need this principle, but Physics and Mechanics do, and Archimedes made use of it.

There is an essential distinction between necessary or eternal truths, and truths of fact or contingent truths, and they differ from one another in much the same way as do rational numbers and surds. For necessary truths can be resolved into identical truths, as commensurable quantities can be resolved into a common measure, but in contingent truths, as in irrational numbers, the resolution proceeds to infinity, and never comes to an end. And so the certainty of and perfect reason for contingent truths is known only to God, who grasps the infinite in one intuition. And once this secret is known, the difficulty about the absolute necessity of all things is eliminated, and it is clear what the difference is between the infallible and the necessary.[6]

The[7] true cause of why these things exist rather than those is to be derived from the free decrees of the divine will. Of these the primary one is the will to do everything as well as possible, as befits the wisest being. Thus although the more perfect may occasionally be excluded by the more imperfect, nevertheless all in all that way of creating the world is chosen which involves more reality or perfection, and God acts like a first-rate **1617** geometer who prefers the best constructions of problems.[8] Thus all beings, insofar as they are involved in the first being, have, in addition to bare possibility, some propensity for existing in proportion to their goodness; and, if God wills it, do exist, unless they are incompatible with more perfect beings, or with a greater number of beings. The latter occurs if they have too great a volume in proportion to their potential, so that they occupy more space than they fill, like angular or sinuous things. An example will make the matter clearer. Hence also determinate things are preferred to indeterminate ones, in which no reason for a choice can be understood. Thus if a wise person decided to assign three points in some space, and there were no reason for one kind of triangle rather than another, he would choose an equilateral triangle, in which the three points are similarly disposed. And if three equal and similar globes are to be arranged together, and no further condition is attached, they will be arranged so as to touch each other.

A real definition is one according to which it is established that the defined thing is possible, and does not imply a contradiction. For if this is not established for a given thing, then no reasoning can safely be undertaken about it, since if it involves a contradiction, the opposite can perhaps be

tasse pari jure de eodem concludi potest. Atque hoc defuit demonstrationi Anselmi, a Cartesio renovatae, quod Ens perfectissimum, seu maximum, quia existentiam involvit, existere debeat. Assumitur enim sine probatione Ens perfectissimum non implicare contradictione, eaque occasione a me agnitum est quae sit natura definitionis realis. Itaque definitiones causales, quae generationem rei continent, reales quoque sunt. Ideas quoque rerum non cogitamus nisi quatenus earum possibilitatem intuemur.

Ens necessarium, si modo possibile est, utique existit. Hoc est fastigium doctrinae modalis, et transitum facit ab essentiis ad existentias, a veritatibus hypotheticis ad absolutas, ab ideis ad mundum.[L1]

Si nullum esset Ens necessarium, nullum foret Ens contingens, ratio enim reddenda est cur contingentia potius existant quam non existant, quae nulla erit, nisi sit ens quod a se est, hoc est cujus existentiae ratio in ipsius essentia continetur; ita ut ratione extra ipsum opus non sit. Et licet in rationibus contingentium reddendis iretur in infinitum, oportet tamen ex-
**1618** tra ipsorum seriem (in qua sufficiens ratio non est) reperiri rationem totius seriei. Unde etiam sequitur Ens necessarium esse Unum numero, et Omnia virtute, cum sit ultima ratio rerum, quatenus realitates seu perfectiones continent. Et cum ratio rei plena sit aggregatum omnium requisitorum primitivorum (quae aliis requisitis non indigent) patet omnium causa re-solvi in ipsa attributa Dei.

Si nulla esset substantia aeterna nullae forent aeternae veritates. Itaque hinc quoque probatur Deus; qui est radix possibilitatis, eius enim mens est ipsa regio idearum sive veritatum. Valde autem erroneum est, veritates aeternas rerumque bonitatem a divina voluntate pendere, cum omnis voluntas judicium intellectus de bonitate supponat, nisi quis commutatis no-

---

L1. FIRST INTERLEAVED NOTE (Aiv315): Haec propositio: *si possibile est Ens necessarium, sequitur quod existat* est fastigium doctrinae modalis, et primum facit transitum a posse ad esse, seu ab essentiis rerum ad existentias. Et quia necessarius est talis transitus, alioqui nihil existeret, vel hinc sequitur Ens necessarium esse possibile, adeoque existere. Et sane nisi esset ens necessarium nulla reddi posset ratio existentiae rerum, nec causa esset cur aliquid existeret. Seu ut brevius dicam: Necesse est aliquid existere, atque ideo datur Ens necessarium. Videndum an haec consequentia sufficiat. Videtur enim hinc saltem sequi Entia quaedam alternative necessaria esse, verum alternativa necessitas tamen debet fundari in aliqua necessitate absoluta.

concluded about the same thing with equal right. And this was the defect in Anselm's demonstration, revived by Descartes, that a most perfect or greatest being must exist, since it involves existence. For it is assumed without proof that a most perfect being does not imply a contradiction; and this gave me the occasion to recognize what the nature of a real definition is. So causal definitions, which contain the generation of the thing, are real definitions as well. The ideas of things, too, we only think of insofar as we intuit their possibility.[9]

A necessary being certainly exists, provided only that it is possible. This is the pinnacle of modal theory, effecting the transition from essences to existences, from hypothetical to absolute truths, and from ideas to the world.[L1]

If there were no necessary being, there would be no contingent being either. For a reason must be provided why contingents should exist rather than not exist. But there will be no such reason unless there is a being which exists in itself, that is, the reason for whose existence is contained in its essence, so that there is no need for a reason outside it. And even if one were to go on to infinity in providing reasons for contingents, a reason for their whole series (in which there is not a sufficient reason) would still have to be found outside the series.[10] From this it also follows that the necessary being is numerically one, and potentially all things, since it is the ultimate reason for things, insofar as they contain realities or perfections. And since the full reason for a thing is the aggregate of all primitive requisites (those which do not need other requisites), it is clear that the causes of all things are resolved into God's attributes themselves.

If there were no eternal substance, there would be no eternal truths. So from this too we have a proof of God, who is the root of possibility, since his mind is the very region of ideas, i.e. truths. But it is highly erroneous to make eternal truths and the goodness of things depend on divine will, since every act of will presupposes a judgment of the intellect concerning

L1. FIRST INTERLEAVED NOTE (Aiv315): This proposition: *if a necessary being is possible, it follows that it exists,* is the pinnacle of modal theory, and makes the first transition from possibility to being, that is, from the essences of things to existences. And since such a transition is necessary, for otherwise nothing would exist, it follows from this that a necessary being is possible, and therefore exists. And to be sure, unless there were a necessary being, no reason could be provided for the existence of things, nor would there be a cause why anything should exist. Or, to say it more concisely: It is necessary for something to exist, and therefore there is a necessary being. It must be seen whether this inference is sufficient. For it seems to follow from this at least that certain beings are conditionally necessary; yet conditional necessity must be founded on some absolute necessity.

1618

minibus omne judicium ab intellectu ad voluntatem transferat, quanquam
ne tunc quidem dici possit, voluntatem esse causam veritatum; cum nec
judicium sit. Ratio veritatum latet in rerum ideis, quae ipsi divinae essentiae involvuntur. Et quis dicere ausit, veritatem existentiae divinae a divina voluntate pendere.

Unaquaeque substatia habet aliqua infiniti quatenus causam suam,
Deum, involvit, nempe aliquod omniscientiae et omnipotentiae vestigium: nam in perfecta notione cuiusque substantiae individualis continentur omnia eius praedicata tam necessaria quam contingentia, praeterita
praesentia et futura; imo unaquaeque substantia, exprimit totum Universum secundum situm atque aspectum suum, quatenus caetera ad ipsum
referentur, et hinc necesse est quasdam perceptiones nostras etiamsi
claras, tamen confusas esse, cum infinita involvant, ut coloris, caloris et
similium. Quin imo substantiae finitae multiplices nihil aliud sunt quam
diversae expressiones ejusdem Universi, secundum diversos respectus et
proprias cuique limitationes. Quemadmodum una ichnographia infinita⟨s⟩
habet sce⟨nographias⟩. Itaque quod Hippocrates de corpore Humano dixit,
de ipso universo verum est, omnia conspirantia et sympathetica esse, seu
nihil in una creatura fieri, cuius non effectus aliquis exacte respondens ad
caeteras omnes perveniat. Neque ullae in rebus dantur denominationes absolute extrinsicae.

**1619**    Tolluntur ex his difficultates de Praedestinatione, et de Causa Mali. Intelligi enim potest Deum non decernere, utrum Adamus peccare debeat,
sed utrum illa series rerum cui inest Adamus, cuius perfecta notio individualis peccatum involvit, sit aliis nihilominus praeferenda. Vidit hoc etiam
Hugo a S. Victore, qui quaerenti cur Deus Jacobum dilexerit, non Esavum,
nihil aliud respondit quam quia Jacob non est Esau. Nempe in notione perfecta substantiae individualis in puro possibilitatis statu a Deo conside-
ratae, ante omne existendi decretum actuale, jam inest quicquid ei eventurum est si existat, imo tota series rerum, cuius partem facit. Itaque non
quaeratur an Adamus sit peccaturus, sed an Adamus peccaturus ad existentiam sit admittendus. Nam hoc interest inter substantias universales et
individuales, quod in harum notione et praedicata contingentia involvuntur, neque enim dubium est quin Deus viderit quid Adamo eventurum esset, antequam eum creare decrevit atque ideo nihil hinc libertati officitur.
Et notio Adami possibilis etiam decreta liberae voluntatis divinae hu-
manaeque sumta ut possibilia, continet. Et unaquaeque series universi

goodness—unless one were to transfer every judgment from the intellect to the will by interchanging their names, although even then it could not be said that the will is the cause of truths, since a judgment is not one either. The reason for truths lies in the ideas of things, which are involved in the divine essence itself. And who would dare say that the truth of divine existence depends on the divine will?

Each substance has something of the infinite insofar as it involves its cause, God: namely, some vestige of omniscience and omnipotence. For in the perfect notion of each individual substance are contained all its predicates, necessary as well as contingent, past, present, and future; indeed, each substance expresses the whole universe according to its own situation and point of view, inasmuch as everything else is related to it. Hence it is necessary that some of our perceptions, even though clear, are nonetheless confused, since they involve infinitely many things—for instance, our perceptions of color, heat, and the like. In fact, the manifold finite substances are nothing but different expressions of the same universe according to the different respects and limitations proper to each one, just as one ground plan has infinite ⟨ly many lateral perspectives.⟩[11] Thus what Hippocrates said of the human body[12] is true of the universe itself, that all things harmonize[13] and are in sympathy, i.e. that nothing happens in one creature for which some exactly corresponding effect does not reach all the others. Nor are there any absolutely extrinsic denominations in things.

**1619** These considerations eliminate the difficulties concerning predestination and the cause of evil. For it can be understood that God does not decree whether Adam should sin, but whether that series of things in which there is an Adam whose perfect individual notion involves sin should nevertheless be preferred to other series. Hugo of St. Victor[14] also saw this: when he was asked why God favored Jacob and not Esau, he simply replied, "Because Jacob is not Esau." That is to say, already contained in the perfect notion of an individual substance, considered by God in a pure state of possibility before every actual decree about what is to exist, there is whatever will happen to it if it should exist, and indeed the whole series of things of which it forms a part. Thus it should not be asked whether Adam will sin, but whether an Adam who will sin should be admitted into existence. For there is this difference between universal substances and individual ones, that in the notion of the latter contingent predicates are also involved. For there is no doubt that God would have seen what would happen to Adam before he decided to create him, and so there is no obstacle to freedom on this account. And the notion of a possible Adam also contains the decrees of free will, divine and human, considered as possible. And each possible series in the universe is supported by certain particular free

possibilis certis quibusdam decretis liberis primariis sibi propriis sub possibilitatis ratione sumtis innitur. Nam quemadmodum nulla linea duci potest, utcunque temeraria manu, quae non Geometrica sit certamque habeat naturam constantem, omnibus suis punctis communem; ita nulla est series rerum possibilis, nullaque ratio creandi mundum fingi potest, tam perturbata, quae non suo quodam fixo et determinato ordine et progressionis legibus constet, licet ut lineae ita et series aliae plus aliis habeant et potentiae et simplicitatis, atque adeo et perfectionis minoreque apparatu ampliora praestent. Ex his etiam apparet causam mali non esse a **1620** Deo, sed ab essentiali limitatione creaturarum, sive ab imperfectione originali ante omnem lapsum, quemadmodum alicui impetus corpori impressus minorem producit velocitatem, si major sit corporis moles sive inertia naturalis.

Ex notione Substantiae individualis, sequitur etiam in Metaphysico rigore, omnes substantiarum operationes, actiones passionesque esse spontaneas, exceptaque creaturarum a Deo dependentia, nullum intelligi posse influxum earum realem in se invicem, cum quicquid cuique evenit ex eius natura ac notione profluat, etiamsi caetera alia abesse fingerentur, unaquaeque enim universum integre exprimit. Verum ea cuius expressio distinctior est agere, cuius confusior pati judicatur, nam et agere perfectionis est, pati imperfectionis. Eaque res censetur esse causa ex cuius statu ratio mutationum facillime redditur. Quemadmodum si unus ponat solidum in fluido motum varios excitare fluctus; alius intelligere potest eadem evenire, si solido in medio fluido quiescente certi motus aequivalentes ⟨fluctibus variis⟩ fluidi ponantur, imo infinitis modis eadem phaenomena explicari possunt. Et certe motus revera res respectiva est, illa tamen Hypothesis quae Motum solido tribuens hinc fluctus liquidi deducit, caeteris infinites simplicior est, atque ideo solidum causa motus censetur. Et causae non a reali influxu, sed a reddenda ratione sumuntur.

Haec adeo vera sunt ut in physicis quoque re accurate inspecta appareat, nullum ab uno corpore impetum in aliud transferri; sed unumquodque a vi insita moveri, quae tantum alterius occasione sive respectu determinatur. Jam enim agnitum est a viris egregis, causam impulsus corporis a corpore esse ipsum corporis Elastrum, quo ab alio resilit. Elastri autem causa est motus partium Elastici corporis intestinus, licet enim a fluido quodam

primary decrees appropriate to it, considered under the aspect of possibility. For just as no line can be drawn, by however rash a hand, which would not be geometrical and have a certain constant[15] nature common to all its points, so also there is no possible series of things so disordered, nor can any reason be imagined for creating a world so disordered, that it would not come with its own fixed and determinate order and laws of progression. But just as some lines have more power and simplicity than others, so also do some series, and so exhibit greater perfection with less wherewithal. From these considerations it is also clear that the cause of evil does

**1620**  not come from God but from the essential limitation of his creatures, i.e. from an original imperfection before every lapse, just as the impetus impressed on a body produces a smaller velocity if the bulk, i.e. natural inertia of the body, is greater.

From the notion of individual substance it also follows in metaphysical rigor that all the operations of substances, both actions and passions, are spontaneous, and that with the exception of the dependence of creatures on God, no real influence of them on one another is intelligible. For whatever happens to each of them would flow forth from its own nature and notion even if all the others were imagined to be absent, since each one expresses the entire universe. However, that whose expression is more distinct is deemed to act, and that whose expression is more confused to be acted upon, since to act is a perfection, and to be acted upon is an imperfection. And that thing from whose state a reason for the changes is most readily provided is adjudged to be the cause. Thus if one person supposes that a solid moving in a fluid stirs up various waves, another can understand the same things to occur if, with the solid at rest in the middle of the fluid, one supposes certain equivalent motions of the fluid (in various waves); indeed, the same phenomena can be explained in infinitely many ways. And granted that motion is really a relative thing, nonetheless that hypothesis which attributes motion to the solid, and from this deduces the waves in the liquid, is infinitely simpler than the others, and for this reason the solid is adjudged to be the cause of the motion. Causes are not derived from a real influence, but from the providing of a reason.

These things are true to the extent that in physics too, on careful investigation of the matter, it is evident that no impetus is transferred from one body to another, but each body moves by an innate force, which is determined only on the occasion of, i.e. with respect to, another. For it has already been acknowledged by eminent men that the cause of the impulse one body gets from another is the body's elasticity itself, by means of which it recoils from the other. The cause of the elasticity, however, is the internal motion of the parts of the elastic body; for although elasticity may

generali derivetur, tamen partes fluidi permeantis dum transeunt, insunt.

**1621**  Sed haec ut recte intelligantur, proprius cujusque corporis motus, qui ictum facit, discernendus est a communi; qui semper et ante ictum intelligi potest, et post ictum servatur, proprius autem, qui solus obstaculum alteri facit, effectum non habet in alterius corpore nisi per ipsius Elastrum.

Similiter ex nostra notione substantiae ipsa Unio Animae et Corporis plenam explicationem recipit. Nam alii crediderunt transire nescio quid ex anima in corpus, et vicissim, quae est *Hypothesis influxus realis;* aliis visum est Deum in anima cogitationes excitare respondentes motui corporis, et vicissim in corpore motus respondentes cogitationibus animae, unum occasione alterius, quae est *Hypothesis causae occasionalis.*[L2] Sed non est opus Deum ex machina evocare in re quae manifeste ex nostris principiis consequitur. Unaquaeque enim substantia singularis exprimens idem universum pro modulo suo, ex propriae naturae legibus, ita se habet, ut mutationes ejus et status perfecte aliarum substantiarum mutationibus et statibus respondeant,[L3] maxime autem Anima et Corpus inter se invicem, quarum unio intima in perfectissimo consensu consistit. Et nisi hoc demonstrationem haberet a priori, Hypotheseos maxime plausibilis locum tueretur. Quid ni enim ponere liceat, Deum ab initio tanto artificio creasse Animam et corpus, ut unoquoque suas leges proprietatesque atque opera-

L2. SECOND INTERLEAVED NOTE: Systema causarum occasionalium partim admitti, partim rejici debet. Unaquaeque substantia est causa vera et realis suarum actionum *immanentium*, et vim habet agendi, ac licet divino concursu sustentetur, fieri tamen non potest, ut tantum passive se habeat, idque verum est tam in substantiis corporalibus quam incorporalibus. Sed rursus unaquaeque substantia (Deo solo excepto) non est nisi causa occasionalis suarum Actionum *transeuntium* in aliam substantiam. Vera igitur *Ratio unionis inter animam et corpus*, et Causa cur unum corpus sese accommodet ad statum alterius corporis non alia est, quam quod diversae substantiae ejusdem systematis mundani ab initio ita creatae sunt, ut ex propriae naturae Legibus conspirent inter se.

L3. IN THE MARGIN: Ad temporis naturam intelligendam requiretur ut consideretur mutatio seu contradictoria praedicata de eodem, diverso respectu qui respectus est nihil aliud quam consideratio temporis.

Spatium et tempus non sunt Res, sed relationes reales. Nullus est locus absolutus, nec motus, quia nulla sunt principia determinandi subjectum motus.

be derived from a kind of general fluid, nevertheless the parts of the permeating fluid, as long as they are passing through the body, are contained **1621** in it. But to understand these things correctly, one must distinguish the proper motion of each of the colliding bodies from their common motion. The latter is always conserved, both before the collision can be conceived, and after the collision; proper motion, on the other hand, which is all that creates an obstacle to another thing, has no effect on the body of the other thing except through that thing's elasticity.

Similarly, the very union of soul and body receives a full explanation from our notion of substance. For some have believed I know not what to pass from the soul into the body, and conversely: this is the *hypothesis of real influence;*[16] and to others it has seemed that God excites thoughts in the soul corresponding to the motion of the body, and, conversely, motions in the body corresponding to the thoughts of the soul, one on the occasion of the other: this is the *hypothesis of the occasional cause.*[L2] But there is no need to summon a *deus ex machina* in a matter which manifestly follows from our principles.[17] For each individual substance, expressing the same universe in its own measure according to the laws of its own nature, behaves in such a way that its changes and states correspond perfectly to the changes and states of other substances;[L3] but most especially correspondent to each other are soul and body, whose intimate union consists in a most perfect agreement. Even if this is not considered an a priori demonstration, it should hold its ground as the most plausible hypothesis. For why may we not suppose that God created soul and body from the begin-

L2. SECOND INTERLEAVED NOTE (Aiv320): The system of occasional causes ought to be partly accepted, and partly rejected. Each substance is the true and real cause of its *immanent* actions, and has a force of acting, and although it is sustained by divine concurrence, it is impossible for it to behave merely passively, and this is true in corporeal substances as well as incorporeal ones. But again each substance (excepting God alone) is but the occasional cause of its own *transient* actions on another substance. Therefore the true *reason for the union between soul and body,* and the cause of one body's accommodating itself to the state of another body, is simply that the different substances of the same world system were so created from the beginning as to harmonize with one another as a result of the laws of their own individual nature.

L3. IN THE MARGIN: In order to understand the nature of time it is essential for us to consider change, that is, the contradictory predicates of the same thing in a different respect, which respect is nothing but the consideration of time.

Space and time are not things, but real relations. There is no absolute place or motion, since there are no principles for determining the subject of motion.

tiones prosequente omnia pulcherrime conspirent inte se, quam ego *Hypothesin concomitantiae* appello, ut neque perpetua quadam peculiari operatione Dei opus sit in progressu, quae consensum efficiat, neque influxus aliquis realis adhibeatur, qui certe explicari non potest.

Ex notione substantiae singularis, sequitur etiam substantiam generari **1622** aut corrumpi non posse, nec nisi creando aut annihilando oriri vel destrui; unde immortalitas animae tam necessaria est, ut nisi miraculo interverti non possit. Sequitur etiam aut nullas esse substantias corporeas et corpora esse tantum phaenomena vera sive inter se consentientia, ut iris, imo ut somnium perfecte cohaerens; aut in omnibus substantiis corporeis inesse aliquid analogum Animae, quod veteres formam aut speciem appellarunt. Nam cum una substantia vel Unum Ens non sit, quod sola aggregatione constat, ut acervus lapidum; nec vero Entia intelligi possint, ubi nullum est verum Ens, sequitur aut Atomos dari (quod hoc ipso argumento Cordemoius voluit) ut initium aliquod unius Entis habeamus, aut potius quia pro demonstrato habendum est, omne corpus in alias partes actu subdivisum esse (ut mox dicetur pluribus), realitatem corporeae substantiae in individua quadam natura, hoc est non in mole, sed agendi patiendique potentia consistere.

Et vero quod paradoxum videri possit, sciendum est Extensionis non esse tam liquidam notionem quam vulgo creditur. Nam ex eo quod nullum corpus tam exiguum est, qui[n] in partes diversis motibus incitatas actu sit divisum, sequitur nullam ulli corpori figuram determinatam assignari posse, neque exactam lineam rectam, aut circulum, aut aliam figuram assignabilem cuiusquam corporis reperiri in natura rerum, tametsi in ipsa seriei infinitiae deviatione regulae quaedam a natura serventur. Itaque figura involvit imaginarium aliquid, neque alio gladio secari possunt nodi quos nobis ex compositione continui male intellecta nectimus.

Idem dicendum est de Motu, nam uti Locus, ita et Motus in solo respectu consistunt, quod recte agnovit Cartesius, neque ulla datur ratio determinandi exacte quantum cuique subjecto absoluti motus sit assignan- **1623** dum. At vis motrix sive potentia agendi reale est quiddam, discernique in corporibus potest. Itaque essentia corporis non in extensione et ejus modificationibus, figura scilicet et motu (quae imaginarii aliquid involvunt non minus quam calor, et color, et aliae qualitates sensibiles), sed in sola vi

ning with so much ingenuity that, whilst each pursues its own laws and properties and operations, all harmonize with one another most beautifully? This I call the *hypothesis of concomitance*. According to it, there is no need for a kind of perpetual and special operation of God in the process which brings about the agreement, nor should one introduce some real influence which is quite inexplicable.

From[18] the notion of individual substance it also follows that substance **1622** cannot be generated or corrupted, and can only originate or be destroyed by creation or annihilation; hence the immortality of the soul is so necessary that it could only be thwarted by a miracle. It also follows either that there are no corporeal substances and bodies are only true or mutually consistent phenomena, such as a rainbow or a perfectly coherent dream; or that in all corporeal substances there is something analogous to the soul, which the ancients called form or species. For one substance or one being is not what is constituted by mere aggregation, such as a heap of stones, nor can beings even be understood where there is not truly one being; from this it follows that either there are atoms (which is what Cordemoy wanted to establish by this very argument), so that we may have some first principle of one being, or rather—since it is to be taken as demonstrated that every body is actually subdivided into further parts (as will presently be stated at greater length)—the reality of a corporeal substance consists in a certain individual nature; that is, not in bulk, but in a power of acting and being acted upon.

Indeed, even though this may seem paradoxical, it must be realized that the notion of extension is not as transparent as is commonly believed. For from the fact that no body is so very small that it is not actually divided into parts excited by different motions, it follows that no determinate shape can be assigned to any body, nor is a precisely straight line, or circle or any other assignable shape of any body, found in the nature of things, although certain rules are observed by nature even in its deviation from an infinite series. Thus shape involves something imaginary, and no other sword can sever the knots we tie for ourselves by misunderstanding the composition of the continuum.

The same thing should be said about motion, since, like place, motions too consist only in relation, as Descartes correctly recognized. Nor is there any way of determining precisely how much absolute motion should be assigned to each subject. But motive force, i.e. the power of acting, is **1623** something real, and can be discerned in bodies. Thus the essence of body must be located not in extension and its modifications, namely, shape and motion (which involve something imaginary no less than heat and color and other sensible qualities), but solely in the force of acting and resisting,

agendi resistendique collocanda est, quam non imaginatione, sed intellectu percipimus. Incorporea etsi actio illis tribuatur, resistentiam tamen non habent. Substantia autem omnis agendi patiendique vi continetur.

Porro nullas esse Atomos, sed omnem partem rursus habere partes actu a se divisas et diversis motibus incitatas, vel quod hinc sequitur, omne corpus utcunque exiguum habere partes actu infinitas; et in omni pulvisculo esse Mundum quendam innumerabilium creaturarum, cum multis aliis modis constat, tum ex eo etiam sequitur, quod omnis portio materiae totius universi motibus agitatur, et ab omnibus aliis materiae partibus utcunque distantibus proportione distantiae aliquid patitur, cumque omnis passio habeat effectum quendam, necesse est particulas massae hujus diversa ratione aliarum actionibus expositas diverse agitari, atque ideo subdividi massam.

Sed neque vacuum rationibus rerum consentaneum est, nam ut taceam spatium reale nullum esse, certe vacuum repugnat perfectioni rerum, cum ergo necessarium non sit (quid enim prohibet in vacuo loco aliquod rursus poni corpus, et in residuo rursus aliquid, et sic in infinitum), utique locum non habet. Praeterea commercia corporum interrumpit, atque illam mutuam omnium cum omnibus luctam.

Sed superest dubitatio de Animabus sive formis (animae analogis), quas in substantia corporea agnovimus. Nam ut de aliis substantiis corporeis non dicamus (ut quibus videtur aliquis esse gradus perceptionis et appetitus), si in brutis saltem reperiuntur animae, sequetur ex nostris principiis etiam bruta immortalia esse. Et quidem quemadmodum statuere quidam, omnem generationem animalis esse transformationem tantum animalis ejusdem jam viventis, et velut accretionem, ut sensibile redderetur, ita videtur pari ratione defendi posse, omnem mortem esse transformationem 1624 viventis in aliud minus animal, et velut diminutionem qua insensibile redditur. Et haec videtur fuisse expressa sententia autoris *libri de Diaeta,* qui Hippocrati ascribitur, nec abhorruere Albertus Magnus et Joh. Baco, qui neque productionem neque destructionem naturalem formarum admisere. Quodsi igitur viventia generationis pariter atque mortis expertia sunt, etiam animae si quas habent perpetuae atque immortales erunt, et (quod omnium est substantiarum) non nisi creatione aut annihilatione incipient aut finientur. Et pro transmigratione animarum (male opinor intellecta) tenenda erit transformatio animalium. Sed a caeterarum animarum sorte

which we perceive not by the imagination but by the intellect. Incorporeals, even if action is attributed to them, still do not have resistance. But every substance is comprised by a force of acting and being acted upon.

Moreover, there are no atoms, but every part again has parts actually divided from each other and excited by different motions, or what follows from this, every body however small has actually infinite parts, and in every grain of powder there is a world of innumerable creatures. And while this is established in many different ways, it also follows from the fact that every portion of matter is agitated by the motions of the whole universe, and is acted upon by all the other parts of matter, however distant, in proportion to their distance. And since every case of being acted upon has some effect, it is necessary for the particles of this mass that are differently exposed to the actions of other particles to be set in motion in different directions, and thus for the mass to be subdivided.

Nor is a vacuum in accordance with the reasons for things, for, not to mention the fact that space is nothing real, a vacuum certainly conflicts with the perfection of things. Since, then, a vacuum is unnecessary (for what prevents some body from being put back again into the empty place, and another again in the remaining space, and so on to infinity?), it has no place, in any case. Besides, it interrupts the interactions among bodies, and the mutual struggle of all against all.

But there remains a doubt about the souls or forms (analogous to the soul) that we have acknowledged in corporeal substance. For, not to speak of other corporeal substances (such as those in which there seems to be some degree of perception and appetite), if souls are found in the lower animals at least, it will follow from our principles that the lower animals too are immortal. Indeed, just as some people have proposed that every generation of an animal is a mere transformation of the same animal now living, and a kind of accretion that renders it sensible,[19] so by parity of reason it seems defensible to hold that every death is a transformation of the living **1624** animal into another smaller animal, and is a kind of diminution by which it is rendered insensible. And this seems to have been the express opinion of the author of the book *De diaeta,* ascribed to Hippocrates, nor was it repugnant to Albert the Great and John Bacon, who accepted neither the natural production nor destruction of forms.[20] But if, therefore, living things are free from generation and death alike, so also their souls, if they have them, will be perpetual and immortal, and will (as is the case for all substances) only begin or end by creation or annihilation. And instead of the transmigration of souls (a misunderstanding, in my opinion) it will be necessary to maintain the transformation of animals. But minds must be excepted from the fate of other souls, for not only are they created by God,

excipiendae sunt Mentes, quas et creari a Deo, et solutas corpore peculiares habere operationes sapientae divinae consentaneum est, ne per innu-
merabiles materiae vicissitudines frustra jactentur. Est enim Deus ut causa
rerum, ita Rex Mentium, et cum ipse mens sit, peculiarem cum illis soci-
etatem colit. Quin imo cum Mens unaquaeque sit divinae imaginis expressio (nam dici potest caeteras substantias magis universum exprimere,
Mentes magis Deum) manifestum est Mentes esse potissimam partem
Universi, omniaque condita esse ipsarum causa, hoc est in eligendo ordine
rerum maximam ipsarum habitam esse rationem, ita institutis omnibus ut
tanto apparitura sint pulchriora, quanto magis intelligentur. Itaque pro
certo habendum est summam a Deo justitiae habitam esse rationem, et
quemadmodum perfectionem rerum, ita mentium felicitatem quaesitam
esse. Quare mirari non debemus Mentes a brutorum animabus et in origine
animalis quod hominem appellamus, et in extinctione distingui, et licet
omnes sint immortales, illis tamen solis reminiscentiam datam esse, in
quibus conscientia est, et praemiorum poenarumque intellectus.

Equidem in brutis esse animas, inclinor ut credam, vel ideo quia pertinet ad perfectionem rerum, ut cum omnia adsint quae conveniunt animae, etiam anima adesse intelligatur. Nam animae vel certe formae sese
non impediunt, itaque multo adhuc minus videtur dari *vacuum formarum*
1625 (etiam veteribus rejectum) quam corporum. Ne quis autem pari jure concludi posse putet, etiam mentes brutis inesse debere, sciendum est, neque
ordinem rerum passarum fuisse, ut omnes animae vicissitudinibus materiae eximerentur, neque justitiam, ut aliquae mentes jactationi relinquere-
ntur; itaque satis fuit brutis animas dari, praesertim cum nec corpora brutorum ad ratiocinandum sint facta sed variis functionibus destinata, ut
bombyx ad texendum, apis ad mellificandum, alia aliis quibus universum
distingueretur.

Porro ne quis queratur non satis claram esse animae notionem, quatenus
a mente distinguitur, et formae multo minus; sciendum est haec pendere a
Notione Substantiae supra explicata, substantiae enim singularis natura
est ut habeat notionem completam, cui omnia ejusdem subjecti praedicata
involvantur; licet enim de notione circuli non sit, ut ligneus vel ferreus sit,
est tamen de notione huius circuli praesentis non tantum ut sit ferreus, sed

but it is also in accordance with divine wisdom that when released from the body they have their own particular operations, so that they are not pointlessly agitated by the countless alternations of matter. For as God is the King of Minds as well as the cause of things, and since he himself is a mind, he cultivates a special fellowship with them. In fact, since every single mind is an expression of the divine image (for it can be said that whereas other substances express the universe more, minds express God more), it is manifest that minds are the most important part of the universe, and everything has been established for their sake. In other words, in choosing the order of things, the greatest account was taken of minds, and all things were so constructed that they would appear the more beautiful the better they are understood. So it is to be held for certain that God took the greatest account of justice, and that just as he sought the perfection of things, so he sought the happiness of minds. Therefore we should not be surprised that minds are distinguished from the souls of lower animals both in the origin of the animal we call man, and in his extinction; and that although all souls are immortal, the only ones that are endowed with memory are those in which there is consciousness and an understanding of rewards and punishments.

For my part, I am inclined to believe that there are souls in the lower animals, on the grounds that it is conducive to the perfection of things that whenever all those things that are in keeping with a soul are present, a soul should also be understood to be present. For souls, or at any rate forms, do not impede one another, and so it seems that a *vacuum in forms* (rejected even by the ancients) is even less viable than one of bodies. But lest someone think it could be concluded with equal right that there ought to be minds in the lower animals too, it must be realized that the order of things would not have let all souls be released from the alternations of matter, nor would justice have let some minds be abandoned to being tossed around. So it was enough for the lower animals to be given souls, especially since their bodies were not made for reasoning, but destined for various functions, as a silkworm is for weaving, a bee for making honey, and others for the other functions by which the universe is distinguished.

Moreover, lest someone should complain that the notion of the soul, to the exent that it is distinguished from the mind, is not sufficiently clear, and the notion of form much less so,[21] it must be realized that this notion depends on the notion of substance explained above. For it is the nature of a singular substance to have a complete notion, in which all the predicates of the same subject are involved; thus although it does not belong to the notion of a circle that it should be, for example, wooden or iron, it does belong to the notion of this existing circle, however, not only that it is iron,

1625

etiam quicquid ipsi est eventurum. Cum vero omnia cum aliis mediate aut
immediate commercium habeant, consequens est omnis substantiae hanc
esse naturam, ut vi sua agendi aut patiendi, hoc est serie suarum operationum immanentium exprimat totum universum. Estque Ens vere unum,
alioqui non erit substantia, sed substantiae plures. Atque hoc principium
actionum, seu vis agendi primitiva, ex qua series statuum variorum consequitur, est substantiae forma. Patet etiam quid perceptio sit, quae omnibus
formis competit, nempe expressio multorum in uno, quae longe differt ab
expressione in speculo, vel in organo corporeo, quod vere unum non est.
Quodsi perceptio sit distinctior, sensum facit. Sed in Mente praeter ex-
pressionem objectorum conscientia sive reflexio reperitur, in qua consistit
expressio sive imago quaedam ipsius Dei, eaque res facit, ut solae Mentes
sint felicitatis miseriaeque capaces. Verum licet formas aut animas statua-
mus, sine quibus generalia naturae recte intelligi non possunt, in ipsis
tamen Phaenomenis corporum specialium explicandis, non magis utemur
anima, aut forma, quam in functionibus humani corporis tradendis hu-
**1626**   mana mente. Vel ideo quod ostendimus, talem esse harmoniam rerum, ut
omnia quae fiunt in anima ex solis legibus perceptionis explicari possint,
quemadmodum omnia quae fiunt in corpore ex solis Legibus motus; et
tamen omnia ita inter se consentiant, ac si anima corpus aut corpus animam moveri posset.

Sed jam tempus est, ut paulatim ad tradendas Naturae Corporeae Leges
progrediamur. Et primum omne corpus magnitudinem et figuram utcunque habet. Ut unum corpus non est in pluibus locis, ita nec plura in uno.
Eadem massa majus aut minus quam antea volumen non occupat, neque
aliud est rarefactio et condensatio quam immissio, aut expressio fluidioris.
Omne corpus mobile est, et recipit quemcunque velocitatis aut tarditatis
gradum, sed et quamcunque directionem. Omnes motus componi possunt
inter se, lineaque erit, quam designabit Geometria, unde corpus quod fertur in linea curva directionem habet pergendi in recta tangente, nisi im-
pediqatur, quemadmodum facile demonstrari potest, quod primus obser-
vavit Keplerus. Praeterea omnis locus corpore plenus est, et omne corpus

but also whatever will happen to it. But since all things interact with others, either mediately or immediately, it is consequently the nature of every substance to express the whole universe by its force of acting or being acted upon, that is, by the series of its immanent operations. And it is truly one being, otherwise it would not be a substance, but several substances. And this principle of actions, or primitive force of acting, from which a series of various states results, is the form of the substance. It is also clear what perception should be if it is to be applicable to all forms, namely, the expression of many in one. This is very different from an expression in a mirror or in a bodily organ, which is not truly one. If the perception is fairly distinct, it constitutes a sensation. In the mind, however, apart from the expression of objects, we also find consciousness or reflexion, in which there is a kind of expression or image of God himself, and this is what brings it about that only minds are capable of happiness and misery. Yet even though we are proposing forms or souls, without which natures in general could not be correctly understood, nevertheless, in explaining the phenomena of specific bodies we do not use souls or forms, any more than we would use the human mind in treating the functions of the human body.

1626  The reason for this, as we have shown, is that the harmony of things is such that everything that happens in the soul can be explained by means of the laws of perception alone, just as everything that happens in a body can be explained by means of the laws of motion alone; and yet all things are in such mutual accord that it is as if the soul could move the body or the body the soul.

### [Laws of Corporeal Nature]

But it is now time for us to proceed gradually to a statement of the Laws of Corporeal Nature. First, every body has some magnitude and shape or other. As one body is not in several places, so neither are several bodies in one place. The same mass does not occupy a greater or smaller volume than before, and rarefaction and condensation are only the absorption and expulsion of a more fluid body. Every body is movable and receives some degree of speed or slowness, but also a tendency in some direction. All motions can be compounded with each other, and their line of motion will be designated by geometry. Hence a body that moves in a curved line has a tendency for continuing its motion in the direction of a straight line tangent to the curve unless it is impeded, as can easily be demonstrated—something that Kepler was the first to observe. Furthermore every place is filled by body, and every body is divisible and transfigurable, since no rea-

dividuum est et transfigurabile cum nulla ratio Atomorum assignari possit. Atque haec quidem dudum constituta habentur.

His adjicio, in omni corpore vim aliquam sive motum esse. Nullum corpus tam exiguum esse, quin rursus in partes diversis motibus incitatas sit actu divisum; et proinde in omni corpore actu inesse corpora numero infinita. Omnem mutationem corporis cujuscunque effectum suum ad corpora utcunque, distantia propagare, sive omnia corpora in omnia agere, et ab omnibus pati. Omne corpus ab ambientibus coerceri ne partes ejus avolent, ac proinde corpora omnia inter se invicem colluctari, et unumquodque corpus resistere toti corporum universitati.

1627      Omne corpus habet aliquem firmitatis et fluiditatis gradum, fluiditatis quidem seu divisibilitatis per se, firmitatis vero ex corporum motu.

Non potest firmitas explicari nisi ex consideratione systematis. Nam omne corpus est divisibile, seu per se alteri non cohaeret, et omne corpus conatum impressum recipit praeter suum, itaque non video, cur non pars una peculiarem impressionem recipiens ab alia recedat. Nisi forte consideremus omnem motum directum esse simul obliquum,[L4] et ita vicina turbare, ut si ipsius corporis *ABC* duae partes sint *AB, BC,* tendat autem corpus a *B* in *F,* et globulus aliquis *H* longe celeriori motu *HG* insequens propellat partem *AB,* quaeritur an et propellat *BC,* ajo in quantum ictus *HG* compositus est ex ictu *HL* et *LG,* seu *DE* ex *DM* et *ME,* impelli etiam *BC,* et cum variae aliae innumerabilibus modis intelligi possint compositiones, multis modis impelli totum, parte impuls[a], etsi motus in se consideratus ut simplex nil videatur cum *AC* commune habere. *Experiendum*[L5] quid fiat in juxta se positis Elatere carentibus, politissima superficie se contingentibus, ut *AB* et *BC.* Videndum an et quantum solo *AB* impulso in *HG* impellatur et *BC.*

An potius dicemus corpora cohaesionem habere per se, fluiditatem per accidens, cohaesionem ex eo quod omnes substantiae universi conspirant

L4. IN THE MARGIN: non puto, quia revera corpus non fertur in latus
L5. IN THE MARGIN: NB

son can be assigned for atoms. And these things, at least, are held to have been long established.

To these considerations I add the following: In every body there is some force or motion. No body is so very small that it is not in turn actually divided into parts excited by different motions; and therefore in every body there are actually infinitely many bodies. Every change of any body propagates its effect to bodies however distant; that is to say, all bodies act on and are acted upon by all others. Every body is confined by those surrounding it so that its parts do not fly away, and therefore all bodies are engaged in a mutual struggle among themselves, and every single body resists the whole universe of bodies.

**1627**    Every body has some degree of firmness and fluidity, that of fluidity or divisibility it has through itself, that of solidity from the motion of bodies.[22]

## [Note on firmness and fluidity][23]

Firmness cannot be explained except by consideration of a system. For every body is divisible, that is, does not in itself cohere with another, and every body receives an impressed endeavour in addition to its own; and so I do not see why one part, on receiving an impression of its own, would not recede from another. Unless perhaps we were to consider every direct motion to be at the same time oblique,[L4] and thus to disturb neighboring bodies. Suppose, for example, a body *ABC* has two parts *AB, BC,* but the body tends from *B* towards *F;* and some ball *H* following it with a much faster motion *HG* knocks the part *AB* forwards, and it is asked whether it also knocks *BC* forwards. I say that inasmuch as the blow *HG* is composed of the blows *HL* and *LG,* or *DE* of the blows *DM* and *ME, BC* is also impelled; and since various other compositions can be conceived in countless ways, the whole is impelled in many ways when the part is impelled,[24] even though the motion, considered in itself as a simple one, seems to have nothing in common with *AC. One must find out by experiment*[L5] what happens when things lacking elasticity are placed next to each other, making contact along a highly polished surface, such as *AB* and *BC.* It must be seen whether, and how much, *BC* is also impelled when *AB* alone is impelled along *HG.*

Or should we rather say that bodies have cohesion through themselves, and fluidity accidentally: cohesion from the fact that all the substances in the universe are in harmony with one another, and fluidity insofar as they

L4. IN THE MARGIN: I do not think so, since in reality a body is not carried laterally.

L5. IN THE MARGIN: N.B.

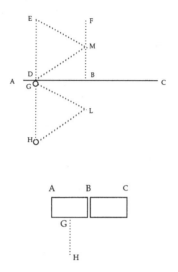

inter se, fluiditatem, quatenus diversis motibus sunt concitatae.$^{L6}$ Cohaerent autem non quae simul quiescunt, sed quae in motu parum a se invicem digrediuntur, magna enim vi opus est, ut digrediantur a se invicem motu **1628** majore, itaque fluida debent varios ipsa motus habere, quia facile sejunguntur. Hoc tamen non opus in arena, sunt enim jam disjuncta corpora, quanquam omnia tenui aliquo gradu cohaereant. Exempli gratia arenula quaevis est systemation aliquod per se, ita et duo globuli aenei separatis itaque jam constant motibus, neque ideo nisi tenuissime cohaerent, nisi forte in contactu elastrum unius propellat alterum. Nihil nocebit tamen si intus ponatur, ut hoc modo: Circulum *ab* intus tangat globulus *c*. Percutiatur *ab* in *d* non secum auferet *c*, quia recedit ab eo versus *b*; videtur hoc obstare cohaesioni corporum naturali, quod facilius flectuntur quam moven-

L6. IN THE MARGIN: Ex *motu* quatenus conspirat oriri *cohaesionem*, duobus habemus experimentis gypsi fusi, quod bullas agit, et limaturae chalybis cui admovetur magnes quae abit in fila. Ut nil dicam de vitrificatione, at cur firmitas major post refrigerationem cessante motu, an quod facieculae consentientis redditae?

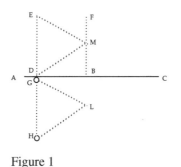

Figure 1

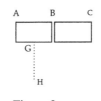

Figure 2

are agitated with different motions?[L6] Yet cohering things are not those that
are at rest together, but those that hardly separate from one another in their
motion, since, in order for them to separate from one another with an ap-
**1628**    preciable motion, a great force is needed. Thus fluids must themselves
have various motions, since they are easily separated. There is no need for
this in the case of sand, however, for there the bodies are already discon-
nected, although all of them cohere to some slight degree. For example,
any grain of sand is a kind of small system in itself. So too, two brass balls
are already established by separate motions, and therefore cohere only
very slightly, except perhaps that the elasticity of one propels the other
when they are in contact. Nor will it matter even if one is put inside the other,
as for example in the following way: Let the globule *c* touch the circle *ab* on
the inside. If *ab* is struck at *d,* it will not take *c* with it, since the latter will recede from it towards *b*.[25] It seems to be an objection to the natural cohesion
of bodies that they are more easily bent than moved; but on the other hand

L6. IN THE MARGIN: That *cohesion* arises *from motion* insofar as it is harmonious, we have from two experiments: that of plaster when poured, which forms
bubbles; and that of iron filings, which, when a magnet is moved towards them,
turn into threads—to say nothing of vitrification. But why is the firmness greater
after refrigeration, when motion has ceased? is this because the facets [of the component parts] have been brought into agreement?

tur, sed videtur tamen utrumque semper fieri simul, utrumque enim vi indiget. Quicquid sit videtur inter prima Dei decreta circa corporum naturam referendum, ut omne corpus alteri cohaereat, nisi quatenus *ab* eo per peculiares motus separatur.

Instituamus et tale experimentum corpora *a* et *b* superficiebus *cd* se perfecte contingant, eam in rem perfecte erunt polita, et flatibus follium, *eb*, et *fa*, versus se invicem premantur, interim quiescente *b*, moveatur *a*, videndum an *b* secum impellat. Considerandum et [experiendum], ubi videtur apparere corpora solida quibus nullum intercedit fluidum, difficulter a se separari. Verum video tantum id contingere cum magnus contactus, quando fluidum se facile insinuare nequit. Si velimus derivare cohaesionem a pressione ambientis ut in tabulis, haeremus in eo, quod tabularum prius firmitas stabilienda est.

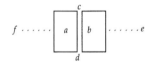

Cohaesio est in corpore per se, quatenus omnia unum sunt continuum, fluiditas est a motu in existente, quatenus enim partes jam diversis motibus incitantur, sunt separabiles. Universum considerari debet ut fluidum continuum sed partibus [diversae] tenacitatis constans, ut ex aqua, oleo, pice liquida et similibus varie invicem diversis compositum. Nec quicquam tam fluidum est quin cohaesionem habeat partium, nec tam firmum respectu nostri, quin revera habeat gradum fluiditatis.

Etsi nulla sit summae fluiditatis, nec summae firmitatis in universo, fingi tamen potest ad res declarandas omnia constare ex globulis quantumvis

it seems that both [sc. being bent and being moved] occur at the same time, for both need force. Whatever the case, it seems that it should be reckoned among the primary decrees of God concerning the nature of bodies that every body coheres with another except insofar as it is separated from it by its own motions.

Figure 3          Figure 4

Let us also set up an experiment of this kind. Let the bodies *a* and *b* make a perfect contact along their surfaces *cd;* to this end, they will be perfectly polished. Let them be pressed together by winds from bellows *eb* and *fa*. Meanwhile, with *b* at rest, let *a* be moved: it must be seen whether *b* is pushed along with it. What must be considered, and put to experimental test,[26] is the case where it seems that solid bodies with no fluid between them appear difficult to separate from one another. In fact, I observe that this happens only when the contact is great, and the fluid cannot easily insinuate itself. If we wish to derive cohesion from the pressure of the surroundings, as in the case of tablets, we are stuck, in that the firmness of the tablets needs to be established first.

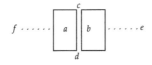

Figure 5

Cohesion is in body through itself insofar as everything is one continuum, fluidity comes from motion within it; for insofar as its parts are excited by already differing motions, they are separable. The universe ought to be considered as a continuous fluid, but one containing parts of [differing][27] tenacity, like a composite of water, oil, pitchwater, and similar things differing from each other in various ways. There is nothing so fluid that it does not have a cohesion of parts, nor so firm with respect to us that it does not really have some degree of fluidity.

Even if there is nothing in the universe of the utmost fluidity, nor of the utmost firmness, one may still imagine for purposes of clarification that every-

parvis infinitae firmitatis, et ex fluido intercurrente moto, infinitae fluiditatis uti in Geometria fingimus lineas infinitas et infinite parvas.

Difficultas: quod omnia corpora libertatem nacta evolvare conantur seu recedere per tangentes, non ergo retinetur nisi a resistentia ambientis. **1629** Quomodo ergo cohaesio ab ipsorum motu intestino? An dicemus non omnino avolatura si nihil retineret, sed tantum se longius diffusura, et extensura (*außthenen*).

An nunquam separatur corpus a corpore, quin maneat connexio, *une traisnée de fumée,* tanto subtilior et inefficacior, quanto major distantia et diutior, aut quanto corpus minus agitatis habet partes. Omnium vestigia odoresque quasi ubi transeunt aliqui relinquuntur.

Ad explicandum corpora pressione cohaerere, prius firmitas in partibus statuenda. Ponatur enim motus vorticum in *ab* et in *lm* quos volumus non permittere transitum ex uno in aliud. Fingamus aliquid transire, licet plane incohaerens tamen, quia prius conspirant omnium motus ad instar unius solidi, vel saltem accedentis ei vorticis ubi aliquid ingreditur, necesse est ea quae consentienter movebantur magis quam antea perturbari. Sed dici potest, quid tum? Omnia sunt ad omnes motus indifferentia. Si ergo cohaesionem non habent, nil refert. Ergo naturae pugna contra perturbationem pendet a cohaesione naturali. Si fluidum perfecte habeat motas partes ad instar solidi, habaebit aliquam tenacitatem, ita ut aliud ingredi non falicle patiatur magnas mutationes, nisi paulatim.

Eadem potentia servatur in natura rerum, seu causa et effectus sunt aequivalentes. Potentiam voco, quae agendo consumitur seu effectum producendo.

thing consists of globules of any desired smallness and infinite firmness, and of a fluid running between them of infinite fluidity, just as in geometry we imagine lines that are infinite and infinitely small.

A difficulty: that all bodies that have become free endeavour to fly away, that is, to recede along their tangents, and are therefore held back only by **1629** the resistance of their surroundings. How, then, can cohesion arise from their internal motion?[28] Should we say that they would not fly away entirely if nothing held them back, but would only become much more diffused and further extended (distended)?

Is one body never separated from another without a connection remaining, a "trail of smoke," which is subtler and more inefficacious the greater the distance and time of separation, or the less the body's parts are agitated?—just as all things leave behind some traces and odors, as they pass by.

In order to explain bodies' cohering by pressure, one must first establish firmness in the parts. For suppose vortical motions in *ab* and in *lm,* which we wish to forbid passing from one to the other. Suppose we imagine some [motion] to pass across, even if this is clearly incoherent; since earlier the motions of all [the parts] harmonize into the likes of one solid, or at least into the likes of a vortex resembling one, then when some [motion] enters in, those [parts] would have to move more harmoniously than before they were disturbed. But, it may be said, what then? All things are indifferent to all motions. So if they have no cohesion, it doesn't matter. Therefore nature's resistance to perturbation depends on a natural cohesion. If a perfect fluid has parts that move like a solid, it will have some tenacity, such that it will not readily endure something else entering it that would change all its motions. This is for the general reason that nature does not readily endure great changes, unless they occur gradually.

Figure 6

Figure 7

[Continuation of the Laws of Corporeal Nature]

The same power is conserved in the nature of things, that is, cause and effect are equivalent. I call "power" that which is consumed in acting, that is, in producing an effect.

Eadem quantitas progressus seu directionis servatur in natura rerum, sed non eadem quantitas motus, sed interdum eadem summa, interdum eadem differentia.

Eadem manet semper quantitas ex aggregatis motuum successivis. Aggregatum motuum est summa omnium motuum quae in corpore fuere inde a quiete, detractis illis quae in aliud corpus sunt translata.

Natura generalis semper scopum suum assequitur.

Omnis motus cuivis alteri componi potest.

Et quivis motus ex quibusvis aliis compositus intelligi potest.

Natura aequabiliter tendit ad easdem partes seu regiones universi et tota natura aequaliter progreditur ad easdem parallelas. Hinc tota natura aequaliter progreditur et ad parallelas contrarias, et tota natura aequaliter progreditur in recta quacunque et parallelis, seu in quamcumvis regionem. Imo amplius conatus totius naturae versus quodlibet punctum in mundo assumtum semper idem est. Et semper aequalis est conatus ad centrum et a centro.

**1630**

Cohaesionis principium est motus conspirans, fluiditatis varius. Etiam in perturbationibus specialibus est conspiratio generalis in certas systematis universi Leges. In omni systemate est conspiratio quaedam motibus variis partium salvis. Omnis perturbatio perpetua est ut oscillationes, sed nunc dividitur in plura, nunc ex pluribus in unum recolligitur, et in hoc consistit vicissitudo rerum. Principium cohaesionis facit, ut natura perturbationibus repugnet. Necesse est enim in perturbatione, ut quae ante simul mota erant, postea superveniente perturbante multipliciter a se divortium faciant.

Omnes restitutiones ejusdem perturbationis sunt aequidiuturnae.

Omnis massa universi aliquam habet cohaesionem.

Totum universum est unum fluidum continuum, cuius partes diversos habent tenacitatis gradus, ut si quis liquor ex aqua, oleo, pice liquida, et similibus varie agitatis constaret.

The same quantity of progress or direction is conserved in the nature of things,[29] but not the same quantity of motion, but sometimes the same sum, sometimes the same difference.

Figure 8

The quantity of successive aggregates of motions always remains the same. An aggregate of motions is the sum of all the motions that have been in a body from the time it was at rest, subtracting those which have been transferred into another body.

Nature in general always pursues its own end.

Every motion can be composed with any other. And any motion can be understood to be composed of any others.

Nature tends equably towards the same parts or regions of the universe, and the whole of nature progresses equally towards the same parallels. Hence the whole of nature also progresses equally towards contrary parallels, and the whole of nature progresses equally along any straight line and its parallels, i.e. into any region. Furthermore, the endeavour of the whole of nature towards any point whatever that we assume in the world is always the same, and the endeavour towards the center is always equal to the endeavour away from the center.

**1630**

The principle of cohesion is harmonizing motion, and that of fluidity is varying motion. Even in specific disturbances there is a general harmony in certain laws of the system of the universe. In every system there is a sort of harmony, which does not violate the various motions of the parts. Every disturbance is perpetual, like oscillations[30]: now it is divided into several parts, and now it is gathered back out of its several parts into a unity again, and it is in this that the alternation of things consists. The principle of cohesion brings it about that nature opposes disturbances. For in a disturbance it is necessary that those things that previously moved together must, after coming upon the disturbing factor, split apart from each other in many directions.

All restitutions of the same disturbance last an equal length of time. Every mass in the universe has some cohesion.

The whole universe is one continuous fluid, whose parts have differing degrees of tenacity, as if someone were to make up a liquid out of water, oil, liquid pitch, and similar things variously stirred up together.

Omne corpus dum movetur circa se vorticem excitat subtilium partium ambientis, ut locus ante ipsum evacuetur, post ipsum repleatur. Sed antea jam habet proprium systema.

Nullus datur transitus per saltum ad quietem, nec quicquam a motu transit as quietem vel contrarium motum, nisi per omnes intermedios gradus. Et quemadmodum nec motus a loco in locum, ita nec mutatio a gradu in gradum, fit in instanti.

Rigorose loquendo nulla transfertur vis a corpore in corpus, sed omne corpus insita vi movetur.

Motus et quies sunt aliquid respectivum et absolute assignari in natura non possunt, sed vires, sive causae mutationum.

In omni ictu corporum aequalis utrinque actio et passio est.

Omnis effectus propagatur in indefinitum, tempore pariter et loco; sed imminutus.

Cohaesio corporum nostrorum quae systemata non sunt sed structurae, explicari potest pressione ambientis ad instar Tabularum politarum. Sed ipsius structurae firmitas, sumenda est a systematio[n]um collocatione conspirante, qualis est in magnetibus, et in fixis. Systemata ipsa a motu conspirante.

## Motum non esse absolutum quiddam                          Aiv317

**1638** Motum non esse absolutum quiddam, sed relativum Aristoteles et Cartesius consentiunt, ille dum locum definivit a superficie ambientis, hic dum motum a mutatione vicinitatis. Spatium absolutum non magis res est quam tempus, etsi imaginationi blandiatur; imo demonstrari potest talia non esse res, sed tantum relationes mentis omnia ad hypotheses intelligibiles, hoc est motus uniformes et loca immota revocare conantis; atque inde deductas aestimationes.

Porro nec influxus substantiae in substantiam ullus est in Metaphysico rigore, (praeterquam quod in dependentia creaturarum, quae continua productio est) nec revera a corpore in corpus ullus transfertur impetus sed ut phaenomena quoque confirmant, omne corpus vi proprii Elastri ab alio recedit quod est a motu partium ipsi inexistentium. Et vero unaquaeque substantia est vis quaedam agendi, seu conatus mutandi sese respectu caeterorum omnium secundum certas suae naturae leges. Unde quaelibet substantia totum exprimit universum, secundum aspectum suum. Et in

Every body while in motion stirs up a vortex around itself of subtle parts of the surrounding matter, in such a way that the place in front of it is emptied and that behind it is filled up. But prior to this it already has its own system.

There is no transition to rest by a leap, and nothing passes from motion to rest or to a contrary motion without passing through all the intermediate degrees of motion. And just as no motion from place to place occurs in an instant, so no change from degree to degree occurs in an instant.

Rigorously speaking, no force is transferred from one body to another, but every body moves by an innate force.

Motion[31] and rest are something relative, and cannot be absolutely assigned in nature; but forces, that is, the causes of the changes, can.

In every collision of bodies, the action and passion is equal on both sides.

Every effect is propagated indefinitely in time as well as in place, but is diminished.

The cohesion of our bodies, which are not systems but structures, can be explained by pressure of the surrounding matter, on the model of polished tablets. But the firmness of this structure is to be derived from a harmonious collocation of little systems, as in magnets and the fixed stars. Systems themselves are to be derived from harmonious motion.

## 38. Motion Is Not Something Absolute[1]                          Aiv317

[c. 1686?][2]

**1638**   That motion is not something absolute, but relative, both Aristotle and Descartes agree, the former in defining place by the surface of the surrounding [matter], the latter in defining motion as change of vicinity.[3] Absolute space is no more a thing than time is, even though it is pleasing to the imagination; indeed, it can be demonstrated that such entities are not things, but are merely relations of a mind trying to refer everything to intelligible hypotheses—that is, to uniform motions and immobile places—and to values deduced on this basis.

Furthermore, in metaphysical rigor there is no influence of one substance on another[4] (apart from that in the dependence of creatures, which is continuous production). Nor is any impetus really transferred from one body into another, but as the phenomena also confirm, every body recoils from another by its own elastic force, which is by a motion of the parts existing in it. And indeed each substance is a kind of force of acting, or an endeavour to change itself with respect to all the others according to certain laws of its own nature. Whence any substance whatever expresses the

phaenomenis motuum res egregie apparet, unumquodque enim corpus ibi supponi debet habere motum communem cum altero quovis, quasi in eadem navi et proprium moli reciprocum; quale quid fingi non posset, si motus essent absoluti, nec corpus unumquodque omnia alia exprimeret.

## De tempore locoque, duratione ac spatio                    Aiv321

**1641** Tempus et Locus, seu duratio et spatium sunt Relationes reales, seu existendi ordines. Earum fundamentum in re est Divina magnitudo, aeternitas scilicet et immensitas. Nam si spatio seu magnitudini addatur appetitus vel quod eodem redit conatus, adeoque et Actio, jam aliquid substantiale introducitur, quod non in alio est quam in Deo, seu Uno primario. Spatium scilicet reale per se aliquid Unum est indivisibile, immutabile; nec tantum continet existentias sed et possibilitates, cum per se demto appetitu sit indifferens ad diversos secandi modos. Appetitus vero spatio accedit, facit substantias existentes atque adeo materiam seu aggregatum infinitarum Unitatum.

whole universe, according to its own point of view. And in the phenomena of motions this fact is especially apparent, for there every single body must be supposed to have a motion in common with any other, as if they were in the same ship, as well as its own motion, reciprocal to its bulk; how this could be so could not be imagined if motions were absolute and each body did not express all others.

### 39. On Time and Place, Duration and Space[1]                Aiv321

[c. 1686?][2]

1641   Time and place, or, duration and space, are real relations, i.e. orders of existing. Their foundation in reality is divine magnitude, to wit, eternity and immensity.[3] For if to space or magnitude is added appetite, or, what comes to the same thing, endeavour, and consequently action too, already something substantial is introduced, which is in nothing else than in God, or the primary unity. That is to say, real space in itself is something that is one, indivisible, immutable; and it contains not only existences but also possibilities, since in itself, with appetite removed, it is indifferent to different ways of being dissected. But if appetite is added to space, it makes existing substances, and thus matter, i.e. the aggregate of infinite unities.

## Appendix 1
## Excerpts from Leibniz's Early Writings
## on the Continuum (1669–71)

### (a) from a Letter to Thomasius,
### 30 April 1669[1]                                          A VI.ii N54

. . . Even if both the Scholastics' and the Moderns' explanations were possible, the clearer and more intelligible of two possible hypotheses must always be chosen, and without any doubt this is the hypothesis of the moderns, which, rather than supposing incorporeal entities within bodies,
assumes nothing apart from magnitude, shape, and motion. For I cannot
better show the possibility of a reconciliation [between Aristotle and the
Moderns] than by asking for any principle of Aristotle to be given me that
cannot be explained by means of magnitude, shape, and motion.

Primary matter is mass itself, in which there is nothing but *extension*
and antitypy, i.e. impenetrability. It has extension from space it fills. The
very nature of matter consists in the fact that it is something gross and im-
penetrable, and consequently *movable* if something else strikes it (as long
as it must give way to the other). Now this continuous mass which fills the
world is, as long as all its parts are at rest, primary matter; everything is
produced out of it through motion, and everything is dissolved back into it
through rest. For regarded in itself there is no diversity in it, but only homogeneity, except as a result of motion. Hence all the knots of the Scholastics are now untied. First they ask about its entitative actuality prior to all
form. And it must be replied that it is an entity prior to all forms, since it
has its own existence. For everything which is in some space exists, and
this cannot be denied of this mass, even though it lacks all motion and *discontinuity.* But the essence of matter, or the very form of *corporeality,* consists in antitypy or impenetrability. Matter has *quantity* too, but this is *interminate,* as the Averroists call it, or indefinite. For so long as matter is
continuous, it is not cut into parts, and therefore does not actually have
boundaries in it (I am not speaking of the inside boundaries of the world or
whole mass, but those of its parts), although it does have extension or
quantity in it.

From matter let us proceed to form on an orderly basis. Here if we suppose *form* to be nothing other than shape, again everything is in wonderful
accord. For since shape is the boundary of a body, boundary will be needed
for introducing shapes into matter. Therefore in order for various boundaries to arise in matter, there is a need for a discontinuity of its parts. For by
the very fact that the parts are discontinuous, each of them will have separate boundaries (for Aristotle defines continuous things as ων τα εσχατα

εν, those whose extremities are one). But *discontinuity* can be introduced in this formerly continuous mass in either of two ways: first, in such a way that contiguity is at the same time destroyed, which happens when they are forced apart in such a way as to leave a *vacuum;* or second, in such a way that contiguity remains intact, which happens when they remain immediately next to each other but move in different directions. For example, two spheres, one contained within the other, can be moved in different directions, yet they remain contiguous, even though they cease to be continuous. From this it is clear that if in fact mass were created discontinuous or interrupted by vacuities from the beginning, then some forms of matter would immediately have been created with them. But if it is continuous from the beginning, then forms would have to arise through motion (for I am not talking about obtaining vacuities in matter by annihilating certain of its parts, since that is supernatural). For from motion comes division, from division the boundaries of parts, from the boundaries of parts their shapes, and from shapes forms; therefore forms are the result of motion. From this it is clear that every arrangement into form is motion; and we have a clear solution to the vexatious controversy over the origin of forms . . . .

## (b) from *A New Physical Hypothesis*

*THE THEORY OF CONCRETE MOTION*[2]                                         **A VI.ii N40**

[Winter 1670–71][3]

43. For it should be recognized, as those celebrated *Micrographers, Kircher* and *Hooke* have observed,[4] that most of the qualities that we are sensible of in larger things, a sharp-eyed observer will detect in proportion in smaller things. And if this proceeds to infinity—which is certainly possible, since the continuum is divisible to infinity—any atom will be of infinite species, like a sort of world, and there will be *worlds within worlds to infinity.* And those who consider this more profoundly will be unable to stop themselves being carried away by a certain ecstasy of admiration, which should be transferred to the Author of things.

44. Hence now there appears to be a reconciliation between *Anaxagoras's* infinitely many homeomeries [ομοιμερειας] and our opinion about the small number of elements of things. For even if it were true that *putrefaction* is an insensible infestation with worms, and *mold* an insensible sprouting, that *air* is insensible water, and *cold* is frozen air, that *fire* is a subtle sulfur, and *water* a subtle nitre, and that the little animals that cause putrefaction could be resolved again into other smaller ones, and so on as

you please to infinity; I say even if these things were true, as they are perhaps in part, they would not suffice for providing the causes of things, since an example or analogy is advanced rather than a cause. For there will remain a question everywhere without end, and there will be no less difficulty explaining why secondary or subtle nitre reacts with subtle sulfur than in explaining why primary or gross nitre reacts with gross sulfur. However, we have provided reasons that will suffice even for those explanations, if there are any, that form an infinite regress.

### (c) from *A New Physical Hypothesis*

*The Theory of Abstract Motion*[5]                                 **A VI.ii N41**

[Winter 1670–71]

#### *Predemonstrable Foundations*

(1) *There are actually parts in the continuum,* contrary to what the most acute Thomas White believes,[6] and

(2) *these are actually infinite,*[7] for Descartes's "indefinite" is not in the thing, but the thinker.[8]

(3) *There is no minimum in space or body,* that is, nothing which has no magnitude or part.[9] For such a thing has no situation, since whatever is situated somewhere can be touched by several things simultaneously that are not touching each other, and would thus have several faces; nor can a minimum be supposed without it following that the whole has as many minima as the part, which implies a contradiction.[10]

(4) *There are indivisibles or unextended things,* otherwise neither the beginning nor the end of a motion or body is intelligible. This is the demonstration: any space, body, motion, and time has a beginning and an end. Let that whose beginning is sought be represented by the line *ab,* whose midpoint is *c,* and let the midpoint of *ac* be *d,* that of *ad* be *e,* and so on. Let the beginning be sought to the left, on *a*'s side. I say that *ac* is not the beginning, since *dc* can be taken away from it without destroying the beginning; nor is *ad,* since *ed* can be taken away, and so on. Therefore nothing is a beginning from which something on the right can be taken away. But that from which nothing having extension can be taken away is unextended. Therefore the beginning of a body, space, motion, or time (namely, a point, an endeavour, or an instant) is either nothing, which is absurd, or is unextended, which was to be demonstrated.

(5) *A point is not that which has no part,*[11] nor that whose part is not

considered;[12] but that which *has no extension,* i.e. whose parts are indistant, whose magnitude is inconsiderable, unassignable, is smaller than can be expressed by a ratio to another sensible magnitude unless the ratio is infinite, smaller than any ratio that can be given. But this is the basis of the *Cavalierian Method,* whereby its truth is evidently demonstrated, inasmuch as one considers certain rudiments, so to speak, or beginnings, of lines and figures smaller than any that can be given.[13]

(6) The ratio of rest to motion is not that of a point to space, but that of nothing to one.

(7) Motion is continuous, i.e. not interrupted by any little intervals of rest.[14] For

(8) once a thing comes to rest, it will always be at rest, unless a new cause of motion occurs.

(9) Conversely, that which is once moved always moves, insofar as it is able,[15] with the same velocity and in the same direction.

(10) Endeavour is to motion as a point is to space, i.e. as one to infinity, for it is the beginning and end of motion.[16]

(11) Whence, *whatever moves*—however feebly, and however great the obstacle—*will propagate an endeavour through all obstructions in the plenum* to infinity, and will therefore impress its endeavour on everything else.[17] For it cannot be denied that even when it ceases to continue moving, it at least endeavours to do so; and therefore that it endeavours—or what is the same thing, begins—to move any obstacles, however large, even if it is overcome by them.

(12) Thus there can *be several contrary endeavours in the same body simultaneously.* For if there is a line *ab,* and *c* tends from *a* to *b,* and *d,* in turn, tends from *b* to *a,* and they collide; then at the moment of collision *c* will endeavour towards *b,* even though it be thought to have stopped moving, since the end of a motion is an endeavour; but it will also endeavour in the reverse direction, if the opposing body be thought to prevail, for it will begin to move backwards. But it will be all the same even if neither body prevails, since every endeavour is propagated through obstructions to infinity, and thus the endeavour of each will be propagated into each; and if it makes no difference when their speeds are equal, then neither will it when one is double or however much greater than the other, since twice nothing is nothing.

(13) *One point of a moving body in the time of its endeavour,* i.e. in a time smaller than can be given, *is in several* places or *points of space,* that is, it will fill a part of space greater than itself, or greater than it fills when it is at rest, or moving more slowly, or endeavouring in only one direction; yet this part of space is still unassignable, or consists in a point, although

the ratio of a point of a body (or of the point it fills when at rest) to the point of space it fills when moving is as an angle of contact to a rectilinear angle, or as a point to a line.

(14) But in general, too, *whatever moves is never in one place while it moves,* not even at an instant or minimum of time; since that which moves in time, endeavours to move in an instant, that is, it begins and ceases to move, i.e. to change place. And it is no good saying that what endeavours at any time smaller than can be given is really at a minimum in place: for there is no minimum part of time, otherwise there would also be one of space. For whatever completes a line in a time will, in a smaller time than can be given, complete a smaller line than can be given, that is, a point; and in an absolutely minimum time, will complete an absolutely minimum part of space; but there is no such thing (*by Foundation 3*).

(15) On the other hand, *at the time of collision,* impulse, or impact, the two extrema or endpoints of the colliding bodies mutually penetrate, i.e. *are in the same point of space:* for since one of the colliding bodies endeavours to move into the other's place, it begins to be in it, i.e. it begins to penetrate, or be united. For endeavour is a beginning, penetration is a union: thus they are at the beginning of a union, i.e. their bounds are one.

(16) Therefore *bodies which press against* or impel *one another, cohere:* for their bounds are one, and those things whose extremities are one [ων τα εσχατα εν] are, by Aristotle's definition too,[18] continuous, i.e. cohering, since if two things are in one place, one cannot be impelled without the other.[19]

(17) *No endeavour lasts longer than a moment without motion, except in minds.* For that which in a moment is an endeavour, is in time a motion of a body. And here a door is opened for pursuing the true distinction between bodies and minds, till now explained by no one. For every body is a momentaneous mind, i.e. a mind lacking *recollection,* since it does not retain its own endeavour and a contrary one together for longer than a moment. (For two things are necessary for *sensing pleasure* or pain: namely, action and reaction, that is to say, comparison and thus *harmony*—and there is no sensation without these). Therefore body lacks memory, it lacks a sense of its own actions and passions, it lacks thought.

(18) *One point is greater than another, one endeavour is greater than another, but one instant is equal to another,* whence time is expounded by a uniform motion in the same line,[20] although its parts do not cease in an instant, but are indistant. In this they are like the angles at a point, which the Scholastics (whether following Euclid's example, I do not know) called *signs,* as there appear in them things that are simultaneous in time, but not simultaneous by nature, since one is the cause of the other. Like-

wise in accelerated motion, which, since it increases at any instant, increases at once from the beginning; but to increase presupposes an earlier and a later; so in this case it is necessary for there to be one sign prior to another in a given instant; though without distance or extension (add *problems 24, 25*).[21] The inequality of endeavours no one will easily deny, but the inequality of points follows from it. It is clear that one endeavour is greater than another, i.e. that a body which moves more quickly than another already covers more space from the beginning: for if it covers just as much space at the beginning, it will always cover just as much, since as a motion begins, so it continues, unless there is some extrinsic cause changing it (*by foundation 9*). . . . Therefore the faster covers more space than the slower in a given instant, but in one instant no endeavour can traverse more than a point, or a smaller part of space than can be expounded, otherwise in a time it would traverse an infinite line. Therefore there is one point greater than another. Whence the unassignable arc of a bigger circle is greater than that of a smaller one: and any line whatever, drawn from the center to the circumference, commensurable with the circle, that is, the line by whose rotation the circle is generated, is a perpetually increasing *minimum sector,* but extensionless within. Hence one also solves the difficulties about the two *concentric wheels* rotating on a flat plane,[22] about *the angle of contact,* and as many others, which the most eloquent *Belin* challenged all the philosophers on earth to explain,[23] and from which the *Skeptics* derive the most triumph. An *angle* is the quantity of a point of intersection, i.e. a portion of a circle smaller than can be assigned, i.e. of a *center*—the whole doctrine of angles is about quantities of unextended things. An *arc* smaller than any that can be given is still greater than its chord, although this is also smaller than can be expressed, i.e. consists in a point. But that being so, you will say, an *infinitangular polygon* will not be equal to a circle: I reply, it is not of an equal magnitude, even if it be of an equal extension: for the difference is smaller than can be expressed by any number. Whence from Euclid's definition: *a point is that which has no part,* no error could creep into demonstrations concerning extension, . . . provided a part of extension, i.e. a part distant from another part, is understood. . . .

(19) *If two endeavours occurring at the same time are conservable, they are composed into one, and the motion of each is conserved,* as is clear in the case of a sphere rotating in a straight line on a plane, where the motion of some specified point on its surface is composed through minima, i.e through endeavours, out of straight and circular motions combined into a Cycloidal one. . . . This argument deserves to be treated more diligently by Geometers, so as to make clear which lines will produce which new

lines by the combining of their endeavours; and in this way they will perhaps be able to demonstrate many new Geometrical Theorems.

. . .


USES

Even if these [sc. the General and Special Problems Leibniz has just
outlined] or other problems are not solvable by means of the abstract reasons for motions in bodies considered absolutely; still, in sensible bodies,
at least if the insensible Aether is assumed, it can easily be explained how
it comes about that no sensible error disturbs our reasons, which suffices
for the phenomena. For Nature (insofar as it is sensible, for otherwise it is
not only possible, but even necessary, that the accurate figures in its inte-
riors be constructed from the abstract laws of motion, according to the
problems premised, a kind of construction that I call *Physical*) . . .[24]
solves these problems very differently than does the Geometer, namely,
mechanically, with motions that are not continuous, but in fact interrupted; as when Geometers describe the quadratrix by means of points,
and Archimedes squares the circle by means of polygons, disregarding an
error that will not disturb the phenomena. For sensation cannot discriminate whether some body is a continuous or contiguous unit, or a heap of
many discontiguous ones separated by gaps; whether [a body's] parts are
wholly at rest, or redound on themselves by an insensible motion; whether
an angle of intersection is very slightly oblique, or exactly a right angle;
whether the angle of contact is made at a point, or a line or surface; to what
extent speed is a true curvity, or fabricated from broken lines, by the variation of which the motions are also varied, as is clear from our theory . . . .


## (d) On Primary Matter[25]                    A VI.ii N42₃

[Winter 1670–71][26]
Aristotle's primary matter is the same as Descartes's subtle matter. Each is
divisible to infinity. Each lacks form and motion in itself, each acquires
forms through motion. Each receives its motion from a mind. Each is
formed in certain whirls, and Aristotle's vortices have no greater solidity
than do Descartes's. Each kind of vortex gets its solidity from motion,
since nothing disturbs it, although Descartes did not himself give this as
the cause of solidity. Each whirl propagates its action onto another whirl
through impressed motion, on account of the continuity of matter. For
Aristotle too, no less than Descartes or Hobbes, derives all particular

whirls solely from the motion of the universal whirls. Whence Aristotle imparted intelligences only to the principal whirls, since from the collisions of these whirls the actions of the others follow. Aristotle erred in making the earth the center of the world and of all the gyrations. But this error should be pardoned, since philosophy had not yet been sufficiently equipped with observations.

To these remarks I now add that *primary matter is nothing if it is at rest.* And this is what certain Scholastics said obscurely when they said that primary matter even obtains its existence from form. There is a demonstration of this. For whatever is not sensed is nothing. But that in which there is no variety is not sensed. Similarly: *If all primary matter were to move in one direction, that is, in parallel lines, it would be at rest,* and consequently would be nothing. *Everything is a plenum,* since primary matter and space are the same. Therefore *every motion is circular,* or is composed of circular motions, or at least joins back up with itself. The several circulations will mutually obstruct each other, or act one upon another. *Several circulations will endeavour to unite into one,* that is, all bodies tend towards rest, i.e. annihilation. *If bodies are devoid of mind, it is impossible for motion to have been eternal.*[27] *The conflicting universal circulations give rise to the particular ones, i.e. bodies. Matter is actually divided into infinite parts. There are infinitely many creatures in any body whatever. All bodies cohere to one another. Yet every body separates from every other, although not without resistance. There are no Atoms,* i.e. bodies whose parts never separate. There are two principles by which motion is varied: compositions of endeavours and compositions of {——}[28]

## (e) from *A Hypothesis of the System of the World*[29]                              A VI.ii N44

[Spring–Fall 1671?][30]

I *suppose* as demonstrated: that the world is not a plenum, for if it is a plenum, there is no action of one body on another, no diverse centers of motions, and all things are either equally solid or equally fluid.

I *suppose* as demonstrated, secondly, that this aspect of the world has not existed from eternity, nor will it endure forever.

. . .

7. We may suppose the whole space of the world to be filled with globes, touching each other only at a point, so that the interstices cut out between them (*intercepta*) are vacua. But all integral bodies, i.e. those lacking an interposed vacuum, are uniform, i.e. spherical.

9. Bodies are either integral or fractured. *Integral* bodies are those with no vacuum interposed, *fractured* ones, those with an interposed vacuum. The only integral bodies are Atoms.

10. Bodies are either mundane, i.e. enduring for a while, or momentaneous.

11. The surfaces of Mundane bodies are equidistant from the center, even if they are not continuous, for example, if they are crowned with globes of equal size.

12. Bodies are either naturally dissoluble, or they are indissoluble, i.e. atoms. Integral bodies are atomic, fractured ones are dissoluble.

13. There are three grades of bodies: atomic, mundane, momentaneous.

14. It is impossible that being at rest makes a body cohesive, and undissolved by the impulse of another body, unless the body impinging on it makes contact with it at a point, and has a motion which is not about its own center.

15. It suffices for a body to be integral in its surface. For inside it is again composed of infinite[ly many] globes, and new worlds can be contained in it without end.

. . .


### (f) from *On the Nature of Corporeal Things: A Specimen of Demonstrations from the Phenomena* (Second Draft)[31]      A VI.ii N45$_2$

[late 1671?][32]

[After giving an a priori demonstration of the difference between space and body based on the propositions: "Whatever is clearly and distinctly perceived is possible," and "Whatever is immediately sensed is true," Leibniz continues:]

Another demonstration taken from the phenomena will be given in its own place, which people accustomed to figures will understand more easily. For it will be shown from the motions we sense that there is a vacuum;[33] now if there is a vacuum, there is certainly a distinction between space and body.

Since we have posited space in the definition of body, and extension in the definition of space, we must explain extension. Likewise distance, since mention is made of indistance in the definition of body.

*Extension*, seeing as it is applied so broadly as to be attributed to time as well, is the magnitude of the continuous.

*Magnitude* is the multiplicity of parts.

A *continuum* is a whole between any of whose parts other parts of the same thing are interjected.[34]

Something is *interjected* between two things if the sum of its distances from each of them is the distance apart of the two things.[35]

. . .

All worlds are contiguous. It follows from the same thing that everywhere there is a world. For otherwise that which is surrounded by a vacuum on all sides will soon be dissipated by having its parts forced out. But in case someone should not admit this, a better reason can be found: this is that otherwise there would be no resistance in the world, since everywhere there would be space for yielding.

. . .

To be demonstrated: Every body is in motion.

There is no minimum in the continuum.

In every continuum there are unextended parts.

Every continuum has infinite parts.

Body is divided in such a way that it is impossible for any of its parts to fall away from or become more distant from any other, in other words, into infinite parts.

Two bodies cannot be in the same place.

The same body cannot be in several places.

The same body cannot fill unequal spaces at different times.

The same space cannot hold unequal bodies at different times.

There are more bodies than vacuum. Otherwise there would be space for yielding, and thus no resistance in the world.

Everything consists of globules.

Some globes move around their own center; but otherwise they do not move, or are fixed.

All other globes engage in both locomotion and motion around their own center at the same time.

There are whirls which are not parts of another whirl, that is, planets.

## Appendix 2
## Leibniz's Predecessors on the Continuum

### (a) Aristotle

Aristotle discusses the continuum in a number of different places in his works, most notably in the *Physics* (Books 5 and 6), before this in the *Categories* (4b 20–5a 14), and afterwards in *On Coming to Be and Passing Away* (*De Generatione et Corruptione*) (316a 15–317a 26). In what follows I give selections from and synopses of these. There are also shorter passages in *On the Heavens* (268a 6–7) and the *Metaphysics* (1068b 26–1069a 14), the discussion of which I have relegated to footnotes.[1]

For the translations I had initially intended to give adaptations of those in the Barnes and Loeb editions. But in an effort to render all the technical terms consistently, I found it necessary to provide fresh translations from the Greek. For these I am much indebted to Don Adams for invaluable assistance. Some key terms (and their cognates) are translated as follows: διωρισμένον: discrete; διώρισται: are separate; συνεχής: continuous; ἅπτεσθαι: to be in contact; ἐφεξῆς: consecutive; ἐχόμενος: contiguous; ἔσχατον: extremity; ὅρος: limit; περας: boundary, bound; απείρον: unbounded, infinite; πεπερασμένον: bounded, finite; ἄκρον: extremum; αμερὲς: partless thing; διαρετὸν: divided, divisible; ἀδιαίρετον: indivisible; διῃρημένον: divided.

CATEGORIES

In this work Aristotle distinguishes all quantities into the *discrete,* such as number and speech, and the *continuous,* such as lines, surfaces, bodies, time, and place (4b 20–21, 4b 23–26). Number is discrete because there is no common limit at which its parts are joined together: "although five is a part of ten, the two fives are not joined together at any common limit, but are separate" (4b 26–29); and similarly for the syllables in speech (4b 33–38). In contrast, a line is continuous, since its parts are joined together at a common limit, namely, a point. Similarly, the parts of a surface have as common limit a line, and those of body a line or plane. The parts of a place are joined at the same common limit as the parts of the body occupying them, and past and future time are joined together at the present, or "now" (το νυν) (5a 1–14), conceived by Aristotle as a durationless instant (see *Physics,* 6, ch. 3).

PHYSICS

The theoretical foundation for this understanding of continuity is provided by Aristotle in Books 5 and 6 (i.e. E and Z) of the *Physics.* In Book

5, chapter 3 (226b 18–227 b2), and again in summary form at the start of Book 6 (231a 21–24), Aristotle lays down a series of definitions: things are "*in contact* if their extrema are together" (226b 23), "*consecutive* if there is nothing of their own kind between them" (226b 34–227a 5, 231a 23), and "*contiguous* if they are consecutive and in contact" (227a 6). This sets up the definition so often quoted by Leibniz: "things are *continuous* if their extremities are one" (231a 22). Thus:

> What is *continuous* is contiguous, but I say one thing is continuous with another when the bounds at which they are in contact become one and the same,[2] and (as the word signifies) hold together;[3] but if these extremities are two, continuity is impossible. This definition makes it plain that continuity belongs to things that have grown to be one by virtue of their mutual contact. And in whatever way that which holds them together is one, so too will the whole be one, whether, e.g., by a rivet, or glue, or contact, or grafting (227a 7–17).

On the basis of these definitions Aristotle argues in Book 6 that this precludes the composition of the continuous out of indivisibles, e.g. a continuous line out of indivisible points:

> For the extremities of two points can neither be *one* (since an indivisible can have no extremity distinct from some other part), nor *together* (since a partless thing can have no extremity, for the extremity and that of which it is the extremity are different things) (231a 26–29).

Nor can the continuous be composed of indivisible parts that are merely *in contact* with one another. For indivisibles, being partless things, would have to be in contact as whole to whole; but then they would not be distinct and spatially separable parts, as befits the parts of the continuum (231b 1–6). Nor, again, can the continuous be composed of indivisibles that are *consecutive*. "For things are consecutive if there is nothing of their own kind between them, whereas what is between two points is always a line, and what is between two nows is always a time" (231b 8–10).

Another very important property of the continuous that Aristotle derives from these definitions, and one that is often used to define it, is *infinite divisibility:*

> Moreover it is clear that everything continuous is divisible into parts that are ever divisible;[4] for if it were divisible into indivisibles, an indivisible would be in contact with an indivisible, since the extremities of things that are continuous with one another are one and in contact (231b 15–18).[5]

Aristotle then proceeds to argue that time, magnitude, and motion are on a par in this regard: "either all of these are composed of indivisibles and divisible into indivisibles, or none of them are" (231b 18–20). For example,

> Since every motion is in time, and within any time it is possible for something to be moved, and since any moving thing may move faster or slower, in any time there may be a faster or slower motion. This being so, it necessarily follows that time also is continuous. *By 'continuous' I mean that which is divisible into parts that are ever divisible;* for if continuity is assumed to be this, it follows that time must be continuous (232b 20–26; my italics).

The infinite divisibility of time, magnitude, and motion was, of course, the crucial property that Zeno had appealed to in formulating his paradoxes. So it is natural that Aristotle should discuss it first in preparation for his treatment of those paradoxes. But a curious feature of the discussion (as I have signaled by the above italics) is that he takes the property of being "ever divisible" to *define* the continuous, i.e. to be logically equivalent to his previous definition.[6] Since he has already proved that the latter implies the former, this means that he is implicitly assuming that the former implies the latter: that is, that the ever divisible must be such that any two adjacent parts into which it is divided must share their boundary. It is hard to see how this would be so if the parts and the divisions in question were actual, where each part would have its own boundary. But it seems to follow if being ever divisible, or infinitely divisible, means being potentially divisible into parts in arbitrarily many ways, but not actually divided into them. Each point would then mark a place of possible division. That is, although Aristotle does not explicitly say so, the equivalence of his definition seems to presuppose his account of the *infinite* earlier in the *Physics,* where he formulates his famous distinction between the *potential* and the *actual* infinite.

According to Aristotle's interpretation of infinity, "What is infinite is not that of which there is nothing outside, but that of which there is always something outside" (206b 33–207a 1). "In general," he says, "the infinite exists through one thing always being taken after another, what is taken being always finite, but always different" (206a 28–29). Hence nothing infinite can exist all at once. This condition is satisfied directly by the temporally infinite, but only indirectly by the spatially infinite: "in spatial magnitudes, what is taken always persists, while in the succession of time and men it takes place by the passing away of these in such a way that the source of supply never gives out" (206b 1–2). This implies that "there

cannot be an infinite by addition, at least not one that exceeds every determinate magnitude" (207a 35). There can, however, be an infinite by division, since this amounts to saying only that no matter how many divisions one makes it is always possible to make more. But this means that "this infinite is potential, never actual" (207b 12–13). The one kind of infinite by addition that is possible is that which we get as the inverse to such a process of infinite division. For if we divide a finite magnitude infinitely, and then add its parts together, "the sum of the parts taken will not exceed every determinate magnitude" (206b 18–19). Thus:

> What is continuous is divisible to infinity, but it is not infinite with respect to the greater. For however much bigger it may be in potentiality, it may be in actuality. Hence, since no sensible magnitude is infinite, it is impossible for it to exceed every limited magnitude; for then something would be greater than the heavens (207b 16–21).

These considerations allow Aristotle to give a neat resolution of Zeno's dichotomy paradox, intended to establish the impossibility of motion. Zeno had argued that before one could traverse a given distance in a finite time, one would first have to cover half this; and before the half, half of this, or a quarter; and before this, an eighth; and so on to infinity. Thus one would have to traverse (and so make contact with) an infinity of subintervals in a finite time, which is impossible. Therefore motion is impossible. But, replies Aristotle, this is to confuse the two ways in which a continuous thing may be said to be infinite: infinite in respect of divisibility (which any continuous quantity is potentially) and infinite in extent (literally, "in respect of its extremities"), which no sensible magnitude may be:

> So while in a finite time a thing cannot make contact with things infinite in respect of quantity, it can make contact with things infinite in respect of divisibility: for in fact time itself is infinite in this way. And so it turns out that the thing traverses the infinite in an infinite [time], and not in a finite one, and it makes contact with the infinite [spatial divisions] by [temporal divisions] not finite but infinite. . . . Hence Zeno's argument makes a false assumption in asserting that it is impossible for a thing to traverse or come in contact with infinite things one by one in a finite time (233a 26–31, 21–23).

Now to this it might be objected that Aristotle is not entitled to say, as he does here, that an infinity of things can be traversed. He cedes this criticism later in the *Physics* (263a 4–b 9), explaining that the above was sufficient to refute Zeno on his own terms. In his later discussion Aristotle gives a more accurate solution, pointing out that on his own view the divi-

sions of the continuum are potential rather than actual (263a 28). Thus "if someone asks whether one can traverse an infinity either in time or in length, it must be said that in a way one can, and in a way one cannot. For an infinity of actually existing [divisions] cannot be traversed, but an infinity of potential ones can" (263b 4–6).[7]

Finally, in his treatment of infinity Aristotle is at pains to point out that insofar as his account "denies that the infinite is actually inexhaustible with respect to increase" (207b 28–30), it is in conformity with the usage of the mathematicians:

> In point of fact, they neither need the infinite nor use it, but need only [posit] that a finite line may be produced as far as they wish, and that any magnitude whatsoever may be cut in the same ratio as the greatest magnitude may. Hence for the purposes of proof, it makes no difference to them whether the infinite is to be found among existent magnitudes (207b 31–34).

### ON COMING TO BE AND PASSING AWAY

There is much else of great subtlety in Aristotle's thought on the continuum, and which may well have influenced Leibniz.[8] An illustration is his discussion of atomic magnitudes and the divisibility of bodies in *De Generatione et Corruptione* (316a 15–317a 26), in which he develops the following objection to his doctrine of *potentially divisibility:*

> It is in no way absurd that every perceptible body should be divisible at any and every point and also indivisible, since it will be divisible potentially, and indivisible in actuality. Nevertheless it would seem impossible for a body to be, even potentially, simultaneously divisible throughout. For if this were possible, it might indeed occur, with the result, not that it would simultaneously be both—indivisible and divided—but that it would be divided simultaneously at any and every point. . . . [Hence, it is urged] if you divide a body part by part, the process of dissolution cannot go to infinity, nor can a body be simultaneously divided at every point, for that is not possible, but there is a limit beyond which the dissolution cannot proceed. It is necessary, then, that there must exist in a [perceptible] body atomic magnitudes that are invisible, especially if coming-to-be and passing-away are to take place by association and dissociation respectively (316b 20–26, 30–35).

The fallacy in this argument, Aristotle explains, is that it proceeds on the assumption that being divisible throughout means that there is not only a

point anywhere in it, but everywhere within it. But "no point is contiguous to another point," so that the body is divisible throughout only in the sense that "there is one point *anywhere* within it and all its points are *everywhere* within it if you take them singly one by one. But there are not more points than one *anywhere* within it, for the points are not consecutive" (317a 2–9).

## (b) Galileo Galilei

### TWO NEW SCIENCES

The following extracts are from the *Discorsi e dimostrazioni matematiche, interno a due nuove scienze* ("Discourses and Mathematical Demonstrations Concerning Two New Sciences"), Dialogue 1, where Galileo gives an extended discussion of indivisibles, indivisible voids, and the problem of the continuum. The translations were made jointly by myself and Gabriella Colussi Arthur, to whom I am much indebted for her collaboration. They are from the Leiden edition of 1638 (for which I thank the Centre for Reformation and Renaissance Studies at the University of Toronto for the loan of their copy), although the text is (as far as I could determine) identical to the definitive Edizione Nazionale, to which I have keyed it.

Having introduced the possibility of voids in matter with his explanation of the cohesion of the marble slabs in terms of nature's repugnance to a vacuum (see GLOSSARY entries on *cohesiveness* and *tabula*), Galileo declares (through his spokesman Salviati):

> SALV.: . . . Experiencing firsthand how repugnance to the vacuum is undoubtedly what prevents the two slabs from being separated without the use of great violence, with even more being needed to separate the two large parts of the marble or bronze column, I cannot see how this repugnance would not take place and equally be the reason for the coherence of the smaller parts, and even of the ultimate minima of the same material . . . (EN 66).

Then when the question is raised as to whether these ultimate particles and the voids that separate them might not be infinite in number, Galileo suggests that they "see whether it might in some way be demonstrated how in a continuous finite extension it is not unreasonable that there could be found infinite voids" (EN 68). The demonstration begins by asking us to imagine two concentric, regular polygons—for the sake of example,

two regular hexagons—rotating on a smooth plane, as in the figure below. As they rotate, the side of the larger one will touch *AB, BQ, QX*, etc. successively, while the smaller one's sides will touch *HI, OP*, etc., skipping over the gaps *IO, PY*, etc., while Galileo will equate with voids. After one complete revolution, "it may be understood that the space passed over by the smaller polygon is almost equal to that passed over by the larger," being "smaller only by the chord of one of these arcs, provided we understand the line *HT* to include the spaces of the five [skipped] arcs" (EN 69). If now the same thing is imagined with two concentric circles in place of the two hexagons, one obtains the conundrum known as "Aristotle's Wheel," first proposed by someone of the Aristotelian school in *Mechanical Questions*.[9] For both circles will trace out approximately equal lines, smoothly, and without skipping any gaps.[10] But "how, without skipping, can the smaller circle run through a line so much greater than its circumference?" (EN 70). Galileo responds as follows:

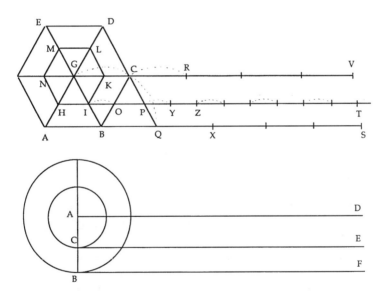

SALV.: . . . Just as I say that in polygons of one hundred thousand sides, the line traversed and measured by the perimeter of the greater—that is, by its hundred thousand sides extended continuously—is equal to that measured by the hundred thousand sides of the smaller, but with the interposition of a hundred thousand void spaces placed between; so, I shall say, in the circles (which are poly-

gons of infinite sides) the line traversed by the infinite sides of the greater circle, arranged continuously, is equal in length to the line traversed by the infinite sides of the smaller circle, but in the latter with the interposition of just as many voids between them. And just as their sides are not quantified [*non quanti*], but properly infinite, so the interposed voids are not quantified but infinite; that is to say, the former [line's components] are infinite points, all of them full, the latter['s components] are infinite points, some full and some void.

And here I would like it to be noted how, on resolving and dividing a line into parts that are quantified [*parti quante*], /EN 72/ and consequently numbered, it is not possible to arrange them into a greater extension than they occupied when they were continued and conjoined, without interposing as many void spaces. But on imagining it divided into unquantified parts [*parti non quante*]—that is, into its infinite indivisibles—we can conceive it as expanded beyond measure without there being interposed any quantified void spaces, but rather infinite indivisible voids.

And what is thus said of simple lines will be understood to hold for surfaces and solid bodies, considering them as composed of infinite unquantified atoms: when we wish to divide them into quantified parts, there is no doubt that we will not be able to arrange them into spaces greater than those formerly occupied by the solid without interposing quantified void spaces—void, I mean, at least of the material of the solid. But if we understand there to be made the highest and ultimate resolution into prime components, unquantified and infinite, we will conceive such components expanded into immeasurable space without interposing quantified void spaces, but only infinite unquantified voids; and in this way expansion would not be inconsistent . . . (EN 71–72).

Here Galileo warns through Simplicio of the profound difficulties attendant on "composing the line from points, the divisible from indivisibles and the quantified from the unquantified"; not to mention that of "the need to assume the void, so conclusively refuted by Aristotle" (EN 72–73); Salviati concurs, reminding them that "we are among infinities and indivisibles, the former incomprehensible to our finite intellect because of their largeness, the latter because of their smallness" (EN 73). Still, he notes, "human reason cannot refrain from dealing with them," and proceeds to expound his "reverie" (*fantasticheria*) about the cone, the bowl, and the cylindrical razor, according to which the ultimate section of the cylindrical razor, a circle, will be equal to the ultimate section of the cone,

a point (EN 73–77). Galileo had sent this argument to Bonaventura Cavalieri as a caution concerning his Method of Indivisibles (see Stillman Drake's edition of *Two New Sciences*, p. 35). Leibniz's summary of the argument (minus Galileo's demonstration) in Aiii11 above is sufficiently accurate to obviate the need for repetition here. Galileo then resumes his "capricious" musings, as he calls them in (tongue-in-cheek) contrast with the "supernatural doctrines" that "are our unerring guides along our obscure and dubious paths, or rather Labyrinths" (EN 77):

> SALV.: Among the first objections usually raised against those who compose the continuum out of indivisibles is that one indivisible added to another indivisible does not produce a divisible thing. For if that were the case, it would follow that the indivisible too would be divisible; for, if two indivisibles, for example, two points, made a quantity when conjoined, which would be a divisible line, then one composed of three, five, seven, or some other odd multiplicity [of indivisibles], would be even more divisible. But these lines would then be bisectible into two equal parts, making the indivisible that is located in the middle also bisectible. In this and other objections of this kind, satisfaction is given to the other side by telling them that not only do two indivisibles not compose a divisible and quantified magnitude, but neither do ten, nor a hundred, nor a thousand, but rather an infinity of them.

> SIMP.: Here there immediately arises a doubt which to me appears insoluble; and this is that since we surely do find lines one greater than the other, each time both containing infinite points, one has to admit that there would be, in one and the same kind, a thing greater than the infinite; because the infinity of points of the greater line will exceed the infinity of points of the smaller. Now, this being the case, an infinite greater than the infinite seems to me a concept that cannot be understood in any way.

> SALV.: These are the sort of difficulties that derive from our engaging in discussion about infinites with our finite intellect, giving them the attributes that we give finite and bounded things, which is, I think, not fitting. For I believe that these attributes of greatness, smallness, and equality do not befit infinities, about which it cannot be said that one is greater than, smaller than, or equal to another. To prove this I recall a similar discussion I once had, which, in order to explain it more clearly, I will propound by interrogating S. Simplicio, who raised this difficulty (EN 77–78).

At this point Galileo gives the argument reproduced by Leibniz in the *Pacidius Philalethi* concerning the comparison of the number of all numbers with the number of all squares. Since there are numbers that are non-squares, it follows that (i) "all numbers, comprising the squares and the non-squares, are greater than the squares alone" (EN 78); and yet, (ii) "there are as many square numbers as there are their own roots, since every square has its own root, and every root its own square, nor is there any square that has more than one root, nor any root that has more than just one square" (EN 78). But, again, (iii) "if I were to ask how many roots there are, it cannot be denied that there are as many as all the numbers, because there is no number that is not the root of some square. That being so, it must be said that the square numbers are as many as all the numbers, because they are as many as their roots, and all numbers are roots" (78). So the multiplicity of squares is apparently both less than that of numbers, and also equal to it. To avoid the contradiction, Galileo says,

> SALV.: I do not see how it is possible to come to any decision other than to say that all the numbers are infinite, the squares are infinite, and their roots are infinite; the multiplicity of squares is neither less than that of all the numbers, nor is the latter greater than the former. And in final conclusion, the attributes of equal, greater, and less have no place in infinities, but only in bounded quantities (EN 79).

Actually this is the penultimate conclusion. For Sagredo interjects that the larger the number to which we go, the fewer of the numbers contained in it are squares, and therefore the farther we get from infinity, where the squares cannot be less than the number of numbers; from which Salviati concludes that greater, less, and equal are out of place not only in comparing infinites, but in comparing infinites with finites. (He will later conclude on the same basis that "if any number may be called infinite, it is unity" [EN 83].) Then this line of argument is transferred to the case of continuous quantities:

> SALV.: Given that the line, and every continuum, are divisible into ever divisibles, I do not see how to escape their composition being from infinite indivisibles. For a division and subdivision that can be performed perpetually supposes that the parts are infinite, since otherwise the subdivision would be terminable. And the existence of infinitely many parts entails as a consequence their being unquantified, since infinitely many quantified things make an infinite extension. . . . The very ability to perform perpetual division into quanti-

fied parts implies the necessity of composition out of infinitely many unquantified things" (EN 80).

### (c) René Descartes

PRINCIPLES OF PHILOSOPHY, PART 2[11]

**33. How in every motion an entire circle of bodies moves simultaneously.**

Now it was observed above that all places are full of bodies, and that the same parts of matter always take up equal places. But from this it follows that no body can move except in a circle: that is, in such a way that one body expels another from the place it enters, and this again expels another, and another, and so on until the last, which enters the place that was left by the first one at the very moment of time that the first one leaves it. And this we readily understand in the case of a perfect circle, since we see that no vacuum, and no rarefaction or condensation are required in order for part $A$ of the circle to move towards $B$, provided at the same time part $B$ moves towards $C$, $C$ towards $D$, and $D$ towards $A$. But the same thing may be understood even in the case of a circle that is not perfect, and is as irregular as you please, provided we observe how all the inequalities of the places can be compensated by the unequal speeds of the motions. Thus all the matter contained in the space $EFGH$ can move in a circle without any condensation or vacuum, and the part of it which is at $E$ can pass towards $G$ in the same time that the part that is at $G$ passes towards $E$: provided only that, if we suppose the space at $G$ to be four times wider than at $E$, and twice as wide as at $F$ and $H$, then the matter also moves four times faster at $E$ than at $G$, and twice as fast as at $F$ or $H$; and so in all the remaining places, the speed of motion compensates for the narrowness of the place. For in this way, in any determinate time, the same amount of matter will pass though one part of this circle as through another.

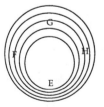

### 34. From this there follows a division of matter into actually indefinite[12] particles, although these are incomprehensible to us.

It must be admitted, however, that in this motion something is found which our mind perceives to be true, even though it does not comprehend how it occurs: namely, a division of certain particles of matter to infinity—that is to say, a division that is indefinite, and into so many parts that we can distinguish in thought none so minute that we do not understand it to be actually divided into parts still smaller. For it is not possible that the matter which now fills the space $G$ should successively fill all the spaces that are between $G$ and $E$, which are smaller by degrees beyond number, unless some part of it adapts its own shape to the innumerable measures of those spaces: but, for this to happen, it is necessary that all the imaginable particles of this part of matter—which are in fact beyond number—be to some degree mutually displaced from each other; and such a displacement, however slight, is a genuine division.

### 35. How this division occurs; and that it is not to be doubted that it occurs, even though this cannot be comprehended.

It should be noted, however, that here I am not talking about the whole of matter, but only a certain part of it. For although we may suppose two or three of its parts at $G$ to be as wide as the space $E$, and likewise that there are also several smaller parts that remain undivided; nevertheless, they can still be understood to move in a circle towards $E$, provided that, mixed in with these parts that adapt only their speed of motion to the place that is to be occupied, there are certain other parts which somehow bend and change their shapes in such a way that, when they are joined to those not changing their shapes in this way, they completely fill all the crevices that these others will not occupy.[13] Moreover, although we are unable to comprehend in thought how this indefinite division occurs, we must not for that reason doubt that it does occur: for we clearly perceive that this necessarily follows from the nature of matter that we know most evidently, and we also perceive it to be one of those things which our mind, inasmuch as it is finite, is unable to grasp.

## (d) Thomas Hobbes

CONCERNING BODY [14]
CHAPTER 8: ON BODY AND ACCIDENT

### 9. What contiguous and continuous are.

Two bodies are said to be *contiguous* and *continuous* with one another in the same manner as two spaces are: namely, *those are contiguous between which there is no space.*[15] Now, by space we understand, as explained above, an idea or phantasm of a body. And so
even if no other body is placed between two bodies, and consequently no magnitude oir, as they call it, real space, is placed there,
nevertheless if a body could be placed between them, i.e. if there is
between them a space capable of receiving a body, then those bodies
are not contiguous. And this is so easy to recognize that I wonder that
people, whenever they are philosophizing more subtly, judge otherwise, and affect a kind of metaphysical subtlety, as if led astray by a
will-o'-the-wisp of words. For who, using his natural sense, would
think that two bodies must necessarily touch one another just because
there is no other body between them? Or that there is no vacuum because a vacuum is nothing, or a non-being? This is as if someone
were to argue that no one can fast, because to fast is to eat nothing, but
nothing cannot be eaten.

Now *two bodies are continuous with each other when they have a
part in common; and several are continuous when any two that are
next to each other are continuous;* in a word, in the same way as two
spaces were defined to be continuous above.[16] . . .

### 12. What a point, a line, a surface, and a solid are.

If the magnitude of a body that moves be not considered (even
though there always is some magnitude), the path along which it
passes is called a *line,* or *one single dimension,* the space through
which it passes, a *length,* and the body itself, a *point;* in the sense that
the earth is usually called a point, and its annual path, the line of the
ecliptic. But if the body that moves be now considered as *long,* and it
is supposed to be moved in such a way that every single one of its parts
is understood to make a single line, then the path of every single part
of the body is called a *breadth,* and the space that is made a *surface,*
consisting of the twofold dimensions of *length* and *breadth,* of which
the whole of one is applied to all the individual parts of the other. . . .

CHAPTER 15. ON THE NATURE OF MOTION

## 2. Other principles added to these.

[Having summarized in 15.1 the eleven principles he has given so far, Hobbes adds six more, beginning:]

First I define ENDEAVOUR *to be motion through less space and time than is given; i.e. less than is determined, or assigned by a representation or number; i.e. motion through a point [and in an instant or point of time].*[17] In explanation of this definition it must be remembered that by a point I do not mean that which has no quantity, or which cannot be divided by any means (for there is nothing of this kind in the nature of things); but that whose quantity is not considered, that is, that of which no quantity or part is computed in a demonstration; so that a point is not to be regarded as an indivisible, but as an undivided thing. So also an *instant* is not to be taken for an indivisible, but for an undivided time.

Similarly, an endeavour is to be understood in such a way that it is indeed a motion, but one such that neither the quantity of time in which it is made, nor the quantity of the line through which it is made, has any comparison with the quantity of time or the line of which it is a part; yet, just as one point can be compared with another, so can one endeavour be compared with another, and one can be found to be greater or smaller than the other. For if the vertical points of two angles are compared with one another, they will be equal or unequal in the ratio of the angles; or if a straight line cuts the circumferences of several concentric circles, the points of intersection will be unequal in the ratio of the circles' perimeters. In the same way, if there are two motions that both begin and end together, their endeavours will be equal or unequal in the ratio of the velocities; just as we see a ball of lead descend with a greater endeavour than a ball of wool.[18]

## (e) Pierre Gassendi

CRITICAL OBSERVATIONS ON THE TENTH
BOOK OF DIOGENES LAËRTIUS
PART 2. ON EPICURUS'S PHYSICS[19]

### There is no magnitude that is infinitely divided, according to Epicurus[20]

. . . Meanwhile, however, the force of the explanation used by Epicurus consists principally in these words: that, when a finite body is as-

sumed, if the number of parts into which it is divided is nonetheless
not finite, we may then understand there really to be in it infinite
parts; whence the whole resulting from these parts is infinite, which
is contrary to the supposition.

. . .

Let us now investigate what is usually objected to Epicurus: it is
really a wonder not only that there should have been some in antiquity who attacked Epicurus as if he had believed that the division of
magnitude is terminated in certain mathematical points; but also that
there have been learned men from more recent times who have inveighed against him in whole tomes[21] as if he had said that bodies
were constituted from surfaces, surfaces from lines, lines from points,
and accordingly bodies and indeed all things, from points, into which,
accordingly, bodies and all things were resolved. This is a wonder, I
say, since if they had been willing to pay the least attention, they
would have been able to observe that the indissectibles into which
Epicurus held divisions to be terminated are not mathematical points,
but the meagerest bodies; since, moreover, he not only gave them
magnitude, when it is acknowledged that there is nothing of this kind
in a point; but he also gave them incomprehensibly variable shapes,
such as cannot be conceived in a point, which lacks magnitude and
parts.

*not points*
*L 8*

> **On magnitude and figure [and their consequents],**
> **subtlety, bluntness, smoothness, and roughness** where
> it is specifically mentioned that nothing concrete is
> absolutely continuous, nothing is absolutely smooth

Now something will have to be said concerning the continuity of
magnitude; but the matter will be well nigh understood after we have
discussed the admixing of things. For from this it will be evident that
each body must be said to be continuous insofar as its parts are conjoined, cohering with, and unseparated from one another, and are
such that, even though they are only contiguous with each other, their
joints cannot be distinguished by any of the senses. That is to say,
magnitude, or as they [the Schoolmen] call it, continuous quantity,
differs from multiplicity, i.e. discrete quantity, in the fact that *the
parts of a continuous quantity can indeed be separated, but are not in
fact separated,* whereas *the parts of a discrete quantity are actually
or really separated.* This is not to say that the parts of a multiplicity
are not also contiguous with each other, as, for example, are many
stones in one pile; but that they do not mutually grip each other, bind
together, and hold onto one another by their own angles or little

hooks. . . . Thus in a word, all bodies that may be broken apart by the force of heat, or by something else, have parts which are only in mutual contact, and which separate when this bond is severed and their continuity is broken.

Thus it is that, if we are asked what is so continuous that it does not on any account consist of the contiguous, the only thing we can specify in reply is the *Atom*. And we should understand Democritus to have been talking about this when, according to Aristotle, he wrote: "And neither can one become two, nor two one," since, of course, one atom is not dissectible in such a way that two should emerge, nor are two penetrable by each other in such a way that they might coalesce into one. But this does not prevent every body that is not really divided into parts from being called continuous, in accordance with common usage, and inasmuch as the senses cannot reach as far as atoms or their joints.

Aristotle, however, says that a continuum is "a thing whose parts are conjoined at a common boundary." This is physically true, to the extent that it has no two assignable parts which are not conjoined at some intermediate part, either a *sensible* part—as in a magnitude of three feet, the outermost feet are conjoined by the middle one—or an *insensible* one—as in a magnitude of two feet, these two feet have an item lying between them that evades the senses, as will be established in what I shall have to say later. There I shall declare that it is impossible for any continuous thing to be dissected with such great subtlety that middle-sized conglomerates of innumerable atoms are not expelled from it. Of course, accepting with Aristotle that the common boundary is a mathematical individual (for he asserts that the parts of a line are conjoined by a point, the parts of a surface by a line, and the parts of a body by a line or a point), this insensible boundary cannot be a physical reality, insofar as there do not exist in the nature of things indissectible things of this kind, which are instead only imagined or supposed, as we already mentioned above, and will further discuss below. . . .

### What motion is, and whether it exists

[In this section, Gassendi examines the problem of "Aristotle's Wheel" previously discussed by Galileo (see 2b above), although without mentioning either (pseudo-)Aristotle's *Mechanical Questions* or Galileo. He prefaces his analysis with the remark that a motion that appears to the senses as continuous may in reality be discontinuous, as, for instance, the apparently smooth line drawn by a pen is revealed by the microscope to

have been interrupted by gaps, owing to the imperfections of the paper. This allows him to give a solution to the problem that is in keeping with the Epicurean doctrine of the discontinuity of atomic motions, and is reminiscent of Galileo's, but with finite voids instead of the latter's infinite voids *non quanti.*[22]]

Should I add, because of the difficulty where, when a slower moving body is compared with a swifter one, each can be transferred in physical indissectibles—namely, that if each of the two motions is continuous, then while the slower body moves in a unique instant and traverses a physical indissectible, the swifter must simultaneously and without succession run through many indissectibles set in order, which is something that cannot be grasped at all—should I add, I repeat, that slowness arises from the intermixture of rests?

Certainly, just as we conceive the light of the midday sun to be the brightest, and then the various degrees of light down to pure darkness to be created by the intermixture of more or less darkness, so may we conceive the motion by which we infer Atoms are carried through the Void—or, if you prefer, the motion attributed to the Primum Mobile—to be the swiftest; then all the degrees there are from this to a pure rest, are made up of more or fewer particles of rest intermixed. By this account, from the whiteness of snow or milk one arrives at the blackness of a raven, carbon, or pitch; from the heat of fire to the cold of ice, and so on for the rest: with Aristotle not denying that these changes come from the admixing of contraries.

Accordingly, when there are two moving bodies, one of which is going twice as fast as the other, it must be conceived that for every two moments during each of which the faster is moving, the slower moves in only one and remains at rest in the other; and, by the same reasoning, when the motion is three times as fast, for every three moments during which the former moves, the latter moves for one and rests for two, and so on for the rest.

Nor may you object that a motion of this kind will not then be continuous in itself; for it will still be continuous to the senses—in the same way as when a fire-brand is spun around rapidly, it appears to the senses that the fire is circular, or that the fire-brand is continuously in any part of the circle you please, whereas it is not, except in an interrupted way. It is the same as when, on drawing a line with a pen on a clean sheet of paper, you see yourself drawing it straight and continuous, and yet that line is marvelously and ineffably divided up, as a result of the sharpness of the pen and the unevenness of the sur-

face of the paper; which is not only argued by what we deduced above, but also demonstrated by discriminating Engyscopes;[23] as are many other things of this kind besides. . . .

As a kind of postscript, it is very curious to note that neither of Gassendi's chief disciples, François Bernier (1620–88) in France, and Walter Charleton (1619–1707) in England, subscribed to his doctrine of the interruption of motion by rests. In his *Physiologia,* Charleton reproduces almost all Gassendi's other arguments from the *Animadversiones* (and helpfully reorders them), but this doctrine he ascribes only to Arriaga: "Such was the contumacy of *Arriaga,* that in hopes to elude this insoluble difficulty, he pretends to discover a new kind of Motion, distinguished by certain *Respites,* or *Pauses,* intercedent; thereupon inferring that all things are moved, during their motion, with equal Celerity, but because the motion of one thing is interrupted with many pauses, and the motion of another with few, therefore doth the motion of this seem swift, and the motion of that slow. . . . If this be true than must a Pismire[24] move slower than an Eagle only because this distinguisheth its motion by shorter pauses, and that by longer. . . ." Further sarcastic examples (a Falcon and a Partridge, a Sloth and the fleetest Courser in the Hippodrome of Alexandria) apparently establish that "*Arriaga's Quiet,* imagined to be in motions, is not part of Motion."[25]

Bernier, for his part, repeats Gassendi's argument in full in the 1678 edition of his *Abridgement of the Philosophy of Gassendi.*[26] But in the revised edition of 1684, he disowns this doctrine. In Doubt XI, "Whether Slowness of Motion Has Its Origin in the Interception of Little Rests,"[27] he writes: "Thus it ought to be ridiculous to imagine that in these different motions there should be little pauses[28] or rests intermingled, and that a slow motion and a fast one differ in that in the slow there are more of them, and in the fast, fewer. . . ." Indeed, his refutation rests on thoroughly Gassendian principles and terminology, including that of the "physical point," also appealed to by Leibniz. The difficulty, he explains, "pertains only to those who compose the continuum out of mathematical points, and time out of mathematical instants, and not to those who like us recognize only physical points and instants." The slower body "traverses a physical point successively and continuously" in the same time a body moving twice as fast traverses its physical point in the same way.

# Notes

### Introduction

1. The quotation is from *De usu geometriae* of 1676 (Aiii54: 449). See also G.ii.262, G.ii.451, G.vi.29, as well as below.

2. G. W. Leibniz, *Theodicy,* ed. A. Farrer, trans. E. M. Huggard (La Salle: Open Court, 1985), p. 53; G.vi.29. Cf. also "On Freedom" (c. 1689): "There are two labyrinths of the human mind: one concerns the composition of the continuum, and the other the nature of freedom, and both spring from the same source—the infinite" (PW 107).

3. These descriptions are from a manuscript prospectus for an encyclopedic work entitled "Guilielmus Pacidius's *On the Secrets of Things*" (*Guilielmi Pacidii De rerum arcanis*) (Aiii77, in DSR 88–91).

4. "I shall have perchance at another time an opportunity to declare myself on the second, and to point out that, for lack of a true conception of the nature of substance and matter, people have taken up false positions leading to insurmountable difficulties, difficulties which should properly be applied to the overthrow of these very positions" (preface to the *Theodicy,* p. 53).

5. Many of these passages were included by Bertrand Russell in the excellent selection of translations of "leading passages" he appended to his *Critical Exposition of the Philosophy of Leibniz* (London: Routledge, [1900], 1992: pp. 205–305). To these should be added his correspondence with Princess Sophie (G.vii.541ff.), as Glenn Hartz and Jan Cover point out ("Space and Time in the Leibnizian Metaphysic," *Noûs* 22 [1988], 493–519: 500); they translate four key passages from Leibniz's letter of 1705 (500–501). Perhaps the fullest account Leibniz wrote of his travails in the labyrinth can be evinced from his "autobiographical" remarks in the *Phoranomus* of 1689, extracts of which were published by Gerhardt (in their original Latin) in 1888, of which a snippet was translated by Russell (pp. 84–85). Now the complete Latin text has been made available by André Robinet in an annotated critical edition: G. W. Leibniz, *Phoranomus seu De potentia et legibus naturae, Dialogus I* in *Physis,* 28, 3, 1991, pp. 429–541; *Dialogus II* in *Physis,* 28, 23, 1991, pp. 797–885.

6. See G.ii.98, G.ii.262, G.ii.267–68, G.ii.278, G.ii.282, G.ii.379, G.iii.583, G.iv.394, G.iv.491, reproduced in Russell's *Critical Exposition* on pp. 108 and 245–46.

7. I have examined some of these efforts—those of Leonhard Euler, Bertrand Russell, Nicholas Rescher, and J. E. McGuire—in my "Russell's Conundrum: On the Relation of Leibniz's Monads to the Continuum," pp. 171–201 in James Robert Brown and Jürgen Mittelstraß, eds., *An Intimate Relation: Studies in the History and Philosophy of Science* (Boston: Kluwer Academic Publishers, 1989).

8. The metaphor of the labyrinth, as Catherine Wilson has observed (in her *Leibniz's Metaphysics* [Princeton: Princeton University Press, 1989], p. 8), was a common one in seventeenth-century rhetoric, and the figure of the labyrinth had already been used to describe the problem of the continuum by Galileo Galilei in *The Assayer* (1631) and *Two New Sciences* (1638), and by Libert Froidmont in the title

of his book *Labyrinthus de compositione continui* (The Labyrinth of the Composition of the Continuum, 1631).

9. Although we should allow for the conventions of modesty, the papers of the Paris period are described by Leibniz's spokesman Pacidius in the dialogue in Part II below as "a few sheets of paper and some poorly expressed vestiges of hasty reflections, which were only ever saved for the sake of my memory."

10. As André Robinet has observed, the style of these pieces is characterized by the typical lead-in phrase, *Videndum est . . .* , "It must be seen whether . . . ": "Ce reclassement des structures est obtenu à suite d'hypothèses éphémères, toutes ces pièces restant sur le style du *'videndum est'*," Robinet, *Architectonique disjonctive, automates systemiques et idéalité transcendentale dans l'oeuvre de G. W. Leibniz* (Paris: J. Vrin, 1986), p. 189.

11. "To me, a barbarous Englishman, has been entrusted the revelation of this diaphanous mystery. . . . T'sui Pên must have said once: *I am withdrawing to write a book.* And at another time: *I am withdrawing to construct a labyrinth.* Everyone imagined two works; to no one did it occur that the book and the maze were one and the same thing" (Jorge Luis Borges, "The Garden of Forking Paths," quoted from Donald Yates and James Irby, eds., *Labyrinths* [New York: New Directions Books, 1964], p. 25).

12. See Gilles Deleuze, *Le Pli: Leibniz et le baroque* (Paris: Les Editions de Minuit, 1988), translated by Tom Conley as *The Fold: Leibniz and the Baroque* (Minneapolis: University of Minnesota Press, 1993).

13. The problem of the continuum is captured very neatly in Stuart Brown's succinct formulation: it is "the problem of how anything that is extended in space or time can be real if each of its parts is further divisible *ad infinitum*" (Stuart Brown, "The Seventeenth Century Intellectual Background," pp. 43–66 in Nicholas Jolley, ed., *The Cambridge Companion to Leibniz* [Cambridge: Cambridge University Press, 1995], p. 51).

14. They had also been much discussed by a whole tradition of earlier thinkers in antiquity and the Middle Ages. See in particular Norman Kretzmann, ed., *Infinity and Continuity in Ancient and Medieval Thought* (Ithaca: Cornell University Press, 1982), and Richard Sorabji, *Time, Creation, and the Continuum: Theories in Antiquity and the Early Middle Ages* (Ithaca: Cornell University Press, 1983). But Leibniz does not allude to this rich medieval tradition in any of his writings here.

15. See Lynn Sumida Joy, *Gassendi the Atomist* (Cambridge: Cambridge University Press, 1987), pp. 83–105, 255–61. The problem, translated from the Latin text given by Joy, is "whether there is a demonstration, perfectly mathematical, perfectly logical, or perfectly sensible, by which it could be proved that there is such a thing as a magnitude not lacking in extent, which is contained at a certain time and place in a genuine mathematical point having no parts, yet which itself has at the same point parts beyond parts" (255).

16. Joy, *Gassendi the Atomist,* p. 105.

17. In a letter to Nicolas Rémond in January 1714, Leibniz recalls: "On becoming emancipated from the Trivial Schools, I fell upon the moderns, and I remember

walking alone in a copse near Leipzig called the Rosenthal, at the age of fifteen, to deliberate whether I should keep Substantial Forms." (GP.iii.606). Loemker reports that "Kabitz has shown that [Leibniz's] memory was in error here, and that his decision could not have been made earlier than 1664" (L 84).

18. In a further letter to Rémond in 1714 in July, Leibniz wrote: "As for Gassendi, . . . I am not as content with his meditations at present as I was when I was starting to abandon the opinions of the school, while still myself a schoolboy. Since the doctrine of atoms is satisfying to the imagination, I gave myself over to it completely, and the void of Democritus or Epicurus, together with the impregnable corpuscles of these authors, appeared to me to relieve all difficulties." (GP.iii.620).

19. This, I believe, very much understates the influence of Gassendi's views on Leibniz's understanding of the continuum. At any rate, the distinction between mathematical and physical points, the distinction of both from incorporeal indivisibles, the characterization of mathematical points as fictions, the emphasis on how the problem of the continuum is underdetermined by what is perceivable to the senses, are all doctrines that are as characteristic of Leibniz's thought as of Gassendi's; though see Philip Beeley's criticisms of my claims for Gassendian influence on Leibniz in the symposium on his book in the *Leibniz Society Review* 7 (1997): 79–81.

20. See in particular Christia Mercer, "The Seventeenth Century Debate Between the Moderns and the Aristotelians: Leibniz and *Philosophia Reformata,*" *Studia Leibnitiana Supplementa* 27 (1990): 18–29. Leibniz's teachers were of course hardly alone in trying to reconcile Aristotle with the moderns. As Leibniz himself points out in a letter to Thomasius, Julius Caesar Scaliger had "paved the way," and in his own time Kenelm Digby, Thomas White, Jean de Raey, and Abdias Trew were in harmony with Thomasius and Weigel on this (L 97–98).

21. See Christia Mercer and R. C. Sleigh, Jr., "Metaphysics: The Early Period to the *Discourse on Metaphysics,*" pp. 67–123 in *The Cambridge Companion to Leibniz.*

22. For insightful analyses of this early metaphysics, see Daniel Garber, "Motion and Metaphysics in the Young Leibniz," pp. 160–84 in Michael Hooker, ed., *Leibniz: Critical and Interpretive Essays* (Minneapolis: University of Minnesota Press, 1982); Mercer and Sleigh, "Metaphysics: The Early Period"; and Mercer, *Leibniz's Metaphysics: Its Origins and Development* (forthcoming).

23. For instance, in the *Nouveaux Essais,* he writes: "To tell the truth, I believe that perfect fluidity is only appropriate to *primary matter,* that is to say, in abstraction and as an original quality, in the same way as rest, not to *secondary matter,* such as is found in actuality, reinvested with its derivative qualities, for I believe that there is no point of mass which would be of ultimate subtlety" (222).

24. "Meanwhile I have penetrated much more deeply, I think, into both problems, for you will not read there [sc. in the *Confessio*] what I have found out since about the perpetual creation involved in motion, and about the innermost nature of a thinking being or a mind" (L 102).

25. "I have demonstrated instead that whatever moves is continuously created,

and that bodies are something at any instant in assignable motion, but nothing at any time midway between the instants in motion—a view that has never been heard of till now, but which is clearly necessary, and will silence the atheists" (A II.i: 23–24; L 102). Leroy Loemker took Leibniz's reference to continuous creation here "merely to mean the source of all motion in God," construing Leibniz's position simply as a variant of Descartes's (L 104). But that would render Leibniz's claim for originality very odd, since both he and Thomasius would have been familiar with the Cartesian view. I would hazard the guess that the theory is more Gassendian in inspiration: in apparently continuous motion, the body is in successive discrete places at successive assignable times, being at rest at the unassignable times in between; Leibniz's original contribution being the claim that when the body is at rest, it is therefore "nothing." Philip Beeley suggests an Ockhamist reading (*Mechanismus und Kontinuität,* Stuttgart, Franz Steiner, 1996, p. 133).

26. In addition, as Mercer points out in her article with Sleigh, since the cause of motion (and thus of shape and magnitude too) is God, it is not clear in what sense shape and the other mechanical properties belong to the body rather than God ("Metaphysics . . . ," *Companion,* p. 77). For "nothing ought to be supposed in bodies whose cause cannot be discovered in their first or constitutive principles" (L 101). Mercer calls this the Principle of Causal Self-sufficiency (p. 72).

27. See Thomas Hobbes, *Leviathan,* part 1, chs. 1–3 and 6, in e.g. the edition of C. B. MacPherson (London: Penguin, 1968).

28. See John Watkins, *Hobbes's System of Ideas* (London, 1973), pp. 87–94; Howard Bernstein, "*Conatus,* Hobbes and the Young Leibniz," *Studies in History and Philosophy of Science* 11 (1980): 25–37; and especially Daniel Garber, "Motion and Metaphysics in the Young Leibniz."

29. The *Theory of Abstract Motion* (hereafter TMA) is the abstract part of the *Hypothesis physica nova* (hereafter HPN); relevant sections are reproduced in Appendix 1c.

30. Cf. Joseph Hofmann, *Leibniz in Paris, 1672–1676* (Cambridge: Cambridge University Press, 1974); John Earman, "Infinities, Infinitesimals and Indivisibles: The Leibnizian Labyrinth," *Studia Leibnitiana* 7 (1975): 236–51.

31. See Appendix 2a. As I mention in a note there, however, Aristotle's arguments in *Physics,* 5 and 6, are such that Leibniz might have read him as denying the actual infinite only to the infinite by extent, not the infinite by division. See also Beeley, *Mechanismus und Kontinuität,* ch. 1, esp. pp. 37ff.

32. The Aristotelian character of Leibniz's later construal of continuity has been discussed with particular clarity in a series of papers by Herbert Breger, especially "Das Kontinuum bei Leibniz," pp. 53–67 in *L'infinito in Leibniz, Problemi et terminologia,* ed. Antonio Lamarra (Rome: Edizioni dell'Ateneo, 1990). See also Enrico Giusti, "Immagini del continuo," pp. 3–32 in the same volume.

33. Relevant quotations from Aristotle and Descartes are given in Appendix 2a and 2c.

34. This crucial difference between Leibniz's indivisibles and Galileo's has been lucidly emphasized by Eberhard Knobloch. See his "L'Infini dans les mathématiques de Leibniz," pp. 33–51 in Lamarra, *L'infinito in Leibniz.*

35. Compare the TMA with "Infinite Numbers" (Aiii69) of April 1676.

36. "Therefore space is composed of parts smaller than any determinable by us . . . time is composed of moments, i.e. parts smaller than any determinable by us" (Aiii3: 81).

37. Hobbes also justifies his unequal points ("whose quantity is not considered") in terms of points of intersection between a radius and the circumferences of ever-bigger circles (see Appendix 2d). Interestingly, this justification in terms of horn angles was offered by the Augustinian friar Fulgence Vauville as a solution to Poysson's challenge problem, discussed in Section 2 above. But I have found no explicit evidence that Leibniz had read the literature on Poysson's problem.

38. Compare Appendix 1c, Aiii5, and Aiii4 below.

39. TMA, Appendix 1c (A VI.ii: 266). Cf. "In the mind all endeavours endure, and none is chosen for addition or subtraction unless it is harmonious (ἁρμονιχώτατος)" (A VI.ii: 282).

40. See the quotations from Huygens's paper in the July 1672 *Journal des sçavans* given in footnote 8 to Aiii4 below.

41. These two quotations are from Leibniz's letter to Hobbes of 23 July 1670 (A II.i: 57) and his letter to Oldenburg of 28 September 1670 (A II.i: 64), resp.

42. *Julii Caesaris Scaligeri Exotericarum exercitationum libri XV de subtilitate ad Hieronymum Cardanum* (i.e. "Fifteen Books of Exoteric Exercises on Subtlety, for Hieronymum Cardano," by Julius Caesar Scaliger), Paris, 1557; *Ex. 101: mistio est motus corporum minimorum ad mutuum contactum, ut fiat unio* (quoted from Andrew G. van Melsen, *From Atomos to Atom,* Pittsburgh: Duquesne University Press, 1952; New York: Harper, 1960). Scaliger's book was a polemical reply to Cardano's *De subtilitate libri XXI* ("Twenty-One Books on Subtlety"), Basel, 1554. In chapter 12 of his *De chymicorum cum Aristotelicis et Galenicis consensu ac dissensu, Liber I* (i.e. "On the Agreement and Disagreement of the Chemists with Aristotelians and Galenists, Book I"), Wittenberg, 1619, Sennert wrote, "I confess I am now won over by the opinion of Scaliger, who defines mixtion to be the motion of minimum bodies towards mutual contact so that a union is made" [Scaliger's definition from Ex. 101]; quoted from James Riddick Partington, *A History of Chemistry* (London: Macmillan; New York: St. Martin's Press, 1961–70), p. 274.

43. Scaliger, op. cit., quoted from van Melsen, *From Atomos to Atom,* p. 76; translation slightly altered.

44. Leibniz to Hobbes, 23 July 1670; A II.i: 57. As Catherine Wilson observes (draft of "VORTEX: The Significance of Inertial Circular Motions in Leibniz's *Paris Notes* with reference to Aristotle, Hobbes and Descartes," given at the Dibner Symposium on Leibniz and the Sciences, December 1984), Hobbes's actual explanation of hardness or *consistentia* was, like Leibniz's, in terms of very swift motion in small circles. Perhaps the reason for this mistake is that, since Leibniz himself gives a unified explanation of gravity, magnetism and cohesion, he is thinking of Hobbes's explanation of gravity.

45. "For whenever subtle things endeavour to break through dense ones, and there is some obstruction, dense things are formed in certain hollow bubbles, and

an internal motion of parts, and thus a consistency or cohesion, is produced. . . . The same thing is established in the workshops of glassmakers, where, by a circular motion of fire and a straight one of spirit, glasses, the simplest artificial kind, are produced; similarly, by a circular motion of the earth and a straight one of light, bubbles are produced" (TMC: A VI.ii: 226).

46. In the account of origins in the PQP, the whirls stirred up by the conflict of the larger vortices in the planetary system may be either full, in which case they are globules (*globulae*), or hollow (i.e. full of a more subtle fluid), in which case they are bubbles (*bullae*) (Aiii2: 29). Globes and bubbles collectively are called *terrellae*. See GLOSSARY.

47. Echoes of these early attempts to explain the cohesion of *bullae* persist in the later writings. See for instance Leibniz's explanation of the connection of bodies at Aiii76: 525, and the following passage from "A Chain of Wonderful Demonstrations about the Universe" of December 12, 1676: "Cohering bodies arise from the fact that if certain bodies are composed into an arch that is hollow inside, that is, full of more subtle matter, this arch would be difficult to break up, because the pores left by the component bodies are too small to be penetrated by the surrounding matter so as to fill the place" (Aiii85: 585; DSR 108–9).

48. "Hence it follows that whatever endeavours to move into another's place already at its boundary begins to exist in the other's place, i.e. their boundaries are one, i.e. penetrate each other; and consequently one cannot be impelled without the other. And consequently these bodies are continuous" (Aiii4: 96).

49. There is a serious difficulty with this construal of cohesion as motion in common that does not seem to have occurred to Leibniz. This is that if any two bodies (or parts of bodies) are co-moving, then they will be mutually at rest. But in that case they will have no endeavour to penetrate one another.

50. One might even say that Leibniz comes full circle. After his flirtations with a neo-Hobbesian theory of cohesion and with a revised atomism, he returns to something much more like his early theory of substance as a union of body with mind or substantial form.

51. "I have always [!] believed that whatever may be said about atoms having various figures, . . . about hooks, crooks, globules and so much other apparatus proper to the game of the learned, is too remote from the simplicity of nature and from any experiments, and too naïve to be connected in any obvious way with the phenomena" (A VI.ii: 248).

52. "Supposing plenitude, *atoms* are demonstrated;—no, even without plenitude, from the mere consideration that every flexible body is divided into points" (Aiii85: 585; DSR 106–11).

53. Thus Leibniz writes to Oldenburg: "for indivisibles are boundaries of things . . . therefore the two points or extremities of body, that of the one pushing and that of the one pushed, penetrate one another (for there is such a thing as a penetration of points, although not of bodies)" (A II.i: 64).

54. Strictly speaking, Gassendi's atoms differed from the classical ones in being created, rather than eternal, and in possessing a motive force. Magnen's atoms were

also not standardly Democritean: although they were physically indivisible, finite in number and finitely extended, Magnen claimed that a single atom, while retaining the same area and mass, "may, without rarefaction, without inflation or reproduction, naturally occupy a greater and greater place to infinity" by changing its shape (translated from the Latin given by Partington in his *History,* p. 457). Magnen (Jean Chrysostôme Magnen or Magnenus, professor of medicine at the University of Pavia) published his views on atoms in *Democritus reviviscens sive De atomis,* Pavia, 1646. Leibniz cites this work in his *De arte combinatoria,* A VI.i: 216.

55. "Whatever is divided, is divided into parts that are further divisible; or, there is no minimum divisible thing" (*De corpore,* VII, §13); "Therefore there is no tininess of a body that is impossible. . . . For we know there to be some animalcules so tiny that we can scarcely discern the whole of their bodies, so that we are capable of assuming no magnitude so tiny that our supposition is not exceeded by nature herself" (XXVII, §1).

56. Cf. Hobbes, *De corpore,* XXVI, §4: "In the first place, I suppose that the immense space we call the world is an aggregate of bodies: both of those that are cohesive and visible, the earth and the stars; and of those that are invisible, the very minute atoms which are scattered between the earth and the stars; and finally, of a very fluid aether, occupying every remaining place, wherever it is in the universe, in such a way that no place is left empty."

57. Daniel Sennert (1572–1637) was a major natural philosopher of the early seventeenth century who outlined his views on atoms and corpuscles in his *De chymicorum cum Aristotelicis et Galenicis consensu ac dissensu* (Wittenberg, 1618), and his *Opera omnia* (Paris, 1641; Lyons, 1650, 1654–56). Joachim Jungius (1587–1657), a professor of mathematics and of medicine at various German universities, was held in the highest esteem by Leibniz. I am indebted here to Partington, *History of Chemistry,* to which one should refer for further details concerning these authors' views.

58. According to Jungius's *syndiacritic* version of atomism, published in two *Disputationes* of 1642, chemical change arises from the separation (*diacrisis*) or conjunction (*syncrisis*) of the smallest parts of bodies, or atoms. See Partington (op. cit.) for details. Partington suggests that Sennert (272), and perhaps Jungius too (417), were initiated into atomism by a medical tradition originating with Asklepiades of Prusa (272).

59. Thus Sennert: "[atoms or minima of nature] owe their names to the fact that they cannot be further divided through natural processes, and, reversely, form the building blocks of all natural bodies. They are, however, so small that they escape detection by the senses" (*Opera,* I, 151; quoted from van Melsen, *From Atomos to Atom,* p. 85). But even Descartes wrote that "No one ever rejected Democritus' atomic theory because it admitted particles that are so small that they elude the senses, . . . but [inter alia] because it supposed the atoms to be indivisible" (*Principles,* IV, §202; AT VIII.1 325).

60. Thus see Aiii36: 393: "it is necessary that as many vortices are stirred up as

there are firm bodies in nature, solely by the motion of the firm bodies. And there are as many minds, or little worlds, or perceptions, as there are vortices in the world." But in "On the Union of Soul and Body" of February 1676 (Aiii62: 480; DSR 34–37) Leibniz explicitly asserts that the soul itself stirs up its own vortex, causing gyrations in the cavities of the brain.

61. This is a quotation from Gassendi, given by Richard S. Westfall, *The Construction of Modern Science* (New York: Wiley, 1971), p. 99. For Malpighi, see Marcello Malpighi, *De pulmonibus observationes anatomicae,* Bologna, 1661.

62. This organic model of the body, together with the conception of the mind as a kernel that can spread throughout a body or draw itself into an invisible center, is already broached by Leibniz in a letter to Duke Johann Friedrich of May 1671 (A II.i 108ff.; see Mercer, *Companion,* p. 82).

63. Cf. Aiii71: 510; DSR 60–61: "It is my opinion that . . . minds will be withdrawn within themselves for a long time, and will perhaps at some time return to a sensation of external things, perhaps of a far different nature."

64. "Every corporeal substance has a soul. Every soul is immortal. . . . Corporeal substance has no definite extension. There are as many souls as there are substantial atoms or corporeal substances" ([1683], Aiv279: 1466).

65. "If all organic bodies are animate, and all bodies are either organic or collections of organic bodies, it follows that indeed every extended mass is divisible, but that substance itself can neither be divided nor destroyed" (Aiv346: 1798).

66. There he says: "it is all the same whether you affirm or deny the *vacuum,* since I freely acknowledge that whatever is exhausted of air is filled up with aether; in short, whether little empty spaces are left is irrelevant to the gist of our hypothesis" (TMC, A.VI.ii N40: 246).

67. Here Leibniz appears to owe a debt to Gassendi, who had claimed that bodies whose joints cannot be distinguished by the senses must be said to be continuous (see Appendix 2e).

68. Spinoza (op. cit., SC 265–66) makes this proportionality explicit as his axiom 14: If two pipes, A and C, are of the same length, but the bore of C is twice that of A, and some fluid matter passing through them goes twice as fast through A as C, the quantity of matter passing through them in any given time is equal. The continuity equation is still an axiom of Fluid Mechanics, nowadays expressed as Div $v$ $= -\partial\rho/\partial t$: the divergence of the velocity $v$ of a fluid is equal to its rate of decrease of density $\rho$. Descartes's is the earliest formulation of this law I know of, although he is not normally credited with its discovery.

69. Again, Spinoza provides an explicit axiom from which this may be derived: "Axiom 16: Matter that moves in various ways has at least as many parts into which it is actually divided as the different degrees of speed that are observed in it as the same time" (SC 266).

70. This quotation is from Leibniz's *De quadratura arithmetica* (Fall 1675– Summer 1676), recently edited by Eberhard Knobloch. See fn. 5 of Aiii52 below for the full reference, and a more extensive quotation.

71. Here Leibniz assumes it is contradictory for anything to be smaller than the

infinitely small. But to this one could object (i) (as the early Leibniz might have) that some infinitely small entities are bigger than others; (ii) (as Galileo would have) that "greater" and "smaller" do not apply to the infinite; or simply (iii) that *zero* is smaller than the infinitely small—why shouldn't the error be zero at infinity? The proof might also be criticized for assuming without proof that a result that holds for any finite *n* still holds when *n* is infinite.

72. This paragraph was prompted by the probing questions of Sam Levey in private correspondence.

73. In Aiii5 Leibniz had argued that the only way to define a point so that it does not reduce to a minimum is in terms of endeavour: bodies with differing endeavours will traverse unequal points in the same instant; although the points are infinitely small, they will be in proportion to the endeavours. Actually, as the astute reader may have noticed, the finiteness of endeavours does not automatically invalidate this proportionality, since the two unequal points could just as well be in proportion to two finite endeavours as two infinitely small ones.

74. This sounds like Descartes's argument against indivisibles, that so long as they are imaginable, they will be extended and therefore divisible. But Leibniz does not need to appeal to the dubious question of what is imaginable, but only to his calculus of differences, where every differential is an infinite sum of differentials of the next higher order. Thus there is no line, not even an infinitely small one, that cannot be regarded as an infinite sum of infinitely smaller lines.

75. Actually, the word "finally" is a bit premature. For in "A Chain of Wonderful Demonstrations About the Universe" (Aiii85), Leibniz (bizarrely, in my view) returns to his previously held views that an infinite division would issue in points, and that this necessitates atoms, despite his having demolished them a month earlier. Thus if the dating of that piece is secure, as I am assured it is, there must be something amiss with my reconstruction.

76. Cf. also Leibniz's claim that "all bodies are necessarily flexible" in "On Motion and Matter" (Aiii58: 468).

77. In Bacon's Latin: *Inter terminos densi et rari est plica materiae, per quam se complicat et replicat absque vacuo.* This is the sixth of the *Canones mobiles of Historia Densi et Rari; from The Works of Francis Bacon*, vol. 3 (A. Millar in the Strand, London 1753), p. 408. In Canon 4 he had written: "There is a bound of denseness and rarity beyond which things cannot go, but not in any entity known by us" (*Est terminus, sive non ultra, densi et rari, sed non in ente aliquo nobis noto*).

78. Here I am again very much indebted to Sam Levey for his sharp formulation of this difficulty in our e-mail correspondence.

79. "There is an actual infinite in the mode of a distributive whole, not of a collective whole. Thus something can be enunciated concerning all numbers, but not collectively. So it can be said that for every even number there is a corresponding odd number, and vice versa; but it cannot therefore be accurately said that the multiplicities of odd and even numbers are equal" (G.ii.315; Russell, *Philosophy of Leibniz*, 244).

80. "By infinity," Leibniz writes in his *De quadratura arithmetica* of 1676, "I understand a quantity . . . greater than any that can be assigned by us or that can be designated by numbers" (p. 133, op. cit. n. 5 of Aiii52).

81. The one disanalogy between aggregates of minds and aggregates of places, Leibniz notes, is that the minds endure whilst the places, being continually changed by the motions of matter, are continually destroyed and recreated.

82. For a comprehensive review and interpretation of Leibniz's highly ramified position on relations, see Massimo Mugnai, *Leibniz' Theory of Relations,* Studia Leibnitiana Supplementa XXVIII (Stuttgart: Franz Steiner Verlag, 1992); and my modest footnote to this, "Relations of Time and Space," pp. 25–31 in *Leibniz und Europa* (VI Internationaler Leibniz-Kongreß, Hanover: Gottfried-Wilhelm-Leibniz-Gesellschaft, 1994).

83. Compare also Leibniz's critique of Cordemoy: "It is necessary that situation or relation be founded on something; if you say, on a possible interposition, then I say this possible interposition must in turn be founded on something already then actual"—by which Leibniz presumably means divine magnitude, which contains all possible situations, and is for him the foundation of space.

84. Cf. Leibniz's statement in the *New Essays:* "space, time and motion are of the nature of rational entities, and are true and real, not of themselves, but insofar as they involve divine attributes—immensity, eternity, operation—or the force of created substances" (NE 684: Russell, *Philosophy of Leibniz,* 233).

85. "These two orders—space and time, that is—relate not only to what actually is, but also to anything that could be put in its place. . . . This inclusion of the possible with the existent makes a continuity which is uniform and indifferent to every division" (G.iv.490; L 583).

86. "For every finite substance is actually acted upon . . . ; every passion of a body, on the other hand, is by division" (Aiv267: 1398); ". . . is acted upon by all the other parts of matter . . . in proportion to their distance. And since every case of being acted upon has some effect" (Aiv312: 1623).

87. Robert Merrihew Adams makes this argument in his fine recent book (*Leibniz: Determinist, Theist, Idealist,* New York: Oxford University Press, 1994; p. 236–38). Although I do not agree that Aiv316 can be definitively concluded to represent a phenomenalist position, I do however agree with Adams that Leibniz is unable to rule out phenomenalism except by reverting to atomism until he adopts substantial forms (although he seems to do this not in the summer of 1679, but in 1678—see Aiv365, fn. 2). I also agree with Adams's dating of this piece as near the beginning of the Hanover period.

88. See Leibniz's letter to Arnauld, 30 April 1687; quoted from PW 67.

89. Leibniz does not explicitly conclude that there are no actual infinitesimals. But it seems implicit in remarks such as "for the rest, it must be seen whether there are not other things that are infinitely small, such as angles," right after the discussion of the fictitious nature of the circle, and his conclusion that there are not; and the later remark that "the unbounded . . . is something, the infinitely small is not."

90. See his "On the Nature of Corporeal Things" of 1671, Appendix 1 v: "*Magnitude* is the multiplicity of parts" (A VI.ii N45$_2$).

91. Cf. "Whenever the whole is prior to the parts, then it is a maximum, as for example in space and in the continuum. If matter, like shape, is that which makes a modification, then it seems that there is not a whole of matter, either" (Aiii74: 520).

92. Cf. Leibniz's "Remarks on the Objections of M. Foucher" (1695): "And as everything is indefinite in the abstract line, one takes into account there everything that is possible, as in the fractions of a number, without troubling oneself over the divisions actually made, which designate these points in an entirely different manner" (G.iv.491).

93. For a treatment of this point, see my "Russell's Conundrum," pp. 171–201 in Brown and Mittelstrass, *An Intimate Relation,* esp. pp. 179–80.

94. This law is also worth quoting in the more formal version: "When the difference *in the given quantities* of two cases, i.e. those assumed, can be diminished below every given quantity, it is necessary that the difference *in the quantities sought,* i.e. the consequences that result from the assumed quantities, be simultaneously diminished below every given quantity" (ibid.).

95. As Leibniz notes, "if one body is carried by another in a certain direction, but is moving of its own accord equally in the contrary direction, it will certainly come to rest, i.e. it will not leave its place" (Aiii68: 493).

96. "Assuming motion is a reproduction of distance into distance, then it is now exceedingly clear, very much more so, how God is the immediate cause of all things, how conservation is continuous production . . . , since otherwise, if we assume continuous motion, things would produce themselves. . . . Hence, the cause of things is at last made clear in an admirable way, as well as production out of nothing. Yet mind always persists" (Aiii68: 494).

97. At least, that is my interpretation. Leibniz's words are: "For there seem to arise from them infinite straight lines bounded at both ends, as I will show at another time; which is absurd" (Aiii78: 564–65).

98. Cf. Leibniz's discussion of the obvious attractions of the Copernican System in his "Mechanical Principles" (Aiii6: 105), concluding: "The beauty and simplicity of the Copernican System easily attracted all the most talented people onto its side."

99. "An attribute is either a state or a change; although in fact a change is an aggregate of two opposite states in one stretch of time, with no moment of change existing, as I demonstrated in a certain dialogue" (Aiv76: 307). The Akademie editors date this manuscript (titled *Definitiones: Aliquid, Nihil* [Definitions: Something, Nothing]) as Spring–Summer 1679 (?).

100. "I have proved elsewhere that there is no middle moment, or moment of change, but only the last moment of the preceding state and the first moment of the following state" (Aiv310: 1613).

101. Cf. Leibniz's remark to de Volder in June 1703: "You doubt, distinguished sir, whether an individual simple thing would be subject to changes. But since only simple things are true things, the rest being mere entities by aggregation, and thus phenomena, . . . it is obvious that unless there is change in the simple things, there will be no change in things at all" (G.ii.252; L 531).

102. "Accurately speaking, though, matter is not composed of these constitutive

unities, but results from them. . . . Substantial unities are not parts, but foundations of phenomena" (G.ii.268; L 536).

## 1. A Demonstration of Incorporeal Substances

1. LH XXXVII 4, leaves 65–66, 1 sheet in folio; ⅔ page on leaf 66 verso. This is one of several interesting drafts that Leibniz composed on the same sheets of folio, in which he takes up a problem dear to him, that of proving that incorporeal substances are necessary for a satisfactory definition of bodies (cf. the "Confession of Nature Against the Atheists" of 1668 (A VI.i 491–92), and Proposition 36 of "Certain Physical Propositions" (Aiii2: 72); cf. also "On the Minimum and Maximum . . ." (Aiii5, below), where he finally proves this to his apparent satisfaction). It is the fourth of seven drafts, all of which save part of the sixth and the whole of the seventh Leibniz had canceled by crossing them out. Apart from the reworkings of his theory of cohesion, it is noteworthy for the demonstrations that the spatial continuum is composed of parts smaller than any determinable by us, the second of which assumes as a premise that time is composed of moments—although, in view of the fact that the draft is canceled, we cannot assume that Leibniz found these demonstrations satisfactory.

2. Leibniz's original title.

3. As the Akademie editors note, there are no traces in either this or any of the other drafts of this piece of Leibniz's first trip to England (mid-January to beginning of March 1673), so that "they may all have been composed in 1672, and were probably already abandoned after his first conversation with Huygens in the Fall of 1672."

4. I have inserted proposition and definition numbers, according to Leibniz's apparent intent.

5. —reading *extremo* for *extremi*.

6. It may be useful to compare these definitions with those beginning the first draft: "| (1) A *substance* is whatever acts. (2) A *body* is a substance whose unique action is to move or change its place (or at least to endeavour or begin to move). Thus a heavy body that is suspended, even if it isn't moving, still endeavours to move. (3) An *incorporeal substance* is that whose action is something more than a change of its place. |"

7. Leibniz left this blank, perhaps realizing that it does not accord with any of the propositions he has proved so far.

8. Again Leibniz left this blank, presumably with the intention of inserting the needed definition in a final draft.

9. In using the Greek terms συγκίνητα and συμπαθεῖν for 'co-moving' and 'sympathize', Leibniz is signaling the ancient Greek sources for his doctrine of universal sympathy, which was promulgated particularly by the early Platonists and Stoics. They read this view back into Hippocrates, whom Leibniz also mentions in this connection. In the sixth draft of this *Demonstration* (Aiii3$_6$: 87), not reproduced here, where he writes: "And what Hippocrates asserted of the human body,

that πάντα σύρροια καὶ σύμπνοια εἶναι (everything flows together and con-spires/is in harmony), is true in the world." Cf. similar remarks in *A Specimen of Discoveries* (Aiv312, below).

## 2. Notes on Galileo's *Two New Sciences*

1. LH XXXVII 5, leaves 205–6, 1 sheet of folio, 1 page on leaf 206 verso; on the two pages of leaf 205, and in a different writing, are two pages of notes by Leibniz on the second dialogue (Aiii11₁). These are not directly relevant to the continuum problem, so I have not included them here. Leibniz gives his references to the sec-ond volume of the 1656 Bologna edition of Galileo's *Opere;* pages 21–24, 82–83, 102–3 of this edition correspond to pages 73–78, 152–54, 174–77 in volume VIII of the Edizione Nazionale of his *Opere,* Florence, 1898; I have inserted references to the latter in square brackets [EN] in the text. A synopsis of Galileo's discussion of the continuum in the *Two New Sciences,* with quotations, is given in Appendix 2b.

2. The Akademie editors note that the two fragments, written by Leibniz in the order given, but at different times, "cannot be given a reliable dating by means of watermarks"; but "his remarks on the method of indivisibles and the infinite (Aiii11₂) must have been written before the *Accessio ad arithmeticam infinitorum,* which Leibniz had composed for Gallois at the end of 1672 (see A III.i 3, 10–13; II.i 223, 226 ff.)." One might add that there are numerous references to Galileo's *Two New Sciences* in the *Certain Physical Propositions* (Aiii2, dated Spring–Fall 1672?), so that if the notes given here date from his first thorough reading of the first dialogue of the *Two New Sciences,* they would have preceded that work, and also Aiii3 above.

3. Galileo's term was *braccio* (corresponding to the Latin *ulna*), a seventeenth-century measure that varied between 58 and 70 cm. Stillman Drake informs us that "the Florentine braccio of Galileo's time was 58.4 cm., or about an inch less than two feet" (Galileo Galilei, *Two New Sciences,* ed. and trans. Stillman Drake, Madi-son: University of Wisconsin Press, 1974; p. xxxiii). This presents a difficulty, since 18 *braccia* would then be some 34½ feet (or, for *braccia* of between 58 and 70 cm., between 34 and 41 feet). But the maximum height of a column of water that is even theoretically sustainable by the pressure of the atmosphere is only some 34 feet; and practically, due to the imperfection of the vacuum obtainable in a suction pump, it is hard to get it to work at much more than 26 feet above the surface of the water. A more realistic figure is obtained if we suppose that by *braccio* Galileo in-tended the *cubito* (cubit), a unit of approximately 18 inches (or about 46 cm), for 18 cubits is some 27 feet (or a little over 8 meters).

4. Cf. *Two New Sciences,* EN 65: "And since a copper rod can support itself up to a length of 4801 cubits, the resistance it encounters that is dependent on the vac-uum, compared with the remaining resistance, is as much as the weight of a rod of water, eighteen cubits long and as thick as the copper rod; and if we find, for exam-ple, that copper is nine times as heavy as water, the resistance to breaking of any

copper rod, insofar as it depends on the vacuum, is as much as the weight of two cubits of this same rod. By a similar reasoning and procedure one may find the maximum lengths to which wires or rods of all solid materials can sustain themselves, as well as the part the vacuum plays in their resistance."

5. See Appendix 2b for a synopsis of Galileo's explanation.

6. Halfway through the proof summarized by Leibniz below, Galileo says: "Note, by the way, the nature of mathematical definitions, which consist in the mere imposition of names, or, if you prefer, abbreviations of speech, established and introduced in order to remove the tedious drudgery you and I experienced before we agreed to call this surface the 'circular band', and that sharp solid portion of the bowl a 'round razor'."

7. In a passage in his *Traité du triangle arithmetique* (1665), Pascal writes, "This is how one can vary the expressions. What I show in this proposition should be understood of all the others, . . . for if you do not know how to shape the propositions to every sense, and if you make use only of the first bias that you envisaged, you will never get very far; it is these diverse routes which open up new consequences, and which, by expressions suited to the subject, link together propositions which seemed to have no connection in the terms by which they were first conceived." *Oeuvres de Blaise Pascal,* ed. Léon Brunschvig and Pierre Boutroux, III, lxiv, p. 511.

8. Having given the above proof only for areas, Galileo refers the reader interested in the corresponding proof for volumes to "the twelfth proposition of the second book of *De centro gravitatis solidorum,* by Signor Luca Valerio, the new Archimedes of our age." According to Stillman Drake (*Two New Sciences,* p. 38), Valerio (1522–1618) met Galileo at Pisa in about 1590, and later corresponded with him. The book cited was published in Rome in 1603/4.

9. The views of Galileo alluded to here by Leibniz are quoted in translation in Appendix 2b.

10. Galileo and Leibniz both mean the natural numbers, of course. If negative numbers are included, there are twice as many roots as squares (although the argument can of course be adjusted to accommodate this).

11. At EN 78, Salviati says: "for in my estimation the attributes of greatness, smallness and equality are not suitable for infinities, of which one cannot be said to be greater than, smaller than, or equal to another"; and again at the end of the ensuing proof: "in final conclusion, the attributes of equal, greater, and smaller have no place among infinites, but only among bounded quantities" (EN 79). For Gregory of St. Vincent's opinion, the Akademie editors refer us to his *Opus geometricum,* 1647, lib. 8, pr. 1, theorema, p. 870 ff. (See A III.i 11.)

### 3. On Minimum and Maximum; On Bodies and Minds

1. LH XXXVII 4, leaves 45–46; 1 sheet in folio; 2⅓ pages.

2. The Akademie editors note that the watermark is registered twice, for November and December of 1672; they also note the thematical connection between

this piece and two earlier pieces of the same period, *Certain Physical Propositions* and *A Demonstration of Incorporeal Substances* (Aiii2 and 3), all three of which would have been written before Leibniz left for his first trip to England in mid-January 1673. Also it was probably written after his notes on Galileo's *Two New Sciences* (Aiii11$_2$), since one of the demonstrations is taken from the latter.

3. Leibniz's identification here of indivisibles with minima represents a significant change from the doctrine expounded in the *Theory of Abstract Motion* (Appendix 1c), where he had identified them with the infinitely small parts of the continuum. For here, as there, he asserts that the infinitely small parts do exist, but that minima do not.

4. Before deciding to treat minima in space and body separately from minima in time and motion, Leibniz had originally begun this piece "| There is no minimum in the continuum. |," and had continued with the following second paragraph: "| If there are no minima in time and space, then there will be none in motion and body either: and consequently none in the universe. For I suppose that whatever is capable of being greater or smaller, is comprised by space, time, body, and motion. But if someone doubts this position, he may formulate the proposition as follows: there is no minimum or indivisible in the continuum. First of all |"

5. This is a classical argument against the composition of a line out of points on the basis of the incommensurability of the side and diagonal of a square. Libert Froidmont, for example (see Aiii60, n. 12 below), gives a version of it in one of his arguments against the heretical opinions of Epicurus, proving (to his own satisfaction, at any rate) that the diagonal is either equal to or twice as long as the side, depending on whether there is a further point in the diagonal between the points of intersection of two neighboring transverse lines (*Labyrinthus de compositione continui,* ch. XII, pp. 43–44). But Leibniz's argument is more sophisticated in that it does not presuppose that the lines are composed of points; but it still presupposes that all the points in a line are assignable, an assumption Galileo explicitly denies.

6. Compare with Leibniz's remark prompted by his reading of Galileo's *Two New Sciences* (Aiii11$_2$ above): "the most infinite, i.e. all the numbers, is something that implies a contradiction." The demonstration which follows here is derived from Galileo's, which he summarized in Aiii11$_2$, after describing it as "worth noting."

7. It is noteworthy that now Leibniz does not claim that these infinitesimals are actual parts of the continuum, as he had in the *Theory of Abstract Motion.* This perhaps represents another advance in his understanding of the continuum; for his argument only demonstrates that there are such things in the continuum, not that they compose it.

8. Cf. Proposition III.16 of *Euclid's Elements:* "the angle between a circle and a tangent is less than every rectilineal angle." This proposition is the topic of a fascinating discussion by S. K. Thomason, "Euclidean Infinitesimals," *Pacific Philosophical Quarterly* 63 (1982): 168–85, in which he defends the consistency of such curvilinear angles.

9. This otherwise rather surprising suggestion that motion is essential to the definition of body is consonant with Leibniz's reflections in *Certain Physical*

*Propositions* written around July 1672. There he argued that it follows from his principle that *existere esse sentiri,* "to exist is to be sensed" (cf. "On Primary Matter," Appendix 1d), that "for a body to exist, to be, to act on the senses, it is necessary that it move or at least endeavour, since if everything were at rest, not even God could distinguish it from nothing. Whence it can be understood that matter and motion, or rather endeavour, are the same" (Aiii2: 56). Cf. Leibniz's discussions in Aiii58, Aiv316, and Aiv277 below.

10. Concerning the *mode of thought,* Leibniz had deduced that "thought consists in endeavour, as body consists in mind," so that, since "endeavour in the mind is indestructible with respect to degree of velocity," it is impossible to cease to think (A II.i 173); the *immortality of the soul* follows from the fact that "mind can no more be destroyed than a point" since "a point is indivisible" (A II.i 113); the existence of tiny *worlds within worlds to infinity* follows from the infinite divisibility of the continuum (A VI.ii 241–42; Appendix 1b), and occurs without the *penetration of dimensions* that the Stoics were accused of using to explain rarefaction and condensation—see Andrew Pyle, *Atomism and Its Critics* (Bristol: Thoemmes, 1997), pp. 127–28—an idea "which results from a false notion of matter" (Aiii2: 55); and, finally, the *propagation of minds by minds* seems to refer to the production of new whirls in the collision of existing whirls: at any rate, Leibniz had written that "A new mind can originate in a place of rectilinear collision of the actions of all suns; certainly as a result of the actions of stars" (A VI.ii 285).

## 4. On the Cohesiveness of Bodies

1. LH XXXVII 4, leaf 44. 1 sheet in folio; 1⅓ pages. Leibniz had been in the process of reworking his views on the cohesion, hardness, and continuity of bodies ever since publishing his earlier neo-Hobbesian account in the *Hypothesis physica nova,* A VI.ii 250 ff. (see Appendix 1b). This particular revision seems to have been prompted by his reading of Huygens's letter to the Abbé de Gallois, published in the *Journal des sçavans* in July 1672.

2. In terms of content, this appears to have been composed after Aiii3 above, perhaps after Leibniz's first meeting with Huygens in Paris. Certainly it is later than 25 July 1672, the date of Huygens's letter in the *Journal des sçavans,* which Leibniz obliquely alludes to within. The Akademie editors note as well that the implicit references to *Certain Physical Propositions* (Aiii2) (written between spring and fall of 1672)—whose 24th proposition he appears to have intended to adopt as the conclusion of this fragment—make the probable date of composition "not long afterward, but at the latest the winter of 1672–73." If the items noted in footnotes 3 and 4 are indeed marks of Galileo's influence, this piece would probably have been composed after Leibniz's reading notes on the *Two New Sciences* (Aiii11$_2$).

3. 'Cohesiveness' is my translation of *consistentia* (see GLOSSARY), a scientific term of the time meaning the degree to which a body holds together, its power of cohering. Leibniz had originally written *resistentia* ('resistance' = *resistenza* in Galileo's Italian), before crossing it out and replacing it with *consistentia.*

4. Leibniz had begun to write *necessarium ad continui⟨tatem contiguitatis⟩?*, (needed for the continu⟨ance of their contiguity⟩). Compare the end of the third paragraph below. The identification here of *consistentia* with the force needed to destroy the contiguity of a body's parts—i.e., with *resistentia*—may well be a mark of Galileo's influence.

5. See the *Theory of Abstract Motion* (Appendix 1c), as well as Leibniz's earlier work on accelerated motion in 1671 (A VI.ii 284), and in "Summary of a New Physical Hypothesis" (A VI.ii 349): "If a new endeavour equal to the first were always added, the motion would be accelerated in the ratio of the square numbers starting from unity, as has been demonstrated by Galileo. But it is impossible for this acceleration to be uniform. For the following endeavour is always feebler than the previous one, since the endeavour now has a smaller ratio in the aether, for [the body] is already less disturbed when it begins to move, as a result of the fact that it starts to push away the disturbing fluid."

6. This paragraph replaces the following attempts deleted by Leibniz: "I In sum continuous things are either *tenacious* or *hard*. Tenacious things are those which {can be broken into parts, hard things those which are simply wholes together—DELETED} *are transformed rather than broken up,* hard things those which are broken up rather than transformed. *Ductile things* are {those which can only be broken up into parts, even if for the whole to be [broken up]—DELETED} those of which only certain parts are separated from one another, without breaking their connection with the whole, even though there is an endeavour tending to break up the whole. *Contiguous things at rest are not continuous, or what is the same thing, they lack cohesiveness. Rest is not the cause of cohesiveness.* For the definition of *cohesiveness,* however it is resolved [into other notions], cannot be generated from the definition of rest, however that is resolved. For to rest I."

7. —reading *contiguitatis* for *contiguitas*.

8. As observed by the Akademie editors, this refers to Huygens's Letter to Gallois of 25 July 1672, "touchant les phénomènes de l'Eau purgée d'air," published in the *Journal des sçavans* (Christiaan Huygens, *Oeuvres,* VII, *Correspondance* No. 1899, pp. 201–6). Huygens ends his letter speculating that experiments may show that the force due to the pressure of his hypothesized subtle matter is perhaps "great enough to cause the union of the parts of glass and of other kinds of bodies, which hold together too well to be joined only by their contiguity and by their being at rest, as M. Descartes wanted."

9. Cf. Descartes, *Principles,* II, §44.

10. Cf. Descartes, *Principles,* II, §54: "Hence one may conclude that bodies divided into many tiny particles, agitated by diverse motions away from each other, are fluid; whereas those bodies all of whose particles are at rest against each other are hard"; and §55, "The parts of two bodies are joined by no other glue than their rest" (AT VIII.1, 71).

11. See the *Theory of Abstract Motion,* Appendix 1c.

12. Instead of this sentence Leibniz had originally written: "I For endeavour is change of place, but through a space and time infinitely less than any given perceptible one, i.e. at a moment, through a point. Some quantity, however, belongs to this

point (for elsewhere we have expelled indivisibles, i.e. things lacking parts, or minima, from the nature of things l" Given the identification of indivisibles with minima, the "elsewhere" very likely refers to "On Minimum and Maximum ..." (Aiii5) above.

13. —reading *experimentis* for the Akademie's *experti mentis.*

14. This is another indirect reference to Huygens's letter to Gallois in the *Journal des sçavans* of 25 July 1672.

15. These statements refer to Huygens's reported experimental results in the above-mentioned letter. According to Expt. 5 (pp. 205–6), titled "Two polished metal plates remain strongly attached in the void, without having anything between them," Huygens claimed to have duplicated Boyle's earlier report of the failure of the plates to separate in a vacuum, using plates—more accurately, tablets—formed from "one-inch squares of the kind of material they use to make mirrors," with a three-pound lead weight attached to the bottom one; but he does not mention Boyle's announcement in 1669 that he had succeeded in separating them after all. According to Expt. 6 (p. 206), titled "The effect of the siphon works in the void," Huygens claimed that, despite the accepted explanation of the operation of an ordinary siphon of two unequal legs in emptying a vessel of water as being due to the pressure of the atmosphere on the surface of the water, he had "found a way to make the water flow in the siphon after the receiver has been emptied of air, and I have seen that, with the water purged of air, it had its effect just the same as if it had been outside the receiver." See Steven Shapin and Simon Schaffer, *Leviathan and the Air-Pump: Hobbes, Boyle, and the Experimental Life* (Princeton: Princeton University Press, 1985), for an illuminating discussion of Huygens's criticisms of Boyle.

16. This is one of Leibniz's favorite criticisms of atomist accounts of the hardness or cohesion of bodies. Ultimately it derives from Hobbes: "Therefore [Epicurus] ought first to have shown that some bodies are maximally hard, not only relatively to soft ones, but absolutely, i.e. infinitely, hard; but this is not true." Hobbes, *De corpore,* ch. 26, §3.

17. The Akademie editors suggest that Leibniz probably has in mind Proposition 24 from version 3 of *Certain Physical Propositions* (Aiii2: 42–47): "*Heterogeneous or disturbing matter is collected into one by a general motion, even when it is outside the center of the general motion.*" In his discussion of this, Leibniz says "this proposition and its demonstration . . . is of the greatest importance for providing the reason why even different bodies cohere to one another" (43), and he proceeds to use it in explaining the results of Boyle's and Huygens's experiments with polished marble tablets in the exhausted chamber of a "Torricellian Tube."

### 5. Notes on Descartes's *Principles of Philosophy*

1. LH XXXV, 14, 2, leaves 54–55; 1 sheet in folio, 2 pages. These criticisms of Descartes are extremely interesting in revealing the maturity of Leibniz's thought on substance, extension, and the relativity of motion at an early stage of his devel-

opment. Critical remarks by Leibniz that I have not reproduced here are those on Part 1, §13 (on the mind's doubting the certainty of a demonstration), §29 (dissatisfaction with Descartes's demonstration that God cannot err), §41 (incomprehension at Descartes's claim that the freedom of the will is indubitable because clearly comprehended, after having admitted that he did not know how to reconcile it with divine providence), §§47 & 48 (on Descartes's enumeration of his "simple notions"), and §50 (on the need to demonstrate eternal truths) (Aiii15: 213–14).

2. Although Leibniz had already acquired a copy of Descartes's *Opera philosophica* in the fall of 1671, the Akademie editors note, he would have had to leave this behind in Mainz with other books, and in 1675 he writes to Simon Foucher (A II.i 247; L 153) that he has gleaned his understanding of Descartes almost entirely from other authors "who disclose his meaning 'un peu plus familierement.'" But he must already have written the present notes by 28 December 1675, when he opposes Oldenburg concerning Descartes's proof of God (A II.i 250 ff.). This is consistent with the watermark, registered for December 1675. On the evidence of contents, it was likely penned earlier than the next piece (Aiii58), which Leibniz explicitly dates as December 1675.

3. As can be seen by comparison with Descartes's Latin (AT VIII.1 9 ff.), Leibniz's quotations are by our standards more nearly accurate paraphrases.

4. The intended reference is §§34–35; see Appendix 2c.

5. Leibniz had already formulated this criticism five years earlier in the *Theory of Abstract Motion* (Appendix 1c).

6. In this comment, Leibniz appears to equate eternity with unbounded duration. Cf. Aiii33: 385, Aiii63: 481, Aiii60: 475; Aiii69: 503–4, and the GLOSSARY note on *aeternitas*.

7. Leibniz alludes to (but does not reproduce) *Figure 1* to §30 of Part 2 of Descartes's *Principles* (AT VIII.1 56; CSM.i.235), a picture of two bodies AB and CD on the Earth's surface, translated in opposite directions.

8. This could be seen as a fascinating anticipation of Mach's response to Newton's thought experiment with the rotating bucket. Newton had argued that the observable centrifugal effects of the water in the pail entailed the reality of circular motion. To this Mach replied: "Newton's experiment with the rotating vessel of water simply informs us that the relative rotation of the water with respect to the sides of the vessel produces *no* noticeable centrifugal forces, but that such forces *are* produced by its relative rotation with respect to the mass of the earth and the other celestial bodies." Ernst Mach, *The Science of Mechanics,* trans. Thomas McCormack (La Salle: Open Court, 1960), ch. 2, section 6, ¶5).

But the argument is an old one, and with the phrase *si omnia circa ipsum agantur* Leibniz is implicitly alluding to a classical source. This is revealed in a letter he wrote at about this time to Claude Perrault (1613–88), one of the founding members of the Académie des Sciences in Paris, in response to the manuscript of the *Discourse on the causes of the heaviness, resilience and hardness of bodies* that Perrault had sent him for his inspection. There Leibniz reiterated the view he had stated in the *Hypothesis physica nova:* "I believe that the motion of the aether comes from the daily motion of the light surrounding the earth, without troubling

myself whether it is the sun or the earth that turns: *circa nos omnia Deus an nos agat* [whether God moves everything around us, or moves us around], as Seneca said" (quoted from Gerhardt, "Zu Leibniz' Dynamik," p. 569). The quoted phrase occurs at the end of a passage in Seneca's *Natural Questions* (X, II, Loeb Philosophical Library, Cambridge: Harvard University Press, 1972; pp. 230–31), in which he alludes to the heliocentric hypothesis of Aristarchus of Samos.

9. This echoes the criticism expressed above in Aiii4: 95.

10. Leibniz will later systematize his criticisms of Descartes's rules of collision, showing how they violate simple continuity considerations when the relativity of motion is properly taken into account. With this in mind, this earlier critique is of some interest, in that it is given from a standpoint that presupposes both relativity of motion and elasticity.

### 6. On Matter, Motion, Minima, and the Continuum

1. From LH IV, 3, 9, leaf 7; 1 sheet of folio, 2 pages; previously published and translated by Parkinson, DSR 10–21. This piece is mainly concerned with the demonstration of the conservation of the quantity of motion, a question raised by Leibniz's reading of Descartes's *Principles of Philosophy* (see the preceding piece, Aiii15). This is connected with the issue of distinguishing matter and the void, which Leibniz had discussed with Malebranche earlier in the year, where Malebranche had argued that an extended void would have distinct parts, which would therefore be separable and movable, and therefore be parts of matter (see the exchange in G.i.321–27, reproduced in Malebranche, *Oeuvres complètes,* Tome XVIII: *Correspondance et actes 1638–1689,* ed. André Robinet, Paris: J. Vrin, 1961, pp. 96–104). In rejecting this, Leibniz had declared his belief that "it is necessary to maintain that the parts of the continuum only exist insofar as they are effectively determined by matter or motion" (Letter to Malebranche, March–April 1675 ?: G.i.322; Malebranche, *Oeuvres,* 97). The relevance of motion to the continuum problem is further explored in the present piece, giving invaluable insight into Leibniz's thinking on the continuum at the time when he was laying down the mathematical foundations of his calculus.

2. Cf. what Leibniz calls his "Herculean argument" in Aiv316: that "all those things which are such that it is impossible for anyone to perceive whether they exist or not, are nonexistent." We might call this the Principle of the Nonexistence of Imperceptibles; when it is applied to differences, we obtain the Principle of the Identity of Indiscernibles as a special case (since indiscernible things are those whose difference is in principle imperceptible, and therefore nonexistent).

3. An early version of this argument appears in "On Primary Matter," Appendix 1d: "whatever is not sensed is nothing. But that in which there is no variety is not sensed. Similarly: *If primary matter were to move in one direction, that is, in parallel lines, it would be at rest,* and consequently would be nothing." Cf. also Proposition 36 of the index of *Certain Physical Propositions* (probably composed in the fall of 1672): "If matter were left to itself (i.e. if there were no minds), every-

thing in the world would approach more and more nearly to a universal equilibrium, i.e. uniform motion, i.e. universal rest, i.e. annihilation" (Aiii2: 72).

4. Leibniz will later return to both lines of argument, the impossibility of minima and the impossibility of distinguishing a perfect fluid and empty space; see in particular "Matter and Motion Are Only Phenomena" (Aiv278) and "A Body Is Not a Substance" (Aiv317).

5. In both his *De motu* and his *Discourse on Bodies in Water,* Galileo had explicitly used the analogy with a balance to claim that "weights absolutely unequal are reciprocally counterpoised and rendered of equal momenta whenever their weights are inversely proportional to their speeds of motion" (Drake, *Two New Sciences,* p. xxix; see also R. S. Westfall, *Force in Newton's Physics,* New York: American Elsevier, 1971: pp. 27ff.); a similar formula recurs in the *Two New Sciences* (EN 217). It is presumably with the balance in mind that Leibniz ascribes the principle to Archimedes too—although he may be misremembering Galileo's attribution of it to (Pseudo-)Aristotle's *Mechanical Problems.* For Descartes, see *Principles of Philosophy,* II, §§36–37 (and Leibniz's discussion in his reading notes [Aiii15] above); for Hobbes, *De corpore,* II, ch. 8, §18.

6. Cf. Descartes, *Principles,* part II, §§36–37. Leibniz will amplify this criticism in the dialogue *Pacidius to Philalethes* (Part II below).

7. —interpreting *ipsa* as 'that', i.e. 'the quantity'. The Akademie editors instead interpolated a *natura,* which would give the reading: "But if it should be shown from the very nature of matter and the plenum that a quantity of motion is necessary, then what I want will be granted more readily."

8. By a fast-moving part of matter's "alternating," Leibniz appears to mean its alternately moving more and less slowly (reminiscently of Aristotle's interpretation of Empedocles as proposing an alternation of motion and rest [*Physics,* VIII, 1, 250b23–251a5]). For as it slows down it must become correspondingly heavier in order for the same quantity of motion to be conserved, as Parkinson suggests (DSR 127).

9. The sense of this principle appears to be that matter or body *as a whole* occupies the same amount of space in equal times, since it is granted that any particular body can occupy more or less space by speeding up or slowing down; but in the latter case, according to the principle, this must be compensated by another body slowing down or speeding up in proportion. If the change in velocity of the second body is of opposite sign to the first's and in inverse proportion to their bulks, then the Huygens-Wallis-Wren version of Descartes's conservation of quantity of motion (bulk or *moles* times velocity) will hold.

10. Cf. Descartes's argument in his *Principles,* II, §33, AT VIII.1 59; reproduced in Appendix 2c.

11. Cf. the proof of this in "On Minimum and Maximum . . ." (Aiii5) above.

12. A version of this argument, which is from Lucretius's *De summa rerum* (Book 1, 921–1051), was repeated by Descartes in his *Principles,* and recorded by Leibniz in his reading notes on that work: see Aiii15 above.

13. This accords with Huygens's explanation of the terrestial gravity of a body as resulting from the deficit of its centrifugal tendency in comparison with that of

the surrounding ether particles, which, Leibniz tells Huygens in a letter of 1690, "always seemed very plausible to me" (GM.iv.189–93; AG 310). For, on this view, rather than there being a centrifugal motion outwards of the many ether particles, there is a downward tendency of the single massive object.

### 7. An Infinite Line Is Immovable

1. LH IV 5, 10, leaf 8; written on a slip of paper; previously published by Couturat, 1903, p. 149. Leibniz's motivation for writing this piece can be understood in the light of his exchange with Malebranche the previous year (G.i.321–27; Malebranche, *Oeuvres*, XVIII, 96–104). Leibniz had objected to Malebranche's thesis that separable things are movable, giving as a counterexample an extended thing which is separated by one of its parts being destroyed (322; 97–98). To this Malebranche replied that "this does not prevent one part from moving away [*s'éloigner*] from the other, unless one wants the extended always to be represented as immovable, that is to say, to suppose what is in question" (324; 100). In reply to this, Leibniz conceded that "you [sc. Malebranche] would be right to want an adversary to prove to you himself that there is some immovable extended thing [*étendue immobile*], if you were dealing with an adversary; but you will not find one in me"; and that "at least the presumption is that everything that is extended is movable, until it is proved that there is some immovable extended thing" (103). If the extended is conceded to be unbounded—as in "Unbounded Extension" (Aiii66) below—the demonstration given here would constitute such a proof.

2. Leibniz's original title.

### 8. On Spinoza's *Ethics;* and On the Infinite

1. LH IV, 8, leaf 20; the annotations concerning Spinoza's ethics (Aiii33$_4$) are on the front of this scrap of paper, and the observation concerning the infinite (Aiii63) on the back. Although much of what Leibniz relates is not directly relevant to the continuum problem, it seemed preferable to give his notes in full rather than as a patchwork of excerpts, especially because of the importance usually attached to Spinoza as a formative influence on Leibniz's thought in this period.

2. Through the mediation of Tschirnhaus, Leibniz had long been seeking to get Spinoza's permission to look at the *Ethics,* which had existed in manuscript form for some time. Spinoza, perhaps not entirely sure of Leibniz's trustworthiness, gave permission sometime in the winter of 1675–76 for him to be apprised of some of its contents only. The Akademie editors ascribe the annotations made here to around February 1676. The further abstracts communicated to him through Ehrenfried Walther von Tschirnhaus by G. H. Schuller along with Spinoza's Letter on the Infinite (Aiii19 below), and his notes on them, appear to date from around April.

3. Leibniz elaborates on this tripartite distinction among infinities in his notes on Spinoza's Letter on the Infinite: see the "Annotated Excerpts from Spinoza" (Aiii19) below.

4. See Leibniz's explanation of this at Aiii19: 282, where he correctly states that the area comprised between the hyperbola and its asymptote is given by the sum of the (diverging) infinite series $\frac{1}{1} + \frac{1}{2} + \frac{1}{3} + \frac{1}{4} + \ldots$, which he equates to "$\frac{1}{0}$."

5. This was presumably written around the same time as the notes on Spinoza on the same sheet.

6. The addition of this 'not' seems necessary in order to make sense of the example.

### 9. On the Secrets of the Sublime

1. LH IV 3, 9, leaf 8; 1 sheet of folio, 2 pages. Previously translated in part by Loemker, L 157–60; and rendered in its entirety in Latin and English by Parkinson as DSR 20–33—to which I refer the reader for the passages not included here, as well as for Parkinson's valuable footnotes. The title given this piece by the Akademie editors is suggested by Leibniz himself in a paragraph I have not reproduced here (474–75): "God is not something metaphysical, imaginary, incapable of thought, will, or action . . . but rather a kind of substance, a person, a mind. Meditations of such a kind could be entitled *On the Secrets of the Sublime,* or even *On the Supreme Being (de summa rerum)."*

2. The Akademie editors note changes of tint and flow which perhaps indicate that this piece was not written in one go; they suggest Leibniz entered the date after writing it.

3. See GLOSSARY entry on *terrella.*

4. This is a reference to the argument in Descartes's *Principles* for the actually infinite division of matter into indefinitely small parts. See the discussion in the Introduction (Section 6); see also Appendix 2c, Aiii15 above, and especially the discussion in the *Pacidius* (Part II) below.

5. In this passage one can see many possible influences on Leibniz's thinking about the continuum. The idea of a *physical* plenum as consisting in contiguous parts whose joints "cannot be distinguished by any of the senses" is reminiscent of Gassendi (see Appendix 2e). The notion of the infinite division of a liquid plenum by the motion of a solid in it is due to Descartes, as explained above; but the interpretation of this infinite division as a division into "perfect points" echoes Galileo's argument in *Two New Sciences* (see Appendix 2b, EN 71–72), save that Galileo's indivisibles *non quante* as are for Leibniz "unassignable" points. For the latter, see the *Theory of Abstract Motion,* Appendix 1c, and Aiii3 and Aiii5 above.

6. Leibniz had first speculated about the center of the universe in "On Mind, the Universe, and God" (Aiii57: 465; DSR 8–9), concluding that there must be one "if the greatest line that can be drawn from one given point through another is a quantity."

7. See Leibniz's remarks on the "universal whirls" (i.e. those carrying the planets), the "particular whirls" (i.e. bodies), and the necessity of mind for motion, in "On Primary Matter" (Appendix 1d) below.

8. By the time he wrote "On the Origin of Things from Forms" (2nd half of April 1676?), Leibniz had abandoned this heretical opinion. See also "On the Present World" (Aiv301: 1509 below) for Leibniz's reasons why "God cannot be understood as the *World Soul*."

9. This claim that an infinite whole is one contradicts Leibniz's previous proofs that it is rather comparable to *nothing* (cf. Aiii5: 98). As discussed in Sections 6 and 7 of the Introduction, Leibniz soon repudiates the claim again. Cf. Aiii69: 503–4, Aiv301: 1509.

10. This principle that the consistency of sensations is the criterion for existence is further explored by Leibniz in a piece dated 15 April 1686 (Aiii71: 511–12, DSR 62–63).

11. The line of reasoning Leibniz is alluding to here—that the division of lines into actual points seems to entail that the circle, if it exists, has a rational quadrature—is investigated by him in detail in the piece "Infinite Numbers" below (Aiii69). See Introduction, Section 7.

12. Froidmont's book, *Labyrinthus de compositione continui* (1631), is a reactionary scholastic diatribe against atomism, on the part of Aristotelianism and the Church. Insofar as Leibniz, too, saw the wholesale abandonment of Aristotle as a mistake and a threat to piety, he would have found common ground with it. Also, of course, he agreed with Froidmont's judgment as to the centrality of the problem of the continuum. Beyond these general points of agreement, however, it is hard to see how Leibniz would have found much of value in it beyond the figure of the labyrinth itself, given the shallowness of its arguments. For an excellent study of Froidmont in relation to Leibniz, see Philip Beeley, *Kontinuität und Mechanismus* (Stuttgart: Franz Steiner, 1996), ch. 12, pp. 285–312.

13. In his *Theory of Abstract Motion* (Appendix 1c) and in "On Minimum and Maximum . . ." (Aiii5) Leibniz had defended a construal of infinitesimals as parts smaller than any that can be assigned, using the Angle of Contact as a concrete example. See GLOSSARY entries on *angulus contactus* and *infinitesimalis.*

14. The notion of the Immensum is further discussed by Leibniz in his metaphysical notes of March 18 (Aiii36: 391, DSR 43) and also in those of April (Aiii71, 74; DSR 67, 77, 79, 81, 85), all given below; so that by the time he made his notes on Spinoza's Letter on the Infinite (late April 1676?), Leibniz was able to say, "I have always distinguished the Immensum from the Unbounded, i.e. that which has no bound" (Aiii19: 281, below).

15. This is related to a classical objection to Aristotle's denial of the actual infinite, first raised by Philoponus. For Aristotle had also argued that neither time, motion, the world, nor the generations of man, had a beginning. Will there not then, Philoponus asked, already have been an actual infinity of days at any given time? See Richard Sorabji, *Time, Creation, and the Continuum: Theories in Antiquity and the Early Middle Ages* (Ithaca: Cornell University Press, 1983), pp. 214 ff. Leibniz's remark is also evocative of the "Noteworthy Observation on Infinity" he made in Aiii63 above, apparently under the stimulus of Spinoza.

16. This again refers to Descartes's argument in the *Principles* for the actually

infinite division of matter, coupled with a construal of a (perfect) liquid as one composed of actually infinitely small parts, or "perfect points."

17. Leibniz's allusion here is to his success in developing a calculus of infinitesimal sums and differences. What is in question is not the soundness of the hypothesis in geometry, but whether there could be such things in nature.

18. Again, an instance of Galilean influence. Galileo had identified the number one with the infinite, on the ground that each is equal to all its powers. See Aiii11 above.

## 10. Unbounded Extension

1. LH IV, 5, 10, leaf 63; written on a strip of paper, on the back of which there is a mathematical draft on proportions that mentions Sluse; previously published by Couturat, C 149–50.

2. The Akademie editors find no external criteria for dating, such as watermarks, but suggest that it belongs with Leibniz's other discussions of the unbounded in April 1676, especially Aiii65. It should be noted, however, that these meditations began with his reflections in "On Mind, the Universe, and God" of December 1675 about "the greatest line produced in both directions," and whether either it or eternity can be said to have a midpoint (Aiii57: 465; DSR 9); and were continued in Aiii59 (3 Jan. 1676), Aiii60 (11 Feb. 1676) and Aiii63 (Feb. 1676?), as well as more systematically in Aiii65 and Aiii69 in April. So this piece might conceivably have been composed at any time between December and April, but I believe most likely just after Leibniz had explicitly distinguished the unbounded from the infinite on 11 February (Aiii60: 475).

3. Parkinson notes (DSR 127) that Leibniz seems to understand straight lines as intrinsically unbounded when he says in "On Mind, the Universe, and God": "From a given point to a given straight line, a greatest line cannot be drawn" (Aiii57: 465; DSR 9).

## 11. Notes on Science and Metaphysics

1. LH XXXVII 6, leaves 14–16; one sheet in folio, on which the second entry (Aiii$36_2$) is also written; 1½ pages on leaf 14 recto and verso. Previously published by Parkinson (DSR 42–49), with selections from the second entry too, but with less extensive excerpts from the first. These notes appear to be fragments from a kind of diary or commonplace book that Leibniz had kept in Paris, in which he had written down anything that caught his interest. The entry of 18 March begins with sundry unconnected notes, written in French and Latin, which I have not reproduced. These include observations on acquaintances in Paris; mention of alchemical information received from one Mons. Adriano Nicosanti; a note on a letter that Tschirnhaus had shown him from Dr. Schuller of Amsterdam, reporting that "a mechanical philosopher from Delpht has improved the microscope to such an extent

that one can see even the changes which happen every day in the growth of plants, and distinguish the shapes of the gross parts of the air"; a brief note on anatomy; and some reflections on moral philosophy.

2. This remark seems to refer to Leibniz's proof of 3 January 1676 that "An Infinite Line Is Immovable," thus demonstrating (in response to Nicolas Malebranche's presumption in their correspondence of 1675 that the extended is always movable) that an unbounded body, at any rate, is not. See Aiii59 and notes. Again, if space is identified as the greatest of all extended things, and thus infinite, as in Leibniz's note on Spinoza and the infinite (Aiii33 above), it will be immovable. The possibility that extension is unbounded is explored in "Unbounded Extension" (Aiii66 above).

3. Cf. the conclusion of "On Motion and Matter" below: "there is no number of relations, which are true entities only when they are thought about by us . . . ; for they can always be multiplied by constantly reflecting on them, and so they are not real entities, or possibles, except when they are thought of"; and the opening paragraph of "Notes on Metaphysics" (Aiii39: 399–400; DSR 114–15): "It is no wonder that the number of all numbers, or that all possibilities, or all relations or reflections, are not distinctly understood; for they are imaginary, and have nothing corresponding to them in reality."

4. This has interesting similarities with the view expressed by Newton in an unpublished manuscript written a few years earlier: "Space is the affection of an entity insofar as it is an entity. No entity exists or can exist which is not related in some way to space. God is everywhere, created minds are somewhere, and body is in the space it fills; and whatever is neither everywhere nor anywhere does not exist. Hence it follows that space is the emanative effect of an entity's existing in the first place, since when the entity is posited, space is posited" (Isaac Newton, "De gravitatione et aequipondio fluidorum," pp. 89–121 in Rupert and Marie Boas Hall, ed. and trans., *Unpublished Scientific Papers of Isaac Newton,* Cambridge: Cambridge University Press, 1962, p. 103; my translation.)

5. Aristotle, *De anima,* III, 5. Cf. Alexander of Aphrodisias, *De anima,* 88, 24.

6. As the Akademie editors observe, Leibniz is referring to the dissertation he wrote as a student in Leipzig in 1663, *De principio individui,* sections 15, 25 (A VI.i 15, 18). He was to return to this theme two weeks later with the important "Meditation on the Principle of the Individual" of 1 April (Aiii67: 490–91; DSR 50–53).

7. Most of this seems directed at Spinoza: cf. Leibniz's notes on Spinoza's views about God alone being substance, on "infinite affirmative attributes," on space as "infinite in its own kind," as well as his comments on them, in Aiii33$_4$ above. But Parkinson notes that the reference to those who make God material is probably to Conrad von dem Vorst (Vorstius) and his *Tractatus theologicus de Deo* (1610), to whose thesis of God's corporeality Leibniz had referred in Aiii60: 475 (see DSR 129, 132).

8. The referents of Leibniz's pronouns here are obscure, and my interpretation is quite tentative.

9. This remark shows that Leibniz still subscribed to the doctrine of mind he had advocated in his *Theory of Abstract Motion* (Appendix 1c below; see also A VI.ii 281–85 and Aiii4 above). Building on Hobbes's idea of the mind as a kind of storehouse of endeavours, Leibniz had proposed that the distinction between body and mind lay in mind's being able to conserve endeavours (hence memory) without breaking out into motion. As he claimed in a letter to Arnauld in November 1671: "thought consists in endeavour as body consists in motion . . . every endeavour in bodies is indestructible with respect to determination, and in mind it is also indestructible with respect to degree of velocity; . . . as body consists in a stretch of motions, so mind consists in a harmony of endeavours; the present motion of a body arises from the composition of preceding endeavours; the present endeavour of a mind, i.e. its will, arises from the composition of preceding harmonious endeavours into a new one" (Aiii II.i.173).

10. Leibniz apparently again has Spinoza in mind here; cf. his remark about the latter's believing "in a kind of Pythagorean transmigration, at least that minds go from body to body" (Aiii33: 385). The "new experiments" that refute this are those of the famous microscopist Marcello Malpighi of 1673, which were thought to establish preformation (see Parkinson's note in DSR 132).

### 12. On the Plenitude of the World

1. LH IV 1, 14c, leaf 8; 1½ pages. Previously published (in part) by Couturat in C 10 ff., and in complete edition and translation by Parkinson as DSR 84–89.

2. Leibniz entered '1676' at the head of this piece at some later time, but precisely when in that year it was written is uncertain. (There is no watermark on the paper.) The discussion of atoms and the plenum in the second, third, and last paragraphs seem to recapitulate the arguments of "Secrets of the Sublime" of 11 February, but it is not clear whether what is said about atoms and vortices was written after the similar discussions in the notes of 18 March (Aiii36). The themes of the first paragraph are closely connected to ones sounded in papers of *De summa rerum* written in the second half of April (Aiii71–75, DSR 56–85), suggesting it was written at about that time. Against this, though, his claim here that "there are as many different relations in the universe as there are minds" is refuted by his arguments on 10 April that "there is no number of relations," in contrast to "the multiplicity of things[, which] is something determinate" (Aiii58: 495). Moreover, here he upholds an unassignable vacuum, from which it follows that "an unassignable quantity is something" (Aiii.525). But in "Infinite Numbers" (c. 10 April) he claims that he has "shown that the unassignable is nothing other than [a point, an extremum]" (Aiii69: 498), which may refer to Aiii52 of 26 March. These considerations suggest that the piece was composed earlier in March.

3. Here *confusas* ("fused together") echoes the earlier *confuse* ("confusedly"), as does *confusas in unum* further on. The literal translation is intended to bring out Leibniz's meaning: the perceptions are not confused in the sense of being disturbed

or thrown into disorder, but are *fused together* from an infinite aggregate of smaller and smaller perceptions, none of which is consciously discerned. See GLOSSARY note on *confuse*.

4. Cf. "On Forms, or on the Attributes of God" (Aiii72: 514; DSR 68–69): "The reason why those things in which there is some variety, such as color, are not perceived distinctly by us is that we perceive a color at some definite time; yet this time can be subdivided into infinitely many parts, and in any of its parts we will have acted in a way pertinent to the case, but will not remember, because of a defect of our organs."

5. Compare "A Chain of Wonderful Demonstrations About the Universe" of 12 December 1676: "It seems very much in accord with reason that primitive *bodies* should all be spherical, but that their directions should all be rectilinear" and "Hence all things are made of globes, and even if globes were not the most basic elements, there would still always be a reduction to globes; therefore it would be useless for there to be a variety of shapes among atoms, so that it suffices for atoms all to be globular" (Aiii85: 585; DSR 109).

6. This evokes Leibniz's remarks in the HPN about the "hooks, crooks, globules and so much other apparatus" ascribed to atoms being "too remote from the simplicity of nature and from any experiments, and too naive to be connected in any obvious way with the phenomena" (A VI.ii 248).

7. Again, compare with Aiii85: "Cohering bodies arise from the fact that if certain bodies are composed into an arch that is hollow inside, that is, full of more subtle matter, this arch would be difficult to break up, because the pores left by the component bodies are too small to be penetrated by the surrounding matter so as to fill the place" (585).

8. The first hypothesis—that atoms all move with equal velocity—is that of the classical atomists: "through undisturbed vacuum all bodies must travel at equal speed though impelled by unequal weights"—Lucretius, *De rerum natura,* Book II, 1. 270 ff. (in Ronald Latham's translation, *On the Nature of the Universe,* Harmondsworth/Baltimore: Penguin, 1951, p. 67). The second hypothesis—that velocities are inversely proportional to magnitudes—is established a priori by Leibniz in Aiii58 above.

### 13. On the Infinitely Small

1. LHXXXV, 13, 3, leaves 22–25; on one of two strips cut off from the top of a sheet, on which Aiii51 is also written. Although short, this piece is of the greatest importance. The proof given here that the differentials of his calculus are not infinitely small actuals but "nothing at all" is relevant to Leibniz's attempts over the next two weeks to construe infinitesimals (and also last members of converging series, and limit-figures such as circles and parabolas) as fictions (cf. Aiii68, 69, below).

2. The Akademie editors note that Leibniz obviously inserted the date above the text after writing the note.

3. For an insightful analysis of Leibniz's construal of differentials as "nothings," see Herbert Breger, "Le Continu chez Leibniz," in Jean-Michel Salanski and Hourya Sinaceur, eds., *Le Labyrinthe du continu* (Paris: Springer-Verlag France, 1992), pp. 76–84.

4. Leibniz is referring to his construal of curves as (circumscribed or inscribed) polygons with infinitely many infinitely small sides (the differentials). As he will argue in "Infinite Numbers" below, this means that a curve can be construed as an ideal limit of a sequence of such polygons, so that its length $L$ will be the limit of a sequence of sums $ns$ of their sides $s$ as their number $n \to \infty$. Although he does not give the proof, if the error $L - ns$ is less than $s$ for every $n$, then it will be so as $n \to \infty$. Similarly, the sum of an infinite series is construed by Leibniz as a limit of a sequence of partial sums. In the case of a converging alternating infinite series, like the series $\pi/4 = 1 - \frac{1}{3} + \frac{1}{5} - \frac{1}{7} + \dots$, the absolute value of the $n$th term is always greater than or equal to the remainder (i.e. to the sum minus the $n$th partial sum). Thus the error in terminating the series at the $n$th term is always less than the $n$th term. This is standardly called "Leibniz's alternating series test"—see, e.g., M. A. Munem and D. J. Foulis, *Calculus and Analytic Geometry* (New York: Worth, 1984), p. 670.

5. It is interesting to compare this with what Leibniz says in his masterwork on the calculus, the *De quadratura arithmetica,* written between the end of 1675 and fall 1676, recently published in a critical edition with commentary by Eberhard Knobloch (*De quadratura arithmetica circuli ellipseos et hyperbolae cujus corollarium est trigonometria sine tabulis,* Göttingen: Vandenhöck & Ruprecht, 1993), especially the Scholium to Prop. 23, p. 69: "Nor does it matter whether there are such quantities [as infinities and infinitesimals] in the nature of things, for it suffices that they be introduced by a fiction, since they allow abbreviations of speech and thought in discovery as well as in demonstration. . . . [M]y readers . . . will sense how much the field has been opened up when they correctly perceive this one thing, that every curvilinear figure is nothing but a polygon with an infinite number of sides, of an infinitely small magnitude. And if Cavalieri or even Descartes himself had considered this sufficiently, they would have produced or anticipated more."

6. See T. L. Heath, ed., *The Works of Archimedes,* reprint of 1897 ed. (New York: Cambridge, 1953), pp. 221–32.

## 14. Unbounded Lines

1. LH IV 3, 9, leaves 11–12; this is written on the front and back of leaf 11 of this sheet of folio (on leaf 12, whose bottom half is cut off, are Aiii72 and 73; DSR 11 and 12). Motivationally, this piece seems connected with Leibniz's desire to prove that even a spatially and temporally unbounded universe has a midpoint, and his belief that "It is necessary for us to be in the middle of the universe, and at the middle instant of eternity" (Aiii57: 465; DSR 9). Ellipses replace Leibniz's "*etc.*"

2. In the first part of "On Motion and Matter" (Aiii68), written between 1 and

10 April, Leibniz apparently refers to a demonstration from this piece (that it is impossible for an unbounded line to move along its own path), implying that this was the earlier of the two. After writing the date, Leibniz originally began this piece as follows, before crossing it out and beginning again: "⌐ If an unbounded line is a kind of unity and whole, endowed with magnitude, let us see what follows. First, whatever can be made greater or less certainly seems to be endowed with magnitude. But to the unbounded line *CB . . . , DC* can be added, or *CE* can be taken away. If then *DB . . . , CB . . .* and *EB . . .* are wholes endowed with magnitude, one of them, at any rate, will be greater than another, so that ⌐."

3. Before 'once' Leibniz had written 'recently': he presumably had in mind the proof he had given the previous December that the universe has a midpoint by equating the greatest straight lines drawn in opposite directions from the same point (Aiii57: 465).

### 15. On Motion and Matter

1. LH IV 1, 8: leaves 1–2; 1 sheet of folio. This piece is the second of four (Aiii67–70), all written on the same sheet of folio. The first 46 lines are on leaf 1 r° and v°, and the piece "Infinite Lines," reproduced below, straddles its conclusion, dated 10 April, on leaf 2 v°. It comes immediately after the *Meditation on the Principle of the Individual* (Aiii67; DSR 50–53); there, on the premise that two different things must always differ in themselves in a certain respect, Leibniz had argued that any two apparently perfectly similar material things must differ in retaining the effect of their prior states, which can only happen by the persistence in each of them of a mind. This "proves that matter is not homogeneous, and that we cannot really think of anything by which it differs except mind" (Aiii67: 491). In this paper one can see this consideration playing upon his thought, as Leibniz struggles to come to terms with the metaphysical implications of his calculus. His recent discovery that "endeavours are true motions, not infinitely small ones," coupled with his mathematical construal of the circle as an infinite polygon with infinitesimal sides, seems to lead him immediately into the exploration of a discretist conception of motion and matter.

2. This fragment follows immediately after Aiii67 of 1 April 1676, and its conclusion is dated 10 April.

3. Like the Akademie editors, I have been unable to locate the demonstration Leibniz refers to here. It may refer to a demonstration in the differential calculus. For if the endeavour of a body, or element of its velocity $dv$, is defined as the quotient of the differential of space $ds$ by the differential of time $dt$, Leibniz may have proved that this quotient ($ds/dt$) differs from a finite velocity by a quantity less than any assignable. More geometrically, this means that the slope $dv$ of the characteristic triangle $ds$-$dt$-$dv$ at a given point on a graph of distance against time for a moving body differs from that of the tangent to the curve at that point by an infinitesimal, and thus null, amount. If so, the body could be regarded as having a finite velocity directed in a straight line tangent to the curve at any point. The curve,

meanwhile, is regarded as composed of a certain infinite progression of infinitely small straight lines. See Aiii52 above.

4. Hippocrates' lunule is a figure like the crescent or gibbous moon: it is a section bounded by the arcs of two circles, the first being a semicircle whose diameter is the chord of a segment of the second. The source of Leibniz's knowledge of Hippocrates' squarable circular lunule is Léotaud's *Examen circuli quadraturae,* which he read in Nuremberg in 1667. See Joseph E. Hofmann, *Leibniz in Paris, 1672–1676* (Cambridge: Cambridge University Press, 1974), pp. 5 ff., for a brief but illuminating discussion.

5. See Hobbes, *De corpore,* ch. 21, "On Circular Motion."

6. Leibniz seems to be alluding to his demonstration in "Unbounded Lines" that the motion of the unbounded line *LH* along its own path is impossible (Aiii65: 489), implying that that piece was written earlier in April.

7. The Akademie editors suggest that Leibniz is referring to prop. 3. of *A Demonstration of Incorporeal Substances* (Aiii3$_1$: 75) of the fall of 1672: "*All perceivable bodies in the world are continued from one to another,*" i.e. form a series of contiguous bodies. There he claims that "This proposition can also be admitted by those who find the interspersed vacuum pleasing; for the continuity and connection of the sea is not interrupted by the fact that islands are seen to be scattered in it here and there. . . . I say therefore that the parts of the plenum are interspersed by a vacuum . . . , by which fact the propagation of actions and motions is not interrupted, even if it happens by circuitous paths, as when, for example, we sense sound insinuating itself along curves in the air that are spread out in all directions."

8. In classical mathematics, one was only allowed to take ratios of quantities of the same kind, e.g. a volume to a volume, a speed to a speed. Equating ratios of magnitude and speed in a proportion violates the requirement of homogeneity. For Leibniz's notion of homogeneity see "Infinite Numbers" (Aiii69 below), and the discussion in his Preface to the *New Essays* (NE 63–64; AG 302–3). The "marvelous secret" referred to here—concerning the mutual compensation of speed and magnitude—was demonstrated in Aiii58 above.

9. Here Leibniz first had "of the relative speed [*celeritate respect⟨iva⟩*]," and then "of the force, or a⟨ction⟩," before finally settling on "of the action, i.e. relative motion."

10. The significance of this is further examined below in "Motion Is Something Relative" (Aiv360).

11. —reading *eiusque* for *eumque*.

12. This difficult task is taken up by Leibniz later in the year in the dialogue *Pacidius to Philalethes* (Part II below).

13. In his *De corpore,* ch. 8, § 19, Hobbes had argued: "*Whatever is moved will always be moved, unless there is some other body outside it which causes it to come to rest;* for if we suppose there is nothing outside it, there will be no reason why it should come to rest now rather than at some other time; thus its motion would cease in every point of time together, which is unintelligible" (pp. 102–3).

14. It is hard to follow Leibniz's reasoning here; I take him to be arguing that, on the hypothesis of continuous motion, one can prove both that motion is perpetual

and that it is possible for it to stop when opposed by an equal and opposite motion; therefore the hypothesis is false.

15. In Book VIII, ch. 1 of the *Physics,* Aristotle claims that Empedocles' account of motion is that "Love and Strife alternately predominate and cause motion, while in the intermediate period of time there is a state of rest" (252a 7–9), basing this on his reading of a fragment (Diels-Kranz Fragment 26, lines 8–12) that concludes: "But since their motion must alternate be, / Thus have they ever Rest upon their round." Aristotle explains that "we must suppose that by 'alternate' he means that they change from the one motion to the other" (251a 1–5).

16. Here Leibniz probably has in mind his spherical atoms (see Aiii36, Aiii76) which will no longer be properly spherical if all circles are polygons with arbitrarily many straight sides.

17. This argument is elaborated in greater detail in *Pacidius to Philalethes* (Part II below).

18. Cf. Aiii36: 391 above, and Aiii39: 399–400; DSR 114–15.

### 16. Infinite Numbers

1. LH IV 1, 8: leaves 1–2; 1 sheet of folio. As remarked above, these reflections continue those of the preceding piece, whose concluding paragraph they straddle. The two pieces together are vital for understanding the profound changes affecting Leibniz's thinking on the continuum at this time, and of how the foundation of the continuum in terms of endeavours gives way to the discontinuist doctrine explored in the *Pacidius* later in the year. Particularly important in this connection is Leibniz's new understanding of the differentials or infinitesimals of his calculus as fictions, rather than infinitely small (but unassignable) actuals (cf. Aiii52 above), which characterization Leibniz had extended in Aiii68 to precise geometric figures such as circles. Here he reaffirms this, and one can see his doctrine of *petites perceptions* emerging from it as a corollary. The main theme of this piece is the nonexistence of infinite number and the infinitely small actual. The scene is set by his earlier remark (Aiii60: 474 above) that their existence would entail the commensurability of all parts of matter, so that "the circle, if it exists, would have a ratio to its diameter as number to number." This is what Leibniz begins by investigating here, whence he proceeds to an anticipation of Legendre's conjecture that pi is transcendental, to a replacement of his earlier characterization of angles as infinitely small actuals by one in terms of a ratio still existing in the limit, to a correct conception of the sum of a converging infinite series as a limit of partial sums, a redefinition of magnitude, and the denial that an infinite aggregate is one whole. The first four of Leibniz's notes consist of the word 'error' written by each statement that two commensurable lines will be "as finite number to finite number," an assumption that he was led to question after reaching the end of the second paragraph (see para. 3 below: "And now I see the reason for the error . . ."). Ellipses replace Leibniz's "*etc.*"

2. This piece follows Aiii67, dated 1 April 1676, and the beginning of Aiii68; it ends after the conclusion of Aiii68, which is dated 10 April.

3. Leibniz had denoted the rectilinear figure QRST and "QSTR," and the infinitely small square αβγ of the curvilinear figure as "αβ." I have also added a point 'U' to his figure 3, so that the square he denoted "XQZ" becomes "XQZU." I have also tacitly adopted corrections by the Akademie editors of other minor errors of this kind.

4. Thus $QT$, the abscissa common to the two figures, is drawn vertically, and the ordinates $ZY$ and $Z\omega$ are drawn horizontally on either side of it. This is the inverse of the modern convention, where abscissae are drawn horizontally and ordinates vertically.

5. To have assumed that "two finite commensurable lines are as finite number to finite number" is not really an "error." But Leibniz has seen that his quadrature of the circle depends not on the ordinates of the figures being equal to a finite number of finite common measures, but to an infinite number of infinitesimal common measures. So he defines an extended commensurability in terms of a ratio of infinite whole numbers.

6. Leibniz's idea appears to be that that two infinite primes would still have 1 as a finite common measure, even though they would not be expressible as finite number to finite number. Correspondingly, he argues, if circle and square are commensurable in this extended sense, they could have an infinitely small common measure.

7. Leibniz was aware that although the "rational quadrature" of the hyperbola—that is, the expression of the ratio between the area under a hyperbola and that under the corresponding square as a rational fraction—had been accomplished by Gerardus Mercator and William Brouncker, no one had managed this for the circle. The "approximations" referred to here are undoubtedly those of John Wallis (in terms of an infinite product) and Brouncker (in terms of an infinite continued fraction), of which Leibniz was aware. See Joseph E. Hofmann, *Leibniz in Paris,* p. 95; Leibniz to Oldenburg, 16 October 1674 (*BG:* 107).

8. In asserting that the magnitude of a unit circle "cannot be expressed by an equation of any degree," Leibniz is effectively asserting that $\pi$ is a transcendental number.

9. Here Leibniz presumably has in mind the inscribed and circumscribed polygons by means of which Archimedes was able to find the area of a circle by a double *reductio.*

10. Thus the area $A$ of an $n$-sided regular polygon, whether inscribed or circumscribed, is made up of $n$ triangles of base $b$, height $h$, and area $\frac{1}{2}bh$, so that $A = \frac{1}{2}nbh$. As $n$ increases, the perimeter of the polygon, $nb$, approaches more and more closely to the circumference of the limiting circle ($2\pi r$), and the height $h$ closer and closer to $r$, so that $A$ approaches more and more nearly to $\frac{1}{2} \cdot (2\pi r) \cdot r = \pi r^2$. This "the mind declares to be perfectly so in the ultimate polygon," the circle.

11. Here Leibniz is reiterating his earlier views, as expressed in Aiii5: 99 above.

12. Although Leibniz's mature doctrine of *petites perceptions* is prefigured in other passages in his early writings, nowhere else is its intimate connection with his reflections on the status of unassignables, infinitesimals, and limits revealed so

clearly as here. For his mature views, see the *New Essays on Human Understanding,* and Remnant and Bennett's note on "minute perceptions" (NE 1v–1vi).

13. This resumes Leibniz's discussion where he had left off in "Unbounded Lines" (Aiii65 above).

14. The two points '1' and '2' were inadvertently omitted in figure 4; I have inserted them accordingly. I have also renamed the two parts of the unbounded line "*C2 etc.*" and "*C1 etc.*," where Leibniz mistakenly had "*C etc.*" and "*1 etc.*"

15. Here Leibniz continues his exploration of the idea that motion is strictly discontinuous, begun in "On Motion and Matter" above. The new term he coins here, "transcreation," reappears in the dialogue *Pacidius to Philalethes* below, where the idea is discussed more thoroughly. See also the discussion of "transproduction" below (503).

16. Here Leibniz returns to a problem that had troubled him in "Unbounded Lines," concerning the oblique motion of such lines. Having been unable to reach a conclusion there, he gives it another try here.

17. The converging infinite series cited, whose sum is $\pi/4$, is now known as "Leibniz's Series" in honor of Leibniz's discovery of it in 1674. See his own account of this discovery in *Historia et origo calculi differentialis* (ed. C. I. Gerhardt, Hanover, 1846), translated as pp. 22–58 in J. M. Child, *The Early Mathematical Manuscripts of Leibniz* (Chicago: Open Court, 1920): p. 42. The square is circumscribed about the circle so that the diameter $d$ of the circle is the side of the square, and the ratio of their areas is $\pi d^2/4 : d^2$, or $\pi/4 : 1$.

18. Compare to the definition in "On Magnitude" (Aiii64: 482; DSR 36–37): "magnitude is that through which it is recognized whether a thing is a whole." A little further on in that piece, he gives a more sophisticated definition: "*Quantity or Magnitude* is that according to which some thing (which is called *so much*) is said to be capable of being *congruent* with a certain other thing (i.e. capable of being brought within the same boundaries)." This is good evidence that Aiii64 is the later of the two.

19. This is a close anticipation of the modern definition of the sum of a converging infinite series as the limit of its partial sums $S_n$ as $n \to \infty$.

20. Leibniz had mistakenly corrected *in serie interminata* to *in serie linea.* The Akademie editors altered this to read *in linea interminata,* but the original *in serie interminata* gives the proper sense.

### 17. Annotated Excerpts From Spinoza

1. LB 886, leaves 5–6, 1 sheet of folio of $3\frac{2}{3}$ columns; previously published by Gerhardt, G.i.131–38. As Leibniz's own title for this piece indicates, these excerpts from Spinoza's writings (on which his annotations are almost as long as the original) were taken from a letter by G. H. Schuller, who had presumably communicated them to him with Spinoza's permission through the mediation of Walther von Tschirnhaus. Schuller was an Amsterdam doctor of Spinoza's acquaintance, and Leibniz was already indebted to Tschirnhaus for information on the *Ethics* (see

Aiii33$_4$). The fragments in the first two sections are drawn from a draft of Spinoza's *Ethics,* Propositions 8, 13, and 14, and Definitions 3 and 6. These fragments may be compared to the canonical versions in Gebhardt, SO.ii (Latin), and Curley SC 408–9 (English); although as usual I give my own translations here. The third section reproduces the philosophical part of Spinoza's famous "Letter on the Infinite" (Letter 12 in his edited Correspondence), written by him on 20 April 1663 to his longtime friend Lodewijk Meyer. Leibniz's version of the main text of this letter is published by Gebhardt on the bottom halves of pages 53–62 of SO.iv, and the edited version of it from the *Opera posthuma* on p. 52 and the top halves of pp. 53–62. Gebhardt says that Leibniz's copy "perhaps gives the original of the letter, at any rate a version again deviating from the edition of the *Op. Posth.*" (SO.iv.390). Curley translates the latter version in his SC 200–205, as does Shirley in his translation (Baruch Spinoza, *The Ethics and Selected Letters,* trans. Samuel Shirley & ed. Seymour Feldman, Indianapolis: Hackett, 1982), pp. 231–35.

2. The watermark of the paper used by Leibniz is registered for February 1676. But the Akademie editors note that Leibniz's extracts "were presumably written not long before 2 May 1676," since Tschirnhaus—perhaps prompted by Leibniz—raised a question concerning the "Letter on the Infinite" (from which he quotes) in a letter to Spinoza of this date (see n. 13 below), in which he also mentions "mijn Heer Leibnits" (SO.iv.331). In support of this late April dating, it appears that Schuller communicated these extracts some time after 18 March, for on that date Leibniz describes the contents of a (presumably different) letter from Schuller shown him by Tschirnhaus, without mentioning Spinoza (in Aiii36$_1$: 390). Lastly, certain phrasings in Leibniz's "On Magnitude" (Aiii64; DSR 36–43) show signs of possible influence from his reading of Spinoza here (see n. 11 below). It is not known when "On Magnitude" was written, but it seems to have been written not long after "Infinite Numbers" (Aiii69), which was finished after 10 April.

3. Leibniz's original title.

4. This refers to Spinoza's Prop. 8: "Every substance is necessarily infinite"; Prop. 13: "An absolutely infinite substance is indivisible"; and Prop. 14: "No substance can be or be conceived besides God"; and their accompanying demonstrations, from Book I of the *Ethics* (SO.ii.49, 55–56; SC 412, 420).

5. This differs slightly from Definition 3 of the official version in the *Ethics:* "By substance I understand that which is in itself and is conceived through itself, that is, that whose concept does not require the concept of another thing, from which it must be formed" (SO.ii.45, SC 408).

6. This is identical with Definition 6 from Spinoza's *Ethics,* except that the last phrase of the definition in Leibniz's copy, "and is thus immense," is missing from the published version.

7. This is identical with the gloss on Definition 6 appearing in the *Ethics,* except that the last qualification given in the latter is missing from Leibniz's excerpt: "but if something is absolutely infinite, whatever expresses essence and involves no negation pertains to its essence" (SO.ii.45–46, SC 408).

8. Boethius (480–525/6) denied that it was proper to ascribe duration to eternity: see Richard Sorabji's discussion in *Time, Creation, and the Continuum,* pp.

115 ff. In his *Consolation of Philosophy,* 5.6, Boethius wrote: "What is subject to the condition of time is not yet such as to be judged eternal, even if, as Aristotle believed of the world, it never began to exist, and does not cease, but has its life stretched out with the infinity of time" (quoted from Sorabji, ibid., pp. 119–20). Perhaps even more pertinent is the view of Philoponus: "Eternity . . . should not be cut, like time, into discrete segments. . . . Rather, [Plato] thinks eternity is some single, uniform extension ( *paratasis*), not cut by any differentiation, but staying always (*aei*) the same, and remaining without change in itself" (ibid., p. 118).

9. Thomas White argued this in detail in his *Quaestio praevia: Utrum in continuo sunt partes actu* (A Leading Question: Whether There Are Actually Parts in the Continuum), §§ 1 and 2; Sir Kenelm Digby in his *Two Treatises* (Paris: Gilles Blaizot, 1644), "A Treatise of Bodies," chapter 2, especially § 4 ("If partes were actually in theire whole, Quantity would bee composed of indivisibles") and § 5 ("Quantity cannot be composed of indivisibles"). Leibniz had criticized the doctrine (as set forth by White in his first preface to Digby's *On the Immortality of the Soul*) some years previously, in his *Demonstration of the Possibility of the Mysteries of the Eucharist* (1668?; A VI.i n.15), where he declared White's opinion "that the parts of a thing are not in it actually" to be "in hersesy" and "absurd" (504).

10. Leibniz added then crossed out the '*non*' ("not"); but it is necessary for the sense, and is there in the canonical edition of Spinoza (cf. SC 202).

11. There are perhaps echoes of this in Leibniz's "On Magnitude," where he writes: "Time is not duration, any more than space is collocation. . . . Time is a certain continuum with respect to which something is understood to endure. . . ." (Aiii64: 484).

12. See Hobbes, *De Corpore,* II, ch. VII, § 2: "*space is the phantasm of an existing thing, insofar as it is existing,* that is, with no other accident of the thing considered beyond the fact that it appears outside the person imagining"; § 3: "*time is the phantasm of motion, insofar as we imagine in motion an earlier and a later, i.e. succession.*"

13. Here "divided in continuous proportion" means that each two successive terms are in the same ratio, here 1:2; and a "double geometrical progression" means a geometrical series in which each term is twice its successor. The "no book can be found" argument is reminiscent of AIII52 above.

14. In his letter to Spinoza of 2 May 1676, Tschirnhaus raises precisely this objection: "I was desirous to learn from you how one is to understand what you remind us of in the Letter on the Infinite with these words: 'Yet they do not conclude that such things exceed every number because of the multiplicity of their parts.' For it seems to me that, concerning such infinities, all mathematicians always demonstrate that the number of parts is so great that they exceed every assignable number, and with respect to the same matter in the example employed concerning the two circles, you do not seem to prove exactly what you had undertaken to. For there you show merely that they do not draw the conclusion in question from the excessive magnitude of the intervening space, 'and the fact that we do not know its maximum and minimum'; but you do not demonstrate, as you wanted to, that 'they do not conclude it from the multiplicity of the parts'" (Tschirnhaus to Spinoza, Letter 80,

SO 331). Spinoza replied that if the infinity of the parts were concluded from their multiplicity, the latter "would have to be greater than any given, which is false. For in the whole space between the two non-concentric circles we conceive the multiplicity of parts to be twice as great as in half the space, and yet the number of parts in both the half-space and the whole is greater than any assignable number" (Spinoza to Tschirnhaus, 5 May 1676; Letter 81, SO 332). I do not believe that Leibniz would have been persuaded by this reply, if he saw it. For it is hard to see how one multiplicity can be twice the other if no number is assignable to either of them.

15. Cardano maintained the doctrine that one infinity is greater than another in "Arithm. Pract. c. 66. n. 165 and 260," according to Leibniz in his dissertation *De arte combinatoria* of 1666 (A VI.i 229). As for Leibniz's own view, see "Infinite Numbers" (Aiii69: 497) above, where he concluded that "there can be two infinite commensurable numbers which are not as two finite numbers, if their greatest common measure is a finite number—for example, if both are prime." That is, for Leibniz two infinite numbers are not only not necessarily equal: they may not even have a finite ratio.

16. Leibniz had articulated this distinction concerning the three degrees of infinity in much the same terms in his notes on Spinoza (Aiii33$_4$) above.

17. See Leibniz's discussions of the unbounded above, especially in Aiii66, 65, and 69.

18. Chasdaj (or Hasdai) Crescas (c. 1340–1410), a Spanish-Jewish critic of Aristotle and Maimonides, published this argument in his *Or Adonai,* 1555, book I, proposition 3. See H. A. Wolfson, *Crescas' Critique of Aristotle* (Cambridge: Harvard University Press, 1929).

19. The '*nisi*' ('unless') is Leibniz's addition, and is not found in Gebhart or Curley (SC 205). Yet it seems necessary to give the correct sense.

## 18. On Body, Space, and the Continuum

1. LH IV 3, 9: leaf 8; 1 sheet of folio, 2 pages; written on the back of this sheet in parts over figures and calculations. Previously translated in part by Loemker, L 161–162; and rendered in its entirety in Latin and English by Parkinson in DSR 21–33—to which I refer the reader for the passages not given here.

2. The Akademie editors note that Leibniz probably added the date after writing the piece.

3. Cf. the discussion of the equinumerousness of minds, solid bodies, and the vortices they stir up, in Aiii36: 393 above.

4. Leibniz had argued that on the supposition that "the more our sensation is scrutinized, the more consistent it will be," and given that "our sensation has always been consistent," it follows that space and the world are infinite, and the world is eternal. "So the thesis of the eternity and infinity of the world depends upon the probability of the perpetual consistency of things for us; in other words, on the probability of our always being able to discover and agree upon their cause, providing we have enough time to inquire into it." Yet there could be "another

world or other minds that are consistent with each other in another way, yet not consistent with us." This notion of consistency (*congruentia*) of perceptions as "the mark of existence" is a recurrent theme of the Paris notes (see Aiii60: 474); and this notion, as well as the conception of space as "that which brings it about that several perceptions cohere with each other at the same time," is taken up again later in this piece (DSR 62–65).

5. Cf. Leibniz's remarks about space being only a consequence of God's immensity, and also about its undergoing continuous change, in Aiii36: 391 above.

6. Here Leibniz wrote and crossed out "*Ideo praeter liquidum et*": perhaps "Therefore besides liquid ⟨there must⟩ also ⟨be space⟩."

7. Descartes's account of the cohesiveness of bodies is considered by Leibniz in "On the Cohesiveness of Bodies" (Aiii4) above.

8. LH IV 3, 9: leaf 9; 1 leaf of folio, 2 pages on both sides of the sheet; also on this sheet are Aiii37, *Exemplum obtrectationis* (An Instance of Spiteful Treatment); and Aiii75, *De formis simplicibus* (On Simple Forms; DSR 82–85). Previously translated in part by Loemker, L 163 ff.; and rendered in its entirety in Latin and English by Parkinson as DSR 74–83, to which I refer the reader for the passages not given here.

9. This is on the same sheet as Aiii75, "On Simple Forms," which continues the same themes, and is dated by Leibniz April 1676.

10. Leibniz had already called it this in "On the Secrets of the Sublime" (Aiii60: 475) above. Cf. also Aiii36: 391 and Aiii71 above.

11. Cf. Leibniz's remarks on the motion of a body as an "expansion," and on the equivalence of conservation of motion and conservation of matter, in "On Matter, Motion, and the Continuum" (Aiii58: 469) above.

12. This metaphor of the net presages that of the "folds of matter" outlined in the *Pacidius Philalethi* later in the year. For a fascinating exploration of Leibniz in terms of this metaphor see Gilles Deleuze, *Le Pli: Leibniz et le baroque* (full reference at n. 12 of the Introduction).

### 19. Pacidius to Philalethes

1. LH XXXV 10, 11. A Latin edition was published by Couturat, C 594–627. There is a rough draft of the manuscript in Leibniz's hand (here symbolized $L^1$) on leaves 35–46 (6 sheets of quarto, 23 pages); a corrected partial fair copy of the beginning of $L^1$ (symbolized $L^2$) on leaves 31–32 (2 sheets of quarto, 4 pages); and a corrected fair copy of $L^2$ and most of $L^1$ in the hand of a secretary (symbolized $l$) on leaves 1–30 (15 sheets of quarto, 59 pages). The Akademie edition follows $l$ on pp. 529–67—occasionally corrected by reference to $L^2$ (up to p. 533) and $L^1$—and is based on $L^1$ alone from p. 568 to the end (p. 571). I have adopted the Akademie editors' corrections of obvious errors and omissions in $l$, usually made by reference to $L^1$, without recording them (save in the one or two cases where I have demurred). Of the marginal notes by Leibniz recorded in the Akademie edition, I have left out two that are irrelevant to the piece's contents (having to do largely with nautical

matters relevant to his journey), and two others that are mere marks I have recorded in my footnotes.

2. See Eric Aiton, *Leibniz: A Biography* (Bristol: Adam Hilger, 1985), pp. 67ff.

3. *Guilielmi Pacidii de rerum arcanis,* Aiii77: 526–27; Latin and English translation in Parkinson, DSR 88–91. For Leibniz's evolving conception of the encyclopedia, see Catherine Wilson's *Leibniz's Metaphysics,* esp. pp. 16–19, 266.

4. In his first draft, the labyrinth of the continuum was the only labyrinth, numbered (5); then, having inserted the other labyrinth and renumbered, his description of this "second labyrinth" in his second draft was the same as in the third and final draft.

5. See Parkinson's excellent note, DSR 136, n. 1, for this explanation, as well as other suggestions and references.

6. On Schütz, see Hoffmann, *Leibniz in Paris,* pp. 46, 164–65. Neither he nor Aiton say whether he is related to Baron Ludwig Justus Sinold von Schütz, who later gave Leibniz assistance in his capacity as Brunswick ambassador in London; see Aiton, pp. 171, 260, 318.

7. For Schelhammer, again see Hoffmann, *Leibniz in Paris,* pp. 147, 362; and Aiton, *Leibniz,* p. 235.

8. Leibniz's original title.

9. Before deciding on this neutral last ascription after naming Galen, Leibniz had written and crossed out first "or of Paracelsus," then "or of the Hermeticists," then "or of the Democrit⟨eans⟩."

10. In the light of my conjecture that "Charinus" is modeled on Tschirnhaus, compare Pacidius's "it is easy for me to tell from this what can be expected of you if you get the right guidance" with what Leibniz wrote to Oldenburg the previous December: "Your sending Tschirnhaus to us is a token of your friendship, for I take great delight in his company and recognize outstanding ability in the youth. His discoveries are very promising, and he has shown me a number of elegant ones in analysis and geometry. *I can easily judge from this what may be expected of him*" (GM.i.83; quoted from L 165, my emphasis).

11. According to Aristotle, Plato posited "intermediate natures" in addition to, and between, sensible things and Forms; these are "mathematical objects, differing from sensible things in being eternal and immobile, and from the Forms in that they are many and alike, whereas the Form itself is only one in each case" (*Metaphysics,* I 6, 987b 14–18; see also I 9, 991b 27–29; II 2, 997a 34–b3, 12–14; 998a 7–9).

12. Perhaps Leibniz is thinking of the following passage in Galileo's *Two New Sciences,* EN 175: "*Sagredo:* Shouldn't we confess that the virtue of Geometry is that it is the most potent instrument of all for sharpening one's wits and disposing them to reason and speculate with perfection? and that there was a grain of reason in Plato's wish that his students be well grounded in Mathematics first? . . . In my view, Logic teaches one to recognize whether reasonings and demonstrations already completed and discovered are conclusive, but I very much doubt whether it teaches one to discover conclusive reasonings and demonstrations."

13. Here the partial fair copy $L^2$ ends.

14. Here Leibniz had originally written "Phaedo and Cebes," Socrates' collocu-

tors in the *Phaedo*. Alcibiades is his principal collocutor in the *Theaetetus*. Leibniz had written Latin synopses of both of these dialogues earlier in the year. See Aiii20: 283–311.

15. See Plato, *Theaetetus*, 148 e6–149 a4, and 151 b7–c1.

16. This definition of motion avoids the question of whether place is absolute or only with respect to something else. Thus, as Leibniz observes in his note appended to the subtitle above, the discussion here does not take into account the relativity of motion, which he had acknowledged the previous year in his notes on Descartes (see Aiii15 above). The metaphysical implications of this relativity are explored by Leibniz in a piece written on his return to Hanover in February 1677, "Motion Is Something Relative" (Aiv360 below).

17. This may be a subtle irony for those familiar with Aristotle's *Physics,* for a substantial portion of Books IV and V are taken up with his elaborations of the different meanings of 'place', 'being in', and 'change' (208a–13a, 224a–26b).

18. The problem of the instantaneous state of change has a distinguished and ancient lineage, perhaps going all the way back to Parmenides and Zeno. At any rate, Plato attributes it to them in his *Parmenides,* which Leibniz had been reading at about this time (see his *Quod Ens perfectissimum sit possible* [That a Most Perfect Being Is Possible, Aiii79: 572–74; DSR 90–95], which the Akademie editors date as [probably] November 1676). Plato asks: "Then when does it change? For it does not change when it is at rest, nor when it is in motion, nor when it is in time" (156c–d).

19. The illustration of the problem in terms of the instant of death is due to the Sophists, according to Alexander of Aphrodisias. In a quotation from his lost commentary preserved by Simplicius, he attributes the argument to them in the form: "At what time did Dion die? For it was either when he was living or when he was dead; but not in the time in which he was living (for at that time he was living), nor in the time in which he was dead (for he was dead in all that time)" (quoted from *Simplicius on Aristotle's Physics 6,* trans. and ed. David Konstan, Ithaca: Cornell University Press, 1989: 983, 1: 26–30; p. 82). Leibniz would doubtless also have been familiar with Sextus Empiricus's version of this argument, couched in terms of Socrates (Sextus Empiricus III, *Against the Physicists,* I, 269–70). Aristotle too had introduced his discussion of the continuity of motion through a consideration of states of a person's body. He reasoned that if it is one and the same health that a person has at different times of the day, "then it must be possible for that which is one and the same to come to be and to cease to be many times." However, his conclusion about motion was that "A motion that includes intervals of rest will not be one but many," and will accordingly be "neither one nor continuous." (*Physics,* V, 4, 228a 7–19; 228b 4–6).

20. *Tertium nullum est* (or, as Leibniz had originally written, *Tertium non datur*) is the traditional name for the Law of Excluded Middle in Logic: "P or not-P."

21. Aristotle, *Physics,* V, 3, 227a 10–b2. See Appendix 2a.

22. Leibniz's conclusion about the impossibility of a state of instantaneous change appears to contradict Plato's, who asked of the moving thing at an instant: "does it not pass into an intermediate stage between certain forms of motion and

rest, so that it neither is nor is not, neither comes into being nor is destroyed?" "Yes, so it appears." (*Parmenides,* 157a; translation of H. N. Fowler, Loeb Classical Library, vol. VI, p. 301.) But the dialectical nature of Plato's argument should be taken into account, and its influence on Leibniz should not be underestimated.

23. In the margin, Leibniz has annotated this sentence with the symbol ♃. As the Akademie editors of VI.ii explain, this alchemical sign for distillation is used by Leibniz as an indicator that the problem is to be further worked on.

24. Leibniz had originally begun this paragraph by identifying the source of this argument: (a) "This was a sophism of the Stoics', which they called the Sorites (*Acervus*)," (b) "This type of argument, which the ancients called the Sorites, is not entirely useless if you use it correctly. For now let us transpose the argument." See GLOSSARY entry *acervus.*

25. There is no point *D* on Leibniz's diagram, but it is clearly supposed to be between *C* and *E,* where I have inserted it accordingly.

26. Postliminy is the right of a returned prisoner, exile, etc., to resume his or her former status.

27. For this interpretation of Empedocles, see Aristotle, *Physics,* VIII, 1, 252a 7–10 and 20ff., discussed in note 15 of "On Motion and Matter" above. The "certain learned men of more recent times" are probably the Spanish scholastic Rodrigo de Arriaga, and Gassendi and some of his followers (see Appendix 2e)—including Leibniz himself as a teenager (see Introduction, Section 2). Conceivably, the phrase might also be intended to refer to the views of the Mutakellamim reported by Maimonides (on whom Leibniz comments later), but there is no definite evidence for this. See Philip Beeley, *Koninuität und Mechanismus* (Stuttgart: Franz Steiner, 1996), pp. 298–301, for further discussion and references.

28. Here '*EF*' is a correction for '*EG*' in *l,* which itself appears to be a mistaken correction for the '*FG*' of *L¹.*

29. Here '*CE*' is a correction for '*CF*', which is clearly wrong.

30. Cf. Aristotle's discussion in *Physics* V, 6, where he concludes that "everything that is in motion must have been in motion before" (236b 20–237a 4); and then argues, in the remainder of the chapter, that the same goes for all types of change and becoming. For Proclus, the Akademie editors refer us to *Elementatio physica,* I, 17–27.

31. Again, compare with Aristotle's account in his *Physics,* where he says "the 'now' is the link of time, as has been said (for it connects past and future time), and it is a limit of time (for it is the beginning of the one and the end of the other)," 222a 10–12.

32. The Akademie edition has "*nullum . . . punctum C*" here; the *C* appears to be a mistake.

33. The precise referents of these critical remarks are not clear. Perhaps by charging the first thinker with "pretending not to see" the problem, Leibniz is accusing Aristotle of failing to explain how something could be infinitely divided without being composed of infinitely small things. As for the second's "abandonment of the problem as hopeless," this may refer to Descartes's denial that the actually infinite division of matter can be grasped by our finite minds; whereas the

claim that the third "severed the knot" might be an allusion to Galileo's denial that greater, equal, and less have a place in the infinite. But other interpretations are certainly possible. See Appendix 2 for the views of these three authors.

34. This refers to Proposition 4 of Book VI of Euclid's *Elements;* pp. 180–81 in the Everyman edition of Isaac Todhunter (J. M. Dent & Sons: London, 1933).

35. There is an error in Leibniz's text here, in that Charinus is given three consecutive speeches, beginning "Without doubt . . . ," "I think I can see . . . ," and "You have driven me . . . ." The simple expedient of ascribing the middle one of the three to Pacidius leaves Charinus putting forward Pacidius's argument, and Pacidius trying to anticipate how the argument will go, which does not seem a very happy solution. I have followed Couturat's suggestion of ascribing all but the first sentence of Charinus's first speech to Pacidius. This still leaves Charinus with two consecutive speeches (a fact apparently unnoticed by Couturat); see the next note but one.

36. '*NM*' is the Akademie editors' correction for '*NP*' in both $L^I$ and *l*, which was clearly a mistake.

37. The section of this paragraph up to the last sentence (*Unde . . . componi.*) was added by Leibniz in the fair copy *l* to replace a section of $L^I$ that occurs after that sentence. It is more succinct than the previous version, which made essentially the same point by a continuation of the dialogue between Pacidius and Charinus, and by reference to the lines in the triangle of the preceding figure, the part *CF* of *CD* being made equal to *AB*. In making this replacement, though, Leibniz has failed to realize that it again gives Charinus two consecutive speeches. As a simple expedient for rectifying this, I have assigned the newly added passage together with the last sentence to Pacidius.

38. The continuation of the dialogue at this point in $L^I$ (in the deleted passage referred to in the previous footnote) begins with a drawing of the same consequence for time: "| *Pa.:* Nor, you might therefore add, are times composed of moments. *Ch.:* For the same reason, since a line is traversed in a certain time, and the parts of time correspond to the parts of the line . . . |"

39. See Galileo Galilei, *Two New Sciences* (EN VIII, 78–79); translated in Appendix 2b, below.

40. Again, see Appendix 2b for Galileo's text.

41. As has often been pointed out, developments in the history of mathematics over the past hundred years—especially Cantor's theory of transfinite numbers— have vindicated Galileo over Leibniz on this point. For Cantor demonstrated that a consistent theory of the infinite can be based on the idea of a one–one correspondence, with the result that the infinite number of squares (the part) is equal to the infinite number of positive integers (the whole), in contradiction to the part–whole axiom that Leibniz took to be constitutive of quantity. This does not in itself prove any inconsistency in Leibniz's approach, based on the primacy of the part–whole axiom: but it would entail an abandonment of the idea of the infinite as a collection, and with it, most of the point-set theoretic foundation of mathematics. Of course, Leibniz, like many distinguished mathematicians since his day (including Her-

mann Weyl and L. E. J. Brouwer), might well have seen this as an advantage, given the paradoxes of the infinite still besetting set-theory!

42. This characteristic Leibnizian doctrine that there is no such thing as a fastest motion is consonant with the views of Hobbes: cf. *De corpore,* IV, ch. 26: "If, however, there is in hard things no hardest—just as there is no such thing in magnitudes as the greatest, nor in motions a maximum velocity—then . . ." But the subsequent proof of this from the example of the wheel spinning with a greatest velocity is even more reminiscent of Spinoza, who discussed it in his geometric exposition of *Descartes' "Principles of Philosophy"* (SO.i.192–94; SC 270–72). Spinoza attributes the spinning wheel argument to Zeno of Elea (SC 270), an error perhaps originating with Arriaga and the Spanish scholastics. Zeno is purported to have argued that the points on the rim, moving infinitely fast, would remain continuously in the same place, and would therefore be at rest. Leibniz may, of course, have derived the example from Arriaga directly. But whereas, according to Bayle, Arriaga "admits that [the difficulty] of the wheel is insoluble" (n. 82 to his article "Zeno of Elea," VI, p. 271, in Pierre Bayle, *Historical and Critical Dictionary: Selections,* trans. Richard Popkin, Hackett 1991), Spinoza argues that Zeno's argument refutes the possibility of a *fastest* motion, rather than of motion itself. It rests he says, on two false assumptions, that there is a fastest motion, and that time is composed of moments. "For we can never conceive a motion so fast that we do not at the same time conceive a faster one" (SC 271). This fact, which also entails that there is no shortest time, he then proves by arranging for the supposed fastest wheel to drive another wheel half its size twice as fast by means of a belt looped around them (SC 272).

43. Two drafts of a passage suppressed by Leibniz here are worthy of note. In his rough draft $L^1$, he wrote:

"| *Ga.:* Similarly it should be concluded that there is no number of all possible analytic curved lines. For you know, Pacidius, what curves I call analytic, namely, those whose nature can be expressed in an equipollent rational, that is, one which is such that its equation, i.e. the relation between its ordinate and abscissa, is expressed by a simple equation that is expoundable in terms of numbers, that is to say, is such that by means of an abscissa given in numbers and a straight edge, the ordinate can also be expressed in numbers. I call two things equipollent, on the other hand, when from the quadrature of one we may obtain the quadrature of the other. See what follows from this: Every analytic curve can be transformed into an equipollent rational. Therefore the number of analytic curves is no greater than the number of rationals. Which is absurd, for there certainly are some non-rational analytic curves. *Pa.:* I am forced to agree. |"

In the fair copy this passage was crossed out, and replaced by the following passage, which was also subsequently crossed out:

"| *Ga.:* Similarly, it should be concluded that there is no number of all possible analytic curved lines. For you know that I call curves analytic when for each of them we can find an equipollent rational, i.e., one whose ordinate is rational if the abscissa is assumed to be rational; so that, to wit, a given quadrature of a rational an-

alytic curve will also be the quadrature of a given analytic curve; therefore there are as many rational curves as analytic ones. But it is clear on other grounds that there are more irrational analytic curves: for to any rational one, there corresponds an infinity of irrational ones. Therefore their number will be at once equal and unequal, and thus impossible, since an impossibility follows from this. *Pa.:* l" (—BREAKS OFF).

44. This is a recapitulation of Descartes's argument in his *Principles of Philosophy,* II, §§33–35; given in translation in Appendix 2c.

45. For Descartes's actual words, see Appendix 2c.

46. The section of dialogue between here and "*Pa.:* With your permission, then, I'll get back under way . . ." (Aiii78: 552, l.22), (including the inspired passage giving the analogy with folds), replaces an altogether more pedestrian first draft in *L¹* that ran as follows: ". . . from points. | *Ch.:* Then what if we take it as demonstrated that a perfect liquid that fills space perfectly is impossible?—especially since Descartes has no demonstrations in favor of the liquid and the plenum. *Pa.:* There is some truth to what you say, Charinus. Still, it seems to me that this does not entirely repudiate the plenum and the liquid in equal measure. There is something of subtlety here, which might also readily come to your aid if a reason for accepting it were at this point clearly set before you. But it will suffice if any self-evident obstacles are razed to the ground, lest, in running off at a tangent everywhere, we reach our proposed goal too late. *Te.* [i.e., *Ga.*]: On condition that you will satisfy us more fully at another time, we will let you off now. For you see that the description of the vacuum and plenum, liquid and solid, is of great importance, and the establishment of a true and certain hypothesis about the nature of things depends on it. You will see that we now have a hope of resolving this controversy with a demonstration. | *Pa.:* With your permission, then, . . . ."

47. As mentioned in Section 6 of the Introduction, this doctrine of the "folds of matter," whose elastic deformations require neither extreme of the dense and the rare, was quite possibly Baconian in inspiration.

48. '*MN*' replaces Leibniz's '*M sive N*' ("*M* or *N*") in *L¹* and *l,* which seems to be a mistake.

49. The following canceled text from *L¹*—enclosed between the horizontal lines ' ❖ ❖ ❖ ' and presented in a different font—together with its accompanying footnotes, was discarded by Leibniz immediately after the beginning of it had been written in fair copy *l.* It was replaced in *l* by the text following it (560–67), beginning "Anyone advocating these leaps . . . ," and ending ". . . since the succeeding state does not necessarily follow from the preceding one." I have indicated the end of the rewritten passage with the mark ' ❖ ❖ ❖ ❖ ❖ ❖ ❖ ❖ ❖ ❖ ❖ '.

50. In the margin Leibniz tagged this statement with a question mark '?'.

51. End of the secretary's fair copy *l:* from here to the mark ˮ—crossed out in *L¹*.

52. Here Leibniz casually introduces the term 'transcreation' that he had coined earlier in the year in "Infinite Numbers" (Aiii69 above); in the text that replaces this section, however, he introduces it more carefully—in fact, he introduces it twice by mistake (see Aiii78: 560, 567 below).

53. Leibniz himself had explained the firmness of atoms in terms of God's concurrence eight years previously in his *Confession of Nature Against the Atheists* (1668): "In providing a reason for Atoms, then, it is right to have recourse to God, who is responsible for these ultimate foundations in things" (A VI.i 492). See the Introduction, Section 5.

54. See Aristotle, *Physics,* V, 3, 227a 10–b2; Appendix 2a.

55. Perhaps Leibniz means that if infinitesimals are taken to be actuals, then the length of a line segment, expressed as a definite integral, will be the sum of an infinite number of such infinitesimals: it will be bounded, but consist in an infinity of parts, and will thus be simultaneously both determinate and indeterminate.

56. Leibniz seems to be alluding to his differential calculus, in which an $n$th order differential, itself infinitely small, can be expressed as the sum of an infinity of differentials of order $n + 1$. But he might also be referring to the fact that the same integral may be performed, with the same result, by taking a different "progression of the variables"; something he had realized at about this time.

57. This phrase is echoed almost forty years later in a famous passage from Leibniz's *Monadology* (¶ 69): "Thus there is nothing waste, nothing sterile, nothing dead in the universe; no chaos, no confusions, save in appearance" (quoted from PW 190).

58. Leibniz appears to have forgotten that he already introduced his newly coined term at the beginning of this rewritten section (560, top).

59. See Aristotle, *Physics,* IV, 8, 215a 19–22.

60. This refers to Gassendi's interpretation of what we call the law of inertia, according to which causes are only necessary for changes in the state of a body's motion (or other qualities), God having imbued each atom with a motive force at its creation. Descartes, to the contrary, maintained that all qualities and states require the constant creative activity of God to remain in being. See my "Continuous Creation, Continuous Time: A Refutation of the Alleged Discontinuity of Cartesian Time," *Journal of the History of Philosophy,* xxvi, 3, 349–75, July 1988; esp. pp. 360–63.

61. It is not clear whether this is intended as a swing at Hobbes; but there were certainly those close to his circle, the Duchess of Newcastle, for one, who drew this radical atheistic consequence, as had the English philosophers Thomas Harriot and Walter Warner before him. See Robert Hugh Kargon, *Atomism in England from Hariot to Newton* (Oxford: Clarendon, 1966).

62. In $L^1$ Leibniz had continued this sentence by adding the following passage, which he then cancelled: "for change among things. | Whence you will understand that if it is a miracle for a man to be transferred from Paris to Rome in a moment, then it is a continual natural miracle, even if it is credible that the spaces through which these leaps occur are smaller than can be explicated by their ratio to magnitudes known by us. {Whence motion will be geometrically continuous, even if it is}—CROSSED OUT. {And these kinds of spaces are taken in geometry to be points or null spaces, so that motion, although metaphysically interrupted by rests, will be geometrically continuous—just as a regular polygon of infinitely many sides cannot be taken metaphysically for a circle, even though it is taken for a circle in geom-

*191*

etry, on account of the error being smaller than can be expressed by us. It is not at all to be defended, lest the reasonings of geometry or mechanics are subverted by metaphysical speculations.}—CROSSED OUT. Indeed leaps occur in other things ever smaller and smaller. But nonetheless it seems that from this there follows an absurdity, that at some time here a leap could be noticed by a thinking being. Therefore, in order to avoid this, we must always consider that the bigger the body is, the smaller is the interval of the leap. |"

63. I have made two changes in this passage to preserve its sense: *minores* (smaller) for Leibniz's *majores* (greater), in "the greater are the leaps they make," which is not compatible with the position he is advocating (cf. his preliminary wording in the preceeding footnote); and *pauci* (few) for *parvi* (small), as the context seems to require.

64. 'Alethophilus' is a poetic inversion of 'Philalethes', both meaning "lover of truth."

65. Leibniz had Theophilus attribute his mysteries first to "the Ancients," then to "the Pythagoreans," then "the Platonists," before deciding on "the theologians."

66. The bracketed phrase was canceled in the rough draft, but I have reinserted it to give the letter a less abrupt ending.

### 20. Space and Motion Are Really Relations

1. LH XXXVII, 4: sheet 88, a slip of paper, 2 pages; edited by Ursula Franke for the Vorausedition as Ve503: 2384 (Fascicule 9, 1990). This piece explores the first of the outstanding problems of motion that Leibniz had noted were left unexamined in the *Pacidius Philalethi,* namely, "the subject of motion, to make clear which of two things changing their mutual situation motion should be ascribed to." It contains the first clear statement of his mature view that space is not absolute but consists solely in relation, and shows how Leibniz conceives this to follow from the relativity of motion. It is also closely related in content to the piece following it, in which the metaphysical implications of the relativity of motion are further explored.

2. Although the piece has no watermark, its close relation in content to the *Pacidius* and to "Motion Is Something Relative" strongly indicate a date right at the beginning of the Hanover period.

3. Here Leibniz is referring to his *Theory of Abstract Motion* of 1671 (A VI.ii N41), some excerpts of which are given in Appendix 1c below.

4. This paragraph, with its accompanying figure, were suppressed by Leibniz in favor of those following it.

### 21. Motion Is Something Relative

1. LH XXXVII, 5: sheet 122, a slip of paper, 1⅓ pages; edited for the Vorausedition by Ursula Franke as Ve145: 654 (Fascicule 3, 1984). The Akademie title is *Quod Motus sit Ens Respectivum,* "That Motion Is a Relative Entity," from the

fourth paragraph of the piece; I have instead used the (equivalent) opening phrasing. This piece is closely related in content to the previous piece, "Space and Motion Are Really Relations" (Aiv359: 1976 = Ve503: 2384).

2. This picks up on the conclusion reached in "On Motion and Matter" above, that since the conservation of the quantity of motion can only be asserted "of the action, i.e. relative motion, by which one body is related to another or acts on another" (Aiii68: 493), it cannot be guaranteed by the minds of the individual bodies, but only by a universal mind, i.e. God.

3. Contrast with "Secrets of the Sublime" above: "nor do intelligences seem absurd" (Aiii60: 477).

4. Leibniz is probably alluding to Galileo's discussion of the cause of cohesion in his *Two New Sciences.* See Appendix 2b, as well as Leibniz's "Notes on Galileo's *Two New Sciences*" (Aiii11$_2$) and "On the Cohesiveness of Bodies" (Aiii4) above, the Introduction, Seciton 4, and the GLOSSARY notes on *tabula* and *consistentia.*

5. This is a fascinating early example of Leibniz's application of his Principle of the Identity of Indiscernibles, or perhaps more accurately, what I have called his Principle of the Nonexistence of Imperceptibles: cf. Aiii58, n. 1, and Aiv316, n. 4.

### 22. Chrysippus's Heap

1. LH IV 8, leaf 80; 1 slip of paper, 2 pages. Previously edited for the Vorausedition by Ursula Franke as Ve110: 426 (Fascicule 2, 1983). Here Leibniz outlines a solution to the Paradox of the Heap—the *Sorites* of the Stoics—eloquently described in the *Pacidius* above (Part II, Aiii78: 539ff.). Although he does not here apply it to shape or motion, it seems clear that it would solve the problem of the continuity of motion raised in the *Pacidius,* so that "nearness" would be a "vague imaginary notion" and we would simply stipulate when something approaching a second thing becomes "near from having not being near." Comparisons of distance and magnitude, however, would still be immune from the paradox, indicating the inherently relational nature of the notions of distance and magnitude. Cf. Aiii69.

2. Leibniz's original title.

3. This is a quotation from Persius, *Satires,* 6, 80, as is noted beside it in someone else's hand.

4. The Akademie editors plausibly suggest that Leibniz had written *obolo adjecto* (by the addition of a penny) in error for *obolo abjecto* (by throwing away a penny).

### 23. Conspectus for a Little Book on the Elements of Physics

1. LH XXXVii 3, leaves 9–10; 1 sheet of folio, 3 pages; loss of text at the end, supplemented after the edition of Ernst Gerland, *Leibnizens nachgelassene Shcriften physikalischen, mechanischen und technischen Inhalts,* Leipzig 1906, pp. 110–13. Edited for the Vorausedition by Ursula Franke as Ve144: 649–53 (Fascicule 3,

1984). English translation by Leroy Loemker of all but the last two paragraphs (L 277–80). I have excerpted only those sections having most to do with the continuum problem.

2. The watermark is registered for July 1678 to June 1682. That time frame is further reduced, as the Akademie editors note, by a reference to this piece in the *Aphorismi* of "Summer 1678–Winter 1678/79" (Aiv496), yielding the same dating for this piece. This early date is significant, since here Leibniz attributes "souls or kinds of forms" to bodies, entailing that he reintroduced substantial forms earlier than had previously been supposed.

3. Leibniz had originally written: "a description of phosphorus, or the fire that is harmless and needs no fuel." I have made explicit the literal meaning of *noctiluca,* "nightlight," in my translation. Robert Boyle published two works on phosphorescence, *The Icy Noctiluca* of 1672, and *The Aerial Noctiluca* of 1680, and Leibniz's use of the same word prompted Gerland to speculate (*Leibnizens nachgelassene Schriften,* 113) that it was occasioned by the apppearance of Boyle's later work. However, Leibniz's keen interest in phosphorus dates from the time of its discovery by Heinrich Brandt in Hamburg in 1677. He published an announcement of its discovery in the *Journal des sçavans* of 2 August 1677, wrote a well-regarded Latin poem about it as a eulogy to Duke Johann Friedrich (16 July 1678; A II.i N.65), and corresponded with Brandt from the middle of 1678 until the end of 1682; see also the description of phosphorus he gives in a letter to Christiaan Huygens of 8 September 1679 (accompanying a prepared sample of the substance; L 249), and Loemker's valuable notes at L 176, 277, 289–90.

4. Leibniz's deletions here are worth recording. He first had "The extended is a continuous whole whose parts are simultaneous," then "The extended is a substance which has parts similar to the whole," before deciding on this definition.

5. Compare Leibniz's definitions of magnitude at Aiii69: 503 and at Aiii64: 482 (DSR 36–37), which I give in footnote 17 to Aiii69.

6. Again two prior tries: "Situation is the form of a thing", and "is a mode according to which several [entities] can be perceived simultaneously."

7. This argument from the Principle of Sufficient Reason is essentially the same as that given in *A Chain of Wonderful Demonstrations About the Universe* of December 1676: "we may demonstrate that space is infinite from the fact that whatever space is supposed, there is no reason why it may not be made bigger. Yet it is clear that no reason can be provided, since there is the utmost homogeneity in space, and its existence does not stand in the way of other things. That there was some space to be made is clear from the fact that some has been made, and since there is no reason determining or limiting its size, it will be the greatest it can be, i.e. absolutely infinite" (Aiii85: 585; DSR 109). The same form of argument is applied to perfection at Aiii36: 392.

8. See in particular the arguments of Aiv278 below.

9. The arguments that souls result from God thinking of things, and that minds are immortal because they never forget themselves, are both spelled out in Aiv275 above.

10. Cf. Leibniz's exposition of this in "On the Plenitude of the World" (Aiii76: 524).

11. Leibniz had discovered that the quantity conserved in collisions is quantity of power ($mv^2$) in January–February of 1678, in his *De corporum concursu*. See Michel Fichant, *Gottfried Wilhem Leibniz. La Réforme de la dynamique: De corporum concursu (1678) et autres textes inédits* (Paris: J. Vrin, 1994).

## 24. Created Things Are Actually Infinite

1. LH I, 20, leaf 210; on 2 sides of a slip of paper; edited for the Vorausedition by Gerhard Biller as Ve254: 1129 (Fascicule 6, 1987).

2. There are no external points of reference for dating. The Akademie editors suggest that it could be a forestudy for the following piece, dating it in the same time frame of Summer 1678–Winter 1680/81.

## 25. Metaphysical Definitions and Reflections

1. LH XXXV 11, 14, leaves 16–21 (¾ sheet of folio, 9¾ columns). Previously edited for the Vorausedition by Heinrich Pfannkuch as Ve445: 2035–45 (Fascicule 8, 1989).

2. The watermark is registered for July 1678–June 1682. It is on the same paper as Aiv365 (dated by Aiv as Summer 1678–Winter 1678/79), to which it is closely related in content, although to the Akademie editors these reflections "no longer appear very early, leaving one to assume a time of origin probably no earlier than Spring of 1679."

3. At first Leibniz had defined body as an *extensum* without resistance, only to make this his definition of a vacuum instead: "⌐ Body is an extended thing, but endowed with no resistance. But whether such a thing is to be found is another question. {The *organs of sense* are bodies whose resistance we perceive as other bodies} If two bodies resist each other absolutely, without the addition of anything else ⌐."

4. This is a more formal exposition of the principles Leibniz had expounded in Aii60: 472–73 above. The figure of God as an excellent geometer recurs in Aiv312 below.

5. There is some text missing in the copy of Aiv here. Where the Vorausedition had *Hinc jam obitur consideratio spatii cujusdam generalis dum* . . . (Ve445: 2038), the new edition has *Hinc jam or dum.* . . . I have surmised that the mistake occurred in the course of correcting *obitur* ("is met with") to *oritur* ("arises"), which makes slightly better sense. On "generic space," see GLOSSARY under *genus, generalis.*

6. After "Body is . . . "this passage had originally continued: "⌐ . . . an extended thing that is in motion. For since body is a substance capable of being acted upon; and since every substance, on the other hand, is actually operating, as is demon-

strated in its own place, and every thing being acted upon has several things at the same time, i.e. is extended; and since, moreover, the passion of an extended thing is by division, i.e. local motion: and also actually the cause of the passion of an extended thing is in another extended thing, and thus so is the cause of local motion, but the cause of local motion is local motion; it follows that every body is an extended thing in motion. And conversely, every extended thing in motion will be a body. This therefore we demonstrate if we define *body* to be a substance which can act and be acted upon. |"

7. A first version of this sentence continued: "these definitions coincide; | likewise every extended thing is movable, and every movable thing is extended. And so *body, movable thing,* and *extended thing* are equivalent. |" But they are not equivalent: for space and vacuum are both extended, but neither movable nor bodies; which is presumably why Leibniz deleted this. However, it is not clear to me why he abandoned the definitions of the first section of this piece, *body* as "an extended thing that resists," and *vacuum* as "an extended thing without resistance."

8. This sentence was originally continued: "| and soul is the same as substantial form, i.e., the principle {of action, whereas matter is the principle of passion} of unity, whereas matter is the principle of multiplicity, i.e. of change. |"

9. This is an interesting variation on Leibniz's more usual definition, with which he had begun, before crossing it out: "| Substantial form . . . is the principle of action, and matter that of passion |"; the second version had "| . . . is the principle of unity and constancy. |"

10. These statements follow from his discussions in the first section, where "generic space" arises from the assignment of situations to all phenomena, and "generic time" is a way of relating changes of situation to one another.

11. At first sight it might seem strange for Leibniz to claim that an atom cannot be acted upon when it could, for instance, be moved. But since all motion is relative, it cannot be an absolute attribute of a body (see Aiv360). There must be some real change in the body, so that if all change in body is by local motion, then "the principle of passion (or being acted upon)" must be *division.* A perfectly rigid body would be incapable of *registering* any action on itself, and thus of sensing.

12. The objections referred to are the classical ones of the atomists, namely, that if everything were full, motion would be impossible. Leibniz's solution is along the lines of Descartes's, given in Appendix 2c below. See Aiii58; see also the Introduction, Section 5, for a discussion.

13. This echoes the passage in *Pacidius to Philalethes* at Aiii78: 566, and the corresponding passage in the *Monadology.*

14. Compare with the definitions of 'organ' and 'object' in the first section above (1394).

15. Leibniz continued this "and the whole world is one continuum," before crossing it out.

16. Leibniz originally had: "For a unity always lasts as long as it can, since every division is a passion, i.e. a change, but every change is always as small as can be, since nothing happens without a reason."

17. This passage on the best republic, of which God is King, echoes sentiments

expressed (in passages I did not translate) in "On the Secrets of the Sublime" at Aiii60: 476; DSR 29, and in Aiv365: 1989 above.

18. "In laughable imitation of the master dissembler, perhaps" (*ridicula dissimulatoris fortasse magistri imitatione*) appears to be a rare derogatory reference to Descartes and his followers.

19. The reference to Plato's *Phaedo* is to the passage at 97b–101b, and the revivers of Democritus are, above all, Descartes, Gassendi, and Magnen, who published *Democritus Reviviscens sive De Atomis* in Pavia in 1646.

20. In the first of three deleted attempts to continue this passage, Leibniz wrote: "⎡Whence Fermat's demonstration about reflection and refraction, which is drawn from final causes, is right, and Descartes's demonstration from efficient causes is wrong. ⎦"

21. This seems to be an implicit criticism of Descartes's account in Discourse 2 of his *Dioptrique* (AT VI, 93–96; English translation in *Descartes: The World and Other Writings,* ed. and trans. Stephen Gaukroger (Cambridge: Cambridge University Press, 1998), 76–78; although, if so, it seems misplaced, since Descartes adequately accounts for the composition from these two components.

22. As the Akademie editors inform us, in a letter to Christiaan Huygens of 5 February 1680 (A III.iii N.22), Leibniz mentions Hero of Alexandria (who expounded the Law of Shortest Path in chapter 4 of his *Catoptrica*) and Ptolemy (to whom the work *Sphaera* is attributed, in which Hero's work was reprinted under the title *De speculis*).

### 26. Matter and Motion Are Only Phenomena

1. LH IV 6, 12f, leaf 22; 1 slip of paper, 1¼ pages. Edited for the Vorausedition by Gerhard Biller as Ve416: 1911 (Fascicule 8, 1989). Previously published by Louis Couturat at C 185ff.

2. There are no external clues for dating. The Akademie editors suggest that the concerns of this piece (and Aiv278) with the phenomenality of extension, motion, and matter, considered purely extensively, link it in content with "Mira de Natura Substantiae Corporeae" (Aiv279 below), setting it in the same time frame, winter 1682–83. But Leibniz had already sounded these concerns in 1676 (see Aiii68, 69), 1677 (see Aiv360), and 1678 (Aiv365), and to me the close linkage in themes and language with those pieces suggests soon after the Paris period, around 1678–79.

3. See, for instance, Aiv360 above.

4. The argument for this is given in Aiii58 above. See also Aiv365: 1988.

### 27. There Is No Such Thing as One Body

1. LH I, 20, leaf 209, on 2 sides of a slip of paper; edited for the Vorausedition by Gerhard Biller as *Nullum dari ullum corpus,* Ve253: 1127–28 (Fascicule 6, 1987). I have retained this title in preference to the new title in Aiv, *An corpora sint mera phaenomena,* "Whether Bodies Are Mere Phenomena."

2. There are no external clues for dating. The Akademie editors place it in the same time frame as Aiv277 and Aiv279 (Winter 1682–83?) on the basis of similarity of contents. Essentially, though, it is no more than a formal demonstration for the claim in Aiv365 that, because of the indefinite division of the extended, "nothing could be assigned in body which could be called *this something,* or *some one thing,*" and so could equally well have originated in the same period, summer–winter of 1678–79. But then again, it could as well have been prompted by Leibniz's rereading of Cordemoy in 1685 (see Aiv346 below).

3. Leibniz originally had the second and third suppositions in reverse order, but switched them after he realized that the argument succeeded without this supposition, originally numbered (2).

4. This example is reminiscent of the argument concerning a square composed from two triangles in *Meditatio de principio individui* (Aiii67: 490–91; DSR 50–53). There Leibniz argued that a square would be indiscernible from one formed from two rectangles, so that the principle of individuation of each would have to be outside the thing, contrary to the principle that the effect must involve its cause. "But if we admit that two different things always differ in themselves in some way as well, then it follows that in any matter there is something which retains the effect of its prior states, namely, a mind" (491).

## 28. A Body Is Not a Substance

1. LH IV 1, 14b, leaf 1; 1 sheet in octavo, 1½ pages. Previously published by Foucher de Careil, *Nouvelles lettres et opuscules,* 1857, p. 171ff.; edited for the Vorausedition by Heinrich Pfannkuch as Ve402: 1872 (Fascicule 8, 1989).

2. There are no external clues for dating. The Akademie editors date it as from Leibniz's Italian journey, on the grounds of similarity of content with Aiv314, citing Leibniz's reference to the labyrinth of the continuum in connection with the establishing of the phenomenality of merely extended bodies. To me the contents suggest a date not long after the Paris period, since it continues not only the themes but also the language of the *De summa rerum* and the *Pacidius.* It is closely linked in content to Aiv277 and Aiv 278, so I have assigned it to the same period of around 1678–79. One could argue that it was written after Aiv267 (*Definitiones cogitationesque metaphysicae;* 1678–79?), however, since there a body is defined as extended substance (albeit one containing sensation and appetite): but in both pieces Leibniz is offering an account of body that is distinguished from the purely extensive notion of the "Democriteans." Robert Merrihew Adams believes this piece belongs to a putative period during which Leibniz entertained phenomenalism, prior to his rehabilitation of substantial forms, "a decision he apparently made in summer 1679" (*Leibniz: Determinist, Theist, Idealist,* New York: Oxford University Press, 1994; p. 236); see my argument against this in the introductory essay. Leibniz explicitly rejects phenomenalism in Aiv267, and seems to have reintroduced substantial forms by the winter of 1678 (see Aiv365, especially n. 2).

3. Leibniz's original title.

4. 'Bulk' translates '*molem*'; see GLOSSARY under *moles*. Leibniz had originally written *extensum,* an extended thing.

5. Leibniz had begun to write *corporem,* body, but crossed it out.

6. Cf.Aiv365: 1988, and Aiv278, "There Is No Such Thing as One Body."

7. Cf. Aiii58: 466 above: "According to certain ways of reasoning it follows that to be is nothing other than to be capable of being perceived"; in the accompanying footnote, I dubbed this the Principle of the Nonexistence of Imperceptibles. Cf. also Aiv360 above.

8. Cf. "On the Secrets of the Sublime," Aiii60: 474: "conforming sensations are the mark of existence," and the accompanying footnote.

### 29. The Origin of Souls and Minds

1. LH IV, I, 14c: sheet 10. 1 slip of paper, two sides. Edited for the Vorausedition by Ursula Franke as Ve81: 292–93 (Fascicule 2, 1983).

2. The watermark gives March–June 1681. In it, Leibniz presents an interpretation of the substantial form of a body as what results from God thinking of "all the appearances or relations of things to this body considered as immobile" (in addition to its being endowed with sensation and appetite). This is strongly suggestive of the views and language of Aiv360, Aiv267, and Aiv277.

3. Leibniz's original title.

4. Leibniz's attribution of understanding (*intellegere*) to God, but intellect (*intellectus*) to us, is deliberate. He elaborates this distinction in the next paragraph.

### 30. Wonders Concerning the Nature of Corporeal Substance

1. LH IV, I, 14c: sheet 11. This piece is scrawled on the back of a small bill (3.5 × 19 cm), folded twice. Edited for the Vorausedition by Ursula Franke as Ve82: 294–95 (Fascicule 2, 1983).

2. The bill is dated 29 March 1683.

3. Leibniz's original title.

4. This argument, implicit in Aiii69, is spelled out particularly clearly in "There Is No Perfect Shape in Bodies" of c. 1686 (Aiv310).

5. In a similar vein, Leibniz writes in *De modo distinguendi phaenomena realia ab imaginariis* (dated Summer 1683–Winter 1685–86 by watermark): "Concerning bodies I can demonstrate that not only light, heat, color, and similar quantities are apparent, but also motion, and shape, and extension. And if anything is real, it is only the force of acting and being acted upon, and so the substance of body consists in this (as if in matter and form). But those bodies which do not have a substantial form are merely phenomena, or at any rate aggregates of true bodies" (Aiv299: 1504).

6. Here the Akademie edition mistakenly has *infinitum* (infinite) for Leibniz's *illimitatum* (unlimited), which I have corrected by reference to the microfilm copy at Hanover.

7. The first part of this echoes what Leibniz earlier said of minds in 1676 in Aiii76: 524 above.

8. Cf. "There Is No Such Thing as One Body" (Aiv278) and "A Body Is Not a Substance" (Aiv316) above.

## 31. On Substance, Change, Time, and Extension

1. LH IV, 7C, leaves 105–6, 1 sheet in folio, 4 pages. Edited for the Vorausedition by Heinrich Pfannkuch as *Terminus, Possibile, Ens. Divisiones* (Term, Possible, Entity, Divisions), Ve294: 1298–1305 (Fascicule 6, 1987); renamed in Aiv as *Divisio Terminorum ac enumeratio attributorum* (A Division of Terms and Enumeration of Attributes). In this piece Leibniz works in a systematic fashion from the most general categories to the more particular, beginning with definitions of Term, Possible, and Entity, before dividing the latter into Concreta and Abstracta, concreta into Substantives and Adjectives, substantives into those that are complete, which he calls Supposita and those that are incomplete, the Attributes, taking us to the first passage excerpted here. Between this and the second passage, Leibniz gives a discussion of attributes; and after the account of time excerpted here, moves on to definitions of Coincidents, Quality, Congruents, Quantity, Homogenes, Bound, before the definitions of Extension and Extended given here.

2. The watermark gives August 1680–February 1685; in Aiv this is dated as Summer 1683 at the earliest.

3. This interesting first draft, given in a different font, was canceled by Leibniz and replaced by the paragraph following.

4. The passage from the beginning of the paragraph to this point is almost identical with one in Aiv97, *Enumeratio terminorum simpliciorum,* "An Enumeration of Simple Terms" (= Ve93, *De terminis simplicibus,* "On Simple Terms"), a manuscript dated in Aiv as Summer 1680–Winter 1684–85 (?), where it occurs as a footnoted gloss to the definition "An extended thing is a continuous whole whose parts coexist." The only differences are clarifying editorial expansions (such as the additions of *et, est,* etc., left implicit in Aiv97) and *quaedam* for the impossible *quatenus* of the latter.

5. Leibniz does not manage to carry out this plan. Instead, after an interesting definition of *ratio* in terms of similarity or indiscerniblility with respect to magnitude, the fragment breaks off. The analysis in Aiv156 (= Ve104), however, seems a natural continuation of the above remarks on the extended.

## 32. On Part, Whole, Transformation, and Change

1. LH IV, 7B, 4, leaves 13–14, 1 sheet in 2°, 3 pages. Edited for the Akademie by Martin Schneider, as *Definitiones Notionum Metaphysicarum atque Logicarum* (Definitions of Metaphysical and Logical Notions), Ve284: 1251–55 (Fascicule 6, 1987). As in the previous piece (Aiv132/Ve294), Leibniz begins with the most

general categories, working toward the more particular by division. He begins with definitions of Entity, Nothing, Complete Term, Substantive Term, Adjective, Proper Vocable of a thing, Individual Substance, Impossible, Possible, (an Existent cannot be defined), Similars, Congruents, before proceeding to the definitions of Requisite, Condition, Parts, and Whole with which this selection begins.

2. The dating of mid-1685 is made on the basis of well-confirmed watermarks. This is consistent with the contents.

3. Leibniz does not enter into this here; the piece ends instead with a series of clarifying definitions of various types of causes in terms of requisites.

### 33. Annotated Excerpts from Cordemoy's *Treatise*

1. These two pieces contain extracts made by Leibniz from Gerauld de Cordemoy's *On the Distinction Between Body and Mind,* together with Leibniz's comments on them. The treatise was originally published in French as *Six discours sur la distinction et l'union du corps et de l'ame* in 1668, and then in the Latin edition of 1679 as the first of "Two Treatises on Physics," *Tractatus physici duo. I. De corporis et mentis distinctione,* from which Leibniz is here excerpting. (The second Latin treatise, *II. De loquela* [On Language], does not concern us here.) The first of Leibniz's pieces is a précis, with dissenting comments, of the First Discourse of Cordemoy's treatise (titled "On Bodies and Matter"); the second concerns a point in the Third Discourse. I have broken the first piece into paragraphs, and supplied emphases, in accordance with Cordemoy's original.

2. The well-confirmed watermark of the first piece gives 1685, and the second piece appears to be a direct continuation of it. Also, see Leibniz's comments on Cordemoy's treatise in a letter to Arnauld of 8 December 1686 (G.ii.78)

3. Leibniz's original title. LH IV 6, 12f, leaf 5. 1 leaf in quarto, 1¾ pages; edited for the Vorausedition by Martin Schneider as Ve157: 695–97 (Fascicule 4, 1985). Previously edited by Pierre Clair and François Girbal in *Gerauld de Cordemoy: Œuvres philosophiques,* Paris; Presses Universitaires de France, 1968: Latin text: pp. 362–64; French translation pp. 364–67.

4. "Extended mass" here translates *moles* (see GLOSSARY); Leibniz had originally written *extensionem* (extension).

5. In the original, Cordemoy says "none of its extremities is separable from it" (*Six Discours sur la distinction et l'union du corps et de l'ame; Premier discours: Œuvres philosophiques,* ed. Clair and Girbal, p. 98).

6. Sc. *actiones sunt suppositorum.* See note under *suppositum* in GLOSSARY.

7. Here Cordemoy is referring to the Cartesians.

8. —reading *lumini naturali* with Clair and Girbal for the Akademie's *menti naturali.* For Descartes's doctrine of the "natural light which is in our souls," see his *Principles of Philosophy,* I, §§ 11, 18, 20, 28.

9. See Descartes, *Principles,* I, §§ 33–35, given in Appendix 2c.

10. This is almost identical to the argument Leibniz put forth in *Meditatio de principio individui* (DSR 8; Aiii67: 490–91): "it is impossible for two squares of

this kind to be perfectly similar, since although they will consist of matter, that matter will have a mind, and the mind will retain the effect of the prior state." See also the similar argument in Aiv278: 1464–65 above, and accompanying footnote (3).

11. The full sentence from Cordemoy's treatise précised here by Leibniz is: "However, it seems to me that we have a very clear and very natural idea of a body perfectly at rest among other bodies, none of which is in motion, and that what I say of each body accords perfectly well with this idea" (Cordemoy, *Six discours,* Clair and Girbal, p. 99).

12. This is an extremely difficult passage to translate. I have interpreted Leibniz's *creare* as an error for *constare.* I take the gist of this criticism of Cordemoy to be that he mistakes a clear image for a clear concept (in this connection cf. Aiii19); one can conceive a body as something whose nature it is to be moved and still perceive the same thing (and have an image of it in one's mind) as if rest were its natural state.

13. Descartes supposed in his *Principles* that some bodies remain undivided (see Appendix 2c); but Leibniz's reasons for denying that one is forced to suppose this are well expounded in Aiv278 above.

14. Cordemoy gives as examples "a horse, a slave."

15. Leibniz had mistakenly inserted a ' + )' here. This is the first of three errors he made with his parentheses in this part of the text. He also forgot closing parentheses after the remarks ending "*et quantitas extensionis.*" and "*sunt correquisitae.*" (The Akademie editors wrongly corrected the last error by omitting the opening parenthesis of "( + *Necesse est situm*", thus attributing Cordemoy's statement '*Distantia non erit substantiae, sed situs.*' to Leibniz.)

16. Again, Cordemoy's target is the Cartesians. In Part 2 of his *Principles,* Descartes wrote: "if someone asks what would happen if God were to take away every single body contained in a vessel, without allowing any other body to take the place of what had been removed, the answer must be that the sides of the vessel would, in that case, have to be in contact. For when there is nothing between two bodies, they necessarily touch each other" (AT VIII.1, 50; CSM.i.231).

17. Cordemoy had written: "And although one might say that between two bodies which are not touching one could put other bodies of a length of so many feet, one should not conclude on that account that there were any there. One should only say that they are situated in such a way that one could place between them bodies which, when joined together, would compose one extension of so many feet. Thus one conceives only that one could place bodies: but one does not conceive on that account that they are there" (Cordemoy, *Six Discours,* Clair and Girbal, p. 103).

18. Leibniz had continued, "| Animam introducunt ex illo: *dispositionem habenti non denegatur forma* |," "| They introduce the soul from the fact that *form cannot be denied to something having an orderly arrangement* |," and then crossed it out—presumably because the extract and commentary is continued instead in the note that follows here.

19. LH IV 6, 12f, leaf 13; a slip of paper 5 by 8 cm.; 1¾ pages. Edited for the Vorausedition by Martin Schneider as Ve157$_2$: 698 (Fascicule 4, 1985).

### 34. On the Present World

1. LH IV 7C, leaves 111–14, on 2 sheets of quarto. Edited by Martin Schneider for the Vorausedition as Ve107: 416–23 (Fascicule 2, 1983).

2. The watermark gives July 1683–March 1686. The reference to Cassini's discovery of "more" moons of Saturn is not specific enough to allow us to decide whether it was made some time after Cassini's announcement in March 1684 of his discovery of two further moons to add to the two he had discovered in 1671 and 1672. But the contents are consistent with such a later date, especially the discussion of the complete concept of Peter on 417, which echoes that of the *Generales inquisitiones,* completed in 1686. See Walter O'Briant, ed., *Gottfried Willhelm Leibniz's General Investigations Concerning the Analysis of Concepts and Truths* (Athens: University of Georgia Press, 1968); pp. 1 (dating), 51–52 (complete concept of Peter).

3. Above the *Ens* of both *Ens per se* and *Ens per accidens* Leibniz had written the word *unum* (a unity); I have instead set it in parentheses afterwards.

4. Alphonso X of Castile, under whose patronage a group of Jewish, Arabian, and Christian scholars completed the astronomical charts known as the Alphonsine Tables in 1252.

5. Cf. Spinoza's definition of substance as "that whose idea or concept does not arise from the idea or concept of another thing," and of God as "an *absolutely* infinite being," in his *Ethics,* reproduced by Leibniz in Aiii19 above. The phrase *ex vi essentiae ipsius* (by dint of its very essence) also evokes Spinoza's distinction in his Letter on the Infinite between what has no limits *ex vi suae essentiae,* "by dint of its own essence," and what has no limits "by dint of its cause."

6. Compare the final paragraph of "The Origin of Souls and Minds" (Aiv275) above.

7. After "representation of external things in a certain individual thing," Leibniz had written then deleted "I conjoined with an endeavour to act (*conatu agendi*) I."

8. This argument would appear to rule out substantial forms altogether. For Leibniz is adamant that every body has an infinity of parts. Thus if "an infinite body cannot be understood as one entity," so that "it has no substantial form and therefore no soul," then no body will have a substantial form. Gregory Brown has argued just this since I first wrote the preceding two sentences: see his discussion note on an article by Laurence Carlin, "Who's Afraid of Infinite Numbers? Leibniz and the World Soul," *Leibniz Society Review* 8, December 1998, 113–25. I have since written a defense of the consistency of Leibniz's position, "Infinite Numbers and the World Soul: In Defence of Carlin and Leibniz," in *Leibniz Review* 9, December 1999, 105–16; which Brown has responded to in painstaking detail in his "Leibniz on Wholes, Unities and Infinite Number," in *Leibniz Review* 10, 21–51.

9. The Akademie editors refer us to Martianus Capella, *De nuptiis Philologiae et Mercurii,* lib. IX; see Leibniz's notes on Capella in Aiii13: 201–2.

10. Huygens's discovery of Saturn's largest satellite, Titan, in March 1655 was to launch his career as one of the top astronomers of his day. He published his dis-

covery the following year, and followed this up in 1659 with his *Systema Saturnium,* in which he correctly identified the problematic *anses* or "handles" of Saturn as projections of a hypothesized ring. Giovanni Cassini, equipped with the fine telescopes of Giuseppe Campani, subsequently discovered Iapetus in 1671, Rhea in 1672, and Dione and Tethys in 1684. See "Huygens and the Astronomers," Albert van Helden, pp. 147–65 in Bos et al., *Studies in Christiaan Huygens,* Lisse, 1980.

11. —reading *innumerabilium* for *innumerabilem.* Cf. "A Specimen of Discoveries": "in every grain of powder there is a kind of world of innumerable creatures" (Aiv312: 1623).

12. See Descartes, *Principles,* III, § 48.

13. Leibniz had *flexum,* pliable, but the sense seems to require the opposite, *fragile,* brittle.

14. A quotation from the Bible: *Genesis* 1:2.

15. This is a reference to Descartes's theory of light, according to which light is a kind of pressure or tendency to move, a *conatus,* and no real motion is required. See Descartes, *Principles,* III, §§ 55–64. According to Leibniz's "New Physical Hypothesis," on the other hand, light must be an actual motion of a subtle fluid or aether. See *Hypothesis physica nova,* VI.ii.235–6: "*Light* is a very fast rectilinear motion of the aether propagated to the senses at any sensible point around and about" (see also §§ 7 and 56).

16. Here I have inserted a sentence break (. . .*exercetur. Perspicuum est* . . . in place of . . . *exercetur perspicuum est* . . . ) in order to make sense of this last passage.

### 35. There Is No Perfect Shape in Bodies

1. LH IV, 3: 5 pages. Edited for the Akademie by Gerhard Biller as Ve321: 1478–79 (Fascicule 7, 1988).

2. The provisional dating is based on the watermark, which gives April to October 1686.

3. This refers to the proof in the *Pacidius* in Part II above (Aiii78: 566–67).

4. Leibniz had originally continued: "| One can even doubt whether that happens *in an instant* at least, for with each body being acted on by all the others in the universe, it cannot at all be the case that these infinitely variable impressions accord with one another precisely to place. |"

### 36. There Can Be Infinite Degrees of Souls

1. LH IV 2, 11, leaves 10–11, 1 sheet of 8°, 4 pages. Edited for the Vorausedition by Heinrich Pfannkuch as Ve404: 1876–77 (Fascicule 8, 1989).

2. As a reference point for dating, the Akademie editors cite the article Leibniz published in June 1686 of the *Acta Eruditorum* (pp. 289–92), *Meditatio nova de natura anguli contactus et osculi, horumque usu in practica mathesi, ad figuras fa-*

*ciliores succedaneas difficilioribus substituendas,* "A New Meditation on the Nature of the Angle of Contact and the Osculum, and Their Use in Practical Mathematics for Substituting Easier Figures for More Difficult Ones," which might have occasioned this piece.

3. In the Vorausedition the editor Pfannkuch reports Leibniz as having replaced *discreto* by *discreta,* a change not recorded in the final edition.

### 37. A Specimen of Discoveries

1. LH IV 6, 9, leaves 1–4; 2 sheets of folio, 7⅓ pages, together with two interleaved slips of paper. Edited for the Vorausedition by Gerhard Biller as Ve125: 482–95 (Fascicule 2, 1983). The first part (up to the end of p. 1626) was previously edited and transcribed by Gerhardt (G.vii.309–18); the second part by G. W. R. Parkinson as an appendix to his "Science and Metaphysics in Leibniz's 'Specimen Inventorum,'" *Studia Leibnitiana* VI/1, 1–27: pp. 17–27.

Of the two small sheets inserted among the folio leaves, Gerhardt transcribes only the second, that dealing with occasional causes (5 recto and verso: G.VII. 313–14n); this is edited as a separate piece by the Akademie (Ve126 = Aiv320), *De Systemate Causarum Occasionalium* (On the System of Occasional Causes), but I have followed Gerhardt in including it as an elaborative note to the *Specimen.* The first (on 6 recto), which deals with possibility and the necessary being, is transcribed by Parkinson but also edited by the Akademie as a separate piece (Ve414 = Aiv315). It appears to be an elaboration on the fifth and sixth paragraphs of the *Specimen,* and I have included it there as a note. The *Specimen* is very much a work in progress, and it is difficult to tell whether a given marginal jotting is intended as an inclusion, a revision, a suggestion for revision, or a footnote. I have interpreted the first two passages given as footnotes by the Akademie editors (and Gerhardt) as intended insertions, and have included them in the main body of text.

2. Parkinson notes that the work "is full of theses and arguments that are reminiscent of the *Discourse on Metaphysics* and the correspondence with Arnauld, and it may therefore be said with reasonable confidence [to have been] written in about 1686" (op. cit., p. 1). This is also consistent with the resonance of themes with "On the Present World," and the greater maturity of their expression here; as well as with the new themes sounded here, especially the idea that contingent truths require an infinite analysis, first expounded in the *General Investigations* of 1686 (Aiv165: 741–90); see following note. The Akademie editors, however, place it in the Vienna period (1688), on the basis of weakly confirmed watermark evidence.

3. Leibniz's original title.

4. For the full argument that contingent truths require infinite analysis, see Leibniz's *General Investigations,* §§ 60–61; pp. 45–46 in Walter O'Briant's edition.

5. Leibniz has not yet settled on a name for this principle (later to become famous as his Principle of Sufficient Reason), although he has already been employing it for some years (see Mercer and Sleigh, "Metaphysics: The Early Years," *The*

*Cambridge Companion to Leibniz,* pp. 72ff.). In the manuscript, he first wrote *principium rationis praesuppositae,* the "Principle of a Presupposed Reason," before changing it to the "Principle of Providing a Reason."

6. This is expounded particularly clearly in Leibniz's "Necessary and Contingent Truths" (c. 1686; C 16–24; PW 96–105), and the short essay "On Freedom" (c. 1689; PW 106–11; L 263–66).

7. This explanatory paragraph was written down on the manuscript next to the preceding one, on leaf 2v°.

8. Cf. the *Discourse on Metaphysics,* §5: "he who acts perfectly is like an excellent geometer who knows how to find the best constructions of a problem" (G.iv.430; L 305).

9. This passage is amplified upon in the *Discourse on Metaphysics,* §24: Aiv306; G.iv.449–50.

10. Compare the version of this argument Leibniz gave in his annotations on Spinoza's Letter on the Infinite (Aiii19: 282–83).

11. The passage from *Quin imo* to *scenographias* was added by Leibniz in the margin. As Parkinson notes (PW 77–78), the figure alluded to here of the *plan géométral* (or ground plan) and its infinitely many projections from the sides—or variations on this such as the bird's-eye view of a town, and the points of view of approaching travelers—is one of Leibniz's favorites, and is given by him on numerous occasions, e.g. in Aiii76 above, and the letters to Arnauld of 12 April 1686 (G.ii.19; PW 50) and 9 October 1687 (G.ii.112; PW 72, L 339), in "Primary Truths" (C 518; PW 90, L 269), and in the "Monadology" §57 (PW 187; L 648).

12. Hippocrates, *De alimento,* §23; cf. n. 8 in Aiii3 above.

13. *Omnia conspirantia esse,* literally, "all things conspire." This theme of universal sympathy reverberates through the essay: at 492 l.25 cohesion is explained in terms of the fact that *omnes substantiae universi conspirant inter se,* "all substances in the universe harmonize with one another," and at 494 l.3 the principle of the cohesion of bodies is identified as *motus conspirans,* harmonizing motion.

14. Hugo of St. Victor was a German scholastic philosopher, 1096–1141. The reference is to his *Quaestiones et decisiones in epistolas D. Pauli,* I, qu. 237.

15. The *constantem* ("constant") in *certamque . . . naturam constantem* was omitted in the Vorausedition. It accords with the "notion constante" of the *Discourse on Metaphysics* (§6; Gi.iv.431), where this whole comparison with the line is treated by Leibniz at greater length.

16. This refers to Francisco Suárez's theory of causation, where *cause* is defined as "what flows [*influere*] being into something else"; which Leibniz (in his critical reflections on Nizolius of 1670) described as "a most barbarous and obscure expression" (Loemker, p. 126). See GLOSSARY note on *influxus.*

17. The Hypothesis of Occasional Causes is also depicted as bringing in a *deus ex machina* (a god brought on stage by mechanical device to resolve some difficulty in plot) in *Primary Truths* and in Leibniz's letter to Arnauld of 9 October 1687. In the latter Leibniz alleges that its "authors . . . consider it a *nodus vindice dignus, cui Deus ex machina intervenire debeat* (a knot worthy of a champion, for which God should intervene *ex machina*)," an allusion to Horace, *Ars poet.* 191–

92, which he quoted in *Confession of Nature Against the Atheists:* "*Nec deus intersit, nisi dignus vindice nodus inciderit* (And let not a god intervene, unless a knot should occur worthy of a champion)" (G.ii.113; L 119, 349).

18. Leibniz had originally begun this paragraph: "⌐ From the same notion of substance it is a consequence that neither a vacuum nor an atom exists. Instead there follows from it something even more important, that either there exist no ⟨corporeal⟩ subst⟨ances⟩ ⌐."

19. In his letter to Arnauld of 9 October 1687, Leibniz cites both Antoni van Leeuwenhoek and Jan Swammerdam in support of his transformationism: "I learned some time ago [presumably when he met them on his way to Hanover in 1676–77] that Mr. Leeuwenhoek holds opinions very close to mine, in that he maintains that even the largest animals originate by a kind of transformation . . . and Mr. Swammerdam, another great observer and anatomist, gives enough evidence of also inclining towards it" (G.ii.122–23; L 345). A more obvious proponent of transformation is Malpighi, whom he mentions in his "New System of Nature" (1695), citing in addition Nicolas Malebranche, Pierre Sylvain Régis, and Niklaas Hartsoeker as "being not very far removed from this opinion" (G.ii.480; AG 140).

20. For the work ascribed to Hippocrates, see *The Regimen,* I.4: "So of all things, nothing perishes and nothing comes into being that did not exist before" (quoted from AG 141). The Akademie editors give Pseudo-Hippocrates, *De dieta,* §23. Albert the Great (c. 1207–80) was a scholastic philosopher and Bishop of Ratisbon; "John Bacon" is John of Baconthorpe (d. 1348), a medieval commentator on Aristotle with Averroistic leanings famous for his *Commentary on the "Sentences."* Leibniz alludes to the first two thinkers in the same connection his letter to Arnauld of 8 December 1686 (G.ii.75), and to all three in that of 9 October 1687 (G.ii.116; L 342).

21. This very complaint has been made by Arnauld in his correspondence with Leibniz in September 1686: "6. Finally it will be said that it is not worthy of a philosopher to admit entites of which we have no clear and distinct idea; and that we do not at all have one of substantial forms" (28 September 1686: G.ii.67); to which Leibniz makes much the same reply as here (8 December 1686: G.ii.77; AG 80).

22. This sentence is marked off by two strokes of the pen, and from here on Leibniz's writing is smaller. Gerhardt did not transcribe the rest, regarding it as a hasty jotting down of "a large number of remarks having to do with the firmness and cohesion of bodies" (G.vii.318). But as G. H. R. Parkinson first discovered (op. cit. in note 1, p. 2), this is "only half the truth," in that after the long note on firmness and fluidity, Leibniz in effect resumes his "laws of corporeal nature." As Parkinson explains (17), the order of composition seems to have been as follows: after marking off the above sentence on 4 recto, Leibniz left the remainder of the page free for further reflections on firmness and fluidity, and proceeded with the "Laws of Corporeal Nature" in the left-hand column on 4 verso. Halfway down the column, he turned back to write the note on firmness and fluidity, which then spilled over onto 4 verso underneath the "Laws," and back onto 4 recto in the margin. After he had finished the note, he returned to an elaboration of the "Laws" in the right-hand column of 4 verso.

23. Title suggested by Parkinson for this digression on the explanation of the firmness of bodies in terms of harmony of motions.

24. Reading with Parkinson and Biller *parte impulsi* as a slip of the pen for *parte impulsa.*

25. Leibniz surely means *d.*

26. Leibniz had written *experimendum* for *experiendum,* "it must be put to experimental test."

27. Leibniz had crossed out *diversae* ("of *differing* tenacity"); but as Parkinson points out, the sense seems to require it (or something synonymous). Cf. "the whole universe is one continuous fluid, whose parts have differing degrees of tenacity *(partes diversos habent tenacitatis gradus)*" at 1630 below.

28. This is indeed a difficulty for Leibniz's account, and one that he does not resolve in this note. On the one hand, all free bodies will fly away along the tangent unless constrained by the pressure of their surroundings; but on the other hand, one cannot explain firmness or cohesion in terms of the pressure of surrounding bodies, on pain of an infinite regress ("in order to explain bodies' cohering by pressure, one must first establish firmness in the parts"). Thus "firmness cannot be explained except by consideration of a system," i.e. a system of harmonious internal motions that would constitute the body as a real or apparent whole.

29. See GLOSSARY notes on *direction* and *progress.* Leibniz had originally written "The same quantity of endeavours is conserved in the nature of things," then "The aggregate of endeavours," then "The aggregate of existing motions and," before settling on this wording.

30. Or perhaps (as Parkinson renders it), "Every perpetual disturbance is like oscillations." But it seems to me that Leibniz's meaning is not that there is a well-defined class of particular disturbances that are perpetual, but that, because of the elasticity of all matter, the effect of any disturbance on the universe as a whole is never entirely dissipated, but alternates back and forth.

31. This sentence replaces: "Truly every body is to be understood as having a motion in common with every other body whatsoever."

### 38. Motion Is Not Something Absolute

1. LH XXXV 12, 2, leaf 22. 1 bill (6 by 10 cm.), 2 pages; on the remainder of the reverse side of a geometric figure. Edited for the Akademie by Ursula Franke as Ve447: 2047 (Fascicule 8, 1989).

2. The Akademie editors date this piece (together with Aiv315–16 and 318–24) as belonging to Leibniz's Italian journey, March 1689 to March 1690 (?), on the basis of similarities in content to Aiv314, *De ratione cur haec existant potius quam alia* (The Reason Why These Things Should Exist Rather Than Others). They cite in particular the assertion of the relativity of motion and rejection of the *influxus physicus.* But concerning the first, Leibniz was aware of the relativity of motion as early as 1676 (see Aiii15 above), and since 1677 had affirmed the phenomenal nature of motion and non-absoluteness of space as consequences (see Aiv359,

Aiv360, Aiv277). So it cannot be assumed that his remarks on the non-absoluteness of space here are consequent on his reading of Newton's *Principia*. The metaphysics in the second paragraph, however—particularly the assertion of the lack of influence of one substance on another, and the connection of this with the non-transference of impetus in collisions—suggests a date of around the same time as the *Specimen*, i.e. about 1686 or some time thereafter.

3. See Aristotle, *Physics*, IV, 2, 209 a32–b2; Descartes, *Principles of Philosophy*, II, §28.

4. Leibniz had originally written "there is no *action* of one substance on another."

### 39. On Time and Place, Duration and Space

1. LH IV 8, leaf 91, 1 slip of paper (10 by 11.5 cm.), 1 page. Edited for the Vorausedition by Gerhard Biller as Ve440: 2022 (Fascicule 8, 1989).

2. This date is highly speculative. The notion of appetite or endeavour introducing something substantial when added to space, as well as that of space containing "not only existences but possibilities," to me suggest composition at around the same time as Aiv310 and Aiv317. The Akademie editors suggest that, given the closeness of the formulations to metaphysical discussions Leibniz penned while on his Italian journey (1689–90), all three may have been written then; but that this piece, with its mature terminology, could have been penned as late as 1700 (Aiv314: 1634).

3. Cf. Aiii74 above. Cf. also Aiv147: 629: "whatever is real in space and time consists in God comprising everything" (Ve284: 1255).

### Appendix 1: Excerpts from Leibniz's Early Writings

1. In 1669 Leibniz had sent two letters to Jacob Thomasius, his former professor at Leipzig, giving an outline of his philosophical position at that time. He thought sufficiently highly of the synopsis in the second that he published it—with some revisions—as a supplement to his introductory essay in his edition of Marius Nizolius's *De veris principiis et vera ratione philosophandi, contra pseudophilosophos, Librus IV* (On the True Principles and True Reason for Philosophizing; against the Pseudo-philosophers, Book IV), Frankfurt: Hermann a Sande, 1670. My translation is from this published edition, as reproduced in A VI.ii 435–36. The earlier version is given at A II.i 16–17, which Loemker translates (L 95–96).

2. The (full) title on the cover page is: *A New Physical Hypothesis; by which the causes of most of the Phenomena of Nature are derived from a certain unique universal motion, supposed in our world, without disdaining either the Tychonians or the Copernicans;* whereas the (full) title at the beginning of the text is *Theory of Concrete Motion; or, A Hypothesis About the Reasons for the Phenomena of Our World.* Thus *A New Physical Hypothesis* is often taken to be an alternative title for the *Theory of Concrete Motion*. But I take it to be the title of the whole work in-

cluding the *Theory of Abstract Motion*, since the physical hypothesis is invoked in the theorems and special problems of the TMA, if not in the theoretical foundation. The fragment translated is from pp. 241–42.

3. Leibniz had formulated the leading ideas of this piece in the spring of 1670, at the time of his most profound study of Hobbes. But after receiving a request from Oldenburg in August (10/20 August, A II.i 60) to send an exposition of the gist and grounds of his hypothesis for the Royal Society, it took him till the end of the following April before he had the whole of it (including the *Theory of Abstract Motion*) ready for publication.

4. Athanasius Kircher, *Scrutinium physico-medicum contagiosae luis, quae dicitur pestis* (Physico-Medical Examination of the Contagious Pestilence which is called the Plague), 1659, pp. 25–28; Robert Hooke, *Micrographia, or Philosophical Description of Minute Bodies,* 1665, (see II, I, pp. 17 and 47).

5. The full title is *Theory of Abstract Motion, or, The Universal Reasons for Motions, Independent of Sense and the Phenomena,* by the author G.G.L.L. (sc. Gottfried Wilhelm Leibniz of Leipzig), and it is dedicated to "the recently established Illustrious French Royal Society, for the promotion of Mathematics, Physics, Medical Studies, and for increasing the conveniences of the human race." It is the companion piece to the *Theory of Concrete Motion,* as explained above. I have translated most of the "Predemonstrable Foundations" (264–67; also translated by Loemker, L 139–42), and the beginning of the "Uses" (273), but not the preface or the "Definitions" preceding them (261–64), nor the "Theorems," "General Problems," or "Special Problems" between (268–73).

6. Thomas White, *Quaestio praevia: Utrum in continuo sunt partes actu* (A Leading Question: Whether There Are Actually Parts in the Continuum), §§ 1 and 2.

7. Cf. Axiom 4 from the *Dissertatio de Arte Combinatoria* of 1666: "Every single body has infinite parts, or, as is commonly said, the Continuum is divisible to infinity" (A VI.i 169). The "parts" here might be thought to be merely potential parts, in keeping with the standard Aristotelian analysis (see Appendix 2a), but as Philip Beeley has established, the context makes clear that these parts are conceived by Leibniz as actual parts of the continuum. See Philip Beeley, *Kontinuität und Mechanismus* (Stuttgart: Steiner, 1996), pp. 56–57.

8. This was a common reaction to the distinction between the infinite and the indefinite which Descartes had elaborated in his *Principia philosophiae,* part 1, § 26–27, and applied to the infinite division of matter in part 2, § 34–35 (see Appendix 2c).

9. Cf. Euclid's definition, "*A point is that which has no part, or has no magnitude,*" *Elements,* Book 1, Definition 1.

10. Presumably Leibniz is here thinking of any of the standard geometrical demonstrations that a shorter line contains the same number of assignable points as a longer one, such as could be found, for instance, in Froidmont's *Labyinthus de compositione continui.* In "On Minimum and Maximum . . . " (Aiii5) above, Leibniz gives a version of the argument that Galileo Galilei had presented in his *Two New Sciences.*

11. As noted above, this is Euclid's definition of a point.

12. This is Hobbes's definition: "*a point is that whose quantity is not considered*"; cf. the definitions from *De corpore* given in Appendix 2d below. It is defended by him in his *Six Lessons to the Savilian Professors of the Mathematics* as equivalent to Euclid's, which he gives as *Signum est, cujus est pars nulla* (*The English Works of Thomas Hobbes,* vol. 7. London, 1845; reprinted by Scientia Verlag Aalen, Germany, 1966; pp. 200–202).

13. Leibniz is here referring to Bonaventura Cavalieri's *Geometria indivisibilibus continuorum nova quadam ratione promota,* 1635 and 1653. See GLOSSARY notes on *indivisibilis, infinitesimalis.*

14. This is the Arriagan analysis of motion popularized by Gassendi (see Appendix 2e), which Leibniz himself had subscribed to some years earlier. Here he gives his reason for abandoning it as its incompatibility with (8), the "inertial" principle for rest, subscribed to by Aristotle, Descartes, and Gassendi himself. See the discussion in the *Pacidius,* Part II above.

15. Leibniz's Latin here is *quantum in ipso est,* close to the *Quantum in se est* of Newton. See I. Bernard Cohen, "'Quantum in se est': Newton's Concept of Inertia in Relation to Descartes and Lucretius," *Notes and Records of the Royal Society of London* 19 (1964): 131–55.

16. See Hobbes's definition in *De corpore,* given in Appendix 2d.

17. Compare with Hobbes, *De corpore,* part II, ch. XV, §7: "All endeavour is propagated to infinity."

18. See Aristotle, *Physics,* VI, 1, 231a 19; given in Appendix 2a.

19. That Leibniz was proud of this demonstration is clear from his attempt to urge it on Hobbes himself. In his letter to Hobbes of 28 July 1670, he wrote: "I would have thought that the endeavour of the parts towards one another—i.e. the motion by which one presses upon another—would suffice to bring about the cohesion of bodies. For those things which *press upon* each other are in an endeavour to penetrate. Endeavour is a beginning, penetration is a union. Therefore they are at the beginning of a union. But those things are at the beginning of a union whose beginnings or boundaries are one. Now things whose boundaries are one, or τα εσχατα εν, are, by Aristotle's definition too, not only contiguous but continuous, and truly one body, movable in one motion" (A II.i 57). See also his letter to Oldenburg of 28 September 1670 (A II.i 63–64), where he gives another lengthy rendition of this account of cohesion.

20. This Gassendian doctrine has its origin in Galileo's analysis of falling bodies. Since the time of fall is divided into equal parts, it is assumed that when the division is continued indefinitely, the equality still holds even for the infinitely small parts or moments. Uniform motion is thus that in which equal infinitesimals of space are accrued in equal moments; uniform acceleration that in which equal infinitesimals of velocity are accrued in equal moments. See Gassendi, Letters on Motion, *Opera omnia,* III (Anisson: Lyon, 1658; reprinted by F. Frommann: Stuttgart, 1964), pp. 478ff.; esp. 564b–65a.

21. Problems 24 and 25 are respectively to *accelerate* and to *retard* a given con-

tinuous motion in a given ratio. Leibniz conjectures: "I think this can occur at different instants of the same *sign* (see *foundation 18*) different endeavours are impressed on the same body." But he concludes with the confession that "these last three problems [sc. 23–25] I have not yet adequately weighed or exactly constructed" (A VI.ii 273).

22. This is the problem of "Aristotle's Wheel," which Galileo used to support his theory of voids in matter, and may have led Gassendi to propose his theory that the slower motion is one interrupted by intervals of rest. See Appendices 2b and e, and notes therein.

23. The Akademie editors identify Belin as the author of the anonymously appearing books *Les Aventures du philosophe inconnu en la recherche et en l'invention de la pierre philosophale*, Paris 1646, and *Apologie du grand oeuvre*, Paris, 1659, but they could not locate the challenge referred to by Leibniz.

24. Here the Akademie text has '*et Ars*' ('and Art'), which does not seem to fit either syntactically or semantically.

25. Only the slip of paper containing the first paragraph (LH IV 1, 4k, leaf 37; cut off to the right of and beneath the margin) has been preserved and catalogued by Eduard Bodemann. But Gerhardt had a second manuscript before him, now missing, which he interleaved with the first in the edition he made; re-edited by the Akademie, pp. 279–80.

26. On the basis of the style of the handwriting, the Akademie editors assign the first paragraph to the second half of Leibniz's stay in Mainz. The second paragraph was probably written somewhat later, but, on the basis of its contents, the editors ascribe it to the same period.

27. According to Gerhardt, above "for motion to have been eternal," Leibniz had written "it can be diminished without end."

28. According to Gerhardt, here a word and a couple of lines were unreadable due to destruction of the paper. It is not clear what the second principle is: the composition of motions was generally accepted at this time, but Leibniz analyzes this in terms of the composition of endeavours.

29. This is taken from a folio of two pages (LH XXXVII 3, leaf 167), which sustained considerable loss of text through damage to the right and bottom margins.

30. In dating this piece, the Akademie editors note that "it can hardly have been written before spring 1671," since "the 'doctrine of *the system of the world*' was explicitly excluded from the problematic of the *New Physical Hypothesis*" (see A VI.ii N40: 225 ll.20–22). Likewise a remark near the end "about the 'composition of endeavours' is evidence that the present piece was written earlier than N42$_4$ ("On Endeavour and Motion, Sense and Thought") yet later than the *Theory of Abstract Motion*." Together with the watermark for Summer–Fall 1671, this indicates a time of composition of between spring and fall 1671.

31. LH XXXVII 3, leaves 154–55. 1 sheet of folio; 5 columns. Previously published by Willy Kabitz, *Philosophie der jungen Leibniz,* 1909, pp. 141–44. The Akademie editors observe that the motivation for Leibniz's attempts in this and the preceding draft to demonstrate the *Predemonstrable Foundations* of his *Theory of*

*Abstract Motion* "might have been the consideration which John Wallis had expressed against him" (see Oldenburg to Leibniz, 22 June 1671, A II.i N68). My extract (pp. 306–7, 308–9) continues where Loemker's translation of pp. 303–6 (L 142–44) leaves off.

32. The Akademie editors note: From the name of J. Rouhault, whose *Traité de physique* Leibniz had studied in the summer or fall of 1671 (see A VI.ii N49), in the first draft, and from the letter from Leibniz to Oldenburg of 15/25 Ocotber 1671, in which he offered to send the Royal Society demonstrations of some of the foundations of his theory of motion, it may be supposed that both drafts would have been composed in the second half of the year. In particular, however, this can be supported by the date on the watermark of both sheets, which is identical with those of pieces N46, 48.1, 48.3 (partly), 48.4 and 50, originating at the same time."

33. Although in what follows Leibniz does "demonstrate from the phenomena" that "every body moves," he does not give such a demonstration of the vacuum. Perhaps he has in mind the reasons against the plenum he gave at the beginning of the *Hypothesis of the System of the World* above.

34. A similar definition had been used by Leibniz in an earlier piece on colleges (of all things!), the *De collegiis* of 1665(?): "The determination of the time of the college's physical operation is either continuous or discrete. But I do not mean continuous in the most rigorous sense, for in that way no society would be able to exist but an absolute one according to the laws, i.e. a Republic. . . . A continuous time is one between whose parts no time is interjected at which [the college] is not in operation in the respect in which it is called continuous. However, intervals of discrete time, whether certain or uncertain, are determined in such a way that when certain conditions are in existence, the college will assemble" (A VI.ii.10).

35. The consistency of Leibniz's thought with respect to the continuum and its definition can be judged from the fact that he consistently reiterates very similar definitions whenever he returns to the subject, culminating in the almost identical ones of the *Initia rerum metaphysica mathematicarum* of 1715, some 44 years later! See GLOSSARY note on *interjectum*.

## Appendix 2: Leibniz's Predecessors on the Continuum

1. Those interested in seeing the relevant passages complete may of course consult any standard edition of Aristotle's works. They are also given in full in a very useful appendix in Norman Kretzmann, ed., *Infinity and Continuity in Antiquity and the Late Middle Ages* (Ithaca: Cornell University Press, 1982), pp. 309–21, to which book I refer the reader interested in Aristotle and his impact on medieval and renaissance thought.

2. This definition of the continuous is repeated verbatim (with the exception of λέγω δὲ συνεχὲς for λέγω δ᾽ εἶναι συνεχὲς) in the *Metaphysics* at the end of Book 11 (K), (1069a1–15).

3. The Greek verb συνέχηται corresponding to συνεχής, like the Latin verb

*continere* (i.e. *con-tenere*) from which "continuous" is derived, has the root meaning "to hold together"—cf. the dual meanings of "continent": a continuous land mass; or being able to "hold oneself toegher."

4. The Greek could equally well be rendered "divided into parts that are ever divided," an ambiguity that should be held in mind in what follows. For it is conceivable that Leibniz derived his early commitment to the actually infinite division of the continuum from reading Aristotle this way, i.e. as having countenanced the actual infinite by division, whilst denying the actual infinite by extent. This, at any rate, is suggested by Aristotle's discussion in Book 6, where all his denials of the actual infinite seem to apply only to the second type of infinite, and his refutation of Zeno's dichotomy seems to allow for an actual infinity of divisions of both space and time. But see the discussion below.

5. The *reductio* proof is completed by taking into account that Aristotle had already proved above (321b 1–6) that the continuum cannot be composed of indivisibles in contact.

6. Similarly, in *On the Heavens* Aristotle appears to use divisibility as the defining property of the continuous: "Now a continuum is that which is divisible into parts that are ever divisible, and a body is that which is divisible in every way" (268a 6–7).

7. Richard Sorabji objects that Aristotle is not even entitled to say, on his own principles, that one can "traverse more than a finite number of potential divisions" (*Time, Creation and the Continuum*, p. 210–13, 323), since to do so would yield an actually infinite collection. But Aristotle would reply, I believe, that whereas actually made divisions remain in existence, potential ones do not, so that at no time would there be an infinity of them existing all at once. This seems to accord with his reply in *On Coming to Be and Passing Away* given below. Clearly, however, this is too delicate an issue to be decided in a footnote.

8. The problem of the continuum is, of course, discussed in detail in *On Indivisible lines* (968a 1–972b 32), traditionally ascribed to Aristotle: but probably composed by someone of his school. I have not included selections from that here.

9. See for example the edition and translation of W. S. Hett in *Aristotle: Minor Works* (Harvard University Press, 1936), where Problem 24 concerns the *rota Aristotelis:* "A difficulty arises as to how it is that the greater circle, when it revolves, traces out a path of the same length as the smaller circle, if the two are concentric. When they are rotated separately, the paths along which they travel are in the same ratio as their respective sizes."

10. As Crew and De Salvio point out (71), it is now accepted that the smaller circle will slide and not just roll smoothly.

11. These are my translations from the Latin of AT VIII.1 59–60.

12. —*revera indefinitas.* Here *indefinitas* could be understood as "indefinitely many" or "indefinitely small," just as *partes infinitas* is ambiguous between "infinitely many parts" and "infinitely small parts." As for *revera,* Descartes uses this adverb, as well as its synonyms *reipsa* and *reapse* (all meaning "actually," "in fact") in preference to the Aristotelian *actu* ("actually," "in act"); the latter forms a

pair of opposites with *in potentia* ("potentially," "in potency"). This distancing of himself from Aristotelian terminology is understandable given the likelihood that his "indefinite division" would be assimilated by many to Aristotle's "potential division" (with some epistemological gloss), rendering *revera indefinitas* as *actu infinitas in potentia,* a contradiction in terms. Cf. Descartes's scathing remarks about the Scholastic definition of motion as *actus entis in potentia, prout est in potentia* as "so obscure that I am compelled to leave them in Latin because I cannot interpret them" (*The World,* ch. 7, CSM.i.94), and as "magic words" (Rule 12 of his *Rules for the Direction of Mind,* CSM.i.49).

13. In other words, mixed in with the solid particles (those not changing their shape, but only their speed) are particles of liquid (which alter their shape to fill the gaps between the solids). Under the influence of this argument, Leibniz interprets liquids (at any rate, perfect liquids) as divided all the way down into physical points; see in particular Aiii60 and Aiii78 above.

14. The following selections are translated from Hobbes's Latin works, *Thomae Hobbes Malmesburiensis opera philosophica, quae Latine scripsit, omnia* (Amsterdam: Joannem Blaev., 1668): vol. 1, *De corpore,* pp. 96–97, 98–99, 178. The corresponding sections received a nineteenth-century translation in *The English Works of Thomas Hobbes of Malmesbury,* vol. 1, *Concerning Body,* collected and edited by Sir William Molesworth (London: John Bohn, 1839); pp. 108–9, 111, 206–7.

15. In Part II, Ch. 7, § 10, Hobbes had written: "Two spaces are said to be *contiguous* with each other between which there is no other space" (87).

16. In Part II, Ch. 7, § 10, Hobbes had written: "Two spaces or times are said to be *continuous* with each other when they have some part in common" (87).

17. The added phrase in brackets follows Molesworth (*English Works,* p. 206), and seems to be necessary.

18. This is a very unfortunate example, since, as Galileo argued (and Boyle showed), if a ball of lead and a ball of wool are dropped together through a certain distance in a vacuum, their velocities at the end of the fall will be equal. Therefore, if their endeavours are in the same ratio as the velocities, as Hobbes supposes, they too will be equal—contrary to what Hobbes is trying to illustrate!

19. Translated from *Animadversiones in decimum librum Diogenis Laertii, pars II: Physicam, ac imprimis nobilem illius partem metereologiam* (Guillelmus Barbier: Lyons, 1649). The selections are from pp. 411, 414, 306–7, and 455–56, resp.; these may also be found (with some interpolations of text from elsewhere in the *Animadversiones*) in *Opera omnia,* vol. 1, *Syntagma philosophicum, pars secunda, seu Physica,* pp. 262b, 263b–65a, 381b–82a, and 341b–42b, resp.

20. In his *Physiologia* (a translation and expansion of Gassendi's *Animadversiones*), Walter Charleton rendered this as: "No Physical Continuum, Infinitely Divisible" (Walter Charleton, *Physiologia Epicuro-Gassendo-Charltonia: or a Fabrick of Science Natural upon the Hypothesis of Atoms,* Sources of Science no. 31, New York/London: Johnson Reprint Co., 1966; reprint of the London edition of 1654: Bk. II, ch. II, p. 90).

21. An example of someone who inveighed against Epicurus by the tome would certainly be Libert Froidmont, whose *Labyrinthus de compositione continui* was mentioned in the Introduction, note 8.

22. In her fascinating book on Gassendi, Lynn Sumida Joy presents Gassendi as coming up with the example of the two concentric wheels by himself, as a modification of an argument of Sextus Empiricus's against atomism involving a rotating ruler, with which he had previously wrestled (*Gassendi the Atomist,* Cambridge: Cambridge University Press, 1987: pp. 176–77, 157).

23. An "engyscope" was a kind of reflecting microscope, now obsolete.

24. A "pismire" is an old word for an ant.

25. Charleton, *Physiologia,* II, ch. III, "Atoms, the First and Universal Matter," pp. 107–8.

26. François Bernier, *Abrégé de la philosophie de Gassendi,* 7 vols., Lyons, 1678, I: 296–99. See Michel Blay, *Reasoning with the Infinite,* Chicago: Chicago University Press, 1998, p. 95, for an English translation.

27. This is translated from François Bernier, *Abrégé de la philosophie de Gassendi,* 7 vols. Lyons: Anisson, Pousel, and Rigaud, 1684; vol. II, *Doutes: Sur quelques-uns des principaux chapitres de ce tome: Doute XI: Si la lenteur du mouvement tire son origine des petits repos interceptez,* pp. 311, 313–14.

28. Notably, the word used by Bernier here is *morules,* the same word used by Arriaga.

# Glossary-Index

Early on in my translating I decided to keep a record of Leibniz's Latin usage in order to ensure consistency in translation. A total consistency, of course, is not possible, nor is it always stylistically or semantically apt. So my notes record the reasons for my choices, discussions of troublesome terms, as well as connections and resonances of meaning in the original language (particularly among cognates) that cannot be preserved in the translation. The idea of presenting this information for readers in a Glossary-Index derives from Edwin Curley, in his *Collected Works of Spinoza,* volume 1 (SC). I have departed from his arrangement of material, however, in giving my notes in the Latin–English glossary, where Curley has his in the English–Latin–Dutch section; for it is the difficulties in translating these Latin words, as well as the various correspondences among them, that the notes concern. Accordingly, I have organized the Glossary-Index as follows:

1. *Latin-English Glossary.* This is more a glossary than an index. It does not list all Latin terms used by Leibniz, but only those that are noteworthy with regard to issues of translation or the development of Leibniz's thought. Nor does it give an exhaustive list of all the occurrences of a term, but rather indicates how the term is translated differently in different contexts. French equivalents in the one passage (Aiii36: 391) and one piece (Aiv310) in French are noted where appropriate. The indexing here is to the piece- and page-numbers in the Akademie and Vorausedition where the Latin (or French) word appears.
2. *Index and English-Latin Glossary.* This functions as a regular index, as well as a glossary indicating in parentheses the Latin (and where applicable, French or Greek) terms that the English word translates. The indexing here is to the pages where the English word appears.
3. *Index of Names.*

## 1. Latin-English Glossary

A PRIORI, A POSTERIORI: a priori, a posteriori.
I leave these terms untranslated. However, as Curley notes in his edition of Spinoza's works (SC 624), in the seventeenth century these still had the meaning given them by Ockham: an *a priori* proof proceeds from cause to effect; an *a posteriori* one from the effects to a cause.

ABSOLUTUS: absolute.

> *motus absolutus:* absolute motion. "Motion is not something absolute, but relative" (Aiv317; Aiv312: 1620); it is not a "true attribute of things containing a certain absolute nature," but is only something with respect to us (Aiv279); thus absolute motion is not a being in its own right, but "an affection of our soul [when we regard] other things as immobile" (Aiv360).

> *spatium absolutum:* absolute space. See under SPATIUM.

ABSTRACTUS: abstract.

> *motus abstractus:* abstract motion. Opposed to *motus concretus,* concrete motion.

ACCIDENS: accident.

> This is equated with a mode by Leibniz at Aiv301: 1506. Examples: heat, motion; contrasted with substance (see SUBSTANTIA).

> *ens per accidens:* an accidental entity. This is something existing only as long as certain accidental conditions hold; opposed to an *ens per se* (q.v.), something existing in its own right. In "On the Present World" Leibniz equates it with a *unum per aggregationem:* "an *accidental entity (unity)*—for instance, a woodpile, a machine—is what is only a unity by aggregation, and there is no real union in it other than a connection: perhaps a contact or even a running together into the same thing, or at least an agreement observed by a mind gathering it into a unity" (Aiv301: 1506).

> *per accidens:* accidental, accidentally; contrasted with PER SE, through itself (q.v.). Thus *corpora cohaesionem habere per se, fluiditatem per accidens,* "bodies have cohesion through themselves, and fluidity accidentally" (Aiv312: 1627).

ACERVUS: heap.

> The Acervus is the Paradox of the Heap, or Sorites, made famous by the Stoics: see Aiii78: 539ff., & n. 24; Aiv23. See also CONGERIES, CUMULUS, STRUES.

ACTIO: action.

> In his "Definitions: Something, Nothing" dating from about 1679, Leibniz defines an action as "a state from which there immediately follows a change in another thing, which change is called a *passion*" (Aiv76: 308). A substance is a thing which acts, and acts continuously. A body, however, does not, strictly speaking, act. "For by moving a body would act, and by acting it would change or be acted upon; but there is no moment of being acted upon, that is, of change or motion, in a body. . . . From this it follows that proper and momentaneous actions belong to those things which by acting do not change"

(Aiii78: 566). "However, that whose expression is more distinct is deemed to act, and that whose expression is more confused to be acted upon, since to act is a perfection, and to be acted upon is an imperfection" (Aiv312: 1620). In this sense, "all bodies act on and are acted upon by all others" (Aiv312: 1626).

Contrasted with PASSIO, q.v.

ACTUALIS (*actuel*): actual.

*actu infinite divisum:* actually infinitely divided. See DIVISIO.

*actu ipso:* an emphatic form of *actu,* "actually," used at Aiv267: 1398, 1400; thus *Omnis corpus actu ipso movetur:* "Every body is actually in motion," *actu ipso divisum est:* "is actually divided."

AEQUABILIS: equable, uniform.

*aequabilitas,* uniformity: Aiv301: 1513.

*aequabiliter,* uniformly: Aiv301: 1513.

AETERNITAS: eternity.

In a comment on Descartes, Leibniz appears to equate eternity with unbounded duration (Aiii15: 215). Similarly, in his notes on Spinoza's *Ethics* he describes eternity as "the greatest of all successives" (Aiii33: 385). But in "On a Notable Observation Concerning the Infinite," eternity is described as absolutely infinite, and distinguished from infinite duration, which is only infinite in relation to us (Aiii63: 481). Leibniz upholds this distinction in "On the Secrets of the Sublime," and in "Infinite Numbers" (Aiii60: 475; Aiii69: 501). See also "On Magnitude" (DSR 36–43, Aiii64: 482–84), where Leibniz distinguishes both unbounded time and unbounded duration from eternity, perhaps under the influence of his reading of Spinoza's Letter on the Infinite (see Aiii19 below).

AFFECTIO: affection

Leibniz appears to use this word to mean a *disposition* of a body or soul, a quality rather than an emotion. Thus in Aiv360 he calls motion "an affection of the whole world," and absolute motion "an affection of our soul when we regard other things as immobile." This usage puts him in line with Descartes and Spinoza (see the note in Curley's Glossary, SC 625).

AGGREGATUM: aggregate.

*ens per aggregationem:* an entity by aggregation. See *ens per accidens* under ACCIDENS.

ANGULUS: angle.

*angulus contactus:* angle of contact. This is the angle between a straight line and a curve (as, for example, that between a circle and its tangent), and is thus curvilinear; it is therefore opposed to *angulus recti-*

*lineus,* a rectilinear angle, i.e. one subtended by two straight lines (Aiii5: 99). Every angle of contact is smaller than any rectilinear angle, and thus by comparison, unassignable and infinitesimal: see INASSIGNABILIS, INFINITESIMALIS.

ANIMA: soul (in the sense of the principle of life).

*anima mundi:* world soul, soul of the world. In Aiii60: Leibniz commits himself to God as a "mind exist[ing] as a whole soul in the whole body of the world"; but he soon repudiates this heretical opinion in Aiii74: 521. See also Aiv301: 1509 for his reasons why "God cannot be understood as the *World Soul.*"

*animalia:* animals. This means animals in the sense of all *living beings,* and might well have been so translated.

*animatus:* animate. Leibniz believed that all substantial individuals in the world are, to a greater or lesser degree, animate, or alive; for him that is equivalent to believing that they are *ensouled,* which is the literal meaning of the word. Thus "Every corporeal substance has a soul" (Aiv279: 1466). But contrast "Every body is animate, i.e. has sensation and appetite" (Aiv267: 1398) with the more precise formulation "all organic bodies are animate, and all bodies are either organic or collections of organic bodies" (Aiv346: 1798).

ANIMUS: soul.

This is the principle of intellection or sensation, as opposed to ANIMA, q.v. The expressions in which Leibniz uses it have a distinctly archaic sound: "souls imbued with the truth through familiar conversation," "knowledge emerge spontaneously in the soul," and so forth (Aiii78: 529, 530, 532, etc.). Clearly, more modern renderings could be found, if one did not mind masking Leibniz's allusions to the soul. But it also seemed to me that perhaps the archaic style was deliberate, intended to evoke Plato and his doctrine of reminiscence. So I have generally opted for archaic sounding accuracy over modern style. An exception is at Aiii78: 534: *quid animo observatum sit,* "what you see in your mind's eye."

ANTITUPIA (ἀντιτυπία): antitypy.

This is a body's resistance to penetration, and is loosely equivalent to ELASTRUM (q.v.), its elasticity or spring.

ANTLIA: the air-pump.

This is the *antlia pneumatica,* the air-pump or "pneumatical engine" pioneered by Otto Guericke in an attempt to demonstrate the possibility of a vacuum. Robert Boyle's subsequent elaborations and improvements on the instrument were such that it came to be known as the *machina Boyleana* (see Steven Shapin and Simon Schaffer,

*Leviathan and the Air-Pump,* Princeton: Princeton University Press, 1985). Leibniz had read Boyle's work (see Aiii4) and would also presumably have possessed an intimate knowledge of the views on the subject of Christiaan Huygens, who had built several versions of the pump and been at the forefront of experimental enquiry into it.

APPARENTIA: appearance.

This is in general equivalent to PHAENOMENON (q.v.). In his note "On Transubstantiation" of 1668(?), Leibniz says "I call appearance whatever can be thought of in a real body deprived of substantial form, that is, matter taken with its accidents" (Aiii VI.i.510; L 117).

APPROPINQUATIO: approximation.

*quod minime conciliabile arbitror cum appropinquationibus,* "which I judge to be completely irreconcilable with approximations" (Aiii69: 497).

ASPECTUS: point of view.

(Aiv312: 1618): this corresponds to the French *face* in the *Discourse,* and is roughly equivalent to *respectus* (see under RESPECTIVUS).

ASSIGNARE: to assign.

*assignabile:* assignable. The notion of points being either assignable or unassignable is an essential ingredient of Leibniz's whole philosophy of mathematics. See DESIGNARE, INASSIGNABILIS, and *punctum metaphysicum.*

ATOMUS (το ἄτομον): (n.) atom; (adj.) atomic.

This Latin noun is borrowed from the Greek, where it is typically το ἄτομος, the uncuttable; it is feminine. But also, as in the Greek, *Atoma* can be short for *corpora atoma* (ἄτομα σώματα), "atomic bodies"; in this case it is neuter, in agreement with both σώμα and *corpus;* hence Leibniz's το ἄτομον. For a commentary on Leibniz's complex and changing views on the status of atoms in this period, see the Introduction.

BRUTUM: lower animal (Aiv 312: 1623, 1624).

BULLA: bubble.

For a discussion of *bullae* in relation to Leibniz's theory of cohesion, and to atoms, see the Introduction, Sections 4 and 5, respectively.

CAUSA (*cause*): cause; reason.

'Reason' is a standard nontechnical sense of *causa* in Latin, as noted by Curley (SC 628). Thus *Nulla autem causa intelligi potest, cur* (Aiii78: 559) could be "but no cause can be conceived for," *or* "but no reason can be understood why." So Leibniz's tendency to use the words interchangeably would not sound so strange to his contemporaries as it does to us. (See Mario Bunge's insightful discussion of the

identification of reasons and causes in the seventeenth century in his study *Causality and Modern Science* (3d ed., New York: Dover, 1979): pp. 226–32). See also RATIO.

CELERITAS: speed.

*celer; celeriter:* fast; fast, quickly.

COGITATIO: thought (Aiii36: 393, Aiv301: 1507).

COGNITIO: knowledge, cognition.

This is generally knowledge in the sense of being aware, as opposed to SCIENTIA, q.v., knowing as a fact. But for Leibniz every corporeal substance has a certain *cognitio,* and is thereby "confusedly omniscient" (Aiv279: 1465–66, Aiv301: 1508, Aiv312: 1618).

COHAESIO: cohesion.

For Leibniz's changing views on cohesion in this period, see the Introduction, Sections 4 and 6. See also CONSISTENTIA.

*cohaerentia:* cohering (Aiv301: 1512).

COLLECTANEUM: collection (Aiv346: 1798).

COMMERCIUM: interaction.

—as in *commercia corporum:* the interactions of bodies (Aiv312: 1623).

*commercium habeant:* interact (Aiv312: 1625).

COMPAGES: assembly (Aiv346: 1798).

COMPENDIUM: abbreviation.

Galileo's remark that mathematical definitions are abbreviations of speech (*compendia loquendi*) (Aiii11: 167), as well as the similar remarks by Pascal, were taken to heart by Leibniz. Thus in his notes on Descartes (Aiii15: 215) he says that "we humans are accustomed to attributing rest to larger bodies, for the sake of the abbreviation or ordering of thought" (*compendii seu ordinatae cogitationis causa*); and in Aiii68 and 69 he develops a similar construal of geometrical figures generally, angles, and infinitesimals, as "abbreviations for expressions" (*enuntiationum compendia*) (Aiii69: 499). *compendiosarum enuntiationum cause:* "for the sake of abbreviation" (Aiii69: 498).

CONATUS, CONARI (*l'effort, tacher*): endeavour.

Here I am bucking the recent trend among Leibniz translators (Parkinson excepted) to leave the term 'conatus' untranslated ('conatus' does exist in English, but it is extremely rare). In favor of that strategy, the Latinate word aptly marks it as a technical term. But this does not work so well for the corresponding verb, *conari,* which must then be rendered "to have a conatus" when it is being used in this technical sense (otherwise it is simply "to try"); and the plural of the noun is either the ugly 'conatuses', or 'conatûs' with long 'u,' invisible in writ-

ten English. 'Endeavour', on the other hand, works equally well for the noun and the verb, and seems preferable for a technical term to 'strive' and 'striving', the choices made by Curley in his translation of Spinoza. Also in favor of 'endeavour', it was how Hobbes (who had a powerful command of language) rendered *conatus* into English, and since Leibniz inherited the concept from him, I think this is reason enough to prefer it. (I have also retained Hobbes's spelling, which is the standard spelling in English, but rarer in American.) See also Remnant and Bennett's note on *tendance,* a French equivalent, which they translate 'endeavour' (notes, xxxix); and the very Hobbesian passage in the *New Essays,* 172–73, where Leibniz equates *tendance* and *conatus.* In the French passages translated in the present volume (Aiv310), Leibniz uses *'effort'* as the equivalent of *'conatus',* and *'tacher'* for *'conari'* (as he had previously in Aiii2: 4–5, 37–38).

*conatus ad motum* (Aiv301: 1513): an endeavour to move.

CONCRETUM: a concretum, concrete thing.

CONCURSUS: concurrence; collision.

Thus *divino concursu sustentetur,* "sustained by divine concurrence" (Aiv320); *Resistentia seu concursus,* "resistance or collision" (Aiv365: 1987); more literal is *aut etiam concursus ad idem,* "or even a running together into the same thing" (Aiv301: 1506).

CONFUSE: confusedly.

"It seems to me that every mind is omniscient, confusedly" (Aiii76: 524). "There are as many universal mirrors as minds, for every mind perceives the whole universe, but confusedly" (Aiv365: 1989).

*confusas:* confused, fused together.

According to Leibniz's doctrine of *petites perceptions,* any given perception is fused together from an infinite aggregate of smaller and smaller perceptions in such a way that they cannot be distinguished: see Aiii76: 524, and note 3; cf. also "On Simple Forms" (Aiii75: 522–23; DSR 83). See DIFFUSE, COGNITIO, PERCEPTIO, REFRINGERE, SENSUM.

CONGERIES: conglomeration.

This corresponds to Cordemoy's French *amas* at Aiv346: 1800. At Aiv301: 1508, *congeries lapidum* is translated "a heap of stones," but *partium congeries* is a "conglomeration of parts."

CONSENTIRE: to accord with, be consonant with.

Although this can be translated by the weaker "agree with," I have preferred to preserve the hint of harmony (see CONSPIRARE), especially in *inter se consentiant:* "are consonant with one another" (Aiv312: 1626).

CONSEQUENTIA: consequence (Aiii5: 98, 100; Aiii36: 383; Aiii78: 550, 551), (Aiv266); inference (Aiii60: 474, Aiv315), argument.

In the logic of Leibniz's time, this denotes the inference from the premise (or conjoined premises) of an argument to the conclusion, with the argument stated in the form of a conditional; it is thus also the relation of the antecedent of that conditional to its consequent. See William of Ockham, *Philosophical Writings,* ed. and trans. P. Boehner (Indianapolis and Cambridge: Hackett, 1990); pp. 84–88.

CONSERVARE, CONSERVATIO: to conserve; conservation.

In Aiii58 Leibniz attempts to derive the conservation of the quantity of motion from that of quantity of matter. Five months later he realizes it applies only to relative motion: "the conservation of the quantity of motion must be asserted of the action, i.e. relative motion, by which one body is related to another or acts on another" (Aiii68: 493). Finally, he realizes that this must be supplemented by conservation of power: "the same quantity of motion cannot be conserved, but . . . the same quantity of power is conserved" (Aiv365: 1989). "So I say that matter is divided not even into parts of equal bulk, as some have supposed, nor into parts of equal speed, but into parts of equal power, but with bulk and speed unequal in such a way that the speeds are in inverse ratios to the magnitudes" (Aiv267: 1401–2).

*conservari:* is conserved.

Some translators translate this as "is preserved," but this loses the extremely important connection with the laws of *conservation* of quantity of motion and of power, and thus the conservation laws of modern physics.

CONSISTENTIA: cohesiveness; a cohesive thing.

This is a technical term of seventeenth-century physics meaning the degree to which a body holds together, its power of cohering. It occurs in Galileo's discussion of the cause of cohesion (*consistentia* is the Latin equivalent of his *consistenza,* EN 86), and in Hobbes's *De corpore,* where Molesworth renders it as 'consistency'. It is closely related to what Leibniz (again following Galileo, cf. EN 65) called 'resistance' (*resistentia, resistenza*), a body's resistance to being broken up into parts. See Aiii4, especially nn. 3 and 4. Curley (SC) translates it as "coming to rest, solidification" in his edition of Spinoza, the first of which terms presupposes the correctness of Descartes's analysis of its cause, rejected by Leibniz, and the second of which does not seem appropriate here. There is an English noun *consistence,* meaning degree of density, which Newton uses in describing how the ether surrounding bodies "must crowd and press their parts together, much af-

ter the manner that air surrounding two marbles presses them together if there be little or no air between them" in his "Hypothesis
Explaining the Properties of Light Discoursed of in My Several Papers" of 9 December 1675 (Isaac Newton, *Newton's Philosophy of
Nature,* ed. H. Thayer, pp. 87–88). But Newton clearly uses it to describe the degree of density of the ether—which "may be the principal cause of the cohesion of the parts of bodies," but is not the degree
of that effect. Individual *consistentiae* I have rendered as "cohesive
things," as at (Aiii4: 95): *nulla consistentia erit separabilis,* "no cohesive thing will be separable"; but *omnes consistentiae erunt inter
se aequales,* "all things will be equally cohesive." The one instance
of *consistentia* simply translating as 'consistency' is at (Aiv301:
1513): *sed major consistentiae aequabilitas, qualis est lactis ante coagulum,* "but of a more equable consistency, like milk before coagulation."

CONSPIRARE: to harmonize.

*omnia pulcherrime conspirent inter se:* "all harmonize with one another
most beautifully" (Aiv312: 1621); *cohaesionem ex eo quod omnes
substantiae universi conspirant inter se,* "cohesion from the fact that
all substances in the universe harmonize with one another" (Aiv312:
1627); *Cohaesionis principium est motus conspirans,* "the principle
of cohesion is harmonizing motion, that of fluidity is varying motion" (Aiv312: 1630). See SYMPATHICUM.

CORPUS (*corps*): body.

*corpora firma:* firm bodies (see FIRMUS).

CREATURA: creature (Aiv310: 1510, 1512; Aiv312: 1623); created thing
(Aiii69: 501, Aiv266, Aiv301: 1507).

CUMULUS (*tas*): a pile.

In Cordemoy, *cumulus* corresponds to the French *tas* at Aiv346: 1798;
*un tas de pierres,* "a pile of stones," Aiv310.

DARI: to be given, to be (such a thing as), to exist.

As Parkinson notes in DSR 131, Leibniz normally uses *dari* in the sense
of "to be given for consideration," to exist conceptually, as opposed
to *existere,* to exist actually. Cf. *si quod detur Ens necessarium existet, ostendum solum est dari, scilicet in numero rerum possibilium
sive intelligibilium,* "if what is given as a necessary entity exists, all
that has to be shown is that it is given, namely, in the number of possible things or intelligibles" (Aiii80: 576: DSR 99); and *Datur ergo
sive intelligi potest Ens . . . ,* "Therefore there is given, i.e. can be understood, an entity . . . " (577). Accordingly, where it needs to be
made explicit that intelligible existence is concerned, I have rendered

*non dari* and *nullum datur* as "there is no such thing as" (Aiv278 and elsewhere).

DEMONSTRATIO: demonstration.

This means a formal proof, usually either by syllogism or *reductio ad absurdum.* See PROBARE.

DESIGNARE: to designate.

Leibniz uses this more or less synonymously with ASSIGNARE (q.v.), and likewise their cognates.

*designabile:* designatable (Aiii5: 100, Aiii52, Aiii69: 496, Aiii78: 543). In "On the Infinitely Small," Leibniz defines an undesignatable quantity as one "whose magnitude cannot be expressed by any character signs detectable by the senses," since "every designatable magnitude whatsover will always be writable in a sufficiently small book with the aid of abbreviations and representations" (Aiii52).

DETERMINARI: to be determined; to be terminated or bounded.

Literally, to determine means to set limits or bounds to a thing, and this literal sense must always be borne in mind. Spinoza, for instance, in his Letter on the Infinite, uses 'determine' in this sense when he talks of "determining duration and quantity," i.e. of assigning them finite times and measures. Likewise Leibniz: *Sed quoniam [series] non determinatur quomodo?* "But seeing as the series is not bounded, how can this be the case?" (Aiii69: 502); "since there is no reason determining or limiting its size" (Aiii85: 585). See also INTERMINATUM.

DIFFERENTIA: difference; differential; differentia.

The differential is the linchpin of Leibniz's differential calculus. The rate of change of quantity $y$ with respect to $x$ is given by the ratio of their differentials, $dy$ and $dx,$ namely, $dy/dx.$ Here $dy$ and $dx$ are the infinitely small differences, $y$ and $x$ being conceived as sums of infinitely many such differences. See Henk Bos, "Differentials, Higher-Order Differentials and the Derivative in the Leibnizian Calculus," *Archive for the History of the Exact Sciences,* 14, no. 1 (1974): 1–90, for an admirably clear account of Leibniz's calculus. Leibniz's success in formulating the calculus in terms of these entities did not automatically resolve the problem of their status, which is clearly crucial in the problem of the composition of the continuum. In Aiii52, Aiii68, and Aiii69 Leibniz makes some important advances in clarifying this status. See INFINITESIMALIS.

An instance of *differentiae* being the "differentiae" of a species, that is, the properties distinguishing different species, is at Aiv301: 1508. In "On the Origin of Things from Forms" an idea is equated with "a differentia of thoughts" (Aiii74: 518, 521; DSR 75, 81).

DIFFUSE: diffusedly.

Every substance is "diffusedly omnipotent"; "omnipotent" because it acts on all others, "diffusedly" because "its action is diffused by things acting in contrary ways" (Aiv267, Aiv279); "every substance has in itself a certain participation in divine omniscience and omnipotence, even though its knowledge is confused, and its action is diffused by things acting in contrary ways" (Aiv267: 1400). See CONFUSE.

DIRECTIO (*direction*): direction; tendency in a given direction.

Although Leibniz uses this word in its standard sense (as in Aiii58, Aiii68, Aiv267: 1404, Aiv304: 1525, and elsewhere), it often seems to be used as a contraction of "tendency in a given direction." Thus: *directionem habet pergendi in recta tangente,* "has a tendency for continuing its motion in the direction of a straight line tangent to the curve" (Aiv312: 1626); *si le point A tend dans le droite AB, le point B ait une autre direction,* "if the point A tends along the straight line AB, the point B should have a tendency in another direction" (Aiv310); . . . *an omnes directiones debeant esse aequiveloces. An forte . . . sint directionum velocitates in reciproca ratione magnitudinis:* "whether tendencies in all directions ought to be of equal velocity; or whether perhaps . . . the velocities of bodies tending in different directions are inversely proportional to their magnitude" (Aiii76: 525). It differs from the Cartesian *determinatio,* the determination of a body's motion in a given direction, in that Descartes held *determinatio* to be a distinct component of motion from *celeritas,* speed (see Descartes, *Principles,* II, § 41; and Letter to Clerselier, 17 February 1645, CSMK: 247); for Leibniz's critique, see Aiii15: 216.

In the "Laws of Corporeal Nature" in the *Specimen of Discoveries* (Aiv312: 1629), the *directio* seems to be understood as the directed motion (or quantity of motion understood as a vector quantity) that was established as the quantity conserved in collisions by Wren, Wallis, Huygens, and Marriotte. There Leibniz coins a new technical term for it, PROGRESSUS (q.v.).

DISPOSITIO: orderly arrangement, disposition.

*disponere,* to give an orderly arrangement to (Aiv346: 1800). Thus *dispositionem habenti non denegatur forma,* "form cannot be denied to something having an orderly arrangement" (Aiv346: 1800); *a dispositione nostri et medii,* "as a result of the disposition of ourselves and the medium" (Aiv301: 1506).

DISSOLVI: to be dissolved, broken up.

*nulla mens naturaliter dissolvi possit,* "no mind can be naturally dis-

solved" (Aiii36: 393); *qui fornix difficulter dissolvetur,* "which would be broken up with difficulty" (Aiii85: 585).

DIVIDUUS: divisible.

Lost in the translation is that this is the opposite of INDIVIDUUS (q.v.). Every real substance is *individua;* all things that are *dividua* are not complete things (Aiv132: 560).

DIVISIO *(division)*: division.

*la division actuelle des parties a l'infini:* "the actual division of the parts [of matter, shape] to infinity," is one of Leibniz's most characteristic doctrines, and of central importance to the continuum problem (see the Introduction, passim).

*divisibilis:* divisible.

DURATIO: duration.

In "On Magnitude" (late April 1676), Leibniz distinguishes duration from time as follows: "*Duration* is continuity of existing. Time is not duration, any more than space is collocation. And it would be inappropriate to say that a day is a duration, since on the contrary we say that the ephemerids endure for a day. Time is a certain continuum according to which something is understood to endure" (Aiii64: 484; DSR 41).

DURUS: hard.

Leibniz's doctrine that "there are no *atoms* in things, i.e. no things having an infinite degree of hardness" (Aiv301: 1510) derives from Hobbes. See the Introduction, Section 5.

ELASTRUM, ELATERIUM, ELASTICUS: elasticity, elastic.

*Sciendum est autem in omnibus esse aliquem et Elastri gradum:* "it should be realized, though, that there is some degree of elasticity in everything" (Aiv301: 1512). Each body gets an impulse from another body through its own elasticity, but the cause of the elasticity "is the internal motion of the parts of the elastic body" (Aiv312: 1620).

ENS: entity, being.

Literally, an *Ens* is a being, and this is how the word is most often translated in Leibniz. But whilst this is unproblematic in contexts where real existents are being referred to, as in Leibniz's references to the *necessary being* in Aiv312, the Latin word has a wider connotation than the English word 'being'customarily bears, embracing not only "accidental beings" (like a heap of stones or even a pair of diamonds located far apart), but even purely conceptual entities like infinite-sided polygons. The strain of this Scholastic usage was felt by Spinoza, who, in claiming that "Fictitious Beings and Beings of Reason are not beings," pointed out that "dividing being into real being and

being of reason" is hardly proper, since it amounts to the division of "being into being and non-being" (Spinoza, Appendix Containing Metaphysical Thoughts, part 1, SC 299–310). But Leibniz, distinguishing the possibly existing from the actually existing (*existens*), could embrace the wider connotation of *ens* with no such qualms, as he does in a series of definitions probably dating from 1688–89, where *Ens* is equated with *possibile*, and *non-Ens* with *impossibile* (Aiv196: 930). Similarly, in "On the Present World" (Aiv301): "An *Ens* is that about which something can be affirmed" (1506), i.e. which has at least one positive attribute. The translation of *Ens* as *entity* seems more conformable to these conceptions, and I have so rendered it wherever possible. Thus "motion is a relative entity" (Aiv360), "a circle is a fictive . . . entity" (Aiii68: 492, Aiii69: 498); but *Corpus non est substantia sed modus tantum Entis,* "A Body is not a Substance, but only a mode of being" (Aiv316), and *necesse est aliquid existere, atque ideo datur Ens necessarium,* "it is necessary for something to exist, and therefore there is a necessary being" (Aiv315).

*ens per se:* an entity in itself (opposed to *ens per accidens, ens per aggregationem:* see under ACCIDENS).

*ens reale:* a real entity, *ens imaginarium:* an imaginary entity.

*ens rationis:* an entity of reason.

*non-ens:* a nonentity (Aiv301: 1506).

*entia ficta:* fictive entities (Aiii69: 498).

*entia fictitia:* fictitious entities (Aiii68: 492; Aiii69: 499).

ENTITAS: entity.

This is entity in the sense of "beingness." It occurs only twice: in the Letter to Thomasius (Appendix 1a), and (Aiii19: 282): *quicquid OMNIA continet, est maximum in entitate,* "Whatever contains *everything* is maximum in entity."

EQUABILE: equable.

EXPERIENTIA: experience (the general concept) (Aiii68, Aiii78: 532).

EXPERIMENTUM: (a particular) experience (Aiv132: 1300, 1302); an experiment (Aiii78: 529, 531, 534, 537; Aiii19; Aiv312: 1627, 1628); an empirical fact (Aiii19).

*experiri:* to test, to put to experience, to find out by experiment Aiv312: 1627, 1628.

EXTENSIO: extension.

At Aiv132: 565, *extensio* is defined as "whatever we observe as common to all simultaneous perceptions." It does not, *contra* Descartes, belong to the substance of a body: only matter and form do (Aiv279: 1465).

EXTENSUM (*l'étendue*): the extended, that which is extended, an extended thing.

This is a particular extended thing as opposed to EXTENSIO (q.v.), extension in general, the quality of extendedness. Thus it corresponds to Descartes's extended substance, shorn of the status of substance. At Aiv132: 565, the extended is said to be "a continuous whole whose parts are simultaneous and have a situation among themselves," which "behaves as a part with respect to another whole."

*extensum absolutum:* "the absolute extended" (Aiii74: 519); this is a maximum and indivisible, and thus differs from space. Similarly, in his "Meditations on Knowledge, Truth, and Ideas" of 1684, Leibniz claims that "it is necessary that there actually be in God an idea of absolute and infinite extension," of which the various shapes of matter are modifications, rather than parts (AG 27; L 294). But at Aiv267: 1393 *extensum, absolute, sine alio addito* defines space.

*ipsum per se extensum:* that which is extended in itself (Aiii74: 519).

EXTREMUM: extremum (Aiii69: 498, Aiii78: 537, 541, 546, 548, 553, 555, 557); [of a line:] endpoint (Aiii65: 488, Aiii78: 562, 564, 566); [of the universe:] extremity (Aiv277).

FIGURA (*figure*): figure, shape.

This has the sense of 'geometrical figure', and could have been translated 'figure' throughout. But this occasionally sounds forced in English, so I have forgone consistency for style, using 'figure' only in obviously geometrical contexts, and 'shape' elsewhere.

FINGERE: to imagine (Aiv346: 1799; Aiv312: 1619, 1620, 1628).

This is the cognate verb to the noun *fictio,* a fiction. In his edition of Spinoza, Curley chose to preserve this correspondence between the cognates by using the now archaic 'feign'. But as he notes, "it is important to realize that the English terms have connotations which may be misleading. A feigned or fictitious idea is not necessarily a false one . . . " (SC: 637). Given this, 'imagine' seems to me a good synonym, and I can find no cases where this translation is misleading.

FIRMUS: firm.

This is Leibniz's preferred term, as he makes clear in the *New Essays:* "many philosophers attribut[e] hardness to their atoms. . . . However, rather than the word 'hardness' I would prefer 'firmness', if I may be allowed to use it in this sense, for there is always some firmness even in soft bodies. I would even look for a broader and more general word such as 'stability' or 'cohesion'. Thus I would contrast hard with soft, and firm with fluid; for wax is soft, but unless melted

by heat it is not fluid and retains its boundaries; and even in fluids
there is usually some cohesion, as can be seen in drops of water or
mercury. My opinion is that all bodies have a degree of cohesion; just
as I think that there are none which are entirely without fluidity or
possessed of a cohesion that cannot be overcome; so that in my view
the atoms of Epicurus, which are supposed to be insuperably hard,
cannot exist, any more than can the rarefied and perfectly fluid
matter of the Cartesians." *New Essays,* II, iv, 125–26. Cf. CONSIS-
TENTIA.

*firmitas:* firmness. (Aiv301, esp. 1510, Aiv312 passim.) *corpora firma:*
firm bodies.

FLEXUM: bending (Aiv304: 1525, 1526).

*flexum osculi,* curve of osculation (1527).

GENUS: kind (Aiii19: 276, Aiii33: 385, Aiii68: 495, Aiii69: 498, Aiii78:
522); genus (Aiv275).

*generalis:* general, generic.

*tempus locumque generalem,* generic place and time (Aiv267: 1397). In
this piece of the late 1670s, Leibniz uses these terms for space and
time in general. The terminology is used by Descartes in his *Princi-*
*ples,* II, §10, 12, 18, as Newton notes (*Unpublished Scientific Papers*
*of Sir Isaac Newton,* p. 131).

*natura generalis:* see under NATURA.

GLOBULUS: a globule, small sphere, ball.

In Cartesian physics, a *globulus* is a one of the "spherical particles" into
which the second of the "three primary elements of this observable
world" is divided. These *globuli* "are exceedingly minute compared
with the bodies we can discern with our eyes, but"—unlike the
minute parts of the first element or subtle matter (*materia subtilis*),
which are indefinitely small and of changeable shape—"they are
of a certain and deteminate quantity, and divisible into other much
smaller ones" (Descartes, *Principles,* III, §52: AT VIII.1, 165). In his
*Propositiones Quaedam Physicae,* Leibniz defines *globuli* as "particular whirls, or terrellas" (q.v.) that are solid (Aiii2: 31, 29); but he
writes disparagingly of the "globules of the second element" that
Descartes "was forced to suppose as having arisen by being worn
away from the innumerable cubes moving around their own centers
that he implausibly supposed right at the beginning of his *Principles*"
(Aiii2: 33). See Aiv301: 1510; see also TERRELLA.

GUTTA: drop (Aiv301: 1513).

HARMONICUM: harmonious (Aiii60: 474; Aiii4: 95).

*harmonicωtaton* (Aiv316): most harmonious.

HYPOTHESIS: hypothesis.

Leibniz gives this noun a semi-Greek declension: [nom, acc, gen, dat/ abl] (sing.) *hypothesis, hypothesin, hypotheseos, hypothesî* (corresponding to the Greek ὑποθεσις, ὑποθεσιν, ὑποθεσεος, ὑποθεσει); (plur.) hypotheses, hypotheses, hypothesum, hypothesibus (Greek ὑποθεσεις, ὑποθεσεις, ὑποθεσεων, ὑποθεσεσι).

ICTUS: a blow, impact, collision.

*cujusque corporis . . . , qui ictum facit:* of each of the colliding bodies (Aiv312: 1621).

IDEA: idea.

In his "Definitions: Something, Nothing" of 1679, Leibniz defines as *Idea* as "a concept in the mind of an agent, to which he wants to render a similar effect" (Aiv76: 309).

IMAGINARE: to imagine.

*imaginarius (imaginaire):* imaginary.

IMMENSITAS: immensity.

*immensum:* (n.) the immensum, (adj.) immense, beyond measure.

Parkinson translates these as "immeasurability" and "immeasurable" (see DSR 122, n. 92), to avoid the modern connotation of "immense" as "very large." But *immensum* does have a spatial connotation not captured by "immeasurable," immensity being to extension what eternity is to duration. *Immensum* can be synonymous with "infinite" or "beyond measure," as at Aiii4: 95; and at Aiii60: 475 Leibniz distinguishes this species of the infinite from the unbounded. But at Aiii74: 519 Leibniz seems to be trying to establish a special technical sense of *immensum* as "that which persists during continuous change of space, . . . and is one and indivisible"; for this I have left the word untranslated, "the immensum." As Leibniz explains in Aiii36: 391– 92, Aiii74: 519, divine immensity is the "basis of space," an attribute that is "one, indivisible, and immense," just as divine eternity is the basis of duration. See also Aiv321, and the discussion in the Introduction, Section 7.

IMPELLERE: to impel.

*impulsus:* impulse.

IMPLICARE: to involve, to imply.

*contradictionem implicare* (or often, by ellipsis, simply *implicare*): to imply or involve a contradiction. Thus *antequam dicatur perfectam fluiditatem implicare,* "before it is said that a perfect fluidity implies a contradiction" (Aiii58: 466).

*implicantia (contradictionem):* a contradiction.

INASSIGNABILIS: unassignable.

In the TMA Leibniz defines a point as "unassignable," i.e. as that which is "smaller than can be expressed by a ratio to another sensible magnitude unless the ratio is infinite, smaller than any ratio that can be given" (Appendix 1c). The doctrine of unassignable points, lines, and bodies is a crucial ingredient in his philosophy of mathematics (see Introduction, Sections 3, 5, and 6).

INCONCINNITAS: disproportion, lack of proportion (Aiii78: 560).

INDESIGNABILIS: undesignatable.

In "On the Infinitely Small," Leibniz defines an undesignatable quantity as "one whose magnitude cannot be expressed by any perceivable character signs" (Aiii52: 484). Cf. DESIGNARE, INASSIGNABILIS.

INDISTANS: indistant.

Two contiguous points are not identical, but lack distance from one another: *indistantia sunt, non distant:* are not distant, are indistant (Appendix 1c; Aiii78: 567); not "are dense," as Loemker indefensibly translates it (L 141).

INDIVIDUUS: individual; indivisible.

"Individual" is the usual meaning, and is the meaning clearly intended in "On the Present World" and "A Specimen of Discoveries." But at Aiv132: 560 it contrasts with DIVIDUUS and SUBDIVIDUUS (q.v.), and therefore has its root meaning of "indivisible."

INDIVISIBILIS: indivisible.

Galileo Galilei speculated in his *Two New Sciences* of 1638 that the continuum is composed of an infinity of indivisibles, or unquantified parts, separated by indivisible voids (see Appendix 2b). Thus the indivisibles of a line would be points, those of a surface, lines, and so on. (Gassendi and Descartes, on the other hand, followed Aristotle in regarding these as mathematical entities, or modes of things, having no physical existence; see Appendix 2 a, c, d). But Galileo was preceded in print in his use of the term by Cavalieri, who published his *Geometria indivisibilibus continuorum nova quadam ratione promota* ("Geometry, advanced in a new way by the indivisibles of continua") in Bologna in 1635. Cavalieri compared plane figures by comparing "all the lines" of each, but stopped short of asserting that the figures were actually composed of the lines. The lines, in fact, are generated by the motion or transition through the figure of a specific line, the *regula;* and only figures effected by the same transition and same regula may be regarded as equal. Leibniz has been accused of great naïveté in assimilating Cavalieri's indivisibles to *infinitesimals*

and to the *method of exhaustion.* But in his defense it must be said that Roberval, who was pioneering methods based on composing rectangles of infinitely small rectangles, saw little difference between his method and Cavalieri's, even adopting Cavalieri's term "indivisible"; and Blaise Pascal, much influenced by Roberval, and (in Paris) one of Leibniz's sources on indivisibles, completed this assimilation of the two different foundations: he asserted that "the indivisibles of a plane figure constitute an infinity of infinitesimal rectangles, whose sum differs from the figure only by a quantity smaller than any given one" (Pascal, *Oeuvres,* vol. 8, p. 352), and also said that it is only in a manner of speaking that the method of indivisibles differed from the ancient method of exhaustion. See Enrico Guisti, *Bonaventura Cavalieri and the Theory of Indivisibles,* Bologna 1980; Kirsti Andersen, "Cavalieri's Method of Indivisibles," *Archive for the History of the Exact Sciences,* vol. 31, no. 4, 1985, pp. 291–367.

INFINITESIMALIS: infinitesimal.

An infinitesimal is an infinitely small part of a continuous quantity, and infinitely many of them make up the whole. In its standard acceptation, an infinitesimal is a part smaller than any assignable (see INASSIGNABILIS), a definition to which Leibniz frequently has recourse. The sense of this is that it is not a minimum or absolutely least element or indivisible, but a divisible part such that, however small a finite part may be given, it is still smaller.

INFINITUS (*infini*): infinite.

*numeri infiniti:* infinite numbers, but also *an infinity of* numbers: the Latin is ambiguous in a way that can be misleading, as in Gassendi's estimate of Epicurus's best argument against infinite division (Appendix 1e). On occasion Leibniz also seems tempted in this direction, but eventually decides that although there are infinitely many numbers, there are no *infinite numbers,* i.e., infinitely large ones: see "Infinite Numbers" (Aiii69). For his distinction among three different types of infinity, see Aiii63, Aiii19: 282.

*infinite parva:* infinitely small, *infinities minus:* infinitely smaller (Aiii5: 98–99).

INFLUXUS: influence (Aiv312: 1620; Aiv317).

The term *influxus* has both scholastic and astrological connotations. Francisco Suárez (1548–1617) had proposed that efficient causes could be understood in terms of an *influxus physicus* of one substance on another (*Disputationes metaphysicae,* XII, ii, 4). Leibniz had rejected this as early as 1666 in his *Dissertatio de arte combinatoria:*

"what is the word *influxus* beyond a mere word?" (L 75, 83; see also his criticisms on L 126). Likewise, as a modern he would have dismissed the idea of the *influxus astrorum* of the astrologers. Nevertheless, he accepted the idea of the *influxus divinus* of the Thomist theologians. That is, like Descartes, he approved the idea of an "inflow/influence of the first cause into/on" each individual substance—which is equivalent to God's continuous production of that substance—but rejected as unintelligible Suárez's thesis that any created substance can "flow into"—i.e. have influence on, or act on—any other. See Aiv312: 1620 and Aiv317 for classic statements of this position. See also his correspondence with Burcher de Volder (L 521, 525, 529).

*influere:* to flow into, influence.

INSECABILIS: indissectible.

INSENSIBILIS: insensible (Aiv301: 1512); see *sensibilis* under SENSUM.

This term has an Aristotelian pedigree: the pseudo-Aristotelian *De lineis insecabilibus* is usually translated "On Indivisible Lines." But Leibniz's use of the term to describe bodies may derive from Gassendi (see Appendix 2e). Cf. *unum corpus atque insecabile, sive ἄτομον* (Aiii36: 393; cf. also Aiii76: 524,5).

INSTANS (*instant*): instant.

INTELLIGERE: to understand; to conceive (of).

Although the former is preferable, idiomatic English will sometimes allow only the latter, as at Aiii15: 215: *semper spatium ultra intelligere liceat,* "one may always conceive another space beyond."

*intelligi posse:* to be intelligible.

*intellectio:* understanding.

*intellectus:* intellect.

INTERCEPTUS: intercepted, cut off between.

This is a technical term from geometry (cf. Heath, *The Works of Archimedes,* clxxi). *Spatium interceptum,* the space intercepted (Aiii5: 99, Aiii65: 488), is the space cut off by, and comprehended between, two lines or figures, as the space between the legs of an angle.

INTERJECTUS: interjected, intervening, lying between.

This functions as a technical term for Leibniz, and is defined by him in "On the Nature of Corporeal Bodies" (Appendix 1f) as follows: "Something is *interjected* between two things if the sum of its distances from each of them is the distance apart of the two things." It is often used nontechnically, however. Thus *spatium interjectum:* intervening space (Aiii59: 471); *coalescere in unum has duas mentes, quia vacuum nullum interjectum est,* "these two minds

would coalesce into one, because there is no vacuum between them" (Aiii36: 393).

INTERMINATUS: unbounded.

An exception is the Letter to Thomasius (Appendix 1a), where I have rendered *interminata* as "interminate," to mark it as an Averroist term.

*linea interminata,* or sometimes just *interminata,* an unbounded line (Aiii65, Aiii66, Aiii69, *passim*). See also DETRIMINARI, TERMINUS.

INTERRUPTUS: broken up, interrupted by gaps.

For example, Aiii69: 501: *lineam eiusmodi materialem interminatam non-interruptam implicare,* "that for an unbounded material line of this kind to be *uninterrupted by gaps* implies a contradiction."

LEX: law.

*leges Mechanicae:* the Laws of Mechanics.

LINEA (*ligne*): line.

See also RECTA, INTERMINATUM.

MACHINA: machine.

But note *machinas ratiocinationis* (Aiii78: 558), *machinas rationum* (Aiii78: 567): logical stratagems.

MAGNITUDO: magnitude, size; greatness.

Although "size" is more colloquial, *magnitudo* almost always carries a mathematical connotation in Leibniz and so is better translated by "magnitude." Exceptions are *magnitudo aut parvitas nihil ad rem faciat,* "size has nothing to do with the matter" (Aiii78: 560); and *magnitudini divinae,* "to divine greatness" (Aiii78: 566).

MASSA (*masse*): mass.

In his Letter to Thomasius, Leibniz equates *massa* with *materia prima,* primary matter (see under MATERIA); whereas in his mature work he equates it with *materia secunda,* secondary matter, as distinct from MOLES (q.v.). See in particular his correspondence with Johann Bernoulli in fall 1698 (GM.iii.537, 539f., 541f.; AG 167ff.).

MATERIA: matter.

*materia prima:* primary matter. Leibniz adopts this Aristotelian term, equating it in his Letter to Thomasius with "mass itself," the purely material aspect of bodies, consisting in a pure potential for receiving forms. From the 1680s on, it is primitive passive force, which, together with *substantial form,* or primitive active force, constitutes a corporeal substance.

*materia secunda:* secondary matter. As distinct from *materia prima* (q.v.), this is existing matter, divided into its individual parts, or bod-

ies (which in turn are either *corporeal substances,* or aggregates of such substances). See Aiv278, Aiv267, Aiv279.

METAPHYSICUS: metaphysical.

For the contrast with the *physical* see PHYSICUS; see also *punctum metaphysicum* and *vacuum metaphysicum* under PUNCTUM, VACUUM.

MOBILE (*mobile*): moving point (Aiii78: 557f.), moving thing (Aiv310), moving body (Aiii78: 566).

*corps mobile:* moving body (Aiv310).

MOLES: bulk, extended mass.

This is the term used by the Cartesians and other contemporaries of Leibniz in their physics for quantity of body: *moles* × speed = quantity of motion. As Curley notes, 'bulk' is the translation given by (Leibniz's probable source) Boyle in his contemporary English (SC 628, c.1): thus (Aiv316). But as a singular term (rather than a mass term) I have translated it as an 'extended mass' (e.g. at Aiv346: 1798). Leibniz equates it with natural inertia at Aiv312: 1620. See also MASSA.

MOMENTUM (*moment*): moment.

*momentaneum:* momentaneous (Aiii78: 566).

In Leibniz's usage, these seem to be entirely synonymous with instant and instantaneous.

MOTUS (*mouvement*): motion.

*moveri:* to be moved, to move, to be in motion (Aiii58: 470).

Leibniz consistently uses the passive forms of the verb *movere* and *mutare* when applied to bodies, in keeping with the doctrine that bodies are entirely passive, and that motion and change are their *passions.* Since this reads awkwardly in modern English, I have rendered these verbs in active mood when bodies are the subject, trusting the reader to keep the passive nature of bodies' motions and changes in mind.

MULTITUDO: multiplicity.

This is synonymous with plurality, but not, according to Leibniz's considered view developed in this period, with number: for infinite multiplicities, according to that view, have no corresponding numbers. See Aiii19, Aiii69.

MUNDUS: world (Aiii58: 467; Aiv301: 1509–13).

This is synonymous with 'cosmos' (or its Latin equivalent, *ornatus*), an ordered universe. In an undated manuscript, titled by Couturat "Resumé de métaphysique" (C 533–35), Leibniz writes: "*Sequiturque in universum, Mundum esse κόσμον, plenum ornatûs; seu ita factum ut maxime satisfaciat intelligenti,* "And it follows in general that the

world is a cosmos, a full and ordered universe; i.e. that it is so made that it is maximally satisfying to the intelligent." Similarly, here in Aiv301 he writes: *Corporum omnium Aggregatum dicitur* MUNDUS, "the aggregate of all bodies is called the *world*" (1509). If there is any difference in Leibniz's use of the words 'world' and 'universe' (see UNIVERSUM), the latter has the broader meaning, incorporating all entities thought by anyone, as well as the things in the world. *De Mundo universo,* "concerning the whole world" (Aiv301: 1508).

*anima mundi:* see under ANIMA.

*spatium mundanum,* the mundane space, i.e. the space occupied by this world, as opposed to *spatium extramundanum,* the extramundane space, or space beyond the limits of this world.

*systema mundanus:* the world system (Aiv320: 1641).

*corpora mundana:* mundane bodies (Aiii76: 525). Cf. also *globos mundanos,* mundane globes (Aiii60: 477). Parkinson suggests (DSR 136) that these might be bodies which are on our earth, as opposed to extramundane ones. More likely, given Leibniz's philosophy of worlds within worlds *in infinitum,* it refers to all bodies (globes) of our world system, both insensible globes and planetary spheres alike. In *Hypothesis de systemate mundi* (Appendix 1e), it refers to enduring bodies: "10. Bodies are either mundane, i.e. enduring for a while, or momentaneous."

MUTATIO (*changement*): change.

*mutari:* to be changed, to change. See note on *moveri.*

NATURA (*nature*): nature.

*natura generalis:* nature in general. Thus "A Specimen of Discoveries" concerns *admirandis naturae generalis arcanis,* "the admirable secrets of nature in general" (although also possible is Parkinson's "marvellous secrets of a general nature," in his "Science and Metaphysics in Leibniz's 'Specimen Inventorum,'" p. 1). In the same piece Leibniz opposes *generalia naturae* (natures in general), which cannot be correctly understood without souls or forms, to the *Phaenomenis corporum specialium* (phenomena of specific bodies), which must be explained without them (Aiv312: 1625); and at 1629, it is said of *Natura generalis* (Nature in general) that it "always pursues its own end," which appears to entail that the world has a soul, contrary to Leibniz's express prouncements on the subject in the period (see under ANIMA).

*tota natura:* the whole of nature. This usage is to distinguish it from the nature of a thing; it seems equivalent to *natura rerum,* for which see RES.

NECESSITAS: necessity.

*ens necessarium:* a necessary being (see ENS).

*necessitas alternativa:* conditional necessity (Aiv315).

OBOLUS: penny.

This is a conventional translation for a small coin; it occurs in Leibniz's discussions of the Stoics' Paradox of the Heap (Aiii76: 539, Aiv23). The *obol* was a small ancient Greek coin, corresponding to the Latin *denarius.* In the Middle Ages the name was applied to various small coins, as to the English halfpenny. See also SOLIDUS.

OMNIA: (n.) everything, all things; (adj.) all.

There is much to commend in translating the noun *omnia* as "all things," as Parkinson consistently does in DSR. But it often seemed to me more natural to translate it as "everything" *(alles)* as in *plena esse omnia intelligo* (Aiii58: 467), where I prefer "I understand everything to be a plenum" to Parkinson's more literal "I take it that all things are full."

OPERATIO: operation.

This is the noun corresponding to *operare,* "to work on," "to be active," and English lacks a good one-word translation like the German *Wirkung.* Operations comprise both actions and passions, and *in Metaphysico rigore, omnes substantiarum operationes, actiones passionesque esse spontaneas,* "in metaphysical rigor all the operations of substances, both actions and passions, are spontaneous" (Aiv312: 1620). The unity in itself *(unum per se)* that is the subject of a thing's attributes and operations is called a soul if it is in us, and a substantial form in every body that is a unity in itself (Aiv301: 1506); and "every substance has within it a kind of operation, and this operation is either of the same thing on itself, in which case it is called reflection or thought, and such a substance is spiritual, i.e. a *mind;* or it is the operation of its various parts, and such a substance is called *corporeal*" (Aiv301: 1507).

*operare:* to operate, work on. (Aiv267: 1398: *omnis substantia actu ipso operatur,* "every substance is actually operating"; see ACTUALIS.

ORGANON: an organ.

*organicus:* organic. The original semantic connection among 'organ', 'organic', and 'organized'—lost in the mists of metaphor to us—is very much alive in Leibniz. In "Metaphysical Definitions and Reflections," he writes: "If two bodies resist one another, and we perceive the action and passion of one as pertaining to us, and those of the other as foreign to us, the former body is called an *organ,* the latter is called an *object*" (Aiv27: 1394). Later in the same piece he

writes, "Every body is organic, i.e. is actually divided into smaller parts endowed with their own particular motions" (1398); and further explains, "Even though everything is animate, nonetheless everything acts according to the laws of mechanics, for sensation and appetite are determined by organs (i.e. parts of a body) and objects (i.e. by surrounding bodies)" (1400). But not only bodies are organic: "Every mind is organic, and learns something, . . . in proportion to the periods of the things it senses" (Aiii36: 394).

OSCULUM: osculation.

A mathematical term, coined by Leibniz in 1686 but now in current usage, meaning a contact between two curves that consists in three or more coincident points. See Leibniz's article cited in note 2 in Aiv304.

*circulus osculans:* osculating circle. This is the "kissing circle," the circle touching a curve at a given point that has the same tangent and same radius of curvature as the curve at that point.

PASSIO: passion; (an instance of something's) being acted upon.

In these writings Leibniz always uses *passio* in the sense of a fact or condition of being acted upon, of experiencing an action. The corresponding adjective is *passivum* (passive), and verb, *pati* (to be acted upon). The absence of a cognate verb in English presents major difficulties for the translator trying to preserve the connections in the Latin, and with them, Leibniz's meaning. I was sorely tempted to translate every case of *passio, passivus,* and *pati* consistently by 're-action', 'reactive', and 'react'—especially since Leibniz equates the *principium passionis* with *vis resistendi primitiva,* the primitive force of resisting at Aiv301: 1507; for it is hard to see how "being acted upon" could be a source of resistance; whereas *reacting,* as in resisting penetration, could be so construed. But (i) in many cases this expedient simply will not work; (ii) it loses the connection with the Scholastic tradition that Leibniz is drawing on, as well as with the *vis primitiva passiva* or "primitive passive (—not 'reactive'—) force"; and in any case, (iii) it is the *principle* of passion, i.e. *matter,* rather than passion itself, that Leibniz goes on to equate with *reactione seu conatu sive appetitu* in the continuation of the above passage (Aiv301: 1508).

Thus: *realitatem corporeae substantiae in individua quadam natura, hoc est non in mole, sed agendi patiendique potentia consistere:* "the reality of corporeal substance consists in a certain individual nature, i.e. not in bulk, but in a power of acting and being acted upon" (Aiv312: 1622); *Substantia omnis agendi patiendique vi continetur,*

"every substance is comprised by a force of acting and being acted upon" (Avi312: 1623); *ab omnibus aliis materiae partibus . . . proportione distantiae aliquid patitur, cumque omnis passio habeat effectum quendam . . . ,* "is acted upon by all the other parts of matter . . . in proportion to their distance. And since every case of being acted upon has some effect, . . . " (Aiv312: 1623).

PER SE: through itself, in itself, per se.

I had left this untranslated throughout; but in deference to some criticisms from readers, reverted to the literal translation "through itself" wherever possible. Still, in my view this is not always possible: "entity (or being) through itself" is hardly transparent, and it is similar with certain other expressions (see UNUM PER SE, and *ens per se, ipsum extensum per se* under ENS, EXTENSUM, resp.).

PERCEPTIO: perception.

See CONFUSE, SENSUM.

PERIODUS: period.

Aiii76: 525. Leibniz appears to have assumed (presciently) that all things have characteristic periods. On the one hand this is related to his doctrine of minds/worlds/vortices, on the other to the idea that we can only sense what has the same kind of periodicity as our sensory organs: "Every mind is organic and learns something, but with difficulty and over a very long time, in proportion to the periods [of repetition] of the things it senses" (Aiii36: 394).

PHAENOMENUM: phenomenon.

This is phenomenon in the sense of thing which appears, equivalent to APPARENTIA, q.v. One mark of the reality of a phenomenon is its consistency or coherence with all other simultaneous phenomena; the mutual relations of all simultaneous phenomena constitute an extended space. See the excellent note of Remnant and Bennett in their edition of Leibniz's *New Essays* (NE lxiii).

PHORONOMIA: Phoronomy.

Phoronomy is the science of pure motion; it is concerned with the analysis of motion in the abstract, and thus involves the consideration of time and instantaneous motion as well as the laws of geometry. The epitome of a phoronomical law would be the Law of Compositions of Motions, which, together with the concept of endeavour, forms the basis for Leibniz's early study in phoronomy, *The Theory of Abstract Motion* (see Apendix 1c). The Law of Conservation of Quantity of Motion might also be considered phoronomical, if mass be not taken as primitive: Leibniz attempts a phoronomical derivation of it in Aiii58. Although Hobbes is the major influence on Leib-

niz's early phoronomy, his initial impetus comes from Erhard Weigel
and Joachim Jungius, from whom he probably acquired the term and
his estimation of its importance (see A VI.ii.228, 248, 268, 274f.,
299, 314, 333, 335f.)

PHYSICUS: physical.

What is physical is part of nature, and thus accessible to the senses. For
Leibniz's peculiar Platonic way of contrasting this with the metaphysical, the reality underlying the senses, see *vacuum physicum* and
*punctum physicum* under PUNCTUM, VACUUM.

PLENUM: (n.) the plenum; (adj.) full.

Leibniz was committed to a plenistic physics from the beginning,
largely under the influence of Hobbes. But this was the dominant
view of his contemporaries, shared by the Cartesians and even atomists like Huygens (see Introduction, Section 5). It was not displaced
in continental Europe until the spread of Newtonianism in the latter
part of the eighteenth century.

*plenum physicum:* a physical plenum; i.e. a world in which there is no
assignable or observable vacuum (though there may be an unassignable one: see *vacuum metaphysicum*).

PORTIO MATERIAE: a portion of matter.

(Aiii36: 392, 393; Aiii58). Cf. Cordemoy's distinction between a part of
matter (one body) and a portion of matter (several bodies considered
together and separately from all the others). At Aiv301: 1513, *an alia
sit Mundi portio,* "whether there is another region of the world."

POTENTIA: power.

Even though Leibniz appears to use *vis* and *potentia* almost interchangeably, "power" seems a preferable translation to "force," because the term is part of an older tradition. The "five powers" are five
simple mechanical principles (the wheel, the lever, the wedge, the
pulley, and the windlass), rather than forces in the abstract sense.

Leibniz clarifies what he means by *potentia* in Aiv312: 1629, in a passage which is of great interest in showing how the conservation of *vis
viva* has its origins in Leibniz's principle of the equivalence of cause
and effect: *Eadem potentia servatur in natura rerum, seu causa et effectus sunt aequivalentes. Potentiam voco, quae agendo consumitur
seu effectum producendo:* "The same power is conserved in the nature of things, or, cause and effect are equivalent. I call 'power' that
which is consumed in acting, that is, in producing an effect."

PRINCIPIUM: principle.

*principium actionis:* principle of action. In Aiv312, the *principium ac-*

*tionum* is identified with the "primitive force of acting," and thus with is the form of the substance. See also SUPPOSITUM.

*principium passionis:* principle of passion: see PASSIO.

*principium contradictionis:* the principle of contradiction, *quod scilicet omnis propositio identica vera, et contradictoria ejus falsa est,* "which is that every identical proposition is true, and its contradictory false" (Aiv312: 1616)

*principium reddendae rationis:* the principle of providing a reason, *quod scilicet omnis propositio vera quae per se nota non est, probationem recipit a priori, sive quod omnis veritatis reddi ratio potest, vel ut vulgo ajunt, quod nihil fit sine causa,* "which is that every true proposition which is not known through itself receives an a priori proof, i.e. that a reason can be provided for every truth, or as is commonly said, that nothing happens without a cause" (Aiv312: 1616). This is, of course, what Leibniz will later term his Principle of Sufficient Reason; see Aiv312, n. 4.

PROBARE; PROBATIO: to prove; a proof, evidence.

A *probatio* is weaker than a DEMONSTRATIO (q.v.); it is a proof in the sense of the adage "the proof of the pudding is in the eating."

PROGREDI, PROGRESSUS: to progress; progress.

In the "Specimen of Discoveries," Leibniz introduces the technical term *progressus* as an equivalent to his previous term DIRECTIO (q.v.): *Eadem quantitas.*

PUNCTUM (*point*): point.

*punctum consursus anguli:* vertex of an angle (Aiii5: 99).

*punctum extremum:* endpoint (Aiii65: 485).

*punctum mathematicum:* mathematical point. "Mathematical points could be called Cavalierian indivisibles, even if they are not metaphysical points," (Aiii60: 473). But by April 1676 Leibniz has decided that they are equivalent to mere endpoints (see EXTREMUM).

*punctum medium:* midpoint (Aiii65: 486).

*punctum metaphysicum:* metaphysical point. Equated with a *minimum* at (Aiii60: 473), and thus with a *punctum perfectum,* q.v. By analogy with a *vacuum metaphysicum,* this would appear to be a point smaller than any that can be assigned, yet true and real.

*punctum perfectum:* perfect point (Aiii60: 473): *divisam esse in puncta perfecta, seu in omnes partes in quas dividi potest:* "divided into perfect points, i.e. into all the parts into which it can be divided." Apparently equivalent to *punctum metaphysicum,* q.v.

*punctum physicum:* a physical point. Many defenders of atomism (among

them Gassendi and Magnen) distinguished a physical point from a mathematical one. Cf. Gassendi, Appendix 2e. Also contrasted with *punctum metaphysicum,* q.v.

PYRIUM EXPLOSUM: blasting powder.

This occurs in these writings only as one of Leibniz's example of a sudden transition from dense to rare in (Aiv301: 1513). Leibniz presumably became familiar with blasting powder as a result of his experience with the mines in the Harz mountains in the late 1670s and early 1680s (on the latter, see Eric Aiton, *Leibniz: A Biography,* (Bristol: Adam Hilger, 1985); pp. 87f., 107f.). (I am indebted to my erstwhile colleague at IHPST, Bert Hall, for this translation and explanation.)

QUIES: a rest, interval of rest.

*quiescere:* to be at rest, to come to rest.

*quietulus:* a small (interval of) rest.

RATIO: reason; explanation, account; method, way; cause; ratio.

The many distinct senses of this common word, and particularly its near synonymy with CAUSA, q.v., make it one of the most troublesome for a translator. Two quite distinct senses of *ratio,* and the use of *cause* as reason, all occur in this passage: *eademque ratione ostendi potest, nec rationem posse exprimi fractione numeris finitis assignabili media, inter 2 et 3 eandem ob causam* (Aiii69: 500): "and by the same method it can be shown that the ratio cannot be expressed by an assignable fraction of a finite number intermediate between 2 and 3, for the same reason." In Leibniz's worldview, every thing has its *ratio* or *causa* for existing and being the way it is (his Principle of Sufficient Reason—see *principium reddendae rationis* under PRINCIPIUM), as in Aiv312: 1623: *neque vacuum rationibus rerum consentaneum est,* "Nor is a vacuum in accordance with the reasons for things." But in the sentence before this, particles are said to be exposed to the actions of other particles *diversa ratione,* i.e. in a different way, differently—or perhaps "in a different ratio"? The deliberate equation of "reason" and "ratio" in passages such as Aiv267: 1401–2 gives a very Pythagorean content that is impossible to capture adequately in translation.

*ratio* as cause or explanation: *quorum ratio a pressione äeris reddi non potest* (Aiii4: 96): "which cannot be accounted for by the pressure of the air." *Mechanicas potentiarum rationes* (Aiii78: 569), "mechanical explanations of powers." Again, *rationem quae fecit eam esse paulo ante adhuc existere* (Aiii78: 569n): "a reason which makes what existed a little while before still exist," shows that Leibniz un-

derstood reasons as efficacious. Note also: *ratione causae* (Aiv360),
"with respect to cause."

*esse rationalis:* to be in rational proportion to (Aiii69: 497).

RECEPTACULUM: receptacle.

RECEPTUM: recept.

In the absence of a word in English that would be a good correlative for
receptacle, I have coined the word 'recept' for the thing that occupies
a receptacle. See Aiv301: 1509.

RECTA (*droit*): straight line.

These expressions are of course aphetic for *linea recta, ligne droite.*

REFRINGERE: to diffuse, break up.

*semper refringitur actio [substantiae finitae] sive nonnihil impeditur,*
"[a finite substance's] action is always diffused, or to some extent impeded" (Aiv267: 1398). *omnis substantia corporea omniscia confuse
et omnipotens refracte,* "every corporeal substance is confusedly omniscient and diffusedly omnipotent" (Aiv279).

REPASSIO: (undergoing) reaction.

*posse aliquid agere sine repassio,* "it is possible for something to act
without undergoing reaction" (Aiii78: 571).

RES: thing, fact (Aiii58: 466; Aiv360).

*ab initio rerum:* "from the beginning of things" (Aiv279), *de origine rerum,* "concerning the origins of things" (Aiv279), *rerum primordia
ac velut summas:* "the first and as it were highest principles of
things" (Aiii78: 561). Likewise I have rendered *creator rerum* and
*rerum autor* (Aiii78: 560, 561, 566) as "creator of things" and "the
Author of Things," despite their sounding somewhat archaic; and
*natura rerum* as "the nature of things," echoing the title of Lucretius's poem. *Summa rerum:* the whole universe (Aiii78: 561).

RESPECTIVUS: relative (Aiii68, Aiv360).

There is an English adjective 'respective', but it does not quite carry the
connotation of the Latin that *motus respectivus,* for example, is motion *with respect to* something else. On the other hand, my translation
of this as "relative motion," loses the connection of *respectivus* with
RESPECTUS (q.v.), respect, point of view. Cf. Aiv360: *Motum esse
quiddam respectivum:* "motion is something relative," i.e. it is only
motion with respect to (from the point of view of) something considered as at rest.

RESPECTUS: respect, point of view, relation.

*respectus* as relation: *hic rerum inter se respectus dicitur* TEMPUS, "this
relation of things to each other is called *time*" (Aiv267: 1397); *Motus*

*in solo respectu consistunt:* "motions consist only in relation" (Aiv312: 1622).

SCIENTIA: knowledge, science.

This is knowledge as in the sense of what has been learned or can be taught, as opposed to COGNITIO, q.v. Thus *scientiarum omnium semina,* "the seeds of all knowledge," and *sponte in animis nascatur scientia,* "knowledge might grow spontaneously in the soul" (Aiii78: 529); but *Scientiam Mechanicam,* "Mechanical Science" (Aiii78: 530).

SCLOPETUM: a musket.

This occurs only in Leibniz's example of a sudden transition from dense to rare in (Aiv301: 1513) in the phrase *sclopeto ventaneo.* A *sclopetum ventaneum,* or "wind musket," was apparently an early version of the air rifle. See Hobbes, *De corpore,* IV, § 30, 11, for a description and diagram; Hobbes calls it a "gun of recent invention." At the end of the fourteenth century, a *sclopette* was a hand-culverine or arquebus, that is, a lighter gun than the musket (which required a strong man to bear it), but the latter name gradually came to be applied to a lighter handgun. The word still survives in Friuli in northeast Italy, where "*un sclop*" or "*une sclope*" is a shotgun for hunting. (I am indebted here to Professor Bert Hall, and to my Friulian in-laws.)

SENSUM: sense, sensation.

*sentire:* to sense, to have sensation (Aiv267: 1398).

*sensibilis:* sensible, detectable by the senses (Aiii52: 434, Aiv301: 1513). The sensible qualities of body are those we perceive confusedly (Aiv365: 1986).

SERVARI: is conserved.

See CONSERVARE, *conservari* above.

SEU, SIVE: or, i.e., that is (to say).

This is the Latin "or of equivalence," as distinct from the disjunctive 'ors'—*aut* (exclusive disjunction) and *vel* (inclusive disjunction, "and/or," "or perhaps"). Initially it had seemed desirable to preserve this distinction in English, and I had followed Curley in using a notation to mark the 'or' as one of equivalence. But I became persuaded that in cases where it was necessary to mark the equivalence, this was achieved neatly enough by 'i.e.' or some equivalent.

SIMUL: simultaneous, together.

"*Simultaneous* things are those that are connected; either by necessity, or if a reason can be given for the connection with certainty"

(Aiv132: 563). "Those things are simultaneous one of which is the condition for the other absolutely" (Aiv147: 628).

SITUS: situation.

Every body has a situation with respect to other bodies around it, determined by angles and distances. In 1679 Leibniz began to develop his *Analysis Situs,* or Analysis of Situations, a kind of generalized geometry. See, for instance, L 248ff.

SOLIDUS: solid; shilling.

This latter is a conventional translation. The *solidus* was a Roman gold coin introduced by Constantine, later called the *bezant.* In the Middle Ages in England the solidus was a silver coin of 12 denarii or pence, the sign '/', or solidus, representing the lengthened form of the initial 's', so that £/d., or £.s.d. (until recently), represented *librae, solidi, denarii,* pounds, shillings, and pence.

SPATIUM (*espace*): space.

"Space and time are not things, but real relations." (Aiv312: 1621); see also Aiv359, Aiv321).

*spatium absolutum:* absolute space. In Aiv317, Leibniz describes this as "no more a thing than time is, even though it is pleasing to the imagination; indeed, it can be demonstrated that such entities are not things, but are merely relations of a mind trying to refer everything to intelligible hypotheses." Space is rather a "real relation" (Aiv359; Aiv321; Aiv312: 1621).

*spatium reale nullum esse:* "space is nothing real" (Aiv312: 1623). Nevertheless, Leibniz insists that "whatever is real in space and time consists in God comprising everything" (Aiv147: 629), i.e. that space, insofar as it is something real, is divine immensity. Thus "real space in itself is something that is one, indivisible, immutable; and it contains not only existences but possibilities" (Aiv321).

*spatium generale:* see *generalis,* under GENUS.

SPECIES: species; specific kind; appearance.

This is a troublesome word to translate, as it has several specific (no pun intended) and quite distinct meanings. Different *species* are included in a GENUS, q.v., and it is thus a type or specific kind of thing: thus *[motus] species seu modus,* "Specific motions or modes of motion" (Aiii68: 494), *[Mentis] diversas species,* "different species of mind" (Aiv304: 1526). At Aiv312: 1622 Leibniz writes that "in all corporeal substances there is something analogous to the soul, which the ancients called form or species"; but at (Aiv301: 1507–8), he says the consideration of whether bodies have substantial forms or not is ir-

relevant to "the species of body," so that this probably means their specific kinds. But it could perhaps mean "appearance," as in *machinam, quae forte externa specie no satis examinanti hominem mentiretur,* "a machine which would perhaps remind you of a man by its outward appearance" (Aiv346: 1801). Finally, see the legal definition of species mentioned by Leibniz in correction of Cordemoy (Aiv346: 1800).

   *specialis:* specific; as at Aiv312: 1625: *in ipsis tamen Phaenomenis corporum specialium explicandis,* "in explaining the phenomena of specific bodies," as opposed to "generic natures" (see *natura generalis*).

SPIRITUALIS: spiritual.

   *substantia spiritualis:* spiritual substance.

STATUS (*estat*): state.

   *estats durables:* enduring states (Aiv310).

STRUES, STRUIX: a pile.

   *strues lignorum,* a woodpile (Aiv132: 559, Aiv301: 1506). See also
   ACERVUS, CONGERIES, CUMULUS.

SUBDIVIDUUS (Aiv132: 559): subdivisible.

   *sousdivision:* subdivision.

SUBSTANTIA: substance.

   *substantia singularis = substantia individualis* (Aiv132: 559–60, Aiv301: 1506–7; Aiv312: *passim*): individual substance.

   *substantias universales:* (Aiv312: 1619): the difference between universal and individual substances is "that in the notion of the latter contingent predicates are also involved."

   *substantia corporea:* corporeal substance (Aiv316; Aiv312: 1622, 1623); this is not corporeal substance in the sense of Cordemoy and other moderns, pure extension or bulk (MOLES, q.v.); for Leibniz a "pile, or entity by aggregation, such as a heap of stones should not be called a corporeal substance, but only a phenomenon"; rather, "every corporeal substance has a soul," "has [probably] always existed from the beginning of things," and "has no definite extension" (Aiv279).

SUPPOSITUM: (n.) subject (Aiv346: 1799); (adj.) supposed (Aiii11$_2$).

   Literally, this means 'subordinate', but in Scholastic philosophy it meant 'subject' or 'substance', as in the doctrine established by Suárez (in his *Disputationes metaphysicae,* Disp. 34) that *actiones sunt suppositorum,* "actions belong to subjects," to which Leibniz often declares his assent, and by reference to which in later writings he often justifies his doctrine of force (e.g. in *De Ipsa Natura,* §9; Loemker, p. 502). In his note "On Transubstantiation" of 1668(?), Leibniz says "a

*suppositum* is a substantial individual—as, for instance, a person is a
rational substantial individual—or a certain substance in particular.
Moreover, the School has generally established it as a property of
*suppositum* that it is itself denominated by action; hence the rule that
actions belong to *supposita*. It is clear from this that the *suppositum,*
substance, or entity which subsists in itself—which are all the same
thing—is defined correctly in the Scholastic sense as that which has
a principle of action with itself, for otherwise it would not act but be
an instrument of some agent." (A VI.i 510; L 117; see also Loemker's
notes on pp. 119–20). At Aiv132: 559, however, Leibniz defines a
*suppositum* as either an individual substance or a real phenomenon
(q.v.).; here I have left the term untranslated.

SYMPATHICUM, SYMPATHETICUM: sympathetic (Aiii3: 80–81, Aiv312:
1618).

Leibniz's advocacy of a form of the doctrine of universal sympathy is
evident particularly in Aiii3 and Aiv312, although he only mentions
Hippocrates in this connection: see Aiii3, n. 7, Aiv312, ns. 11 & 12;
see also CONSPIRARE.

*sympathisant:* sympathizing (Aiv310).

SYSTEMA: system

*systemation:* little system. *Exemplia gratia arenual quaevis est systemation aliquod per se:* "For example, any grain of sand is a kind of
little system in itself" (Aiv312: 1628); *ipsius structrae firmitas,
sumenda est a systemationum* [for *systematiorum*] *collocatione conspirante,* "the firmness of this structure is to be derived from a harmonious collocation of little systems" (Aiv312: 1630).

TABULA: slab, tablet.

The example of the smoothly polished marble slabs had a prominent
place in seventeenth-century discussions of cohesion, and consequently occurs several times in these writings. Galileo introduced it in
his *Two New Sciences:* "If one takes two exquisitely smooth, clean
and polished slabs (*piastre*) of marble, metal or glass, placed one on
top of the other, then when one is moved, it will effortlessly slide over
the other (a sure argument that there is no glue conjoining them); but
whenever one wants to separate them, keeping them equidistant, there
is such a repugnance to this that the upper one will lift the other behind
it, and keep it up indefinitely, even when the lower one is very large
and heavy. Evidently this shows nature's aversion (*orroro*) to having
to admit an empty space, even for the brief moment it would remain
before the onrush of the parts of the surrounding air occupied it and
filled it up" (NE 59). He uses this example to buttress his theory that

the vacuum is the cause of the cohesion not only of the slabs, but even
of the very smallest particles composing it (see Appendix 2b).

*tabula rasa:* blank tablet.

TEMPUS (*temps*): time.

> *Tempus est Ens imaginarium* "Time is an imaginary entity" (Aiv147:
> v1255). See DURATIO, SPATIUM.

TENACITAS: tenacity.

> This functions as a technical term meaning the capacity of an object to
> hold itself together. Thus *habet . . . omne liquidum aliquid tenaci-*
> *tatis,* "every liquid has some tenacity" (Aiii78: 555). Cf. Aiii2: 13:
> *Scio Galilaeo aquae tenacitatem displicuisse sed eam tamen multis*
> *experimentis confirmari posse arbitror,* "I know that Galileo did not
> favor the tenacity of water, but I believe it can be confirmed by many
> experiments."

*tenax:* adhesive. Thus *neque enim ulla tenax in primis originibus,* "for no
adhesive can be allowed in the primary origins of things" (Aiii36: 393).

TERMINUS: bound (Aiii78: 565, Aiv267: 1399), boundary (A VI.ii 435–
36, Aiii58: 469).

> This preserves the correspondence with *[linea] interminata,* an un-
> bounded line. See especially Aiii69: 502: *Adeoque interminatum,*
> *[prius] habente terminum, cum terminus sit accessio quaedam:*
> "And so is the unbounded prior to what has a bound, since a bound is
> a kind of addition."

TERRELLA: terrella.

> The modern meaning of terrella (literally, a "little earth") is "a magnetic
> model of the earth," and both senses are present in Leibniz's use of
> the word. Thus in his *Propositiones quaedam physicae,* which con-
> cerns *terrellae* centrally, he says: "*Sensible bodies are aggregates of*
> *innumerable terrellas,* i.e. corpuscles that are arched or enclosed by
> the motion of matter along the meridians in every region" (Aiii2: 32).
> But as he says earlier in this treatise, "Gilbert said that the Earth is a
> magnet, [but] I have demonstrated that all bodies made firm by the
> circulation of matter along the meridians are magnetic, . . . and ac-
> cordingly sensible bodies contain innumerable tiny terrellas . . . "
> (Aiii2: 61–62). See also BULLA, GLOBULUS.

TRANSCREATIO: transcreation.

> A term of Leibniz's own coinage (Aiii78: 560, 567): a moving body is
> "transcreated" if it is annihilated at a given moment, then recreated at
> a point "indistant" (see INDISTANS) from the first at a neighboring or
> contiguous moment. This is synonymous with TRANSPRODUCTIO, q.v.

*transcreari:* to be transcreated (Aiii69: 500).

TRANSFORMATIO: transformation.

See the discussion at Aiv147: v1254: "we may call it a transformation when one thing becomes another without any part being added or taken away."

TRANSITIO: transition.

*transire:* to pass.

TRANSPRODUCTIO: transproduction (Aiii69: 503); synonymous with TRANS-CREATIO, q.v.

ULNA: cubit.

*Ulna* in Leibniz's Latin correctly translates Galileo's *braccio,* an Italian measure of some 58–70 cm. However, as pointed out in a note to Aiii11 above, this gives far too big a value for the maximum height above the surface that a pump will work, for Galileo's reported 18 *braccia* would translate into between 34 ft., 3 in. and 41 ft., where 26 feet would be a more likely practical maximum. My translation reflects my surmise that Galileo might have meant *cubito* (Latin *cubitum*), a cubit being some 18 inches. (*Cubito* is the anatomical counterpart of *ulna*).

UNIVERSUM (*l'univers*): the universe.

*in universum:* in general (Aiii5: 99, Aiii69: 502, etc.); overall (Aiii76: 526).

UNUM PER SE: a unity in itself. See *ens per se, ens per accidens,* under AC-CIDENS.

VACUUM: vacuum, void; empty.

*vacuum interspersum:* an interspersed vacuum (Aiii68, Aiii85: 585): i.e. a vacuum scattered about in the interstices of a solid, as opposed to an extramundial vacuum, i.e. one existing beyond the sphere of the fixed stars. For Leibniz's changing views on the status of the interspersed vacuum, see Appendix 1, Aiii60, Aiii68, Aiii78, and the Introduction, Section 5.

*vacuum metaphysicum:* A metaphysical vacuum; perhaps inspired by Galileo's "unquantifiable voids," to which they are equivalent if Galileo's and Cavalieri's indivisibles are interpreted as infinitesimals. Cf. Aiii60: 473: "A metaphysical vacuum is an empty place however small, only true and real. A physical plenum is consistent with an unassignable metaphysical vacuum."

VESTIGIUM: trace, footstep, vestige (Aiv312: 1618).

*per sua vestigia,* along its own path (Aiii65: 489, Aiii668: 493).

VIOLENTIA: violation of proportion (PP7 560).

VIRTUS: virtue; potential.

*potentia seu virtus agendi patiendique,* "a power of potential of acting

and being acted upon" (Aiv346: 1799). *proportione virtutis,* "in proportion to their potential (Aiv312: 1617).

*virtute:* potentially (Aiv301: 1507; Aiv312: 1618; Aiv147: v1255).

VIS: force.

I have consistently rendered *vis* as "force," POTENTIA (q.v.) as "power," even though Leibniz appears to use them as equivalents, e.g. at Aiv365: 1989. Note, however, that Leibniz sometimes uses the plural *vires,* as at Aiii4: 94: *quantitas virium,* quantity of force.

VOLUNTAS: will.

This is the faculty of the will, as opposed to *volitio,* a particular act of willing.


## 2. Index and English-Latin Glossary

## 3. Index of Names

# The Labyrinth of the Continuum
*Writings on the Continuum Problem,*
*1672–1686*

## G. W. Leibniz
Translated, Edited, and with an Introduction
by Richard T. W. Arthur

This book gathers together for the first time an important body of texts written between 1672 and 1686 by the great German philosopher and polymath Gottfried Leibniz. These writings, most of them previously untranslated, represent Leibniz's sustained work on a problem whose solution was crucial to the development of his thought, that of the composition of the continuum.

The volume begins with excerpts from Leibniz's Paris writings, in which he tackles such problems as whether the infinite division of matter entails "perfect points," whether matter and space can be regarded as true wholes, whether motion is truly continuous, and the nature of body and substance. Comprising the second section is *Pacidius Philalethi,* Leibniz's brilliant dialogue of late 1676 on the problem of the continuity of motion. In the selections of the final section, from his Hanover writings of 1677–1686, Leibniz abandons his earlier transcreationism and atomism in the favor of the theory of corporeal substance, where the reality of body and motion is founded in substantial form or force.

Leibniz's texts (one in French, the rest in Latin) are presented with facing-page English translations, together with an introduction, notes, appendixes containing related excerpts from earlier works by Leibniz and his predecessors, and a valuable glossary detailing important terms and their translations.

**Richard Arthur is professor of philosophy at Middlebury College.**

The Yale Leibniz

Daniel Garber and Robert C. Sleigh, Jr., general editors

*De Summa Rerum: Metaphysical Papers, 1675–1676*
Translated with an Introduction and Notes by G. H. R. Parkinson

XXVI    Composition of the continuum

XXX    continual creation

fiction XXXIV

XXXIII    unassignably small

359    space between bodies    Hobbes